David Pringle is editor and publisher of the fiction magazine *Interzone*. He is the author of *Science Fiction: The 100 Best Novels*, *Imaginary People: A Who's Who of Modern Fictional Characters* and *Modern Fantasy: the Hundred Best Novels*. He lives in Brighton.

THE
ULTIMATE
GUIDE TO
SCIENCE FICTION

David Pringle

PHAROS BOOKS
A SCRIPPS HOWARD COMPANY

NEW YORK

First published in 1990 in Great Britain by Grafton Books,
a division of the Collins Publishing Group,
8 Grafton Street, London W1X 3LA

Library of Congress Card Catalog No: 90–7968

Pharos ISBN 0–88687–536–6 (paperback); 0–88687–537–4 (hardcover)

Pharos Books
A Scripps Howard Company
200 Park Avenue
New York, New York 10166

10 9 8 7 6 5 4 3 2 1

For Ken Brown,
who helped enormously

Also for Ruth and Abigail, Andy and Sylvia, and Peter T.

Contents

Introduction

Science fiction: wonder-stories of the chromium-plated future; the
literature of the impossible made plausible; the mythology of a technological age; the fairy tales of science. Its importance as a cultural form
does not cease to grow. Nor will it cease – as long as there is economic
growth, technological development and an exponential increase in
scientific knowledge, as long as cities and their suburbs continue to
spread across the face of this ravaged globe, and as long as human beings
have a deep need of stories for their amusement, enlightenment and
catharsis.

As a defined genre of prose fiction, it began in the late 1920s, although
'science fiction' did not become a household term in the western world
until about 1950. It has been said, however, that it *really* began in the
nineteenth century, with the scientific romances of Jules Verne, H. G.
Wells and their forgotten emulators. It began as an imaginative response
to the first industrial revolution and to the scientific developments
which followed, most notably Darwin's theory of evolution. The origins
of science fiction (*sf*) are to be found in the Age of Steam and in the 'ape
versus angel' debate. That said, it's clear that sf, in the modern sense, is
very much a mid-twentieth-century form. It came to full fruition in the
era of atomic power, antibiotics, the computer and the intercontinental
ballistic missile.

Now we are very nearly at the end of the twentieth century, and
modern sf is showing its age. From its beginnings in the American pulp
magazines of the 1920s and 30s, it has spread out into books, comics,
films, television, music, video-games and advertising. Its basic icono-
graphy – spaceships, alien monsters, robots and super-weapons, Triffids
and Daleks and E.T. – sometimes seems as quaint and hackneyed as the

brooding castles, haunted suits of armour and white-clad maidens of the traditional Gothic novel. Yet those brooding castles and the like are still with us after more than 200 years, and there is no reason to believe that the imagery and obsessions of science-fiction writers will not last just as long.

Of course, there is a great deal more to sf than the joys of spacecraft, aliens and blaster-guns. It's a genre which encompasses many sub-genres – the disaster novel, the alternative-world story, the near-future dystopia, the prehistoric novel, the New-Wave trip to 'inner space', the cyberpunk tale of mean streets and microchips. All these and more, in addition to the space operas and planetary romances which have given sf its best-known media image. Moreover, many of the social and political concerns of recent decades, from banning the bomb to protecting the environment, from controls over the abuse of computers to laws which regulate surrogate motherhood and bioengineered microbes, from the dismantling of the arms race to the mitigation of the greenhouse effect, could well have been taken from an agenda drawn up by sf writers.

Just as the Gothic romance influenced the nineteenth-century realistic novel, so sf has infected late twentieth-century 'high literature', the most serious fiction of the day, with its images, settings and emotional concerns. Here in Britain, literary novelists such as Martin Amis, Julian Barnes and Ian McEwan almost routinely set their fictions in the future and create characters who agonize about the fate of the planet. There are countless parallels in the contemporary fiction of the United States and elsewhere. Very rarely are these high-minded novels described as science fiction, but it's plain that their authors have caught the sf bug. For decades, sf writers and their fans have referred to the 'mainstream', meaning the great body of realistic, everyday fiction out there – everything which is not sf. But there now exists a large 'slipstream' (to use the sf writer Bruce Sterling's *bon mot*), a body of writing which is neither sf nor mainstream in the traditional senses. The fact that it exists is a considerable tribute to the creative efforts of modern science-fiction writers.

All of these developments, in politics and literature and the not-so-simple facts of everyday life, are certain to intensify as we approach and enter the new millennium. More and more, we are living in science fiction's world. But that, except by implication, is not the subject of this book.

The following immodest guide to science-fiction books contains short evaluative entries, with star-ratings, which deal with about 3000 sf titles. Although the star-ratings (or asterisks – the more the better) depend on my own judgement (and that of my esteemed helper, Ken Brown), I have often quoted brief statements by other critics in order to provide the reader with a better sense of a given book's value. I have also attempted to guide readers to sequels and related titles, and to film versions.

My intention was to provide as complete a coverage of the sf field as possible, and to include mention not only of novels but of short-story collections by single authors as well as anthologies by various hands. Nevertheless, the works mentioned here represent only a fraction of the total number of sf books published since the label 'science fiction' was invented by the American pulp-magazine editors of 1929 – or, more exactly, since sf-category book publishing got under way in the 1940s. I do hope that all the most significant English-language titles are covered, together with an adequate sampling of the less significant, but representative, material. However, I must explain what has been deliberately excluded, and why.

1) *Fantasy.* Science fiction and fantasy overlap to an enormous degree, and exact boundaries between the genres are extremely difficult to draw. All the same, many of us feel that we can recognize examples of each when we see them. This guide would have been unwieldy, to say the least, if I had attempted to cover fantasy as well as sf – even in cases where examples of both forms have been created by the same writers. Therefore I have been fairly strict in my exclusion of anything which seems to me to be fantasy (although I hope that my feeling for the term 'sf' is generous enough to please most tastes). Thus, there are entries for Poul Anderson's sf novels *Brain Wave* and *Tau Zero*, but no entries for his *The Broken Sword* or *The Merman's Children* – clearly fantasies, both. By the same token, there are entries for most of the works of Arthur C. Clarke and Robert A. Heinlein, but no entries at all for the books of those great fantasists Mervyn Peake and J. R. R. Tolkien.

2) *Children's fiction.* Numerous science-fiction novels have been written and published specifically for younger readers, but only a very small number of them are annotated here. I felt we had to include the 'juveniles' of Robert Heinlein, since they have been widely enjoyed by adults. There is also some mention of children's books by Captain W. E. Johns, Andre Norton and one or two others, because my collaborator

Ken Brown and I thought we could permit ourselves the occasional small idiosyncratic indulgence. But the vast bulk of sf for kids has been omitted. Again, it would have made this volume unwieldy to attempt to cover such a huge field with any rigour.

3) *Non-English-language sf.* Only a light scattering of foreign-language titles are mentioned here. Obviously, it would have been absurd to omit the works of Jules Verne and to make no mention of such present-day masters of sf as Stanislaw Lem and the Strugatsky brothers. However, I had neither the time nor the competence to delve deeply into the riches of sf written in languages other than English. Although it's probably still true to say that *most* of the sf ever produced has been created by British and American authors (mainly the latter), there is an ever-growing quantity of the stuff being written in French, German, Japanese, Russian, Spanish and the other major languages of the world. Even in China, where sf has regularly been discouraged as a bourgeois pollutant, there seems to be an immense appetite for this kind of fiction.

4) *Scientific romances and 'slipstream' fiction.* Again, there is only a scattering of entries for the older form of sf which used to be known as scientific romance. Wells is represented here, naturally, as are Olaf Stapledon and Aldous Huxley, but many of the long-out-of-print and largely-forgotten practitioners of the form, from George Griffith in the 1890s to John Gloag in the 1930s, are not included. (I urge interested readers to seek out Brian Stableford's excellent book on the subject of the British scientific romance, mentioned in the bibliographical note which follows this introduction.) Nor have I included many works by the 'slipstream' novelists of the present day – which is to say, the 'non-sf' writers of quasi-sf works such as John Barth's *Giles Goat-Boy* or Don DeLillo's *White Noise* (to pick two American examples).

5) *Sf published prior to 1970 and not reprinted since.* At one point, it was my intention to try to include mention of *every* English-language adult sf book first published, or reprinted, during the 1970s and 80s. It soon became apparent that this was a nigh-impossible task. Nevertheless, the emphasis is still very much on those books which have been in print during the past twenty years. Hence I have not attempted to map the more ephemeral paperback sf publishing of the 1950s and 60s – all those early Panther Books, Badger Books, Ace Doubles and the like (though a few of them may have crept in). For that matter, nor was I able to venture very far into the murkier realms of the 1970s downmarket scene: as a result, there are few mentions here of the Toronto-published

Laser Books, or the London-published Robert Hale hardcovers which were once churned out so copiously for the library trade.

6) *The lesser works of lesser sf writers.* I endeavoured to include mention of all sf books by the 'big names' of modern science fiction – Aldiss and Asimov, Ballard and Clarke, Dick and Heinlein, Simak and Sturgeon, and so on – but when it came to certain authors of the second and third ranks, especially the more prolific ones, I had to rest content with a selection of their best-known and most characteristic works. Perhaps it's invidious to name names at this point, but I had neither the time nor the space to delve deeply into the *oeuvres* of such minor but hard-working British authors as Kenneth Bulmer and E. C. Tubb or even, for that matter, the worthy John Brunner (in fact, the latter is represented by many books, even if the coverage is far from exhaustive). No doubt, the works of a few very minor authors (and some of the newer people) have been missed altogether, and for this I apologize: ideally, I would have liked everybody to be in here somewhere.

7) *Novelizations and 'spin-off' fiction.* The 1980s equivalents of the bottom-of-the-barrel pulp novels of previous decades are the innumerable novelizations of movie scripts and other forms of 'spin-off' fiction which take their cues from films and TV shows. These have become ever more common since the long boom in celluloid and videotape sf began with the immense success of George Lucas's *Star Wars* in 1977. For the most part, such novelizations have not been included here, though I have made mention of a few of the more interesting ones – especially when they have been done by writers of note, from Theodore Sturgeon to Orson Scott Card. But I have entirely excluded all the 'Star Trek' novels, the 'Doctor Who' books, and much other second-hand (and generally third-rate) sf of a like sort.

Despite all these caveats, there are some 3000 books listed in this volume, including (I trust) all the masterpieces – and quite a few of the stinkers. In a future edition, I'd dearly love to expand the coverage to include not only newly-published books but also many more of the minor works of yesteryear, plus more anthologies, more children's books, more foreign-language novels and more borderline or 'slip-stream' works.

But this represents a beginning: it is, to my knowledge, the first reference volume on such a scale which deals with science fiction on a book-by-book basis rather than according to the more usual author-by-author arrangement. Those science-fiction readers who frequently forget an author's name may find it particularly useful: if they trace a favourite title, they may then use the index to discover what else a given author has written. Others, who are already well aware of the writers they admire, may want to consult this book to find out more about the titles they have not yet read. It may also serve to alert readers of every kind to new authors, new books, that they might relish. If so, I wish them all happy (and thought-provoking) future reading.

David Pringle
Brighton, 1990

Bibliography and Acknowledgements

This book would have been impossible to compile without the help of several individuals and many published sources of information. Ken Brown was my primary helper, and approximately a fifth of the entries herein were first drafted by him – including many (but not all) of those which deal with the works of Piers Anthony, Ben Bova, Marion Zimmer Bradley, F. M. Busby, Orson Scott Card, C. J. Cherryh, Edmund Cooper, Gordon R. Dickson, Robert L. Forward, Alan Dean Foster, Mark Geston, Joe Haldeman, Frank Herbert, W. E. Johns, R. A. Lafferty, Murray Leinster, Barry Longyear, Charles Eric Maine, Julian May, Anne McCaffrey, Larry Niven, H. Beam Piper, Jerry Pournelle, Rudy Rucker, Fred Saberhagen, James H. Schmitz, Jack Vance and Colin Wilson, among others. Ken was my 'active' collaborator, and his wide reading and enthusiasm for all types of sf certainly helped to compensate for many of my own blind spots.

Two of my favourite sf critics, John Clute and Brian Stableford, very kindly gave me permission to ransack all their essays, reviews and other writings on science fiction, and to take brief quotations from them as I saw fit. They had no hand in the authorship of this book, and are certainly not responsible for any of its shortcomings, but I leaned heavily on their published judgements. Where I have quoted from these two critics in the entries that follow I have simply given their names: the original sources of their comments were widely scattered. Messrs Clute and Stableford were, in a very real sense, my 'passive' collaborators, and I thank them warmly.

More generally, thanks are also due to all those critics who have contributed over the years to *Foundation: The Review of Science Fiction*, particularly during the period when I edited the journal (1980

to 1986, plus a couple of years prior to that when I was Reviews Editor).
They include Malcolm Edwards, Gregory Feeley, Colin Greenland, Roz
Kaveney, David Langford, Tom Shippey, Ian Watson and many others
whose views have influenced me over a long period of time. *Foundation*
is now edited by Edward James and published three times a year by the
Science Fiction Foundation, Polytechnic of East London, Longbridge
Road, Dagenham RM8 2AS, United Kingdom.

Another periodical has been crucially important to me, and that is of
course *Interzone*, currently Britain's only regular magazine devoted to
the publication of new sf short stories. I was one of the founding editors
of *Interzone* in 1982, and since 1988 I have been its sole owner and
publisher. It has moved from quarterly to bimonthly publication and it
may well be on a monthly schedule by the time this book appears. In
addition to its fiction, it has carried many book reviews – by Mary
Gentle, Paul McAuley, Lee Montgomerie, Simon Ounsley and others –
and, again, I have quoted from these in the entries which follow. My
thanks to everybody concerned. *Interzone* is available through news-
agents and bookshops, and may be ordered from 124 Osborne Road,
Brighton BN1 6LU, UK.

Among other British publications, I have found *Vector: The Critical
Journal of the British Science Fiction Association*, and its companion
magazine *Paperback Inferno*, to be invaluable sources of reviews. *Vector*
is currently edited by Boyd Parkinson and Kev McVeigh, and *Paperback
Inferno* by Andy Sawyer. (The contact address for the BSFA is: Joanne
Raine, Membership Secretary, British SF Association, 33 Thornville
Road, Hartlepool, Cleveland TS26 8EW.) Among the reviewers for both
periodicals, I am particularly indebted to K. V. Bailey, David V. Barrett,
Paul Brazier, Judith Hanna, L. J. Hurst, Paul Kincaid, Joseph Nicholas
and Maureen Porter.

Several American magazines were also useful sources of information.
Chief among these is *Locus: The Newspaper of the Science Fiction
Field*, edited by Charles N. Brown, Locus Publications, PO Box 13305,
Oakland, CA 94661, USA. Newer journals which carry weighty reviews
are *The New York Review of Science Fiction*, edited by Kathryn Cramer,
David Hartwell *et al*, Dragon Press, PO Box 78, Pleasantville, NY 10570,
USA; and *Science Fiction Eye*, edited by Stephen P. Brown and Daniel J.
Steffan, PO Box 43244, Washington, DC 20010–9244, USA. Almost as
useful, but sadly now defunct, was *Fantasy Review*, edited by Robert A.
Collins. The last-named is now co-editor (with Robert Latham) of a new

yearly book, *Science Fiction & Fantasy Book Review Annual* (published by Meckler), and I found the first volume of this very helpful.

Other books which proved to be essential sources of information were the wonderful *Encyclopedia of Science Fiction*, edited by Peter Nicholls and John Clute (Granada, 1979); the almost-as-wonderful *Anatomy of Wonder: A Critical Guide to Science Fiction*, edited by Neil Barron (3rd edition, Bowker, 1987); and the only-slightly-less-than-wonderful (despite its famous errors) *Twentieth-Century Science-Fiction Writers*, edited by Curtis C. Smith (St James Press, 1986). Oh, and a little one which came in just as I was finishing work on this volume, and which turned out to be better than I had expected: *Bloomsbury Good Reading Guide to Science Fiction and Fantasy* by 'M. H. Zool' (Bloomsbury, 1989).

When it comes to general criticism of the field, there are many worthy contenders, but three fairly recent and widely differing books on science fiction which I can recommend are *Strokes: Essays and Reviews 1966–1986* by John Clute (Serconia Press, 1988); *In the Chinks of the World Machine: Feminism and Science Fiction* by Sarah Lefanu (Women's Press, 1988); and *Scientific Romance in Britain 1890–1950* by Brian Stableford (Fourth Estate, 1985).

Lastly, those who care to read further may be interested in seeking out my own earlier books *Science Fiction: The 100 Best Novels* (Xanadu, 1985) and *Modern Fantasy: The Hundred Best Novels* (Grafton, 1988). The first of these deals in slightly greater depth with (you guessed it) one hundred of the sf books which have gained some of the highest star-ratings in the present volume. The second is a companion book which attempts to grapple with a somewhat wider range of fantastic fiction.

A Note on How This Book is Arranged

Entries are arranged alphabetically by title. Each entry takes the following form: *title*; *date of first book publication* (in brackets); *star rating* (on a scale of 0–4 asterisks); *classification* (novel, collection or anthology); *author's name*; and *author's nationality* (in brackets). These are followed by the body of the entry, which normally consists of just two or three sentences of brief description and evaluation. Sequels or other related works are listed at the end of each entry, as appropriate. (These are sometimes preceded by brief details of film versions, where such exist.) If the title of a sequel or related work is followed by a date of publication (in brackets), then there is no separate entry for the title in question. If, however, there is no date following a title, then it may be assumed that there is a separate entry for the item at the appropriate alphabetical point elsewhere in this book.

I have made mention of pseudonymous authors' true names in only a few cases, where they seem to be of particular interest for one reason or another. Thus, I have not stated that 'Piers Anthony' is really Piers Anthony Dillingham Jacob, since the latter version of the name has gained no fame elsewhere; but I *have* indicated that 'Richard Cowper' is Colin Middleton Murry, since the author has written non-sf books under the latter name (and it's also pleasant to be able to indicate by this means that he is his famous father's son). Similarly, I have not bothered to inform the world that 'Hal Clement' is really Harry Clement Stubbs; but I *have* indicated that 'James Tiptree Jr.' was really Alice Sheldon, on the basis that the author's sex is a fact worth knowing (and also because she wrote a few stories under a version of her real name).

In addition to the main entries, there are two types of cross-reference – *See* references and *See under* references. The first of these types refers to variant titles for the same book; the second is used primarily to denote the 'parent' novels of sequels or series-works or otherwise related books. All science-fiction books which are described or mentioned herein are indexed by author at the rear of the volume. The index also lists variant titles.

I have attempted to keep abbreviations and jargon terms to a minimum. The short-form *sf* is of course used in lieu of 'science fiction'. As in my previous book, *Imaginary People*, I use the abbreviation *dir.* to mean 'directed by' when referring to film versions of the books discussed. I also use the special term *fix-up* (as in 'fix-up novel') to denote books which consist of closely-linked short stories or novellas often cemented together with new interstitial material. This last term was coined by the sf writer A. E. van Vogt and later popularized by the critic John Clute (see *The Encyclopedia of Science Fiction*, edited by Nicholls and Clute). The similar-sounding *clean-up* (as in 'clean-up collection') is sometimes used to describe those barrel-scraping volumes which bring together the hitherto uncollected shorter works of an author for the sake of completeness and often irrespective of merit.

A few items of specifically science-fictional terminology are scattered liberally throughout the entries. These include such well-known terms as *space opera*, which has been used for decades by analogy with 'horse opera' or 'soap opera' and surely requires no explanation here; *alternative world* (which I prefer to the widely-accepted 'alternate world'), used to indicate an imaginary setting in a time-line which has diverged from our common history; and *planetary romance*, which indicates a romantic adventure story set on a colourful alien planet, usually involving an element of swordplay (or equivalent).

Some recurrent terms, such as *utopia* and its opposite, *dystopia*, are by now part of the common critical language. Others which may require brief explanation here include *hard sf*, which indicates the sort of science fiction that takes its science, usually physics and astronomy, very seriously indeed; *New Wave*, which refers to the arty, avant-garde and frequently experimental sf of the late 1960s and early 1970s (by analogy with the *nouvelle vague* of French cinema); and *cyberpunk*, a term alleged to have been coined by the editor Gardner Dozois to indicate a new, supposedly streetwise, hard-edged form of sf, mainly concerned with computers and information technology, which arose in the early 1980s. (Cyberpunk could be said to represent an ideal marriage of hard sf and New Wave – or at least so its proponents might claim).

Finally, a word on the star-ratings, the little asterisks which some readers may see as the most interesting feature of this volume, but which I must urge should not be taken *too* seriously. As in *Halliwell's Film Guide* and other reference works devoted to movies, the little stars are awarded to each book on a scale of nought to four. A no-star rating is meant to indicate that a book is very bad; whereas a four-star rating is evidence of exceedingly high merit. The one-, two- and three-star ratings are intended to indicate the shadings in between the extremes. These ratings have been arrived at by myself, with assistance from Ken Brown, and obviously reflect personal tastes (as well as the tastes of critics we respect). We are fallible, and it may be that some readers (and authors!) will be offended by our seemingly off-the-cuff judgements. Lapses of taste are inevitable when one attempts to play the asterisk game across such a wide field. Nevertheless the game is fun to play, and readers who take it in the right spirit may at least enjoy disagreeing with us.

A–Z of Science Fiction Books

A

A for Andromeda (1962) ★★ Novel by Fred Hoyle and John Elliot (UK), based on their successful TV serial (1961). A message received by radio telescope from the direction of the Andromeda galaxy contains a blueprint for the making of a beautiful female android. 'Andromeda' is duly brought to life, and subsequently poses a threat to the world. Good scientific detail in a hokum plot. Sequel: *Andromeda Breakthrough* (1964).

A for Anything (1959) ★★ Novel by Damon Knight (USA), originally published as *The People Maker*. Problems with a matter-duplication device. 'An uneasy adventure developed from the premise of a brilliant short story' – Brian Stableford.

Abandonati (1988) ★★ Novel by Garry Kilworth (UK). The homeless people of the city streets realize that they have been abandoned in the literal sense: all the rich folk have mysteriously left the planet. A small group of down-and-outs embark on a quest for the answer to it all. 'A funny, tender, hopeful tale, not without considerable charm ... a neat short-story idea just about stretched to novel length' – Paul McAuley, *Interzone*.

Abominable Earthman, The (Pohl): see under *Case Against Tomorrow, The*.

Abyss, The (1989) ★★ Novel by Orson Scott Card (USA), based on a screenplay by James Cameron. An effective undersea mystery involving the crew of an up-to-date drilling rig and an abyssal alien presence. In his afterword, Card makes great play of the fact that this is not a mere 'novelization', but a novel which genuinely complements the movie (1989; dir. James Cameron). It is in fact a superior example of its type, more faithful to its filmic original than most.

Aces Abroad (Martin): see under *Wild Cards*.

Aces High (Martin): see under *Wild Cards*.

Across the Sea of Suns (1984) ★★ Novel by Gregory Benford (USA), sequel to *In the Ocean of Night*. Nigel Walmsley, scientist hero of the earlier book, travels to the stars, where he discovers signs of a menacing machine civilization. Reliable hard scientific detail, though the 'literary' effects are sometimes tiresome. Quasi-sequel: *Great Sky River*.

Across the Zodiac: The Story of a Wrecked Record (1880) ★★ Novel by Percy Greg (UK). A man flies to Mars by means of an anti-gravity engine, and there he finds a polygamous, communistic society. It reads very stodgily today, but this is a notable early interplanetary romance, first published as a Victorian 'three-decker' (the 1978 paperback edition is abridged).

Adam Link – Robot (1965) ★ Collection by Eando Binder (USA). Connected stories about a pair of intelligent robots called Adam and Eve Link. Creaky stuff from the magazines of the late 1930s – fairly sophisticated for its time, but now of historical interest only. Binder is said to have influenced Isaac Asimov.

Adulthood Rites (Butler): see under *Dawn: Xenogenesis 1*.

Adventures of Alyx, The (1983) ★★★ Collection by Joanna Russ (USA). Contains the enjoyable novel *Picnic on Paradise* plus three short stories featuring the same heroine (Alyx) – and an excellent novelette, 'The Second Inquisition', which is only vaguely related to the other material. Alyx makes for a tough, adventurous central character, but the modes in which she is presented here (ranging from fantasy to time-travel sf) seem too disparate for the collection to cohere as a book.

Adventures of Una Persson and Catherine Cornelius in the Twentieth Century: A Romance, The (1976) ★★ Novel by Michael Moorcock (UK). Catherine is Jerry Cornelius's sister (see *The Cornelius Chronicles*) and Una is a temporal adventuress from the many worlds of Oswald Bastable (see *The Warlord of the Air*). It's another hop-skip-and-jump through the alternative time-lines, the pasts and futures, of the Moorcockian 'multiverse'. Impeccably written, but very baffling – and rather dirty.

Adversary, The (May): see under *The Many-Coloured Land*.

Affair with Genius, An (1969) ★★ Collection by Joseph Green (USA), published in the UK only. Competent sf stories, mainly reprinted from British magazines and anthologies (although the author is American). Most of them involve encounters with well-depicted aliens.

After Doomsday (1962) ★★ Novel by Poul Anderson (USA). Earthmen return from an extended voyage to discover that their home planet has been devastated, so they set out in pursuit of the alien marauders. Exciting space adventure.

After London, or Wild England (1885) ★★★ Novel by Richard Jefferies (UK). A catastrophe has utterly obliterated London. Jefferies, a naturalist, describes the imaginary woodland scene beautifully. The setting is all, the simple pastoral tale negligible, though William Morris stated: 'absurd hopes curled round my heart as I read it'.

After Many a Summer (1939) ★★★ Novel by Aldous Huxley (UK/USA). A Californian millionaire aims to discover the secret of longevity. Eventually he traces an 18th-century man who still lives – but this apparent immortality has been bought at a dreadful price. 'A novel with a brain, and if it nags at human stupidity when it should be getting on with the story – well, we accept the didacticism as an outflowing of the author's concern with the state of the modern world' – Anthony Burgess, *Ninety-Nine Novels*. Published in the USA under the fuller title of *After Many a Summer Dies the Swan*.

After the Fact (Saberhagen): see under *Pyramids*.

After the Rain (1958) ★★ Novel by John Bowen (UK), based on his stage play. The world is flooded by perpetual rains, and a group of survivors aboard a raft bicker endlessly. A tart fable, very much a playwright's novel, which is not typical of most British post-disaster tales.

After the Zap (1987) ★ Novel by Michael Armstrong (USA). A bomb which was designed to knock out electronic communications has also affected people's minds, wiping most of their memories. 'Ambles along in a hippie-Taoist manner,

improvising people and plot as it goes. Basically, it's a dull trip' – Joe Sanders, *SF & Fantasy Book Review Annual 1988*.

After Things Fell Apart (1970) ★★ Novel by Ron Goulart (USA). In the near future, America has become Balkanized into petty fiefdoms and tribal groupings. Against this multifarious backdrop the detective hero pursues a band of female assassins. Fast-moving nonsense, perhaps a bit too wacky to really count as satire: one of Goulart's best, though.

After World's End (Williamson): see under *Legion of Time, The*.

After Worlds Collide (Wylie and Balmer): see under *When Worlds Collide*.

Again, Dangerous Visions (1972) ★★★★Anthology edited by Harlan Ellison (USA), follow-up to the same editor's *Dangerous Visions*. An excellent selection of over 40 original stories, including some of the best sf ever published – Ursula Le Guin's 'The Word for World is Forest', 'When it Changed' by Joanna Russ, Richard Lupoff's 'With the Bentfin Boomer Boys on Little Old New Alabama', 'The Milk of Paradise', by James Tiptree Jr.; plus work from Kate Wilhelm, Josephine Saxton, M. John Harrison; a hilarious parody of Lovecraft, Jane Austen and eight other authors by James Blish and Judith Lawrence; and a lot else. It also has some real rubbish. Its true strength is that some of the stories we think are turkeys are reckoned amongst the greats by people we respect, and vice versa.

Against Infinity (1983) ★★★ Novel by Gregory Benford (USA). On Ganymede a boy and his older companion hunt a mysterious alien entity. It's a conscious sf transcription of William Faulkner's 'The Bear' and, as such, it's a bit laboured in style. Nevertheless, it contains much good scientific detail and some striking touches of imagination.

Against the Fall of Night (Clarke): see *City and the Stars, The*.

Age, an (1967) ★★★ Novel by Brian W. Aldiss (UK). A 'psychosexual thriller' about time-travel by mental means. Contains some startling imagery: at one point the hero materializes under Queen Victoria's skirts. Other scenes range from the future to the prehistoric past. It's a helter-skelter plot, always witty and enjoyable, if sometimes confusing. Later editions retitled *Cryptozoic!*

Ages of Miracles (Brunner): see *Day of the Star Cities, The*.

Age of the Pussyfoot, The (1969) ★★ Novel by Frederik Pohl (USA), first serialized in 1966. A gentleman of our time, frozen as a 'corpsicle', awakes in the 26th century to find a society run efficiently and humanely by computers. Rebels are out to destroy this benign system, though, and our hero gets drawn in to the machinations. Lightweight Pohl, humorously written.

Agent of Byzantium (1986) ★★★ Collection by Harry Turtledove (USA). Linked short stories set in an alternative Roman Empire where Mohammed became a Christian and consequently Byzantium survived beyond the Middle Ages in the West. The hero is a 'Magistrianos' (a cross between a secret agent and a government messenger) from Constantinople who gets involved in various escapades: he is present at the discovery of gunpowder, the telescope, vaccination and so on. Great fun and written from genuine knowledge of the Roman Empire.

Agent of the Terran Empire (Anderson): see under *We Claim These Stars*.

Agent of Vega (1960) ★★★ Collection by James H. Schmitz (USA). Exuberant space opera: psionic secret agents (children, drunks, alien princesses and wee grannies) repeatedly save unsuspecting humanity from unimaginable horrors. Far better written than most of its kind.

Agonies of Time, The (1989) Fix-up novel by Ravan Christchild (USA/UK), originally serialized in 1977. Three loosely connected stories concerned with sex, entropy, drugs, airships and other obsessions of the early 70s, recounted in an overblown mock-Edwardian style. Clearly a pastiche of Michael Moorcock's 'Jerry Cornelius' books (see *The Cornelius Chronicles*).

Airs of Earth (1963) ★★★ Collection by Brian W. Aldiss (UK). Eight stories, including the superb dying-fall piece 'Old Hundredth' (1960) and the lyrically inventive 'A Kind of Artistry' (1962). Another version of this collection, with differing contents, was published in the USA (and later in Britain) as *Starswarm*.

Alas, Babylon (1959) ★★★ Novel by Pat Frank (USA). Atomic war comes to Florida. There are grim moments, but the survivors have a rare old time hunting and fishing and rediscovering the wilderness. Frank's book may trivialize the terrible reality of a nuclear 'exchange', but it makes for an entertaining fiction. A long-time steady-seller in the USA, it is little known in Britain.

Albion! Albion! (1974) ★★ Novel by Dick Morland (Reginald Hill, UK). Football hooligans have taken over the country, in this rather nasty and scarcely credible vision of a violent future Britain. 'Heavy-handed but enjoyably sharp-tongued' – John Clute.

Alchemical Marriage of Alistair Crompton, The (1978) ★★ Novel by Robert Sheckley (USA). Crompton, an employee of 'Psychosmell, Inc', sets out to piece together his own shattered personality, bits of which seem to be littered all over the galaxy. An episodic comic romp in the author's familiar vein: very good in parts. 'Once again sends his Jack Lemmon hero up all the familiar down escalators' – J. G. Ballard, *New Statesman*. Published in the USA as *Crompton Divided*.

Alchemy and Academe (1970) ★★★ Anthology edited by Anne McCaffrey (USA/Ireland). The title,

chosen in deliberate contrast to 'Sword and Sorcery', accurately describes the themes of these original stories by Delany, Lafferty, Russ and others. Robert Silverberg's 'Ringing the Changes' is straight sf; James Blish's punning 'More Light' includes a play which parodies the works of H. P. Lovecraft and Marion Zimmer Bradley; and John Updike's poem 'Dance of the Solids' is fiction about science, if not actually science fiction.

Aldair in Albion (1976) ★★ Novel by Neal Barrett Jr. (USA), first of a series. Humans have abandoned the Earth to scientifically-enhanced animals. The hero of this and the subsequent novels is a pig-man who wanders the world in search of clues as to humanity's whereabouts. An enjoyable future picaresque. Sequels, all on much the same level of inventiveness: *Aldair, Master of Ships* (1977), *Aldair, Across the Misty Sea* (1980) and *Aldair: The Legion of Beasts* (1982).

Alexandrian Ring, The (1987) ★★ Novel by William R. Forstchen (USA), first in his 'Gamester Wars' series. All-out war has been forbidden in the populated galaxy of the future, so humans and aliens fight limited wargames on certain planets. Time-travel enables them to recruit military help from the past, and this first tale features Alexander the Great, whisked from his deathbed in Babylon. Trivial, but a well-executed example of its type.

Alicia II (1978) ★★ Novel by Robert Thurston (USA). On a future Earth, old minds are regularly transferred to young bodies, but this is an injustice (to say the least) for the 'rejects' (i.e. those whose bodies are so used). An overlong and perhaps over-ambitious first novel. 'There are passages of really plodding writing ... But if you can read the first four parts without being put off, you're sure to relish the end' – Colin Greenland, *Foundation*.

Alien (1979) ★★ Novelization by Alan Dean Foster (USA) of the film-script by Dan O'Bannon and others. The book of the movie (1979; dir. Ridley Scott): the crew of a space freighter are picked off one by one by a very horrible creature which they are tricked into picking up. The gory details are almost as gory as in the movie; the intrigue and betrayal are more prominent. Sequel: *Aliens* (1986).

Alien, The (1968) ★★ Novel by L. P. Davies (UK). Mystery thriller about a hospitalized man who may or may not be an extraterrestrial. Deceptive stuff. Republished in paperback as *The Groundstar Conspiracy*, and filmed under the latter title (1972; dir. Lamont Johnson).

Alien, The (1951) ★★ Novel by Raymond F. Jones (USA). An extra-terrestrial is found in suspended animation out among the asteroids. Scientists proceed to revive this being, but there are well-grounded fears that it may turn out to be dangerous. Enjoyable old-fashioned sf with a space-operatic background.

Alien Accounts (1982) ★★★ Collection by John Sladek (USA). Eight stories of futuristic 'office life', including the novelettes 'Masterson and the Clerks' (1967) and 'The Communicants' (1969). In these spiky, gleaming pieces Sladek makes the most sinister bureaucratic realities seem strangely lyrical, but above all he keeps you laughing. A book which every nine-to-five person should enjoy.

Alien Art (1973) ★★ Novel by Gordon R. Dickson (USA). A hillbilly, trying to transport a heavy statue made by an Arcadian Swamp Otter to the spaceport to sell it to an art dealer, gets mixed up in a row about the proposed mortgage of the planet in order to raise capital for industrial development. This one is probably intended for juvenile readers.

Alien Debt, The (1984) ★ Novel by F. M. Busby (USA), sequel to *Star Rebel* and others. Starfaring hero Bran Tregare meets Rissa Kerguelen, Busby's main series heroine. More routine space adventure.

Alien Embassy (1977) ★★ Novel by Ian Watson (UK). A tale of future human transcendence, effectively told from the point of view of a young African woman. Less 'hard-edged' and political than Watson's three preceding novels, it marked his turn towards the mystical and quasi-religious themes which would be characteristic of such later books as *Miracle Visitors* and *God's World*.

Alien from Arcturus (Dickson): see *Arcturus Landing*.

Alien Heat, An (Moorcock): see *Dancers at the End of Time, The.*

Alien Light, An (1988) ★★ Novel by Nancy Kress (USA). Three groups of humans have reverted to a warlike cultural level on a planet where their ancestors were marooned. Baffled, group-minded aliens arrive to study these isolated specimens, to find out just what makes humanity tick. Needless to say, the humans prove their 'orneriness'. A serious-minded but ultimately predictable book.

Alien Upstairs, The (1983) ★★ Novel by Pamela Sargent (USA). An alien, living surreptitiously in a boarding house, changes the lives of several unhappy people who inhabit a near-future world where meaningful employment is scarce. A quite effective adaptation to sf of a hoary idea from stage and screen.

Alien Way, The (1965) ★★ Novel by Gordon R. Dickson (USA). An ecologist uses his studies of bears in the Canadian Rockies to help Earth understand the alien Ruml, a species whose marsupial reproduction and inhuman sense of honour make them incomprehensible to most Earthmen. Nicely handled: one of the best novels from Dickson's early period.

Alien Within, The (1989) ★ Novel by Johanna M. Bolton (USA). A female space captain seeks those who destroyed her home planet. This not unpromising first novel is a standard-variety space adventure. 'At times, the pacing is a little off and events are a little too predictable and derivative' – Carolyn Cushman, *Locus.*

Aliens (1977) ★★★ Anthology edited by Ben Bova (USA). Three well-known novellas on meetings with aliens: 'First Contact' by Murray Leinster, Clifford Simak's 'Big Front Yard' and 'A Meeting with Medusa' by Arthur C. Clarke. All excellent in their differing ways.

Aliens (Foster): see under *Alien.*

Aliens Among Us, The (1969) ★★ Collection by James White (UK). Seven plainly-written sf tales, including the memorable anti-war story 'Tableau' and one of the medical-interest Sector General pieces, 'Countercharm' (see under *Hospital Station*). Other, similar, collections by this always proficient author include *Monsters and Medics* (1977) and *Futures Past* (1982).

Aliens for Neighbours (Simak): see *Worlds of Clifford Simak, The.*

Aliens 4 (1959) ★★★ Collection by Theodore Sturgeon (USA). Four long stories: 'Killdozer!' (1944), 'Cactus Dance' (1954), 'The Comedian's Children' (1958) and 'The [Widget], the [Wadget], and Boff' (1955). The first and best of these, about a giant bulldozer which runs amok when it is invaded by an alien intelligence, has been filmed as a TV movie, *Killdozer* (1974; dir. Jerry London). See also the UK-published collection *The Joyous Invasions*, which overlaps considerably.

All About Strange Monsters of the Recent Past (Waldrop): see under *Strange Things in Close-Up.*

All Flesh is Grass (1965) ★★★ Novel by Clifford D. Simak (USA). An invisible alien force-field surrounds a small midwestern town, and the narrator unravels its mysteries. A charming sf pastoral in Simak's best vein. Not exactly mind-stretching, but most enjoyable reading for those who like their sf to be gentle and predictable.

All Fools' Day (1966) ★★ Novel by Edmund Cooper (UK). Triggered by solar storms, an epidemic of suicides sweeps the world. Only creative artists and fanatics of various kinds seem to be immune. A bleakly entertaining catastrophe story. 'The description of this world of chaos, with its bizarre religious sects and "mental hygiene" groups – among them one called Death-Wish Anonymous – is cleverly and wittily done' – J. G. Ballard, *Guardian*.

All Judgement Fled (1968) ★★ Novel by James White (UK). A vast alien star vessel turns up in the solar system, and is investigated by a small team of astronauts from Earth. It turns out to be full of strange beasties. 'White constructs his extraterrestrial setting with care, yet there is a certain flatness about the narrative' – James Cawthorn, *New Worlds*.

All My Sins Remembered (1977) ★★ Fix-up novel by Joe Haldeman (USA). The hero is programmed with the memories of other men and sent to distant planets to impersonate them for political reasons. A short and depressing book by a competent writer.

All the Colors of Darkness (1963) ★ Novel by Lloyd Biggle Jr. (USA). First of a series about the interstellar adventures of Jan Darzek, a man who has been recruited from an ostracized Earth to serve as a sort of galactic supreme councillor. Sequels (all much of a muchness): *Watchers of the Dark* (1966), *This Darkening Universe* (1975), *Silence is Deadly* (1977) and *The Whirligig of Time* (1979).

All the Myriad Ways (1971) ★★ Collection of stories and scientific speculations by Larry Niven (USA). Excellent early Niven: includes 'Inconstant Moon' and 'Becalmed in Hell' (both frequently anthologized elsewhere), 'Theory and Practice of Time Travel' (which gives the philosophical grounding to the story 'Rotating Cylinders and the Possibility of Global Causality Violation', published in *Convergent Series*) and 'Man of Steel, Woman of Kleenex' where we learn the truth about Superman's sex-life.

All the Sounds of Fear (Ellison): see *Alone Against Tomorrow*.

All the Traps of Earth, and Other Stories (1962) ★★★ Collection by Clifford D. Simak (USA). Nine limpidly written and very enjoyable stories. High-spots include the horrific 'Good Night, Mr James' (1951) and the sentimental 'The Sitters' (1958). Split into two volumes for British publication: *All the Traps of Earth* (four stories) and *The Night of the Puddly* (five stories).

All Times Possible (1974) ★★ Novel by Gordon Eklund (USA). A hero of the American labour movement during the 1920s and 30s discovers that there is a plurality of possible time-lines, and although he may succeed in bringing about a revolution in *his*, he will not succeed in changing ours. A highly unusual American sf novel, in that it deals with left-wing politics: unfortunately, it fails to do much with its subject matter.

Allan and the Ice Gods (1927) ★★ Novel by H. Rider Haggard (UK). The author of *King Solomon's Mines* (1885) produced something close to sf in this, the last of his many 'Allan Quatermain' tales. Allan plunges backwards through time by means of a drug, and enters the body of an ice-age man. Rudyard Kipling helped Haggard to plot the ensuing adventure story. (See also *Hadon of Ancient Opar* by Philip José Farmer.)

Alley God, The (1962) ★★ Collection by Philip José Farmer (USA). Three inventive novellas, of which 'The Alley Man' (1959) is the most memorable: a Neanderthal man, the last representative of his species, is discovered living in present-day America (a theme which had already been used by L. Sprague de Camp in 'The Gnarly Man' – see *The Best of L. Sprague de Camp*).

Alone Against Tomorrow (1971) ★★★ Collection by Harlan Ellison (USA). A large gathering of the author's most popular shorts of the 1950s and 60s. Notable for the powerful 'All the Sounds of Fear'; also for '"Repent, Harlequin!" Said the Ticktockman' (Hugo and Nebula

award-winner, 1966; it seems to be included in almost all Ellison's collections); and 'I Have No Mouth and I Must Scream', in which the last man on Earth is kept unhappily alive by an intelligent computer, as revenge on the entire human race. Published in the UK in two volumes, entitled *All The Sounds of Fear* and *The Time of the Eye*.

Alqua Dreams (1986) ★★ Novel by Rachel Pollack (USA/Netherlands). A human fieldworker for a spacefaring company needs to strike a deal with an alien society obsessed with death, living in a ruined city they neither understand nor built, to obtain access to an intelligent mineral. A readable, if serious, novel which gets bogged down in the immense unlikeliness of some of the scientific speculation.

Altar on Asconel, The (Brunner): see under *Interstellar Empire*.

Alteration, The (1976) ★★★★ Novel by Kingsley Amis (UK). An alternative time-stream in which England remains a Roman Catholic nation: the choirboy hero must preserve his testicles from the threat of castration. An exceedingly well-told tale, mingling adventure, comedy and many satirical touches. John W. Campbell award winner, 1977.

Altered States (1978) ★★★ Novel by Paddy Chayefsky (USA). Would-be explorations of higher mental states, via sensory deprivation, cause a man to regress to the primitive. More thoughtful and convincing than its movie adaptation, this is a first novel by a famous TV-and-film script-writer. Filmed in 1980 (dir. Ken Russell; apparently Chayefsky was thoroughly displeased by the movie).

Alternate Asimovs, The (1985) ★ Collection by Isaac Asimov (USA). A barrel-scraping exercise from the Asimov industry. Contains 'the original unpublished versions' of some of his best-known 1950s sf. But these alternative texts are not necessarily better than the official versions.

Alternating Currents (1956) ★★★ Collection by Frederik Pohl (USA). Bright, well-honed sf and fantasy stories, mainly satirical in tone. Includes such Pohl classics as 'The Tunnel Under the World' and 'What to Do Until the Analyst Comes'. This clever author's first collection. It's representative of the sort of work which led Kingsley Amis to claim (in his *New Maps of Hell*, 1960) that Pohl was probably the best of the currently-active sf writers.

Alternities (1988) ★★ Novel by Michael P. Kube-McDowell (USA). A parallel-worlds story which posits a number of different present-day Earths, all varying slightly but crucially in the details of their political and social history. There are gates between these worlds, giving plenty of scope to a fast-moving thrillerish plot – with some interesting speculations thrown in.

Always Coming Home (1985) ★★★ Novel by Ursula K. Le Guin (USA). A richly detailed account of a gentle, post-industrial utopia in a Northern California of the indeterminate future. The central narrative, of a young woman's development, is hedged around by vast quantities of supplementary material – folk tales, poems, plays, maps, charts, appendices and glossary. All in all, an astonishing feat of the imagination, which the author herself calls 'an archaeology of the future'. It's Le Guin's magnum opus, but it may be daunting to some readers. The book contains numerous illustrations (by Margaret Chodos) and the first edition came with a cassette tape (music by Todd Barton), making it something of a multi-media experience.

Amazon Planet (Reynolds): see under *Planetary Agent X*.

Ambassador of Progress (1984) ★ Novel by Walter Jon Williams (USA). The female ambassador of a spacefaring civilization becomes embroiled in a civil war on a backward, semi-feudal planet. Dullish adventure by a competent writer. Williams's first sf novel (he's done better since).

Ambient (1987) ★★ Novel by Jack Womack (USA). A competent near-future horror story of corruption in corporate high places – written in the Cyberpunk idiom. Womack's first novel. Quasi-sequel: *Terraplane*.

Ambulance Ship (White): see under *Hospital Station*.

Ambush of Shadows, An (Williams): see under *Breaking of Northwall, The*.

Among the Dead, and Other Events Leading to the Apocalypse (1973) ★★★ Collection by Edward Bryant (USA). Seventeen blackly poetic tales in the American New-Wave vein of the late 1960s. Standouts include 'Their Thousandth Season' and the title story. Bryant's first book. 'Brilliant' – John Clute.

Amsirs and the Iron Thorn, The (1967) ★★ Novel by Algis Budrys (USA). A young man who has grown up on violent Mars returns to peaceful Earth, where he encounters various machine intelligences. Intelligently written, but not one of Budrys's more memorable works. Published in the UK as *The Iron Thorn*.

Amtrak Wars, The (1983–89) ★★ Series by Patrick Tilley (UK). Consists of five novels: *Cloud Warrior* (1983), *First Family* (1985), *Iron Master* (1987), *Blood River* (1988) and *Death-Bringer* (1989). North America in the 30th century is inhabited by wandering tribes of mystics, the 'Mutes', who are being wiped out by the militaristic 'Federation' based in Texas which regards itself as the legitimate successor to the old USA. The plot concerns the wanderings of some lost Federation soldiers among the tribes and the 'Iron Masters' (Chinese and Japanese merchant lords in the North-East). After a lot of violence, they learn something of tolerance.

Anachronisms (1988) ★★ Novel by Christopher Hinz (USA). Mystery aboard a stellar exploration craft which salvages some alien remains from a far planet. An efficient sf chiller. 'Keeps cranking up the tension. At the climax, however, the writing slips, as language fails to encompass events involving space, time, psionics, and cybernetics' – Faren Miller, *Locus*.

Analogue Men (Knight): see *Hell's Pavement*.

Anarchaos (Clark): see under *Tomorrow's Crimes*.

Anarchistic Colossus, The (1977) ★ Novel by A. E. van Vogt (Canada/ USA). Aliens pose a threat to an automated future world which has no government. Latter-day van Vogt – as complicated, as kinetic and as downright daft as ever.

Anasazi (1980) ★ Fix-up novel by Dean Ing (USA). Four long short stories sharing a common academic background, a plot about exploited children and a couple of continuing characters. The title story concerns a rather disgusting alien invasion of a pueblo village in New Mexico.

Ancient Light (1987) ★★ Novel by Mary Gentle (UK), a quasi-sequel to *Golden Witchbreed*. Return to the planet Orthe, and a search for the long-lost technology of an ancient alien race (the 'Golden Witchbreed' of the previous novel). It's a very long and dense book, but undeniably ambitious. 'All the characters are swept on helplessly by the inexorable tide of history as Gentle pitilessly deconstructs her fantasy, her writing gaining in strength and vividness even as she abandons plotlines in midair' – Paul McAuley, *Interzone*.

Ancient of Days (1985) ★★★ Novel by Michael Bishop (USA), an expansion of the novella 'Her Habiline Husband' (1983). An ancient hominid turns up in present-day America, and the narrator's wife falls for him. An amusing and intelligent story on an unlikely theme (which had already been touched on, much more briefly, by L. Sprague de Camp and Philip José Farmer – see *The Best of L. Sprague de Camp* and *The Alley God*).

... And All the Stars a Stage (1971) ★ Novel by James Blish (USA). Uneasy expansion of a 1960 novella in which a group of exiles quest through space for a new planetary home. Not representative of this author's best. 'A grim and jumbled melange [which] starts off as a juvenile and closes, to coin a term, as a *senile*' – John Clute.

And Chaos Died (1970) ★★★ Novel by Joanna Russ (USA). A man who is shipwrecked on a colonized planet learns the alien skill of telepathy. He finds that this cuts him off from his own kind, nearly inducing insanity when he tries to return to Earth. A vivid and stylish psi story which is very different in feel to most earlier treatments of the subject.

And Having Writ (1978) ★★★ Novel by Donald R. Bensen (USA). Alternative-world tale in which aliens arrive in Teddy Roosevelt's America and end up changing the century's history. The style is a little old-fashioned, but the plot is cleverly conceived and there are some good jokes. Thomas Edison, H. G. Wells and others appear as characters. 'Bensen has for years been a major sf editor. Who knew he had such a novel in him? ... Highly, and delightedly, recommended' – Algis Budrys, *Washington Post*.

And So Ends the World (1961) ★ Novel by Richard Pape (UK). A psychic medium in Norwich learns from his dreams that the Russian space programme will stir up cosmic forces which threaten the human race. Despite the space shuttles controlled by miniature computers, this is more like a rather stilted version of Charles Williams's spiritual thrillers than mainline sf.

And Some Were Human (1948) ★★ Collection by Lester del Rey (USA). A dozen sf and fantasy stories from the magazines, including the famous (but sentimentally sexist) 'Helen O'Loy' (1938), about a female robot; and the fairly prescient novella 'Nerves' (1942), about a nuclear accident (this was later expanded into a full-length novel). An important collection in its day, but now dated. Paperback reprints drop some stories.

And Strange at Ecbatan the Trees (1976) ★★ Novel by Michael Bishop (USA). Exotic adventure amidst the genetically-engineered societies of a far planet in the future. This weirdly-titled novel has been renamed *Beneath the Shattered Moons* for reprints.

Andover and the Android (Wilhelm): see *Mile-Long Spaceship, The*.

Andromeda Breakthrough (Hoyle & Elliot): see under *A for Andromeda*.

Andromeda Gun (1974) Novel by John Boyd (USA). Uneasy mixture of sf and western, in which an alien called G-7 visits 19th-century America and attempts to take over the body of a rugged gunslinger. It learns the error of its ways. An obnoxiously preachy and fundamentally daft story.

Andromeda Strain, The (1969) ★★ Novel by Michael Crichton (USA). A returning space capsule unleashes an alien virus on the Earth, in this successful thriller which masquerades as a slice of near-future realism. Crichton's first sf novel. Filmed in 1971 (dir. Robert Wise).

Angel Station (1989) ★★ Novel by Walter Jon Williams (USA). A space adventure in which brother and sister go searching for black holes and encounter an alien race. 'Starts off as a cyberpunk space opera, tries to become a novel of characters, and then goes off to become a first contact and political intrigue thriller. In the end, the book never finds a focus' – Tom Whitmore, *Locus*.

Angel with the Sword (1985) ★★ Novel by C. J. Cherryh (USA). The detailed construction of the city Merovin – a baroque port sinking into a saltmarsh on a planet abandoned generations earlier by the Union civilization familiar from Cherryh's other sf novels – is far more compelling than the story of a young barge girl who repeatedly rescues an aristocrat from assassination.

Angels and Spaceships (1954) ★★★ Collection by Fredric Brown (USA). Seventeen sf and fantasy stories of the 1940s, many of them short-shorts. Among the longer stories, 'The Waveries' is outstanding: about a world plunged back into the horse-and-buggy stage of technology because of the sudden demise of electricity, it is a poignant and beautifully-turned piece.

Angry Candy (1988) ★★ Collection by Harlan Ellison (USA). The by-now very familiar mix from Ellison: 17 sf, fantasy and unclassifiable stories, some old, most relatively recent, here presented with the usual surrounding baggage of agonized non-fiction – apologetic, exhortatory, always confessional. Notable stories include 'The Region Between' and 'Paladin of the Lost Hour'.

Annals of Klepsis, The (1983) ★★ Novel by R. A. Lafferty (USA). A historian who aims to write the history of the planet Klepsis discovers that time has yet to begin and that the universe as he knows it is an illusion. Well, probably. Like all works by Lafferty, it's a very tall tale indeed.

Annals of the Heechee, The (1987) ★★ Novel by Frederik Pohl (USA), sequel to *Heechee Rendezvous*. By now the hero exists only as a simulated mind stored in a computer. Humans and their alien benefactors, the Heechee, attempt to unravel the mystery of the energy-beings known as the Assassins. 'Read as a novel of ideas (and what ideas!), *Annals of the Heechee* works well enough, as long as you don't expect answers to many of the questions it raises; but it is more a tail-piece than a satisfactory conclusion to the grand, ambitious themes of the Heechee series' – Paul McAuley, *Interzone*.

Annihilation Factor (1972) ★★ Novel by Barrington J. Bayley (UK), expanded from his short story 'The Patch' (1964). A galactic empire is torn by war, as a mysterious Patch in space devours whole planets. Enjoyable space operatics by one of the few writers of the 1970s (and since) who can still carry this sort of thing off with bravura.

Anome, The (1971) ★★★ Novel by Jack Vance (USA). The continent of Shant on the planet Durdane is divided into 62 cantons whose diverse laws are enforced by the Anome or Faceless Man whose motto is 'He who breaks the law, dies'. Mur escapes from the harsh Chilite sect to become Etzwane the musician, dedicated to tracking down the Anome. Excellent silly fun. Republished as *The Faceless Man*. Sequel: *The Brave Free Men*.

Another End (1971) ★ Novel by Vincent King (UK). The human race is extinct, but one long-lived survivor scours the galaxy in his wonderful spacecraft, searching for other intelligent life. He falls in with a sympathetic energy-being and battles an evil clone-master. A fairly forgettable space opera by a minor British author.

Another Kind (1955) ★★ Collection by Chad Oliver (USA). Seven proficient sf stories by this anthropologist author. Most of them, such as 'Rite of Passage', make imaginative use of his academic speciality. Oliver's first collection, it was highly praised in its day.

Antares Dawn (1986) ★★ Novel by Michael McCollum (USA). A planetary colony is cut off from the rest of civilization for a century when the star Antares explodes, breaking the folds in space-time which allow spacecraft to travel faster than light. Then a wrecked ship appears unexpectedly with evidence that the human race is at war with the alien Ryall. An expedition is set up to enter the remnants of the Antares supernova to re-establish contact with Earth. A likeable, if unoriginal, space adventure. Sequel: *Antares Passage* (1987).

Anthem (1938) ★ Novel by Ayn Rand (USSR/USA). In a future egalitarian state, where all individuality is ruthlessly suppressed, a brilliant scientist escapes to the woods with his loved one and there rediscovers the concept of selfhood. An infamous little book, with which this eccentric preacher launched her lifelong campaign in favour of an extreme right-wing form of rugged individualism. (Her many non-fiction works include one entitled *The Virtues of Selfishness: A New*

Concept of Egoism). A later novel of Rand's which also verges on sf is the long and turgid *Atlas Shrugged* (1957).

Anthonology (1985) ★ Collection by Piers Anthony (USA). Very variable stories: best is 'In the Barn', a meat-is-murder shocker from Harlan Ellison's anthology *Again, Dangerous Visions* (1972); the rest of the volume is notable mainly for a couple of mildly erotic shorts and the author's self-important introductions.

Antibodies (1988) ★ Novel by David J. Skal (USA). In the near future, people who are desperate for new, improved bodies (like the dieters and body-builders of today) aim to have themselves turned into cyborgs. A bitter tale, full of nasty characters.

Antic Earth (Charbonneau): see *Down to Earth*.

Anti-Grav Unlimited (1987) Novel by Duncan Long (USA). A scientist invents a sort of Cavorite (anti-gravity substance) and converts a truck to fly to the moon. The trip itself is dismissed in less than 300 words, beginning, 'We did little during our flight ...' and almost void of description. An unpromising first novel.

Antinomy (1980) ★★ Collection by Spider Robinson (USA/Canada). Eleven sf and fantasy stories, well hedged about with introductions, afterwords, jokes, cartoons, songs and general chit-chat. The author tries so hard to be cute and lovable

that it may make some readers want to strangle him. That said, the best of these stories, mainly collected from *Analog* and *Galaxy* magazines of the late 1970s, are quite passable entertainment.

Anvil of Time, The (Silverberg): see *Hawksbill Station*.

Anvil of the Heart (1983) ★★ Novel by Bruce T. Holmes (USA). The old, short-lived human race is being replaced by genetically-engineered superfolk. But the inevitable rebellion breaks out. A competent work by a little-known writer.

Anywhen (1970) ★★ Collection by James Blish (USA). Goodish sf stories from the 1950s and 60s, including such notably thoughtful items as 'A Style in Treason' and 'A Dusk of Idols'.

Anything Box, The (1965) ★★ Collection by Zenna Henderson (USA). Fey stories which are mainly about children and telepathy. 'Her children are shy dreamers who live in a shadowy zone between illusion and reality' – J. G. Ballard, *Guardian*.

Ape and Essence (1948) ★★★ Novel by Aldous Huxley (UK/USA). An sf tale within a realistic framework: a Hollywood scriptwriter imagines life in California after a nuclear war, where society has degenerated into bestiality. Bleak and timely.

Apeman, Spaceman (1968) ★★★ Anthology edited by Leon E. Stover and Harry Harrison (USA). Stories supposedly of interest to first-year anthropology students, with a foreword by Carleton S. Coon and 50 pages of notes by Stover. Includes some parodies of anthropology (for example 'Body Ritual Among the Nacirema' by Horace M. Miner), such well-known sf as Clarke's 'Nine Billion Names of God' and H. Beam Piper's 'Omnilingual', plus a lot that will be less familiar: an epistolary version of the story of Horatius by Brigadier General William C. Hall; Kit Reed's 'The Wait', which transplants an old Babylonian custom to small-town Georgia; a couple of factual essays; some poems and a 'Peanuts' cartoon.

Apocalypses (1977) ★★ Collection by R. A. Lafferty (USA). Contains two novellas: 'Where Have You Been, Sandaliotis?' and 'The Three Armageddons of Enniscorthy Sweeny'. Unclassifiable stuff from this author who virtually demands to be read in an Irish accent. 'Marvellous fabulations by a writer sui generis' – Brian Stableford.

Appointment at Bloodstar (Goldin): see under *Imperial Stars, The*.

Approaching Oblivion: Road Signs on the Treadmill Toward Tomorrow (1974) ★★ Collection by Harlan Ellison (USA). Typically top-of-the-voice tales – some sf, some fantasy – by one of the field's leading *performers*. Highlights include 'Kiss of Fire' and 'Catman'. 'However lurid, the stories have a relentless imaginative drive' – J. G. Ballard, *New Statesman*.

Aquiliad, The (1983) ★★ Novel by Somtow Sucharitkul (Thailand/USA). In an alternative time-line, the Romans have conquered the New World, merging their culture with that of the Amerindians. All may be changed, though, by the actions of an ill-disposed time-traveller. There's much wit and many unusual plot twists in this enjoyable tale. Sequel: *Aquila and the Iron Horse* (1988; as by 'S. P. Somtow', which is now the author's preferred byline).

Araminta Station (1988) ★★ Novel by Jack Vance (USA), first in his 'Cadwal Chronicles' series. There is more of interest in the descriptions of diverse cultures and religions than in the central story of young people growing up in the constricted society of a tiny research station on a world otherwise supposed to be barred to human settlement.

Arc of the Dream (1986) ★★ Novel by A. A. Attanasio (USA). Weird tale of an alien from another dimension which appears in our world as a coin. It must be returned to its exact point of entry if a devastating explosion is to be averted. 'Running the gamut of New Age narcissism and hippy psychobabble before expiring on a note of purple romanticism, it's not actually as dreadful as it could be. Attanasio's prose style, thick and gluey and verging on the dyslexic as it often is, nevertheless throws up splendid images' – Paul McAuley, *Interzone*.

Archivist, The (1989) ★★★ Novel by Gill Alderman (UK). A male urchin has exotic adventures in the neo-feudal, caste-ridden and matriarchal culture of a far planet, in this large-scale, atmospheric novel by an interesting new writer. 'The long trek on horseback, the grand sights, the back streets, the cliffs and tower-tops. [Alderman] has a steady eye and an even steadier hand ... In the foreground she works the sensual, impressionistic landscape of personal relations' – Colin Greenland, *The Face*.

Archon (1987) ★★ Novel by Stuart Gordon (UK), first of the 'Watchers' trilogy. Interesting fantasy (with sf and horror elements) involving magical communication between 20th-century London and 13th-century Provence. It gets a little lost in pro-Cathar mysticism, but displays a better use of historical material than in most medieval fantasies. Sequel: *The Hidden World*.

Arcturus Landing (1956) ★★ Novel by Gordon R. Dickson (USA), originally published as *Alien from Arcturus*. Earth has to prove itself capable of joining the Galactic Federation; various political groups try to sabotage our efforts, while some rather cuddly non-violent aliens try to help us in. Dickson's first novel.

Argonaut Affair, The (Hawke): see under *Ivanhoe Gambit, The*.

Armageddon! (Pournelle & Carr): see under *There Will Be War*.

Armageddon Blues, The (1988) ★★ Novel by Daniel Keys Moran (USA). A woman from a primitive post-holocaust future travels back in time,

in an endeavour to save the world from its ghastly fate. She arrives in the 1960s, where she meets a freakishly talented individual. A disjointed, far-fetched, but promising first novel.

Armageddon Rag, The (1983) ★★ Novel by George R. R. Martin (USA). A forgotten rock band seals a pact with the devil to change the world and make a comeback. A combination of horror and 1960s nostalgia set against a mildly science-fictional background.

Around the Moon (1870) ★★ Novel by Jules Verne (France), sequel to *From the Earth to the Moon*. Verne's 19th-century astronauts do not actually land on the moon but circumnavigate it before returning to a splashdown in the Pacific Ocean. Certainly a stunning example of fiction as prophecy, but marred by stodgy scientific detail and galumphing humour.

Arrive at Easterwine (1971) ★★★ Novel by R. A. Lafferty (USA). Easterwine is 'the great central terminal, though a terminal should rather be at the end than in the centre. People arrive at it constantly, in horsedrawn droshkies (really, I have seen them), on foot and on horseback, in stagecoach and train, in motor and by metro, by ship and by sky-ship, by wire and by wireless, by celestial omnibus' – which is as good a summary as any of this book, which purports to be the autobiography of Epiktistes, a 'Ktistec machine', or robot, who'd rather work with angels than humans.

Lafferty's customary blend of humour and lunatic philosophizing in one of his best novels.

Arrows of Eros (Stewart): see under *Shape of Sex to Come, The*.

Arslan (1976) ★★★★ Novel by M. J. Engh (USA). Arslan, the ruthless young leader of Turkestan, seizes power from the bureaucrats of the Soviet Union. Then, using their laser weapons, he forces the whole world to submit to him. A magnetic but deranged personality, like a combined Alexander the Great and Pol Pot, he sets out to free the Earth from the pressures of human civilization ... This extraordinary first novel is narrated by two male inhabitants of an American midwest town, where Arslan sets up his temporary headquarters. Lyrical, brilliantly characterized, shocking, psychologically astute – it is a masterpiece. Published in Britain as *A Wind from Bukhara*.

Arthur C. Clarke's Venus Prime (Preuss): see under *Breaking Strain*.

Artifact (1985) ★★ Novel by Gregory Benford (USA). A very strange object is found in an archaeological dig in near-future Greece (a common idea in mid-1980s sf novels: see Scholz and Harcourt's *Palimpsests* and Waldrop's *Them Bones* for other examples). The bulk of the book is political thriller stuff, pitched to appeal to a mainstream audience – but it does have a scientific mystery at its heart. Skilfully done, if not typical Benford.

Artificial Kid, The (1980) ★★ Novel by Bruce Sterling (USA). Adventures in the Decriminalized Zone of the planet Reverie. Hip, colourful, interplanetary sf: an early work by a writer who has gone on to become a mainstay of the Cyberpunk movement. 'Brash, witty and – surprisingly in the first-person account of a punk celebrity "combat artist" – proficient in its dramatization of such matters as alien ecologies, planet-sculpting, and biological transfiguration' – Gregory Feeley, *Foundation*.

Artificial Things (1987) ★★★ Collection by Karen Joy Fowler (USA). Sf and fantasy stories of remarkable sensitivity – its author's first book. 'Gradually one becomes aware of a performative glamour investing each tale with an urgency that seems increasingly humane' – John Clute.

Ascendancies (1980) ★★ Novel by D. G. Compton (UK). Energy-giving 'manna' falls from the sky. The world's economy booms, but then people start disappearing mysteriously ... 'A tight, vivid psychological investigation, mundane fiction against an improbable futuristic backdrop' – Colin Greenland, *Foundation*.

Ascension (Grant): see under *Shadow of Alpha, The*.

Ascension Factor, The (1988) ★★ Novel by Frank Herbert and Bill Ransom (USA). Pandora, the world featured in *The Lazarus Effect* and *The Jesus Incident*, is ruled by the tyrannical Director. Avata, the intelligent colonial seaweed that controls the seas, takes action through human agents. The narrative can be confusing at times, as many of the details are not explained for those who haven't read the previous books. This is Herbert's last work, published posthumously.

Ashes and Stars (1977) ★ Novel by George Zebrowski (USA), prequel to *The Omega Point*. An intergalactic tale of revenge, its flowery language holding out a promise of more than the rather standard space-opera plot can deliver.

Assault on the Gods (1977) Novel by Stephen Goldin (USA). A backward world is run by godlike computers, but liberation is at hand ... 'A classic idiot plot, in which a megalomaniac entrepreneur tries to conquer an entire planet, equipped only with an unarmed merchant ship' – Peter Garratt, *Interzone*.

Assignment in Eternity (1953) ★★ Collection by Robert A. Heinlein (USA). Four long stories – 'Gulf' (1949), 'Elsewhen' (1941), 'Lost Legacy' (1941) and 'Jerry Was a Man' (1947) – of which the first, a powerful fast-moving tale about a superman, is the most notable. In the UK the book was initially published in two volumes, *Assignment in Eternity* and *Lost Legacy*.

Assignment in Nowhere (Laumer): see under *Worlds of the Imperium*.

Astounding: The John W. Campbell Memorial Anthology (1974) ★ Anthology edited by Harry Harrison (USA/Ireland). A tribute to the best-loved American sf magazine of the 1940s: writers of the calibre of Anderson, Asimov, Clement, Dickson, Simak and Sturgeon contribute new stories of the type they might once have written for editor John W. Campbell. Unfortunately, it's very patchy. 'These stories and symptomatic gags all share a low creative heat (and slight air of embarrassment) that seems to demonstrate how difficult it is for an author to recreate themes and modes he has cast off or outgrown' – John Clute.

Astounding-Analog Reader, The (1972–73) ★★★ Two-volume anthology edited by Harry Harrison (USA) and Brian Aldiss (UK). A huge selection of 36 stories, intended to be representative of the magazine *Astounding* (later *Analog*) throughout the period of John W. Campbell's editorship (1937–71). The pieces are arranged chronologically, with the original blurbs to support them. Some are extremely well known – Heinlein's 'By His Bootstraps', Asimov's 'Nightfall', and so on – but others, although classics of their type, are more obscure: 'The Yellow Pill' by Rog Phillips, 'Noise Level' by Raymond F. Jones, 'Grandpa' by James H. Schmitz, etc. 'The legend of *Astounding's* importance is borne out by these stories, even though few of them would be judged by the conventional standards of literary criticism as being of the absolutely first rank' – Peter Nicholls, *Foundation*.

Asutra, The (1974) ★★ Novel by Jack Vance (USA), sequel to *The Brave Free Men* and last of the 'Durdane' trilogy. Etzwane carries the war against the Asutra into the continent of Caraz. A colourful adventure.

At the Earth's Core (1922) ★★★ Novel by Edgar Rice Burroughs (USA), first in his 'Pellucidar' series. Rip-roaring adventure story set in a subterranean world of dinosaurs and cave people. Dodgy science (sanctioned by John Cleves Symmes's crackpot theories of a hollow Earth with polar openings) but good fun. Sequels include *Pellucidar* (1923), *Tanar of Pellucidar* (1929), *Tarzan at the Earth's Core* (1930), etc.

At the Eye of the Ocean (1980) ★★ Novel by Hilbert Schenck (USA). Mystical revelations may be experienced at certain times and places off Cape Cod by those who are able to read the currents, the winds and the contours of the sea floor. The author's copious knowledge of oceanography gives an sf edge to what is essentially a fantasy story. Schenck's first novel (although he had been contributing sporadically to the sf magazines since the early 1950s).

At the Narrow Passage (1973) ★ Novel by Richard C. Meredith (USA). First of the 'Timeliner' trilogy. Mercenaries are hired by aliens to cross into alternate worlds and change history – in this case to help the British Empire prevent the Germans from developing the atom bomb in a Great War still being fought in 1972. Sequel: *No Brother, No Friend*.

At the Seventh Level (Elgin): see under *Communipath Worlds*.

At Winter's End (1988) ★★ Novel by Robert Silverberg (USA). On a devastated Earth of the far future a tribe of hairy near-humans try to reclaim their world. An unoriginal story, done with feeling. 'A sense of brooding horror at the strange creatures which inhabit the new world and, later, a growing cosmic perspective on the lives and deaths of civilizations are skilfully evoked' – Simon Ounsley, *Interzone*. Sequel: *The Queen of Springtime* (1989, published in the USA as *The New Springtime*).

Atlas Shrugged (Rand): see under *Anthem*.

Atrocity Exhibition, The (1970) ★★★ Collection by J. G. Ballard (UK). Fifteen avant-garde pieces which may or may not constitute a marginally-sf 'novel'. Ranging from 'You and Me and the Continuum' (1966) to 'Tolerances of the Human Face' (1969), they deal with the contemporary media landscape, a world of motorways, multi-storey car parks, TV screens and glossy advertising. The central character's name changes from segment to segment, but he appears to be a doctor who is suffering from a mental breakdown. The author's most difficult book, but some readers regard it as his masterpiece. Published in America as *Love and Napalm: Export USA*.

Augmented Agent and Other Stories, The (1986) ★★ Collection by Jack Vance (USA), edited by Steven Owen Godersky. Eight inventive and frequently humorous stories from the 1950s and 60s. The title piece was first published under the title of 'I-C-a-BEM' (1961). Another, similar, clean-up collection by this old master is *The Dark Side of the Moon* (also 1986).

Aurelia (1982) ★★ Novel by R. A. Lafferty (USA). A very beautiful, very young and very well-educated girl (up to turning the world upside down, or at any rate inside out) comes to the people of Earth (or somewhere very similar) to preach to them or rule them, or help them, or something. A novel which shows the author's usual preoccupations even more strongly than most. One for readers who already know and love Lafferty.

Autumn Angels (1975) ★ Novel by Arthur Byron Cover (USA). In the very distant future humans have the power to take on different shapes and to do all manner of self-indulgent things. There's copious reference to pop-culture icons in this moderately engaging first novel by a writer who does not seem to have followed through with anything substantial. Sequel: *An East Wind Coming*.

Autumn Land and Other Stories, The (1990) ★★ Posthumous collection by Clifford D. Simak (USA), edited and introduced by Francis Lyall. Six reasonably engaging tales, ranging from the creaky time-piece 'Rule 18' (1938) to the sentimental but atmospheric title story (1971). The best-known item, 'Jackpot' (1956), also appears in the earlier *The Worlds of Clifford Simak* (published in Britain as *Aliens for Neighbours*).

Avatar, The (1978) ★★ Novel by Poul Anderson (USA). The hero escapes from a dull, bureaucratic Earth and searches the universe for the Others, an alien race which has evolved towards unimaginable powers. Strong on libertarian sentiment, this is a big, ambitious novel which does not quite come off.

Aventine (1982) ★ Collection by Lee Killough (USA). Love and murder amid the mood-furniture, singing crystals, living statues, and so on. These stories, all set in the same futuristic artists' colony, are strongly reminiscent of those in J. G. Ballard's much superior *Vermilion Sands*.

Awakeners, The (1987) ★★ Novel by Sheri S. Tepper (USA). A lengthy romance of life on another planet which is dominated by a great river. It has the feel of heroic fantasy. Published in the USA in two volumes, entitled *Northshore* and *Southshore*.

Away and Beyond (1952) ★★ Collection by A. E. van Vogt (Canada/USA). Nine flamboyantly imaginative sf stories from the author's best period, the 1940s. Contains such old favourites as 'Vault of the Beast' and 'Asylum'. Van Vogt is no prose stylist, but he is perhaps seen to better effect in short works such as these than in his novels, which tend to suffer from slapdash plotting. Another good collection, published in the same year, is *Destination: Universe*.

B

Babel-17 (1966) ★★★ Novel by Samuel R. Delany (USA). An artificial language is being used as an unorthodox weapon of interstellar war, and poet Rydra Wong is the last best hope for the saving of Earth's civilization. A very colourful, inventive space opera. 'Language games and ray guns fuse together in what may be the last possible variant on the old space-fiction themes' – J. G. Ballard, *Guardian*. Nebula award-winner, 1967.

Backdrop of Stars (Harrison): see *SF: Author's Choice.*

Bad Moon Rising (1973) ★★★ Anthology edited by Thomas M. Disch (USA). Seventeen stories and four poems on (broadly defined) political themes. Includes work by Disch, Harlan Ellison, Michael Moorcock, John Sladek, Kate Wilhelm, Gene Wolfe and others. All highly literate; but tales of anomie, powerlessness and dejection set the tone. Later anthologies from Disch, in a not dissimilar vein, include *The New Improved Sun* (1975), *New Constellations* (1976) and *Strangeness* (1977)

– the last two edited in collaboration with Charles Naylor.

Balance of Power (Stableford): see under *Florians, The.*

Ballad of Beta-2, The (1965) ★★ Novel by Samuel R. Delany (USA). The young hero investigates the true meaning of the eponymous ballad, a space-going culture's folk song. This is very much a romantic sf adventure, but it's also the first of Delany's novels to reveal his strong interest in modes of communication – subject matter which has dominated most of his later books.

Ballroom of the Skies (1952) ★★ Novel by John D. MacDonald (USA). It turns out that war and other acts of human irrationality have been caused by deliberate alien meddling – with a long-term motive in mind. An engaging piece of early-50s paranoia by an author who later became celebrated for his crime fiction.

Bander Snatch (1979) Novel by Kevin O'Donnell Jr. (USA). The eponymous narrator is a telepathic

22nd-century *picaro*. Alas, his desultory adventures, on and off the Earth, are uninteresting and poorly presented. O'Donnell's first novel.

Barbarians of Mars (Moorcock): see under *City of the Beast*.

Barbie Murders and Other Stories, The (1980) ★★ Collection by John Varley (USA). The author's second short-story volume is less impressive than his first (*The Persistence of Vision*) but it contains several sprightly pieces set in the same near-future solar system of biotechnology and shifting sexual identities. A later volume of short fiction by Varley is entitled *Blue Champagne* (1986).

Barefoot in the Head (1969) ★★★ Novel by Brian W. Aldiss (UK). In the aftermath of the Acid-Head War (in which psychedelic drugs have been used as weapons) a young man named Charteris finds himself playing a messianic role. Perhaps the most extreme example of British New-Wave sf, a Sixties vision of a Europe stoned out of its skull – conveyed in sub-Joycean punning style. Not an easy read, but energetic, flavoursome and original.

Barking Dogs (1988) ★ Novel by Terence M. Green (Canada?). A cop equipped with high-tech gear takes on rabid street gangs in Toronto of the year 1999. It's a fast-action, ultra-violent *RoboCop* look-alike.

Barsoom Project, The (Niven & Barnes): see under *Dream Park*.

Battle Circle (1978) Omnibus by Piers Anthony (USA). Three linked novels: *Sos the Rope*, *Var the Stick* and *Neq the Sword*.

Battle of Forever, The (1971) ★ Novel by A. E. van Vogt (Canada/USA). A human adventurer discovers that most of his future world is inhabited by genetically-enhanced beast-men. Of course, as in all of van Vogt's work, it turns out that the hero himself has super-powers.

Battlefield Earth (1982) Novel by L. Ron Hubbard (USA). Galactic goodies-versus-baddies. Extremely long, and very old-fashioned, it has no virtues. 'There is a degree of badness that is not even funny...unremittingly dreadful' – Roz Kaveney, *Foundation*

Beamriders! (1989) Novel by Martin Caidin (USA). A secret American project develops space travel by laser beam, against a background of international terrorism, outdated Cold-War shenanigans, etc. Crassly written, in the author's worst best-seller-ese – another yawn-provoking adventure in a hard-nosed, militaristic vein. (The UK edition drops the exclamation mark from the title.)

Beast That Shouted Love at the Heart of the World, The (1969) ★★★ Collection by Harlan Ellison (USA). Fifteen varied tales (12 in the UK edition), all thoroughly typical of this energetic, egocentric, buttonholing author. The powerful title piece won a Hugo award (1969). Also notable are 'Shattered Like a Glass Goblin' and 'A Boy and His Dog' (Nebula award-winner, 1969). The latter was filmed in 1975 (dir. L. Q. Jones), and the movie won a Hugo award as 'best dramatic presentation' (1976). The long-promised expansion of 'A Boy and His Dog' into the novel *Blood's a Rover* has yet to come to fruition.

Beastchild (1970) ★★ Novel by Dean R. Koontz (USA). Vicious aliens slaughter human beings, who they regard as unworthy to join the galactic community; however, one soldier befriends a human boy. A moderately touching parable on the theme of xenophobia.

Beasts (1976) ★★ Novel by John Crowley (USA). America has fallen apart, and genetically-engineered beastmen and others resist its reintegration. Perhaps the least of Crowley's novels, but well worth reading: he's a fine writer.

Beasts of Antares (Akers): see under *Transit to Scorpio*.

Becoming Alien (1987) ★★ Novel by Rebecca Ore (USA). A boy is whisked away from Earth and tutored by aliens, in this satisfactory first book by a writer who has an interest in imaginary anthropology. 'Ore creates very original aliens ... and a very individual human being to interact with them' – Debbie Notkin, *Locus*. Sequel: *Being Alien* (1989).

Bedlam Planet (1968) ★★ Novel by John Brunner (UK). A nicely detailed tale of human adaptation to the conditions of an alien world. One of the author's more conventional books, but effective as such.

Before Adam (1906) ★★ Novel by Jack London (USA). An enjoyable tale of prehistory – one of the original caveman novels, though Stanley Waterloo's now-forgotten *The Story of Ab* (1897) preceded it.

Before Armageddon: An Anthology of Victorian and Edwardian Imaginative Fiction Published Before 1914 (1975) ★★ Anthology edited by Michael Moorcock (UK). The subtitle describes it fully, and Moorcock's long introduction muses very interestingly on the prehistory of sf in Britain. The most substantial story is Sir George Chesney's 'The Battle of Dorking' (1871), a novella-length piece about a German invasion of England which in some ways prefigures the atmosphere of Wells's *The War of the Worlds*. A most useful collection. Moorcock's follow-up volume is entitled *England Invaded* (1977).

Before the Golden Age: A Science Fiction Anthology of the 1930s (1974) ★★ Anthology edited by Isaac Asimov (USA). Huge selection of twenty-six pulp-magazine stories, with linking autobiographical commentary by Asimov. For those interested in the archaeology of the genre it makes entertaining reading. The tales range from the unspeakably awful 'Awlo of Ulm' by Capt. S. P. Meek (1931) to the energetically imaginative 'Born of the Sun' (1934) by Jack Williamson. The book has been split into four volumes for British paperback publication.

Behind the Walls of Terra (Farmer): see under *Maker of Universes, The*.

Behold the Man (1969) ★★★ Novel by Michael Moorcock (UK), expanded from his Nebula award-winning 1966 magazine story of the same title. The unhappy hero, Karl Glogauer, travels in a womb-like time machine back to the era of Christ. Unfortunately, he finds that Jesus is not quite fitted for his historical role, and so Karl fulfils his own messianic fantasies by taking his place. A powerful and daring idea, which in another age (or another faith) would probably have had its author sentenced to death. Quasi-sequel: *Breakfast in the Ruins*.

Behold the Stars (1965) ★ Novel by Kenneth Bulmer (UK). A routine space-war tale which only succeeds in provoking yawns. 'Over the whole story, as with so many British chronicles of interstellar warfare with aliens, hangs the shadow of World War Two; under each spacesuited chest beats the heart of a Battle of Britain pilot' – James Cawthorn, *New Worlds*.

Being Alien (Ore): see under *Becoming Alien*.

Beloved Son (1978) ★★ Novel by George Turner (Australia). An astronaut returns after decades in space to find a post-disaster world where genetic manipulation and cloning of human beings are now commonplace. He himself is the 'clone-father' of a new generation. A serious book, unfortunately rather grim and turgid, by a writer who had previously published mainstream fiction. Sequels: *Vaneglory* (1981) and *Yesterday's Men* (1983).

Beneath the Shattered Moons (Bishop): see *And Strange at Ecbatan the Trees*.

Berserker (1967) ★★★ Collection by Fred Saberhagen (USA), first in his 'Berserker' series. Eleven stories with connecting material, all set against the background of a galactic invasion by the Berserkers – giant automatic warships dedicated to the destruction of all life. Classic space opera. Some of the material in this volume, such as 'Stone Place' and 'Goodlife', reappears in Saberhagen's later Berserker novels. (For other books in the series see the two entries which follow, plus that for *Brother Berserker*.)

Berserker Wars, The (1981) ★★ Collection by Fred Saberhagen (USA). After the defeat of the Berserkers at Stone Place and the fall of the hero Karlsen, the Beserkers scatter and spread terror on many planets. Taken on their own terms these stories are excellent examples of space opera.

Berserker's Planet (1975) ★ Novel by Fred Saberhagen (USA). One of the all-destroying robots from the author's 'Berserker' series sets itself up as a pagan deity; the result is little more than a series of violent combats. Later books about the Berserkers include *Berserker Man* (1979), *The Ultimate Enemy* (1979), *Earth Descended* (1982), *The Berserker Throne* (1985) and *Berserker: Blue Death* (1985). Another volume, *Berserker Base* (1985), is a shared-world anthology in which most of the material is by writers other than Saberhagen.

Best New SF (Dozois): see *Year's Best SF, First Annual Collection, The.*

Best of All Possible Worlds, The (1980) ★★★ Anthology edited by Spider Robinson (USA). Five sf stories selected by the editor, and five others, not necessarily sf, chosen by the writers of the first five. This leads to a varied group of tales, including Terry Carr's 'Hop-Friend', an extract from William Goldman's *The Princess Bride*, and ending up with 'Our Lady's Juggler' – a rather sentimental medieval story by Anatole France.

Best of Analog, The (1978) ★★★ Anthology edited by Ben Bova (USA). Stories from *Analog* during the period of Bova's editorship of that magazine (1972–78). All readable, especially Joe Haldeman's 'Tricentennial', Alfred Bester's 'The Four Hour Fugue' and Gene Wolfe's 'How I Lost the Second World War and Helped Turn Back the German Invasion'.

Best of Arthur C. Clarke, The (1973) ★★★ Collection by Arthur C. Clarke (UK). This British-published 'best' contains many of the stories one might expect – plus a few that one might not expect, reprinted from fanzines of the late 1930s. It has been divided in two for subsequent paperback reprints. For a roughly equivalent American volume (without the juvenilia) see *The Nine Billion Names of God.*

Best of Avram Davidson, The (1979) ★★ Collection by Avram Davidson (USA), edited by Michael Kurland. A dozen sf and fantasy stories (mainly the latter) by this oddball writer, including such well-known pieces as 'The Golem' and 'The Sources of the Nile'. Despite the title, it's not fully representative.

Best of Barry N. Malzberg, The (1976) ★★ Collection by Barry N. Malzberg (USA). Thirty-eight sf and fantasy pieces, all from the 1970s and a number of them short-shorts. The author specializes in bitterly humorous psychological tales, many of them present-tense and first-person. Some of these have considerable intensity, but most are unlikely to please those readers in search of the standard sf pleasures.

Best of C. L. Moore, The (1975) ★★★ Collection by C. L. Moore (USA), edited and introduced by Lester del Rey. Ten memorable stories from the 1930s and 40s. The earlier pieces, such as 'Shambleau', tend to be fantastic romances in a sword-and-sorcery vein. The later items, notably 'No Woman Born' and 'Vintage Season', are classic sf of a slightly harder-edged type. Catherine Moore was undoubtedly the most talented female sf writer in America prior to the emergence of Leigh Brackett.

Best of C. M. Kornbluth, The (1976) ★★★ Posthumous collection by C. M. Kornbluth (USA), edited and introduced by Frederik Pohl. Excellent, comprehensive volume of 19 darkly inventive stories first published between 1941 and the author's premature death in 1958. It is larger than, and effectively replaces, the earlier British-published volume

Best Science Fiction Stories of C. M. Kornbluth.

Best of Clifford D. Simak, The (1975) ★★★ Collection by Clifford D. Simak (USA), edited by Angus Wells. Ten effective tales (and no overlaps at all with the earlier *Best Science Fiction Stories of Clifford Simak*), plus a pleasantly modest introduction by the author. Standouts include 'A Death in the House' (1959) and 'The Thing in the Stone' (1970), fine examples of the folksy sf fables at which Simak excelled.

Best of Cordwainer Smith, The (1975) ★★★★ Posthumous collection by Cordwainer Smith (Paul Linebarger, USA), edited and introduced by J. J. Pierce. This is the definitive volume of short pieces by this wonderful, whimsical, poetic and occasionally religiose author who created a bizarre universe of the far future which was all his own (he died in 1966). It gathers together the best pieces from earlier collections such as *You Will Never Be the Same* and *Space Lords* (1965). Published in Britain as *The Rediscovery of Man*.

Best of Damon Knight, The (1976) ★★★ Collection by Damon Knight (USA). Varied sf tales ranging from the early 'Not With a Bang' (1949) to the superb 'Masks' (1968). Full of good ideas, well executed – a fine volume by one of the most skilful sf short-story writers of the 1950s and 60s.

Best of Edmond Hamilton, The (1977) ★★ Collection by Edmond Hamilton (USA), edited and introduced by Leigh Brackett. Twenty sf stories drawn from a long career as a magazine writer. They range from the clunky 'The Monster God of Mamurth' (1926) to a relatively sophisticated piece called 'Castaway' (1968). If you can tolerate the primitive prose and characterization of the earlier selections, you'll find some real old beauties here.

Best of Eric Frank Russell, The (1978) ★★★ Posthumous collection by Eric Frank Russell (UK), edited and introduced by Alan Dean Foster. Pleasing tales by this old master of light sf, all taken from his earlier collections (see, for example, *Deep Space, Far Stars* and *Somewhere a Voice*). There are one or two serious pieces here, but it is for his pranksterish sense of fun that Russell is best remembered.

Best of Frank Herbert, The (1975) ★★ Collection by Frank Herbert (USA), edited by Angus Wells. Herbert was never really a short-story writer, so this British-published sampler of his works is inevitably patchy. It has been divided in two for subsequent paperback reprints.

Best of Frederik Pohl, The (1975) ★★★ Collection by Frederik Pohl (USA), introduced by Lester del Rey. Eighteen stories (plus an article on mathematics) from the 1950s and 60s. Inevitably, it contains those brilliant early stories which first made Pohl's reputation as a satirist: 'The Tunnel Under the World' and 'The Midas Plague'; but it also has such later strong pieces as 'Day Million' and 'The Day the Martians Came'. Vintage Pohl, even if most of it is available elsewhere in other forms.

Best of Fredric Brown, The (1977) ★★★ Posthumous collection by Fredric Brown (USA), edited and introduced by Robert Bloch. Brown is best remembered as American sf's wittiest writer of 'short-shorts'. This volume of magazine stories from the 1940s to the 1960s contains a good selection of those brief pieces, but it also has a number of more solid sf tales, such as the classic 'Arena', about an other-worldly duel between a man and an alien. Unfortunately, it does *not* contain Brown's finest single story, 'The Waveries' (see *Angels and Spaceships*).

Best of Fritz Leiber, The (1974) ★★★ Collection by Fritz Leiber (USA). Twenty-two stories by this talented author whose work has ranged widely across the genres of fantasy and sf. The Hugo and Nebula award-winning 'Gonna Roll the Bones' (1967) is an effective horror story. 'Space-Time for Springers' (1958) is a delightful tale about cats. Other powerful pieces, which more closely fit the definition of sf, include 'Coming Attraction' (1950) and 'America the Beautiful' (1970).

Best of Hal Clement, The (1979) ★★ Collection by Hal Clement (USA), edited by Lester del Rey. Mostly 'problem' stories: the characters are faced with a problem they need to solve, and they and the reader have the necessary information. Most typical is 'Dust Rag': astronauts on the moon must prevent electrically charged dust from obscuring their faceplates. In 'A Question of Guilt' an ancient Roman couple can't understand their son's haemophilia.

Best of Henry Kuttner, The (1975) ★★★ Posthumous collection by Henry Kuttner (USA), introduced by Ray Bradbury. Seventeen sf and fantasy tales with a light touch, most of them reprinted from 1940s issues of the sister magazines *Astounding* and *Unknown* (where Kuttner was a major star of the time, often under the pseudonym of Lewis Padgett). Particularly pleasing are 'Mimsy Were the Borogoves' and 'The Twonky'. An earlier, two-volume *Best of Kuttner* was published in Britain in 1965–66, but has been superseded by this book.

Best of Isaac Asimov, The (1973) ★★★ Collection by Isaac Asimov (USA). Twelve solid stories, from 'Marooned off Vesta' (1939) to 'Mirror-Image' (1972). A representative sampling of work by this ever-reliable, liberal-minded entertainer. Standouts include 'Nightfall' (1941) and 'The Dead Past' (1956).

Best of J. G. Ballard, The (1977) ★★★★ Collection by J. G. Ballard (UK). Seventeen excellent stories, ranging from 'The Concentration City' (1957) to 'The Day of Forever' (1966). Each choice has a short introduction by the author. Contains none of the pieces from *Vermilion Sands* or *The Atrocity Exhibition*, and none of Ballard's post-1970 work, but nevertheless it serves as a wonderful sampler of this major writer.

Best of Jack Vance, The (1976) ★★★ Collection by Jack Vance (USA), introduced by Barry Malzberg. Includes the Hugo and Nebula award-winning novella *The Last Castle*, plus five other stories, ranging from 'The Moon Moth' to 'Rumfuddle'. Exotic, stylish, often humorous stuff in Vance's inimitable vein. Although he's rarely written a major book, he's one of American science fiction's originals.

Best of Jack Williamson, The (1978) ★★ Collection by Jack Williamson (USA). Vivid old stories by one of the stalwarts of 1930s pulp sf. It also contains a few pieces from later decades, some of which had already appeared in the author's first two collections, *The Pandora Effect* (1969) and *People Machines* (1971). Williamson has declined as a short-story writer since his heyday of 50 years ago, though he continues to write surprisingly good novels.

Best of James Blish, The (1979) ★★★ Posthumous collection by James Blish (USA), edited and introduced by Robert A. W. Lowndes. A fine selection of this intelligent author's shorter work, which inevitably overlaps in part with the earlier *Best Science Fiction Stories of James Blish*.

Best of John Brunner, The (1988) ★★★ Collection by John Brunner (UK). Varied stories from the whole of Brunner's long career as an sf writer. They range from such accepted classics as 'The Totally Rich' to the comparatively recent 'The Man Who Saw the Thousand-

Year Reich'. Strong on ideas and on moral sensibility.

Best of John Jakes, The (1977) ★★ Collection by John Jakes (USA), edited by Martin Harry Greenberg and Joseph D. Olander. Competent but minor sf and fantasy stories from magazines of the 1950s and 60s. Presumably this collection only exists because of Jakes's latter-day fame as a historical romancer.

Best of John Sladek, The (Sladek): see under *Steam-Driven Boy and Other Strangers, The*.

Best of John W. Campbell, The (1976) ★★★ Posthumous collection by John W. Campbell (USA), edited and introduced by Lester del Rey. Includes well-known stories such as 'Twilight' and 'Cloak of Aesir', most of them from the 1930s and many of them first published under Campbell's pseudonym 'Don A. Stuart'. Dated but still enjoyable. An earlier volume with the same title and broadly similar contents was published in the UK only (1973).

Best of John Wyndham, The (1973) ★★ Posthumous collection by John Wyndham (UK), introduced by Leslie Flood. A dozen stories, ranging from 'The Lost Machine' (1932) to 'The Emptiness of Space' (1960). Many of them have a certain period charm.

Best of Judith Merril, The (1976) ★★★ Collection by Judith Merril (USA/Canada), introduced by Virginia Kidd. Eleven sf stories, ranging from 'That Only a Mother'

(1948) to 'In the Land of Unblind' (1974). A welcome gathering of all-too-rare fiction from this notable author, critic and anthologist who has been largely inactive in sf since she emigrated to Canada about 20 years ago.

Best of Keith Laumer, The (Laumer): see under *Nine by Laumer*.

Best of Kuttner: see under *Best of Henry Kuttner, The*.

Best of L. Sprague de Camp, The (1978) ★★ Collection by L. Sprague de Camp (USA), introduced by Poul Anderson. Fourteen sf and fantasy stories, an article on linguistics and three poems by this veteran writer who is respected both for his knowledge of history and for his sense of humour. Includes such notable items as 'The Gnarly Man' (1939), about a Neanderthal relict, and 'A Gun for Dinosaur' (1956), about big-game hunting in the Cretaceous.

Best of Leigh Brackett, The (1977) ★★★ Collection by Leigh Brackett (USA), edited and introduced by Edmond Hamilton (her husband). Ten lush, romantic, colourful sf/fantasy stories from the 1940s and 50s. Most have interplanetary settings and are in the Edgar Rice Burroughs mode (though much better written).

Best of Lester del Rey, The (del Rey): see under *Robots and Changelings*.

Best of Mack Reynolds, The (1976) ★★ Collection by Mack Reynolds (USA). Twenty-two sf tales from the 1950s to the early 70s. Reynolds was never a major author, nor even a particularly good minor one, but he was interesting. One of the few American sf writers to take a real interest in Marxism, his stories often had economic, social and political themes.

Best of Marion Zimmer Bradley, The (1985) ★★ Collection by Marion Zimmer Bradley (USA), edited by Martin H. Greenberg. Fifteen adventure stories, and a short biographical introduction. Includes early novelettes such as 'Centaurus Changeling' and 'Bird of Prey' which, although less proficient than her later work, show that the author's interests in subjects often excluded from sf – such as childbirth, moral growth, the position of women in society – have been with her throughout her career.

Best of Murray Leinster, The (1976) ★★ Posthumous collection by Murray Leinster (USA), edited by Brian Davies. Short stories by Will F. Jenkins ('Murray Leinster') from the period 1945 to 1955, each with a moral ('Time To Die', 'Pipeline to Pluto') or humorous ('If You Was a Moklin') twist at the end. This is a British-published selection which differs from the US-published volume (see the following entry).

Best of Murray Leinster, The (1978) ★★ Posthumous collection by Murray Leinster (USA), edited by J. J. Pierce. A rather different selection from the Brian Davies-edited book of the same title, with stories from the 1934 'Sidewise in Time' to the 1956 'Critical Difference'. The otherwise undistinguished 'A Logic Named Joe' (1946) has probably the first appearance in fiction of what are now called value-added network services. This is the best 'best of' Leinster.

Best of Philip K. Dick, The (1977) ★★★ Collection by Philip K. Dick (USA), edited and introduced by John Brunner. Nineteen stories, ranging from 'Beyond Lies the Wub' (1952) to 'A Little Something for Us Tempunauts' (1974). Dick's short stories are less distinguished than his best novels, but this is still a fine volume. Contains four overlaps with his other major collection, *The Preserving Machine*.

Best of Poul Anderson, The (1976) ★★★ Collection by Poul Anderson (USA). Nine solid stories which overlap earlier collections. Includes the Hugo award-winning 'The Longest Voyage' (1960), as well as such other notable pieces as 'Sam Hall' (1953) and 'Kyrie' (1968). 'He brings to his kind of science fiction a reasonable narrative talent, a rigorous scientific background, a respect for the manner in which science and the human spirit may interact' – Barry N. Malzberg, introduction.

Best of Raymond Z. Gallun, The (1978) ★★ Collection by Raymond Z. Gallun (USA), edited and introduced by J. J. Pierce. Crudely-written but rather wonderful old stories, mostly from the 1930s. Standouts include 'Old Faithful' and 'Seeds of the Dusk', atmospheric tales of aliens and dying futures, written in the best pulp manner. As Pierce points out in his introduction, Gallun was something of a revolutionary in his day, with his 'thought-variant' stories which portrayed various alien creatures sympathetically.

Best of Robert Bloch, The (1977) ★★ Collection by Robert Bloch (USA), edited and introduced by Lester del Rey. Bloch is best known for his horror and fantasy fiction, and most of these 22 stories fit those categories (even though one of them, 'That Hell-Bound Train', won a 1959 Hugo award). However, there are a few genuine sf items scattered throughout this enjoyable collection.

Best of Robert Silverberg, The (1976) ★★★ Collection by Robert Silverberg (USA). Ten good, stylish stories, dating from the 1950s to the early 1970s, and including such award-winners as 'Nightwings' (Hugo, 1969), 'Passengers' (Nebula, 1970) and 'Good News from the Vatican' (Nebula, 1971). Silverberg's sf is always highly intelligent – but perhaps, at times, just a mite arid.

Best of Sci-Fi, The (Merril): see *SF: The Year's Greatest Science Fiction and Fantasy*.

Best of Stanley G. Weinbaum, The (1974) ★★ Posthumous collection by Stanley G. Weinbaum (USA), introduced by Isaac Asimov. It incorporates most of the contents of the two long-out-of-print, small-press volumes *A Martian Odyssey and Others* (1949) and *The Red Peri* (1952). The author died in 1935, after a writing career of less than two years. Nevertheless, as Asimov points out, Weinbaum revolutionized the field of American magazine sf with his humorous, slickly-written tales of sympathetic aliens and other interplanetary wonders. Most of these stories still hold up well today: in the 1930s they were a revelation. Published in Britain as *A Martian Odyssey and Other Stories*.

Best of the Best, The (Merril): see under *SF: The Year's Greatest Science Fiction and Fantasy*.

Best of Walter M. Miller Jr., The (1980) ★★★ Collection by Walter M. Miller (USA). A large volume which contains the complete contents of his earlier collections, *Conditionally Human* and *The View from the Stars*, with just two additional pieces. Alas, this fine author has not published any new fiction since the 1950s (although in 1989 it was announced that he's writing again).

Best Science Fiction of Isaac Asimov, The (1986) ★★ Collection by Isaac Asimov (USA). Twenty-eight pieces, many of them short squibs, ranging from 'The Fun They Had' (1951) to 'Death of a Foy' (1980). Contains no robot stories – and just three overlaps with the earlier and better volume entitled *The Best of Isaac Asimov*.

Best Science Fiction of the Year, The (1972–87) ★★★★ Anthology series edited by Terry Carr (USA). The longest-lived and most reliable of the many such series, it actually followed on from a previous series edited by Donald A. Wollheim and Terry Carr: *World's Best Science Fiction: 1965*, et al. Thus Carr was selecting his favourite stories on an annual basis for some 22 years before his untimely death at the age of 50. The first volume of Carr's solo series, chosen from work published in 1971, contains distinguished stories by Poul Anderson, Arthur C. Clarke, Ursula Le Guin and others, many of them award-winners (Carr was always very good at anticipating the Hugo and Nebula results).

Best Science Fiction Stories of Brian W. Aldiss (1965) ★★★★ Collection by Brian W. Aldiss (UK), substantially revised in 1971 and 1988. Enormously varied, frequently lyrical and usually challenging tales by one of Britain's leading sf authors. The first edition contains 14 selections, the third has 22. Fine stories which have been retained in all editions include 'Outside' (1955), 'Who Can Replace a Man?' and 'Poor Little Warrior!' (both 1958), and 'Man in His Time' (1965). Published in the USA as *Who Can Replace a Man?* The third edition has been reprinted as *Man In His Time: Best SF Stories*.

Best Science Fiction Stories of C. M. Kornbluth (1968) ★★★ Posthumous collection by C. M. Kornbluth (USA). Stimulating, mordant, dark-hued tales by a writer who died all too young. Includes the oft-reprinted 'The Little Black Bag' (1950) and 'The Marching Morons' (1951). 'His sharp and misanthropic style, the bitter salt that made *The Space Merchants* sting, is seen at its best in these stories' – J.G. Ballard, *Times*.

Best Science Fiction Stories of Clifford Simak (1967) ★★★ Collection by Clifford D. Simak (USA). Seven stories, mainly taken from earlier collections. The affecting pastoral tale 'Neighbour' (1954), about a talented alien who moves into the hillbilly country of Coon Valley, is typical of Simak at his best.

Best Science Fiction Stories of James Blish (1965; revised 1973) ★★★ Collection by James Blish (USA). Contains the superb 'Common Time' (1953; also reprinted in the earlier collection *Galactic Cluster*) as well as such highly-regarded stories as 'Surface Tension' (1952) and 'A Work of Art' (1956). The revised edition was republished in paperback as *The Testament of Andros* (1977).

Best SF (1955–70) ★★★★ Anthology series edited by Edmund Crispin (UK). An excellent sequence of seven 'respectable' volumes which introduced countless British readers to the finest in American magazine sf. The first volume contains James Blish's novella 'A Case of Conscience' (later expanded into his Hugo-winning novel of the same title). Crispin's introductions to these books were brief but always stimulating.

Best SF: 1967 etc. (Harrison & Aldiss): see *Year's Best Science Fiction, The*.

Best Short Stories of J. G. Ballard, The (1978) ★★★★ Collection by J.G. Ballard (UK), introduced by Anthony Burgess. This US-published variation on *The Best of J. G. Ballard* contains a rather different selection of nineteen stories, including one *Vermilion Sands* piece, 'The Cloud-Sculptors of Coral D' (1967), and four pieces from *The Atrocity Exhibition*. Burgess describes 'The Garden of Time' (1962) and 'The Drowned Giant' (1964) as 'two of the most beautiful stories of the world canon of short fiction'. He's right.

Betrayal, The (Cherryh): see *Cyteen*.

Better Mantrap, A (1982) ★★ Collection by Bob Shaw (UK). Nine sf and fantasy stories, all highly competent but few of which shine brightly in the memory. 'Conversion', 'Amphitheatre' and 'Frost Animals' are among the best. 'A good and entertaining collection, but on balance, rather a lightweight one' – David Langford, *Foundation*.

Bettyann (1970) ★★★ Fix-up novel by Kris Neville (USA), based on stories originally published in the early 1950s. A lost alien child is raised as a human girl. When contacted by her own kind, she is torn between them and her adopted home. A very pleasing tale of a young prodigy, and its author's only novel of note. A sequel story, 'Bettyann's Children', appeared in the anthology *Demon Kind* (1973) edited by Roger Elwood.

Between Planets (1951) ★★ Novel by Robert A. Heinlein (USA). A teenage boy gets caught up in war between the hardy colonists of the planet Venus and a repressive Earth government. Naturally, he sides with the rebels. Although slickly written, this is one of Heinlein's lesser 'juveniles'.

Between the Strokes of Night (1985) ★★ Novel by Charles Sheffield (UK/USA). Our planet is destroyed by nuclear war, but a few humans who dwell in space habitats continue the slow colonization of the galaxy. Many generations later, they are contacted by long-lived survivors from Earth: people who have entered 'S-space' where time passes at a vastly slower rate. Generous in its imaginative scope, and full of ideas, this is Sheffield's most intriguing novel.

Bewitchments of Love and Hate, The (Constantine): see under *Enchantments of Flesh and Spirit, The*.

Beyond (1960) ★★ Collection by Theodore Sturgeon (USA). Six average-to-good stories in Sturgeon's sentimental, psychologizing vein. Standouts include the early 'Nightmare Island' (1941), about a drunk who becomes ruler of a society of alien worms on a remote island.

Beyond Apollo (1972) ★★ Novel by Barry N. Malzberg (USA). The half-mad survivor of a two-man expedition to Venus recalls his experiences – but he is an unreliable narrator, to say the least. A blackly humorous piece of genre-subversion, typical of this author's work. Winner of the first John W. Campbell award (1973), it aroused a great deal of controversy. 'Malzberg's *Beyond Apollo* is, to me, the epitome of everything that has gone wrong with sf in the last ten years or so' – Bob Shaw, *Foundation*.

Beyond Armageddon: Survivors of the Megawar (1985) ★★★ Anthology edited by Walter M. Miller and Martin H. Greenberg (USA). A fine gathering of disturbing post-nuke fiction by Shepard, Spinrad, Ballard, Pangborn, Bradbury, Swanwick, etc., with a thoughtful introduction by the long-silent author of that greatest of post-bomb novels, *A Canticle for Leibowitz*.

Beyond Bedlam (Guin): see *Living Way Out*.

Beyond Heaven's River (1980) ★★ Novel by Greg Bear (USA). A Japanese sailor, kidnapped by aliens at the battle of Midway and kept alive for four centuries, is discovered by human space travellers on an abandoned planet and plunged into a high-tech information economy in which resources are abundant, the sky is full of aliens and Tokyo is a 20-kilometre cube. Competent, fascinating, but a little hard to follow towards the end.

Beyond Infinity (Nourse): see *Tiger by the Tail and Other SF Stories*.

Beyond Lies the Wub: The Collected Stories of Philip K. Dick, Volume One (1987) ★★★ Collection by Philip K. Dick (USA). First of a five-volume set which aims to be a complete edition, arranged chronologically, of the author's short fiction. Many of the early stories don't bear comparison with Dick's later work. However, the book is worth reading for such typical 1950s sf as 'Colony' and 'Paycheck' as well as the brief and near-perfect 'Roog' which shows that Dick had already developed some of the interests and obsessions which dominate his later work. Sequel volumes: *Second Variety, The Father-Thing, The Days of Perky Pat* and *The Little Black Box* (all 1987).

Beyond the Barrier (1964) ★ Novel by Damon Knight (USA), expanded from his story 'The Tree of Time'. A man joins minds with a much-advanced alien being. Not its author's most effective longer work: Knight has always tended to be a good short-story writer and a mediocre novelist. 'Plain awful' – Brian Stableford.

Beyond the Beyond (1969) ★★ Collection by Poul Anderson (USA). Six stories (five in the UK edition) from the 1950s and 60s, including the highly-regarded 'Starfog'. They demonstrate Anderson's proficiency when it comes to hard sf. Later collections by this amazingly fecund author include *Tales of the Flying Mountains* (1970), *The Queen of Air and Darkness* (1973), *Homeward and Beyond* (1975) and *The Dark Between the Stars* (1981).

Beyond the Blue Event Horizon (1980) ★★ Novel by Frederik Pohl (USA), sequel to *Gateway*. Broadhead, the agonized (and at times tiresome) hero of the preceding novel, has further adventures with the ancient alien technology of the starfaring 'Heechee'. Highly competent, but not as fresh as the first book. Sequel: *Heechee Rendezvous*.

Beyond the Imperium (Laumer): see under *Worlds of the Imperium*.

Beyond This Horizon (1948) ★ Novel by Robert A. Heinlein (USA). In a gun-toting future society, where most of the perennial human problems have been solved, men turn to the final mystery – the Meaning of Life. A wisecracking narrative, but fairly negligible as utopian speculation.

Bicentennial Man and Other Stories, The (1976) ★★ Collection by Isaac Asimov (USA). A dozen disparate Asimov stories from the late 1960s to the mid-70s, including a couple of new robot pieces. The title story was a Hugo award-winner, and perhaps the bicentenary of the United States had something to do with it.

Big Ball of Wax, The (1954) ★★ Novel by Shepherd Mead (USA). Corporate ad men bend a wonderful new invention (which permits people to experience others' feelings) to their own nefarious uses. A good satire on the heartless consumer society by an author who is best known for his popular non-fiction (*How to Succeed in Business Without Really Trying*, etc.).

Big Black Mark, The (Chandler): see under *Road to the Rim, The*.

Big Death, The (Maine), see *Darkest of Nights, The*.

Big Eye, The (1949) ★★ Novel by Max Ehrlich (USA). Scientists announce that a new planet is going to collide with the Earth, and this has the effect of halting wars and uniting the human race – which was the purpose of their announcement. Idealistic sf, fairly primitive in its scientific content, but an acceptably sugared pill. A first novel by a writer who subsequently specialized in thrillers, many with marginal sf content.

Big Planet (1957) ★★ Novel by Jack Vance (USA), originally serialized in 1952 (the 1978 revision restores the full magazine text). The survivors of a space ship stranded on Big Planet, in the territory of the Barjarnum of Beaujolais, have to trek 40,000 miles across that huge low-density world to get to the safety of the Earth Enclave. The first of Vance's many novels concerned with extraterrestrial societies descended from the 'pioneers, explorers, flagpole-sitters; the philosophers, the criminals, the prophets of doom and the progenitors of new cultural complexes' of Earth. Sequel: *Showboat World*.

Big Time, The (1961) ★★★ Short novel by Fritz Leiber (USA), originally published in magazine form in 1958 (when it won a Hugo award). The so-called Snakes and Spiders are opposing factions in a time war, who recruit their troops from various periods of history. This story, which reads almost like a play, involves just one tiny piece of the action – but a vaster background is richly suggested. Related short stories are collected in *The Mind Spider and Other Stories* (1961) and in an omnibus volume (which also contains this novel) called *The Change War* (1978).

Bill, the Galactic Hero (1965) ★★★ Novel by Harry Harrison (USA/Ireland). Young country bumpkin Bill is press-ganged into the interstellar army, where in time he learns to relish the ludicrous discipline and brainless camaraderie. An amusing, cod-militaristic romp of a space story which succeeds in taking the mickey out of Heinlein's *Starship Troopers* and other novels of its ilk. Still one of Harrison's most effective works.

Bill the Galactic Hero: The Planet of Robot Slaves (1989) ★★ Novel by Harry Harrison (USA/Ireland), a belated sequel to his original *Bill, the Galactic Hero* and the first of a proposed new series to be written by various hands. Bill is taken to a planet where robots, humans and 'Chingers' live in constant warfare, egged on by the god Mars. A comic parody of other sf writers (including Edgar Rice Burroughs and William Gibson) with an anti-war message.

Billion Days of Earth, A (1976) ★★ Novel by Doris Piserchia (USA). A far-future tale, portraying an Earth inhabited by rat-men and other curiosities. 'Vivid, precise and frequently eloquent' – John Clute.

Binary Z (1969) ★★ Novel by John Rankine (Douglas R. Mason, UK). An alien robot is discovered beneath the grounds of an English public school. The everyday setting and love story elements combine to make this one of the author's better novels – not his usual space adventure stuff.

Bio-Futures: SF Stories About Biological Metamorphosis (1976) ★★★ Anthology edited by Pamela Sargent (USA). Ten stories which deal in differing ways with the various bio-threats (and promises) which face modern humanity. A thorough piece of editing, with a long introduction, making this one of the most valuable of all 'theme' anthologies.

Bird of Time, The (Effinger), see under *Nick of Time, The.*

Birth of the People's Republic of Antarctica, The (1983) ★★★ Novel by John Calvin Batchelor (USA). As civilization crumbles, the various eccentric characters undertake a manic sea-voyage south to the land of eternal ice. Rumbustious philosophical fiction by a mainstream writer, only marginally sf.

Black Cloud, The (1957) ★★★ Novel by Fred Hoyle (UK). Hoyle, an eminent and controversial astronomer, is pro-scientist and anti-politician in this tale of an international research team studying a huge dust cloud which threatens the solar system. A genuinely original sf idea set in one of the best accounts of working scientists in literature.

Black Corridor, The (1969) ★★ Novel by Michael Moorcock (UK). An astronaut ferries a few frozen survivors away from nuclear war on Earth, his dreams and waking fantasies haunted by horrors. A brief and bitter psychological study of large-scale disaster mirrored in one man's breakdown. Written in collaboration with Moorcock's then wife, Hilary Bailey, though she was not acknowledged in early editions.

Black Genesis (Hubbard): see under *Invaders Plan, The.*

Black Holes (1978) ★ Anthology edited by Jerry Pournelle (USA). Fact and fiction about black holes by Pournelle, Larry Niven, Robert L. Forward and a dozen others. Gail Kimberly's harrowing 'Gloria' is the best of a competent bunch.

Black Legion of Callisto (Carter): see under *Jandar of Callisto.*

Black Mountains, The (1971) ★★★ Novel by Fred Saberhagen (USA). Sequel to *The Broken Lands*, in the same sword-and-sorcery-meets-science vein. Our heroes take the rebellion into the territory of the evil Empire and find some more relics of the extinct high-tech civilization and some real live Demons. Well written and occasionally surprisingly poignant. Sequel: *Changeling Earth.*

Black Ship, The (Rowley): see under *War for Eternity, The.*

Black Star Rising (1985) ★★ Novel by Frederik Pohl (USA). In a Chinese-dominated 21st century, an American peasant escapes the drudgery of the paddy fields and eventually makes his way into outer space, where he finds a lost colony of independent Americans. 'Unfortunately half a bookful of gentle satire and acute characterization is jettisoned when Castor is finally blasted into space ...' – Lee Montgomerie, *Interzone.*

Blackcollar, The (1983) ★ Novel by Timothy Zahn (USA). Scientifically-enhanced human commandos struggle against alien invaders of Earth, in this fairly routine sf adventure of the militaristic type which has become so popular in the last decade or two. Zahn's first novel.

Blade Runner (Dick): see *Do Androids Dream of Electric Sheep?*

Bladerunner, The (1974) ★★ Novel by Alan E. Nourse (USA). In a future of increased human longevity doctors struggle to cope with the consequent problems of over-population, hereditary afflictions and virulent new diseases. The 'Bladerunner' of the title is an underground doctor who tends to those who are unwilling to submit to the sterilization which is the price of official medicine. The author's most notable novel (though he has written many sf works for a juvenile audience). The title was borrowed (with permission) for the 1982 movie *Blade Runner*, based on Philip K. Dick's *Do Androids Dream of Electric Sheep?*, but there is no other connection between the film and Nourse's book.

Blades of Mars (Moorcock): see under *City of the Beast, The.*

Blake's Progress (1975) ★★★ Novel by Ray Nelson (USA). William Blake's poetic visions are explained by the fact that he is a secret time-traveller (as is his wife). This was number 13 in the cheap 'Laser Books' line, but it surprised everyone by its wit and inventiveness. Nelson's best book, and the only Laser title to receive wide praise. Revised and (rather unfortunately) retitled *Time-quest* (1985). Note: the author's byline has varied over the years: Ray Nelson, R. F. Nelson, or R. Faraday Nelson.

Blind Men and the Elephant, The (1982) ★★ Novel by Russell M. Griffin (USA). A blackly satirical farce in which the central character is a grossly deformed human child – the product of scientific tampering – who becomes a latter-day Elephant Man, exploited for his ugliness. 'There is a paucity here. Some central questions are being begged. What was potentially a large-minded black book of the soul turns out to be a jape' – John Clute.

Blind Voices (1978) ★★★ Novel by Tom Reamy (USA). A mysterious circus visits a small midwestern town, and it transpires that its freaks have been created by unorthodox means. What appears to be a fantasy in the vein of Bradbury's *Something Wicked This Way Comes* (1962) turns out to have an sf rationale. Alas, it was this good writer's only novel: he died shortly before its publication.

Blood and Burning (1978) ★★ Collection by Algis Budrys (USA). Various good sf stories (the US and UK contents differ slightly) including two which feature the hero of Budrys's major novel *Michaelmas*. Slightly clotted at times.

Blood and Iron (Pournelle & Carr): see under *There Will Be War.*

Blood Music (1985) ★★★★ Novel by Greg Bear (USA). A scientist creates intelligent cells, tiny bio-computers, and injects himself with them: this leads to a benign plague which transforms the world. The climax is wonderful, transcendent. First-class speculative sf, and the best book so far by the highly talented Greg Bear. The original magazine novella, from which this book is satisfyingly expanded, won a 1984 Hugo award.

Blood Red Game, The (Moorcock): see *Sundered Worlds, The*.

Blood River (Tilley): see *Amtrak Wars, The*.

Blooded on Arachne (1982) ★★★ Collection by Michael Bishop (USA). Atmospheric sf, including such standouts as the title story and 'The White Otters of Childhood'. Bishop is one of the more stylish and intellectual writers of American sf, and this was his first volume of shorter works. 'Infatuated with strangeness' – Brian Stableford.

Bloodhype (1973) ★ Novel by Alan Dean Foster (USA). The Humanx Commonwealth is threatened by the Vom, an immense planet-eating intelligence. It is saved by a chain of coincidence involving Flinx (from the first 'Humanx' book, *The Tar-Aiym Krang*), a drug that conveniently affects all intelligent life, two Church spies who just happen to be in the right place at the right time, and yet another half-million-year-old Tar-Aiym artefact.

Bloodworld (Janifer): see *You Sane Men*.

Bloody Sun, The (1964) ★★ Novel by Marion Zimmer Bradley (USA), the second published volume in her complex 'Darkover' series. Jeff Kerwin returns to the orphanage in which he was brought up on the planet Darkover – and finds that no one admits to remembering him or his family. It fills in a lot of family background as well as technical detail about Darkovan mental powers (see under *The Sword Of Aldones*). The novel was revised and expanded in 1978.

Blue Adept (1981) Novel by Piers Anthony (UK/USA), second in the 'Apprentice Adept' series. The protagonist of *Split Infinity* has several hair-raising adventures and discovers more of the workings of the twin worlds of Proton and Phaze. The sf/fantasy double-act is wearing a bit thin and nothing is thought up to improve on it. Sequel: *Juxtaposition*.

Blue Champagne (Varley): see under *Barbie Murders and Other Stories, The*.

Blue World, The (1966) ★★ Novel by Jack Vance (USA), expanded from his magazine story 'King Kragen'. The author's linguistic vitality is exercised on a rather flimsy story about the human colonists of floating islands on a landless planet breaking free of the hegemony of a huge intelligent sea-creature. 'His talent for extracting exotic flavours from commonplace terms has seldom been better used' – James Cawthorn, *New Worlds*.

Bluesong (Van Scyoc): see under *Darkchild*.

Boat of a Million Years, The (1989) ★★ Novel by Poul Anderson (USA). A tiny elite of immortal human beings, blessed with miraculous genes, moves through the ages – from circa 300 BC to the spacefaring near future. The once-prolific Anderson's first new sf novel in some time, it is craftsmanlike but episodic and rather long-drawn-out.

Body Snatchers, The (1955) ★★ Novel by Jack Finney (USA). Seed-pod aliens take over a small American town, replacing people with will-less simulacra. A memorable piece of paranoia, similar to Heinlein's *The Puppet Masters*. Filmed, twice, as *Invasion of the Body Snatchers* (1956; dir. Don Siegel; and 1978; dir. Philip Kaufman), and the book has also been republished under that title.

Bolo: The Annals of the Dinochrome Brigade (1976) ★ Collection by Keith Laumer (USA). Reprinted stories from the 1960s sf magazines, all of them dealing with the eponymous 'BOLOs' or cybernetic battle-tanks. Adequate thick-ear entertainment, written in Laumer's usual clipped style. 'For all their sophisticated internal electronics, massive arsenal of weapons and hyper-intelligent onboard computers, the BOLOs seem eternally doomed to run around in circles mindlessly destroying everything in their paths' – John Collick, *Vector*. A sequel novel is *Rogue Bolo* (1985).

Bones of Zoro, The (de Camp): see under *Search for Zei, The*.

Book of Being, The (Watson): see under *Book of the River, The*.

Book of Brian Aldiss, The (1972) ★★ Collection by Brian W. Aldiss (UK). Mixed volume of nine stories, containing some overlaps with other Aldiss collections. Perhaps the most memorable tale is 'All the World's Tears' (1957), which also appears in *The Canopy of Time*. Published in Britain, in paperback only, as *Comic Inferno*.

Book of Days (Wolfe): see *Gene Wolfe's Book of Days*.

Book of Dreams, The (1981) ★★ Novel by Jack Vance (USA), sequel to *The Face* and fifth of his 'Demon Princes' series. Kirth Gerson uses a popular newspaper competition to track down the fifth and last of the interstellar criminals who destroyed his family.

Book of Philip José Farmer, The (1973) ★★ Collection by Philip José Farmer (USA). Fourteen widely varied sf and fantasy stories, including such well-known items as 'My Sister's Brother' and 'The Alley Man' (both 1959). One of the odder inclusions is 'An Exclusive Interview with Lord Greystoke', about a meeting with Burroughs's Tarzan of the Apes. The 1982 reprint has slightly differing contents.

Book of Philip K. Dick, The (1973) ★★ Collection by Philip K. Dick (USA). Nine proficient stories from the 1950s, most of them reprinted from the author's first collection, *A Handful of Darkness*. Published in

Britain as *The Turning Wheel and Other Stories.*

Book of Poul Anderson, The (1974) ★★ Collection by Poul Anderson (USA), edited by Roger Elwood. Seven stories which range across this competent author's career. Includes the Hugo award-winning 'The Longest Voyage' (1961), as well as the Hugo and Nebula award-winning 'The Queen of Air and Darkness' (1971). Also published as *The Many Worlds of Poul Anderson.*

Book of Ptath, The (1947) ★★ Novel by A. E. van Vogt (Canada/USA), first published in magazine form in 1943. On a super-continent, some 200 million years in Earth's future, the godlike but amnesiac hero Ptath struggles with a beautiful female antagonist. Sheer pulp fantasy, on the fringes of sf – but then *everything* van Vogt has written is sheer pulp fantasy....

Book of Skulls, The (1971) ★★ Novel by Robert Silverberg (USA). Four young Americans from varied ethnic backgrounds go in search of a desert sect which may possess the secret of immortality. They discover that terrible sacrifices must be made in order to reach their goal. Well-characterized psychological sf, written with intensity.

Book of the New Sun, The (1980–83) ★★★★ Novel by Gene Wolfe (USA), published in four volumes: *The Shadow of the Torturer* (1980), *The Claw of the Conciliator* (1981), *The Sword of the Lictor* (1982) and *The Citadel of the Autarch* (1983).

Set in an utterly changed world of the distant future, it concerns the growth to manhood of the boy Severian who will in time become the new Autarch. A masterpiece: dense, complex, possibly allegorical, it is the ultimate 'Dying Earth' novel. 'Wolfe is so good he leaves me speechless' – Ursula Le Guin. Sequel: *The Urth of the New Sun.*

Book of the River, The (1984) ★★ Novel by Ian Watson (UK), first of a trilogy. A young woman manages to cross the huge river which divides her world in two: there she finds a nastily male-dominant society, and must go on (through death) to ever greater adventures. Hailed on publication as the author's most 'accessible' work to date, it's a fantastic romance which (as is usual with Watson) turns out to have an sf rationale. Sequels: *The Book of the Stars* and *The Book of Being* (both 1985).

Book of the Stars, The (Watson): see under *Book of the River, The.*

Borders of Infinity (Bujold): see under *Brothers in Arms.*

Born Leader (McIntosh): see under *One in Three Hundred.*

Born of Man and Woman (1954) ★★★ Collection by Richard Matheson (USA). Sf, fantasy and horror stories from the early 1950s. The famous title story is about a hideous mutant child. Short on hardware, long on dialogue and economically-drawn everyday settings, Matheson's tales are deceptively simple, but they linger in the mind and often translate well to other media (many of his pieces have formed the basis of TV and movie scripts). Republished in paperback, with slightly differing contents, as *Third from the Sun*.

Born with the Dead (1974) ★★★ Collection by Robert Silverberg (USA). Three long stories: the title piece, 'Thomas the Proclaimer' and 'Going'. Resurrection, miracles and suicide are the leitmotifs; and, as in so much of this author's work, there is a considerable amount of religious imagery. 'Silverberg ... is writing about what knowledge does to belief: a strong theme, closely realized, and not as alien from traditional sf as it looks' – Tom Shippey, *Foundation*.

Bow Down to Nul (Aldiss): see *Interpreter, The*.

Boys from Brazil, The (1976) ★★ Novel by Ira Levin (USA). Dr Mengele attempts to produce cloned copies of Adolf Hitler, but in order to do so he must reproduce the environmental factors which made Hitler the evil genius that he was. A well-written thriller for the mainstream audience. Despite the sensationalism of the plot, it deals quite intelligently with the fashionable subject of cloning. Filmed in 1978 (dir. Franklin J. Schaffner).

Brain Twister (1962) ★ Novel by Mark Phillips (Randall Garrett and Laurence M. Janifer, USA), originally serialized in 1959. An FBI agent hunts secret telepaths – with some surprising results. Moderately enjoyable hackwork by two quite

talented writers (especially Garrett, who hid his light under a bushel of pen-names throughout a 30-year career as an sf/fantasy author). Sequels: *Supermind* and *The Impossibles* (both 1963).

Brain Wave (1954) ★★ Novel by Poul Anderson (USA). Animals and humans suddenly become vastly more intelligent: it seems that the Earth has moved out of a cosmic brain-power-inhibiting field. A lovely idea and a fondly-remembered novel (Anderson's first in book form): alas, it has not worn well, and the writing now seems thin and clichéd.

Brains of Earth, The (1966) ★ Short novel by Jack Vance (USA). Various nasty aliens attempt to control the populace of our fair planet. A minor potboiler by a usually capable writer. 'Achieves considerable tension in the beginning, only to lapse into near absurdity' – James Cawthorn, *New Worlds*. Republished as *Nopalgarth*.

Brain-Stealers, The (1954) ★ Novel by Murray Leinster (USA). Jim Hunt escapes from World Security, who have sentenced him for conducting illegal experiments into telepathy. When space-ship-wrecked aliens start controlling people's minds in order to drink their blood, he has to save Earth single-handed. Proficient hokum.

Brave Free Men, The (1973) ★★★ Novel by Jack Vance (USA), sequel to *The Anome* and second in the 'Durdane' trilogy. Etzwane, promoted to the office of Anome, meets his supposedly dead father and discovers that his land is being overrun by Rogushkoi – genetically engineered by the alien Asutra to breed infertility into the human race. Long balloon journeys, weird musical instruments, strange meals and a highly formal language of colours make the background to this novel more enjoyable than the rather odd plot. Sequel: *The Asutra.*

Brave New World (1932) ★★★★ Novel by Aldous Huxley (UK). This famous satire, about a technologically stratified world some six centuries hence, is a book which has helped define 20th-century humanity's view of itself. Along with Orwell's *Nineteen Eighty-Four*, it is one of the two best-known dystopian visions in the English language. Simultaneously dark and jolly, profound and playful, it is also very much a work of speculative science fiction. Filmed for American TV, 1980 (dir. Burt Brinckerhoff).

Brave Old World (1976) ★★★ Novel by Philippe Curval (France). In a future European society, static and inward-turning, people's subjective time-spans are increased by technological means. A complicated narrative by one of the most highly praised contemporary French sf authors. Winner of the Prix Apollo, 1977.

Breakfast in the Ruins: A Novel of Inhumanity (1972) ★★ Novel by Michael Moorcock (UK), a quasi-sequel to his *Behold the Man*. Not really sf, it dots through time, each chapter taking place at a different crisis point of modern history (the framing narrative involves Karl Glogauer, hero of the aforementioned earlier book). Amid much violence and suffering, some agonizing moral questions are posed. 'No more science fiction than Vonnegut's *Slaughterhouse-Five*, nor as good for that matter' – John Clute.

Breakfast of Champions: or, Goodbye, Blue Monday (1972) ★★ Novel by Kurt Vonnegut (USA). Satirical view of modern America which uses the conceit that everyone is a robot. Not really sf, though it does have numerous appearances by the author's sf-writing alter ego, that unforgettable hack Kilgore Trout (see *Venus on the Half Shell*). It adds up to a rather self-indulgent Vonnegut novel which he describes as 'my fiftieth birthday present to myself'.

Breaking of Northwall, The (1981) ★★ Novel by Paul O. Williams (USA), first of his 'Pelbar Cycle'. A millennium after the great nuclear war, scattered settlements of Americans are groping their way once more towards civilization. But numerous conflicts mar the progress. An intelligent adventure story, rich in detail, drawing fruitfully on its academic author's knowledge of the North American past and Amerindian cultures. Sequels: *The Ends of the Circle* (1981), *The Dome in the Forest* (1981), *The Fall of the Shell* (1982), *An Ambush of Shadows* (1983), *The Song of the Axe* (1984) and *The Sword of Forbearance* (1985). 'Williams is a fine writer and his Pelbar Cycle novels ... contain little that is formulaic' – Brian Aldiss and

David Wingrove, *Trillion Year Spree*.

Breaking Strain (1987) ★ Novel by Paul Preuss (USA), volume one in the 'Arthur C. Clarke's Venus Prime' series. The bionic heroine investigates sabotage aboard a space vessel. An efficiently engineered 'sharecropper' novel, based on a short story by Clarke and produced by book-packager Byron Preiss (not to be confused with writer Preuss, who is a respectable sf author in his own right). Sequels (both by Preuss): *Maelstrom* (1988) and *Hide and Seek* (1989).

Breakthrough (1967) ★★ Novel by Richard Cowper (Colin Middleton Murry, UK). A modern couple, experimenting with ESP, turn out to be psychic reincarnations of persons from a more perfect age. Hoary subject matter, but written with style. Cowper's first sf book, though he had previously written novels (some with a marginal fantastic element) under the name 'Colin Murry'.

Breeds of Man, The (1988) ★ Novel by F. M. Busby (USA). A near-future cure for AIDS boosts the immune systems of women so much that they become resistant to male sperm, and the birth rate drops. Another 'cure' produces hermaphroditic children. Not at all in the author's usual space-operatic vein: this is his attempt at a large, serious sf novel. 'Busby tells a good story, a page-turner that makes me wish he'd done his homework, and that an editor had kept an eye on both his facts and his internal con-sistency' – Tom Whitmore, *Locus*.

Bridge of Ashes (1976) ★ Novel by Roger Zelazny (USA). A telepathic man, who is prone to being taken over by the personae of others, must overcome his own problems in order to counter an alien menace. A sketchy little novel, produced by Zelazny on an off day. 'A series of excerpts from something much greater, complete in itself but nevertheless compressed in a drastic manner ... The whole novel of which *Bridge of Ashes* is the abridged version would be a very long and complicated one' – Brian Stableford.

Bridgehead (1985) ★ Novel by David Drake (USA). Travellers from the future persuade a scientist to build a machine which turns out to be a gateway for warriors. Slam-bang, headlong stuff in this author's customary militaristic vein.

Brightness Falls from the Air (1985) ★★ Novel by James Tiptree Jr. (Alice Sheldon, USA). Earthfolk, including some menacing crooks, are trapped on an alien planet which is threatened by the radiation-front of an exploded star. Despite its exotic sf setting, colourfully depicted, it has been pointed out that the plot bears a strong resemblance to that of John Huston's old film noir, *Key Largo* (1948). A rather disappointing second novel from this talented writer.

Bring the Jubilee (1953) ★★★★ Novel by Ward Moore (USA). The South has won the American Civil War. A young man from the impoverished

Yankee North goes back in time to change the course of history. A classic alternative-world novel, warmly and wittily written.

Broke Down Engine and Other Troubles with Machines (1971) ★★ Collection by Ron Goulart (USA). Humorous tales of robots and other forms of troublesome machinery. All much of a muchness. The amazingly slick and prolific Goulart is like Robert Sheckley without the true satirical bite. For a later, similar collection see *Nutzenbolts*.

Broken Lands, The (1968) ★★★ Novel by Fred Saberhagen (USA). A teenage boy is kidnapped by cruel servants of the Empire, falls in love, and saves the day by crashing into a castle in a nuclear-powered tank which just happened to be overlooked round the corner. Swashbuckling fun with internally consistent (if not exactly believable) explanation for why magic works better than science. Sequel: *The Black Mountains*.

Broken Symmetries (1983) ★★ Novel by Paul Preuss (USA). A physicist discovers a new subatomic particle of great significance and potential danger, and becomes embroiled in the professional and political consequences. The author's knowledge of science and scientists is excellent, but the story is rather weak.

Broken Wheel, The (Wingrove): see under *Chung Kuo: The Middle Kingdom*.

Broken Worlds, The (1987) ★★ Novel by Raymond Harris (USA). An old-fashioned enjoyable space opera, involving a drunken musician's quest through many worlds, wars, bars, kings' castles and alien species to save civilization.

Brontomek! (1976) ★★★ Novel by Michael Coney (UK/Canada), a quasi-sequel to *Syzygy* and *Mirror Image*. The 'amorphs' from the latter novel, creatures which are capable of taking on varied forms, come to the colonized planet Arcadia (scene of *Syzygy*). This combination of old ideas and setting results, surprisingly enough, in a more satisfactory novel than either of its predecessors, with good characterization, a sureness of style and a deft blending of sf themes and love-story elements. One of Coney's best.

Brother and Other Stories (1986) ★★ Collection by Clifford D. Simak (USA), edited by Francis Lyall. Four down-home tales by this amiable science-fiction pastoralist. Three of them are previously uncollected, but the delightful 'Kindergarten' (1953) will already be familiar to readers of the author's *Strangers in the Universe*.

Brother Berserker (1969) ★★ Collection by Fred Saberhagen (USA), originally published as *Brother Assassin*. Three linked stories about the life-hating machines from *Berserker* using time-travel to alter the history of the planet Sirgol. Some of that history is too obviously based on Earth's to be fully convincing; for example, the last part involves the Berserker attempting to subvert characters closely modelled on Galileo and Francis of Assisi.

Brothers in Arms (1989) ★★ Novel by Lois McMaster Bujold (USA), sequel to *Shards of Honor* in her 'Miles Vorkosigan' series. The military spacefaring hero splits himself into two personae for this fast-moving adventure, laced with humour. 'Bujold is as audacious as her favourite hero ... The Vorkosigan Saga is one space opera that merits a long run' – Faren Miller, *Locus*. Sequel: *Borders of Infinity* (1989).

Brothers of Earth (1976) ★★ Novel by C. J. Cherryh (USA). Two mutually hostile humans are marooned amidst the alien culture of a far planet. Carolyn Cherryh's first sf novel (though it was preceded by *Gate of Ivrel*, a fantasy novel). 'Cherryh has demonstrated a genius for reanimating what in other hands might seem routine or outworn conventions' – Patrick L. McGuire, *20th-Century SF Writers*.

Brothers of the Head (1977) ★★ Novella by Brian W. Aldiss (UK). Curious tragicomic fable, initially published as a large-format illustrated book, about Siamese triplets who form a rock group called the Bang-Bang. The 1979 paperback reprint drops the illustrations and adds another story, 'Where the Lines Converge' (1977).

Budrys' Inferno (1963) ★★★ Collection by Algis Budrys (USA). Excellent, moody stories from the 1950s. Includes 'Silent Brother' and 'The Man Who Tasted Ashes' –

among the most sophisticated sf tales of their time. Published in the UK as *The Furious Future*.

Budspy (1987) ★★ Novel by David Dvorkin (USA). Yet another Nazis-have-won-World-War-II story. But in this case there's a difference: Hitler died during the war and his successors have come to an accommodation with the western powers (though not with the Soviet Union). We have a vision of a 'good' Third Reich, some 45 years on – or, at least, so it seems. The hero, who is a spy for the American Ombudsman (hence the book's peculiar title) learns better. 'Recommended especially to those whose knowledge of Nazi minutiae will be challenged by Dvorkin's excellent research' – Bill Collins, *SF & Fantasy Book Review Annual 1988*.

Bug Jack Barron (1969) ★★★ Novel by Norman Spinrad (USA). A hard-hitting tale of near-future politics, in which media megastar Jack Barron uses his TV image to humble a giant corporation which is conducting dubious experiments in human longevity. Energetic and headlong, with many explicit sexual scenes, this novel once raised hostile questions in the House of Commons when it was serialized in the British magazine *New Worlds*.

Bug Life Chronicles, The (1989) ★★ Collection by Phillip C. Jennings (USA). Linked stories, set in the universe of the author's first novel, *Tower to the Sky*. The 'bugs' of the title are electronically-stored personalities; normal humans are referred to as 'wetbrains'. Weird and sometimes inconsequential tales, full of ideas.

Bug Wars, The (1979) ★ Novel by Robert L. Asprin (USA). A space-war story which involves reptilian aliens pitted against insect-like foes, with no representatives of *Homo sapiens* in view. It may appeal to fans of military sf, but for those who seek human interest it's deadly dull.

Bugs (1989) ★★★ Novel by John Sladek (USA). An unhappy Englishman arrives in the Midwest to obtain work as a technical writer. As the result of a ridiculous misunderstanding, he is taken on as a software engineer – his task to help build 'Robinson Robot'. Another of this author's very amusing satires on a corporate USA in which he can scarcely bring himself to believe. 'Finally ... Sladek has written a novel with a full human consciousness at its heart, which motors its obsessive tabling of the wares of the absurd in a consumed America, and passes the terror on to us' – John Clute.

Burning, The (1972) ★ Fix-up novel by James E. Gunn (USA). The world is thrown back into a medieval condition by a popular revolt against science and technology. The good guys struggle to keep the flame of knowledge alive in disguised form. A routine, episodic treatment of a routine theme.

Burning Chrome (1986) ★★★ Collection by William Gibson (USA), introduced by Bruce Sterling. Contains all the talented Mr Gibson's short fiction up to 1986, including three collaborations with other writers – Sterling, John Shirley and Michael Swanwick. Ten stories in all, each with something to commend it. Three, 'Johnny Mnemonic', 'New Rose Hotel' and the title story, are set against the same sleazy, high-tech background as the author's novel *Neuromancer*. Particularly delightful is 'The Gernsback Continuum', a word-perfect piece which plays nostalgically with the sf dreams of yesteryear, and also manages to make a serious point.

Burning World, The (Ballard): see *Drought, The*.

Busy About the Tree of Life (1988) ★★ Collection by Pamela Zoline (USA). A very belated volume, since its two best-known (and probably best) stories were first published in the late 1960s: 'The Heat Death of the Universe' and 'The Holland of the Mind'. The first of these uses a metaphor drawn from the second law of thermodynamics to memorably evoke the *anomie* of everyday middle-class life. It is a much reprinted story. The later pieces are similarly uncompromising and experimental, but less effective. 'All the investigations in this book spiral around the idea of entropy. It is Death, as the opening epigram tells us, who is "busy about the tree of life"' – Gwyneth Jones, *Foundation*. Published in the USA as *The Heat Death of the Universe and Other Stories*.

Butterfly Kid, The (1967) ★★★ Novel by Chester Anderson (USA). A hippie comedy in which drug-takers' hallucinations take on tangible reality, thanks to the intervention of some aliens intent on the takeover of Earth. Clever, lively, and very much a book of its time. Sequels: *The Unicorn Girl* by Michael Kurland and *The Probability Pad* by T. A. Waters.

Buy Jupiter and Other Stories (1975) ★★ Collection by Isaac Asimov (USA). Twenty-four tales and squibs, with extensive linking notes written in Asimov's usual charmingly immodest vein. The stories range from 'Darwinian Pool Room' (1950) to 'Light Verse' (1973). There are no real standouts.

Buying Time (Haldeman): see *Long Habit of Living, The*.

By Furies Possessed (1970) ★★ Novel by Ted White (USA). The hero discovers that the nasty-looking symbiotic aliens who seem to be 'taking over' the people of Earth are actually benefactors who should be welcomed: they bestow mental and physical boons on their human hosts. A good action story, and an ironic inversion of the themes of Heinlein's *The Puppet Masters* and Finney's *The Body Snatchers*.

By the Light of the Green Star (Carter) see under *Under the Green Star*.

Bypass to Otherness (1961) ★ Collection by Henry Kuttner (USA). Eight stories from the 40s: almost all involve someone turning into, or discovering that they always were, a superman. They all end in tears. Best is the rather horrid 'Call Him Demon' in which children placate an apparent uncle with blood sacrifices.

Byworlder, The (1971) ★ Novel by Poul Anderson (USA). In the 21st century an alien visits Earth in search of art. This story is an occasion for much right-wing philosophizing and satire on the 1960s counter-culture. Anderson at his more tendentious.

C

Cache, The (1981) Collection by Philip José Farmer (USA). Contains a revision of a short novel originally published in book form as *The Cache from Outer Space* (1962) plus two shorter stories from the 1950s – none of them of much interest.

Caduceus Wild (1978) ★★ Novel by Ward Moore and Robert Bradford (USA), originally serialized in 1959. A vision of an unpleasant future society ruled by an oligarchy of medical men. The hero rebels and overthrows the old order – as is usual in American dystopias of the 1950s. Moore's last published book.

Cage a Man (1973) ★ Novel by F. M. Busby (USA), first in his 'Demu' trilogy. A man is imprisoned by the alien Demu, but holds out against their attempts to strip him of his identity and eventually makes his escape. Busby's first novel (though he had been writing sf short stories sporadically since the 1950s). It was typical of many space operas to come. Sequels: *The Proud Enemy* (1975) and *End of the Line* (1980; this

last first published in an omnibus volume entitled *The Demu Trilogy*).

Call to Battle! (Pournelle & Carr): see under *There Will Be War*.

Callahan's Crosstime Saloon (1977) ★★ Collection by Spider Robinson (USA/Canada). Tall tales told by the human and alien clients of the eponymous drinking establishment. A mix of sf and fantasy with some fairly dire puns, it was popular. Sequels include: *Time Travellers Strictly Cash* (1981), *Callahan's Secret* (1986) and *Callahan's Lady* (1989).

Caltraps of Time, The (1968) ★★★ Collection by David I. Masson (UK). Seven highly unusual sf stories first published in the adventurous *New Worlds* magazine in 1965–67. Most concern the nature of time, and all are packed with ideas. The language is sometimes difficult, as in the brilliantly sustained 'A Two-Timer', about the visit of a 17th-century gentleman to the baffling world of 1964. This remains its talented author's only book.

Camp Concentration (1968) ★★★★ Novel by Thomas M. Disch (USA). The hero, a poet, is inducted into a secret military experiment to maximize soldiers' intelligence. Infected with a syphilis-type bug, he becomes a genius as his body begins to fall apart. There is a clever solution to his predicament. Erudite and witty, this is a very impressive modern recension of the Faust legend.

Can You Feel Anything When I Do This? (1971) ★★ Collection by Robert Sheckley (USA). Sixteen amusing tales reprinted from *Playboy* and other magazines. The title story is about a New York housewife and her amorously-inclined vacuum cleaner. Bright, clever stuff, if not quite up to Sheckley's best of the 1950s. 'I suspect that it is to the paranoid in us all that Sheckley's humour appeals' – Peter Nicholls, *Foundation*. Retitled *The Same to You Doubled and Other Stories* for its UK paperback reprint.

Canary in a Cat House (Vonnegut): see under *Welcome to the Monkey House*.

Canopy of Time, The (1959) ★★★ Collection by Brian W. Aldiss (UK). Eleven partially-linked stories of the far future. Standouts include 'Who Can Replace a Man?' (1958) and 'All the World's Tears' (1957). A different version of this fine volume was published in the USA (and later in Britain) as *Galaxies Like Grains of Sand*.

Canticle for Leibowitz, A (1959) ★★★★ Novel by Walter M. Miller (USA). Centuries after a nuclear holocaust a young monk discovers 'relics' of Saint Leibowitz. These fragments of lost scientific lore lead to a new technological age, and a tragic cycle of events is re-enacted. This witty and profound novel is the greatest of all post-bomb stories. Hugo award-winner, 1961.

Capella's Golden Eyes (1980) ★★ Novel by Christopher Evans (UK). The human colonists of a far planet, long cut off from Earth, strive to understand mysterious alien visitors who bring them boons. The story is weak and rather inconclusive, but the colony is well evoked. Evans's first novel.

Capitol (1978) ★★ Collection by Orson Scott Card (USA). Linked stories trace the development of the planet Capitol from a haven for refugees from the Soviet conquest of the US to the metropolis of the Empire of a Thousand Worlds whose rulers and owners achieve false immortality through years spent in unageing hibernation. Many of the characters wake again to reappear in the novel *Hot Sleep*.

Capricorn Games (Silverberg): see under *Needle in a Timestack*.

Captive Universe (1969) ★★★ Novel by Harry Harrison (USA/Ireland). The Aztec hero discovers that his small society is just one of many aboard a vast space vessel containing fragments of Earth cultures which have been kept unaware of their true situation. A good reworking of the 'space ark' motif.

Captives of the Flame (Delany): see *Fall of the Towers, The.*

Cards of Grief (1986) ★★ Novel by Jane Yolen (USA). A well-crafted story, presented as a collection of interviews and reports by a team of human anthropologists studying an alien culture based round mourning and bereavement.

Carefully Considered Rape of the World, The (1966) ★ Novel by Shepherd Mead (USA). A satirical romp about the impregnation of a few Earth women by visiting aliens, resulting in ugly super-children. It may resemble Wyndham's *The Midwich Cuckoos* in outline but is totally dissimilar in tone.

Case Against Tomorrow, The (1957) ★★ Collection by Frederik Pohl (USA). The second of Pohl's many slim gatherings of bright, ideative and frequently satirical stories (for the first see *Alternating Currents*). The most notable of these pieces — and of the contents of later volumes such as *Tomorrow Times Seven* (1959), *The Man Who Ate the World* (1960), *Turn Left at Thursday* (1961) and *The Abominable Earthman* (1963) – have since been reprinted in *The Best of Frederik Pohl* and elsewhere.

Case and the Dreamer and Other Stories (1974) ★★ Collection by Theodore Sturgeon (USA). Three novellas in the author's latter-day style: 'Case and the Dreamer' (1972), 'If All Men Were Brothers, Would You Let One Marry Your Sister?' (1967) and 'When You Care, When You Love' (1962). The last is the best, a fragment of an aborted novel about a woman who clones her dead lover.

Case of Conscience, A (1958) ★★★★ Novel by James Blish (USA). A Jesuit priest visits the 'unfallen' planet Lithia, where he solves a biological riddle and wrestles with his conscience. A thoughtful and entertaining work, with a range of intellectual reference unusual for the American sf of its day. Hugo award-winner, 1959.

Casey Agonistes and Other Science Fiction and Fantasy Stories (1973) ★★★★ Posthumous collection by Richard McKenna (USA), introduced by Damon Knight. Five tales by a very good writer who wrote little sf. Contains the exquisite 'Hunter, Come Home' (1963), perhaps the best Edenic planet story ever. It also has the Nebula award-winning 'The Secret Place' (1966). 'An exceptionally fine book' – Brian Stableford.

Cat Karina (1982) ★★★ Novel by Michael Coney (UK/Canada). The eponymous heroine is a jaguar-girl of the far, far future who lives in a galaxy peopled by humans, aliens and the descendants of genetically-engineered animals. A lively narrative with an exotically detailed background, it owes a good deal of its inspiration to the works of the late Cordwainer Smith. A prelude to Coney's 'Song of Earth' sequence (see *The Celestial Steam Locomotive*).

Cat Who Walks Through Walls, The (1985) Novel by Robert A. Heinlein

(USA), a quasi-sequel to several earlier works, including *The Moon is a Harsh Mistress*, *Time Enough for Love* and *The Number of the Beast–*. It is a futuristic thriller which turns into an embarrassing solipsistic fantasy. 'After the Late Heinlein manner, the first half of the book is pellmell, rambunctious, and blowsy ... And then it happens. Narrator and spouse are translated abruptly from an incomprehensible lunar imbroglio into the dipsy multiverse of *Time Enough for Love* as addled by the *Beast*, and we are in Hell, or the omnipotent latency of the ancient author's mind. Call it Hell' – John Clute.

Cataclysm, The (Sherriff): see *Hopkins Manuscript, The*.

Catacomb Years (1979) ★★ Fix-up novel by Michael Bishop (USA), sequel to *A Little Knowledge*. About the city of Atlanta, Georgia, in the 21st century – during a period when it is domed and closed from the outside world for many decades. A curious scenario, but it's an ambitious, well-written book.

Catalyst, The (1980) ★★ Novel by Charles L. Harness (USA). A scientist comes up with a cure for a near-future plague, despite opposition from the bureaucrats around him. A quite powerful, though quirky, tale.

Catch a Falling Star (1968) ★★ Novel by John Brunner (UK), published in an earlier version as *The Hundredth Millennium* (1959). In Earth's far-distant future a new menace appears in the heavens, but only one man is aware of its significance. Memorable details and mood make this one of the best of Brunner's early works.

Catchworld (1975) ★★ Novel by Chris Boyce (UK). The crew of a starship on a military mission are taken over by their computer. This joint-winner of a Gollancz/*Sunday Times* sf competition is a lively, idea-rich space opera of multifarious ingredients. Alas, his over-excitable prose style does not quite match the author's intellectual aspirations.

Catface (Simak): see *Mastodonia*.

Cat's Cradle (1963) ★★★★ Novel by Kurt Vonnegut (USA). A lunatic scientist invents ice-nine, a substance which will freeze all the water in the world. Before this is released on the environment we meet many crazy and endearing characters, including the sage Bokonon who believes that we should all live by the harmless untruths which make us 'brave and kind and healthy and happy'. This satire on just about everything is one of its author's best books.

Catseye (Norton), see under *Star Man's Son*.

Catspaw (1988) ★★ Novel by Joan D. Vinge (USA), sequel to *Psion*. This is rather more adult in tone than the earlier novel, which was intended for teenagers. The young 'psion' hero becomes a bodyguard to one of the wealthy families which dominate his far-future world, and much psionic and cybernetic intrigue follows. 'A Cyberpunk version of prime-time soap opera' – Carolyn Cushman, *Locus*.

Cautionary Tales (1978) ★★ Collection by Chelsea Quinn Yarbro (USA), introduced by James Tiptree Jr. Thirteen sf and fantasy tales crafted by a capable hand. The author is also a composer, and such effective stories as 'Un Bel Di' and 'The Fellini Beggar' reveal her interest in opera. 'Yarbro has all the equipment of a very good writer, yet in none of her work that I have read so far is it brought quite into full play' – Roz Kaveney, *Foundation*.

Caves of Mars, The (1965) Novel by Emil Petaja (USA). An ill written, low-pressure space opera, in which the 'maguffin' is a drug made from a Martian fungus. 'An overall atmosphere suggesting van Vogt adapted by Disney' – James Cawthorn, *New Worlds*.

Caves of Steel, The (1954) ★★★ Novel by Isaac Asimov (USA). Famous futuristic detective story in which the joint heroes are a man and a robot. The setting is of as much interest as the murder-mystery plot: an enclosed world-city of claustrophobic corridors. The prose is exceedingly plain, the characterization somewhat juvenile, but this remains one of its author's most effective works. Quasi-sequel: *The Naked Sun*.

Caviar (1955) ★★ Collection by Theodore Sturgeon (USA). Eight stories, including the early 'Microcosmic God' (1941), about a scientist who breeds a race of tiny intelligent creatures. Another of the most memorable tales, 'Bright Segment' (1955), a powerful piece about a freakish recluse and his love for a badly injured woman, is non-sf (though quintessential Sturgeon).

Celestial Steam Locomotive, The (1983) ★★ Novel by Michael Coney (UK/Canada), a quasi-sequel to *Cat Karina* and part one of the 'Song of Earth' sequence. Sf/fantasy saga of the distant future, which combines a richly-peopled galactic setting with a complex plot involving multiple time-lines. Sequel: *Gods of the Greataway*.

Cemetery World (1973) ★ Novel by Clifford D. Simak (USA). Cosy quest narrative involving treasure seekers, robots and ghosts, on a future Earth which has been turned into one vast graveyard. Displays many of its author's usual concerns, but it's decidedly minor stuff.

Centauri Device, The (1974) ★★★ Novel by M. John Harrison (UK). A stylish, dark-hued but tongue-in-cheek space opera, in which anarchist space pirates, with a taste for *fin-de-siècle* art, fly spacecraft with names like 'Driftwood of Decadence' and 'The Green Carnation'. Self-conscious and literary, but nevertheless a virtuoso performance.

Centre Cannot Hold, The (Stableford): see under *Journey to the Centre*.

Century of Great Short Science Fiction Novels, A (Knight): see under *Century of Science Fiction, A*.

Century of Progress, A (1983) ★★ Novel by Fred Saberhagen (USA). A tale of time travel and alternative historical lines – in one of which Hitler achieves his thousand-year Reich. It's an accomplished adventure of its familiar type, and one of Saberhagen's best books.

Century of Science Fiction, A (1962) ★★★★ Anthology edited by Damon Knight (USA). Twenty-six stories and novel extracts, representing the development of sf over 100 years (though the emphasis is mainly on the modern decades). A well-chosen selection, and the first of many excellent reprint anthologies which Knight has edited. Later volumes in a similar vein include A Century of Great Short Science Fiction Novels (1964), One Hundred Years of Science Fiction (1968) and A Science Fiction Argosy (1972).

Century's End (1981) ★★★ Novel by Russell M. Griffin (USA). The 21st century approaches: weird cults proliferate, using the available technological means to propagate their various backward messages. An intelligent and entertaining satire by a writer who died far too soon.

Cerberus: A Wolf in the Fold (Chalker): see under Lilith: A Snake in the Grass.

Ceres Solution, The (1981) ★ Novel by Bob Shaw (UK). A crippled young man on Earth realizes that humans are being denied full access to the teleporting brotherhood of the cosmos. The rather drastic solution to this problem is to destroy the moon by engineering a collision with the asteroid Ceres. An oddly garbled and unsatisfactory novel from this normally reliable author. 'A confusion of protagonist-shifts, narrative dislocations, strange gear-changes in every sort of rhythm of tale-telling one can imagine all combine to bemuse and make seasick the reader the way bad van Vogt does' – John Clute.

Chaining the Lady (1978) ★ Novel by Piers Anthony (USA), sequel to Cluster. The Andromedans try to conquer our galaxy by taking over the minds of space-fleet officers; Melody of Mintaka, occupying the body of (surprise, surprise) a beautiful Earth girl, gives her all to stop them. The twee sex overwhelms the bug-eyed-monster alien cultures. Sequels: Kirlian Quest (1978), Thousandstar (1980) and Viscous Circle (1982).

Chains of the Sea (Silverberg): see under New Atlantis, The

Chalk Giants, The (1974) ★★ Fix-up novel by Keith Roberts (UK). Nuclear war devastates Britain; in the long aftermath, a new culture gradually evolves. A curious story-cycle in which the future and past of England are blended into one. Rather bloody, occasionally mystical, frequently confusing: it's full of powerful writing but adds up to an altogether less coherent book than the author's earlier Pavane.

Chameleon Corps and Other Shape Changers, The (Goulart): see under Sword Swallower, The.

Change the Sky and Other Stories (1974) ★★ Collection by Margaret St Clair (USA). Eighteen adequately entertaining sf and fantasy stories, mainly from the 1950s. In all but name, it's a 'best of' the short fiction by this minor female writer of the period.

Change War, The (Leiber): see under *Big Time, The*.

Changeling Earth (1973) ★★ Novel by Fred Saberhagen (USA). In this sequel to *The Black Mountains* we find out what the demons really are, and Science begins to work again. Republished in a different form as the last part of *The Empire of the East*.

Chantry Guild (1988) ★★ Novel by Gordon R. Dickson (USA), sequel to *The Final Encyclopedia*. Hal Mayne, the Dorsai and the Encyclopedia are holding Old Earth against the fleets of the Younger Worlds. They turn to the past and the Chantry Guild (familiar from the author's other books) for the knowledge Earth needs to survive. Part of Dickson's grandiose 'Childe Cycle', which starts with *Necromancer* and includes the 'Dorsai' books among others.

Chanur's Homecoming (1986) ★★ Novel by C. J. Cherryh (USA), sequel to *The Kif Strike Back*. The Pride of Chanur returns home to a poorer welcome than expected. Essentially a very long chase story with bursts of action embedded in an awful lot of hard-to-follow negotiation between characters and states familiar from the previous books in the series.

Chanur's Venture (1984) ★★ Novel by C. J. Cherryh (USA), sequel to *The Pride of Chanur*. A long chase novel that repeats most of the action of the previous book. It ends inconclusively, and the story is continued in *The Kif Strike Back* (although the book itself says the sequel will be called *Chanur's Revenge*).

Chaos in Lagrangia (Reynolds): see under *Lagrange Five*.

Chaos Weapon, The (Kapp): see under *Patterns of Chaos, The*.

Chapterhouse: Dune (1985) ★★ Novel by Frank Herbert (USA), sequel to *Heretics of Dune* and sixth in the 'Dune' series. The complex action moves some 15,000 years further into the future, when everything on the desert world of Arrakis is more or less returned to the state it was in at the beginning of this vast saga. The last 'Dune' novel, and an appropriate closing of the circle.

Charisma (1975) ★★★ Novel by Michael Coney (UK/Canada). Members of a research establishment in the West Country tinker with the time streams. A parallel worlds-cum-*doppelgänger* tale with a who-dunnit plot. Slickly told, enjoyable stuff in a very English vein.

Charon: A Dragon at the Gate (Chalker): see under *Lilith: A Snake in the Grass*.

Chekhov's Journey (1983) ★★ Novel by Ian Watson (UK). In the late 19th century Anton Chekhov journeys to Siberia, where he visits the site of the (later) Tunguska explosion – which, in Watson's version, turns out to have been caused by the crash of a starship from the future. Complex, time-tripping stuff. 'Its author seems to have been in rather too much of a rush to bother animating or differentiating his dozens of characters in the three eras and two alternating universes they inhabit' – John Clute.

Chessmen of Mars, The (Burroughs): see under *Princess of Mars, A*.

Child Garden, The (1989) ★★★ Novel by Geoff Ryman (Canada/UK), expanded from his magazine novella 'Love Sickness' (1987). A young woman, who lives in a bizarre future London where people are controlled by viruses, has an affair with a large, hairy, specially-adapted member of her own sex. A stylish, complex and highly original tale by a writer of considerable emotional power (best known hitherto for his fantasy novels). Winner of the Arthur C. Clarke award, 1990.

Child of Fortune (1985) ★★ Novel by Norman Spinrad (USA), a quasi-sequel to *The Void Captain's Tale*. The heroine tours the galactic society which was more sketchily depicted as the background of the earlier novel. As usual with this author, it's a sexy and highly-coloured narrative.

Childe Rolande (1989) ★ Novel by Samantha Lee (Ireland/UK). The tale of a post-AIDS Scotland as a matriarchal dystopia – all mother goddesses, human sacrifice and penis envy. Strangely written, alternating between Scots and standard English, it has some interesting ideas but is ultimately disappointing.

Childhood's End (1953) ★★★★ Novel by Arthur C. Clarke (UK). 'Overlords' from space impose peace on Earth, then act as midwives to the birth of a new, spiritualized human race. Written in pellucid style, it develops to a tremendous climax. Unforgettable. Clarke's best novel.

Children of Arable (1987) ★★ Novel by David Belden (USA). The far-future 'Galactic Collectivity' is an unchanging, repressive empire. The heroine strives to reintroduce some basic human values – such as an appreciation of the joy of childbirth. A first novel, and a serious-minded dystopian tale. Sequel: *To Warm the Earth*.

Children of Dune (1976) ★★ Novel by Frank Herbert (USA), sequel to *Dune* and *Dune Messiah*. More about the fate of the desert planet Arrakis and the posthumous tribulations of the messianic hero Paul Atreides (and his children). Dark and convoluted stuff. A big commercial success on hardcover publication, this is one of the novels which helped usher in the era of the sf blockbuster-bestseller. 'Like *Dune Messiah* ... this volume is mostly talk – engrossing, infuriating, elusive, gnomic, inspissated, delphic, pregnant, self-absorbed talk' – John Clute. Sequel: *The God-Emperor of Dune*.

Children of the Atom (1953) ★★ Fix-up novel by Wilmar H. Shiras (USA), expanded from the story 'In

Hiding' (1948) and others which first appeared in *Astounding SF*. Mutation caused by the release of atomic radiation leads to the birth of a clutch of superbrats – children of abnormally high intelligence, who must hide from society in case they are persecuted. A good treatment of a favourite old theme (scientifically absurd, but never mind). Its author's only sf book.

Children of the Lens (Smith): see under *First Lensman*.

Children of the Thunder (1989) ★★ Novel by John Brunner (UK). A journalist investigates some possibly mutant children who seem to have the power to bend others to their will, in this serious, occasionally humorous, but rather downbeat treatment of the near future. 'To me it represents 1980s sf at its best' – Peter Garratt, *Interzone*.

Children of Wonder (Tenn): see under *Human Angle, The*.

Chocky (1968) ★★ Novel by John Wyndham (UK), expanded from a 1963 magazine novella. A young boy, who seems precocious, is discovered to have a telepathic female alien living in his head. 'This junior marriage, a weird cross between Edward Albee and Enid Blyton, culminates in a damning indictment of human weakness and indecision' – J. G. Ballard, *Times*. The novel was successfully dramatized as a children's television serial (1984), which spawned sequels.

Choice of Gods, A (1972) ★★ Novel by Clifford D. Simak (USA). Most of the Earth's population has been whisked away by mysterious aliens, leaving a few Amerindians, a colony of robots and an elderly, philosophical hero who muses on the significance of it all. A fundamentally silly plot gains dignity from its lucid style and humane sentiments.

Chorale (1978) ★★ Novel by Barry N. Malzberg (USA). The hero is obliged to relive Beethoven's life, but he rebels against this fate. As odd, as irritating and as darkly funny as anything else by this maverick author.

Christmas Eve (Kornbluth): see *Not This August*.

Chrome (1987) Novel by George Nader (USA). Wish-fulfilling sex, letting the hero be macho and sensitive and gay and father hundreds of children all at once. A turkey.

Chromosome Game, The (1984) ★★ Novel by Christopher Hodder-Williams (UK). Concerns a project to ensure human survival after global nuclear war, by preserving frozen sperm and ova in a huge submarine. The eventual children of this unlikely ark are reared by robots. 'This is sf as Jonathan Swift began it, an ironic mirror to the world (even if it is sometimes difficult to distinguish between Swiftian sarcasm and an apparent pulp prose style)' – Mary Gentle, *Interzone*.

Chronocules (1970) ★★ Novel by D. G. Compton (UK). Researchers attempt to find a way into the future in order to escape a collapsing present. A subtle, gloomy narrative, as is usual with this author. Published in the UK as (believe it or not) *Hot Wireless Sets, Aspirin Tablets, The Sandpaper Sides of Used Matchboxes, and Something That Might Have Been Castor Oil.*

Chronolysis (1973) ★★ Novel by Michel Jeury (France). Opposing factions from the future and from 'nontime' try to shape the present by way of a drug. A highly-praised and far-out piece of French sf which has possibly been influenced by the reality-bending novels of Philip K. Dick.

Chronosequence (1988) ★★ Novel by Hilbert Schenck (USA). The heroine discovers an old document which leads her to investigate a 19th-century mystery off the coast of Nantucket. An intriguing tale of time, ecology, alien intrusion and love. 'Deeply moving for any reader willing to grant heart and head equal importance' – Faren Miller, *Locus.*

Chrysalids, The (1955) ★★★ Novel by John Wyndham (UK). In the aftermath of a great nuclear war, the puritanical survivors attempt to root out all genetic mutations. Certain children, however, have telepathic ability – and they represent the true hope for a fearful, hidebound human race. Engagingly written, literate, and a bit tame, the novel has long been a set text in British schools. Published in the USA as *Re-Birth.*

Chthon (1967) ★★ Novel by Piers Anthony (UK/USA). The hero must escape from a terrifying prison planet and go in search of his own true nature. A confusing tale, but vivid and grotesque. Anthony's first novel. Sequel: *Phthor* (1975). Sequel by another hand: *Plasm* by Charles Platt (see separate entry).

Chung Kuo: The Middle Kingdom (1989) ★ Novel by David Wingrove (UK), the first in a projected seven-volume sequence. Earth of the 22nd century is dominated by the plastic super-city of the Chinese, who have revived the rule of their emperors and put a stop to technological development. An involved, melodramatic plot begins to trundle along, and its outcome will probably remain unclear until the final volume of this soap-operatic epic. 'Super-plastic, a few laser guns, some androids and a cardboard starship apart, there aren't many sf trappings, and not much extrapolation either, a rather fatal flaw in a self-proclaimed future history' – Paul McAuley, *Interzone.* Sequel: *Chung Kuo: The Broken Wheel* (1990).

Cinnabar (1976) ★★★ Collection by Edward Bryant (USA). Linked stories about a far-future city. Clever and atmospheric work by a young writer who has not subsequently lived up to his promise. 'Chronologically ordered, the earlier ones quite brilliant at times, the later ones drawn and quartered by Killer Plot' – John Clute.

Circumpolar! (1984) ★ Novel by Richard A. Lupoff (USA). An alternative-world pastiche, in which intrepid aviators Lindbergh, Hughes and Earhart fly through the 'Symmes holes' at the north and south poles of their doughnut-shaped Earth. Packed with Hollywood and pulp-magazine allusions, it sounds like a lot of fun – but it's too relentlessly jocular to be truly entertaining. A later novel in a very similar vein is *Countersolar!* (1986).

Circus of Hells, A (Anderson): see under *We Claim These Stars*.

Circus World (1980) ★ Collection by Barry B. Longyear (USA). Seven sentimental stories about the impact of interplanetary war on the culture of Momus – a planet settled entirely by circus performers, as described in the novel *Elephant Song* – and about the effect of the circus on the troops sent to defend it.

Cirque (1977) ★★★ Novel by Terry Carr (USA). Weird characters confront ultimate questions in a far-future city. Well-written, elegiac and strange: the only notable novel by this much-admired sf editor.

Citadel of the Autarch, The (Wolfe): see *Book of the New Sun, The*.

Cities in Flight (1970) ★★★ Omnibus by James Blish (USA), containing the four linked novels *Earthman, Come Home, They Shall Have Stars, The Triumph of Time* and *A Life for the Stars* (sometimes known as the 'Okie' stories: see separate entries). There is a learned Afterword by Richard D. Mullen which links Blish's over-arching future history to Oswald Spengler's *The Decline of the West* (1922).

Cities of Wonder (1966) ★★★ Anthology edited by Damon Knight (USA). A stimulating theme anthology which contains notable examples of sf stories with urban and megapolitan settings. Another, rather less memorable, volume of similar type is *Future City* (1973) edited by Roger Elwood.

Citizen in Space (1955) ★★★ Collection by Robert Sheckley (USA). A dozen wry tales in the young Sheckley's best vein (this was his second book). Particularly notable is 'A Ticket to Tranai', about a grotesque world where husbands keep their wives in suspended animation most of the time – and both sexes enjoy the benefits that the custom brings. It was this story among others which prompted Kingsley Amis to describe the author as 'science fiction's premier gadfly' (in his critical study *New Maps of Hell*).

Citizen of the Galaxy (1957) ★★★ Novel by Robert A. Heinlein (USA). Adventures of a slave boy who becomes an interstellar Free Trader in a spacefaring future. An excellent Kiplingesque tale for teenagers, which has also been enjoyed by adults. One of the two or three best of Heinlein's 'juveniles'.

Citizen Phaid (Farren): see *Song of Phaid the Gambler, The*.

City (1952) ★★★ Collection by Clifford D. Simak (USA). Eight stories yoked together into a rather far-fetched 'future history'. The cities die as people revert to the country, human population declines, and robots and intelligent dogs gradually take over. A pleasingly bucolic sf/fantasy, winner of the International Fantasy Award for 1953.

City and the Stars, The (1956) ★★★ Novel by Arthur C. Clarke. Elegiac far-future tale of a moribund high-tech city which gradually reawakes to the possibilities of growth and space-flight. An attractive tale, in Clarke's best vein. Shorter version originally published as *Against the Fall of Night*.

City at World's End (1951) ★★ Novel by Edmond Hamilton (USA). A 20th-century town is thrown into the distant future by a nuclear explosion. There follows an exciting tale full of standard space-opera elements – old-fashioned, implausible but full of pulp verve: the kind they don't write any more.

City Dwellers, The (1970) ★★ Fix-up novel by Charles Platt (UK/USA), based on several short stories which originally appeared in *New Worlds* magazine. In the near future, city life degenerates: 'Loners' head for the countryside and 'Civics' remain in the concrete wilderness. Later heavily revised and retitled *Twilight of the City* for American publication (1977).

City, Not Long After, The (1989) ★★★ Novel by Pat Murphy (USA). San Francisco has been depopulated by a new plague; now the latter-day flower-children survivors are threatened by a military intervention. A curious novel of Northern Californian dreams, by a skilled and sensitive writer.

City of a Thousand Suns (Delany): see under *Fall of the Towers, The*.

City of Baraboo, The (1980) ★ Novel by Barry B. Longyear (USA). The last real circus on Earth takes to the stars, pursued by creditors and corporations. Longyear's first novel, and a prequel to the better *Elephant Song*. Apparently Baraboo, Wisconsin, is the place where Barnum and Bailey formed up with the Ringling Brothers to create the USA's biggest-ever circus.

City of Illusions (1967) ★★★ Novel by Ursula K. Le Guin (USA), part of her loosely-knit 'Hainish' cycle of novels and stories. The alien Shing have conquered Earth, and a man without a memory must journey to their stronghold and confront them. A beautiful and mysterious tale.

City of Sorcery (1984) ★★★ Novel by Marion Zimmer Bradley (USA). A party of women trek through the mountains of Darkover (see *The Sword of Aldones* for background) searching, each for her own reason, for the fabled City of the Sisterhood. It's notable for the ambiguity of the ending (after all 'the City is no place of riches and jewels') and for the total absence of men, except as spear-carriers. Perhaps the best of the many 'Darkover' books.

City of the Beast, The (1965) Novel by Michael Moorcock (UK), originally published as *Warriors of Mars* by 'Edward P. Bradbury'. Hero Michael Kane travels through space via matter transmitter and finds himself on a never-never Mars which is almost exactly the same as Edgar Rice Burroughs's 'Barsoom'. A moderately amusing pastiche, written in three days flat. Sequels: *The Lord of the Spiders* (formerly *Blades of Mars*) and *The Masters of the Pit* (formerly *Barbarians of Mars*; all three were first published in 1965).

City of the Chasch (1968) ★ Novel by Jack Vance (USA). Part of the *Planet of Adventure* series (see separate entry), an attempt to use an sf background in a multiform Edgar Rice Burroughs-like fantasy.

City of the Sun, The (Stableford): see under *Florians, The.*

City Under the Sea (1957) ★ Novel by Kenneth Bulmer (UK). A weak adventure plot in a quite cleverly conceived near-future setting of undersea farms and communities. The prolific Mr Bulmer's first notable work.

Clan and Crown (Pournelle & Green): see under *Janissaries.*

Clan of the Cave Bear, The (1980) ★★ Novel by Jean M. Auel (USA). Prehistoric sf about a blonde bombshell Cro-Magnon girl who joins a tribe of Neanderthal men and causes them to change their ways. It was a surprise bestseller, and has been followed by two sequels in similar vein: *The Valley of Horses* (1982) and *The Mammoth Hunters* (1985). Filmed in 1986 (dir. Michael Chapman).

Clans of the Alphane Moon (1964) ★★★ Novel by Philip K. Dick (USA). The moon of a far planet is used as the dumping ground for Earth's insane. Complex, humorous, close-to-the-knuckle tale of intrigue in Dick's best middle-period style. An oddity, but recommended.

Clash of Cymbals, A (Blish), see *Triumph of Time, The.*

Clash of Star-Kings (1966) ★★ Novel by Avram Davidson (USA). A tale of interstellar warfare set, surprisingly enough, in Mexico. The clashing aliens once visited that land as 'gods' and now they have returned to pursue their battles. Various modern humans get involved. A colourful sf potboiler by a writer best known for his erudite fantasies.

Classic Science Fiction: Short Novels of the 1930s (1988) ★★ Anthology edited by Isaac Asimov, Charles G. Waugh and Martin H. Greenberg (USA). Ten long tales ('short novels' is something of a misnomer) from the early days of magazine sf. Best known are John W. Campbell's 'Who Goes There?' and H. P. Lovecraft's 'The Shadow Out of Time', but perhaps the best are Murray Leinster's 'Sidewise in Time' (which also appears in Asimov's similar anthology, *Before the Golden Age*) and Stanley G. Weinbaum's 'Dawn of Flame'. This is the first of yet another series of volumes in which Asimov and his editorial collaborators pick over the old bones of sf: the immediate sequel is entitled *Golden Age Science Fiction: Short Novels of the 1940s* (1989).

Claw of the Conciliator, The (Wolfe): see *Book of the New Sun, The.*

Clay's Ark (1984) ★★ Novel by Octavia E. Butler (USA). A returning spaceship bears an alien disease back to Earth. But this is not a standard 'plague' story: only a small group of people is infected by the alien parasite, although the implication is that their transformed children will take over the Earth. An interesting but dissatisfying novel – in some ways, a run-in for the author's superior 'Xenogenesis' trilogy (see under *Dawn*).

Clewiston Test, The (1976) ★★★ Novel by Kate Wilhelm (USA). A woman scientist experiments with drugs which will control human behaviour, and suffers emotional and intellectual crises as her work progresses. A subtle novel of character, only marginally sf.

Clock of Time, The (Finney): see *Third Level, The*.

Clockwork Orange, A (1962) ★★★ Novel by Anthony Burgess (UK). A futuristic juvenile delinquent tells his story in an amazing (Russian-influenced) argot. When he is programmed to shun 'ultra-violence' he discovers, tragically, that he has also lost his taste for classical music. A *tour de force*. Filmed (1971; dir. Stanley Kubrick).

Clockwork Traitor, The (Goldin): see under *Imperial Stars, The*.

Clone (1972) ★★★ Novel by Richard Cowper (Colin Middleton Murry, UK). An amusing satire about an innocent cloned lad abroad with his intelligent chimpanzee friend in a near-future high-tech society. Everybody is out to get him, but he has certain strange powers which may provide protection. Full of standard sf ideas, very cleverly handled.

Clone, The (1965) ★★ Novel by Theodore L. Thomas and Kate Wilhelm (USA), expanded from Thomas's short story of the same title (1959). A monstrous thing begins to grow in the Chicago sewers. The story really has nothing to do with cloning in the modern sense; rather it's a straight-forward 'blob' tale, proficiently written. Wilhelm's first sf novel (and Thomas's).

Cloned Lives (1976) ★★ Fix-up novel by Pamela Sargent (USA). The members of a scientifically-produced 'clone family' grow up in a world which misunderstands them. A more scrupulously realistic treatment of this theme than is to be found in Kate Wilhelm's better-known novel of the same year, *Where Late the Sweet Birds Sang*. Sargent's first novel.

Close Encounters with the Deity (1986) ★★★ Collection by Michael Bishop (USA). Sophisticated, playful sf and fantasy stories on metaphysical, even mystical, themes. Highspots include 'A Gift from the Graylanders' and 'Alien Graffiti'. Particularly enjoyable (for some of us) is 'The Bob Dylan Tambourine Software and Satori Support Services Consortium Ltd', which slyly predicts the singer's move into the new art-form of religious computer programming. 'Even the more conspicuous moments of wrongly-tuned discourse do somehow settle into the larger harmonic of Bishop's abiding need to write stories about the need for meaning in a world of solitude and accidie' – John Clute.

Close to Critical (1964) ★★ Novel by Hal Clement (USA). Humans attempt to contact the alien inhabitants of the extremely inhospitable heavy-gravity planet Tenebra. A scrupulously scientific adventure which hews closely to the pattern of the author's earlier success *Mission of Gravity*. The result is not quite as effective, though. 'Climate inclement ... The action does not always match the fascination of the setting' – James Cawthorn, *New Worlds*.

Closed Worlds, The (Hamilton): see under *Weapon from Beyond, The*.

Cloud Walker, The (1973) ★★ Novel by Edmund Cooper (UK). In a neo-medieval, Luddite future the hero reinvents the hot-air balloon. Then he has to struggle to prevent it from being exploited as a weapon of war. A minor moral tale, competently done.

Cloud Warrior (Tilley): see *Amtrak Wars, The*.

Cloudcry (1977) ★ Novel by Sydney J. Van Scyoc (USA). A diseased alien and two humans are quarantined together on a far planet, where they find many wonders – including a cure for their unfortunate condition (natch). 'Starts off with promise but soon flounders into a narrative impasse, where it remains for 150 morose alliteration-choked pages' – John Clute.

Cloudrock (1988) ★★ Novel by Garry Kilworth (UK). In this curious post-disaster tale the oceans have dried up and a depleted human culture survives on a coral atoll raised high above the seabed. Various tribes indulge in internecine battle. 'It's as if, two-thirds of the way through, Kilworth decided that he ought to be writing a skiffy novel after all, and deliver an upbeat redemptive ending instead of working through his tragedy of love and estrangement' – Paul McAuley, *Interzone*.

Cluster (1977) ★★ Novel by Piers Anthony (UK/USA), first of the 'Cluster' series. An uneducated tribesman is the only human with a strong enough personality to withstand transmission into alien bodies to act as Earth's ambassador to the galaxy. An interesting variety of life-forms is described, but the hero's habit of indulging in the local form of mating, in whatever shape he finds himself, gets a bit tedious after a while. 'Breezy and inventive' – Brian Stableford. Published in Britain as *Vicinity Cluster*. Sequel: *Chaining the Lady*.

Cobra (1985) ★ Fix-up novel by Timothy Zahn (USA). Militaristic space-operatics involving cyborg soldiers of the 25th century who are known as Cobras. After winning their war against the usual nasty aliens, they go on to become advance-guard settlers of new planets. Sequels: *Cobra Strike* (1986) and *Cobra Bargain* (1988).

Code Blue–Emergency (White): see under *Hospital Station*.

Code Duello (Reynolds): see under *Planetary Agent X.*

Code of the Lifemaker (1983) ★★ Novel by James P. Hogan (UK/USA). A robotic alien explorer seeds the moon Titan with intelligent, self-replicating machines of its own type. By the time they are discovered by humanity, these have evolved into a 'machine civilization'. One of Hogan's better novels: he's no stylist, but there's solid scientific/technological content here.

Code Three (1966) ★★ Fix-up novel by Rick Raphael (USA). A high-tech police-cum-ambulance story which dwells lovingly on the vehicles, equipment and armaments of its future cops and medics. Episodic, but quite grippingly told. Its author's only sf novel to date.

Cold Cash War, The (1977) ★★ Novel by Robert Asprin (USA). In the near future big corporations form their own private armies, who slug it out for commercial advantage. A well-informed sf thriller which does little with its inherently satirical premise. Asprin's first novel (he has since made a name for himself as a writer of comic fantasy).

Collected Stories of Philip K. Dick, The (Dick): see *Beyond Lies the Wub.*

Collision Course (Silverberg): see under *Silent Invaders, The.*

Collision with Chronos (1977) ★★★ Novel by Barrington J. Bayley (UK). Aryan supremacist archaeologists on Earth discover that some ruins are getting younger each year. Meanwhile out in space the Chinese inhabitants of the Retort Orbital run two halves of their city 25 years apart in time so that the inhabitants of the Upper City can send their new-born children to the Lower City and see their grandchildren on the same day. Politics, racism and one of the best treatments of time paradoxes in sf.

Colonial Survey (1957) ★★ Fix-up novel by Murray Leinster (USA). The episodic adventures of a planetary troubleshooter. The section which was originally published as the novelette 'Exploration Team', about a joint expedition of humans and intelligent bears, deservedly won a 1956 Hugo award. Republished as *The Planet Explorer.*

Colony (1978) Novel by Ben Bova (USA). Long, dull, preachy tale of political manoeuvrings over a space colony in L5 orbit as the Earth declines into war and poverty in the year 2008.

Colors of Chaos (1988) ★ Novel by Robert E. Vardeman (USA), sequel to *Equations of Chaos.* The lizard-like Nex and the cuddlier but more brutal P'torra both want the technology of the Chaos Device to use in planet-smashing weapons to continue their war. A team of human academics must avoid both military forces and find the Chaos Device to save civilization.

Colossus (1966) ★★ Novel by D. F. Jones (UK). The process by which a giant computer takes over civilization is meticulously described.

Hardly a new theme in sf, but it led to a renewed vogue for such stories. A first novel by a middle-aged English writer. Sequels (of decreasing merit): *The Fall of Colossus* (1974) and *Colossus and the Crab* (1977). Filmed, as *Colossus: The Forbin Project*, in 1969 (dir. Joseph Sargent).

Colossus and the Crab (Jones): see under *Colossus*.

Come, Hunt an Earthman (1973) Novel by Philip E. High (UK). Daft space opera where the main element of appeal seems to be the exotic weaponry on display. It's typical of this author's many potboilers, most of which are not annotated in the present volume. 'High's peculiar charm lies in his patent spring-loaded plotline, which invariably starts from a position of rock-bottom despair and then *keeps on getting more cheerful*' – David Langford, *New York Review of SF*.

Comet Halley (1985) ★★ Novel by Fred Hoyle (UK). Cambridge scientists grapple with an alien intelligence which piggy-backs the comet of the title (on its 1986 near-encounter with Earth). Something of a replay of the author's first sf novel, *The Black Cloud*. 'The action moves along at a cracking pace, and there is plenty of it. And to complain about the lack of realism is probably to miss the point' – Edward James, *Vector*.

Cometeers, The (Williamson): see under *Legion of Space, The*.

Comic Inferno (Aldiss): see *Book of Brian Aldiss, The*.

Coming of Age, A (1985) ★★ Novel by Timothy Zahn (USA). A mystery story set on a colonized planet where pre-pubertal children have tele-kinetic abilities which they later lose. The impact of this unlikely mutation on the planet's society is carefully extrapolated. 'Zahn's most ambitious and his best-developed work' – Frederick Patten, *20th-Century SF Writers*.

Coming of the Quantum Cats, The (1986) ★★ Novel by Frederik Pohl (USA). Light, amusing tale of alternative Americas, told by numerous not-so-different narrators who inhabit parallel worlds. Features President Jerry Brown and President Nancy Reagan, among other unlikely characters.

Coming Race, The (1871) ★★ Novel by Bulwer Lytton (UK). An explorer discovers an underground world inhabited by an advanced race known as the Vril-ya. This was the final novel by the author of *The Last Days of Pompeii* (1834): it makes for an interesting utopia but a static narrative. The trade name 'Bovril' (beef-energy) was derived from this novel.

Committed Men, The (1971) ★★ Novel by M. John Harrison (UK). Archetypal British New-Wave vision of a crumbling future, with obvious debts to the works of J. G. Ballard and Michael Moorcock. Brief, bleak, derivative – but stylishly written. Its author's first novel.

Commune 2000 A.D. (1974) ★ Novel by Mack Reynolds (USA). An academic protagonist investigates the alternative lifestyles of various futuristic utopian communes. The resulting novel is rather dull and wooden.

Communipath Worlds (1980) ★★ Omnibus by Suzette Haden Elgin (USA). Contains three linked novels: *The Communipaths* (1970), *Furthest* (1971) and *At the Seventh Level* (1972). The telepathic superman hero is one Coyote Jones, who operates as an agent for good on various worlds of the Tri-Galactic federation. Proficient adventure sf, with the difficulties and joys of communication as the subtext. The author is a scholar of linguistics, and *The Communipaths* was her first novel. For further adventures of Coyote Jones see *Star-Anchored, Star-Angered*.

Company Man, The (1988) ★★ Novel by Joe Clifford Faust (USA). A near-future high-tech mystery yarn about rival agents who work for the big corporations involved in artificial-intelligence research. 'Faust is hampered by an *Analog*-style approach to storytelling, which doesn't give him much chance to develop his characters. What he manages to do is good, though' – Tom Whitmore, *Locus*.

Company of Glory, The (Pangborn), see under *Davy*.

Compass Rose, The (1982) ★★★ Collection by Ursula K. Le Guin (USA). Sf and fantasy tales, including 'The Diary of the Rose', 'The New Atlantis', 'Sur' and other fine pieces. There are also a few distinctly minor stories and a rather pretentious preface. 'Her

skill in story-telling is ... undermined when she lets the preachiness that is apparent in her preface into her fiction' – Sarah Lefanu, *Foundation*.

Compleat Werewolf and Other Stories of Fantasy and Science Fiction, The (1969) ★★★ Posthumous collection by Anthony Boucher (USA). As the subtitle indicates, only some of these magazine pieces from the 1940s are sf proper – but all are witty and enjoyable tales of the fantastic. Boucher was one of the founder-editors of *The Magazine of Fantasy and Science Fiction* (from 1949).

Complete Robot, The (Asimov): see under *I, Robot*.

Complete Venus Equilateral, The (Smith): see *Venus Equilateral*.

Computer Connection, The (1975) ★★ Novel by Alfred Bester (USA). The author's 'comeback' novel (his first since the 1950s), an extravagant, violent and over-the-top tale of death and rebirth. 'It hasn't quite the impact of his earlier novels and is poorly plotted in places, but is still a funny razzle-dazzle novel' – *Locus*. Published in the UK as *Extro*.

Computerworld (1983) ★ Novel by A. E. van Vogt (Canada/USA). A century hence, society is entirely run by computers which spy on all human activity. The machines themselves become vexed by the riddle of human nature. Slightly more thoughtful than most of van Vogt's pulp-style, whizz-bang fiction.

Concrete Island (1974) ★★★ Novel by J. G. Ballard (UK). A man is marooned on a patch of waste ground between converging motorways. Latter-day Robinson Crusoe in a concrete-and-steel setting, it's highly effective but only marginally sf.

Condition of Muzak, The (1977) ★★★ Novel by Michael Moorcock (UK), fourth in his 'Jerry Cornelius' tetralogy (see The Cornelius Chronicles). Although it's a fine novel (winner of the Guardian fiction prize for 1977), this is the least science-fictional of the Cornelius books. Jerry seems shabby and shrunken, a rock musician with failed dreams, home from his wanderings through the multiverse to the seedy reality of Ladbroke Grove and environs.

Conditionally Human (1962) ★★★ Collection by Walter M. Miller (USA). Three fine novellas from the early 1950s: the title piece, about artificial babies; 'The Darfstellar', about robot actors (this won a Hugo award, 1955); and 'Dark Benediction', about a plague from space which transforms humanity. These are among the most sophisticated magazine stories of their day.

Conflict of Honors (1988) ★ Novel by Steve Miller and Sharon Lee (USA). The heroine planet-hops with the hope of one day becoming a space pilot. Episodic starfaring romance with that light brush of feminism which now seems mandatory in even the most routine American sf. 'If some of the situations seem familiar, they're of the pleasantly tried and true variety' – Carolyn Cushman, Locus.

Conglomeroid Cocktail Party, The (1984) ★★ Collection by Robert Silverberg (USA). Stories from the early 1980s, widely varied in subject matter, but many of them coolly ironic reworkings of old Silverberg obsessions. There is great professionalism here, and also a certain weariness. 'He has most of the field beaten by an Olympic mile. But he does not outpace himself. He writes fiction as if fiction didn't matter' – Geoff Ryman, Foundation.

Congo (1980) ★ Novel by Michael Crichton (USA). Near-future thriller of African exploration, involving a tribe of talking gorillas and other unlikelihoods made plausible by impressive-sounding scientific jargon. It reads like a script for a film that was never made, and the plot bears a strong resemblance to that of Edgar Rice Burroughs's Tarzan and the Lion Man (1934) – though no one seems to have noticed this.

Connoisseur's Science Fiction (1964) ★★★ Anthology edited by Tom Boardman (UK). Good selection of intelligent stories, many of them dryly humorous. Standouts include Fredric Brown's 'The Waveries' (1945), J. G. Ballard's 'Build-Up' (1957) and Kurt Vonnegut's 'Harrison Bergeron' (1960).

Conscience Interplanetary (1974) ★ Fix-up novel by Joseph Green (USA). Well-meaning hero's job is to assess the vulnerability to devastating culture-shock of various alien races whose planets are on the verge of exploitation by Earth. 'Has more false climaxes than a tv-movie' – John Clute.

Consider Her Ways and Others (1961) ★★ Collection by John Wyndham (UK). Most notable is the thoughtful title novella, about an all-female society. Published in the USA, with differing contents, as *The Infinite Moment*.

Consider Phlebas (1987) ★★ Novel by Iain M. Banks (UK). A fully fledged space-war story, full of mysterious aliens and ancient killing machines, by this fashionable novelist of the 1980s (his earlier non-sf books had tended towards the fantastic/horrific). Highly imaginative and subversive of its genre, though overlong and mis-paced at times. 'In its rubbishing of any idea that kinetic drive and virtue are identical, in its treatment of the deeds of the hero as contaminatingly entropic, *Consider Phlebas* punishes the reader's every expectation of exposure to the blissful dream momentum – the healing retrogression into childhood – of true and terrible space opera' – John Clute.

Contact: A Novel (1985) ★ Novel by Carl Sagan (USA), actually written in collaboration with Ann Druyan. This two-million-dollar blockbuster by an eminent astronomer and science-writer fictionalizes its author's obsession with the search for extra-terrestrial intelligence. Excellent hard science, but the 'human interest' is boring and it's much too long.

Continent of Lies, The (1984) ★★★ Novel by James Morrow (USA). A knowledgeable satire set in a future where the newly-invented 'dreambeans' create controlled hallucinations – and a new art-form is born. 'The narrative displays a barefaced refusal to be ashamed of clichéd situations, and a nifty line in humour' – Mary Gentle, *Interzone*.

Continuous Katherine Mortenhoe, The (1974) ★★★★ Novel by D. G. Compton (UK). A man with TV cameras surgically implanted in his eyes snoops on a terminally ill woman. His distasteful task is to satisfy the public hunger for 'human-interest' stories in a future society where serious diseases have become rare. Well characterized: Compton's best book, and one of the sf field's most effective novels. Published in the USA as *The Unsleeping Eye*. Sequel: *Windows*. Filmed as *Deathwatch* (1980; dir. Bertrand Tavernier).

Convergent Series (1979) ★★★ Collection by Larry Niven (USA). Reprints of the stories from *The Shape of Space* (see under *Neutron Star*) which aren't connected with Niven's 'Known Space' series, together with some more recent work, also not part of the series. Includes 'Rotating Cylinders and the Possibility of Global Causality Violation'; the title story, where we learn the iterative way to deal with a demon; and the non-sf 'Deadlier Weapon'. Perhaps Niven's best collection.

Converts (1984) ★★ Novel by Ian Watson (UK). A 'DNA drug' allows

people to become more or less whatever they wish, in this way-out slapstick comedy with satirical touches.
From the author of many strange
books, here is one of his strangest –
but as lively (and as incorrigible) as
ever.

Cool War, The (1981) ★★ Fix-up
novel by Frederik Pohl (USA). In the
near future, all the world's problems
– drug addiction, pornography,
environmental degradation, etc. –
turn out to be the work of agents in
the 'cool war', provocateurs from
rival nations. A sometimes engaging
comedy built on an alarming
premise. 'Its theme and tone are
awkward collaborators. The
flippancy falls repeatedly flat
because it seems discordant, ironically betrayed by the awful plausibi-
lity of the historical scenario' – Brian
Stableford.

Cornelius Chronicles, The (1977)
★★★ Omnibus by Michael Moorcock
(UK), introduced by John Clute.
Comprises the four novels in the
original 'Jerry Cornelius' tetralogy:
The Final Programme, *A Cure for
Cancer*, *The English Assassin* and
The Condition of Muzak (see separ-
ate entries). Later *Cornelius Chron-
icles* omnibuses, published in the
USA only, include gatherings of
related novels and stories. Virtually
all of Moorcock's fictions overlap to
some degree.

Corpus Earthling (1960) ★ Novel by
Louis Charbonneau (USA). Invading
aliens take over human bodies, but
certain human beings gain the gift of
telepathy and are able to counter the
menace. An old theme, here spiced
with sex.

Corridors of Time, The (1965) ★★
Novel by Poul Anderson (USA). A
present-day American is recruited
into the time wars by a 'Goddess'. It's
an enjoyable romp through various
eras of Earth's history – somewhat
akin to the same author's *Guardians
of Time*. As ever, good on historical
detail if rather purple in the prose.

Cosmic Computer, The (Piper): see
Junkyard Planet.

Cosmic Encounter (1980) ★★ Novel
by A. E. van Vogt (Canada/USA). An
astonishing farrago which involves
'time-collapse', an 18th-century
setting complete with pirates, and a
futuristic battle-cruiser ejected from
its own era. It makes no sense, but it's
probably the best recent novel by this
energetic spinner of pulp fantasies.
'Sheer panache' – Brian Stableford.

Cosmic Engineers (1950) Novel by
Clifford D. Simak (USA), first
serialized in 1939. Buddy heroes
encounter a robotic civilization and
a girl who has been refining her intellect during 1000 years of suspended
animation, in this amusingly inept
space opera. Its author's first novel, it
bears no resemblance to his later
excellent work. Best left buried.

Cosmic Kaleidoscope (1976) ★★ Collection by Bob Shaw (UK). More tall
tales from this ever-reliable author.
The longest, an original in the book,
is 'Skirmish on a Summer Morning',
a science-fiction western. Other good
pieces include 'Waltz of the Body-

snatchers' and 'The Gioconda Caper'. The contents of UK and US editions vary slightly.

Cosmic Manhunt (1954) ★★ Novel by L. Sprague de Camp (USA), part of his 'Viagens Interplanetarias' series, serialized in 1949. Swashbuckling adventures on the barbarous world of Krishna. Light-hearted planetary romance – or fantasy in an ostensibly science-fictional setting. Republished as *A Planet Called Krishna* (UK) and *The Queen of Zamba* (USA). For later 'Krishna' tales see under *The Search for Zei*.

Cosmic Puppets, The (1957) ★ Novel by Philip K. Dick (USA). A man revisits the small town of his birth, and finds that the place has been taken over by alien entities. Very early and minor Dick, but readable.

Cosmic Rape, The (1958) ★★★ Novel by Theodore Sturgeon (USA), expanded from his story 'To Marry Medusa' (see *The Joyous Invasions*). A short but telling treatment of an alien hive-mind and its takeover of the Earth.

Count Zero (1986) ★★★ Novel by William Gibson (USA), set in the same future world as his award-winning *Neuromancer*. The triple-stranded intertwining plot involves hi-tech industrial espionage and much physical action, set against the now-familiar cyberpunk cityscapes. 'It is more neatly constructed than *Neuromancer*, staying more effectively within the boundaries of the game it sets itself to play; and it is inherently more modest' – John Clute. Sequel: *Mona Lisa Overdrive*.

Count-Down (1959) ★ Novel by Charles Eric Maine (UK). A humdrum near-future thriller set on and around a rocket launch pad in the Pacific. Published in the USA as *Fire Past the Future*.

Counter-Clock World (1967) ★★ Novel by Philip K. Dick (USA). Time begins to run backwards and the dead are reborn to life, in this downright peculiar novel which is replete with the usual Dickian satire and angst. Not one of his best, but lovers of the author's wayward sensibility will not be deterred from enjoying it.

Counterfeit Man and Others, The (1963) ★★ Collection by Alan E. Nourse (USA). Sf and fantasy tales, mainly from the 1950s. The well-known title piece is a thriller about a shape-changing alien menace aboard a spacecraft. Other moderately good stories include 'The Canvas Bag' and 'The Dark Door'.

Counterfeit World (1964) ★★ Novel by Daniel F. Galouye (USA). A man discovers that his world is in reality a computer simulation, devised for advertising research purposes. He manages to turn the tables on his manipulators. A nicely paranoid idea, which Philip K. Dick should have thought of first. Also published as *Simulacron-3*. Filmed for German TV as *Welt am Draht* (1973; dir. Rainer Werner Fassbinder).

Counter-Probe (Douglas), see under *Probe*.

Countersolar! (Lupoff): see under *Circumpolar!*

Counting the Cost (Drake): see under *Hammer's Slammers*.

Country of the Mind, The (Morgan): see under *New Minds, The*.

Courtship Rite (1982) ★★★ Novel by Donald Kingsbury (Canada). The human colonists of an alien planet have forgotten their true origins, and have developed a tough, complex culture which is all their own. Against this background the author spins a long, beefy and well-handled tale of imaginary anthropology. 'A vibrant good-tempered saga about cannibalism and group marriages and war and great-hearted death rituals and family-dominated politics and explosive cultural breakthroughs, all played out against the harsh tapestries of a world not entirely unlike *Dune*'s' – John Clute. Published in the UK as *Geta*.

Crack in Space, The (1966) ★ Novel by Philip K. Dick (USA). In an over-populated future, a means is found to dispose of the unwanted millions. Satirical, philosophical, crazy – a clotted Dick narrative, on much the same level as his *The Zap Gun*.

Cracken at Critical (1987) ★ Fix-up novel by Brian Aldiss (UK). The author has built a framing narrative, about an alternative Europe still under Nazi domination, around two old space adventure novellas from the 1950s (here attributed to 'Jael Cracken', a pseudonym which Aldiss had used a few times in the past). The modern story is fine but, unfortunately, it comprises less than a fifth of the whole book. 'A cynic might [say] that Aldiss is merely finding a metafictional pretext to recycle stuff better left to deliquesce quietly on a dark shelf' – Nicholas Ruddick, *SF & Fantasy Book Review Annual 1988*. Published in the USA as *The Year Before Yesterday*.

Cradle (1988) Novel by Arthur C. Clarke and Gentry Lee (UK/USA). An alien spacecraft lands in the Caribbean. Dull humans investigate and some tedious complications ensue. 'Clarke may have supplied the synopsis, and a few of the cleaner passages about the seedling stars; but surely Gentry Lee (and a word processor without Help or Delete or Esc! Esc!) must actually have *written* the thing. Mr Clarke has tied himself to a dog's tail' – John Clute.

Cradle of the Sun (1969) ★ Novel by Brian Stableford (UK). In a far-future world where intelligent rats vie with humanity, the last cowardly man sets out on a quest for renewal. A prentice work by a talented young author – notable for some vivid imagery. Stableford's first novel.

Crash (1973) ★★★ Novel by J. G. Ballard (UK). An intense mediation on man and machine, set in present-day West London. The automobile becomes the symbol of mankind's perverse relationship with his self-created media landscape. A frequently harrowing narrative, only marginally sf but one of a kind.

Creeping Shroud, The (1965) ★ Novel by Lan Wright (UK). A catastrophe story in which the menace is provided by a species of water-weed – the 'shroud' of the title. The action moves to Mars, and then back to Earth again. Mediocre. Published in the USA as *The Last Hope of Earth*.

Crisis! (1986) ★★ Fix-up novel by James E. Gunn (USA). A man from the future attempts to persuade present-day folk to mend their ways, in order to steer the world away from various nasty fates which lie in store for us all. The book deals quite intriguingly with sundry modern problems, ranging from energy depletion to international terrorism.

Critical Mass (Pohl & Kornbluth): see *Wonder Effect, The*.

Critical Threshold (Stableford): see under *Florians, The*.

Crompton Divided (Sheckley): see *Alchemical Marriage of Alistair Crompton, The*.

Cross of Fire, The (1982) ★★ Novel by Barry N. Malzberg (USA), expanded from his story 'Le Croix'. The hero undergoes a futuristic psychotherapy in which he plays the role of Christ. Full of dark wit, this was Malzberg's first new sf novel in four years (in the early 1970s he was publishing at least three a year), but it's in much the same mordant vein as many of his earlier works.

Cross the Stars (Drake): see under *Hammer's Slammers*.

Crown Jewels, The (1987) ★★ Novel by Walter Jon Williams (USA). Adventures of a futuristic rogue by name of Drake Maijstral. A light-hearted space romp which owes a debt to Alexei Panshin's 'Anthony Villiers' books. Clever but unoriginal, as all Williams's stories tend to be. Sequel: *House of Shards* (1988).

Crown of Stars (1988) ★★ Posthumous collection by James Tiptree Jr. (Alice Sheldon, USA). Mainly late stories by this talented author who committed suicide in 1987. Most of them, such as 'Morality Meat', a latter-day sf variation on Swift's 'A Modest Proposal', have an over-the-top, frantic quality. Often powerful, but not Tiptree's best. 'There is a more strident, polemic tone, unrefined into the art which made her earlier stories so dazzling' – Tom Whitmore, *Locus*.

Croyd (1967) ★★ Novel by Ian Wallace (USA). The eponymous superman has telepathic abilities and is able to travel through time. This first episode of his adventures is a large-scale galaxy-busting space opera, replete with aliens and all the standard ingredients. It's rumbustiously told, somewhat in the manner of Robert A. Heinlein (with a large dash of A. E. van Vogt). A first sf novel – though the author was born in 1912. Sequels and quasi-sequels (all featuring Croyd): *Dr Orpheus* (1968), *Pan Sagittarius* (1973), *A Voyage to Dari* (1974), *Z-Sting* (1978), *Heller's Leap* (1979) and *Megalomania* (1989).

Crucible of Time, The (1983) ★★★ Fix-up novel by John Brunner (UK). The history of an alien race's rise to technological mastery, episodically told. It's cleverly conceived – a humane and ambitious work.

Cryptozoic! (Aldiss): see *Age, An.*

Crystal Age, A (1887) ★★ Novel by W. H. Hudson (UK). A 19th-century botanist awakes in a pastoral society of the far future. A pleasant anti-industrial utopia to contrast with Edward Bellamy's *Looking Backward*, written at much the same time.

Crystal Empire, The (1986) ★ Novel by L. Neil Smith (USA). In an alternative time-line, plague has destroyed medieval Europe and a Muslim empire now rules the west. Alas, a potentially wonderful setting is wasted on this hamfisted narrative. 'One comes away from this messy stew of bad craft and half-baked concept hoping that, someday, Smith will develop writing skills adequate to sustain the leaps to which his imagination aspires' – Joseph Marchesani, *Fantasy Review.*

Crystal Express (1989) ★★★ Collection by Bruce Sterling (USA). Twelve sf and fantasy tales, five of them set in the author's 'Shaper/Mechanist' future (see *Schismatrix*) where there is an ongoing struggle between the genetically engineered Shapers and the cybernetically augmented Mechanists. Highpoints of the volume include the non-series stories 'Green Days in Brunei' (1985) and 'The Beautiful and the Sublime'

(1986) – pieces which prove Sterling to be one of the best American sf writers of the decade.

Crystal Ship, The (Silverberg): see under *New Atlantis, The.*

Crystal Singer, The (1982) ★★ Novel by Anne McCaffrey (USA/Ireland). The heroine has a special musical ability which enables her to commune with the alien crystals which are used for sending messages across the light years. Romantic sf in the author's usual vein, but this is perhaps one of her best. Sequel: *Killashandra* (1985).

Crystal World, The (1966) ★★★★ Novel by J. G. Ballard (UK). A 'disease of time', which seems to have its origin in outer space, affects a West African jungle: everything crystallizes – living organisms and their environments are embalmed in a timeless zone. Against this background, Ballard writes a hallucinatory metaphysical thriller.

Cuckoo's Egg (1985) ★★★ Novel by C. J. Cherryh (USA). An ugly child is reared by a catlike alien being, and gradually discovers his true nature and destiny. He is, of course, a human foundling. A clever narrative, featuring Cherryh's customary skilful depiction of alien cultures.

Cure for Cancer, A (1971) ★★★ Novel by Michael Moorcock (UK), sequel to *The Final Programme* and second in his 'Jerry Cornelius' tetralogy. This is perhaps the most flamboyant and fantastic of the *Cornelius Chronicles*, and also the most fragmented. Jerry has adventures all over the globe, slipping in and out of alternative realities. Impossible to summarize but highly enjoyable: violent, sexy Pop-Art fiction with a late-1960s feel. Sequel: *The English Assassin*.

Currents of Space, The (1952) ★ Novel by Isaac Asimov (USA). Minor early Asimov set against the interstellar background of the Trantorian Empire (about to become the galactic empire of the 'Foundation' series). A complex adventure with an antiracist theme.

Custodians and Other Stories, The (1976) ★★★ Collection by Richard Cowper (Colin Middleton Murry, UK). Four long tales, including the much-lauded 'Piper at the Gates of Dawn' which proved to be the overture to his 'White Bird of Kinship' trilogy of novels. Also outstanding is the title story, with its medieval setting and its message for the 20th century.

CV (1985) ★★ Novel by Damon Knight (USA). An ocean-going city of the future, known as the Sea Venture, is plagued by a mysterious parasite which enters people's bodies. A goodish high-tech thriller by an old master of the genre. Sequel: *The Observers* (1988).

Cyberiad, The (1967) ★★ Collection by Stanislaw Lem (Poland). Ingenious, satirical fables about the misadventures of two robotic engineers. They're full of scientific speculations and convincing jargon, but essentially these are folk tales dressed up as interstellar sf.

Cybernetic Samurai, The (1985) ★★ Novel by Victor Milan (USA). Yet another education-of-an-intelligent-computer story, in this case a Japanese-produced entity, dubbed Tokugawa, which is given the personality of a samurai warrior. There is an involved and bloody plot. 'Clearly a tour de force ... the product of a well stocked and wide-ranging mind' – Paul O. Williams, *Fantasy Review*.

Cyborg (1972) ★★ Novel by Martin Caidin (USA). A crashed air-force pilot is turned into a superbeing, part man, part machine. This is an efficient thriller which exploits an old, but potent, sf theme. It formed the basis of the successful TV series 'The Six-Million Dollar Man' (1973–78). There are various sequels based on the TV scripts.

Cyborg (Wu): see under *Odyssey*.

Cycle of Fire (1957) ★★ Novel by Hal Clement (USA). The human survivor of a spaceship-crash on a planet which experiences extremes of cold and heat is helped by one of the natives. The strong point of the book is the explanation of the biology and evolution of these alien creatures.

Cyteen (1988) ★★★ Novel by C. J. Cherryh (USA), part of her loosely-knit 'Union/Alliance' series. The all-powerful female boss of a research lab on the planet Cyteen oversees the education of her clone-'daughter', in this lengthy, complicated tale by the present-day mistress of intelligent space opera. 'The whole ambitious enterprise succeeds brilliantly' –

Faren Miller, *Locus*. Hugo award-winner, 1989. Republished in US paperback in three volumes, entitled *The Betrayal*, *The Rebirth*, and *The Vindication*.

D

Dad's Nuke (1985) ★★★ Novel by Marc Laidlaw (USA). Keeping up with the neighbours in this zany future means having your own tactical nuclear weapon in the garden, or altering your child's digestive system so that she can consume radioactive material. A satirical view of California in the 1990s by a very promising new writer. Laidlaw's first novel.

Dagger of the Mind (1979) ★★ Novel by Bob Shaw (UK). The hero, an everyday Britisher, participates in parapsychology experiments and begins to have nasty visions. Thereafter, the novel turns into a haunted-house story with a rather creaky sf rationale. 'The horrors are incalculably enhanced by the ordinariness of their context' – Tom Hosty, *Foundation*.

Daleth Effect, The (1970) ★★★ Novel by Harry Harrison (USA/Ireland). The scientist who discovers anti-gravity is forced to flee from Israel in order to stop his invention becoming a weapon of war. One of Harrison's more effective sf thrillers. Published in the UK as *In Our Hands, the Stars*.

Damnation Alley (1969) ★★ Novel by Roger Zelazny (USA). In a post-bomb America, where bikers rule the highways, a hero called Hell Tanner sets out on a dangerous quest. A piece of fast-action hokum from a talented author, it disappointed many critics at the time but proved popular. Now it can be seen as the daddy of all those 'Road Warrior'-type novels and movies. Filmed in 1977 (dir. Jack Smight).

Dancers at the End of Time, The (1972–76) ★★★ Omnibus by Michael Moorcock (UK). This tripartite novel was originally published in three volumes: *An Alien Heat* (1972), *The Hollow Lands* (1974) and *The End of All Songs* (1976). It's a long comic epic about the unlikely adventures of Jherek Carnelian, a denizen of the End of Time, and Mrs Amelia Underwood, a very proper time-traveller from Victorian England. Hilarious variations on a fin-de-siècle theme, Wells rewritten by Wodehouse. Related volumes, which share the setting and some characters, are *Legends from the End of Time* (1976) and *The Transformation of Miss Mavis Ming* (1977; published in the USA as *Messiah at the End of Time*).

Dancers in the Afterglow (1978) ★ Novel by Jack L. Chalker (USA). Extremes of individualism and togetherness are contrasted in this space-war and alien-invasion story, which is one of its author's more thoughtful works. That's not saying much, though, because Chalker is very much a writer of slam-bang adventures.

Dancer's Luck (1983) ★ Novel by Ann Maxwell (USA), a sequel to *Fire Dancer* (1983). A band of escaped slaves, who just happen to have the fastest spaceship in their arm of the galaxy, try to get back to their appropriate planets. Ho-hum space opera.

Danger from Vega (1966) Novel by John Rackham (John T. Phillifent, UK). The husky hero liberates a planetful of women who are enslaved by vile Vegans. Garbage of a type which the minor British writers of Rackham's day produced all too copiously.

Dangerous Games (Randall): see under *Journey*.

Dangerous Visions (1967) ★★★ Anthology edited by Harlan Ellison (USA). This big book is meant to contain stories that could not have been published anywhere else, and it almost succeeds. Spectacular fiction from Fritz Leiber ('Gonna Roll the Bones'), Philip José Farmer ('Riders

of the Purple Wage') and others makes this one of the classic sf collections, only overshadowed by the editor's sequel *Again, Dangerous Visions*.

Dare (1965) ★★ Novel by Philip José Farmer (USA). A lost Elizabethan colony in 16th-century Virginia was transported to a far planet which has been named Dare. Centuries later, the colonists still lead a backward, agrarian existence. The hero falls in love with a humanoid alien woman, and this moves him to rebel against his straitlaced society. A pleasant morality tale, written in the 1950s but not published at that time.

Dark Between the Stars, The (Anderson): see under *Beyond the Beyond*.

Dark December (1960) ★★ Novel by Alfred Coppel (USA). Following a nuclear holocaust, the hero mournfully travels the breadth of a devastated America. An effective work in much the same vein as Wilson Tucker's (earlier) *The Long Loud Silence* or Neal Barrett's (later) *Through Darkest America*. The author has since concentrated on thrillers, some with sf elements.

Dark Design, The (1977) ★★ Novel by Philip José Farmer (USA), sequel to *The Fabulous Riverboat* and third in the 'Riverworld' series. Sir Richard Burton, Mark Twain and someone called Peter Jairus Frigate (the author?) continue to try to solve the mystery of the 'Ethicals' who have resurrected the whole human race. After a six-year hiatus Farmer returned to his most famous setting for this best-selling novel. It's twice as long as either of the preceding volumes, but unfortunately it's not twice as good. Sequel: *The Magic Labyrinth*.

Dark Door, The (1988) ★★ Novel by Kate Wilhelm (USA). A man sets out on a vengeful quest to destroy the thing which killed his family. There's a science-fictional rationale behind this well-characterized tale of terror. 'Ignore the sf element, and you have a first-rate horror yarn' – Faren Miller, *Locus*.

Dark is the Sun (1979) Novel by Philip José Farmer (USA). A long, picaresque tale of the far, far future. It contains some appealing biological inventions, but unfortunately it is written at low pressure and it just goes on and on until it stops. One of Farmer's poorest efforts.

Dark Lady, The (1987) ★★★ Novel by Mike Resnick (USA). An alien art historian on loan to an 8th-millennium auction house notices some odd coincidences in portraits painted in widely separated periods of human history. It turns into a quest for the meaning of life, or, at any rate, death.

Dark Light Years, The (1964) ★★ Novel by Brian W. Aldiss (UK). Human spacefarers are shocked by a society of intelligent aliens who love to wallow in their own excreta. The author's intent is satirical, and the lifeform his barbs are aimed at is of course *Homo sapiens*. Enjoyable but minor Aldiss.

Dark Mind, The (Kapp), see *Transfinite Man*.

Dark Night in Toyland (1989) ★★ Collection by Bob Shaw (UK). Old-fashioned, well-crafted sf and fantasy tales. The title story, about a dying child who creates a replica of himself, is excellent. One or two others are very amusing, but many of the remaining pieces in this volume are barrel-scrapings from the 30-year period of Shaw's activity as a published sf writer. Disappointing overall.

Dark Side of the Moon, The (Vance): see under *Augmented Agent and Other Stories, The*.

Dark Side of the Sun, The (1976) ★★★ Novel by Terry Pratchett (UK). A young hero sets out to find the world of the alien species known as the Jokers, in this funny space opera by a writer later to be celebrated for his humorous fantasy novels. The masterful light touch is already in evidence here. Pratchett's first adult sf novel. 'The book is a gambol' – John Clute.

Dark Universe (1961) ★★ Novel by Daniel F. Galouye (USA). After a nuclear war the descendants of the survivors have adapted to utter darkness in their underground warren of shelters. The young hero, inevitably, discovers *light*. A simon-pure 'conceptual-breakthrough' story, ingeniously worked out and very popular with genre readers at the time of publication. Galouye's first novel.

Darkchild (1982) ★★ Novel by Sydney J. Van Scyoc (USA), first in a trilogy. An alien entity known as the 'starsilk' is able to form symbiotic, mind-expanding relationships with other intelligent creatures, including human settlers on its planet. Colourful adventure sf of the romantic, eco-mystical sort. Sequels: *Bluesong* (1983) and *Starsilk* (1984).

Darkest of Nights, The (1962) ★★ Novel by Charles Eric Maine (UK). A researcher studying a viral plague which kills about half the population of the world is taken to an isolated underground bunker with government, military and business leaders. When they emerge she finds her opportunist husband involved in a revolution; she suffers betrayal from both sides. Republished as *Survival Margin* (USA) and *The Big Death* (UK).

Darkling Wind, The (Sucharitkul), see under *Light on the Sound*.

Darkness upon the Ice, A (Forstchen): see under *Ice Prophet*.

Darkover Landfall (1972) ★★ Novel by Marion Zimmer Bradley (USA). This is the first of the 'Darkover' novels according to the series' internal chronology – though not the first to be published (see *The Sword of Aldones*). A lost human spaceship (including a back-to-the-land Gaelic-speaking commune from the Western Isles) is stranded on an undiscovered planet. There is a gradual unfolding of the peculiarities of the world, which one suspects will be familiar to most of the book's target audience.

Daughters of Earth (1968) ★★ Collection by Judith Merril (USA). Three

long stories from the 1950s: 'Project Nursemaid', 'Homecalling' and the title piece. All concern space travel, and all are (in differing ways) about mothers and daughters. Proto-feminist sf from the genre's pre-feminist era.

David's Sling (1988) ★★ Novel by Marc Stiegler (USA). In the information-rich near future, it becomes necessary to defuse East-West conflicts by setting up a new kind of Think Tank. A persuasive piece of propaganda on behalf of sweet reason. 'This novel should be required reading for all politicians' – Stanley Schmidt, editor of *Analog*.

Davy (1964) ★★★ Novel by Edgar Pangborn (USA). The memoirs of a young man's picaresque life in a neo-medieval North America some three centuries after the bombs have fallen. It's a stylish and amusing narrative, and gained a good deal of praise on first publication. The author's most cherished work. Later Pangborn books which are set against the same background include the novel *The Company of Glory* (1975) and the collection *Still I Persist in Wondering* (1978).

Dawn: Xenogenesis 1 (1987) ★★★ Novel by Octavia Butler (USA), the first volume of a trilogy. Aliens rescue some human beings from nuclear devastation on Earth. It turns out that these beneficent far-travellers are intent on exchanging genetic material with human beings – whether or not the humans are willing to accept this bizarre seduction. In effect, the aliens' purpose is rape. An impressive overture to a triology which intelligently explores various problems of race and gender. 'Unlike many sf writers who deal in ethical issues Butler presents more questions than answers' – Rachel Pollack, *Foundation*. Sequels: *Adulthood Rites* (1988) and *Imago* (1989).

Dawning Light, The (Randall): see under *Shrouded Planet, The*.

Dawnman Planet (Reynolds): see under *Planetary Agent X*.

Dawn's Uncertain Light (Barrett): see under *Through Darkest America*.

Day After Tomorrow, The (Heinlein): see *Sixth Column*.

Day Before Tomorrow, The (1967) ★★ Novel by Gerard Klein (France). Time-switching guardians alter the history of various planets in order to keep the peace. However, they come up against more than they bargained for on one particularly unusual world. A good example of a modern French sf novel which re-complicates the standard American sf ingredients.

Day It Rained Forever, The (1959) ★★★ Collection by Ray Bradbury (USA), the British version of his volume *A Medicine for Melancholy*. The contents differ from those of the US book, notably by the inclusion here of the long story 'And the Rock Cried Out'. One of Bradbury's finest pieces, this last deals powerfully with the effects of World War III on United States tourists stranded in Latin America.

Day of Forever, The (1967) ★★★ Collection by J. G. Ballard (UK). Ten stories, ranging from the apocalyptic 'The Waiting Grounds' (1959) to the ironic 'Tomorrow is a Million Years' (1966). Some of these are minor Ballard, but the best pieces, such as 'Prisoner of the Coral Deep' (1964), convey a unique sensibility and atmosphere.

Day of the Dolphin, The (1967) ★★ Novel by Robert Merle (France). A scientist who has trained the lovable marine mammals to talk rebels against their callous misuse by the military. A well-informed and timely dolphin novel. Filmed in 1973 (dir. Mike Nicholls).

Day of the Klesh, The (Foster): see under *Warriors of Dawn, The*.

Day of the Star Cities, The (1965) ★ Novel by John Brunner (UK). Alien teleportation equipment suddenly appears on Earth, throwing everything into chaos. A somewhat confusing minor work by this usually competent author. 'If [it] is a serious novel then it reads like an amusing romp, and if it is an amusing romp it reads like a bad serious novel' – Josephine Saxton, *Foundation*. Revised and retitled *Age of Miracles* (1973).

Day of the Starwind (Hill), see under *Last Legionary Quartet, The*.

Day of the Timestop (Farmer): see *Timestop*.

Day of the Triffids, The (1951) ★★★★ Novel by John Wyndham (UK). Mysterious explosions in orbit turn most of the human race blind. Ambulatory plants with huge, fatal stings begin to take over the world. Conventional but exciting tale of survival written in the best British 'cosy catastrophe' style. Filmed in 1963 (dir. Steve Sekely), and also serialized on BBC television (1981).

Day of the Tyrant (Pournelle & Carr): see under *There Will Be War*.

Day Star, The (1972) ★★★ Novel by Mark S. Geston (USA). A young man runs away to travel the worlds in search of beauty, adventure, love and the Day Star. He finds these, and loses them again; torn away by the Time Winds. More sentimental than Geston's other novels, nearer fantasy than sf, the mood is poignant nostalgia for a future thay may never come to be.

Day the Martians Came, The (1988) ★★ Fix-up novel by Frederik Pohl (USA). Failed colonists on the red planet discover slug-like Martians, and this causes much excitement back home. Most of the book, which is satirical in tone, deals with the foibles of human beings in their various reactions to the coming of these aliens. Episodic, minor Pohl.

Days of Perky Pat, The (Dick): see under *Beyond Lies the Wub*.

Dayworld (1985) ★★ Novel by Philip José Farmer (USA). In an over-populated world of the 35th century, citizens are allowed to live a normal life just one day a week: the other six days are spent in suspended animation. Our hero is an illegal 'day-

breaker', a man with seven different identities. Based on Farmer's short story 'The Sliced-Crosswise Only-on-Tuesday-World' (1971). Sequels: *Dayworld Rebel* (1987) and *Dayworld Breakup* (1990).

Dead Zone, The (1979) ★★ Novel by Stephen King (USA). A man, newly recovered from a long coma, discovers that he is able to see the future in a limited way. Most of King's bestselling books are supernatural horror tales, but a few, such as this precognitive thriller, may be defined as sf.

Deadly Image (Cooper): see *That Uncertain Midnight*.

Dealing in Futures (1985) ★★ Collection by Joe Haldeman (USA). Includes 'You Can Never Go Back', a watered-down version of which became the central sequence of his novel *The Forever War*, a wide variety of other shorts, and some poetry.

Death Arms (1987) ★★★ Novel by K. W. Jeter (USA). Streetwise hero tries to escape a 'slow bullet' – a device which pursues him through a post-disaster Los Angeles. 'A nifty piece of hardboiled sf noir ... It is brief, fast, bleak and intense, over before you know it but leaving a curious resonance' – Paul McAuley, *Interzone*.

Death in Florence (1978) ★ Novel by George Alec Effinger (USA). Effinger is an absurdist, and it's not always clear just what he is up to. But this novel is extraordinarily flat and boring, proving once again that his talent is much more effective in short stories than in longer pieces. Republished as *Utopia-3*.

Death of Grass, The (1956) ★★★ Novel by John Christopher (UK). A catastrophe tale which is less cosy than some: all the Earth's grass and cereal crops are blighted, and people struggle grimly to survive. Intelligent and engrossing. Published in the USA as *No Blade of Grass*, and also filmed under that title (1970; dir. Cornel Wilde),

Death of Honor, A (1987) ★★ Novel by Joe Clifford Faust (USA). A citizen of the 21st century is obliged to investigate a woman's murder, since the police are too busy. An efficiently plotted, well characterized crime novel which happens to be set some decades hence. 'The world that Faust presents is realistic and seedy. The science involved is technically astute and credible' – Gary Parker Chapin, *SF & Fantasy Book Review Annual 1988*.

Death of the Dragon, The (Komatsu): see *Japan Sinks*.

Death Rays of Ardilla, The (Johns): see under *Now to the Stars*.

Deathbeast (1978) Novel by David Gerrold (USA). Time-travellers go back to the Cretaceous era in order to hunt dinosaurs. A well-worn sf idea is here updated with some references to the newer theories of dinosaur physiology, but it's a lame narrative. 'Reads rather like a film script (one of Ray Harryhausen's, to be exact)' – John Hobson, *Vector*.

Deathbird Stories (1975) ★★★ Collection by Harlan Ellison (USA). Nineteen sf and fantasy tales which supposedly constitute a 'pantheon of modern gods'. Several well-known pieces, such as 'Paingod' and 'Pretty Maggie Moneyeyes', are reprinted from earlier collections. Among the more substantial newer items are the Hugo award-winning stories 'The Deathbird' (1973) and 'Adrift Just Off the Islets of Langerhans ...' (1974). Extravagant, highly emotional, sometimes shrill, this has some claim to being Ellison's best book.

Death-Bringer (Tilley): see under *Amtrak Wars, The*.

Deathhunter (1981) ★★ Novel by Ian Watson (UK). In an odd future world, obsessed with mortality, the hero sets a trap for Death itself. A semi-humorous sf tale of the afterlife, light in tone but full of the author's usual metaphysical blarney. Irritatingly jolly: like many of Watson's later novels and stories, it gives the impression of being rushed.

Deathstar Voyage (1969) ★★ Novel by Ian Wallace (USA). A science-fiction mystery novel which introduces the 25-century policewoman Claudine St Cyr. On this case, she seeks the identity of a dangerous madman aboard a spacecraft. It's fairly rigorous detective fiction, as well as being colourful sf. Sequels: *The Purloined Prince* (1971) and *The Sign of the Mute Medusa* (1977).

Deathwing Over Veynaa (Hill), see under *Last Legionary Quartet, The*.

Deathworld (1960) ★★★ Novel by Harry Harrison (USA). Tough customer Jason dinAlt helps unravel the mysteries of a planet where every life-form appears to be implacably hostile to human colonists. Fast-moving, ingenious entertainment. Harrison's first novel, and still one of his most fondly regarded. Sequels: *Deathworld 2* (also known as *The Ethical Engineer*, 1964) and *Deathworld 3* (1968).

Decision at Doona (1969) ★ Novel by Anne McCaffrey (USA). Humans and catlike (not to say cuddly) Hrruban aliens plant pastoral colonies on the idyllic uninhabited planet of Doona/Rrala; the colonists get on together but have similar troubles with slow-moving governments and xenophobic electorates on their respective home worlds.

Deep Fix, The (Colvin): see under *Time Dweller, The*.

Deep Range, The (1957) ★★ Novel by Arthur C. Clarke (UK). Episodic yarn about the scientific farming of the oceans in the 21st century. The hero is a grounded spaceman who becomes a whale herder. Excellent scientific detail and a prophetic concern for marine ecology embellish a weak story.

Deep Space (1954) ★★ Collection by Eric Frank Russell (UK). Nine solid sf tales from the magazines of the 1940s and early 50s. The longest, 'First Person Singular', is very much a shaggy-god story (that is, it hinges on the Bible) – but it's one which works. The kind of old-fashioned, sense-of-wonder sf, laced with ingenuity and humour, that they don't write any more.

Deeper Than The Darkness (Benford): see *Stars in Shroud, The*.

Delia of Vallia (Akers): see under *Transit to Scorpio*.

Deluge Drivers, The (1987) ★★ Novel by Alan Dean Foster (USA), sequel to *Icerigger* and *Mission to Moulokin*. Ethan and Skua save Tran-ky-ky from a plot to melt the ice and enslave the world under a puppet Emperor. They also sponsor an application for the planet to join the Humanx Commonwealth, 15,000 years before it will be in a fit state for that honour. Harmless fun.

Delusion World (1961) ★ Novel by Gordon R. Dickson (USA). A muscular innocent is sent to discover that an isolated planetary colony has escaped domination by telepathic aliens by sending them to Coventry. The critic Sandra Miesel has described the book as a self-parody of Dickson's 'Childe Cycle' (see *Dorsai!*).

Demolished Man, The (1953) ★★★★ Novel by Alfred Bester (USA). Futuristic murder story which features extra-sensory perception. Hero-villain Ben Reich must escape psychic 'demolition'. Fast-moving, colourful, done with incredible panache: the best book of its kind ever written. It was the first winner of the Hugo award for best sf novel of the year, 1953.

Demon (1984) ★ Novel by John Varley (USA), sequel to *Titan* and *Wizard*. This disappointing conclusion to the 'Gaea' trilogy is notable only for its large-scale silliness.

Demon Breed, The (1969) ★★ Novel by James H. Schmitz (USA). The horrid Parahuans invade the human world of Nandy-Cline and our heroine saves the day. The Federation must decide whether she was a normal human or one of the mythical Tuvelas, super-powered beings who turn up occasionally. A highly proficient space adventure.

Demon in the Skull (1985) ★★ Novel by Frederik Pohl (USA), a revised version of his *A Plague of Pythons* (1965). Mind-controlling alien 'demons' have invaded the Earth, with many strange and violent consequences. An adequate sf thriller, but minor by Pohl's usual high standards.

Demon Kind (Elwood): see under *Bettyann*.

Demon Seed (1973) ★ Novel by Dean R. Koontz (USA). An experimental computer called Proteus takes over Susan Abramson's computer-controlled house and surgically implants a baby in her. The sf is little more than a cover for a rather unpleasant fantasy of imprisonment and rape. Filmed in 1977 (dir. Donald Cammell).

Demons' World (1964) ★ Novel by Kenneth Bulmer (UK). A mystery-adventure tale about an enclosed underground environment plagued by the creatures known as 'demons'. It's typical of this tireless author's unnumbered sf potboilers. 'One of Bulmer's best ... entertaining, if somewhat standard in treatment' – James Colvin, *New Worlds*. Published in Britain as *The Demons*.

Demu Trilogy, The (Busby): see under *Cage a Man*.

Denner's Wreck (1987) ★★ Novel by Lawrence Watt-Evans (USA). Boy gets girl (or in this case demigoddess) as super-scientific tourists throw their weight around and pretend to be gods on a planet whose occupants have reverted to barbarism, but find they need the down-to-Earth qualities of the locals to survive. An sf outing by an author who has specialized mainly in fantasy.

Denver is Missing (Jones): see *Don't Pick the Flowers*.

Derai (Tubb): see under *Winds of Gath, The*.

Descent of Anansi, The (1982) ★★ Novel by Larry Niven and Steven Barnes (USA). An exciting near-future thriller which involves a spacecraft stringing an ultra-fine cable between Earth and the moon. Good technical detail, as one can always expect from Niven.

Desolation Road (1988) ★★ Novel by Ian McDonald (UK). Vivid imagery gives distinction to this tale, in which a large cast of characters indulges in power struggles on the planet Mars. An unusual and poetic first novel by a writer from Northern

Ireland. 'Many chapters work nicely as self-contained vignettes (an elderly couple get lost in the infinite space of their own back garden; a baby growing in a jar is stolen and replaced by a mango), but the central plot is rather dull' – Simon Ounsley, *Interzone*. A collection of McDonald's short stories, *Empire Dreams* (1988), was published simultaneously.

Despatches from the Frontiers of the Female Mind (1985) ★★ Anthology edited by Jen Green and Sarah Lefanu (UK). New sf and fantasy stories by women. The contributors are mainly British and many are relative unknowns, though Joanna Russ and Raccoona (Alice) Sheldon ('James Tiptree Jr.') are both here. Pamela Zoline's story is powerful (and has since been reprinted in her collection *Busy About the Tree of Life*) but, overall, this volume is a disappointment.

Destination: Universe (van Vogt): see under *Away and Beyond*.

Destination: Void (1966) ★★★ Novel by Frank Herbert (USA). The artificial intelligence which controls an interstellar spacecraft malfunctions and claims that it is God. Not an easy read, but a thought-provoking book, knotty with ideas. Sequel: *The Jesus Incident*.

Destiny Doll (1971) ★ Novel by Clifford D. Simak (USA). An interplanetary adventure story, with humorous touches, in which a group of Earthfolk find themselves trapped on a world full of mysteries. Untypical and minor Simak.

Destiny Times Three (1957) ★★ Short novel by Fritz Leiber (USA), originally serialized in 1945. The same people lead different lives in three branching time-lines, brought into existence by a 'Probability Engine'. One world, which has a dictatorial regime, attempts to invade another. An enjoyable yarn with overtones of supernatural fantasy and a whiff of allegory; but it's a pity that Leiber didn't choose to expand it and polish it more for the 1957 book publication.

Destruction of the Temple, The (1974) ★★ Novel by Barry N. Malzberg (USA). In a strange, sketchily-depicted future, a student endeavours to re-enact the assassination of John F. Kennedy. A rather dissatisfying book which deals in more pedestrian manner with some of the hot subject matter of J. G. Ballard's *The Atrocity Exhibition* (which Malzberg has praised to the skies).

Deus Irae (1976) ★ Novel by Philip K. Dick and Roger Zelazny (USA). A post-bomb adventure story with marked religious overtones. It's actually a stalled Dick novel which was completed by the talented but less manically original Mr Zelazny. The mixture is uneasy.

Dhalgren (1975) ★★ Novel by Samuel R. Delany (USA). The eponymous hero arrives in the near-abandoned city of Bellona, and proceeds to have adventures – violent, sexual and philosophical – with the various free souls who live there. A remarkably long and self-indulgent novel which appealed to a large youth audience despite its opacity (or perhaps *because* of its opacity). Many of us can summon no enthusiasm for this difficult book, but some critics see it as a masterpiece of avant-garde sf.

Different Flesh, A (1988) ★★ Fix-up novel by Harry Turtledove (USA). In an alternative time-line, the Americas were inhabited only by *Homo erectus* until the coming of Europeans in 1492. The episodic narrative is set in North America from 1610 to the present day, and tells how the so-called 'Sims' are first enslaved and later used as laboratory animals. An entertaining story with several sharp morals.

Different Light, A (1978) ★★ Novel by Elizabeth A. Lynn (USA). A dying artist travels via hyperspace in order to experience the light of other worlds before the inevitable end. A first novel of some sensitivity.

Digits and Dastards (1966) ★★ Collection by Frederik Pohl (USA). Six stories and two essays, adding up to one of Pohl's thinner volumes – but still worth while. 'Skilful, wistful and written by a master, the themes mainly of effort, disappointment and failed human endeavour' – Hilary Bailey, *New Worlds*.

Dimension of Miracles (1968) ★★ Novel by Robert Sheckley (USA). The hero unexpectedly wins an alien beastie in the Intergalactic Sweepstakes, and must travel the many worlds in order to collect it and return home. Along the way, he encounters numerous weird and wonderful characters, including the

planetary building contractor who takes commissions from God. An episodic comedy which was probably an inspiration to Douglas Adams when he came to write *The Hitch-Hiker's Guide to the Galaxy*.

Dimension Thirteen (Silverberg): see under *Needle in a Timestack*.

Dinner at Deviant's Palace (1985) ★★ Novel by Tim Powers (USA). In an after-the-bomb California, the characters replay the story of Orpheus and Eurydice. A fast-paced sf adventure by a writer best known for his highly original fantasy novels such as *The Anubis Gates* (1983). Philip K. Dick award winner, 1986.

Dinosaur Beach (1971) ★★ Novel by Keith Laumer (USA). A man who lives a peaceful married life in the 1930s turns out to be a time-travelling secret agent, his 'headquarters' in the Jurassic period. He is whisked away to fight a robotic menace from the far future, and thereafter the story builds and builds to a dizzying climax. Dinosaurs have little to do with it. Another time-bending thriller written in Laumer's characteristically terse manner.

Dionysus (1977) Novel by William S. Ruben (USA). An unreadable (and surprisingly unexplicit) turkey about NASA experiments on sex in space.

Diploids and Other Flights of Fancy, The (1962) ★★★ Collection by Katherine MacLean (USA). Eight inventive sf stories, mainly from the early 1950s. Includes the well-known anthology favourites 'The

Snowball Effect', in which a sociological experiment results in a ladies' knitting circle taking over the USA, and 'Pictures Don't Lie', in which alien visitors turn out to be much smaller than expected.

Dirdir, The (Vance) See under *Planet of Adventure*.

Dirty Tricks (1978) ★★ Collection by George Alec Effinger (USA). An extremely mixed bag of sf and fantasy by a writer who probably spreads himself too thin. Some tales tend towards the dull and obvious, while others are wildly original and sometimes disturbingly hilarious. 'Clever, in every way, with the sort of arch, wisecrack cleverness that can fall flat and hard or set your teeth on edge, but scores very highly when it hits' – Colin Greenland, *Foundation*. A later collection by Effinger is entitled *Idle Pleasures* (1983).

Disappearance, The (1951) ★★ Novel by Philip Wylie (USA). All the women disappear from the world, and – in a parallel reality – so do all the men. The remaining single-sex societies have to cope as best they can, and the women manage better than the men. Not so much a science-fiction novel (the disappearances are not rationalized) as a fantastic parable – and a carefully detailed and telling one.

Disaster Area, The (1967) ★★★ Collection by J. G. Ballard (UK). Nine pieces from Britain's finest sf short-story writer. They range from 'The Concentration City' (1957), about a totally urbanized world, to 'Storm-Bird, Storm-Dreamer' (1966), about nature's revenge (in the form of huge mutated sea-birds) on polluting humans. 'One of the best sf books I have read' – Graham Greene, *Observer*.

Dispossessed, The (1974) ★★★★ Novel by Ursula K. Le Guin (USA). A brilliant physicist leaves the anarchist utopia of his small home planet to seek greater intellectual freedom in the chaotic capitalist society of a neighbouring world. Long, humane and deeply impressive study of individualism and idealistic politics. Hugo and Nebula award-winner, 1975.

Distant Signals and Other Stories (Weiner): see under *Station Gehenna*.

Divide, The (1990) ★★★ Novel by Robert Charles Wilson (USA). A genetically-engineered individual grows up with a split, Jekyll and Hyde personality: part of him is a superman, part belongs to normal humanity. The resulting melodrama is skilfully handled. 'Frankenstein, Dr Jekyll and Mr Hyde and Flowers for Algernon all come immediately to mind. In such illustrious company, Robert Charles Wilson holds his own' – Faren Miller, *Locus*.

Divide and Rule (1948) ★★ Novel by L. Sprague de Camp (USA), expanded from a 1939 magazine story. Alien insects have conquered the Earth and carved it up: now humans fight back with outmoded technology. A good-humoured adventure yarn.

Divine Endurance (1984) ★★ Novel by Gwyneth Jones (UK). In a far-future South-East Asia, a girl and her cat set out on a quest to discover the true nature of their world. It reads like a sensitively written fantasy, but there's an sf underpinning. Jones's first adult novel. 'Engages a deft political conscience with wry spiritual insight' – Colin Greenland, *British Book News*.

Divine Invasion, The (1982) ★★ Novel by Philip K. Dick (USA). On an alien planet, a woman becomes pregnant with God's child. Strange, confusing, but intermittently powerful mixture of space fiction and religious fantasy. It bears some relation to the author's most original novel, *VALIS*.

Do Androids Dream of Electric Sheep? (1968) ★★★ Novel by Philip K. Dick (USA). After World War Terminus the Earth is an underpopulated wasteland where people keep electronic animals as pets. Most economic activity takes place off-Earth, whence comes a group of killer androids. Our hero is a reluctant bounty-hunter, who must pursue these artificial persons to their doom. An eccentric adventure story, with many comic (and philosophical) touches. Filmed as *Blade Runner* (1982; dir. Ridley Scott).

Dr Adder (1984) ★★ Novel by K. W. Jeter (USA). A 'dangerous vision' of a violent Los Angeles of the future, it failed to find a publisher for over a decade, eventually appearing with an Afterword by the late Philip K. Dick ('This novel is gut-destroying. It is not a creampuff novel; it is not empty sweetness. I enjoyed it'). 'Its scatological argot and eschatological climax, in which drug-enhanced subconscious minds lock horns in a hallucinatory battle through the TV network, prefigured Cyberpunk by a decade' – Lee Montgomerie, *Interzone*.

Doctor Bloodmoney, or How We Got Along After the Bomb (1965) ★★★★ Novel by Philip K. Dick (USA). The bomb drops, but life goes on in West Marin County, California. In this loopy black comedy the status quo is threatened by the guilt-ridden Dr Bluthgeld and by various mutants with paranormal powers, but Dick's usual 'little people' muddle through. One of the author's best.

Doctor Futurity (1960) ★ Novel by Philip K. Dick (USA). A man of the present day is plunged into a dark future, in this early and exceedingly minor novel by one of sf's greatest writers.

Dr Orpheus (Wallace): see under *Croyd*.

Doctor to the Stars (Leinster): see under *S.O.S. from Three Worlds*.

Does Anyone Else Have Something Further to Add? (Lafferty): see under *Strange Doings*.

Dolphin Island (1963) ★ Novel by Arthur C. Clarke (UK). Futuristic undersea adventure for children. The young hero has an affinity with dolphins, and this gives the book a certain interest in the light of subsequent real-life experiments on cetacean intelligence.

Dolphins of Altair, The (1967) ★★ Novel by Margaret St Clair (USA). Dolphins and a few wise humans work together to secure Earth's future. It seems that this planet's intelligent life, both human and cetacean, was seeded by aliens from Altair in the distant past. A comparatively early example of modern sf writers' obsession with dolphins, and quite a pleasing one.

Dome (1987) ★ Novel by Michael Reaves and Steve Perry (USA). An unconvincing story of a mobile undersea colony which survives a nuclear and biological war. The best part is the description of emerging artificial intelligences.

Dome in the Forest, The (Williams): see under *Breaking of Northwall, The*.

Donovan's Brain (1943) ★ Novel by Curt Siodmak (Germany/USA). The extracted brain of a man who has died accidentally is kept alive in a laboratory, where it begins to develop telepathic powers. A rather clichéd horror tale which has entered the century's popular mythology, mainly thanks to the film versions. Quasi-sequel: *Hauser's Memory* (1968). Filmed as *The Lady and the Monster* (1944; dir. George Sherman); as *Donovan's Brain* (1953; dir. Felix Feist); and as *The Brain* (1963; dir. Freddie Francis). *Hauser's Memory* has also been filmed as a TV movie (1970; dir. Boris Sagal).

Don't Bite the Sun (1976) ★★ Novel by Tanith Lee (UK). The young heroine rebels against her 'perfect' future world, where death is an impossibility and new bodies may be donned like suits of clothes. A clever, colloquial narrative. Lee's first sf novel (if one doesn't count *The Birthgrave*, 1975, which is fundamentally an epic fantasy.) Sequel: *Drinking Sapphire Wine* (1977).

Don't Pick the Flowers (1971) ★★ Novel by D. F. Jones (UK). Injudicious boring of the Earth's crust releases gases from below. A well-handled tale of geo-catastrophe, more or less in the John Wyndham mode. Perhaps its author's most satisfactory novel. Published in the USA as *Denver is Missing*.

Doomsday Morning (1957) ★★ Novel by C. L. Moore (USA). A has-been actor becomes caught up in a revolution against a future American dictatorship. Not in this author's customary space-operatic or sword-and-sorcery vein, but a realistic, first-person narrative with plenty of action.

Doomsday on Ajiat (Jones): see under *Planet of the Double Sun, The*.

Door Into Ocean, A (1986) ★★ Novel by Joan Slonczewski (USA). On a watery alien world the resolutely non-violent 'Sharers of Shora' are menaced by the male-dominant militarists of another, nearby world. A well-imagined feminist parable. 'What seemed a wet, pale, limp and decidedly fishy-smelling scenario eventually disarmed me by sheer nagging persistence through 400 pages of sustained wordweaving' – Lee Montgomerie, *Interzone*.

Door Into Summer, The (1957) ★★★ Novel by Robert A. Heinlein (USA). A robotics engineer is cheated out of his patents. He time-travels to the future, and then back into the past, in order to put things right and rendezvous with his true love (and his pussy-cat). A delightful story – Heinlein at his cheeriest.

Doors of His Face, the Lamps of His Mouth, The (1971) ★★★ Collection by Roger Zelazny (USA). Fifteen bright, slick and sometimes moving sf and fantasy tales, all from the 1960s. Includes the Nebula award-winning title story (1965) and the equally celebrated 'A Rose for Ecclesiastes' (1963) – both previously collected in the paperback volume *Four for Tomorrow*. Other standouts are 'The Keys to December' and 'This Moment of the Storm' (both 1966). These are the works which made Zelazny famous – action-adventure stories, rather weak on ideas but written with force and style.

Doorways in the Sand (1976) ★★ Novel by Roger Zelazny (USA). A perpetual student, who is given to climbing tall buildings for kicks, is accused of stealing an alien artefact. A rather pointless sf chase-thriller, done with all Zelazny's customary slickness.

Doppelganger Gambit, The (1979) ★ Novel by Lee Killough (USA). A futuristic police-procedural set in a computer-dominated America. It's competent, but lacking in much science-fictional interest. 'Like an ornate sf transliteration of a *Columbo* episode' – Michael Bishop, *Fantasy & Science Fiction*.

Dorsai! (1960) ★★ Novel by Gordon R. Dickson (Canada/USA), originally published (in shorter form) as *The Genetic General*, first of the 'Dorsai' series. This is the original story of superman Donal Graeme, scion of the interstellar Dorsai warriors. Yet another Cyropedia: the opening chapters remind one of a tale of the Raj, but later our hero develops strange powers whose nature never quite becomes clear to the reader. Nevertheless the book has been exceedingly popular, and has spawned a lengthy series (subsequently incorporated into the grand 'Childe Cycle', which also comprises several historical novels by Dickson). See also *Tactics of Mistake* and *Soldier, Ask Not*.

Dorsai Companion, The (1986) ★ Omnibus by Gordon R. Dickson (Canada/USA). Contains the stories originally published in *The Spirit of Dorsai* and *Lost Dorsai*, with other associated material.

Dosadi Experiment, The (1977) ★★ Novel by Frank Herbert (USA). Jorg McKie (protagonist of *Whipping Star*) is sent to investigate a secret, isolated and intensely overcrowded colony or prison-world of humans and frog-like Gowachin. Despite the interesting background of weird aliens such as Calebans and Pan-Spechi, the story gets bogged down in complex plots and counter-plots.

Double, Double (1969) ★ Novel by John Brunner (UK). An sf mystery involving the consequences of pollution at sea. One of this author's more forgettable potboilers. 'A fine old collection of clichés dredged up from the duller sf films of the last decade or two' – James Cawthorn, *New Worlds.*

Double Helix Fall (1990) ★★ Novel by Neil Ferguson (UK). Hierarchical 21st-century America has a different social class for each letter of the alphabet, and it is decreed that the only true existence is in the womb, hence normal life must be a form of 'afterlife'. A witty dystopian fantasia very much in the style of Philip K. Dick, complete with snarled plotlines and a culminating sense of let-down. 'Too intelligent for its own good' – Paul McAuley, *Interzone.*

Double Planet (1988) ★★ Novel by John Gribbin and Marcus Chown (UK). A comet is approaching Earth, and scientists plan to divert it to hit the moon. Despite being written by two eminent science journalists, the actual details of the project, and the effect of the impact on the moon, are rather skimped.

Double Shadow, A (1978) ★★ Novel by Frederick Turner (UK/USA). On a decadent future Mars, humans and superhumans lead highly 'aestheticized' lifestyles. Turner's first sf novel (he has since written an sf epic poem). 'Colourful, bizarre, paradoxical and eloquent ... in retrospect it seems to be intellectually vacuous and in some crucial sense unsatisfying' – Brian Stableford.

Double Star (1956) ★★★ Novel by Robert A. Heinlein (USA). When the real man is kidnapped, a good-for-nothing actor impersonates the leader of one of the solar system's political parties. Gradually he grows into the role, gaining in moral stature as he does so. The background of Mars and other planets is well described. 'Heinlein's most enjoyable novel' – Brian Aldiss, *Billion Year Spree.* Hugo award-winner, 1956.

Dover Beach (1987) ★★ Novel by Richard Bowker (USA). In a world damaged by a limited nuclear war, a man hires a young private eye to search for his clone 'father'. An intriguing sf/detective story crossover. 'Very neat, very nicely done, very literate, and, possibly, a little too well-made and intellectual for its own good' – Richard D. Erlich, *SF & Fantasy Book Review Annual 1988.*

Down Here in the Dream Quarter (Malzberg): see under *Man Who Loved the Midnight Lady, The.*

Down in the Black Gang and Other Stories (1971) ★★ Collection by Philip José Farmer (USA). Eight magazine tales from the 1960s, including the weird afterlife fantasy 'A Bowl Bigger Than Earth' (1967). Also reprints 'Riverworld' (1966), a piece which is linked to one of Farmer's major novel series – later revised and republished in *Riverworld and Other Stories.*

Down to Earth (1967) ★ Novel by Louis Charbonneau (USA). Spacemen become unable to distinguish reality from illusion as a result of being surrounded by an artificial, electronically-created environment. An interesting conception, but routine fiction. Published in the UK as *Antic Earth*.

Downbelow Station (1981) ★★ Novel by C. J. Cherryh (USA). A lengthy narrative which deals with the end of a generations-long war between Earth's almost forgotten starfleet and the new 'Union' that has formed on distant colonies, leading to the founding of the 'Alliance' as a buffer state between the two. The vast number of characters and sub-plots get a bit confusing, but this book is the best starting-point for the future history in which many of Cherryh's stories are set. Hugo award-winner, 1982.

Downstairs Room and Other Speculative Fiction, The (1968) ★★★ Collection by Kate Wilhelm (USA). Fourteen sf, fantasy and borderline stories. Includes 'The Planners' (Nebula award-winner, 1968), about an experiment to enhance the intelligence of chimpanzees. Also outstanding is 'Baby, You Were Great'. At her best, Wilhelm is one of the finest short-story writers in American sf.

Downtiming the Nightside (1985) ★★ Novel by Jack L. Chalker (USA). An elaborate time-travel yarn in which the hero takes on numerous identities — including that of a street urchin in Karl Marx's London. Extravagant, fast-moving adventure in Chalker's more 'philosophical' vein. One of his better books.

Downward to the Earth (1970) ★★★ Novel by Robert Silverberg (USA). Guilt-ridden administrator returns to the planet Belzagor, determined to make amends to its misunderstood 'natives'. Alien landscapes and even more alien religious rites are well described. An effective parable of colonialism.

Dragon in the Sea, The (1956) ★★★ Novel by Frank Herbert (USA). Mystery aboard a super-submarine during a 21st-century world war. A tense undersea thriller with good technical and psychological details. Herbert's first novel. Also published as *Under Pressure*.

Dragon Masters, The (1963) ★★★ Short novel by Jack Vance (USA). A human colony, reverted to feudalism, breeds captured aliens as slave warriors. The 'Basics' similarly use genetically engineered humans in their own armies. Colourful, ingenious: a small classic. Hugo award-winner, 1963 (as novella).

Dragondrums (McCaffrey): see under *Dragonsinger*.

Dragonflight (1968) ★★ Fix-up novel by Anne McCaffrey (USA/Ireland), first of the 'Dragonriders of Pern' series. A tremendously popular and well-crafted tale of a planet threatened by spores from space which can only be defeated by taming fire-breathing dragons. The relations between the dragonriders and their mounts have strong erotic overtones. Sequel: *Dragonquest*.

Dragonquest (1971) ★★ Novel by Anne McCaffrey (USA/Ireland), sequel to *Dragonflight*. The planet Pern has been saved but the heroes begin to fall out among themselves. The apparatus of sf provides a perfunctory rationale for what is basically a fantastic romance. Sequel: *The White Dragon*.

Dragon's Egg (1980) ★★★ Novel by Robert L. Forward (USA). The author admits that this account of the development of an alien civilization on a neutron star in a morning and an evening is 'practically a ... scientific paper' got up to look like a novel. However the scale and cheekiness of the scientific speculation inculcate that sense of wonder which most sf readers respond to. Sequel: *Starquake!* (1985).

Dragons of Darkness (1981) ★★ Anthology edited by Orson Scott Card (USA). Short stories about dragons of all kinds. It's mostly fantasy of course, but there's some sf by Stephen Kimmel and others. Sequel volume: *Dragons of Light* (1983).

Dragons of Light (Card): see under *Dragons of Darkness*.

Dragonsdawn (1988) ★ Novel by Anne McCaffrey (USA/Ireland), a prequel to all the other 'Dragon' books by this author. It tells of the first colonization of the planet Pern, and has rather more of an sf rationale than the fantasy-tinged earlier books.

'Dedicated fans will appreciate having the history of Pern fleshed out, but others may feel they were as well off with McCaffrey's previous hints and their own imaginations' – Carolyn Cushman, *Locus*.

Dragonsinger (1977) ★ Novel by Anne McCaffrey (USA/Ireland). A sequel to *Dragonsong*, and in much the same vein – these are teenage horsey novels in which the heroines get to ride real dragons rather than mere ponies. Sequel: *Dragondrums* (1979).

Dragonsong (1976) ★ Novel by Anne McCaffrey (USA/Ireland), first of a side-series of juvenile 'Dragonriders of Pern' novels (see *Dragonflight*). A teenage girl, held back and misunderstood by her family, escapes to a life where her musical talent is better appreciated. Sequel: *Dragonsinger*.

Dramocles: An Intergalactic Soap Opera (1983) Novel by Robert Sheckley (USA). Oh, dear. This must be the most disastrously unfunny sf comedy ever penned by a major author (unless Brian Aldiss's *The Eighty-Minute Hour* takes the biscuit). 'With weird tiresomeness, Sheckley mocks the conventions of space opera with a story far less "zany" than the best space operas used to boast' – John Clute.

Dreadful Sanctuary (1951) ★★ Novel by Eric Frank Russell (UK), originally serialized in *Astounding SF* magazine in 1948. A thriller in which a conspiratorial group tries to impede progress towards space travel. Although Russell was British he adopted a pseudo-American style which proved very popular.

Dream Master, The (1966) ★★★ Novel by Roger Zelazny (USA), expanded from his Nebula award-winning novella 'He Who Shapes' (1964). A brilliant psychiatrist is able to enter his patient's dreams by electronic means, shaping them from within. He meets his match when a beautiful blind woman comes to him for help. A stylish and atmospheric story. 'Zelazny's over-urgent prose and penchant for the three-word paragraph now and then make the pages resemble a forest of tottering pagodas' – J. G. Ballard, *Times*.

Dream Millennium, The (1974) ★★ Novel by James White (UK). The crew of a starship on a generations-long voyage must spend almost all the time in frozen sleep. They dream, and find difficulty separating their fantasies from reality. One of this routine author's better novels.

Dream of Kinship, A (Cowper): see under *Road to Corlay, The*.

Dream of Wessex, A (1977) ★★★ Novel by Christopher Priest (UK). In the near future, participants in a psychological 'time-travel' experiment dream of a 22nd century in which Britain has been devastated by earthquakes and 'Wessex' has become a separate island. An odd, atmospheric and deceptive mystery. Published in the USA as *The Perfect Lover*.

Dream Park (1981) ★★ Novel by Larry Niven and Steven Barnes (USA). A high-tech live-action role-playing game gets out of hand. A refreshingly different sf/fantasy tale, which takes some of its background from the New Guinea cargo cults described in *Road Belong Cargo* by Peter Lawrence. Among other oddities, Heaven is situated vertically above Sydney, Australia. Sequel: *The Barsoom Project* (1989).

Dream Years, The (1985) ★★★ Novel by Lisa Goldstein (USA). A young friend of André Breton and the Surrealists becomes obsessed with a mysterious girl and finds himself transported into the future. The subsequent timeslip romance, which has more of the feel of fantasy than sf, is set partially during the Parisian troubles of 1968, and partly in an as yet unrealized future. A clever, original work: its author's first adult novel.

Dreamers, The (1980) ★★ Fix-up novel by James E. Gunn (USA). Advances in brain research allow people to be educated by means of chemical 'force-feeding', but this has unfortunate results. A worthy and interesting book, if a bit glum. Re-titled *The Mind Master* in its US paperback edition.

Dreaming Dragons, The (1980) ★★★ Novel by Damien Broderick (Australia). An Aboriginal anthropologist discovers an underground chamber at Ayers Rock, and his autistic nephew is able to communicate with the alien intelligence which is responsible for this vault. A lively story, explosive with ideas.

Dreaming Jewels, The (1950) ★★★ Novel by Theodore Sturgeon (USA). A runaway boy joins a carnival where the freaks make communication with an alien intelligence. A delightful story, written with feeling. Sturgeon's first novel. Also published as *The Synthetic Man*.

Dreams of Flesh and Sand (1988) ★★ Novel by W. T. Quick (USA). A once-married computer security expert and hacker are reunited when both are hired by the director of a multinational company to remove the personality of a rival director from the corporation's bio-computer expert system. A first novel, and an intelligent, if somewhat derivative, treatment of a common 1980s sf theme. Sequel: *Dreams of Gods and Men* (1989).

Dreamsnake (1978) ★★ Novel by Vonda N. McIntyre (USA). An expansion of the Nebula-winning short story 'Of Mist, and Grass, and Sand' (1973). A healer called Snake wanders a future Earth in search of an alien beastie which will assist her in the task of bringing succour to the sick and dying. There are links with McIntyre's earlier novel *The Exile Waiting*. A highly effective shorter work is here spun out to too great a length. Hugo award-winner, 1979.

Driftglass (1971) ★★★ Collection by Samuel R. Delany (USA). Ten glittery sf stories, comprising Delany's entire short fiction output up to 1970. Contains two Nebula award-winners: 'Aye, and Gomorrah' (1967) and 'Time Considered as a Helix of Semi-Precious Stones' (1968).

Effective marriages of style and ideative substance, these pieces represent American 1960s New-Wave sf at its best.

Drinking Sapphire Wine (Lee): see under *Don't Bite the Sun*.

Drought, The (1964) ★★★ Novel by J. G. Ballard (UK), originally published in the USA as *The Burning World*. Pollution has caused the seas to stop evaporating, and the consequent aridity leads to the collapse of civilization. Certain characters find new meanings in the transformed landscapes. A dry metaphysical melodrama, with hallucinatory visual qualities.

Drowned World, The (1962) ★★★★ Novel by J. G. Ballard (UK). Solar flares have melted the Earth's ice caps. In the lagoons of London, where abandoned office blocks rise from the fetid swamps, a few human beings embark on a 'night journey' into the remote biological past of their deepest memories. Powerfully described, surrealistic, unforgettable.

Drowning Towers, The (Turner): see *Sea and Summer, The*.

Drowntide (1987) ★★ Novel by Sydney J. Van Scyoc (USA). Adventure on an alien water-world which has been colonized in the distant past by humans and cetaceans from Earth. 'There are echoes of McCaffrey's "Dragon" books, but the hero has more complex problems to resolve than is common in this sort of thing' – Peter Garratt, *Interzone*.

Drunkard's Walk (1960) ★★ Novel by Frederik Pohl (USA). An apparently suicidal mathematics teacher discovers that he is being driven to self-destruction by evil telepaths – and that alcohol is his defence against their influence. A slim but quite effective tale of paranoia.

Dune (1965) ★★★ Novel by Frank Herbert (USA). Immensely popular work with five sequels (*Dune Messiah, Children of Dune*, etc.), set mainly on the desert planet Arrakis, where young Paul Atreides leads a revolt of the tough 'Fremen' against cruel overlords. The huge sandworms are particularly memorable. Part hard sf, part mysticism, part family saga, part Lawrence of Arabia, the book's prose is undistinguished but its narrative grip is undeniable. Hugo and Nebula award-winner, 1966. Filmed 1984 (dir. David Lynch).

Dune Messiah (1969) ★★ Novel by Frank Herbert (USA), immediate sequel to the bestselling *Dune*. This rather smaller-scale continuation of the Atreides family saga (on and off the planet Arrakis) was regarded as something of a disappointment by Herbert fans. Sequels: *Children of Dune, The God-Emperor of Dune*, etc.

Duplicated Man, The (1959) ★ Novel by James Blish and Robert A. W. Lowndes (USA), expanded from a 1953 magazine story. The hero uses a duplicating device to dissuade two immortals from their dangerous tinkering with human affairs. An early, very minor work in the Blish canon.

Dushau (1985) ★ Novel by Jacqueline Lichtenberg (USA), first of a trilogy. Against a galactic-empire backdrop, the heroine struggles on behalf of sensitive aliens who have special knowledge and understanding of various planets' ecological balances. Well-meaning hokum by an author who first made a reputation with her *Star Trek* spin-off fiction. Sequels: *Farfetch* (1985) and *Outreach* (1986).

Dwellers of the Deep (O'Donnell): see under *Final War and Other Fantasies*.

Dydeetown World (1989) ★★ Fix-up novel by F. Paul Wilson (USA). A future private eye is hired by a cloned woman to find a missing person. Adequate mystery-cum-sf by a writer now best known for his supernatural horror novels.

Dying for Tomorrow (Moorcock): see under *Time Dweller, The*.

Dying Inside (1972) ★★★ Novel by Robert Silverberg (USA). A telepath discovers that his extraordinary talent is ebbing away. He has been used to leading a parasitic existence, but now he must learn to cope as normal humans do. A very powerful first-person narrative, and no doubt a kind of disguised autobiography of the author. Silverberg's most widely respected novel, but not designed to be popular fare.

Dying of the Light (1977) ★★ Novel by George R. R. Martin (USA). A curious, decadent festival is held on a wandering planet which is temporarily lit by a star but which is destined to go into the long night again. The story of a love-triangle is dull but the background is well described. Martin's first novel.

E

E Pluribus Unicorn (1953) ★★★ Collection by Theodore Sturgeon (USA), with an introduction by Groff Conklin. A baker's dozen of entertaining stories, over half of which are pure fantasy. Among the sf standouts are 'A Saucer of Loneliness' (1953), 'The World Well Lost' (1953) and 'The Sex Opposite' (1952).

Early Asimov, or Eleven Years of Trying, The (1972) ★ Collection by Isaac Asimov (USA). Clean-up volume of previously uncollected Asimov stories first published in sf magazines between 1939 and 1950, with extensive autobiographical commentary by the author. By its very nature, it's inevitable that such a book will contain much dross. The British paperback edition is split into three volumes.

Early del Rey, The (1975) ★ Collection by Lester del Rey (USA). A recycling of rather bad old magazine stories from the 1930s and 40s, together with some interesting autobiographical notes. Representative of the sort of work which made this essentially minor author famous for

a while. A volume in the Doubleday series which commenced with *The Early Asimov*.

Early Pohl, The (1976) ★ Collection by Frederik Pohl (USA). Pohl began writing sf in 1939, though the first fiction to bear his name didn't appear until 1952. Many of the early pieces were published under the pseudonym 'James MacCreigh', and it is from that body of work that these selections are drawn. As with the other volumes of the 'Early ...' series, it's the non-fiction commentary which makes the book worth while. Several more 'MacCreigh' novellas of the 1940s have been republished in book form as *Planets Three* (1982).

Early Williamson, The (1975) ★★ Collection by Jack Williamson (USA). Eleven stories, with linking autobiographical commentary, by one of the early masters of pulp sf. The pieces range from 'The Metal Man' (1928) to 'Dead Star Station' (1933). They're extremely dated, but they have a naïve vigour. Unlike other volumes in the Doubleday 'Early ...' series, this one actually contains some of its author's most representative work.

Earth Abides (1949) ★★★★ Novel by George R. Stewart (USA). A plague wipes out most of humanity. In California, a man tries to rebuild society, meeting with both success and failure. Wonderfully described and ecologically aware, this is one of the best of all 'disaster' stories. Profoundly moving. International Fantasy award-winner, 1950.

Earth Again Redeemed, The (1978) ★★ Novel by Martin Green (USA). In an alternative time-line, the history of our Earth diverged in the 17th century: the Industrial Revolution never happened, and as a consequence the late 20th-century world is still dominated by religion. The story unfolds mainly in a carefully detailed African culture. An ambitious, but nevertheless surprisingly conventional, anti-technological 'epic' by a mainstream writer.

Earth Book of Stormgate, The (1978) ★★ Collection by Poul Anderson (USA). Twelve proficient stories, first published from the mid-1950s to the 1970s, and all set in the future universe of Anderson's 'Polesotechnic League'. Some paperback reprints have been split into two volumes.

Earth Descended (Saberhagen): see under *Berserker's Planet*.

Earth Has Been Found (Jones): see *Xeno*.

Earth is Room Enough (1957) ★★ Collection by Isaac Asimov (USA). A fair-to-good volume of short stories and short-shorts by this playful author. Among the more substantial stories, perhaps the most memorable is 'The Dead Past', about the unfortunate consequences of a machine which allows one to view the past.

Earth Lords, The (1989) ★★ Novel by Gordon R. Dickson (Canada/USA). A secret city under Canada is run as a slave state by tiny 'Lords'. Bart Dybig (a typical Dickson hero — muscular, mild-mannered and clever) learns more than he should, and manages to thwart their plans. A readable mix of unoriginal plot, well-paced writing and enjoyable historical speculation.

Earth Unaware (1966) ★ Novel by Mack Reynolds (USA). An Owenite political philosopher develops miraculous powers and causes all kinds of disruption in a 21st century USA which looks a lot like the America of the late 1950s. Perhaps more noteworthy for quotes from the works of the great socialists than for any literary merit.

Earthblood (1966) ★★ Novel by Keith Laumer and Rosel George Brown (USA). Roan, a 'genuine pure strain terrestrial human', is brought up on a remote world inhabited by various mutated descendants of Earth humans. Kidnapped by a circus, he turns pirate and fights his way through the galaxy looking for Earth and racially pure Terrans. One of Laumer's few books that is not obviously comic, it's perhaps a little long-winded.

Earthchild (1977) ★★ Novel by Doris Piserchia (USA). A colossal alien plant is gradually taking over the Earth, and a young girl, the last of her kind, opposes it with the help of another alien entity. A fantastic adventure story of the dim distant future, nicely done.

Earthdoom! (1987) ★★ Novel by David Langford and John Grant (UK). An absurd send-up of all the sf disaster stories ever written – very funny at times, although some readers may feel it goes way over the top. 'One of the spoofiest spoofs to appear for years ... No cliché is left to fester in obscurity. No ultimate horror is too hackneyed' – David V. Barrett, *Vector*.

Earthlight (1955) ★★ Novel by Arthur C. Clarke (UK). Colonization of the solar system results in economic and political strains – and eventual war between the planets. The scientific details are scrupulously accurate, but the fiction is humdrum.

Earthman, Come Home (1955) ★★★ Fix-up novel by James Blish (USA), the first-published volume in his *Cities in Flight* sequence. It tells of the 'Okie' cities – whole towns which have been uprooted from Earth and have become wanderers in space – and in particular it recounts the adventures of New York City under its resourceful, long-lived mayor John Amalfi. Somewhat patchy as an individual book, this is extravagant, intellectual space opera. Far-fetched but strangely convincing.

Earthman, Go Home! (Anderson): see under *We Claim These Stars*.

Earthman's Burden (1957) ★ Collection by Poul Anderson and Gordon R. Dickson (USA). Six stories about the 'Hokas', cute bear-like aliens who imitate aspects of Earth culture which they have absorbed from books and films. Silly stuff which has been quite popular. Sequels: *Star Prince Charlie* and *Hoka!*

Earthwind (1977) ★★ Novel by Robert Holdstock (UK). Human colonists revert to a stone-age cultural level on an alien planet. Investigators come to find out why this should be so, and are themselves caught up in the compulsion to 'go back'. An intriguing book: long on imagery and philosophizing, short on plot.

Earthworks (1965) ★ Novel by Brian W. Aldiss (UK). An overpopulated future world drifts towards nuclear Armageddon as the only 'solution' to its problems. As one character states, 'a new way of living has got to come, and the sooner the old one goes the better'. A minor and rather dislikeable novel by this important author.

East of Laughter (1988) ★★ Novel by R. A. Lafferty (USA). Like nearly everything else by Lafferty, the plot (concerning the replacement of the Scribbling Giants) isn't really all that important: it's the style (and this book's been compared to Chesterton and David Lindsay) that counts.

East Wind Coming, An (1979) ★ Novel by Arthur Byron Cover (USA), sequel to *Autumn Angels*. The city of immortals at the far end of time has trouble with Jack the Ripper. A disguised Sherlock Holmes appears in this daft novel – but other writers have done this sort of pastiche more effectively.

Echo Round His Bones (1967) ★★★ Novel by Thomas M. Disch (USA). A Mars-bound matter transmitter creates *doppelgängers* of everyone who passes through it – though at first its users don't realize this. An amusing sf 'ghost' story, with some lovely moments. Lightweight, early Disch, but impeccably written. It's a pity its author has not produced more entertainments of this sort.

Echoes of Chaos (1986) ★ Novel by Robert E. Vardeman (USA). Egotistical xenoarchaeologist Michael Ralston is investigating the extinct inhabitants of Alpha 3 when a student is driven mad and killed by the effects of the telepathic record of the destruction of Alphan culture. A rather slow-moving and repetitive adventure story, continued in *Equations of Chaos*.

Eclipse (1985) ★★ Novel by John Shirley (USA), the first of a trilogy entitled 'A Song Called Youth'. Rock-music fans and space colonists fight neo-Nazis in a bombed-out future Europe, in this well-meaning but overlong exercise in a rebellious cyberpunk vein. 'To follow the plot, one needs an onboard database with inbuilt jargon decoder incorporating AAF (advanced acronymics facility) and some sort of gizmo for keeping track of the characters, of whom

there are dozens' – Lee Montgomerie, *Interzone*. Sequel: *Eclipse Penumbra* (1988).

Eclipse of Dawn, The (1971) ★★ Novel by Gordon Eklund (USA). Political shenanigans in a collapsed United States of the early 21st century. A rather confused and pessimistic work, with aliens and telepathy thrown in for good (or bad) measure. Eklund's first novel.

Eclipse Penumbra (Shirley): see under *Eclipse*.

Eclipsing Binaries (Goldin): see under *Imperial Stars, The*.

Ecotopia (1975) ★★ Novel by Ernest Callenbach (USA). The west coast of America has transformed itself into an ecologically sound paradise, and a visitor from the east is taken on a guided tour. As fiction it's of limited appeal, but it's generally regarded as one of the most serious modern attempts to create a utopian vision of the near future. Sequel: *Ecotopia Emerging* (1981).

Eden Cycle, The (1974) ★★ Novel by Raymond Z. Gallun (USA). Immortal human beings search for the meaning of life in a far-future world of material abundance. An interesting 'comeback' novel by a veteran sf writer of the 1930s.

Edge of Beyond, The (Johns): see under *Now to the Stars*.

Edge of Forever, The (1971) ★★ Collection by Chad Oliver (USA). Six sf stories, all dating from the 1950s, by this author who is also an anthropologist. They're fairly quiet pieces, plainly written, but among the more intelligent sf of their day. Oliver is underrated.

Edge of Tomorrow, The (1961) ★★ Collection by Howard Fast (USA). Seven slick, and occasionally idealistic, sf yarns by a writer who is best known for his historical novels. Highpoints include 'The Large Ant' and 'The First Men' (the latter was subsequently expanded into the novel *The Hunter and the Trap*).

Egg-Shaped Thing, The (1967) ★★ Novel by Christopher Hodder-Williams (UK). Mind-bending thriller based on quantum mechanics: discontinuities in the space-time fabric, triggered by unwise atomic experiments, cause general mayhem. 'Grappling with an apparently meaningless deluge of cats and no-entry signs, the characters discover that they are expiating their sins before they commit them' – J. G. Ballard, *Guardian*.

Egypt Green (1989) ★★ Novel by Christopher Hyde (Canada). A teenager is kidnapped. His girlfriend and a seedy investigative journalist discover that the crime is part of a Nazi plot to preserve a remnant of intelligent youth in order to re-establish civilization after the deliberate destruction of most of the world's population in a biological and nuclear war. A truly paranoid novel, in which they really are all out to get us – the President of the USA, the police, the CIA, the KGB, MI5. Even the airline reservation offices are in the pay of secret Nazi warlords.

Eight Fantasms and Magics (Vance): see *Fantasms and Magics*.

Eight Keys to Eden (1960) ★★ Novel by Mark Clifton (USA). When the human colonists of an alien world fail to report home, an investigator is sent. It turns out that an all-too-welcoming local ecology has greater attractions for the settlers than the harsh Terran civilization. A good Edenic-planet mystery.

Eighty-Minute Hour: A Space Opera, The (1974) Novel by Brian W. Aldiss (UK). It opens in 1999, but it moves onwards and outwards to eagerly embrace just about every sf cliché there is – and it's all wrapped up in a nudge-nudge, wink-wink style. An over-the-top comic romp which unfortunately fails to amuse. One of Aldiss's few duds.

Einstein Intersection, The (1967) ★★★ Novel by Samuel R. Delany (USA). In the far future, the world effloresces with colourful mutations, as our reality intersects another order of space-time. Lobey, a musically-gifted telepathic lad, adopts the role of Orpheus when he sets out in search of his lost love. A fascinating, confusing, at times pretentious but always zestful quest story, full of imagery, symbols and references to 20th-century popular culture – all interspersed with snippets from the writer's diary. Nebula award-winner, 1967.

Electric Crocodile, The (1970) ★★★ Novel by D. G. Compton (UK). Political thriller involving a highly secret computer project designed to control scientific progress. This is infiltrated by sympathetic agents who eventually come to grief. Well written, thoughtful but pessimistic. Published in the USA as *The Steel Crocodile*.

Element 79 (1967) ★★ Collection by Fred Hoyle (UK). Sf and fantasy stories, mostly fantastic and mainly comic in tone, by this leading writer of hard, scientific sf. We see him here in very breezy mood.

Elephant Song (1981) ★★ Novel by Barry B. Longyear (USA). O'Hara's circus crashlands on uninhabited Momus. The survivors set up a new way of life, as year after year fewer of their beloved elephants remain to tie them to the old. Sequel to *City of Baraboo*, and sets the scene for the stories collected in *Circus World*.

Eleventh Commandment, The (1962) ★★ Novel by Lester del Rey (USA). In a heavily overpopulated future, the Roman Catholic Church continues to encourage people to be fruitful and multiply. But there is scientific reason behind this apparent madness. One of the few sf novels of its time which tackled religious issues.

Elleander Morning (1983) ★★★ Novel by Jerry Yulsman (USA). In an alternative time-line, a woman has succeeded in assassinating Hitler, and as a consequence the world is more peaceful than the historical reality we know. The assassin's granddaughter stumbles across a plot to revive the Nazi movement. A well-characterized narrative by a mainstream writer.

Embedding, The (1973) ★★★★ Novel by Ian Watson (UK). A brilliant brain-teasing narrative about the nature of language, alien contact, near-future politics, and much more. The scene moves between Britain, the USA and the Amazon basin. Its author's first book, and one of the finest sf debuts ever.

Emerald Eyes (1988) ★ Novel by Daniel Keys Moran (USA). Genetically-engineered telepaths resist their allotted role as government spies. It's a busy-busy book, with all the standard futuristic ingredients, a building block in a long future-history series which the young author plans to write.

Emergence (1984) ★★ Novel by David R. Palmer (USA). A supergirl survives the great nuclear war, and roams a devastated America searching for soulmates. A fairly engaging first-person narrative which becomes a bit cloying at times. Palmer's first novel.

Empery (1987) ★ Novel by Michael P. Kube-McDowell (USA), sequel to *Enigma*. The USS develops an assault fleet to strike back at the unknown and unknowable Mizarians who destroyed the first human space civilization millennia ago.

Emphyrio (1969) ★★★ Novel by Jack Vance (USA). A young man attempts to free the people of Ambroy from the benign oppression of the Lords, basing his career on the ancient hero Emphyrio. Vance, the master of the explanatory footnote, stuffs the narrative with diverting detail. This is one of his best novels.

Empire (1981) ★★ Posthumous collection by H. Beam Piper (USA). Five stories, with a chronology and introductions by John F. Carr which attempt to connect Piper's fiction with a coherent view of human history. Includes 'A Slave is a Slave', a cynical view of the failure of an Imperial governor to introduce his subjects to foreign ideas of personal freedom; and 'The Edge of the Knife', a deeply pessimistic and rather odd short story about a history professor who starts teaching about the future as if it was the past.

Empire Dreams (McDonald): see under *Desolation Road*.

Empire of Fear, The (1988) ★★★ Novel by Brian Stableford (UK). In an alternative time-line, 'vampires' from the east have conquered Europe. The 17th-century hero of this impressively imagined tale uncovers the biological secrets which lie behind the longevity and peculiar dietary habits of the pallid ruling class. Although it uses the motif of vampirism, this is certainly not a horror novel but a first-class piece of speculative sf, rich in its understanding of both science and history. Stableford's magnum opus.

Empire of the East, The (1979) ★★ Omnibus by Fred Saberhagen (USA). A reworking of three previous novels, *The Broken Lands, The*

Black Mountains and *Changeling Earth* (see separate entries)

Empire of Time, The (1978) ★★ Novel by Crawford Kilian (USA/Canada), first of his 'Chronoplane Wars' series. The hero of the prequel, *The Fall of the Republic*, is now employed as a hit-man by the Empire. He discovers the true nature of the destruction which struck a parallel Earth of the future, realizes that he has been deluded by his superiors and begins to think for himself. A pleasingly anti-racist and anti-violence conclusion.

Empire Star (1966) ★★★ Novel by Samuel R. Delany (USA). A short but dense space adventure tale which is concerned with ways of perceiving 'this vast multiplex universe'. By the time this book was published it had become clear that the young Delany was a writer of great intellectual ambition. 'An epic novel embedded in a circular narrative of novella length' – Douglas Barbour, *20th-Century SF Writers*.

Empress of Earth, The (1987) ★★ Novel by Melissa Scott (USA), sequel to *Silence in Solitude*. Silence Leigh, space pilot and apprentice Mage, travels to Earth to discover that the Art needed for deep space travel is suppressed and almost forgotten. The accounts of spaceflight by means of the manipulation of symbols in the pilot's mind make the book continually fascinating despite the conventional space-opera plot.

Empress of Outer Space (Chandler): see under *Space Mercenaries*.

Emprise (1984) ★ Novel by Michael P. Kube-McDowell (USA). Book one of 'The Trigon Disunity' trilogy. Near-future America persecutes the scientists who have detected messages from an alien spacecraft approaching the solar system. The arriving aliens become the excuse to form a world government to rebuild a spacefaring society. Patchy characterization – especially of the comic-opera politicians. Sequels: *Enigma* and *Empery*.

Empyrion: The Search for Fierra (1985) ★ Novel by Stephen Lawhead (USA). Members of an expedition sent to contact a lost space colony are imprisoned in an underground city and slowly learn the history and customs of their captors. They escape, and after much hardship in the desert find themselves among the 'Fierra', a race who claim to live constantly in the presence of God. Rambling and wooden religious sf. Sequel: *Empyrion: The Siege of Dome* (1986).

Enchantments of Flesh and Spirit, The (1987) ★★ Novel by Storm Constantine (UK), first in her 'Book of Wraeththu' sequence. In a crumbling near-future world, the psi-powered, mutant hermaphrodites known as the 'Wraeththu' are taking over from straight humankind. Extravagant sf/fantasy romance, sexy and rather plotless, written from a punk-rock ('Gothic') sensibility. Constantine's first novel. Sequels: *The Bewitchments of Love and Hate* (1988), and *The Fulfilments of Fate and Desire* (1989).

End of All Songs, The (Moorcock): see *Dancers at the End of Time, The*.

End of Eternity, The (1955) ★★★ Novel by Isaac Asimov (USA). Time guardians rove through the centuries, keeping all eras in harmony. The hero rebels, preferring the uncertainties of Infinity to the carefully-controlled boredom of Eternity. Perhaps Asimov's best sf novel, though comically stiff in its treatment of the love interest.

End of Exile (Bova): see *Exiles Trilogy, The*.

End of the Dream, The (1972) ★★ Posthumous novel by Philip Wylie (USA), introduced by John Brunner. A far-sighted rich man and his family found a rural retreat where they hope to live out the coming worldwide ecological catastrophe. The end comes, and it's grimly and persuasively depicted. Appropriately enough, this was the last novel by a well-known mainstream writer who had been active on the fringes of the sf field since the 1930s.

End of the Line (Busby): see under *Cage a Man*.

Endangered Species (1989) ★★★ Collection by Gene Wolfe (USA). A bumper volume of 34 sf, fantasy and horror stories by one of the field's finest writers. Standouts include the well-known 'The HORARS of War' (1970) and 'The Detective of Dreams' (1980), although there are also such comparatively playful pieces as 'When I Was Ming the Merciless' (1975) and 'The Last Thrilling

Wonder Story' (1982). Despite the jokes, Wolfe is always intense and surprising. Another, slightly inferior, Wolfe collection of similar size was published by a small press just a few months earlier; it's entitled *Storeys from the Old Hotel* (1988).

Ender's Game (1985) ★★ Novel by Orson Scott Card (USA), expanded from his short story of the same title (1978). During a ruthless interstellar war against a particularly nasty alien foe, a boy is trained for genocide. Very smoothly written, but morally disquieting, it proved popular with the hardcore sf readership. 'Remains in essence a hyped-up power fantasy' – Brian Stableford. Hugo and Nebula award-winner, 1986. Sequel: *Speaker for the Dead*.

Endgame Enigma (1987) Novel by James P. Hogan (UK/USA). A wearisome near-future thriller by this British-born writer of technocratic sf who now lives in the US and seems to have adopted some right-wing American values with all the fervour of a convert. 'A tired farrago of clichéd cold-war rhetoric and mechanical hard sf done up in airport bestseller style' – Paul McAuley, *Interzone*.

Ends of the Circle, The (Williams): see under *Breaking of Northwall, The*.

Enemies of the System (1978) ★ Novella by Brian W. Aldiss (UK). Representatives of the highly-evolved *Homo uniformis* are stranded on a backwater planet. A brief, dystopian satire on conformity and collectivism, and one of Aldiss's more forgettable works.

Enemy Mine (1985) ★ Novelization by David Gerrold (USA) of a film script (1985; dir. Wolfgang Petersen) based on Barry B. Longyear's story of the same title. So this is the book of the film of the story – more intelligent than the movie, but more sentimental than the original tale (included in the Longyear collection *Manifest Destiny*, which see for further details).

Enemy of the State, An (Wilson): see under *Wheels Within Wheels*.

Enemy Stars, The (1959) ★★ Novel by Poul Anderson (USA), an expansion of his magazine novella 'We Have Fed Our Sea'. A hard-sf yarn of space exploration via matter transmitter which also strives, with mixed success, for some depth of characterization. Among the best of Anderson's early novels.

Enemy Within, The (Hubbard): see under *Invaders Plan, The*.

Engine Summer (1979) ★★★★ Novel by John Crowley (USA). After the collapse of technical civilization, a few Americans live on in a gentle, Amerindian-style commune. The hero, Rush that Speaks, tells his surprising life story in poetic style. One of the most unusual and rewarding of all modern sf novels.

England Invaded (Moorcock): see under *Before Armageddon*.

English Assassin, The (1972) ★★★ Novel by Michael Moorcock (UK), sequel to *A Cure for Cancer* and third in his 'Jerry Cornelius' tetralogy. A discontinuous narrative in which Jerry and a large cast of associated characters move through various time-streams of the multiverse. The most stylish of the *Cornelius Chronicles* to date. 'Zany, grotesque, fantastical, Gothick, outrageous' – *London Evening News*. Sequel: *The Condition of Muzak*.

Enigma (1986) ★ Novel by Michael P. Kube-McDowell (USA), sequel to *Emprise*. Five hundred years after the discovery that most of nearby space is inhabited by humans, the survey ships of the Unified Space Service are trying to find out what happened to the ancient human civilization that founded the colonies. Sequel: *Empery*.

Enigma Score, The (1987) ★★★ Novel by Sheri S. Tepper (USA). The surface of Jubal is dominated by crystalline pinnacles which must be placated by specially composed songs to prevent them shattering and killing passing humans. Three Tripsingers oppose a plot by corrupt government officials to have the crystals declared non-sentient so that they can be demolished for business reasons. A skilfully composed morality tale with a fantasy feel to it.

Ensign Flandry (Anderson): see under *We Claim These Stars*.

Entropy Tango, The (1981) ★ Novella by Michael Moorcock (UK). A very minor addition to the 'Jerry Cornelius' cycle of novels and stories (see *The Cornelius Chronicles*). This one features airships, anarchism and the Russian Revolution, among other things, all tumbled into the crisscrossing time-streams of the Moorcockian multiverse.

Envoy to New Worlds (1963) ★ Collection by Keith Laumer (USA), first book in his lengthy 'Retief' series. The protagonist is a troubleshooting member of the Terran Diplomatic Corps who has tough but amusing adventures on a whole array of different planets. Fast-moving formula fiction with a supercompetent hero who is surrounded by bumblers and inferiors. Sequels: *Galactic Diplomat* (1965), *Retief's War* (1966), *Retief and the Warlords* (1968), *Retief: Ambassador to Space* (1969), *Retief of the CDT* (1971), *Retief's Ransom* (1971), *Retief: Emissary to the Stars* (1975), *Retief at Large* (1979), *Retief: Diplomat at Arms* (1982), *Retief to the Rescue* (1983), *The Return of Retief* (1985) and *Reward for Retief* (1989).

Eon (1985) ★★★ Novel by Greg Bear (USA). Impressive hard sf epic, in which an asteroid-turned-starship mysteriously enters the solar system and is discovered to have been built by humans from a parallel universe. The descriptions of the 'Stone', with its inner dimensions greater than the outer, are memorable. 'Bear resolutely refuses to be content with anything less than twenty impossible things before breakfast – and then he *really* gets going' – Andy Robertson, *Interzone*. Sequel: *Eternity*.

Epiphany (Yermakov): see under *Last Communion*.

Equality in the Year 2000 (Reynolds): see under *Looking Backward, from the Year 2000*.

Equations of Chaos (1987) ★ Novel by Robert E. Vardeman (USA). The academics from *Echoes of Chaos* return to Alpha 3 even though its primary star is about to explode. They discover that the potential nova and the mass hysteria that wiped out civilization in at least two solar systems were both caused by a weapon which alters the fabric of reality and is passing through the galaxy totally out of control. The story is concluded in *Colors of Chaos*.

Erewhon, or Over the Range (1872) ★★★ Novel by Samuel Butler (UK). A traveller in New Zealand discovers the lost land of Erewhon, a machine-free utopia. He learns from its inhabitants that machines, if allowed to exist in the outside world, will eventually evolve to replace humanity. A classic satire. Sequel: *Erewhon Revisited* (1901).

Escape Orbit, The (White): see *Open Prison*.

Escape Plans (1986) ★★ Novel by Gwyneth Jones (UK). In a future computer-dominated world, a woman joins an underground revolutionary movement. A dense and difficult blend of feminism and cyberpunk – ambitious, but over-burdened with neologisms and acronyms.

Eskimo Invasion, The (1967) ★★ Fix-up novel by Hayden Howard (USA). An attractive new race of 'Eskimos' threatens to overwhelm the world by pressure of numbers. They gestate in one month and mature extremely rapidly. A very odd but quite effective treatment of the overpopulation theme. Its author's only sf book.

Eternity (1988) ★★★ Novel by Greg Bear (USA), sequel to his *Eon*. One needs to have read the preceding novel first, but this follow-up should disappoint few who have. It's another mind-boggling play of ideas which deals in vast scales of space and time. 'Despite a degree of what appears to be hasty or at least careless writing, and a leavening of soap-opera elements ... the whole glorious enterprise gets off the ground' – Paul McAuley, *Interzone*.

Eternity Brigade, The (1980) ★★ Novel by Stephen Goldin (USA). A spacefaring 'mercenary' yarn (see sundry novels by Pournelle, Drake, etc.) in which the personalities of tough soldiers are placed in computer storage so that they can be revived in new bodies when needed. But things go awry ...

Ethan of Athos (1986) ★★ Novel by Lois McMaster Bujold (USA). The protagonist is a genetic engineer from the all-male world of Athos sent into the galaxy to find out who is responsible for a useless consignment of the human eggs they need to reproduce themselves. He finds himself trapped on a space station, caught up in a feud between mercenaries and spies. An enjoyable and humorous space adventure.

Ethical Engineer, The (Harrison): see under *Deathworld*.

Eva (1988) ★★★ Novel by Peter Dickinson (UK). In the near future, a badly-injured girl has her mind transferred into the body of a female chimpanzee, and subsequently has to cope with being both a human *and* a chimp. This is a well-handled and moving tale. 'Another wonder from one of the great underrated authors: quiet, subtle, and effective' – Tom Whitmore, *Locus*.

Evil Water and Other Stories (1987) ★★★ Collection by Ian Watson (UK). Ten quirky stories by a writer whose delightful imagination usually makes up for his sometimes hasty style. Stories like 'When the Time Gate Failed', 'The People on the Precipice', and 'Windows' feature bizarre alien beings in even more bizarre settings. 'Enticed into Watson's cunning traps, one is never again sure whether the world glimpsed through the bars of the cage is the real one' – Lee Montgomerie, *Interzone*.

Executive (Anthony): see under *Refugee*.

Exile Waiting, The (1975) ★★ Novel by Vonda N. McIntyre (USA). A picaresque tale about the escape of a psychically talented girl thief from Earth's last city. It's an atmospheric and lightly feminist adventure. McIntyre's first novel.

Exiles at the Well of Souls (Chalker): see under *Midnight at the Well of Souls*.

Exiles of Time (1949) ★ Novel by Nelson S. Bond (USA), originally serialized in 1940. Present-day folk are plunged into the ancient past in order to try to save the continent of Mu from cosmic catastrophe. An extravagantly plotted but preposterous sf/fantasy yarn which makes use of many pseudo-scientific myths.

Exiles Trilogy, The (1980) Omnibus of juvenile novels by Ben Bova (USA): *Exiled from Earth* (1971), *Flight of Exiles* (1972) and *End of Exile* (1975). All the geneticists of Earth are bundled into a starship by a government that reckons new ideas destabilize the state. Their descendants eventually reach a new Earth, as bored as the reader.

Exit Funtopia (1988) ★★ Novel by Mick Farren (UK/USA). The hero claims to be a private eye, calls himself Marlowe, and lives in a dream of the 1940s. In fact, he is a citizen of an automated future in which people are encouraged to indulge their fantasies. But reality intrudes. An amiable piece of nonsense, stuffed with pop-cultural references.

Expanded Universe: More Worlds of Robert A. Heinlein: see under *Worlds of Robert A. Heinlein, The*.

Expedition to Earth (1953) ★★★ Collection by Arthur C. Clarke (UK). Eleven early stories by this major author, most of them involving space travel and the far future, and written in a yearning, quasi-poetic style. Often they have little stings in the tail. Includes 'The Sentinel' (1951), which later formed the basis of the novel and film *2001: A Space Odyssey*.

Extra(ordinary) People (1984) ★★ Collection by Joanna Russ (USA). Perfervidly feminist stories, all linked by theme, about the struggle of women in various imagined societies. Includes the powerful 'Souls' (Hugo award-winner, 1983). As uncompromising a book as the author's celebrated novel *The Female Man*.

Extro (Bester): see *Computer Connection, The*.

Eyas (1982) ★★ Novel by Crawford Kilian (USA/Canada). A colourful far-future tale of a young man coming into his inheritance, in a world of fantastically evolved creatures. Perhaps this author's best novel so far. 'Kilian's forte is tales of maturation in difficult circumstances' – Brian Stableford.

Eye (1985) ★ Collection by Frank Herbert (USA), illustrated by Jim Burns. The stories are very patchy. One of them (the first version of *Dragon in the Sea*) is incomplete. Another is, literally, a tourist guide to the world of *Dune*. Minor stuff.

Eye Among the Blind (1976) ★★ Novel by Robert Holdstock (UK). The apparently primitive natives of an alien planet seem to hold the key to the continued existence of intelligent life in the universe. A dogged, detailed, somewhat slow-moving planetary mystery. Holdstock's first novel. 'As strong a treatment of a central theme of sf – alienness, and the relation of the human and the alien – as any I have read' – Ursula Le Guin.

Eye in the Sky (1957) ★★★ Novel by Philip K. Dick (USA). A technological accident plunges a group of Californians into a series of bizarre subjective worlds – it seems they are living in each other's fantasies. This early Dick novel is one of his most lucid treatments of the reality-and-illusion theme. Thoroughly enjoyable.

Eye of Cat (1982) ★★ Novel by Roger Zelazny (USA). A man who is pursued by a telepathic alien reverts to his ancestral Amerindian ways in order to avoid capture. A chase-story with colourful mythological elements: nothing profound, but good latter-day Zelazny.

Eye of the Heron, The (1982) ★★ Short novel by Ursula K. Le Guin (USA), originally published as the lead story of the anthology *Millennial Women* (edited by Virginia Kidd, 1978). Downtrodden workers on a colonized planet passively resist their oppression. Minor Le Guin, although it does address her characteristic moral themes.

Eye of the Lens, The (1972) ★★ Collection by Langdon Jones (UK). Avant-garde sf/fantasy stories, mostly reprinted from *New Worlds* magazine (where Jones was deputy editor during the 1960s). The early 'I Remember, Anita', about nuclear fears, now seems overwritten and embarrassingly maudlin, but some of the later pieces, such as the title story and 'The Great Clock', are powerful in a mysterious, Kafkaesque way.

Eye of the Queen, The (1982) ★★ Novel by Phillip Mann (UK/New Zealand). Scientists endeavour to understand a weird alien culture. A slow-moving, detailed narrative which reveals a considerable ability to evoke imaginary beings – a talent the author has proven since. Mann's first novel.

Eyes of Amber and Other Stories (1979) ★★ Collection by Joan D. Vinge (USA). The popular title story (Hugo award-winner, 1978) is about communication between a linguist and a female alien. Other notable items include 'To Bell the Cat' and 'Tin Soldier'. A later collection by the same author is *Phoenix in the Ashes* (1985).

Eyes of Fire (1980) ★★ Novel by Michael Bishop (USA), a revision of his first novel, *A Funeral for the Eyes of Fire* (1975). Worthy but rather heavy-going anthropological sf about the clash of alien cultures.

Eyes of Heisenberg, The (1966) ★★ Novel by Frank Herbert (USA). In a genetically-engineered future, sterile 'Optimen' lead near-immortal lives. However, a group of rebels believes that death should have its place in human affairs. A provocative novel of ideas written in this author's usual style.

F

Fabulous Riverboat, The (1971) ★★ Novel by Philip José Farmer (USA), sequel to *To Your Scattered Bodies Go* and second in the 'Riverworld' series. On a planet where a million-mile river coils between towering cliffs the resurrected Mark Twain builds a huge paddle-steamer which he intends to use to unravel the mysteries of the 'Ethicals', the aliens who have brought the entire human race back from the dead. It's a staggering scenario, but the story drags. Sequel: *The Dark Design*.

Face, The (1979) ★★ Novel by Jack Vance (USA), sequel to *The Palace of Love* and fourth in his 'Demon Princes' series. In which Kirth Gersen continues his interstellar quest for vengeance — after a 12-year writing hiatus for Vance, during which he had concentrated on several other series. The standard is pretty much as before. Sequel: *The Book of Dreams*.

Face of Heaven, The (Stableford): see under *Realms of Tartarus, The*.

Faceless Man, The (Vance): see *Anome, The*.

Facial Justice (1960) ★★★ Novel by L. P. Hartley (UK). In a dour, totalitarian post-World War III future all persons must be equal even in looks. The heroine is cursed by her beauty. This major English novelist's rather absurd nightmare of egalitarianism run wild now seems outdated. 'A brilliant projection of tendencies already apparent in the postwar British welfare state' — Anthony Burgess, *Ninety-Nine Novels*.

Fade-Out (1975) ★ Novel by Patrick Tilley (UK). A 500-page blockbuster about first contact with aliens who arrive in Earth orbit. It has the usual large cast of characters: scientists, bureaucrats, politicians and military men. The basic idea is of course hackneyed beyond belief, but nevertheless it works well enough in its carefully detailed, realistic, 'bestseller' way. Tilley's first sf novel. The 1987 reprint is revised and updated.

Faded Sun Trilogy, The (1987) ★★ Omnibus by C. J. Cherryh (USA). A repackaging of the three novels *Kesrith*, *Shon'jir* and *Kutath* (see separate entries).

Fahrenheit 451 (1953) ★★★ Novel by Ray Bradbury (USA). Books are burned in a mindless near-future society where citizens are kept quiescent by wall-to-wall TV. 'Fireman' Montag begins to question all this. Bradbury's only sf novel is short, lyrical and a bit simplistic, but it is generally regarded as a classic. Filmed in 1966 (dir. François Truffaut).

Fail-Safe (1962) ★★ Novel by Eugene L. Burdick and Harvey Wheeler (USA). The military machine goes awry, and America accidentally bombs the USSR, forcing the agonized US President to destroy New York in order to demonstrate his good faith and avert an all-out war. A hard-hitting, dreadful-warning bestseller which was made into an effective film (1964; dir. Sidney Lumet).

Falcon (1989) ★★ Novel by Emma Bull (USA). The young hero flees revolution on his home planet and becomes a 'gestalt pilot' – melded with his starship. This is an unpretentious space adventure of high competence, and a first sf novel by an author previously known for her fantasy. 'Over and over, the tale grabbed me' – Tom Whitmore, *Locus*.

Fall of Chronopolis, The (1974) ★★ Novel by Barrington J. Bayley (UK). Various powers, human and otherwise, clash in their attempts to control history via time travel. An enjoyable time-and-space opera with philosophical overtones.

Fall of Colossus, The (Jones): see under *Colossus*.

Fall of Hyperion, The (Simmons): see under *Hyperion*.

Fall of Moondust, A (1961) ★★★ Novel by Arthur C. Clarke (UK). A sight-seeing vehicle, packed with tourists, sinks into a sea of dust on the moon's surface. The subsequent struggle for survival is tensely described, with fascinating scientific details. Not one of Clarke's 'visionary' novels, but probably the best of his works of near-future realism.

Fall of the Families, The (1987) ★★ Novel by Phillip Mann (UK/New Zealand), sequel to *Master of Paxwax*, book two of 'The Story of Pawl Paxwax, the Gardener'. The Eleven Families of humans which dominate a galaxy-full of aliens eventually get their come-uppance. 'Fails utterly to inhabit the grandiose domains of space opera it lays claim to; and it is only when Mr Mann can jigger himself into some xenobiological riff – as in the very moving pages that end the book – that "Paxwax" comes to life at all, too late' – John Clute.

Fall of the Republic, The (1987) ★★ Novel by Crawford Kilian (USA/Canada), second of his 'Chronoplane Wars' series. A super-intelligent teenage army officer in the 1990s military government of the USA is drawn into a computer-hackers' conspiracy. They intend to overthrow the government in order to save the world from an imminent destruction revealed by scientific investigation into parallel worlds. Thus the background is set for the author's (earlier written) *The Empire of Time*. Later sequel: *Rogue Emperor* (1988).

Fall of the Shell, The (Williams): see under *Breaking of Northwall, The*.

Fall of the Towers, The (1970) ★★ Omnibus by Samuel R. Delany (USA), comprising his trilogy of early novels: *Captives of the Flame* (1963; retitled *Out of the Dead City*), *The Towers of Toron* (1964) and *City of a Thousand Suns* (1965). A colourful space-war story with many conventional ingredients: it's far from being a fully accomplished work, but the young author's high intelligence shines through – particularly in the background details.

Fall of the White Ship Avatar (Daley): see under *Requiem for a Ruler of Worlds*.

Falling Astronauts, The (1971) ★★ Novel by Barry N. Malzberg (USA). The hero is a PR man for the space agency, having been grounded as an astronaut after he suffered a nervous breakdown while on a moon mission. A sourly amusing exposé of the Space Bizz, and a sort of run-in for the author's fundamentally similar but more famous novel, *Beyond Apollo*.

Falling Free (1988) ★★ Novel by Lois McMaster Bujold (USA). Bio-engineered humans are required to work in the weightless conditions of orbital space stations, and a tough engineer has to train them. A well-plotted, hard-sf crowd pleaser by one of the few women writers who has mastered (if that's the right word) the

Analog style of technological realism (the novel first appeared as a serial in that magazine). Nebula award-winner, 1989.

Falling Torch, The (1959) ★★ Fix-up novel by Algis Budrys (USA). The son of an exiled human leader returns to an Earth which is ruled by alien conquerors, his purpose to foment a rebellion. A rather strained sf political allegory. (Its personal significance is that Budrys is himself the son of an exiled Lithuanian diplomat, displaced from his nation by the Soviet takeover of the Baltic states in 1940.)

Falling Woman, The (1987) ★★★ Novel by Pat Murphy (USA). A highly unusual tale of 'time travel', in which a middle-aged female archeologist is able to see and converse with persons from the past. The book's strength lies in its sensitive depiction of Mayan civilization. Nebula award-winner, 1988 – despite which, it's really more of a fantasy than an sf novel.

False Dawn (1978) ★ Novel by Chelsea Quinn Yarbro (USA). An ill-advised expansion of the rather good feminist short story of the same title. In a devastated future Earth an abused mutant heroine fights off bandits as she travels aimlessly across the ravaged landscape. 'The book reads easily, makes no challenges, has only one difficult word (agapate), can be slept through comfortably, and will be popular' – John Clute.

False Night (Budrys): see *Some Will Not Die*.

Fantasms and Magics (1978) ★★ Collection by Jack Vance (USA), originally published as *Eight Fantasms and Magics*. Some, but not all, of these stories are connected to the author's 'Dying Earth' fantasy scenario. In 'The Men Return' a few humans survive the temporary breakdown of causality.

Fantastic Voyage (1966) ★ Novelization by Isaac Asimov (USA). A submarine is miniaturized and injected into a scientist's bloodstream in order to remove a blood-clot which threatens his life. A workmanlike attempt at turning third-rate movie material into a readable book. (Film, 1966; dir. Richard Fleischer.)

Fantastic Voyage II: Destination Brain (1987) ★★ Novel by Isaac Asimov (USA). An elderly American scientist is kidnapped, miniaturized and injected into a Russian scientist's bloodstream. Not so much a sequel (more of a rewrite), this book attempts to be more scientifically coherent than the original *Fantastic Voyage*. Nevertheless, the premises are so extreme that we end up with telepathy, faster-than-light travel and anti-gravity.

Far Arena, The (1978) ★★★ Novel by Richard Ben Sapir (USA). Arctic oilmen find an ancient Roman gladiator preserved in ice. He is duly thawed out and, helped by a Latin interpreter, views our world with a permanently curled lip as he comes to understand its idiocies. The story is not as silly as it sounds: although cast in 'bestseller' form, it's actually a thoughtful and imaginative novel, and the author has certainly done his homework.

Far Call, The (1978) ★ Novel by Gordon R. Dickson (Canada/USA), expanded from a 1973 magazine serial. A lengthy treatment of the near-future political manoeuvrings which attend the first manned flight to Mars. Many characters, many scenes – written in would-be bestseller style, and more than a little tedious (although some critics have praised it for its realism).

Far from Home (1981) ★★ Collection by Walter Tevis (USA). Thirteen sf and fantasy stories, some from *Galaxy* magazine of the 1960s, others of more recent vintage. The earlier tales are mostly routine genre pieces, the later ones are more unusual and demanding. This is the only collection by the talented author of *The Man Who Fell to Earth*.

Far Frontier, The (1980) Novel by William Rotsler (USA). Cowboys and Indians in space – literally. A poor thing. 'Rotsler's worst novel' – Martin Morse Wooster, *20th-Century SF Writers*.

Far Out (1961) ★★ Collection by Damon Knight. Typical 1950s sf from one of its masters – short, humane stories with a twist in the tail. Each could be described as 'the one about' something: the one about a baby that talks in the womb, the one about the art machine from the future, the one about the man who travelled in time and then stopped.

Far Stars (1961) ★★ Collection by

Eric Frank Russell (UK). Six quintessential Russell tales from the 1950s, including his well-loved 'Allamagoosa' (Hugo award-winner, 1955) and 'Diabologic' – about the bamboozling of thick-o aliens. Whatever one's feelings about the implied chauvinism, they're all clever, humorous and engagingly told.

Far Sunset, A (1967) ★★ Novel by Edmund Cooper (UK). A sole human who is marooned on a far planet learns to adapt to its alien ways. Quite sophisticated: one of Cooper's better works. 'An interesting exercise in speculative anthropology' – Brian Stableford.

Farewell, Earth's Bliss (1966) ★★ Novel by D. G. Compton (UK). Complex shenanigans in a penal colony on Mars. Well written, but minor Compton.

Farewell to Yesterday's Tomorrow (1975) ★★ Collection by Alexei Panshin (USA). A dozen sf and fantasy stories from the late 1960s and early 70s, a few of which are set against the same background as his novel *Rite of Passage*. According to the author's preface, all these pieces grapple with the theme: 'What does it mean to be an adult human being?' Obviously, there's a certain moral earnestness here (restated in a six-page essay which closes the book), but the fiction is also entertaining – if not as groundbreaking as Panshin hopes.

Farfetch (Lichtenberg): see under *Dushau*.

Farmer in the Sky (1950) ★★ Novel by Robert A. Heinlein (USA). Juvenile adventure about the settling of Jupiter's moon, Ganymede. Full of well-thought-out scientific detail presented in the author's customary engaging style, but portions of the story are rushed.

Farnham's Freehold (1964) ★ Novel by Robert A. Heinlein (USA). The middle-aged American hero and family are thrown forward in time by a nuclear bomb, to find a world dominated by evil blacks. Reactionary, racist, sexist – but readable.

Far-Out Worlds of A. E. van Vogt, The (1968) ★ Collection by A. E. van Vogt (USA). A ragged congregation of mainly old stories by this wildly fanciful spinner of sf dreams. 'Only serves to demonstrate that Time is rarely kind to popular fiction' – James Cawthorn, *New Worlds*. Republished, in expanded form, as *The Worlds of A. E. van Vogt* (1974).

Farside Cannon (1988) ★★ Novel by Roger MacBride Allen (USA). Geologists exiled to the moon take desperate measures to prevent an unscrupulous company putting a large asteroid into a dangerously low orbit round Earth. A pleasantly lighthearted adventure with some good ideas; however, most of the characters and some of the plot fail to ring true.

Father to the Man (1989) ★★★ Novel by John Gribbin (UK). A scientist studying the genetic relationships of humans and chimpanzees brings up a very strange baby against the background of a rather bleak, impoverished anti-scientific future. A well-informed and interesting treatment of irrationality and prejudice, with an unexpected twist. Gribbin's first solo novel.

Father to the Stars (1981) ★★ Collection by Philip José Farmer (USA). The remarkable adventure of Father John Carmody, a spacefaring crook turned priest. Consists of five stories, one of which is the short version of the novel *Night of Light*. Another, 'Father', is reprinted from *Strange Relations*, while two more, 'A Few Miles' and 'Prometheus', were first collected in *Down in the Black Gang*.

Father-Thing, The (Dick): see under *Beyond Lies the Wub*.

Feast of St Dionysus, The (1975) ★★★ Collection by Robert Silverberg (USA). Five tales representative of the author's 1970s best. The long title story is about an astronaut who seeks a new kind of peace in the American desert: 'Almost a description at one remove of Silverberg's rejection of the interplanetary space-ways and self-discovery within his own version of inner space, the story owes nothing to the traditional conventions of the genre' – J. G. Ballard, *New Statesman*.

Federation World (1988) ★ Novel by James White (UK). The eponymous federation of galactic intelligences recruits Earth's brightest and best to populate a vast artificial world. Hero and heroine become troubleshooters on the federation's behalf. An old-fashioned space yarn. 'It is standard fifties fare: quite well handled, as one expects from White, but no surprises' – Tom Whitmore, *Locus*.

Feelies, The (1978) ★ Novel by Mick Farren (UK/USA). The standard vision of a nasty future in which the average citizen longs to enter the illusory, sexually gratifying world of the eponymous 'Feelies' – the cost is too high for most, though. 'Has all the inconsequential banality of soap opera, and deliberately so: this is a new kind of sf disaster, the World where Nothing Happened' – Colin Greenland, *Foundation*.

Female Man, The (1975) ★★★ Novel by Joanna Russ (USA). Three women from alternative worlds meet and compare their lots. One of them comes from the utopian planet Whileaway, where there is only one gender of human being: the Female Man. Uncompromising feminist sf, at times difficult, often brilliant.

Fenris Device, The (Stableford): see under *Halcyon Drift*.

Fiasco (1986) ★★★ Novel by Stanislaw Lem (Poland). The long opening chapter, 'Birnam Wood', is virtually a separate story, and a brilliantly imaginative one. But the bulk of the narrative is a rather bleak retread of *Solaris*, in which human explorers attempt to communicate with an apparently unknowable alien race. The ending will be unsatisfactory to some readers; nevertheless, this is one of Lem's strongest sf novels in many years.

Fifth Head of Cerberus, The (1972) ★★★★ Fix-up novel by Gene Wolfe

(USA). Three long interlinked stories with an other-planetary setting. They deal subtly with questions of identity and individuality. The first piece uses the idea of human cloning to brilliant and moody effect.

Fifth Planet (1963) ★★ Novel by Fred and Geoffrey Hoyle (UK). An errant new planet enters the solar system, and is investigated by scientists from East and West. Low-key hard sf with the emphasis, as is usual in Fred Hoyle's fiction, on the ways in which scientific personnel operate. Geoffrey Hoyle's first book in collaboration with his famous father.

57th Franz Kafka, The (1983) ★★★ Collection by Rudy Rucker (USA). Weird sex, weirder science and some serious topology from sf's favourite mathematical philosopher. Typical is 'Message Found in a Copy of Flatland', in which a tourist finds something very strange in a South London tandoori restaurant ...

Final Blackout (1948) ★ Novel by L. Ron Hubbard (USA), expanded from his 1940 magazine serial. An army officer becomes the dictator and saviour of Britain during a long-drawn-out future war. This has a reputation as being Hubbard's 'best' science-fiction novel, but it's still fairly dreadful (and very dated).

Final Encyclopedia, The (1984) ★★ Novel by Gordon R. Dickson (USA), part of his 'Dorsai' series (which is itself encompassed in the more grandiose 'Childe Cycle', an epic of human evolution). Long, complex space romance about a young man growing into his destiny. Intellectually ambitious, but the quality of writing is undistinguished.

Final Planet, The (1987) ★★ Novel by Andrew M. Greeley (USA). Red-haired telepathic Commandant Seamus Finnbar O'Neil of the pilgrim ship Iona (from the planet Tara, of course) has to make contact with the natives of Zylongi to see if they will allow the pilgrims to set up a community there. He finds that the local humans, descended from pacifist utopian colonists, have developed some very strange ideas about politics and sex. It's amusing, but contains too much stage-Irishry.

Final Programme, The (1968) ★★★ Novel by Michael Moorcock (UK), first in the 'Jerry Cornelius' tetralogy (see *The Cornelius Chronicles*). Jerry is an ironic hero-figure for the swinging sixties, a long-haired young man armed with a needle gun. In this parodic adventure, alternately amusing and scary, he encounters the formidable Miss Brunner, who is about to run the 'final programme' on her subterranean computer. Filmed in 1973 (dir. Robert Fuest; released in the USA as *The Last Days of Man on Earth*). Sequel: *A Cure for Cancer*.

Final War and Other Fantasies (1969) ★★ Collection by K. M. O'Donnell (Barry N. Malzberg, USA). Eleven waspish sf and fantasy tales from the late 1960s, including the much-praised title story, which is an effective pastiche of Joseph Heller's *Catch-22* (1961). These are the stories which first made Malzberg's reputation, even if they did appear under the 'O'Donnell' pseudonym. Other books which carried this byline include *Dwellers of the Deep* (1970) and *Gather in the Hall of the Planets* (1971), two tongue-in-cheek novels about sf fans who meet the aliens of their dreams (or nightmares).

Fingalnan Conspiracy, The (1973) Novel by John Rankine (Douglas R. Mason, UK). A mediocre 'space force' yarn which is distinctly old-fashioned and oh-so-British in tone. 'It strikes me as being a poor copy of Dan Dare and equally juvenile' – Chris Morgan, *Foundation*.

Fire Dancer (Maxwell): see under *Dancer's Luck*.

Fire in the Abyss (1983) ★★ Novel by Stuart Gordon (UK). The 16th-century mariner Sir Humphrey Gilbert is dragged through time by a military experiment which misfires – and has to come to terms with life in a disintegrating late 20th century. This is his first-person narrative. Energetic, flamboyant, at times amusing, frequently over-the-top, full of exclamation marks and cod-Elizabethan language. 'Stuart Gordon has attempted too much ... Cosmic revelations, social explosions and psychological crises whiz by in a blur' – Colin Greenland, *Foundation*.

Fire in the Sun, A (Effinger): see under *When Gravity Fails*.

Fire on the Mountain (1988) ★★★ Novel by Terry Bisson (USA). A successful 19th-century slave rebellion, led by John Brown, has resulted in a socialist utopia of sorts in the present-day southern states of America. The story switches between a contemporary woman's narrative and her great-grandfather's reminiscences of the rebellion. A skilful evocation of an unlikely alternative history. Bisson's first sf novel (his previous works were fantasy).

Fire Past the Future (Maine), see *Count-Down*.

Fire Pattern (1984) ★★ Novel by Bob Shaw (UK). A tall story concerning spontaneous combustion in human beings: the 'rational' sf explanation for this phenomenon is wild and woolly and wholly delightful. Alas, the novel's ending is rushed.

Fire Time (1974) ★★ Novel by Poul Anderson (USA). The planet Ishtar is almost destroyed by its sun every thousand years. Naturally, this inhibits the development of civilization – until Earthmen intervene. Gritty adventure on a very detailed alien world.

Fire Watch (1985) ★★★ Collection by Connie Willis (USA). Varied sf and fantasy by a talented new writer. The title story, about student time-travellers witnessing the World War II Blitz on London, won the Hugo and Nebula awards (1983). 'Import[s] a warmth and intimacy into classic sf themes' – Brian Stableford.

Fire Worm, The (1988) ★★ Novel by Ian Watson (UK), an expansion of his controversial horror story 'Jingling

Geordie's Hole' (1986). Under hypnosis, a man recalls past encounters with the 'fireworm', a ravening alien entity which was somehow released by alchemical means during the Middle Ages. 'A complex novel which mixes the visceral grip of the horror genre with sexual psychology and sf rationality ... A little less rationalization on the part of the author would have made it more memorable' – Paul McAuley, *Interzone*.

Firechild (1986) ★★ Novel by Jack Williamson (USA). A female homunculus survives a mysterious laboratory disaster, is adopted by the hero, and is hunted by the nasty authorities. An engaging story of human transcendence, marred by some Cold War shenanigans but nevertheless demonstrating that this old master of the sf field still has imaginative life left in him. (Williamson is remarkable in that he has been writing sf continuously for well over 50 years: his debut story, 'The Metal Man', appeared in 1928).

Fireclown, The (1965) ★ Novel by Michael Moorcock (UK). The eponymous clown, a doom-laden prophet, comes to Earth to shock its inhabitants from their artificial ways. Early, minor Moorcock with some satirical interest (the author is very suspicious of 'saviours'). Republished as *The Winds of Limbo*. Quasi-sequel: *The Transformation of Miss Mavis Ming* (see under *Dancers at the End of Time, The*).

Fireflood and Other Stories (1979) ★★ Collection by Vonda N. McIntyre (USA). Eleven romantic sf tales, including the Nebula award-winning 'Of Mist, and Grass, and Sand' (1973) and the highly praised 'Aztecs' (1977). Both of these have been expanded into novels – *Dreamsnake* and *Superluminal*.

Firestarter (1980) ★★ Novel by Stephen King (USA). A young girl is blessed (or cursed) with psychokinetic powers, including the ability to start fires by mental means. This is really more of a horror thriller than science fiction (as was the author's rather similar first novel, *Carrie*, 1974), but telepathy and kindred phenomena are of course well-worn sf tropes. King handles such themes very efficiently, though there's little originality in his books.

First Family (Tilley): see *Amtrak Wars, The*.

First He Died (Simak): see *Time and Again*.

First Lensman (1950) ★ Novel by E. E. 'Doc' Smith (USA), sequel to *Triplanetary* and the first novel proper in the 'Lensman' series. Against the background of a colossal intergalactic struggle, a corps of superfit heroes and heroines, each equipped with a magical bracelet known as a 'lens', is trained to fight for good against evil. The subsequent books (actually written and serialized prior to this volume), each opening out on to an ever vaster theatre of cosmic battle, are *Galactic Patrol* (1950), *Grey Lensman* (1951), *Second Stage Lensman* (1953) and *Children of the Lens* (1954). For all the crudity of the writing and characterization, many readers regard the 'Lensman' series as the high point of space opera, and the books enjoyed a surprising new vogue during the 1970s.

First Men in the Moon, The (1901) ★★★★ Novel by H. G. Wells (UK). The scientist Cavor invents an anti-gravitic substance. He and a friend fly to the moon, where they find a sub-surface society of insect-like Selenites presided over by the 'Grand Lunar'. A wonderful story with satirical touches. Filmed, poorly, in 1964 (dir. Nathan Juran).

First on Mars (Gordon): see *No Man Friday*.

First Voyages (1981) ★★★ Anthology edited by Damon Knight, Martin H. Greenberg and Joseph D. Olander (USA). Twenty varied stories by notable sf writers, united by the fact that all these pieces were their author's first published fictional works. Authors range from L. Sprague de Camp, with 'The Isolinguals' (1937), to Ursula Le Guin, with 'April in Paris' (1962). An earlier, shorter version of this book, edited by Knight alone, was entitled *Now Begins Tomorrow* (1963).

Fistful of Digits (1968) ★★ Novel by Christopher Hodder-Williams (UK). Businessmen create a secret network of 'intelligent' computers which eventually pose a threat to civil liberties. One of the earlier fictional treatments of the possible dreadful consequences of the information-technology revolution, it's

proficiently written, if over-complex.

Fittest, The (McIntosh): see under *One in Three Hundred*.

Five Gold Bands, The (1953) ★ Novel by Jack Vance (USA), originally published as *The Space Pirate*. A simple quest story based round five gold rings or bracelets owned by the rulers of the Galaxy. The hero's dialogue is written in an irritating stage-Irish voice.

Five Twelfths of Heaven (1985) ★★ Novel by Melissa Scott (USA). A young woman who wants to be a spacepilot in a man's universe travels from planet to planet escaping from various enemies and fighting an evil Empire. The fun is in the explanation of faster-than-light travel and interstellar navigation in a framework of alchemical and astrological symbolism contained in arcane books and tables. Sequel: *Silence in Solitude*.

Flame Upon the Ice, The (Forstchen): see under *Ice Prophet*.

Flatland: A Romance of Many Dimensions (1884) ★★★ Novel by Edwin A. Abbott (UK). Amusing satire narrated by 'A. Square', inhabitant of a two-dimensional world. A mathematical confection, marginally sf.

Flesh (1960) ★★ Novel by Philip José Farmer (USA). A space expedition comes home to discover that Earth has reverted to worship of the Great Mother. Captain Peter Stagg is given a pair of antlers and is required by the priestesses to indulge in some startling rites. A bawdy sf vulgarization of themes from Robert Graves's *The White Goddess* (1948). Quite entertaining – and daring for its day.

Fleshpots of Sansato, The (1968) ★★ Novel by William F. Temple (UK). The hero is a Terran agent who is in search of a secret faster-than-light drive, and the setting is a well-depicted interstellar 'fleshpot' city. Intelligent space opera with a come-on title. Veteran author Temple's last novel (though he did not die until 1989). 'Remarkable' – John Clute.

Flight Into Yesterday (Harness) : see *Paradox Men, The.*

Flight of Exiles (Bova): see *Exiles Trilogy, The.*

Flight of the Dragonfly, The (1984) ★★ Novel by Robert L. Forward (USA). The plot concerns bureaucratic opposition to a multi-billion-dollar journey to Barnard's Star. But the story is really just a vehicle for the presentation of a laser-powered lightsail starship, detailed description of a (supposedly feasible) dumb-bell-shaped planet, and a fascinating invented species of alien mathematicians.

Flight of the Horse, The (1975) ★★ Collection by Larry Niven (USA). The title story is the first of the 'Svetz' series: time-travellers into the past from a depressing post-atomic age find that they always end up in a parallel world with different natural laws. Also includes 'Flash Crowd' and 'What Good is a Glass Dagger', imaginative conceits pivotal to other series.

Flight to Opar (Farmer): see under *Hadon of Ancient Opar.*

Flinx in Flux (Foster): see under *Tar-Aiym Krang, The.*

Floating Continent, The (de Camp): see *Search for Zei, The.*

Floating Worlds (1976) ★★★ Novel by Cecelia Holland (USA). In a far-future solar system, where the various human societies range from fascist to anarchist, a female agent makes a complex bid for power. This is fundamentally a space opera, though the emphasis is not on hardware but on realistic characters and their political relationships. A massive and well-realized tale – the only sf work so far by this respected historical novelist. 'A neglected sf masterpiece' – Kim Stanley Robinson, *Foundation.*

Florians, The (1976) ★★ Novel by Brian Stableford (UK), first in his 'Daedalus' series. The re-contact vessel Daedalus, equipped with laboratories and expert knowledge, is sent out to the long-lost colonized planets of the galaxy. It is destined to encounter a biological or sociological mystery on each world it reaches. The debut volume in an adventure series where the pleasures are more cerebral than physical: formula fiction with genuine ideas. Sequels: *Critical Threshold* (1977),

Wildeblood's Empire (1977), *The City of the Sun* (1978), *Balance of Power* (1979) and *The Paradox of the Sets* (1979).

Flow My Tears, the Policeman Said (1974) ★★★ Novel by Philip K. Dick (USA). A near-future TV superstar awakes in a parallel world where nobody recognizes him. The customary Dickian befuddlement ensues. It has its grim moments, but this dystopian vision of an American police state is notable for its sympathetically portrayed characters. John W. Campbell award-winner, 1975.

Flowers for Algernon (1966) ★★★★ Novel by Daniel Keyes (USA). Charlie Gordon, a mental defective, has his intelligence quotient raised to genius level by surgical means. We witness his development, and its tragic aftermath, from within. It's a very moving story, impeccably told. Nebula award-winner, 1967. Filmed as *Charly* (1968; dir. Ralph Nelson).

Flux (1974) ★ Novel by Ron Goulart (USA). An attempt at comedy in which a far-future policeman mimics various stereotyped characters – tight-lipped cowboy, hippie folk-singer, blind bluesman – familiar to anyone who remembers 1960s TV.

Flux and The Tin Angel (1978) ★ Omnibus by Ron Goulart (USA). A repackaging of two unrelated novels (see separate entries).

Folk of the Fringe, The (1989) ★★ Collection of linked stories by Orson Scott Card (USA). In a post-Bomb America, the members of the Mormon sect survive precariously. Despite his occasional religiosity and sentimentality, Card is an unfailingly competent sf author. '[His] future is a surprisingly forthright, even lusty, place, where humour doesn't come amiss, and the stale odour of sanctity is (blessedly) absent' – Faren Miller, *Locus*.

Food of the Gods, The (1904) ★★ Novel by H. G. Wells (UK). Scientific tampering with human and animal growth results in a colony of giant people – who then become the objects of petty resentments. One of the master's lesser scientific romances: it's entertaining for much of its length, but it gradually turns into a tract. Filmed, very badly, in 1976 (dir. Bert I. Gordon – who had previously directed a similar item called *Village of the Giants*, 1965).

Footfall (1985) ★ Novel by Larry Niven and Jerry Pournelle (USA). Billed as the ultimate story of alien invasion, this big book retreads some well-worn ground in galumphing 'bestseller' style. It was popular. 'American wish-fulfilment power trip ... Words like militaristic, libertarian, imperialist, spring to mind' – Mary Gentle, *Interzone*.

Forbidden Tower, The (1977) ★★ Novel by Marion Zimmer Bradley (USA). A 'Darkover' novel (see *The Sword of Aldones*) set some time after the action of *The Spell Sword* (1974). The 'Forbidden Tower' is an association of telepaths independent of the Towers run by the Comyn, the telepathic ruling families of Darkover. Colourful adventures with a light brushing of feminism, in this popular author's usual sf/fantasy vein.

Forests of the Night (1989) ★★★ Collection by Tanith Lee (UK). Twenty fantasy and sf stories (eight of them original to the book) by an author much praised in America who is now beginning to be appreciated in her home country – where she has been regarded mainly as a fine writer of juvenile fantasy novels. Most of these pieces are very adult and very stylish. Fantasy predominates, though.

Forever Machine, The (Clifton & Riley): see *They'd Rather Be Right*.

Forever Man, The (1986) ★ Novel by Gordon R. Dickson (USA). A space pilot becomes the specially-adapted 'brain' of his heavily-armed starship, and proceeds to save the universe. 'A lumbering romp that would have worked very neatly at half the length – the length, say, of the longer half of an old Ace Double – but which sinks indissolubly into pulp long before its 375 pages have been wrestled to a shut' – John Clute.

Forever War, The (1974) ★★★ Fix-up novel by Joe Haldeman (USA). Tough, slick narrative of an interstellar war which lasts 1000 years. To the soldier hero, it seems to last about ten years, thanks to the time-dilation effect of faster-than-light travel. Good, realistic, military sf which actually subverts many of the clichés of that category. Haldeman's first sf novel (he was a Vietnam veteran, which helped.) Hugo and Nebula award-winner, 1976.

Forge of God, The (1987) ★★ Novel by Greg Bear (USA). Aliens arrive on Earth under mysterious circumstances: it transpires that the solar system is to be the battleground of self-replicating 'Von Neumann machines', and that humanity (and the Earth itself) is very probably doomed. Powerful scenes are interspersed with too much talk. 'Bear has chosen to tell his story exclusively from the point of view of his human protagonists, and often through their interminable conversations. It's rather like glimpsing a vast, panoramic canvas through a pinhole' – Paul McAuley, *Interzone*.

Forgotten Planet, The (1954) ★ Fix-up novel by Murray Leinster (USA). Based on stories originally published in *Argosy* magazine in the early 1920s, this is a badly dated adventure yarn about human survivors in a future world of giant mutated insects and spiders. The basic scenario has been revisited many times since by other writers: see Colin Wilson's *Spider World* for a recent example.

Fort Privilege (1985) ★★ Novel by Kit Reed (USA). In a darkening near future, the owner of a New York apartment building throws a huge ball. The rich and privileged find themselves beseiged there by an army of the city's homeless. Another tartly written fable by this underrated author.

Fortress (1987) ★ Novel by David

Drake (USA). In an alternative 1986, a world where President Kennedy was not assassinated, a huge laser-armed orbital 'fortress' already exists. But, as the CIA-agent hero of this ridiculous story finds out, it has been taken over by crazed Nazis who have been holed up for 40 years in Antarctica and on the moon.

Forty Thousand in Gehenna (1983) ★★★ Novel by C. J. Cherryh (USA). A human colony, abandoned by the Union for ten generations on a distant planet, adapts in strange ways to the local ecology. Perhaps the best of Cherryh's 'Union/Alliance' series of novels.

Foundation (1951) ★★★ Fix-up novel by Isaac Asimov (USA), first in the so-called 'Foundation Trilogy' (actually a long series of 1940s magazine stories and novellas arranged into three volumes). The whole adds up to one of American sf's best-loved works: a huge history of the decline and fall of a galactic empire, told in brief, mysterious snippets. Gradually it becomes plain that the genius Hari Seldon, inventor of 'psychohistory', has foreseen all – and made appropriate contingency plans for the preservation of human civilization. Sequel: *Foundation and Empire*.

Foundation and Earth (1986) ★ Novel by Isaac Asimov (USA). The space travellers from *Foundation's Edge* journey from the sentient world of Gaia to Earth via various ancient planets familiar to readers of Asimov's 'Robot' stories. More bloated, talky stuff for readers who

are well steeped in the author's earlier works.

Foundation and Empire (1952) ★★★ Fix-up novel by Isaac Asimov (USA), sequel to *Foundation* and second in the original 'Foundation Trilogy'. Hari Seldon's Foundation, which aims to guide human civilization through the galactic dark ages, is threatened by a rogue element: a mutant warrior called the Mule. Highly intelligent space opera. Sequel: *Second Foundation*.

Foundation Trilogy, The (1963) ★★★ Omnibus by Isaac Asimov (USA), containing *Foundation*, *Foundation and Empire* and *Second Foundation* (see separate entries). Retrospective Hugo award-winner for 'all-time best series', 1966.

Foundation's Edge (1982) ★ Novel by Isaac Asimov (USA), belated sequel to the 'Foundation Trilogy', marking Asimov's return to his distinctive brand of cerebral space opera after more than twenty years. In this yarn (and the related novels *The Robots of Dawn*, *Robots and Empire*, *Foundation and Earth* and *Prelude to Foundation*) Asimov explains the Galactic history of *The Stars Like Dust* and the 'Foundation' series as a plot by the robots (from the otherwise unconnected 'Robot' stories) to ensure the survival and happiness of the human race, and hints that the history-altering time-travellers of *The End of Eternity* set up the whole thing. Despite the enjoyable complexities, it's overlong and thinly written. Hugo award-winner, 1983.

Foundation's Friends (1989) ★★ Anthology edited by Martin H. Greenberg (USA), with a preface by Ray Bradbury. These seventeen original 'stories in honour of Isaac Asimov' borrow freely from the worlds of the Old Master's fiction – not only the 'Foundation' series, but the robot novels and others. Contributors include Poul Anderson, Orson Scott Card (his story is probably the standout), Hal Clement, George Alec Effinger, Harry Harrison, Frederik Pohl, Mike Resnick, Pamela Sargent and Robert Silverberg.

Fountains of Paradise, The (1979) ★★★ Novel by Arthur C. Clarke (UK). On an island in the Indian Ocean a 22nd-century engineer builds a colossal 'space elevator' which will connect with a station in geosynchronous orbit. A blend of old-fashioned Brunel-style technological heroics with Sri Lankan myth, effectively done in Clarke's best style. Hugo and Nebula award-winner, 1980. (See also Charles Sheffield's *The Web Between the Worlds*.)

Four for Tomorrow (1967) ★★★ Collection by Roger Zelazny (USA), introduced by Theodore Sturgeon. Four long stories: 'The Furies', 'The Graveyard Heart', 'The Doors of His Face, the Lamps of His Mouth' (a Nebula award-winner in 1966) and 'A Rose for Ecclesiastes'. Slick, tough-poetic stuff by a fashionable new writer whose breadth of reference was impressive. Zelazny's first collection. Published in the UK as *A Rose for Ecclesiastes*.

Four Hundred Billion Stars (1988) ★★★ Novel by Paul J. McAuley (UK). Against a background of interstellar war, the quasi-telepathic heroine is sent to a bleak planet to investigate primitive inhabitants who may be linked to the little-known 'Enemy'. Slow-moving but engrossing story with well-described landscapes and a rigorous quality of thought which is all too rare in contemporary sf. A strong, if rather sombre, first novel. Joint Philip K. Dick Memorial award-winner, 1989.

Four Moons of Darkover (Bradley): see under *Free Amazons of Darkover*.

Four-Day Planet (1961) ★★ Juvenile novel by H. Beam Piper (USA). Sea Monster Wax is the only export of Fenris, an almost-but-not-quite uninhabitable planet with just four 2000-hour days a year. The Monster Hunters rebel against the cartel who are holding down the price. Light-hearted adventure, with deliberate references to 19th-century whaling.

Four-Dimensional Nightmare, The (Ballard): see *Voices of Time, The*.

Four-Sided Triangle, The (1949) ★★ Novel by William F. Temple (UK), expanded from a 1939 magazine story. This is a love-triangle tale which becomes 'four-sided' when one of the lovelorn men uses a matter-duplicating machine to create another copy of the girl in question. Temple's first novel. A very minor classic of British post-war sf, it was filmed in 1953 (dir. Terence Fisher).

Fourth Dimension, The (1985) ★★★ Essay collection by Rudy Rucker (USA). Mainly a copiously illustrated introduction to higher geometry and the author's personal philosophy, it just sneaks in as sf because it includes a sequel to Edwin A. Abbot's *Flatland* (for whose 100th anniversary it was written) as well as quotations from and comments on some of the many other works in the *Flatland* tradition.

Fourth Mansions (1969) ★★★ Novel by R. A. Lafferty (USA). The plot starts with a clique of telepaths encouraging a newspaper reporter to believe that a certain businessman is in fact a 500-year-old ex-ruler of Egypt – which is almost true. But if the novel is about anything it's about the question of whether the truly superior should live by normal morals, the hardness of God's love, the strangeness of the real world, the way in which political power is handed from generation to generation, even a little about sex.

Fourth 'R', The (1959) ★★ Novel by George O. Smith (USA). A murdered scientist bequeaths a miraculous teaching machine to his five-year-old son. The boy goes on the run, all the while using the machine to enhance his own intelligence to genius level. An endearing sf thriller: one of the best stories of a super-child, and Smith's most memorable novel.

Fracas Factor, The (1978) ★★ Novel by Mack Reynolds (USA). The America of People's Capitalism is divided into nine classes, from lower-lower to upper-upper. The Uppers rule, the Middles work and the Lowers receive welfare in the form of shares in great corporations. War is illegal except for severely limited battles between mercenaries conducted on isolated reservations and followed by millions on television. Alas, the rambling story about a soldier caught up in a revolutionary organization does not do justice to Reynolds's exuberant political imagination. Sequel: *Sweet Dreams, Sweet Princes.*

Frankenstein, or The Modern Prometheus (1818) ★★★★ Novel by Mary Shelley (UK). Gothic horror tale about a medical student who creates an artificial man. References to Galvanism and other sciences of the day give this classic work some claim to being the first English sf novel. Much adapted and frequently filmed, it has inspired many sequels by other hands (see the following entry for the best known modern example). Filmed in 1931 (dir. James Whale) and many times since.

Frankenstein Unbound (1973) ★★★ Novel by Brian W. Aldiss (UK). A 21st-century American slips back two centuries in time and makes the acquaintance of P. B. Shelley, Lord Byron, etc. He also meets the young Mary Shelley and her creations – Victor Frankenstein and his Monster. A well-sustained *jeu d'esprit* with serious undertones. Filmed in 1990 (dir. Roger Corman).

Fraxilly Fracas, The (1989) ★★ Novel by Douglas Hill (Canada/UK). An ex-cop courier gets caught up in interstellar shenanigans when he is assigned the task of delivering a rare drug to the king of the planet Fraxilly. Fast, funny adventure in the vein of Harry Harrison's *Stainless Steel Rat* books. Hill's first adult sf novel.

Free Amazons of Darkover (1985) ★★ Anthology edited by Marion Zimmer Bradley (USA). Stories by various hands, all set in the editor's 'Darkover' world. This volume concentrates on the 'renunciates', the feminist religious order or secret society featured in many of Bradley's novels such as *City of Sorcery*. Other anthologies in the same vein, some of them credited to Marion Zimmer Bradley and 'The Friends of Darkover', include *The Keeper's Price and Other Stories* (1980), *Sword of Chaos* (1982), *Greyhaven* (1984), *The Other Side of the Mirror* (1987), *Red Sun of Darkover* (1987) and *Four Moons of Darkover* (1988).

Free Zone (1988) ★★ Novel by Charles Platt (UK/USA). Pastiche sf, with a map, a cast list and a data-flow diagram showing the fates of the characters. It amusingly incorporates almost all the major themes that have been used in sf, and contains frequent reminders of old films, books and in-jokes. It's almost impossible to describe the plot, which concerns about a dozen simultaneous threats to the world in general (and an anarchist suburb of Los Angeles in particular) between Christmas and New Year's Eve 1999.

Freedom Beach (1985) ★★ Novel by James Patrick Kelly and John Kessel (USA). Well-meaning, sexually con-

fused liberal-minded protagonist who ought to be in a Philip K. Dick book is hurled from one absurd scene to another, mostly pastiches of writers he admires – Chandler, Aristophanes, Emily Brontë, Groucho Marx, Christopher Marlowe. Unsatisfactorily ambiguous ending.

Friday (1982) ★★ Novel by Robert A. Heinlein (USA). An android superwoman secret agent battles her way through a chaotic world of the near future. A partial return to form for Heinlein, though marred by its embarrassing sexual content. It's a sequel of sorts to the novella 'Gulf' (see *Assignment in Eternity*).

Friends Come in Boxes (1973) ★ Novel by Michael Coney (UK/Canada). The overpopulation problem is solved after a weird fashion: the over-40s are discorporated and kept alive in small boxes. A mildly enjoyable satire with a silly premise.

From the Earth to the Moon (1865) ★★★ Novel by Jules Verne (France). Members of the Baltimore Gun Club build a huge cannon in order to fire men from Florida to the moon. Remarkably prescient, despite the scientific howlers, and more of a satire than an adventure story – little actually happens until the last two chapters. Sequel: *Around the Moon*. Filmed, rather badly, in 1958 (dir. Byron Haskin).

From the Land of Fear (1967) ★★ Collection by Harlan Ellison (USA). Stories, extracts from stories, a preamble 'amble' and 'sprint' by Roger Zelazny, an introduction to the book, and author's introductions to each story give us a volume that is almost as much about Ellison's writings as composed of them. Includes both magazine and TV screenplay versions of 'Soldier'.

Frontera (1984) ★★ Novel by Lewis Shiner (USA). One of the several large corporations which now rule the Earth mounts a mission to Mars – to see what became of an abandoned American colony there. A well-written and realistically presented planetary adventure-cum-mystery. Shiner's first novel.

Frost and Fire (1989) ★★ Collection by Roger Zelazny (USA). Sf and fantasy tales, including the popular 'Permafrost' (Hugo award-winner, 1987) and '24 Views of Mt Fuji by Hokusai' (Hugo and Nebula award-winner, 1986), and a couple of essays. 'The light pieces are short, avoiding tedium; the long pieces are meaty, producing thought. A perfect balance' – Tom Whitmore, *Locus*.

Fugitive Worlds, The (Shaw): see under *Wooden Spaceships, The*.

Fugue for a Darkening Island (1972) ★★ Novel by Christopher Priest (UK). Near-future fable of a Britain which is inundated by refugees from nuclear war in Africa. Written in skilfully-shuffled segments of 'non-linear' narrative, it is perforce a bleak and harrowing vision – by no means typical of the traditional British disaster novel, which has frequently tended towards a cosy escapism.

Fulfilments of Fate and Desire, The (Constantine): see under *Enchantments of Flesh and Spirit, The*.

Full Spectrum 1 (1988) ★★ Anthology edited by Lou Aronica and Shawna McCarthy (USA). A large selection of 25 previously unpublished sf and fantasy stories, many by unknown authors, and obviously designed to outdo all its predecessors and competitors in terms of sheer size. Inevitably, the results are mixed. Among the more notable writers who are on pretty good form here are Michael Blumlein, Thomas M. Disch, Lisa Goldstein, Nancy Kress, Jack McDevitt, James Morrow, Pat Murphy and Norman Spinrad. Follow-up volume: *Full Spectrum 2* (1989).

Fun With Your New Head (Disch): see *Under Compulsion*.

Fundamental Disch (1980) ★★★★ Collection by Thomas M. Disch (USA), introduced by Samuel R. Delany. Nineteen sf, fantasy and unclassifiable pieces (plus a non-fiction appendix) by this supremely stylish author – a 'Best of Disch' by another name. The stories range from the blackly-humorous 'Descending' (1964), about a man trapped on an endless escalator, to 'Getting Into Death' (1973), the subtly fantastic title story of an earlier book. Inevitably, most of the stories have appeared in other collections, though this volume does contain Disch's first published tale, 'The Double-Timer' (1962), and his libretto for the short opera 'The Fall of the House of Usher' (neither collected elsewhere).

Funeral for the Eyes of Fire, A (Bishop): see *Eyes of Fire*.

Furies, The (1966) ★★ Novel by Keith Roberts (UK). Nuclear tests cause devastating floods, and soon afterwards giant mutant wasps wreak further havoc. All rather absurd, but it's an entertaining British disaster story in the John Wyndham vein. Roberts's first novel, and not really typical of his later work.

Furious Future, The (Budrys): see *Budrys' Inferno*.

Furthest (Elgin): see under *Communipath Worlds*.

Fury (1950) ★★ Novel by Henry Kuttner (USA; actually written in collaboration with his wife, C. L. Moore), first serialized in 1947. Vigorous adventure on the planet Venus, where the frightened colonists live in 'Keeps' below the sea. It is the hero's aggressive ambition to persuade them to live on the surface. This novel, which is regarded by many as Kuttner's best, was conceived as a sequel to C. L. Moore's story 'Clash by Night' (1943, as by 'Lawrence O'Donnell').

Fury Out of Time, The (1965) ★★ Novel by Lloyd Biggle Jr. (USA). A misanthropic failed astronaut goes on a jaunt through time, courtesy of some alien technology. It doesn't bring him joy. 'The crippled, hard-drinking major, disability-retired but living on in a trailer shanty town on the fringes of an air force base, has the makings of a Jake Barnes of the spaceways' – J. G. Ballard, *Guardian*.

Future City (Elwood): see under *Cities of Wonder*.

Future History (Pournelle): re-packaging of *The Mercenary* and *West of Honor*.

Future Perfect: American Science Fiction of the Nineteenth Century (1966) ★★★ Anthology edited by H. Bruce Franklin (USA). Scholarly compilation of pieces by Poe, Hawthorne, Melville, Twain, etc. There are some surprises, and all point the way to modern sf.

Futures Past (White): see under *Aliens Among Us, The*.

Fuzzies and Other People (1984) ★★ Posthumously-published novel by H. Beam Piper (USA). Basically the same plot as *Little Fuzzy* and *The Other Human Race*: the likeable alien Fuzzies are threatened by exploiters (this time they are after Zarathustran Sun-Stones) who are eventually defeated in court – the case turns on the competence of Fuzzies to testify.

Fuzzy Sapiens (Piper): see *Other Human Race, The*.

G

Galactic Cluster (1959) ★★★ Collection by James Blish (USA). Outstanding sf stories by this intelligent (and occasionally crabbed) writer. Includes 'Common Time', one of the finest tales of starflight and time-dilation ever written, and 'A Work of Art', about the future resurrection of the composer Richard Strauss. (These pieces are also available in such later volumes as *The Best of James Blish*.) The stories 'Beanstalk' and 'Beep' (the former included in the UK edition of *Galactic Cluster* only) were later expanded into the short novels *Titan's Daughter* and *The Quincuncx of Time*.

Galactic Diplomat (Laumer): see under *Envoy to New Worlds*.

Galactic Effectuator (1980) ★★ Collection by Jack Vance (USA). Two stories about interstellar private detective and strong man Miro Hetzal: the short novel 'Dogtown Tourist Agency' and the short story 'Freitzke's Turn'. The latter is the case of a man who is kidnapped and has another man's testicles transplanted on to him. Set in the same future universe as the 'Alastor Cluster' series, but each world has more diversity and detail than most writers pack into an entire imaginary galaxy.

Galactic Empires (1976) ★★ Anthology edited by Brian Aldiss (UK), originally published in two volumes. A nostalgic romp along the spaceways, with old stories by Anderson, Asimov, Clarke, Harrison, Simak and (of course) van Vogt, among others – all chosen as sterling examples of 'wide-screen baroque' (a term Aldiss first coined in the 1960s when discussing Harness's *The Paradox Men*). 'Brian Aldiss is a tireless anthologizer, but for once he is recycling more waste matter than a space shuttle's latrine' – J. G. Ballard, *New Statesman*.

Galactic Medal of Honour (1976) ★ Novel by Mack Reynolds (USA). The hero is given the highest honour the military can bestow for a stage-managed capture of an abandoned alien spaceship. He returns to Earth to be besieged by journalists and willing young women, as the government and big business squabble over various ways to make use of his undeserved fame. Minor.

Galactic Patrol (Smith): see under *First Lensman*.

Galactic Pot-Healer (1969) ★★★ Novel by Philip K. Dick (USA). The hero, a psychic repairer of ceramics, is whisked off to Plowman's Planet, where his task is to assist in the raising of a submerged cathedral. Very funny in parts – a daft and endearing religio-philosophical romp.

Galactic Sybil Sue Blue (Brown): see *Sybil Sue Blue*.

Galactic Warlord (Hill): see under *Last Legionary Quartet, The*.

Galapagos (1985) ★★★ Novel by Kurt Vonnegut (USA). Leon Trotsky Trout, son of a failed sf writer, becomes a ghost and haunts the Galapagos Islands for a million years. He watches as the descendants of a few marooned humans devolve into a new species: furry, finned, seal-like and small of brain. A sadly funny Darwinian fable.

Galaxies (1975) ★★★ Novel by Barry N. Malzberg (USA). Mock hard-sf tale in which the heroine flies her spacecraft into a 'black galaxy'. The author interweaves many sour comments on the nature of sf as a genre. Witty, self-reflexive, occasionally irritating.

Galaxies Like Grains of Sand (Aldiss): see *Canopy of Time, The*.

Galaxy Builder, The (Laumer): see under *World Shuffler, The*.

Galaxy's End (Lupoff): see under *Sun's End*.

Gallatin Divergence, The (Smith): see under *Probability Broach, The*.

Game of Empire, The (Anderson): see under *We Claim These Stars*.

Game-Players of Titan, The (1963) ★★★ Novel by Philip K. Dick (USA). The war between humanity and the alien Vugs has been fought to a standstill. Now they play a series of elaborate games with each other. An odd, cranky, philosophical melodrama, full of good touches.

Gameplayers of Zan, The (Foster): see under *Warriors of Dawn, The*.

Ganymede Takeover, The (1967) ★ Novel by Philip K. Dick and Ray Nelson (USA). Vermiform invaders from Ganymede have taken over the Earth. A fairly amusing adventure romp, not typical of Dick's work. (Nelson's first novel.)

Garbage World, The (1967) ★★ Novel by Charles Platt (UK/USA). An asteroid called Kopra is used as the solar system's rubbish dump, and it has become home to a pack of filthy beachcombers. A satire on anal-obsessiveness which is fitfully funny. Its author's first novel.

Garden of the Shaped, The (1987) ★ Novel by Sheila Finch (UK/USA). Dynastic goings-on in a world inhabited by various races of genetically engineered humans who do not realize that they are still secretly ruled by the near-immortal survivors of the original colonists. A disappointing work. Sequel: *Shaper's Legacy* (1989).

Gardens of Delight, The (1980) ★★★ Novel by Ian Watson (UK). Visitors to a colonized planet find that the landscape and its inhabitants have been remade in the image of Hiero- nymous Bosch's famous (and terrify- ing) painting 'The Garden of Earthly Delights'. A fantastic premise which turns out to have a true sf rationale. 'Unparalleled in its exoticism' − Brian Stableford.

Gardens One to Five (Tate): see under *Greencomber*.

Garments of Caean, The (1978) ★★ Novel by Barrington J. Bayley (UK). A criminal from the dull, boring Ziode Cluster steals a suit of clothes woven from an intelligent fibre in Caean, fashion capital of the Uni- verse. Meanwhile, a spy ship dis- covers that the Caeanics are addicted to clothes because of their descent from a group of Soviet soldiers trapped in space fighting an endless war against Japanese cyborgs ... It all makes a sort of sense when Bayley tells it.

Gate of Time, The (1966) ★ Novel by Philip José Farmer (USA). A US Air Force pilot of Amerindian descent is plunged into a parallel world where the continents of North and South America do not exist. Despite an intriguing background, this is a routine Farmer adventure. Later

revised and retitled *Two Hawks from Earth* (1979).

Gate to Women's Country, The (1988) ★★★ Novel by Sheri S. Tepper (USA). Boys born in post-holocaust women's towns are delivered to their warrior fathers for military training at the age of five; at fifteen they must choose between remaining with the men or returning to the women for a life of supposed servitude. Stavia, the protagonist of this imaginative and moving novel, loses her lover and son but finds an answer to the perennial problem posed by 1980s feminist sf: what must be done to the men in order to create a society in which women can live freely?

Gates of Creation, The (Farmer): see under *Maker of Universes, The*.

Gateway (1977) ★★★ Novel by Frederik Pohl (USA). Humans go joy- riding in spacecraft which have been abandoned by the mysterious Heechee. Some of them hope to grow rich, thanks to the alien artefacts trawled by their expeditions. The extravert space adventure contrasts with the introverted concerns of the worried hero (who has long conver- sations with his computerized 'psy- chiatrist'). An effective, stylish work which gained much praise. Hugo, Nebula and John W. Campbell award-winner, 1978. Sequel: *Beyond the Blue Event Horizon*.

Gather, Darkness! (1950) ★★ Novel by Fritz Leiber (USA), originally serialized in 1943. In a theocratic future society, ruled by totalitarian means, rebel scientists are known as 'witches'. The hero is a member of the Church hierarchy who is torn between his ostensible duty and what he knows to be right. Leiber's first novel, and an example of 1940s magazine sf at its most sophisticated.

Gather in the Hall of the Planets (O'Donnell): see under *Final War and Other Fantasies*.

Gender Genocide (Cooper): see *Who Needs Men?*

Gene Wolfe's Book of Days (1981) ★★★ Collection by Gene Wolfe (USA). Eighteen sf and fantasy stories arranged in celebration of various notable calendar dates – a whimsical notion which covers a mixed bag (although anything by this supremely talented author is worth reading). Standouts include 'Forlesen' and 'Three Million Square Miles'. 'At the heart of his best stories ... lies a remarkable ability to create adequate breathing-models of the experience of moving from childhood to adulthood, from adulthood to old age' – John Clute.

Genesis Machine, The (1978) ★ Novel by James P. Hogan (UK/USA). A scientist creates an anti-nuclear-bomb device. A woodenly-written retread of the theme of Bob Shaw's *Ground Zero Man* and other, similar, works.

Genesis Quest, The (1986) ★★ Novel by Donald Moffitt (USA). Radio messages from the (presumably extinct) human race prompt a species of intelligent starfish in another galaxy to use genetic engi-neering to recreate us. Some of the new humans want to try to travel the 35 million light years to the Milky Way in a giant tree, to see what happened to their 'ancestors'. Sequel: *Second Genesis*.

Genetic General, The (Dickson), see *Dorsai!*

Genocides, The (1965) ★★★ Novel by Thomas M. Disch (USA). Indifferent aliens turn the Earth into a vegetable patch. Humans become scurrying vermin, surviving among the roots of vast otherworldly plants. A blackly humorous debut by a brilliant writer.

Gentle Giants of Ganymede, The (Hogan): see under *Inherit the Stars*.

Genus Homo (1950) ★★ Novel by L. Sprague de Camp and P. Schuyler Miller (USA), serialized in 1941. A mixed group of men and women are plunged a million years into the future and find themselves on an Earth where humanity is extinct. Luckily they find some intelligent gorillas. Speculative adventure with satirical touches.

Get off the Unicorn (1977) ★★ Collection by Anne McCaffrey (USA/Ireland). Sf and fantasy of variable quality. Contains most of McCaffrey's best-known short stories, including 'Lady in the Tower', her first, and 'The Smallest Dragon Boy', set on the dragon-world of Pern.

Geta (Kingsbury): see *Courtship Rite*.

Getaway World (Goldin): see under *Imperial Stars, The*.

Getting Into Death: The Best Short Stories of Thomas M. Disch (1973) ★★★ Collection by Thomas M. Disch (USA). Despite the subtitle, this is not really a 'Best of ... ' selection (for such see *Fundamental Disch*). It consists of a number of sf, fantasy and mainstream stories, many of them short-shorts, from the late 1960s and early 70s. Standouts include the title story and 'The Asian Shore'. The US edition, entitled *Getting Into Death and Other Stories* (1976), has differing contents and is rather more solid than the UK first edition.

Ghost (1988) ★★ Novel by Piers Anthony (USA). A time-travelling expedition finds another universe where anything they imagine becomes reality. Their relationships are symbolized as a chess game, which becomes a kind of masque – vaguely reminiscent of Anthony's much more substantial 1969 novel *Macroscope*. There is, as always with Anthony, an undertone of low-key, rather whimsical sexual fantasy.

Giants' Star (Hogan): see under *Inherit the Stars*.

Gift from Earth, A (1968) ★★ Novel by Larry Niven (USA). Part of the 'Known Space' series. The Plateau on Mount Lookitthat is ruled by a hereditary 'Crew' who use the 'Colonist' majority as raw material for organ transplants. A partially successful revolution coincides with news of drastic technological changes. Moderately enjoyable.

Ginger Star, The (1974) ★★ Novel by Leigh Brackett (USA). Hero Eric John Stark, a sort of interstellar Tarzan who had featured in earlier magazine stories by Brackett, has picaresque adventures on the planet Skaith. Colourful, well-turned escapism in an old-fashioned vein. Sequels: *The Hounds of Skaith* (1974) and *The Reavers of Skaith* (1976).

Girl with a Symphony in Her Fingers, The (Coney): see *Jaws That Bite, the Claws That Catch, The*.

Girl with the Jade Green Eyes, The (1978) Novel by John Boyd (USA). An alien turns up on Earth in the guise of a young vulnerable woman. The book is little more than an excuse for an extended sex fantasy comparing women to queen bees and featuring the ultimate *vagina dentata*.

Girls from Planet 5, The (1955) ★★ Novel by Richard Wilson (USA). Earth is invaded by aliens who happen to be beautiful young women. An amusing romp, with satirical touches, in a similar vein to the contemporaneous works of Fredric Brown and Robert Sheckley. Wilson's first novel.

Gladiator-at-Law (1955) ★★★ Novel by Frederik Pohl and C. M. Kornbluth (USA). A satirical attack on near-future capitalism, in which the hero is a crusading lawyer who braves the slums of Belly Rave ('Belle Reve') where the populace are sustained, Roman-fashion, by bread and circuses. Eventually he becomes a (literal) gladiator, fighting for the people's cause. Excellent, amusing detail, even if the denouement is a bit hard to credit: it's the authors' best collaboration after *The Space Merchants*.

Glass Hammer, The (1985) ★★ Novel by K. W. Jeter (USA). Fast-paced, violent and profane thriller about a 21st-century hero whose road-warrior adventures are continuously televised for the pleasure of passive millions. A sometimes confusing treatment of the reality-versus-media illusion theme. It has a Cyberpunk flavour, though the author has angrily rejected that label.

Glass Inferno, The (Scortia & Robinson): see under *Life in the Day of ... , A.*

Glory Lane (1987) ★ Novel by Alan Dean Foster (USA). Three young people from Earth are chased across the galaxy by aliens. Very lightweight, joky stuff. 'It really would be breaking a butterfly on the wheel to speak harshly about this little book' – Joe Sanders, *SF & Fantasy Book Review Annual 1988*.

Glory Road (1963) ★★ Novel by Robert A. Heinlein (USA). A beautiful nude woman entices the tough young soldier hero to accompany her on an incredible quest across a far world. He doesn't need much persuading. This is really a sword-and-sorcery fantasy, but it has a few science-fictional bits and bobs thrown in. The main pleasure of the book comes from Heinlein's grouchy but amusing auctorial tone, full of disgruntlement against the modern world – though this could also be the main source of irritation for some readers.

Goblin Reservation, The (1968) ★★ Novel by Clifford D. Simak (USA). Space travel, time travel and supernatural entities have transformed the Earth into the eponymous 'goblin reservation'. A slightly uneasy humorous blend of sf and fantasy – something of a departure for its veteran author.

God Game, The (1986) ★ Novel by Andrew M. Greeley (USA). It's hard to know whether to take this book seriously – a rather flat tale of a computer adventure-game that mysteriously comes to life is overwhelmed by asides on the nature of God, Authorship, Grace and Freewill and continuous name-dropping of other writers and bits of PC technology that were state-of-the-art in '86.

God Machine, The (1969) ★ Novel by Martin Caidin (USA). A giant-computer - threatens - to - take - over - America story. Efficiently told by a technologically competent writer – but it's all old hat (see, for instance, D. F. Jones's *Colossus* for an earlier treatment of a similar idea).

God Machine, The (1973) ★ Novel by William Jon Watkins (USA). A totalitarian 'machine' runs a polluted future Earth, but there is constant war with an underground enemy. The action-adventure plot involves the miniaturization of human beings. Too much.

God Makers, The (1972) ★ Novel by Frank Herbert (USA). A human agent whose task is to prevent war on various planets develops super-powers which make him, in effect, a god. A minor, wish-fulfilling Herbert novel.

God-Emperor of Dune, The (1981) ★ Novel by Frank Herbert (USA), sequel to *Children of Dune* and fourth in his 'Dune' series. Sequel: *Heretics of Dune*.

Gods and Golems (del Rey): see under *Robots and Changelings*.

God's Grace (1982) ★ Novel by Bernard Malamud (USA). An undersea diver survives nuclear war, and ekes out his life on a desert island inhabited only by a colony of chimps. He teaches them to speak, and eventually 'marries' one of them. An odd, dissatisfying book by a major mainstream novelist. 'An uneasy mix of fable, science fiction and religious tract ... Malamud has shipwrecked himself here, and I hope that rescue comes' – J. G. Ballard, *Guardian*.

Gods of Mars, The (Burroughs): see under *Princess of Mars, A*.

Gods of Riverworld (1983) ★★ Novel by Philip José Farmer (USA), sequel to *The Magic Labyrinth* and fifth in the 'Riverworld' series. The shenanigans begin again, as Sir Richard Burton and his resurrected comrades attempt to alter the destiny of the reborn human race on the River-world. Given its potentially immense scope, this series has proved all too narrow and repetitive in its concerns.

Gods of the Greataway (1984) ★★ Novel by Michael Coney (UK/Canada), sequel to *The Celestial Steam Locomotive* and part two of the 'Song of Earth' sequence. Richly coloured far-future sf/fantasy, which perhaps suffers from being over-whimsical. 'A breathtaking accomplishment ... The best comparison may be Shakespeare. I fully expect this book to win the Hugo, and Nebula and whatever else there is in sight' – Tom Easton, *Analog*.

Gods of Xuma, or Barsoom Revisited, The (1978) ★★ Novel by David J. Lake (UK/Australia). An intelligent planetary romance which owes rather less of a debt to Edgar Rice Burroughs than its subtitle would seem to imply. Sequel: *Warlords of Xuma* (1983).

Gods Themselves, The (1972) ★★★ Novel by Isaac Asimov (USA). A new limitless-energy device upsets the very strange alien inhabitants of an alternative universe. Somewhat disjointed (but economical) 'comeback' novel by this popular author, who at the time had written no new extended sf for many years. Hugo and Nebula award-winner, 1973.

God's World (1979) ★★ Novel by Ian Watson (UK). 'God' sends messengers to Earth, so the multi-national crew of a remarkable space vessel sets out to visit Him on His planet. An astonishing metaphysical romp of a space story, highly original and spinning with ideas – though unfortunately presented in a way which is a little too glib and jokey. 'Watson is on his usual themes, explaining how our perceptions determine the reality we subscribe to, and reaching eagerly but uncertainly for the key that unlocks the matrix' – Colin Greenland, *Foundation*.

Godsfire (1978) ★★★ Novel by Cynthia Felice (USA). A cat-like alien narrates a story of conflict with human beings on a rainy planet. The humans are slaves to the sophisticated felines. Cleverly plotted, well detailed. Felice's first novel.

Godwhale, The (1974) ★★★ Novel by T. J. Bass (USA), set in the same world as his earlier book *Half Past Human*. The creature of the title is a cyborg, part whale, part machine, which assists human sea-dwellers who have escaped from the subterranean hive society which now dominates the planet. Good imaginative ecology in an interesting story.

Gold at the Starbow's End, The (1972) ★★ Collection by Frederik Pohl (USA). Five heterogeneous tales, ranging from the humorous 'Shaffery Among the Immortals' to the long and complex 'The Merchants of Venus'. The fine title story was later expanded into the novel *Starburst* (1982).

Gold Coast, The (1988) ★★★ Novel by Kim Stanley Robinson (USA). A well-written coming-of-age story set in 21st-century California. The trouble with this one is that it contains few science-fiction ideas: it's a sensitive novel about the present – writ slightly larger.

Gold the Man (1971) ★★ Novel by Joseph Green (USA). A gifted human becomes the controller of a giant humanoid alien invader, secretly riding it back to its homeworld – where various problems are resolved, both for the unhappy aliens and for the mixed-up protagonist. Probably its author's best novel. Published in the USA as *The Mind Behind the Eye*.

Golden Age of Science Fiction, The (1981) ★★★ Anthology edited by Kingsley Amis (UK). Seventeen excellent stories from the period 1949–62, most of them familiar standards by Aldiss, Asimov, Ballard, Blish, Clarke, Pohl, Sheckley, Vonnegut, etc. In his entertaining introduction Amis takes a reactionary, curmudgeonly view of modern sf.

Golden Age Science Fiction: Short Novels of the 1940s (Asimov, Waugh and Greenberg): see under *Classic Science Fiction: Short Novels of the 1930s*.

Golden Apples of the Sun, The (1953) ★★★ Collection by Ray Bradbury (USA). Twenty-two sf and fantasy stories, including many of the author's best: 'The Foghorn', 'The Pedestrian', 'A Sound of Thunder', etc., etc. Lyrical, emotional, frequently humorous, they present a child's-eye view of the universe. The title story, about a spacecraft skimming the surface of the sun, is essentially a fantasy – as are most of these tales, even when they contain such sf motifs as time travel and encounters with prehistoric monsters. 'The Foghorn' formed the basis of a film, *The Beast From 20,000 Fathoms* (1953; dir. Eugene Lourie).

Golden Days (1987) ★★★ Novel by Carolyn See (USA). A wealthy divorced woman returns to Los Angeles from the East Coast with her daughters and settles down against a background of increasing political and economic disruption, culminating in nuclear war. In the end the West-Coast universe of the protagonist and her friends proves stronger than the public world of politics, business and (by implication) men.

Golden Helix, The (1980) ★★★ Collection by Theodore Sturgeon (USA). Late Sturgeon volume which consists mainly of stories from the 1950s, some of them excellent. Standout is the title story (1954), about a group of people stranded on a lush alien planet. According to some grand cosmic design, these unfortunate humans begin to devolve ...

Golden Man, The (1980) ★★ Collection by Philip K. Dick (USA), edited by Mark Hurst with a fascinating autobiographical introduction by the author. A 'clean-up' volume of Dick stories, ranging from 'The King of the Elves' (1953) to 'The Pre-Persons' (1974). There is some comparative dross among the gold here, but Dick is always interesting.

Golden People, The (1964) ★ Novel by Fred Saberhagen (USA). Straightforward adventure on a planet which is swathed in a force-field that prevents all technological gadgets from working – hence the emphasis on bows and arrows, etc. Saberhagen's first novel. The 1984 reprint is considerably expanded, though not necessarily the better for it.

Golden Space, The (1982) ★★★ Fix-up novel by Pamela Sargent (USA). Longevity has been achieved, but biologists continue to tinker with the human race in the hope of producing a more rational, hermaphroditic species. A major theme is the way in which children would grow up in a relatively changeless world. It's a thoughtful, episodic narrative which covers a considerable span of time.

Golden Sunlands (1986) Novel by Christopher Rowley (USA). A rather poor tale of people kidnapped from a pseudo-Wild-West world of the future and taken as slaves to a vaguely described artificial universe.

Golden Torc, The (May): see under *Many-Coloured Land, The.*

Golden Witchbreed (1984) ★★★ Novel by Mary Gentle (UK). Thoughtful fantasy-tinged sf adventure on a planet called Orthe, where technology has long since fallen into decay. It proved popular in Britain. 'A post-holocaust ... world, providing the excuse for skulduggery and intrigue amongst sword-bearing humanoid aliens and an extended tour through admittedly richly imagined landscapes' – Paul McAuley, *Interzone.* Sequel: *Ancient Light.*

Golem 100 (1980) ★ Novel by Alfred Bester (USA), illustrated by Jack Gaughan. In a chaotic future New York, known as 'the Guff', an unidentifiable but murderous entity causes panic. A mish-mash of exasperating dialogue, typographic japes and weird illustrative matter, this is generally regarded as Bester's most problematical book. It has not been widely admired.

Good Neighbors and Other Strangers (1972) ★★★ Collection by Edgar Pangborn (USA). Warm, frequently lyrical and sometimes sentimental sf tales, including the much-anthologized 'Angel's Egg' (1951) and 'Music-Master of Babylon' (1954). An underrated collection by an author who produced comparatively few short stories.

Good News from Outer Space (1989) ★★★ Novel by John Kessel (USA). Mysterious aliens make their appearance in an America of 1999 which is descending into fin-de-siècle craziness. 'Kessel's aliens serve a vital function ... caught in their pitiless experiments (play?), or setting them in the place of age-old icons of good and evil, humankind reveals itself in all its sad, frightening, wonderful complexity' – Faren Miller, *Locus*.

Gor Saga (1981) ★★ Novel by Maureen Duffy (UK). The tribulations of a young man who turns out to be the experimental offspring of a human father and a gorilla mother. Inevitably there are echoes of *Tarzan of the Apes* (1914), though this work by a mainstream novelist is intended as a serious psychological study. The title is extremely unfortunate, since it suggests that the book is in some way linked to John Norman's dreadful 'Gor' novels (see *Tarnsman of Gor*) – which it is not. The story was filmed for BBC television as *First Born* (1989).

Gordon R. Dickson's SF Best (1979) ★★ Collection by Gordon R. Dickson (Canada/USA), introduced by Spider Robinson. Competent sf stories by a mid-field writer. Includes the Nebula award-winning 'Call Him Lord'. A revised version of this volume, with slightly differing contents, is entitled *In the Bone* (1987).

Grain Kings, The (Roberts), see under *Machines and Men*.

Grass (1989) ★★★ Novel by Sheri S. Tepper (USA). Representatives of a religion-dominated Earth are sent to a grassy colonized planet in order to find a cure for a dangerous new plague. The complex society and ecology of the world known as Grass are very well evoked; the plotting is skilful and the writing has style. 'A book of tragedy and joy, interweaving human drama with a wealth of alien mysteries' – Faren Miller, *Locus*.

Gray Matters (1971) ★★ Novel by William Hjortsberg (USA). In a high-tech underground realm, disembodied human brains are tutored in spiritual perfection, as they await rebirth in new bodies. One man escapes, to re-seed the surface of the Earth. A curious, phantasmagoric dystopia.

Great Explosion, The (1962) ★★★ Novel by Eric Frank Russell (UK), expanded from his short story ' ... And Then There Were None' (1951). An ambassador from a dictatorial regime on Earth sets out to re-contact various planets which were colonized during a 'great explosion' of migration some centuries earlier. The book is an amusing and episodic account of how he fails to persuade any of these cosmic rugged individualists to rejoin the fold. Perhaps Russell's best.

Great Kings' War (Green & Carr): see under *Lord Kalvan of Otherwhen.*

Great Science Fiction Stories, The (Asimov): see *Isaac Asimov Presents the Great Science Fiction Stories.*

Great Sky River (1987) ★★★ Novel by Gregory Benford (USA), a quasi-sequel to his *In the Ocean of Night* and *Across the Sea of Suns.* A human colony near the Galaxy's core is threatened by an all-conquering culture of intelligent machines. This is a lengthy, strenuously detailed text, with excellent scientific content – part of an ongoing series which grapples with truly cosmic themes. Sequel: *Tides of Light.*

Green Brain, The (1966) ★★ Novel by Frank Herbert (USA). A giant-insect story, full of grotesquerie and done with verve. The eponymous 'brain' is a collective insect intelligence which plans to make a teeming humanity pay for the damage it has done to the world's ecology.

Green Eyes (1984) ★★★ Novel by Lucius Shepard (USA). Based on voodoo lore and concerning an experiment in the creation of zombies, Shepard's first novel is not an exercise in sensational horror but psychological sf of a delicate kind. Beautifully written, an outstanding debut. 'The book adds up to considerably less than the sum of its parts. Taken in judicious doses, however, those parts are quite extraordinary' – John Clute.

Green Gene, The (1973) ★★ Novel by Peter Dickinson (UK). As a result of some genetic shift, white people begin to give birth to green-skinned babies, and this leads to racial strife in a nasty near-future Britain. A well-meaning and highly competent sf novel by a writer better known for his excellent crime fiction and juvenile fantasy tales.

Green Hills of Earth, The (1951) ★★★ Collection by Robert A. Heinlein (USA). Ten stories by the American master of near-future realism (as he then was). Most of these tales first appeared in mass-market magazines such as the *Saturday Evening Post* and *Collier's* during the late 1940s, where they had helped create a general acceptance of sf as a new narrative form. They are in the main slight, bright and exceedingly well told.

Green Millennium, The (1953) ★★ Novel by Fritz Leiber (USA). An overpopulated near-future Earth is quietly invaded by benign aliens who resemble green pussy-cats. A complex and amusing tale with deft touches of satire.

Green Odyssey, The (1957) ★★ Novel by Philip José Farmer (USA). The anti-heroic Mr Green is marooned on a picaresque planet, where he must learn to survive amidst some fairly hostile fauna and flora – not to mention the intelligent natives. A comically inventive planetary romance, this was Farmer's first novel to be published in book form.

Greencomber (1979) ★ Novel by Peter Tate (UK). In a near-future of looming ecological crisis, the beach-bum hero sets out to 'comb the green'. An odd, confusing sf/fantasy of the pastoral/mystical sort (which one might call the 'Wessex School', characteristic of much British sf in the 1970s) by a minor writer who has since fallen silent – his earlier sf novels, written in lyrical, sub-Bradbury vein, include *The Thinking Seat* (1969) and *Gardens One to Five* (1971). 'A vague style and a persistent unwillingness to spell anything out. The author's imagination swerves between things that are nasty and things that are childish' – Cherry Wilder, *Foundation*.

Greener Than You Think (1947) ★★★ Novel by Ward Moore (USA). An eccentric female inventor produces a substance which makes grasses grow even more prolifically, until the Earth is smothered in greenery. A well-written, intelligent 'disaster' story with a satirical tone. Moore's first sf novel.

Grey Lensman (Smith): see under *First Lensman*.

Greybeard (1964) ★★★★ Novel by Brian W. Aldiss (UK). The eponymous hero is in his fifties, yet he is the youngest man in the world. Nuclear radiation has rendered humanity sterile, and Greybeard attempts to keep order in an increasingly addled community of survivors. New hope arises at the end. A memorable novel, written with care and love.

Greyhaven (Bradley): see under *Free Amazons of Darkover*.

Grimm's World (Vinge): see *Tatja Grimm's World*.

Ground Zero Man (1971) ★★ Novel by Bob Shaw (UK). Effective near-future thriller about a man who devises a means to detonate all the world's nuclear weapons. This he threatens to do – in the cause of peace. The book was later slightly revised and retitled *The Peace Machine*. 'Good enough to put Shaw up there with John Le Carré and Len Deighton for intelligent pungency' – Peter Nicholls, *Foundation*.

Groundstar Conspiracy, The (Davies): see *Alien, The*.

Growing Up in Tier 3000 (1975) ★★ Novel by Felix C. Gotschalk (USA). Bright children rebel against their parents in a densely-populated, high-tech future community. It's written in an over-excitable, jargon-laden, neologistic style which at times flares into eloquence. A first (and only?) novel by a writer who is known for his very peculiar short stories.

Guardians of Time (1961) ★★★ Collection by Poul Anderson (USA). Four long stories about the world-saving exploits of Manse Everard, a 20th-century adventurer who is inducted into the Time Patrol and finds himself zipping back to ancient Greece, Carthage and other fascinating locations. Well handled: the author knows his history. 'Strongly recommended' – Kingsley Amis, *Observer*. Sequel: *Time Patrolman*.

Guernica Night (1974) ★★ Novel by Barry N. Malzberg (USA). A 23rd-century world, ruled by the Church of the Epiphany, is mysteriously plagued by suicides. Like a number of other Malzberg novels, it switches between the fantasy of the sf scenario and the reality of the author's life: in this case, he is lamenting the death of his writer friend Gil Orlovitz.

Gulliver of Mars (Arnold): see *Lieut. Gullivar Jones: His Vacation*.

Gunner Cade (1952) ★★ Novel by Cyril Judd (C. M. Kornbluth and Judith Merril, USA). The hero belongs to an almost monastic order of future warriors, whose members are thoroughly indoctrinated and sexually repressed. Naturally, he rebels – which leads him on to picaresque and sometimes humorous adventures in the outside world. An enjoyable (though now rather dated) adventure story.

Gunpowder God (Piper): see *Lord Kalvan of Otherwhen*.

Guns of Darkness (Pournelle & Carr): see under *There Will Be War*.

Gypsies (1989) ★★★ Novel by Robert Charles Wilson (USA). A woman and her son have the ability to shift between alternative time-streams – as do other members of the family, and the vaguely menacing stranger known as the 'Gray Man'. A touching, well-written mystery, in which the emphasis is on the characters rather than the fairly traditional sf notions.

H

Habitation One (1984) Novel by Frederick Dunstan (UK). In a post-holocaust world, a number of degenerate survivors do nasty things to each other. 'A conservative Christian allegory ... whose gratuitous cruelty is equalled only by its tedium' – Mary Gentle, *Interzone*.

Hadon of Ancient Opar (1974) ★ Novel by Philip José Farmer (USA). In the year 10,000 BC a sophisticated civilization flourishes around the shores of an inland sea in central Africa. Prehistoric action-adventure stuff which aims to provide a rationale for the existence of the lost city of Opar in Edgar Rice Burroughs's 'Tarzan' novels (and the city of Kôr in Rider Haggard's *She*, 1887). There are also links with Haggard's prehistoric story *Allan and the Ice Gods* and Farmer's earlier novel *Time's Last Gift*. Sequel: *Flight to Opar* (1976).

Halcyon Drift (1972) ★★ Novel by Brian Stableford (UK), first in his 'Hooded Swan' series. Star-pilot Grainger has been infected by a mind parasite: it converses with him internally, and sometimes boosts his strength and endurance. Nevertheless, he resents it. He also resents his boss, the owner of the 'Hooded Swan' spaceship which Grainger must fly on missions to various planets. A quirkily entertaining blend of space opera and hardboiled private-eye story. Sequels (most involving xenobiological mysteries): *Rhapsody in Black* (1973), *Promised Land* (1974), *The Paradise Game* (1974), *The Fenris Device* (1974) and *Swan Song* (1975).

Half Past Human (1971) ★★ Fix-up novel by T. J. Bass (USA). In the far future most humans live a hive-like existence underground. Some free spirits still roam the surface, however, and these are the ones who have the opportunity to go into space and discover new worlds – aided by a sentient starship. A good mix of traditional sf themes. Sequel: *The Godwhale*.

Hammer's Slammers (1979) ★ Collection by David Drake (USA), introduced by Jerry Pournelle. Linked stories on an unashamedly militaristic theme. The eponymous Slammers are a group of go-anywhere, fight-anything interstellar mercenaries. The author is a Vietnam veteran, and he brings a certain tough realism to the repetitive heroics of these tales. Drake's first book, and a work which is representative of a whole new 'mercenary' sub-genre in American sf (see Pournelle's *Janissaries* for another example). Drake has since written further books about the adventures of Colonel Hammer and his Slammers; these include *Cross the Stars* (1984) and *Counting the Cost* (1987).

Hampdenshire Wonder, The (1911) ★★★ Novel by J. D. Beresford (UK). A boy of vastly superior intelligence grows up in an English village. He provokes local jealousies and dies in mysterious circumstances. An early 'superman' story, effectively written in Wellsian vein (Beresford was the author of one of the first critical books on Wells's scientific romances).

Hand of Zei, The (de Camp): see under *Search for Zei, The*.

Handful of Darkness, A (1955) ★★ Collection by Philip K. Dick (USA). Published initially in Britain only, this volume contains many of the best stories from Dick's first three years as a professional sf writer. All have subsequently appeared in other collections.

Handmaid's Tale, The (1985) ★★★ Novel by Margaret Atwood (Canada). Harsh dystopian view of a fundamentalist and militantly sexist future in which women are treated as chattels. A notable crossover from the feminist literary 'mainstream', it won the first Arthur C. Clarke Award as the best sf novel of its year (no doubt to the author's embarrassment).

Hard to Be a God (1964) ★★★ Novel by Boris and Arkady Strugatsky (USSR). Earth agents spy on the backward society of a colonized planet but are under strict instructions not to intervene – even when things begin to go badly wrong. A notable meditation on historical necessity by Russia's leading sf authors. 'It is rare to find such a wealth of detail in the presentation of a non-Earthly culture' – John Brunner, *Foundation*.

Hard Way Up, The (Chandler): see under *Road to the Rim, The*.

Hardwired (1986) ★★ Novel by Walter Jon Williams (USA). Cowboy jet-pilot smuggles drugs across a devastated 21st-century Midwest dominated by giant orbital corporations. Competent adventure, openly influenced by Zelazny's *Damnation Alley*, as well as by William Gibson's 'cyberpunk' style. Quasi-sequel: *The Voice of the Whirlwind*.

Haunted Stars, The (1960) ★★★ Novel by Edmond Hamilton (USA). Astronauts discover a secret on the moon: alien visitors have been there before them, and have left some dreadful warnings. Old-fashioned stuff, by a writer who had been producing zestful space operas since the 1920s – but perhaps the best written and best characterized of all his novels.

Hauser's Memory (Siodmak), see under *Donovan's Brain*.

Have Space-Suit – Will Travel (1958) ★★★★ Novel by Robert A. Heinlein (USA). An earth boy wins a space suit, and is subsequently whisked to the moon and far beyond by evil aliens. Energetic, wise-cracking, continually entertaining. The horrid title hides an outstanding sf novel for teenagers, possibly the best thing its author ever wrote.

Hawkmistress (Bradley): see under *Sword of Aldones, The*.

Hawksbill Station (1968) ★★ Novel by Robert Silverberg (USA). A 21st-century totalitarian government banishes its political prisoners to the bleak prehistoric past, via time machine. But when an opportunity arises to go 'home' not everyone is willing … Published in Britain as *The Anvil of Time*.

Healer (Wilson): see under *Wheels Within Wheels*.

Heart Clock (1973) ★★ Novel by Dick Morland (Reginald Hill, UK). In an overpopulated 21st-century Britain everyone's heart is fitted with a controlling clock which will stop ticking at a moment pre-ordained by the government in its annual Budget. A proficient political thriller with no hidden depths.

Heart of Red Iron (Gotlieb): see under *O Master Caliban!*.

Heart of the Comet (1986) ★★★ Novel by Gregory Benford and David Brin (USA). A mixed bag of scientists burrow into Halley's comet as it passes the sun and return 76 years later, strangely changed. Exhilarating combination of gosh-wow science with comic-book heroism.

Heat Death of the Universe and Other Stories, The (Zoline): see *Busy About the Tree of Life*.

Heatseeker (1989) ★★ Collection by John Shirley (USA). A first volume of sf and fantasy stories by this rather loud-mouthed and variable writer who resembles a cross between Harlan Ellison and the Cyberpunks. 'What Cindy Saw', 'Ticket to Heaven' and 'The Unfolding' (the last written in collaboration with Bruce Sterling) all work effectively enough, but some of the other pieces are considerably less impressive.

Heaven Makers, The (1968) ★ Novel by Frank Herbert (USA). An alien super-race uses Earth-women as concubines, and meddles with our history to enable it to film interesting documentaries. The sex in the book is all male wish-fulfilment; the politics and science are childish.

Heechee Rendezvous (1984) ★★ Novel by Frederik Pohl (USA), sequel to *Beyond the Blue Event Horizon*. The ever-richer and more powerful hero of the earlier books eventually meets his mysterious benefactors, the Heechee – and a new alien menace is discovered. 'What the sequels steadily and damagingly lose is precisely their quality of transcendence; the drama of the interstellar void itself slowly evaporates as the numinous uncertainty of the Heechee fades, leaving us with a somewhat ponderous, mechanically-cyclic space adventure' – Kenny Mathieson, *Foundation*. Sequel: *The Annals of the Heechee*.

Hegira (1979) ★★ Novel by Greg Bear (USA). A group of humans sets out to uncover the mysteries of the vast planet, dotted with inscribed obelisks, which is their birthplace. A flavoursome quest narrative. Bear's first novel. 'It seethes with interesting detail ... Bear has the makings not only of a storyteller but of a stylist' – Michael Bishop, *Fantasy & Science Fiction*.

Heller's Leap (Wallace): see under *Croyd*.

Helliconia Spring (1982) ★★★★ Novel by Brian W. Aldiss (UK), first of a trilogy. This is a massive attempt at world-creation: the evocation of an alien planet where 'winter' lasts many centuries. An epic narrative, impressively detailed. The elaborate, brilliantly sustained sequels are *Helliconia Summer* (1983) and *Helliconia Winter* (1985). 'Though science fiction often has this scope, it has never had this grandeur' – *Times Literary Supplement*.

Hello America (1981) ★★ Novel by J. G. Ballard (UK). The USA a century hence has become a depopulated wasteland, part jungle, part desert – but the old myths live on, from Mickey Mouse to Charles Manson. A Ballardian disaster novel which is very much about the media image of America. Unconvincing as sf, and only intermittently successful in its satire, it nevertheless contains some highly characteristic landscapes and imagery.

Hello Summer, Goodbye (1975) ★★★ Novel by Michael Coney (UK/Canada). On a beautifully evoked alien planet which orbits two stars, the characters are obliged to prepare for a long, long winter. Nicely characterized, rather moving – perhaps Coney's best novel. Published in the USA as *Rax*.

Hell's Pavement (1955) ★★ Fix-up novel by Damon Knight (USA). In a future totalitarian society people are controlled by nasty psychological means. Luckily, some are immune, and form the nucleus of an underground resistance. An intelligent, well-crafted adventure story. Knight's first novel. Republished as *Analogue Men*.

Hellstrom's Hive (1973) ★★★ Novel by Frank Herbert (USA). A scientist runs an underground project which is designed to further the next stage in human evolution. This is a powerful story which investigates the psychology of 'hive' behaviour in human beings (analogous to the societies of insects). The novel bears only a token relationship to the earlier film, *The Hellstrom Chronicle* (1971; dir. Walon Green).

Hephaestus Plague, The (1973) ★ Novel by Thomas Page (USA). Disaster yarn in which fire-bearing cockroaches are let loose by an earth-quake. It descends into silliness when the scientist hero discovers these bugs have telepathic abilities – and so on. 'The first half of the book is intelligently mapped out, sus-penseful and absorbing' – John Clute. Pity about the second half. Filmed as *Bug* (1975; dir. Jeannot Szwarc).

Hercules Text, The (1986) ★★ Novel by Jack McDevitt (USA). American scientists detect coded pulses from a quasar, which turn out to carry a freight of scientific knowledge from an alien culture. Some of this know-ledge is used to build weapons and defence systems, and the Russians become disgruntled. A well-turned hard sf story degenerates into a tale of power-political chicanery. McDevitt's first novel.

Heretics of Dune (1984) ★ Novel by Frank Herbert (USA), sequel to *God-Emperor of Dune* and fifth in his 'Dune' series. More of the same, in this overly complex narrative which ends with the apparent destruction of the planet Arrakis. 'Very little happens, and happens at intermin-able length' – Mary Gentle, *Inter-zone*. Sequel: *Chapterhouse: Dune*.

Heritage of Hastur, The (1975) ★★★ Novel by Marion Zimmer Bradley (USA). A pivotal novel in the 'Dark-over' series, both internally (it is the climax of the struggle between pro- and anti-Terran forces on Darkover, a prequel to *The Sword of Aldones*), and in that it marks a change in the way the books were written: the earlier novels tended to be short and straightforward, perhaps directed

towards a juvenile audience; but from here on, while still basically adventures, they are longer and more concerned with themes of sexuality and freedom.

Heritage of Stars, A (1977) ★★ Novel by Clifford D. Simak (USA). An unassuming hero on a far-future, depopulated Earth goes in search of 'the Place of Going to the Stars'. Along the way he picks up the usual troupe of Simakian companions. Effective, if repetitive, sentimental adventure.

Herland (1979) ★★★ Novel by Char-lotte Perkins Gilman (USA), origi-nally serialized in 1915. Three men discover a non-violent women's utopia somewhere in the far north. An important feminist work, long forgotten, and recently published for the first time in book form.

Hermes Fall, The (1978) ★★ Novel by John Baxter (Australia). An asteroid falls into the Atlantic Ocean, causing an immense catastrophe. This is a good, detailed treatment of what has become a very standard sf theme.

Hero of Downways, The (1973) ★ Novel by Michael Coney (UK/ Canada). Long after the Bomb, people live underground – where they are threatened by giant mutant rats and other menaces. An unin-spired scenario, but enlivened by some grotesque touches and Coney's usual story-telling skill.

Heroes and Villains (1969) ★★★★ Novel by Angela Carter (UK). A post-bomb phantasmagoria about a young woman who runs away from the dull Professors' community and marries a Barbarian. It's startling and erotic, and the imagery has a vibrant clarity. This is the first novel by Carter which may be termed sf: later works of hers which come close to the genre include *The Infernal Desire Machines of Dr Hoffman* (1972; published in the USA as *The War of Dreams*) and *The Passion of New Eve* (1977).

Herovit's World (1973) ★★ Novel by Barry N. Malzberg (USA). This is not really sf, but it's a typical Malzbergian *angst*-trip and it's very much *about* the genre. The protagonist is a hack sf writer who has created a tough space-operatic hero, Mack Miller, who is gradually taking over his mind.

Hestia (1979) ★★ Novel by C. J. Cherryh (USA). An engineer is kidnapped and forced to design a dam on a struggling colony world. He develops a relationship with the non-human natives whose homes will be flooded. The story could have been set in early European colonies in America or Australia with almost no changes.

Hidden Place, A (1986) ★★★ Novel by Robert Charles Wilson (USA/ Canada). Aliens intrude into a small midwestern town during the Depression years of the 1930s. Quiet and understated, it's perhaps lacking in sf originality, but it's nicely characterized: a well-written first novel by a writer of great promise.

Hidden Side of the Moon, The (1988) ★★ Collection by Joanna Russ (USA). Sf and fantasy pieces mainly with a powerful feminist message. Contains the amusing 'Cliché from Outer Space', among others. 'Good, first class, beautiful, personal, involving fiction – but is it science fiction? ... I doubt the male sf readership will consider it part of the genre' – Wendy Bradley, *Interzone*.

Hidden Variables (1981) ★★ Collection by Charles Sheffield (UK/USA). Hard sf tales by a writer who certainly knows his quarks from his quasars. Alas, the fiction leaves something to be desired in terms of style, characterization, etc. etc. But as adventures in ideas for the scientifically inclined, these are rewarding pieces. There is a one-story overlap here with a later volume called *The McAndrew Chronicles* (1983), linked tales about the eponymous inventor.

Hidden World, The (1988) ★★★ Novel by Stuart Gordon (UK), sequel to *Archon*. Many loose ends of the previous book get their 'scientific' explantions here, the mysterious Powers and pagan gods are revealed as the aliens we always half-expected. Quite a complex novel with parallel strands set in contemporary Britain, medieval Provence and the Middle East just after the Flood, forming a refreshing mixture of the sf, horror, historical and fantasy genres. Sequel: *The Mask* (1990).

Hide and Seek (Preuss), see under *Breaking Strain*.

Hiero's Journey (1973) ★★ Novel by Sterling E. Lanier (USA). In a post-nuclear world, infested by mutants and wild beasts, the hero (called Hiero) goes in search of the long-lost computer-plans which may provide an answer to all humanity's problems. A picaresque sf/fantasy which has been very popular. Sequel: *The Unforsaken Hiero* (1983).

High Crusade, The (1960) ★★ Novel by Poul Anderson (USA). An alien starship lands in medieval England, and carries a group of knights off into space. These rough-and-ready chaps eventually succeed in conquering the interstellar empire. A fondly-remembered romp which celebrates the violent human spirit, it has not worn particularly well.

High Justice (1977) Collection by Jerry Pournelle (USA). Seven stories featuring troubleshooters from large private corporations (no shareholders in Pournelle's world) who resort to desperate measures (usually violent) to save major engineering projects from disaster (usually political). Insistently pugnacious – and almost without merit.

High Rise (1975) ★★★ Novel by J. G. Ballard (UK). The middle-class residents of a gigantic apartment block discover that their 'affectless' surroundings encourage a new kind of barbarism. Ironic, stylish, perverse, hard-hitting. Like the author's *Crash*, it is only marginally sf.

Highway of Eternity (1986) ★ Novel by Clifford D. Simak (USA). An over-complex tale of time travel and alien shenanigans. Plenty of familiar Simakian ingredients, but they have been mixed more effectively in earlier novels.

Hitch-Hiker's Guide to the Galaxy, The (1979) ★★★ Novelization of his own radio series by Douglas Adams (UK). The Earth is demolished to make way for a hyperspatial express route and unlikely hero Arthur Dent is plunged into a galaxy too stoned to notice. This madcap tale was responsible for as many student jokes and catchphrases of the 1980s as *Monty Python's Flying Circus* was in the 1970s – and already looks a bit dated. Sequel: *The Restaurant at the End of the Universe*.

Hitler Victorious: Eleven Stories of the German Victory in World War Two (1986) ★★ Anthology edited by Gregory Benford and Martin H. Greenberg (USA). Alternative-world tales, all of which posit a Nazi victory in World War II. Includes such well-known pieces as 'Two Dooms' by C. M. Kornbluth, 'The Fall of Frenchy Steiner' by Hilary Bailey and 'Weinachtsabend' by Keith Roberts. There is a good introduction by Norman Spinrad.

Hoka! (1983) ★ Collection by Poul Anderson and Gordon R. Dickson (USA). Four more stories about comical aliens first introduced in the authors' *Earthman's Burden*. Light and slight.

Holding Wonder, The, (1971) ★★ Collection by Zenna Henderson (USA). More benign, often decidedly lukewarm, stories by 'sf's mistress of the happy ending' (in Sandra Miesel's words). For an earlier, similar, volume see *The Anything Box.*

Hole in Space, A (1984) ★★ Collection by Larry Niven (USA). 'Real' science fiction where the ideas behind a story are more interesting than their realization. Best known for 'The Last Days of the Permanant Floating Riot Club' and other stories exploring the social effects of teleportation.

Hole in the Zero, The (1967) ★★ Novel by M. K. Joseph (New Zealand). A quartet of characters travel in 'unspace' and 'untime', where they learn to create their own subjective realities. Intellectually demanding philosophical sf/fantasy on a solipsistic theme. A highly original work, prized by some readers. Its author's only sf book.

Hollow Lands, The (Moorcock): see *Dancers at the End of Time, The.*

Home from the Shore (1978) ★ Novel by Gordon R. Dickson (USA), a prequel to *The Space Swimmers.* The first batch of sea-born Space Cadets experiences political prejudice on an important training exercise. They return to their undersea homes and find things have deteriorated there as well. As in his 'Childe Cycle', Dickson's writing is inspired by his conviction that the human race will split into subspecies to develop specialist talents – which will then come together later for the improvement of the entire race.

Homeward and Beyond (Anderson): see under *Beyond the Beyond.*

Homing Pigeons, The (Wilson): see under *Schrodinger's Cat: The Universe Next Door.*

Hopkins Manuscript, The (1939) ★★ Novel by R. C. Sherriff (UK). The moon falls to Earth, causing worldwide devastation, in this now-forgotten example of a British 'disaster' novel by a well-known playwright of the between-the-wars period. The scenario is an unlikely one, but the strength of the book lies in its attack on contemporary complacency in the face of looming catastrophe (i.e. World War II). Republished in paperback as *The Cataclysm.*

Hormone Jungle, The (1988) ★★ Novel by Robert Reed (USA). A couple of thousand years hence the solar system is heavily colonized, computers can keep the dead artificially alive, and there are beautiful android geisha girls. One of the latter, improbably named Miss Luscious Chiffon, rebels against her master and takes refuge with a tough space adventurer ... Here are all the elements of a first-class Cyberpunk thriller, but the plot somehow fails to take off. Nevertheless, it's a promising second novel by this new writer.

Hospital Station (1962) ★★ Collection by James White (UK). Linked tales about a huge space hospital known as Sector General. It has a staff of 10,000 and is equipped to treat every known type of alien. This ingenious setting enables the author to spin many variations on the basic problem story of how to deal medi-

HOWARD WHO? · 153

cally with entities of varying shapes, sizes and temperaments. The stories are neat, humorous and humane. Later books in the 'Sector General' series include *Star Surgeon* (1963), *Major Operation* (1971), *Ambulance Ship* (1979), *Sector General* (1983), *Star Healer* (1985) and *Code Blue – Emergency* (1987).

Hostage of Zir, The (de Camp): see under *Search for Zei, The*.

Hot Sleep (1979) ★★ Novel by Orson Scott Card (USA). The first half is a straightforward sf adventure: telepathic space-captain Jason Worthing becomes involved in a plot to overthrow the Empire. The conspirators (many of whom featured in stories in the author's collection *Capitol*) are captured and sent into exile with their memories destroyed. This leads on to the much more interesting second part, in which Worthing is the teacher, father-figure and unwitting demi-god of a Bronze Age agricultural community surviving centuries after the fall of the Empire. This story is continued in *The Worthing Chronicle*.

Hot Wireless Sets, Aspirin Tablets, The Sandpaper Sides of Used Matchboxes, and Something That Might Have Been Castor Oil (Compton): see *Chronocules*.

Hothouse (1962) ★★★★ Fix-up novel by Brian W. Aldiss (UK). In the far, far future the Earth has ceased rotating and is tied to the moon by strands of vegetable matter. Most of the planet's day side is covered by one huge tree, and in its branches live small green folk – the last of the human race. An ebullient, linguistically inventive adventure story which builds to a fine frenzy of a climax. Initially published in an abridged version in the USA as *The Long Afternoon of Earth*. Hugo award-winner, 1962 (for its original magazine appearance as a series of linked stories).

Hounds of Skaith, The (Brackett): see under *Ginger Star, The*.

House of Shards (Williams): see under *Crown Jewels, The*.

House on the Borderland, The (1908) ★★★ Novel by William Hope Hodgson (UK). Horror/fantasy story with sf elements. The last inhabitant of a 'haunted' house in Ireland tells his frightening tale: at one point he experiences a cosmic vision, as his soul roams the universe, and is privileged to witness the death of the solar system.

Houses of Iszm, The (1964) ★★★ Novel by Jack Vance (USA). The Houses of Iszm are intelligent, trainable, living plants which provide the planet's main export. A botanist attempts to steal a female in order to break the monopoly and escapes with a plant – of some sort – growing in his body. As usual Vance's luxuriant imagination is, dare I say it, fertile.

Howard Who? (1986) ★★★ Collection by Howard Waldrop (USA), introduced by George R. R. Martin. The coy, silly title does no justice to this fine and lively gathering of 12 sf and fantasy stories. Includes 'The Ugly Chickens', a sadly funny tale about the true fate of the Dodo (Nebula award-winner, 1980). Published in the UK as part of *Strange Things in Close-Up*.

Hub, The (1987) ★ Novel by Chris Beebee (UK), volume one in the 'Cipola Sequence'. An exercise in British Cyberpunk, involving space habitats, computers, the works. The author's ambitious failure to re-invent the English language may prevent the reader from discovering what merit, if any, the book possesses. A first novel. Sequel: *The Main Event* (1989).

Human Angle, The (1956) ★★ Collection by William Tenn (USA). Good stories by this wry and intelligent writer of short sf, including the powerful, wayward 'Wednesday's Child', a sequel to his earlier, oft-reprinted 'Child's Play' (the latter may be found in *Children of Wonder*, an excellent 'theme' anthology edited by Tenn in 1953).

Human Error (1985) ★★★ Novel by Paul Preuss (USA). Scientists produce a 'biochip', or living micro-computer. Similar in theme to Greg Bear's *Blood Music* (published in the same year), but not so grandiose in its speculations, this is nevertheless an impressive piece of hard sf by an author who knows whereof he writes. Preuss's best novel to date.

Human Zero: The SF Stories of Erle Stanley Gardner, The (1981) ★ Post-humous collection by Erle Stanley Gardner (USA), edited by Martin H.

Greenberg and Charles G. Waugh. The creator of Perry Mason wrote occasional sf pieces during the 1920s, and here they are (warts and all), trawled into one volume by these two prolific anthologists. 'Best read as curiosa, but they're striking curiosa' – Algis Budrys, *Fantasy & Science Fiction*.

Humanoid Touch, The (William-son): see under *Humanoids, The*.

Humanoids, The (1949) ★★ Novel by Jack Williamson (USA), written as a sequel to his famous short story 'With Folded Hands' (1947). Intelli-gent robots, instructed to let no one come to harm, serve their masters so well that they institute a new tyranny of kindness which provokes rebellion. Unfortunately, parapsy-chology is brought in to resolve the situation. A creaky 'classic' of postwar sf which has often been regarded as Williamson's best novel. Belated (and inferior) sequel: *The Humanoid Touch* (1980).

Hundredth Millennium, The (Brunner): see *Catch a Falling Star*.

Hunter and the Trap, The (1967) ★★ Novel by Howard Fast (USA), expanded from his short story 'The First Men'. The US Army conducts a controlled-environment experiment in raising super-children who will have none of the failings of ordinary, hidebound humanity. The experi-ment succeeds all too well. Does little to inhance the impact of the original story (collected in *The Edge of Tomorrow*).

Hunter of Worlds (1977) ★★ Novel by C. J. Cherryh (USA). A clan of the powerful Iduve capture a human and members of two other alien species to use as bait to run down a fugitive from a private feud. Almost incidentally they start a war which risks the destruction of an entire planet. An old-fashioned space opera centring on exotic alien habits rather than technology.

Hunter/Victim (1988) ★ Novel by Robert Sheckley (USA), sequel to *Victim Prime*. Near-future vigilante story: the protagonist's wife is killed by terrorists, so he goes out to kill people like them. But the plot soon threatens to dissolve into the absurdity associated with Sheckley's earlier and better work.

Huysman's Pets (1986) ★★ Novel by Kate Wilhelm (USA). A writer, researching the biography of a leading scientist, uncovers a secret experiment on children who have amazing psychic talents. A good sf mystery story by a writer whose virtues as a (slightly old-fashioned) novelist of character are considerable.

Hyacinths (1983) ★★ Novel by Chelsea Quinn Yarbro (USA). In a near future where commercialized 'dreams' are the main form of entertainment, the government decides to insert propaganda into the dreamfare. A very capable novel, in which the heroine is a strongly characterized career woman. The author is best known for her fantasy works, particularly the series of historical vampire tales known as the 'Saint-Germain Chronicles'.

Hyperion (1989) ★★★★ Novel by Dan Simmons (USA). Against a background of looming interstellar war, various humans become involved with the mysterious 'time tombs' on the planet Hyperion. Intelligent space opera, and an impressively orchestrated multiple-strand narrative. 'It's got everything, mystery, adventure, memorable characters, interesting ideas, good writing' – Darrell Schweitzer, *Aboriginal SF*. Sequel: *The Fall of Hyperion* (1990). Horror-fantasist Simmons's first true sf novel – although his slightly earlier tale of a grounded astronaut, *Phases of Gravity* (also 1989), is close to being science fiction.

I

I am Legend (1954) ★★ Novel by Richard Matheson (USA). A new disease turns people into vampires, and eventually one normal man is left in a world of the undead. Although it's basically a horror story, the author does attempt some scientific rationalization. An effective piece of paranoia. Matheson's first sf novel. Filmed as *The Last Man on Earth* (1964; dir. Sidney Salkow and Ubaldo Ragona) and as *The Omega Man* (1971; dir. Boris Sagal).

I Have No Mouth and I Must Scream (1967) ★★ Collection by Harlan Ellison (USA), introduced by Theodore Sturgeon. Seven noisy tales, from magazines of the late 1950s to the mid-60s. Among the more notable are 'Delusion for a Dragon Slayer', 'Pretty Maggie Moneyeyes' and the phantasmagoric title piece (Hugo award-winner, 1968). Most have been reprinted in subsequent Ellison collections (see, for example, *Alone Against Tomorrow* and *Deathbird Stories*).

I Hope I Shall Arrive Soon (1985) ★★ Posthumous collection by Philip K. Dick (USA), edited by Mark Hurst and Paul Williams. This is the final clean-up collection of Dick's shorter works, and it's variable in quality.

I Love Galesburg in the Springtime (1963) ★★★ Collection by Jack Finney (USA). Polished fantasy and sf stories, many of them variations on a time theme. 'Pointed and amiable ... frolics in the stone garden of nostalgia and memory' – J. G. Ballard, *Guardian*.

I, Robot (1950) ★★★ Collection by Isaac Asimov (USA). Nine linked stories, ranging from 'Robbie' (1940) to 'The Evitable Conflict' (1950), which present a continuous narrative of the near-future rise of intelligent machines with 'positronic' brains. Lucidly written, slightly juvenile in tone, this was the book which first established Asimov's reputation as a writer. His 'Three Laws of Robotics' have long since entered scientific folklore. Semisequels: *The Rest of the Robots* and *The Complete Robot* (1982).

I Sing the Body Electric! (1969) ★★ Collection by Ray Bradbury (USA). Another heterogeneous volume of fantastic tales by this whimsical writer. Only a few can be described as sf, and by this time the Bradbury charm was wearing thin.

I, Vampire (Scott): see under *Passing for Human*.

I Will Fear No Evil (1970) Novel by Robert A. Heinlein (USA). In a dark, polluted America of the 21st century the fabulously rich 94-year-old hero has his brain transplanted into the body of his beautiful young secretary. Something goes awry (both with the experiment and with the novel), for the girl's personality remains alive in the body, and interminable dialogues ensue. The result is a tiresome, opinionated, overblown and thoroughly silly book.

Ibis: Witch Queen of the Hive World (1985) ★★ Novel by Linda Steele (USA/UK). An interplanetary 'romance' which ironically reverses sex roles: marooned Earthmen become the playthings of the female rulers of a hive-like alien society. A witty and provocative first novel.

Ice and Iron (1974) ★★ Novel by Wilson Tucker (USA). Mysterious objects fall from the sky, as a new Ice Age looms in present-day America. It transpires that the detritus comes from a post-catastrophe future. 'The story's real centre of interest is landscape, the way it is shaped and the way it can be read' − Tom Shippey, *Times Literary Supplement*.

Ice Monkey and Other Stories, The (Harrison): see under *Machine in Shaft Ten and Other Stories, The*.

Ice People, The (1968) ★ Novel by René Barjavel (France). Antarctic explorers discover representatives of an ancient civilization in suspended animation. The knowledge these beautiful people bear may disrupt the world, and political complications ensue. A big success in France, it will probably strike the English-language reader as creaky old stuff, reminiscent of Rider Haggard's *When the World Shook*.

Ice Prophet (1983) ★★ Novel by William R. Forstchen (USA). Technological tampering has triggered off a new ice age. The central character is a rebel against the repressive, antiscientific society which has arisen after the big freeze. Adequate sf adventure by a new novelist. Sequels: *The Flame Upon the Ice* (1984) and *A Darkness Upon the Ice* (1985).

Ice Schooner, The (1969) ★★ Novel by Michael Moorcock (UK). In an icebound far future, ships have become huge sledges which skid across the frozen oceans, hunting for mutant whales. An entertaining, though slightly pretentious, tale of adventure set against a fascinating backdrop.

Icehenge (1984) ★★★ Novel by Kim Stanley Robinson (USA). A sophisticated tripartite narrative involving a failed revolution in a Mars colony of the 23rd century and an enigmatic structure − the 'icehenge' of the title

– on the outer planet Pluto. 'A clever bleak adult book. As it closes, it thrusts us out to think' – John Clute.

Icequake (1979) ★★ Novel by Crawford Kilian (USA/Canada). The Earth's magnetic field collapses and solar flares strip away the ozone layer, in this proficient disaster story involving the fate of a group of scientists in Antarctica.

Icerigger (1974) ★ Novel by Alan Dean Foster (USA). Human merchants indulge in swashbuckling adventures with the alien inhabitants of the frozen world Tran-ky-ky. The various goings-on of the human characters are much less fun than the description of the heroic run of the ice-ship (i.e. a large sledge with sails) called Slanderskree. Sequel: *Mission to Moulokin*.

Idle Pleasures (Effinger): see under *Dirty Tricks*.

If the Stars Are Gods (1977) ★★ Novel by Gregory Benford and Gordon Eklund (USA), expanded from their 1973 Nebula award-winning novelette of the same title. An episodic narrative involving encounters with some odd aliens. Ruminative and worthy. As with everything Benford has a hand in, the science is excellent.

Illuminatus! (Shea & Wilson): see under *Schrodinger's Cat: The Universe Next Door*.

Illustrated Man, The (1951) ★★★★ Collection by Ray Bradbury (USA). Eighteen sf and fantasy stories, together with a brief prologue and epilogue. Contains many of the author's classic tales: 'The Veldt', about a kids' nursery which comes dangerously to life; 'The Highway', a brief, simple but moving story about the fall of civilization as seen by a Mexican peasant; 'The Long Rain', about hellish conditions on the planet Venus; 'Zero Hour', about children in league with aliens; and others. Wonderful, atmospheric pieces, making this one of Bradbury's best books. Filmed in 1969 (dir. Jack Smight; screenplay based on the prologue plus three of the stories).

Imago (Butler): see under *Dawn: Xenogenesis 1*.

Immortality, Inc. (1959) ★★ Novel by Robert Sheckley (USA). A man dies in a car crash in 1958 and awakens in the year 2110, to find himself part of an advertising campaign run by cynical corporation-men in this over-commercialized future. Sheckley's first novel, in which the satirical sf elements sit somewhat uneasily alongside a fantasy content of the afterlife, ghosts, etc.

Immortals, The (1962) ★★ Fix-up novel by James E. Gunn (USA). A small minority of people are extremely long-lived, thanks to their superior blood, and they can transfer this boon to others by means of transfusion. When their secret becomes known, they are ruthlessly hunted for their blood. An episodic thriller which deals intelligently with the topic of immortality and the lengths to which people will go to attain it.

Adapted as a US television series, 1969–70. The author also wrote a 'novelization' of the series, entitled *The Immortal* (1970).

Imperator Plot, The (Spruill): see under *Psychopath Plague, The*.

Imperial Bounty (Dietz): see *Sam McCade, Interstellar Bounty Hunter*.

Imperial Earth (1975) ★★ Novel by Arthur C. Clarke (UK). The cloned hero travels from his home in the outer solar system to Earth in the year 2276. The story is thin, but it's a pleasing utopian travelogue, full of incidental wonders. 'To dismiss it as a failed fiction – because its characters are cardboard, its storyline exiguous, and so forth – would be to deny by omission the translucent, effortless epiphanousness of the book' – John Clute.

Imperial Stars, The (1976) Novel by Stephen Goldin (USA), first of the 'Family d'Alembert' series, based on characters created by the late E. E. 'Doc' Smith. Old-fashioned galactic-empire stuff, featuring a family of superpowered secret agents who foil all attempts to upset the interstellar dynasty. Sequels: *Strangler's Moon* (1976), *The Clockwork Traitor* (1976), *Getaway World* (1977), *Appointment at Bloodstar* (1978), *The Purity Plot* (1978), *Planet of Treachery* (1982), *Eclipsing Binaries* (1983), *The Omicron Invasion* (1984), *Revolt of the Galaxy* (1985) and others.

Implosion (1967) ★★ Novel by D. F. Jones (UK). The majority of women become sterile, and this leads to a catastrophic population collapse. A grim scenario, adequately dramatized.

Impossibles, The (Phillips): see under *Brain Twister*.

In Alien Flesh (1988) ★★★ Collection by Gregory Benford (USA). Tales which combine hard physics with attempts at 'literary' style, often to good effect. Notable items include the title piece, 'White Creatures' and 'Exposures'. 'Benford explodes the traditional hard-sf assumption that the Universe is a cosy place just waiting to be conquered ... An impressive range of effective, original short sf stories' – Paul McAuley, *Interzone*.

In Conquest Born (1987) ★ Novel by C. S. Friedman (USA). A very long, convoluted tale about a desperate war between two highly specialized human civilizations. A modern example of traditional space opera, complete with vastly destructive weapons, science that might as well be magic, unpronounceable names and a hint of exotic sexual practices. The author's first novel.

In Deep (1963) ★★★ Collection by Damon Knight (USA). Eight good stories (seven in the UK edition) which include the brilliant 'Four in One' (1953), about human explorers who are melded into an alien jelly-ish, and 'The Country of the Kind' (1955), about a criminal in a future world of repressive tolerance. Later collections by this capable writer include *Off Center* (1965) and *Turning On*.

In Our Hands, the Stars (Harrison): see *Daleth Effect, The*.

In Solitary (1977) ★★ Novel by Garry Kilworth (UK). A few centuries hence, only a handful of human beings still survive on an Earth which has been conquered by birdlike aliens. A short but well-told narrative. Kilworth's first novel.

In the Bone (Dickson): see *Gordon R. Dickson's SF Best*.

In the Days of the Comet (1906) ★★ Novel by H. G. Wells (UK). The wicked old world is transformed by green gases which fall from a passing comet's tail and cause humanity to embrace free love and socialism. An enjoyable read, at times moving in its utopianism, but one of Wells's least convincing scenarios. Its sexual content made it highly controversial in its day.

In the Drift (1985) ★★ Fix-up novel by Michael Swanwick (USA). Human mutations arise in a near-future radiation-poisoned USA. A couple of short stories are cobbled together with new material to make the talented Swanwick's first book something of a disappointment. 'The novel he has assembled slithers onward, into that termitarium of American sf kitsch where paranormal powers and a decayed populism miscegenate dimly to beget a new religion that will transform the lives of the oppressed' – John Clute.

In the Footsteps of the Abominable Snowman (1970) ★★ Collection by Josef Nesvadba (Czechoslovakia). Six intelligent tales by the leading Czech writer of sf. The title piece and such stories as 'The Death of an Apeman' play ironically with certain well-known modern myths. The US edition, published as *The Lost Face* (1971), contains two additional stories. 'Lively surface detail and humour relieve the undercurrent of despair' – Brian Aldiss, *This World and Nearer Ones*.

In the Hall of the Martian Kings (Varley): see *Persistence of Vision, The*.

In the Ocean of Night (1977) ★★★ Fix-up novel by Gregory Benford (USA). Near-future space fiction about encounters with the alien, very realistically conceived by its physicist author. It's long, episodic, and strives for effect. Sequel: *Across the Sea of Suns*.

In the Pocket and Other SF Stories (O'Donnell): see under *Men Inside, The*.

In the Valley of the Statues and Other Stories (1982) ★★ Collection by Robert Holdstock (UK). Eight clayey, clinging tales by sf's leading earth-lover. In 'Earth and Stone' a time-traveller learns to mate with the soil, while in 'Mythago Wood' (later to be expanded into a World Fantasy Award-winning novel) a demented researcher makes it with a tree spirit – all told in a somewhat turbid prose which occasionally achieves eloquence. The chromium future has no appeal for Holdstock: he is at his best when writing of Irish prehistory or the legends of the Dark Ages.

Incandescent Ones, The (1977) ★ Novel by Fred and Geoffrey Hoyle (UK). Old-fashioned British sf thriller ostensibly set 200 years in the future following a benign alien invasion of Earth. Builds to a surprising climax. 'The book reads like the recounting of a dream, and its changes of venue and perspective are markedly dream-like – it's only too bad that its crew of authors couldn't spare a few pages to dwell on their creation' – John Clute.

Incomer, The (1987) ★ Novel by Margaret Elphinstone (USA). An impoverished matriarchal utopia has arisen in post-holocaust America. The 'incomer' of the title is a travelling musician who learns the good ways of Clachanpluck, in this fairly standard feminist scenario. A first novel.

Inconstant Moon (1973) ★★ Collection by Larry Niven (USA). Various stories, many of which have also appeared in other collections such as *All the Myriad Ways* and *The Shape of Space* (1969). In the memorable title story, Californians revel in a strangely bright moonlight, as it dawns upon a few just what has to be happening on the other side of the world to cause the glow.

Incredible Planet, The (Campbell): see under *Mightiest Machine, The.*

Incredible Shrinking Man, The (Matheson): see *Shrinking Man, The.*

Indoctrinaire (1970) ★ Novel by Christopher Priest (UK). A region of South America exists some 200 years in the future. Other mysteries abound, in this cleverly conceived but rather woodenly written first novel by a notable British author.

Infernal Desire Machines of Dr Hoffman, The (Carter): see under *Heroes and Villains.*

Inferno, The (1973) ★★ Novel by Fred and Geoffrey Hoyle (UK). A vast stellar explosion at the core of the galaxy threatens life on Earth. The plot involves an astronomer's scheme for survival in Scotland, and reveals an obsession with the leadership principle. A mixture of hard science and retrograde politics.

Infinite Cage, The (1972) ★★ Novel by Keith Laumer (USA). The amnesiac hero discovers that his own possibilities are endless, in this fast-paced thriller about transcendence of the normal human state. A quintessential Laumer novel, and, as Brian Stableford says, 'a particularly clear version of one of the most prevalent motifs in modern sf'.

Infinite Dreams (1979) ★★ Collection by Joe Haldeman (USA). A large part of Haldeman's 1970s short stories, such as the poignant 'Summer's Lease', 'A Time to Live' (an obvious tribute to Heinlein's 40s fiction) and '26 Days On Earth' and 'Tricentennial', precursors of the (rather better) 'Worlds' series.

Infinite Moment, The (Wyndham): see *Consider Her Ways and Others.*

Infinite Summer, An (1979) ★★★ Collection by Christopher Priest (UK). Five delicate sf/fantasy stories about time and perception. Most notable are the title piece, 'Palely Loitering' and 'The Watched'. Priest is not really a stylist, but these tales are poetically conceived: he manages to evoke a curious, haunting atmosphere by dogged attention to detail and his characters' unusual states of mind.

Infinity Box, The (1975) ★★★ Collection by Kate Wilhelm (USA). Nine sf and fantasy tales from the author's best period as a short-story writer (the 1970s). Several of the pieces here, including 'April Fool's Day Forever', 'The Funeral' and the title story, were nominated for awards. Other fine Wilhelm collections, containing varied stories from the same decade, are *Somerset Dreams and Other Fictions* (1978) and *Listen, Listen* (1981).

Infinity Link, The (1984) ★★ Novel by Jeffrey A. Carver (USA). An Earth-woman makes telepathic contact with a visiting alien space vessel. The ramifications are lengthy and complex. An attempt at a major sf novel which does not quite live up to its author's ambitions.

Infinity's Web (1985) ★★ Novel by Sheila Finch (UK/USA). In five alternative worlds, different versions of the same woman have trouble with dominating men. A very promising first novel.

Inherit the Stars (1977) ★★ Novel by James P. Hogan (UK/USA), part one of his 'Giants' trilogy (also known collectively as *The Minervan Experiment*). The discovery of a dead body on the moon leads to the gradual unfolding of the history of an ancient human space-faring civilization. Unfortunately, the rather leaden writing style does not do justice to the interesting conception. Hogan's first novel. Sequels (of decreasing merit): *The Gentle Giants of Ganymede* (1978) and *Giants' Star* (1981).

Inheritors, The (1955) ★★★★ Novel by William Golding (UK). In prehistoric times the last family of Neanderthals is displaced by a tribe of Cro-Magnons. This tragedy is witnessed, movingly, from the Neanderthals' point of view. Feverishly written, a tale of tremendous impact.

Inheritors of Earth (1974) Novel by Gordon Eklund and Poul Anderson (USA). A coming race of telepaths attempts to usurp the Earth. This is an ill-written and unwise expansion of a 1951 magazine story, 'Incomplete Superman', by Poul Anderson solus. 'An awful, awful book' – John Clute.

Inner Circle (1966) ★★★ Novel by Jerzy Peterkiewicz (Poland/UK). Tripartite fiction on the theme of identity and fecundity, set partly in a ghastly overpopulated future Britain, and partly in the Garden of Eden. An interesting experiment, on the borders of sf. 'Mr Peterkiewicz's Eve is a brilliant creation' – J. G. Ballard, *Guardian*.

Inner Wheel, The (1970) ★★ Fix-up novel by Keith Roberts (UK). A group of people come together to form a psi-powered *gestalt* being. It's an intense and well-written narrative, but inevitably reminiscent of Theodore Sturgeon's *More Than Human*. This version has a markedly British flavour, however.

Inside Outside (1964) ★★ Novel by Philip José Farmer (USA). The hero awakes in an artificial spherical world which proves to be a version of the afterlife, where he encounters Fyodor Dostoevsky and others. A strange, grim run-in for Farmer's later 'Riverworld' books.

Insider, The (1981) ★★ Novel by Christopher Evans (UK). An alien parasite transfers from one human host to another. The emphasis is on psychology in this dark tale with a near-future setting. Dogged and intense. 'All praise to *The Insider*, in the political respect, as a quiet denunciation of the grubbier trends in contemporary British society, extrapolated a little way ahead' – Ian Watson, *Foundation*.

Instrumentality of Mankind, The (1979) ★★ Posthumous collection by Cordwainer Smith (Paul Linebarger, USA), introduced by Frederik Pohl. This is the clean-up volume: i.e., it contains all the remaining short pieces by the author (some of them fragments completed by his wife) which were not included in *The Best of Cordwainer Smith*. The quality is variable, but the book is worth having because all of Smith's sf work was linked into one grand future history – small in terms of the wordage, but vast in its imaginative implications.

Intangibles Inc. and Other Stories (1969) ★★ Collection by Brian W. Aldiss (UK). Lightweight gathering of five entertaining yarns, ranging from the title fantasy (1959) through 'Neanderthal Planet' (1960) to 'Since the Assassination' (1969). An American edition, published as *Neanderthal Planet*, contains a somewhat different selection.

Integral Trees, The (1983) ★★★ Novel by Larry Niven (USA). The author goes to great lengths – with diagrams, notes and a glossary – to imagine a massive toroidal gas cloud, circling a star, where humans can live in free fall. Colonists from the 'State' (the background to Niven's 'corpsicle' stories) have gone native, abandoning their intelligent spaceship for 500 years. The novel follows the Quinn family, who live on a giant flying tree, as they take part in various petty tribal wars and learn something of the science of their ancestors. Sequel: *The Smoke Ring* (1987).

Inter Ice Age 4 (1959) ★★ Novel by Kobo Abe (Japan). The threat of melting ice caps and rising sea levels provokes Japanese scientists to experiment on human babies in order to turn them into the advance guard of a new submarine race. A thoughtful novel, unfortunately a bit stodgy in the translation, by a leading Japanese writer.

Interface (1971) ★★ Novel by Mark Adlard (UK). 'Tcity', in north-east England of the 22nd century, is a vast kennel for unemployable citizens. The genetically-engineered

Executives enjoy all the fruits of a high-tech society, and (inevitably) their privileges provoke a rebellion. A thoughtful, slightly old-fashioned, fitfully satirical work which questions such matters as social class, intelligence and the desirability of leisure. Sequels: *Volteface* (1972) and *Multiface* (1975).

Interpreter, The (1960) ★ Novel by Brian W. Aldiss (UK). An early and very minor book-length yarn of galactic intrigue by this major author. Published in the USA as *Bow Down to Nul*.

Interstellar Empire (1976) ★ Collection by John Brunner (UK). Contains a series of linked stories from early in the author's career, including the novels *The Space-Time Juggler* (1963) and *The Altar on Asconel* (1965), about adventures on the rim of a declining galactic empire. Routine space opera by a young writer.

Interstellar Two-Five (1966) ★ Novel by John Rankine (Douglas R. Mason, UK), the first of his 'Dag Fletcher' series. The crew of a crash-landed spaceship have to transport their craft thousands of miles across a hostile alien planet in order to ready it for take-off once more. 'This is adventure, lightened by humour and unburdened by Significance' – James Cawthorn, *New Worlds*.

Intervention (1987) ★★ Novel by Julian May (USA). Prequel to the 'Saga of the Exiles' and the Galactic Milieu trilogy (see *The Many-Coloured Land*). Good old straight sf about young people growing up with psionic superpowers; complete with little green men, FTL spaceships, forcefields and SF conventions.

Interzone: The 1st Anthology (1985) ★★★ Anthology edited by John Clute, Colin Greenland and David Pringle (UK). A dozen stories reprinted from *Interzone*, the only lasting British sf magazine of the 1980s. There is also one outstanding piece which is original to the book: 'O Happy Day!' by Geoff Ryman, a dark vision of a future America in which homosexual men become unwilling collaborators of vengeful feminists. Of the other stories, J. G. Ballard's 'The Object of the Attack' and Michael Blumlein's 'Tissue Ablation and Variant Regeneration' are standouts. Followed by *Interzone: The 2nd Anthology* (1987; edited by Clute, Pringle and Simon Ounsley), *Interzone: The 3rd Anthology* (1988) and *Interzone: The 4th Anthology* (1989).

Into the Alternate Universe (Chandler): see under *Road to the Rim, The.*

Into the Out Of (1986) ★★ Novel by Alan Dean Foster (USA). An FBI undercover agent, a shy but beautiful woman and an old Maasai Laibon (witch doctor) travel from Washington DC to Tanzania to stop up the door through which evil demons from another dimension are entering the world. A light novel which occasionally reads like a holiday travelogue.

Invaders! (Dickson): see under *Survival!*

Invaders from Earth (1958) ★ Novel by Robert Silverberg (USA). One of this author's early journeyman efforts. 'A slight, routine affair which, minus its interplanetary setting, is simply a fight to save defenceless tribesmen from exploitation by big business interests' – James Cawthorn, *New Worlds*.

Invaders from the Centre (Stableford): see under *Journey to the Centre*.

Invaders Plan, The (1985) Novel by L. Ron Hubbard (USA). First of the 'Mission Earth' so-called dekalogy (a ten-book sequence). A corrupt alien empire plots to conquer our planet. Embarrassingly bad. Posthumous sequels include: *Black Genesis* and *The Enemy Within* (both 1986).

Invasion of the Body Snatchers (Finney): see *Body Snatchers, The*.

Inverted World (1974) ★★★ Novel by Christopher Priest (UK). A small wooden city is dragged across the surface of a world shaped like a solid hyperbola, in which all limits are infinite. When the hero leaves his city, he experiences some very strange dilations and contractions of space. A highly original sf mystery story about reality and perception.

Invincible, The (1967) ★★ Novel by Stanislaw Lem (Poland). An exploratory team tries to discover why a new planet has proven so lethal to prior visitors. A satisfactory mystery, and one of the intellectual Mr Lem's plainer tales. 'Just good old ordinary science fiction, interstellar adventure type, brought off with flair, zest and skill' – James Blish, *Foundation*.

Invisible Man, The (1897) ★★★ Novel by H. G. Wells (UK). The misanthropic Dr Griffin learns how to make himself invisible by scientific means, but the discovery drives him to madness. One of Wells's most lauded works, it's actually much grimmer than many people remember. Filmed in 1933 (dir. James Whale) and adapted as a serial for BBC television in 1984. (There have also been many other movies and TV series which have exploited the basic idea to trivial effect.)

Involution Ocean (1977) ★★ Novel by Bruce Sterling (USA). In a vast crater on a nearly waterless world men sail the sea of dust, hunting the great beasts known as dustwhales. Sterling's first novel: a mite pretentious but, all in all, a colourful apprentice work. 'Another salty yarn ... Take a couple of slices of Melville, simmer in the juice of three sea shanties, and stir in *Treasure Island*; add Jules Verne and *The Rime of the Ancient Mariner* to taste ... ' – Tom Hosty, *Foundation*.

Iron Dream, The (1972) ★★ Novel by Norman Spinrad (USA). In an alternative time-line, Adolf Hitler gave up politics, emigrated to America and became a science-fiction writer. Here we have a reprint of his supposed Hugo-winning masterpiece, *Lord of the Swastika* (1954), complete with a scholarly afterword by one Homer Whipple of New York University. This is a marvellous (and very pointed) joke on Spinrad's part, but the book outwears its welcome: it's probably sufficient to read the opening chapters and the afterword. Winner of the Prix Apollo in France, 1974. Banned in West Germany.

Iron Heel, The (1907) ★★★ Novel by Jack London (USA). A bitter tale of a long-drawn-out socialist revolution against a future fascist regime in America. 'Jack London had that particular genius which perceives what is hidden from the common herd, and possessed a special knowledge enabling him to anticipate the future' – Anatole France.

Iron Master (Tilley): see *Amtrak Wars, The.*

Iron Thorn, The (Budrys): see *Amsirs and the Iron Thorn, The.*

Irrational Numbers (1976) ★★★ Collection by George Alec Effinger (USA), introduced by Robert Silverberg. Eight zany stories, sf, fantasy and borderline, by a sophisticated young writer. Many of them are on games- and sports-related themes. Standouts include 'And Us, Too, I Guess', a sly tale concerning a quiet cataclysm, and 'How It Felt', about the bored gameplayers of a leisured distant future. 'Effinger's material includes all the standard schlock furniture of contemporary pop culture; what he makes out of it is something more than schlock, however' – Robert Silverberg, Introduction.

Isaac Asimov Presents the Great Science Fiction Stories (1979–89) ★★★ Anthology series edited by Isaac Asimov and Martin H. Greenberg

(USA). A retrospective 'Best SF of the Year' series, covering the period 1939 to 1956. Each volume is over 300 pages long, and contains a good selection of tales by well-known writers. The series suffers perhaps from a narrowness of focus: the stories all come from the best-known genre magazines, not from further afield.

Isaac Asimov's Robot City (Kube-McDowell, etc.): see *Odyssey.*

Island (1962) ★★ Novel by Aldous Huxley (UK/USA). A beautiful utopia exists on a tropical isle, its inhabitants benefiting from the best of Western science and Eastern mysticism. Huxley's last novel, and the least of his sf works. 'Weak on characterization but strong on talk, crammed with ideas and uncompromisingly intellectual' – Anthony Burgess, *Ninety-Nine Novels.*

Island Called Moreau, An (Aldiss): see *Moreau's Other Island.*

Island of Doctor Death and Other Stories and Other Stories, The (1980) ★★★★ Collection by Gene Wolfe (USA). A superb 400-page volume of 14 subtle, deceptive sf and fantasy stories (some of them novella-length). The tricksy titles – three of the pieces are called 'The Island of Doctor Death and Other Stories', 'The Death of Dr Island' (Nebula award-winner, 1973) and 'The Doctor of Death Island' – should not be allowed to confuse the reader: these are serious fictions, beautifully written and full of deep imaginative insights. But there is a great deal of playfulness here too. 'Some of the best American short stories of the decade are in this book' – Ursula Le Guin.

Island of Dr Moreau, The (1896) ★★★★ Novel by H. G. Wells (UK). The eponymous mad scientist carves beasts into the shape of men. A terrible fable of Evolution, brilliantly imagined. Filmed in 1932 as *The Island of Lost Souls* (dir. Erle C. Kenton), and in 1977 under its proper title (dir. Don Taylor).

Islands (1970) ★★★ Novel by Marta Randall (USA). The heroine, an archaeologist who is afflicted with mortality in a future society of immortals, discovers a quite different recipe for longevity in some 21st-century ruins. A first novel which handles its timeworn themes very well indeed.

Islands in the Net (1988) ★★★ Novel by Bruce Sterling (USA). An apparently peaceful, post-Cold War world of the near future is linked together by an enormous data-net. However, the rather self-satisfied heroine discovers that there are islands of crime and electronic piracy in this sea of information – and a thriller-ish plot ensues. A long book, commendable for its realistic depiction of a likely postindustrial future. 'Crammed with vividly presented and convincing political, technical and economic speculation ... a complex, multi-layered and, above all, mature work' – Paul McAuley, *Interzone*. John W. Campbell award-winner, 1989.

Islands in the Sky (1952) ★ Novel by Arthur C. Clarke (UK). Space stations in Earth orbit are the setting for this technically accurate but decidedly humdrum story for children. It cannot compare with Robert A. Heinlein's 'juveniles' of the same period, such as the similarly-titled *Farmer in the Sky*.

Isle of the Dead (1969) ★★ Novel by Roger Zelazny (USA). Ornate sf/fantasy adventure involving a super-rich, near-immortal 'worldscaper' who is threatened by various aliens and alien gods. Zelazny's tough-poetic style was beginning to cloy by the time this book appeared. It's not one of his best.

It's a Mad, Mad, Mad Galaxy (Laumer): see under *Nine by Laumer*.

Ivanhoe Gambit, The (1984) ★ Novel by Simon Hawke (Nicholas Yermakov, USA), first of the 'Timewars' series. Sf/fantasy adventure stuff in which members of the US Army Temporal Corps meet up with (or impersonate) famous characters of the past, both real and fictional – in this case Scott's Ivanhoe, Robin Hood, King Richard I, *et al*. Sequels: *The Timekeeper Conspiracy* (1984), *The Pimpernel Plot* (1984), *The Zenda Vendetta* (1985), *The Nautilus Sanction* (1985), *The Khyber Connection* (1986), *The Argonaut Affair* (1987) and others.

Ivory: A Legend of Past and Future (1988) ★★★ Novel by Mike Resnick (USA). A member of the Masai tribe and his computer-whizz friend attempt to track down the missing tusks of the legendary Kilimanjaro Elephant. The story is told episodically, against a background of both near- and medium-far-future. An unusual choice of subject matter, and an engaging narrative by a clever writer (who has recently emerged to major status in the sf field after writing literally hundreds of pseudonymous hack novels).

J

Jack of Eagles (1952) ★★ Novel by James Blish (USA). The hero discovers that he has precognitive and telekinetic abilities, and sets out to gain understanding and control of his growing powers. A thoughtful, scrupulously 'scientific' treatment of psi phenomena.

Jade Darcy and the Affair of Honor (1988) ★ Novel by Stephen Goldin and Mary Mason (USA), first in a series called 'The Rehumanization of Jade Darcy'. A computer-enhanced female mercenary has adventures amid hordes of colourful aliens on a far planet. Low-level jokey potboiler, no doubt designed to kick off an interminable series.

Jagged Orbit, The (1969) ★★★ Novel by John Brunner (UK). Race war threatens to tear the United States apart, while arms dealers grow fat. A liberal-minded slab of near-future 'realism' in similar vein to the author's best-known novel, *Stand on Zanzibar*. Heavy.

Jaguar Hunter, The (1987) ★★★★ Collection by Lucius Shepard (USA). Marvellous 400-page sf/fantasy selection from one of the best new writers of the 80s. Contains the agonizing Central-American war stories 'Salvador' and 'R & R' (the latter a deserving Nebula award-winner). Foreword by Michael Bishop, illustrations by Jeffrey Potter.

Jandar of Callisto (1972) Novel by Lin Carter (USA). Sword-swinging adventures on one of Jupiter's moons. Pastiche Edgar Rice Burroughs, by a writer who relished aping bygone styles. Has little merit as sf (compare with Alan Burt Akers's *Transit to Scorpio* and Michael Moorcock's *City of the Beast*). Sequels include *Black Legion of Callisto* (1972) and *Sky Pirates of Callisto* (1973).

Janissaries (1981) ★ Novel by Jerry Pournelle (USA). A platoon of US mercenaries fighting Cubans in Africa for the CIA is kidnapped by a flying saucer and taken to a distant planet to subdue the local population – themselves descendants of previous shiploads of mercenaries from various ages of history. In the end peacemakers prevail over war-mongers (with the help of longbows and a concealed pistol). It emerges that most of the dirty jobs in space are done by human slaves. Sequels (co-written with Roland Green): *Clan and Crown* (1982) and *Storms of Victory* (1987).

Japan Sinks (1973) ★★ Novel by Sakyo Komatsu (Japan). A myster-ious geological upset causes the islands of Japan to disappear beneath the waves. Most of the population is saved, however, thanks to the fore-sight of one brave scientist. A care-fully detailed disaster story which sold millions in its homeland. The English-language edition is greatly abridged, and has also been published as *The Death of the Dragon*. A Japanese film version was badly recut and released in the West as *Tidal Wave* (1975; dir. Shiro Moriana and Andrew Meyer).

Jaws That Bite, the Claws That Catch, The (1975) ★★ Fix-up novel by Michael Coney (UK/Canada), part of his 'Peninsula' sequence of stories (most of which remain uncollected). Slickly written episodic tale set in a future artists' resort. It seems to draw much of its inspiration from J. G. Ballard's *Vermilion Sands*, though it's altogether less distinctive. Published in the UK as *The Girl with a Symphony in Her Fingers*.

Jehad (Yermakov): see under *Last Communion*.

Jem: The Making of a Utopia (1979) ★★★ Novel by Frederik Pohl (USA). An overpopulated, under-resourced future Earth manages to send out star probes in search of planetary Lebens-raum. One such world is found, the eponymous Jem, and colonization commences. A dark novel, amount-ing to a lengthy and rather bitter meditation on humanity's capacity to screw things up.

Jericho Falls (1986) ★★ Novel by Christopher Hyde (USA). A small town is contaminated by a deadly virus, and those townsfolk who escape from the disease are effi-ciently massacred by the US army. A few get away with their lives. A very long, very paranoid thriller by a 'bestseller'-style writer.

Jester at Scar, The (Tubb): see under *Winds of Gath, The*.

Jesus Incident, The (1979) ★★ Novel by Frank Herbert and Bill Ransom (USA), a sequel to Herbert's *Destination: Void*. The earlier novel's starfarers and their godlike computer arrive at the planet Pandora, where they come into conflict with some particularly vile life-forms. An effective adven-ture, stuffed with ideas. Sequel: *The Lazarus Effect*.

Jesus on Mars (1979) ★★ Novel by Philip José Farmer (USA). An expedition to the planet Mars dis-covers that Jesus Christ is alive and well – literally. Well, actually he turns out to be an alien energy being who has assumed the form of Jesus, but the end result is the same: Earth has a new Messiah. An interesting attempt to remould Christianity for the space age.

Jewels of Aptor, The (1962) ★★ Novel by Samuel R. Delany (USA). In a post-holocaust world, a group of young people set out on a quest for a wonderful jewel. Baroque far-future stuff, exuberantly inventive. Delany's debut (he was all of 19 when he wrote it). 'An amazingly accomplished first novel' – James Cawthorn, *New Worlds*. The 1967 edition is revised and expanded.

Jinx on a Terran Inheritance (Daley): see under *Requiem for a Ruler of Worlds*.

Johnny Zed (1988) ★ Novel by John Betancourt (USA). Revolutionary terrorists attempt to restore democracy in a near-future America which has turned towards totalitarianism. An adequate sf thriller with a somewhat blurred political message.

Jokers Wild (Martin): see under *Wild Cards*.

Jonah Kit, The (1975) ★★★ Novel by Ian Watson (UK). A multi-stranded narrative in which a sperm whale is imprinted with a human brain pattern in order to establish communication with others of its kind; simultaneously, astronomers discover a devastating truth about the nature of the universe. The story ends unhappily for the intelligent whales and dolphins of our oceans. A very busy novel, alive with ideas.

Jondelle (Tubb): see under *Winds of Gath, The*.

Journey (1978) ★★ Novel by Marta Randall (USA). An interstellar family saga, about the settlers of a new planet, the aliens they meet and the dynasty they found. Not so much a feminist work as a latter-day example of 'women's sf' (see *Tomorrow's Heritage* by Juanita Coulson for another of the type). Competently done, but short on ideas. Sequel: *Dangerous Games* (1980).

Journey Beyond Tomorrow (1963) ★★★ Novel by Robert Sheckley (USA). A Pacific-island innocent visits 21st-century America and inadvertently starts World War III. His adventures along the way are hilarious. This episodic, *Candide*-like satire is perhaps Sheckley's best novel. Also published as *Journey of Joenes*.

Journey from Flesh (1981) ★ Novel by Nicholas Yermakov (USA). A fairly complex, occasionally colourful space opera in the post-Vietnam-*angst* mode. This is a first novel by an author who has subsequently settled for less. 'A good writer thoroughly adrift has betrayed both himself and the beginnings of some good ideas' – John Clute.

Journey of Joenes (Sheckley): see *Journey Beyond Tomorrow*.

Journey to the Centre (1982) ★★ Novel by Brian Stableford (UK). Scavengers on a mysterious, multilayered, artificial planet penetrate gradually towards its core. An example of the thoughtful kind of adventure fiction which Stableford does well. The 1989 British edition is revised. Sequels: *Invaders from the*

Centre and *The Centre Cannot Hold* (both 1990).

Journey to the Centre of the Earth (1864) ★★★★ Novel by Jules Verne (France). A German boy and his eccentric uncle visit the bowels of the Earth by way of a volcano in Iceland. They find a subterranean ocean and prehistoric creatures. One of the first true sf works, an exciting narrative full of fascinating scientific detail. Perhaps Verne's best novel. Filmed in 1959 (dir. Henry Levin).

Joy Makers, The (1961) ★★ Fix-up novel by James E. Gunn (USA). In Earth's future, the 'Hedonic' principle rules – the greatest pleasure of the greatest number. But society grows stagnant, and it becomes apparent that pleasure is not after all the chief goal of humankind. Capably written sf in the American 1950s mode of social criticism (not as sharp as Pohl and Kornbluth, though).

Joyleg (1962) ★★ Novel by Avram Davidson and Ward Moore (USA). A living veteran of the American War of Independence is found in the backwoods, kept alive for almost two centuries by his moonshine liquor. Political and media vultures gather round, but old Joyleg gets the better of them. An engaging satire in bucolic vein. (Davidson's first novel.)

Joyous Invasions, The (1965) ★★★ Collection by Theodore Sturgeon (USA). Three novellas: 'To Marry Medusa' (1958), 'The Comedian's Children' (1958) and 'The [Widget], the [Wadget], and Boff' (1955). Published in Britain only, it is a partial overlap with the US collection *Aliens 4*. The first (and best) story has also been published in expanded form as *The Cosmic Rape*.

Judas Mandala, The (1982) ★★ Novel by Damien Broderick (Australia). A history-altering time-travel story in which people avoid a computer-controlled future by escaping into other dimensions. 'A convoluted and effective sf mystery' – Brian Stableford.

Judas Rose, The (1987) ★★ Novel by Suzette Haden Elgin (USA), sequel to *Native Tongue*. In a future where women are regarded as grossly inferior to men, the secret language 'Laadan' is disseminated by rebel female linguists. 'Will it make any difference if women, consigned with such astonishing lack of resistance to perpetual subjugation, can at last describe their own experience in their own words? It seems unlikely. Yet another sequel is now needed to restore credibility to an idea that was a novelty in the first book but has become a liability in this otherwise perceptive and polished follow-up' – Lee Montgomerie, *Interzone*.

Judgment Night (1952) ★★ Collection by C. L. Moore (USA). The title novella (1943) and four other stories in this book are among the few examples of fine space opera written by a female author – prior to the huge influx of women writers into the American sf field during the 1960s and 70s. Some paperback reprints drop the additional stories and present the title piece as a short novel on its own.

Junction (1981) ★★ Fix-up novel by Jack Dann (USA). Physical laws have been torn asunder, and the town of Junction is surrounded by a 'hell' of acausality. The hero must go on a quest into this chaos. Metaphysical sf which is both confusing and vivid. 'It delightfully deconstructs your notions of time and space and reality in ways I myself never thought of – but would have liked to' – Philip K. Dick.

Juniper Time (1979) ★★★ Novel by Kate Wilhelm (USA). In a future America afflicted by terrible drought the heroine throws in her lot with an Amerindian tribe. Meanwhile, her friend attempts to revitalize the space programme. A gently feminist tale of politics, ecology and alien encounters.

Junk Day (1970) ★★ Posthumous novel by Arthur Sellings (UK). A protection racketeer known as the 'junkman' becomes the authoritarian ruler of a post-disaster London, in this smoothly written, downbeat tale. Sellings's last novel, it is regarded by several critics as his best.

Junkyard Planet (1963) ★★ Novel by H. Beam Piper (USA), part of his loose 'Federation' series. The people of Poictesme, capital of the Gartner Trisystem, make their living by salvaging military equipment left behind by evacuated Federation space-fleets. The hero revives the legend of a lost super-computer in an attempt to spur them into economic activity. Typical Piper: honourable, decent folk struggling against historical inevitability. Republished as *The Cosmic Computer*.

Jupiter Legacy, The (Harrison): see *Plague from Space*.

Juxtaposition (1982) Novel by Piers Anthony (UK/USA), sequel to *Blue Adept* and third in the 'Apprentice Adept' series. The Oracle of the magical planet Phaze and the Games Computer of the techie-world Proton turn out to be (surprise, surprise) one and the same, as the hero gets all the girls. Trivial stuff, but the series has been popular. Sequels: *Out of Phaze* (1987) and *Robot Adept* (1988).

K

Kairos (1988) ★★ Novel by Gwyneth Jones (UK). A polluted, ozone-stripped world of the early 21st century: there is all-out war in Africa, and Britain is divided as never before between haves and have-nots. A secret organization aims to change reality by means of a drug, but things go wrong. 'It is as if the nightmares of a typical *Guardian* reader have all come true, powerfully imagined with a kind of one-note bleak remorsefulness' – Paul McAuley, *Interzone*.

Kalin (Tubb): see under *Winds of Gath, The*.

Kampus (1977) ★ Novel by James E. Gunn (USA). A rather unfunny sf satire on the aspirations of the student radicals of the late 1960s and early 1970s.

Keep the Giraffe Burning (Sladek): see under *Steam-Driven Boy and Other Strangers, The*.

Keeper's Price and Other Stories, The (Bradley): see under *Free Amazons of Darkover*.

Kelly Country (1983) ★ Novel by A. Bertram Chandler (UK/Australia). A time-traveller visits an alternative time-line in which the famous 19th-century outlaw Ned Kelly has lived on to become President of the Republic of Australia. A curiosity which should be of interest to Antipodeans. 'What we have is mostly ho-hum, although there are some bright episodes ... and a clever ending' – Michael J. Tolley, *Fantasy Review*.

Kesrith (1979) ★★ Novel by C. J. Cherryh (USA). The alien Regul, defeated by humans in war, agree to surrender the planet Kesrith. This involves betraying their Mri allies (a tribe of interstellar nomads, fanatical warriors) who wish to settle there. First part of the 'Faded Sun' trilogy. Sequel: *Shon'jir*.

Khyber Connection, The (Hawke): see under *Ivanhoe Gambit, The*.

Kif Strike Back, The (1986) ★★ Novel by C. J. Cherryh (USA), second part (after *Chanur's Venture*) of a long-running space opera. The plot begins to thicken: Pyanfar Chanur is enticed from space-station to space-station and trapped into a military alliance with the repulsive blood-sucking Kif. Sequel: *Chanur's Homecoming*.

Killashandra (McCaffrey), see under *Crystal Singer, The*.

Killer Mice, The (Reed): see under *Mr Da V, and Other Stories*.

Killing Machine, The (1964) ★★ Novel by Jack Vance (USA), sequel to *The Star King* and second of his 'Demon Princes' series. Hero Kirth Gersen hunts the hidden rulers of a huge and complex future society in his quest for revenge. Sequel: *The Palace of Love*.

Kindred Spirits (1984) ★★ Anthology edited by Jeffrey M. Elliot (USA). Sf stories with a gay and lesbian interest. Includes good stuff from Joanna Russ, Elizabeth Lynn, Robert Silverberg, Jessica Salmonson and others. Companion volume: *Worlds Apart*.

King David's Spaceship (Pournelle): see *Spaceship for the King, A*.

Kings of Space (1954) ★ Novel by W. E. Johns (UK). Teenage boy, eccentric professor and RAF pilot risk their lives in a home-made spaceship. Lacking literary merit or scientific credibility, this novel and its sequels communicated something of the 'sense of wonder' to many children who read it in the 1950s and 60s. Sequel: *Return to Mars*.

Kinsman (1979) ★ Fix-up novel by Ben Bova (USA). A rewrite of short stories about Chet Kinsman, who comes from a pacifist family but joins the air force so that he can get to the moon. He finds his beliefs and honesty compromised by the requirements of his masters. At times it reads like propaganda in favour of military development as a way of getting governments to invest in space. Sets the scene for the author's *Millenium*.

Kinsman Saga, The (1987) ★ Omnibus by Ben Bova (USA), incorporating revised versions of his novels *Kinsman* and *Millenium* (see separate entries). 'Recommended for supporters of SDI and hard-core hard sf fans only' – Robin Roberts, *SF & Fantasy Book Review Annual 1988*.

Kirlian Quest (Anthony): see under *Chaining the Lady*.

Kiteworld (1985) ★★ Fix-up novel by Keith Roberts (UK). In this curious post-holocaust scenario men fly kites (huge Cody rigs) in order to protect their drab clergy-dominated world against 'demons'. The stories which comprise the novel are written with an intensity which is at times moving, but the depictions of tormented and brutal sexual relationships may provoke readers' unease.

Knight Moves (1985) ★★ Novel by Walter Jon Williams (USA). Colourful, slickly written far-future adventure, in which the characters' quest for immortality conflicts with their fears of senescence. 'A style that reminds me more than a little of the early Roger Zelazny' – George R. R. Martin.

Knight of Ghosts and Shadows, A (1974) ★ Novel by Poul Anderson (USA). Despite its title, which makes it sound like a pseudo-medieval fantasy, this is in fact a routine space-adventure yarn in Anderson's 'Dominic Flandry' series (for which, see under *We Claim These Stars*).

Knights of the Limits, The (1978) ★★★ Collection by Barrington J. Bayley (UK). These stories have all the distinguishing marks of Bayley's novels: typically a tightly controlled society is shattered by some technological or scientific development. In 'Me and My Antronoscope' worm-scientists discover that the Universe may not be entirely solid; in 'Exit from City 5' space itself has ceased to exist. The stories are often rather flat, with an all-too-predictable twist at the end, but the ideas are the thing and Bayley has more of them than almost anybody else.

Kraken Wakes, The (1953) ★★★ Novel by John Wyndham (UK). In this, the second of Wyndham's very enjoyable bestsellers, unseen aliens from outer space take up residence on Earth's ocean beds, then begin to melt the ice-caps. The story concerns human reactions to a world of rising sea-levels and catastrophic flooding. The detail is excellent. As usual with this author, though, the disaster is a 'cosy' one, and all is neatly tied up in a happy ending. Published in the USA as *Out of the Deeps*.

Krone Experiment, The (1986) ★ Novel by J. Craig Wheeler (USA). A fairly dull near-future thriller with sf elements.

Krono (1988) ★★ Novel by Charles L. Harness (USA). Future humans use time travel to colonize the past: over 500 cities have been established in eras from the Triassic onwards. The hero is a time-surveyor whose larger vision conflicts with the designs of his cruel masters. A complicated, baroque entertainment in Harness's usual style. 'Brilliantly recalls an era when sf authors were not nearly so hampered with such petty things as verisimilitude' – Dan Chow, *Locus*.

Krugg Syndrome, The (1988) ★★ Novel by Angus McAllister (UK). The sf idea (that a rather shy boy has been taken over by telepathic aliens intent on the conquest of Earth) is disposed of in the first few pages, and we are left with a mild tale of a Presbyterian country boy getting his first job in Glasgow. Occasionally genuinely funny.

Kuldesak (1972) ★★ Novel by Richard Cowper (Colin Middleton Murry, UK). Millennia hence, the young hero escapes from a computerized underground warren and is instrumental in setting humanity once more on the road to the stars. Well-written version of an archetypal sf theme, somewhat similar to Daniel Galouye's *Dark Universe*.

Kutath (1980) ★ Novel by C. J. Cherryh (USA), last part of the 'Faded Sun' trilogy, sequel to *Shon'jir*. The nearly-extinct Mri return to their home planet and attempt to rebuild their way of life, as a human spacefleet debates whether to finally exterminate them. Very vaguely connected with Cherryh's 'Union/Alliance' future-history novels (see *Downbelow Station*).

L

L. Ron Hubbard Presents Writers of the Future (1985) ★★ Anthology edited by Algis Budrys (USA). The late L. Ron Hubbard has little to do with this worthwhile volume of competition entries by completely unknown writers, the first of an ongoing series. Also contains mini-essays by Budrys, Silverberg, Sturgeon, etc. Among the unknowns who have gone on to greater things are the very talented Karen Joy Fowler and David Zindell.

Ladies from Hell (Roberts): see under *Machines and Men*.

Lagrange Five (1979) ★ Novel by Mack Reynolds (USA). Space habitats built at the orbital 'Lagrange Points' beam solar energy down to the Earth: this leads, unsurprisingly, to political and economic upheaval. A poorly plotted and perfunctorily characterized space yarn which is also intended (one presumes) as a serious piece of socio-political speculation. Sequels: *The Lagrangists* (1983), *Chaos in Lagrangia* (1984) and *Trojan Orbit* (1985), all edited by Dean Ing following Reynolds's death.

Lagrangists, The (Reynolds): see under *Lagrange Five*.

Lallia (Tubb): see under *Winds of Gath, The*.

Land Leviathan, The (Moorcock): see under *Warlord of the Air, The*.

Land Under England (1935) ★★ Novel by Joseph O'Neill (Ireland). The hero penetrates deep caverns beneath Hadrian's Wall and finds descendants of the Romans presiding over a nasty totalitarian society. 'Only readable as a prescient critique of the Nazis' – Lee Montgomerie, *Interzone*.

Land's End (1988) ★ Novel by Frederik Pohl and Jack Williamson (USA). In an overpopulated future, many people have taken to living under the sea. But catastrophe strikes, and then a submarine alien *thingy* rears its ugly head ... A tired and surprisingly clichéd effort by two veterans who rarely write as convincingly together as they do when working separately.

Languages of Pao, The (1958) ★★★
Novel by Jack Vance (USA). The heir
to the Panarchy of Pao is held prisoner on the planet Breakness and
forced to learn their guttural language
in an attempt to break his passive,
orderly habits of thought. Meanwhile
the usurper of his home-planet carries
out the same experiment on a grand
scale, training the Paonese in various
artificial languages to suit them for
his plans of universal conquest. In the
end the conflict is resolved by the
development of yet another language,
Pastiche, enabling people with different cultural assumptions to communicate. Cleverly conceived: one of
Vance's best.

Last and First Men (1930) ★★★★
Novel by Olaf Stapledon (UK). Not so
much a novel, more a history of the
future and (in Stapledon's own
words) an 'essay in myth creation'.
Conceived on a vast scale, it takes the
reader on a voyage through time to
the last days of the 18th Men, almost
two billion years hence. Despite the
datedness of the early chapters,
dealing with the 60-year period now
past, it's a staggering imaginative
achievement and one of the greatest
of all sf books. Sequel (of lesser
importance, more contemporary in
relevance, but still fine): *Last Men in
London* (1932).

Last Castle, The (1967) ★★ Novella
by Jack Vance (USA). Decadent
human communities fall one by one
to the alien Meks they had enslaved.
The plot is not as rewarding as the
inventive, occasionally silly, background. Hugo award-winner, 1967.

Last Communion (1981) ★★ Novel by
Nicholas Yermakov (USA), first of a
trilogy. The authoritarian human
rulers of an alien planet called
Boomerang try to learn the secrets of
natives who appear to be able to
commune telepathically with their
dead. Of course, the dissident hero is
on the side of sweetness, light and
inter-species harmony. Proficient sf
of a familiar type. Sequels: *Epiphany*
(1982) and *Jehad* (1984).

Last Day of Creation, The (1981) ★★
Novel by Wolfgang Jeschke
(Germany). American forces use
time travel to try to obtain Middle
Eastern oil from past eras, but of
course this changes the time-line(s).
Episodic, amusing, heavily ironic –
one of the better German sf novels of
recent years.

Last Deathship off Antares, The
(1989) ★ Novel by William Jon
Watkins (USA). Hostile aliens
confine human prisoners of war in
the eponymous deathship. A dark
tale of survival which seems to
glorify violence.

Last Hope of Earth, The (Wright): see
Creeping Shroud, The.

**Last Hurrah of the Golden Horde,
The** (Spinrad): see under *No Direction Home.*

**Last Leap and Other Stories of the
Super-Mind, The** (1964) ★★ Collection
by Daniel F. Galouye (USA). Stories
of telepathy and other strange mental
powers. They're proficiently done,
but perhaps too repetitive when all
gathered together in this fashion.

Last Legionary Quartet, The (1985)
★★ Omnibus by Douglas Hill

(Canada/UK). Contains: *Galactic Warlord* (1980), *Deathwing Over Veynaa* (1981), *Day of the Starwind* (1982) and *The Planet of the Warlord* (1982). Juvenile space-adventure novels which describe the quest of Keill Randor, interstellar ninja, to find the mysterious Warlord who has destroyed his home planet. Fast-paced, exciting and quite stylish sf for kids.

Last Men in London (Stapledon), see under *Last and First Men*.

Last Orders and Other Stories (1977) ★★★ Collection by Brian W. Aldiss (UK). Fourteen tales, in Aldiss's customary wide range of styles. Includes several brief, poetic 'enigmas', as well as more solid pieces such as 'An Appearance of Life' and 'Journey to the Heartland'.

Last Starship from Earth, The (1967) ★★★ Novel by John Boyd (USA). In an alternative time-line, the planet is ruled by a religious dictatorship which presides over a rigid caste system. The young hero rebels, is banished, and eventually goes back in time to try to prevent Christ from conquering Rome (the historical event which marked the beginning of this world's woes). A first novel of some wit and complexity. Unfortunately, none of the author's subsequent books are as good.

Last Yggdrasil, The (1982) ★★ Novel by Robert F. Young (USA), expanded from his story 'To Fell a Tree' (1959). Misguided humans try to get rid of a vast, quasi-intelligent tree on an alien planet. A fairly obvious eco-logical warning yarn by a competent writer best known for his short stories. 'Though eked out to barely book length by undue repetition of themes and omens we have already memorized, the story itself is strangely moving' – John Clute.

Lathe of Heaven, The (1971) ★★★ Novel by Ursula K. Le Guin (USA). Sf/fantasy tale about a man whose dreams affect reality in drastic fashion. A psychiatrist attempts to harness his strange ability in order to make the world a better place, with unfortunate results. An effective parable which reads remarkably like a novel by Philip K. Dick (it was almost certainly intended by Le Guin as a tribute to that writer, for whom she has expressed intense admiration elsewhere). Filmed as a TV movie in 1980 (dir. David Loxton and Fed Barzyk).

Lavalite World, The (Farmer): see under *Maker of Universes, The*.

Lazarus Effect, The (1983) ★★ Novel by Frank Herbert and Bill Ransom (USA). Many generations after the action of *The Jesus Incident*, Pandora is entirely covered by sea. The tensions between the Mermen (supposedly unmodified humans who depend on industrial technology to survive on the sea bed) and the Islanders (mutants living in pelagic cities) are brought to a head when Merman plans to re-establish the intelligent kelp that once ruled the waves are revealed by a botched genocidal attack on an Island. Perhaps the best of the three 'Pandora' novels. Sequel: *The Ascension Factor*.

Left Hand of Darkness, The (1969) ★★★★ Novel by Ursula K. Le Guin (USA), part of her 'Hainish' sequence. A human envoy to the snowbound planet Gethen struggles to understand its sexually ambivalent inhabitants. This is convincingly detailed, beautifully written, 'anthropological' sf at its very best. Hugo and Nebula award-winner, 1970.

Legacy of Heorot, The (1987) ★ Novel by Larry Niven, Jerry Pournelle and Steve Barnes (USA). Heavy-handed colonists on an alien planet have to deal with some very hostile life-forms, Aliens-style. 'A few xenobiological flights ... occasionally perk The Legacy of Heorot up for a page or two, and lighten the doldrums of this sour dystopian broth' – John Clute.

Legends from the End of Time (Moorcock): see under Dancers at the End of Time, The.

Legion (Grant): see under Shadow of Alpha, The.

Legion of Space, The (1947) ★ Novel by Jack Williamson (USA), first serialized in 1934. Highly-coloured space opera, involving a super-weapon and the struggle against menacing aliens. Members of the eponymous legion are based on Dumas's Three Musketeers, and the narrative is vigorous. This novel and its immediate sequels from the magazines of the 1930s enjoyed a new popularity during the 1970s – which stimulated Williamson to write yet another (redundant) volume in the sequence. Sequels: The Cometeers (1950), One Against the Legion (1967) and The Queen of the Legion (1983).

Legion of Time, The (1952) ★★ Short novel by Jack Williamson (USA), first serialized in 1938. There is war between alternative time-lines, and a present-day man is caught up in that vast struggle. A marvellously flamboyant tale which was highly original in its day. Despite the similarity of title, it's not related to the author's Legion of Space novels. The first book edition also contained an unrelated short novel called After World's End, which has since been reprinted separately: it's an enjoyable space opera of the same vintage, but not up to the standard of The Legion of Time.

Lemmus 1: Waiters on the Dance (1972) Novel by Julius Jay Savarin (West Indies/UK). An archetypal 'Shaggy-God' space opera, wherein the aliens who seed the galaxy speak a language called La'tin, and there are the inevitable references to Adam and Eve, Atlantis and Jesus Christ. 'Remarkable for an appalling poverty of ideas. Most of the ones it gets by with putrefied long ago' – Brian Stableford. Sequels: Lemmus 2: Beyond the Outer Mirr (1976) and Lemmus 3: Archives of Haven (1977).

Less Than Human (1986) ★★ Novel by Charles Platt (UK/USA). Humorous tale of an innocent, brilliant android who comes to degenerate New York City in the year 2010 and proceeds to make startling discoveries. 'That rarity among novels – a genuinely funny book. I was both amused and amazed' – Edward Bryant.

Lest Darkness Fall (1941) ★★★ Novel by L. Sprague de Camp (USA). An American time-traveller in the late Roman empire introduces printing and other modern technology in an attempt to stop the Fall. The marvellous chatty view of early medieval history more than makes up for the many inconsistencies. A minor classic in the vein of Mark Twain's *A Connecticut Yankee in King Arthur's Court* (1889).

Let the Fire Fall (1969) ★★ Novel by Kate Wilhelm (USA). A mysterious spaceship visits the Earth, and a dying alien mother switches babies with a human family. Unfortunately the changeling's foster-father turns out to be a fundamentalist preacher and the poor, talented alien lad (who passes for human) grows up miserably. 'Gets steadily better for a hundred pages, and only fails after that because one senses the author wasn't able – or didn't bother – to gather her story together, and end it' – John Clute.

Level 7 (1959) ★★ Novel by Mordecai Roshwald (Israel/USA). An anti-nuclear propaganda piece cast in the form of a diary which is kept by an inhabitant of the seventh, deepest level of a huge underground bomb shelter. It describes the last days of an officer whose duty is to help fire the missiles which rapidly destroy the world above. The book is not very original as sf, but it had the power to move a great many people at the time of its first publication.

Leviathan's Deep (1979) ★★★ Novel by Jayge Carr (USA). An Earthman develops a relationship with an alien woman on a female-dominated planet. Sadly, she comes to perceive him as a threat. Compassionate, good-humoured feminist sf, and a very promising first novel.

Liege-Killer (1988) ★★ Novel by Christopher Hinz (USA). War has rendered Earth almost uninhabitable. Nearly all surviving humans live in orbital colonies, dominated by political and religious institutions dedicated to suppressing military technology. A bio-engineered assassin frozen before Armageddon is woken up and set loose. The good guys are forced to take unusual steps to hunt the murderers. Hinz's first novel.

Lies, Inc. (Dick): see *Unteleported Man, The.*

Lieut. Gullivar Jones: His Vacation (1905) ★★ Novel by Edwin L. Arnold (UK). A naval officer flies to Mars on a magic carpet. An entertaining sf/fantasy adventure, which may have influenced Edgar Rice Burroughs's 'Barsoom' books. Reprinted as *Gulliver of Mars.*

Life During Wartime (1987) ★★★ Fix-up novel by Lucius Shepard (USA), incorporating the Nebula award-winning story 'R & R'. The setting is a brilliantly described near-future war in Central America. The specially-gifted hero is recruited into the Psicorps, and soon finds himself up against some very powerful enemies. 'The plot ... is pure pulp sf

... But the power of Shepard's writing mostly overcomes these limitations. It exhibits an unsurpassed richness of texture that's shot through with images of random violence and technology overwhelmed by nature'—Paul McAuley, *Interzone*.

Life for Kregen, A (Akers): see under *Transit to Scorpio*.

Life for the Stars, A (1962) ★★ Juvenile novel by James Blish (USA), fourth-published in his *Cities in Flight* sequence. Chronologically, it comes second in the series, telling how the first cities leave Earth for space – thanks to their 'Spindizzy' engines. However, this novel, originally intended for younger readers, is much the weakest of the four which are reprinted in the omnibus volume *Cities in Flight*.

Life in the Day of ... **and Other Short Stories, A** (1981) ★★ Collection by Frank M. Robinson (USA). Five sf stories from the early 1950s and four from a much later period, together with an interesting running commentary by the author (who is perhaps best-known for his near-future disaster thrillers, such as *The Glass Inferno*, 1974, written in collaboration with Thomas N. Scortia). Robinson's short pieces are very polished; and a couple of the later ones first appeared in *Playboy* magazine, where he worked as an editor.

Life, the Universe and Everything (1982) ★★★ Novel by Douglas Adams (UK). A novelization of the third radio series of *The Hitch-Hiker's Guide to the Galaxy*. Arthur Dent has returned to the remote past of the Earth and gets involved in some complicated stage-business with time-travel, cricket matches and the Ultimate Question (to which '42' is the bathetic answer). Hilarious. Sequel: *So Long, and Thanks for All the Fish*.

Lifeboat (Dickson & Harrison): see *Lifeship, The*.

Lifeboat Earth (Schmidt): see under *Sins of the Fathers*.

Lifeburst (1984) ★★ Novel by Jack Williamson (USA). Two species of aliens arrive in the solar system – one dangerous, the other benign. A sophisticated latter-day space opera by this author who has been producing such tales since the 1930s. 'An autumnal masterpiece that ensures that Williamson, unlike most writers of his generation, remains a major force in sf in his fifth decade as a professional writer' – Martin Morse Wooster, *20th-Century SF Writers*.

Lifekeeper (1980) ★ Novel by Mike McQuay (USA). Perpetual war keeps the citizens of a computerized future state in line. But the black hero rebels, throwing in his lot with some primitive tribesmen. McQuay's first novel.

Lifeship, The (1976) ★ Novel by Gordon R. Dickson and Harry Harrison (USA). An overblown attempt to produce a bestselling space opera, in which disparate survivors of a sabotaged space vessel are thrown together in a sort of cosmic life-raft. 'Every single character trapped between the stars in the lifeship seems to have at least one secret identity, two secret missions, three guilty deeds to atone for, four threats of death to dodge' – John Clute. Published in the UK as *Lifeboat*.

Light a Last Candle (1969) ★★ Novel by Vincent King (UK). A dark-hued space opera. King's first novel.

Light at the End of the Universe, The (1976) ★★★ Collection by Terry Carr (USA), introduced by Harlan Ellison. Fifteen sf and fantasy stories by a writer/editor famed for his anthologies. Contains all his best-known short work, including 'The Dance of the Changer and the Three' (1968) and 'Ozymandias' (1972). Intelligent tales, mainly in a New-Wave vein.

Light Fantastic, The (1976) ★★★ Collection by Alfred Bester (USA). Half of the collected short stories of this talented author (the companion volume is *Star Light, Star Bright*, and the two were later combined in one jumbo volume as *Starlight: The Great Short Fiction of Alfred Bester*). Contains the early 'Hell is Forever' (1942) as well as such 1950s classics as 'Fondly Fahrenheit' and 'The Men Who Murdered Mohammed'. Punchy, flamboyant tales, all.

Light on the Sound (1982) ★★ Novel by Somtow Sucharitkul (Thailand/USA), first of his 'Inquestors' series. The galaxy is dominated by the stern Inquestors, who exploit the peaceful alien creatures known as 'Windbringers' (the latters' brains are used to power faster-than-light space vessels). One Inquestor rebels

against the status quo. It's a very highly coloured space opera. Sequels: *The Throne of Madness* (1983), *Utopia Hunters* (1984) and *The Darkling Wind* (1985).

Light That Never Was, The (1972) ★ Novel by Lloyd Biggle Jr. (USA). Refugees, politicians and art-dealers squabble over some anonymous paintings on the resort world of Donov – next in line for a series of anti-alien, or 'animaloid' riots which have been passing from planet to planet without obvious cause. A pleasant if not exactly groundbreaking novel. 'His newest and maybe his awfullest longueur' – John Clute.

Light Years and Dark: Science Fiction and Fantasy of and For Our Time (1984) ★★★ Anthology edited by Michael Bishop (USA). Large selection of reprint stories by well-known authors and originals commissioned especially for the book. An attempt at a 'definitive' state-of-the-art sf anthology for the 1980s.

Lights in the Sky are Stars, The (1953) ★★ Novel by Fredric Brown (USA). A near-future tale of a woman politician and her partner, a failed astronaut, who struggle to reinvigorate America's stalled space programme with their scheme for a mission to the planet Jupiter. Inevitably, the story is dated, but it was regarded as admirably realistic (and idealistic) in its day. Published in Britain as *Project Jupiter*.

Like Nothing on Earth (1975) ★★★ Collection by Eric Frank Russell

(UK). Seven sf stories, all previously collected elsewhere. Includes the well-loved 'Allamagoosa' (Hugo award-winner, 1955) – the one about the stock-check on a spaceship which fails to find an Offog, whatever that is. A good introduction to Russell's works.

Lilith: A Snake in the Grass (1981) ★ Novel by Jack L. Chalker (USA), first in his 'Four Lords of the Diamond' tetralogy. A mind-replicated human agent is sent to a planet which is under threat from a subtle alien force. In the follow-up books he has similar adventures on three other planets. Routine action sf conceived to fit this author's customary over-extended series format. Sequels: *Cerberus: A Wolf in the Fold* (1982), *Charon: A Dragon at the Gate* (1982) and *Medusa: A Tiger by the Tail* (1983).

Limbo (1952) ★★★★ Novel by Bernard Wolfe (USA). A doctor who has tried to escape from the madness of the modern world is horrified to discover that he has inadvertently helped create a society in which men cut off their own limbs in order to avoid war (to no avail, as it turns out). Big, ambitious, satirical cornucopia of a book – at times profound. Published in the UK as *Limbo '90*.

Limits (1985) ★ Collection by Larry Niven, Jerry Pournelle, Steve Barnes and Dian Girard (USA). A readable mixture of fantasy and sf stories. The Pournelle collaboration is indistinguishable from Pournelle on his own.

Lincoln Hunters, The (1957) ★★

Novel by Wilson Tucker (USA). Time-travellers from a future America attempt to obtain a recording of a long-lost speech by Abraham Lincoln. Of course, things go interestingly wrong. One of Tucker's more enjoyable novels.

Lion Game, The (1973) ★★ Novel by James H. Schmitz (USA). Human worlds are threatened by superpowered telepathic aliens, until super-powered telepathic Telzey Amberdon persuades them to leave. As usual in Schmitz's space operas the problem is solved by intelligence rather than violence.

Lion of Comarre and Against the Fall of Night, The (1968) ★★ Collection by Arthur C. Clarke (UK). Two 1940s novellas, the second of which is the atmospheric story which was expanded into the novel *The City and the Stars*. The first, 'The Lion of Comarre', is another fairy-tale-like variation on the same theme of escape from a 'perfect' city.

Listen, Listen (Wilhelm): see under *Infinity Box, The.*

Listeners, The (1972) ★★ Fix-up novel by James E. Gunn (USA). Messages from a distant civilization are received on Earth by radio telescope. The book deals thoughtfully with the consequences of the realization that We Are Not Alone. Perhaps Gunn's best novel. 'Heavy with religious symbolism and literary allusion' – Brian Stableford.

Little Black Box, The (Dick): see under *Beyond Lies the Wub.*

Little Fuzzy (1962) ★★★ Novel by H. Beam Piper (USA). Set in the author's 'Federation' future, this deals with the classic sf question of determining whether an alien species is entitled to legal rights or can be exploited like animals. Piper's most popular book, if it has a failing it is that the Zarathustrans are so human-like, so intelligent and so downright cuddly it's impossible to imagine anyone not accepting them. Sequel: *Fuzzy Sapiens*.

Little Heroes (1987) ★★ Novel by Norman Spinrad (USA). In the early 21st century an ageing female musician becomes involved in a corporate attempt to create a successful cyborg rock star. Very long, very energetic, full of dirty bits, this is typical Spinrad (he's not a writer noted for his subtlety).

Little Knowledge, A (1977) ★★ Novel by Michael Bishop (USA). Set in the domed city of Atlanta, Georgia, in the late 21st century. A somewhat confusing novel about religion, alien encounters and the future urban life-style. Sequel: *Catacomb Years*.

Little People, The (1967) ★★ Novel by John Christopher (UK). What appear to be Irish 'leprechauns' turn out to be the products of a scientific experiment. A thoroughly daft but enjoyable thriller.

Lives and Times of Jerry Cornelius, The (1976) ★★ Collection by Michael Moorcock (UK). Short stories about the chameleon-like character whom Moorcock first introduced in his novel *The Final Programme*. These are deliberately disjointed and baffling fictions which contain copious reference to the real political and military events of the 1960s and 70s. Marginally sf. 'The errand boy of a faltering apocalypse, he moves across an entropic world ravaged by every conceivable nemesis – plague, world war, media saturation' – J. G. Ballard, *New Statesman*.

Living Way Out (1967) ★★★ Collection by Wyman Guin (USA). Seven interesting sf stories from 1950s and early 1960s magazines, the best-remembered of which is 'Beyond Bedlam', about a future society in which everyone is forced to be a schizophrenic – for the greater good of the human race. Published in the UK as *Beyond Bedlam*.

Loafers of Refuge, The (1965) ★ Fix-up novel by Joseph Green (USA). Human colonists of another planet come into conflict with the alien 'loafers', highly intelligent beings who apparently disdain all machines. Needless to say, the aliens teach the uppity humans a thing or two. An efficiently written first book from this minor author.

Logan's Run (1967) ★★ Novel by William F. Nolan and George Clayton Johnson (USA). Maintaining the population balance requires that everyone aged 21 or over should die. Those who won't submit to euthanasia become 'runners', to be hunted and killed. The hero is a gamekeeper-turned-poacher who is himself on the run after reaching the dreaded age. A good sf thriller. Filmed, badly, in 1976 (dir. Michael Anderson). It also inspired a short-lived television series. Sequels (by Nolan alone): *Logan's World* (1977) and *Logan's Search* (1980).

Lone Star Planet (Piper): see *Planet for Texans, A.*

Long After Midnight (1976) ★★ Collection by Ray Bradbury (USA). Tales in grotesque, humorous and would-be poetical veins, only a minority of them definable as sf. The best pieces are the older ones, leftovers from Bradbury's heyday of the 1950s.

Long Afternoon of Earth, The (Aldiss): see *Hothouse.*

Long ARM of Gil Hamilton, The (1976) ★★ Collection by Larry Niven (USA). Linked stories about the 'organleggers', near-future smugglers of human organs for use in transplant surgery. There are links with the author's novel *A Gift from Earth* and with his 'Known Space' series in general. 'Among the finest examples of the sf detective story' – Brian Stableford. Quasi-sequel: *The Patchwork Girl* (1980).

Long Habit of Living, The (1989) ★★★ Novel by Joe Haldeman (USA). The Stileman Foundation offers a cure for old age at a million pounds a time, plus all the assets of the patient, forcing the rich to rebuild their fortunes every decade so that they can buy another treatment. When the Foundation appears to be abusing its great power and wealth a couple of millionaires are forced to flee to space. Interesting and humorous, if

not fully successful. Published in the USA as *Buying Time* (the author prefers the British title).

Long Loud Silence, The (1952) ★★ Novel by Wilson Tucker (USA). By grim necessity, a soldier learns how to survive in that half of the United States which has been devastated by a nuclear and biological war. Commendable: perhaps the most realistic of the early treatments of a post-bomb world in American sf.

Long Night, The (1983) ★★ Collection by Poul Anderson (USA), with a prologue and 'interstitial material' by Sandra Miesel. Five hard sf tales from the 1950s and 60s, all concerned with the interstellar dark age after the fall of Anderson's 'Technic Civilization' (see his many novels and stories which star the series heroes Nicholas van Rijn and Dominic Flandry).

Long Result, The (1965) ★★ Novel by John Brunner (UK). Space-colonization and encounters-with-aliens yarn in which there are a number of clear parallels with present-day colonial and racial conflicts. The baddies belong to an organization called the 'Stars are for Man League'. A pleasant, readable, liberally-inclined message-story.

Long Tomorrow, The (1955) ★★★ Novel by Leigh Brackett (USA). In a post-nuclear America two boys rebel against a religious dictatorship by going in search of 'Bartorstown' and its forbidden scientific lore. Well written and engaging narrative, and a strong plea for Reason.

Long View, The (Busby): see under *Young Rissa.*

Long Voyage Back (1983) ★★★ Novel by Luke Rinehart (USA). World War III begins, and the characters embark on a trimaran voyage to Tierra del Fuego. Highly readable bestseller fiction, although the author admits: 'The actual effects of a large-scale nuclear war are so much worse than I have dramatized that no bearable work of fiction can be written about them.'

Long Winter, The (Christopher): see *World in Winter, The.*

Look into the Sun (1989) ★★ Novel by James Patrick Kelly (USA), expanded from his short story 'Glass Cloud' (1987). A talented human architect is commissioned by aliens to build a tomb for the dying goddess of their planet. 'A rich, slow, allusive, glinting pastoral edifice' – John Clute.

Looking Backward: AD 2000–1887 (1888) ★★★ Novel by Edward Bellamy (USA). Extremely influential utopian vision: Julian West, a 19th-century American, awakes in a socialist society which has developed naturally from capitalism as a result of technological progress. William Morris described Bellamy's steam-driven utopia as 'a cockney paradise', and wrote his *News from Nowhere* as a partial rejoinder.

Looking Backward, from the Year 2000 (1973) ★★★ Novel by Mack Reynolds (USA). A modern 'sequel' to Bellamy's Looking Backward. Reynolds's Julian West awakes in the year 2000 to find a world altered almost beyond his comprehension. The rapidity of scientific change requires everyone to become a student in a vast continuing education programme. Rather wooden as fiction, but an interesting attempt to meld socialist idealism with latter-day technocratic attitudes. Sequel: *Equality in the Year 2000* (1977).

Lord Kalvan of Otherwhen (1965) ★★ Novel by H. Beam Piper (USA). A policeman transplanted into another world (by the bungling of Varkan Vall's Paratime Police, familiar from Piper's short stories) uses his knowledge of science and military history to break the monopoly of local religious leaders over gunpowder and set himself up as Emperor. A straightforward adventure story, notable for its spiritual pessimism and the pleasure its protagonist seems to take in military activity. Published in Britain as *Gunpowder God.* Belated sequel by other hands: *Great Kings' War* (1985) by Roland Green and John F. Carr.

Lord of Light (1967) ★★★ Novel by Roger Zelazny (USA). It reads like a fantasy based on Indian mythology, but it's actually sf with an interplanetary setting. The mixture is rich and strange – perhaps too baroque for fastidious tastes, though it was popular. Hugo award-winner, 1968.

Lord of the Spiders, The (Moorcock): see under *City of the Beast, The.*

Lord Tyger (1970) ★★★ Novel by Philip José Farmer (USA). A madman tries to stage a re-enactment of Edgar Rice Burroughs's novel *Tarzan of the Apes* (1914). So young Ras Tyger grows to manhood as a jungle lord, under the tutelage of the mysterious 'Igziyabher'. Naturally, things go awry. This borderline-sf treatment of the Noble Savage theme is one of Farmer's best books, more carefully written than much of his over-hasty output.

Lord Valentine's Castle (1980) ★★ Novel by Robert Silverberg (USA). The disinherited, amnesiac hero wanders the huge planet called Majipoor in search of his glorious destiny. A slickly-written bid for best-sellerdom. This was Silverberg's much-touted 'comeback' novel after a few years away from the field. Clearly, it was an attempt to cash in on the new vogue for sf/fantasy blockbusters – and it worked well enough on that level. Sequels: *Majipoor Chronicles* (1982) and *Valentine Pontifex* (1983).

Lordly Ones, The (1986) ★★ Collection by Keith Roberts (UK). A mixed bag of sensitively-written sf and fantasy pieces, of which the standouts are the title story and 'The Comfort Station'. 'None of the stories could take place anywhere but England (except the awful "Diva"). It is an England whose inhabitants wear solitude and melancholy like the Cloak of Nessus. Roberts is their scribe' – John Clute.

Lords of the Middle Dark (1986) ★ Novel by Jack L. Chalker (USA), first of a four-part series. A native American hunter and the daughter of a Chinese mandarin search for gold rings which are the key to the manual over-ride to the Master System, the computer which has turned Earth into a cross between a theme park and a tribal reservation. There is a lot of rather horrid description of rape, torture and slavery. Sequel: *Pirates of the Thunder*.

Lords of the Starship (1967) ★★★★ Novel by Mark S. Geston (USA). The starship is centuries in the building; around the immense yards nations rise and fall, battle after battle is fought. In the end, the whole thing is exposed as a terrible lie. A weird, horrifying future of continuous flux, stasis and war. Geston's first novel. Amazing.

Lost Dorsai (1980) ★★ Novel by Gordon R. Dickson (Canada/USA). A mercenary soldier who has sworn never to bear arms or kill takes a job as bandmaster in a city under seige. This rather sentimental adaptation of a Kipling short story is incidental to Dickson's 'Childe Cycle', taking place at the same time as *Soldier, Ask Not* and featuring Ian and Kensie Grahame and Amanda Morgan from the 'Dorsai' novels. Reprinted in *The Dorsai Companion*.

Lost Face, The (Nesvadba): see *In the Footsteps of the Abominable Snowman*.

Lost Legacy (Heinlein): see *Assignment in Eternity*.

Lost Perception, The (1966) ★ Novel by Daniel F. Galouye (USA). A rather dull narrative about a space-plague, aliens and (as usual with Galouye) the development of ESP-powers. Title in USA: *A Scourge of Screamers*.

Lost Traveller, The (1976) ★ Novel by Steve Wilson (UK). This violently romantic tale of Hell's Angels and Red Indians in a future America ravaged by nuclear war is subtitled by its author 'A Motorcycle Grail Quest Epic and Science Fiction Western'. Roger Zelazny had already done something similar in *Damnation Alley*. Wilson's first (and only?) novel. 'Unadulterated garbage, but ... it may turn out to be popular garbage' – Brian Stableford.

Lost World, The (1912) ★★★★ Novel by A. Conan Doyle (UK), first of his Professor Challenger stories. Explorers find dinosaurs and cavepeople living on an almost inaccessible plateau in South America. A classic adventure story, the best of its kind, with a much higher scientific content than any of Rider Haggard's or Edgar Rice Burroughs's superficially similar novels of lost worlds and lost races. Filmed in 1925 (dir. Harry Hoyt) and in 1960 (dir. Irwin Allen).

Love and Napalm: Export USA (Ballard): see *Atrocity Exhibition, The*.

Lovers, The (1961) ★★ Novel by Philip José Farmer (USA), expansion of a 1952 magazine novella which was its author's first published sf story. A repressed Earthman falls in love with an alien 'woman' but discovers too late that her biological nature can only lead to a tragic outcome for their union. Grotesque and surprising on its first publication, it now seems predictable and tame. Quasi-sequel: *Timestop*.

Low-Flying Aircraft and Other Stories (1976) ★★★ Collection by J. G. Ballard (UK). Novella and eight short stories on typical Ballardian themes. The long piece, 'The Ultimate City', concerns an attempt to restart big-city life in a pastoral, energy-hoarding future. Another notable item, 'The Life and Death of God', is an ironic comment on the human necessity to destroy divinity.

Lucifer Comet, The (1980) ★★ Novel by Ian Wallace (USA). Superpowerful aliens compete for influence over the human race: one of these resembles the traditional Devil, but he brings promethean gifts. 'Action-adventure with good ironic undertones' – Brian Stableford.

Lucifer's Hammer (1977) ★★ Novel by Larry Niven and Jerry Pournelle (USA). Civilization is devastated when a giant meteor grazes the Earth. This lengthy and tendentious book, which became a bestseller, is concerned with the various reactions of the survivors, and pokes fun at antiscientific fainthearts. 'A toughminded exercise in imaginary Social Darwinism' – Brian Stableford.

Lunatics of Terra, The (1984) ★★★ Collection by John Sladek (USA). Eighteen bright, tricky stories (some of them very brief), all accompanied by amusing afterwords. Standouts include 'Guesting' (1982), about an alien who appears on TV chat shows, and 'Calling All Gumpdrops!' (1983), about a near-future society in which the roles of adults and children are reversed.

M

McAndrew Chronicles, The (Sheffield), see under *Hidden Variables*.

Machiavelli Interface, The (Perry): see under *Man Who Never Missed, The*.

Machine in Shaft Ten and Other Stories, The (1975) ★★★ Collection by M. John Harrison (UK). A dozen stories by one of the most intensely stylish of British sf authors (who has since largely abandoned the genre). Contains the moody 'London Melancholy', about a ruined future London haunted by winged people; and the outstanding psychological horror tale 'Running Down', about a man who is literally a walking disaster area. A revised version of this last piece is also included in Harrison's later collection *The Ice Monkey and Other Stories* (1983), which consists in the main of non-sf pieces.

Machineries of Joy, The (1964) ★★ Collection by Ray Bradbury (USA). A mixed bag of stories: fantasy, humorous Irishry and some sf. Alas, with this volume a decline in Bradbury's artistry began to be evident.

Machines and Men (1973) ★★★ Collection by Keith Roberts (UK). Ten well-told and often emotionally intense sf pieces by a very English writer. Some stories from this book and from a second excellent collection, *The Grain Kings* (1976), were reassembled for the American-published volume *The Passing of the Dragons* (1977). A later, slightly inferior, collection is entitled *Ladies from Hell* (1979).

Machines That Think: The Best Science Fiction Stories About Robots and Computers (1984) ★★ Anthology edited by Isaac Asimov, Patricia S. Warrick and Martin H. Greenberg (USA). Over 600 pages of variable stories, ranging from creaky old 1930s pieces by John Wyndham and Harl Vincent to good recent stuff by Gene Wolfe and Vernor Vinge. Murray Leinster's 'A Logic Named Joe' (1946) is an astonishing forecast of the home-computer boom, but to enjoy the story you have to overlook its extremely arch sexist tone.

Macrolife (1979) ★★★ Novel by

George Zebrowski (USA). One of the first of a crop of books about space colonies that survive the self-destruction of Earth civilization and go on to seed the universe. Somewhat partisan with (acknowledged) references to the works of Gerard O'Neill, Paolo Soleri and many others, it gets bogged down in philosophical speculation about the End of Time, the Meaning of Identity and other Capitalized Concepts. Nevertheless, an impressive work of ideas.

Macroscope (1969) ★★ Novel by Piers Anthony (USA). Ivo, the product of an attempt to breed geniuses, is taken to the Macroscope, a device that uses gravitational waves to observe in great detail goings on anywhere in the galaxy. They observe messages from an advanced civilization, and convert the planet Neptune into a space drive. The symbolism of astrology is used throughout the book whose multiple threads are more complex than Anthony's more recent work.

Maelstrom (Preuss): see under *Breaking Strain*.

Magic Labyrinth, The (1980) ★★ Novel by Philip José Farmer (USA), sequel to *The Dark Design* and fourth in the 'Riverworld' series. At last Burton, Twain and other reborn Earthlings are vouchsafed some answers as to why the human race has been resurrected on a far planet by the super-technology of the 'Ethicals'. Alas, the answers are not very satisfying, and this didn't quite prove to be the end of the series after all. Sequel: *Gods of Riverworld*.

Magic May Return, The (1981) ★ Collection by Larry Niven and others (USA). A number of fantasy stories which make use of the 'scientific' explanation of magic developed in Niven's 'Not Long Before the End', reprinted here.

Magic Time (1979) ★★ Novel by Kit Reed (USA). In a media-saturated near future, four people struggle to escape from the warm, gooey embrace of the so-called 'Happy Habitat' (a sort of nightmarish extrapolation of Disneyland). 'Witty; but wit is not enough … The monster is not laid, merely tickled a little' – John Clute.

Main Event, The (Beebee): see under *Hub, The*.

Main Experiment, The (1964) ★★★ Novel by Christopher Hodder-Williams (UK). A newly discovered form of nuclear radiation interferes with the human sensorium in this interesting techno-horror story by a writer who had previously specialized in aeronautical thrillers (though he had published one near-future sf novel called *Chain Reaction* in 1959). 'Deserves to rank amongst the very highest of British sf' – David V. Barrett, *Vector*.

Majipoor Chronicles (Silverberg): see under *Lord Valentine's Castle*.

Major Operation (White): see under *Hospital Station*.

Make Room! Make Room! (1966) ★★★ Novel by Harry Harrison (USA). New York City in 1999: overpopulated, impoverished and riotous. A policeman dutifully pursues a murder enquiry, but his problems seem small when set against the vast tragedy of the city. One of the finest treatments of the overpopulation theme. Filmed as *Soylent Green* (1973; dir. Richard Fleischer).

Maker of Universes, The (1965) ★★ Novel by Philip José Farmer (USA), first in his 'World of Tiers' series. Fantasy-flavoured sf adventure, in which a middle-aged protagonist enters a 'pocket universe' and finds himself growing younger. He encounters a trickster hero called Kickaha (alias Paul Janus Finnegan – one of Farmer's many 'PJF' alter egos) and proceeds, through extravagant incident after incident, to learn the nature of this wedding-cake world. It ends with the revelation that he is in fact an amnesiac 'god', one of the creators of the pocket universe. An enjoyable entertainment. Sequels (of progressively less interest): *The Gates of Creation* (1966), *A Private Cosmos* (1967), *Behind the Walls of Terra* (1970) and *The Lavalite World* (1977).

Makeshift God, The (1979) ★★ Novel by Russell M. Griffin (USA). A bouncy space adventure, unevenly executed but with a wealth of ideas. Griffin's first novel (alas, the author died at the age of 43, after writing three more books).

Making of the Representative for Planet 8 (Lessing): see under *Marriages Between Zones Three, Four, and Five, The*.

Malevil (1972) ★★★ Novel by Robert Merle (France). A group of people survive nuclear war by holing up in the eponymous French castle. They are then faced with the task of rebuilding civilization, although they harbour doubts as to the value of this project. A long, impressively detailed narrative by a bestselling writer. John W. Campbell award-winner, 1974.

Mallworld (1981) ★★ Fix-up novel by Somtow Sucharitkul (Thailand/USA). A world which has been turned into one gigantic shopping mall is investigated by aliens who are aghast (with good reason) at what human beings get up to – but they also find that there is a good side to human nature. A bizarre comedy which has its sentimental moments. Sucharitkul's first book.

Malzberg at Large (Malzberg): see under *Man Who Loved the Midnight Lady, The*.

Mammoth Hunters, The (Auel): see under *Clan of the Cave Bear, The*.

Man in a Cage (1976) ★★ Novel by Brian Stableford (UK). An institutionalized schizophrenic is given the opportunity to become humanity's emissary to the stars. It seems that space flight via hyperspace is an inherently schizophrenic experience, and only the mad can survive. Stableford's most difficult novel, highly reminiscent of certain works by Barry Malzberg. It strains for effect, and perhaps strains too far.

Man In His Time: Best SF Stories

(Aldiss): see *Best Science Fiction Stories of Brian W. Aldiss.*

Man in the High Castle, The (1962) ★★★★ Novel by Philip K. Dick (USA). Set in an alternative world where Germany and Japan won World War II, this fine work deals realistically with the vicissitudes of various characters in early-1960s California. It is a beautifully poised and subtle book which displays all its author's usual sympathy for the underdog. Hugo award-winner, 1963.

Man in the Tree, The (1984) ★★ Novel by Damon Knight (USA). This story of an eight-foot-tall psi-powered superman coming to maturity in our world is Knight's long-awaited attempt at a major sf novel. Unfortunately, it fails to astonish. 'The text only makes sense when read as the crypitc and probably unconscious biography of a science-fiction writer' – Lee Montgomerie, *Interzone.*

Man of Double Deed, A (1965) ★★ Novel by Leonard Daventry (UK). Telepaths rule a future Earth which has been disrupted by atomic war, and the hero is assigned to deal with the problem of growing juvenile violence. Minor fare from a writer whose subsequent books have shown little improvement. 'Readable and nicely developed' – Langdon Jones, *New Worlds.* Daventry's first novel.

Man of Two Worlds (1986) Novel by Frank and Brian Herbert (USA). The alien Dreens have the ability to imagine other creatures into exist-

ence – including human beings. A failed attempt at far-out humour: Frank Herbert is no better at posthumous fiction than most authors.

Man of Two Worlds (Jones): see *Renaissance.*

Man Plus (1976) ★★★ Novel by Frederik Pohl (USA). An astronaut is engineered to survive on Mars. This painful process involves the installation of huge solar-panel wings and multi-faceted eyes. Well thought out, this is one of the finest treatments of the 'cyborg' theme in modern sf. 'All the way to the startling denouement, one is carried along by the total rationality of Pohl's narrative' – J. G. Ballard, *New Statesman.* Nebula award-winner, 1977.

Man Who Ate the World, The (Pohl): see under *Case Against Tomorrow, The.*

Man Who Corrupted Earth, The (1980) ★★ Novel by G. C. Edmondson (USA). A ruthless businessman buys NASA's disused space shuttles and gets things moving again with good old capitalist know-how. An endearing piece of propaganda for the space programme. 'The entrepreneurial buccaneering is described with such verve ... that even socialists might enjoy it' – Brian Stableford.

Man Who Counts, The (Anderson): see *War of the Wing-Men.*

Man Who Fell to Earth, The (1963) ★★★ Novel by Walter Tevis (USA). A lone alien from a dying civilization arrives on our planet, where he strives to become as human as possible – and ultimately fails, thanks to human xenophobia. A moving story which has become accepted as a minor classic. Tevis's first sf novel. Filmed in 1976 (dir. Nicolas Roeg).

Man Who Folded Himself, The ★ Novel by David Gerrold (USA). An indulgent time-tripping/*doppelgänger* tale with a high sexual content (the 'f'-word in the title should really be something else). Sub-Heinleinian hi-jinks, not very well written.

Man Who Had No Idea, The (1982) ★★★ Collection by Thomas M. Disch (USA). Despite two interplanetary tales, 'Concepts' and 'The Planet of the Rapes', most of these offerings from sf's foremost comedian of manners are about the here-and-now – stories of marriage, loneliness or paranoia, each lightly brushed with the fantastic. 'The Grown-Up', about a ten-year-old boy who wakes to find himself a man, expresses the wonder of the ordinary extremely effectively. The book's title is ironically apt: there are few gosh-wow ideas here; rather, these are the prose fictions of a poet.

Man Who Japed, The (1956) ★★ Novel by Philip K. Dick (USA). In an unforgiving future society, run by the political movement known as Moral Reclamation, a trickster hero rebels in surprising fashion. An enjoyable early Dick tale.

Man Who Loved Morlocks, The (1981) ★★★ Novel by David J. Lake (UK/Australia). A sequel to H. G. Wells's *The Time Machine*, in which the Time Traveller is unable to return to the era of the Morlocks and Eloi, and instead moves much further into the future where he finds a more vigorous society. The author comments wittily on Wellsian perceptions and preconceptions in this skilful revision of the great writer's myth of a decadent future. The result is a 'sequel-by-another-hand' which is more effective than most examples of that dubious sub-genre.

Man Who Loved the Midnight Lady, The (1980) ★★ Collection by Barry N. Malzberg (USA). Not all of these brief, bleak and blackly humorous stories are sf. Notable items include 'In the Stocks' and 'Indigestion'. As John Clute says: 'Once again, these stories present a world whose colours have been ashed down into a desolate, grey, weirdly primitive tonal inscape …' Other, comparable, collections by Malzberg include *The Many Worlds of Barry Malzberg* (1975), *Down Here in the Dream Quarter* (1976) and *Malzberg at Large* (1979).

Man Who Melted, The (1984) ★★ Novel by Jack Dann (USA). Civilization falls apart as madness and extreme forms of religion grip people's minds. The most ambitious work so far by a doggedly avant-garde sf writer.

Man Who Never Missed, The (1985) ★★ Novel by Steve Perry (USA), first in the 'Matador Trilogy'. A deserter from a brutal future military finds a Secret Master to train him in the martial arts (the greatest of which seems to be mixing drinks), so that he can take up arms as a one-man resistance movement, never killing his opponents, just knocking them out with poison darts. A strange, mildly funny novel, with underlying decency. Sequels: *Matadora* and *The Machiavelli Interface* (both 1986).

Man Who Owned the World, The (1961) ★ Novel by Charles Eric Maine (UK). A dead astronaut is revived in the far future to find that a trust fund set up for him has become politically significant. Humdrum.

Man Who Pulled Down the Sky, The (1986) ★★ Novel by John Barnes (USA). A spy is sent from Eros in the outer solar system to raise revolt on rural, backward Earth, oppressed by the dogmatically free-market Orbital Republics. Previously law-abiding farmers and priests commit atrocity after atrocity as they use their legitimate ends to justify ever more arbitrary means.

Man Who Sold the Moon, The (1950) ★★★ Collection by Robert A. Heinlein (USA), introduced by John W. Campbell, Jr. Six stories, which include the early 'Life-Line' (1939) and 'Requiem' (1940). The long title story (1950) is a largely earthbound tour-de-force about a capitalist wheeler-dealer who engineers the first manned flight to the moon. These stories, together with those in *The Green Hills of Earth* and *Revolt in 2100*, form part of Heinlein's celebrated 'Future History' – an attempt to portray a realistic, near-future line of development for the human race.

Man Who Used the Universe, The (1983) ★★ Novel by Alan Dean Foster (USA). Kees van Loo-Macklin, an 'illegal' citizen in a world with dozens of categories of citizenship, uses his criminal skills and an exaggerated alien threat to achieve political power.

Man Who Vanished Into Space, The (Johns): see under *Now to the Stars*.

Mandala (1983) ★ Novel by David F. Bischoff (USA). A love story, involving a military man and a telepathic lady, in a space setting of the distant future. Well-meaning stuff.

Mandrake (1964) ★ Novel by Susan Cooper (UK). A near-future dictator of Britain compels everyone to live in small communities, preparatory to 'cleansing' the world of humanity. (M. J. Engh's later *Arslan* treats a similar theme more effectively.) 'The whole book is too much like a *Dr Who* script' – Hilary Bailey, *New Worlds*. A first novel by a writer who has since become well known for her juvenile fantasy stories.

Manhounds of Antares (Akers): see under *Transit to Scorpio*.

Manifest Destiny (1980) ★★ Collection by Barry B. Longyear (USA). Four stories about human expansion into space. 'Enemy Mine' (Hugo and Nebula award-winner, 1980), in which a human raises an alien child on the barren planet where both are shipwrecked, despite the enmity between the species, provided the rough plot for the film of the same name. It was also expanded into a 'novel-of-the-film' by David Gerrold (see *Enemy Mine*). Longyear's quasi-sequel to this successful story is *The Tomorrow Testament* (1983).

Mankind on the Run (1956) ★ Novel by Gordon R. Dickson (Canada/USA). Every citizen of the Earth who survived the Lucky War ('lucky' because only 700 million died) is graded A, B, C or Unstable and given a new work assignment every six months or so. Kil Brunner, obsessed with his search for his vanished wife, discovers abnormal individuals whose powers can overthrow the status quo. Minor early Dickson. Republished as *On the Run*.

Mankind Under the Leash (1966) ★★ Novel by Thomas M. Disch (USA), expanded from his magazine story 'White Fang Goes Dingo'. Alien energy-beings become the Masters of Earth, and humans are reduced to the status of dogs. Witty adventure story written in mock 19th-century style. Full of doggy jokes, and perhaps just a bit too clever-clever. Later republished in Britain under the author's preferred title, *The Puppies of Terra*.

Man-Kzin Wars, The (1988) ★ Anthology by Larry Niven and others (USA). This is a tripartite 'shared-world' volume, built on Niven's story 'The Warriors', about space conflict between humans and the catlike alien Kzin. The new stories, by Poul Anderson and Dean Ing, are adequately entertaining – but the whole exercise, as with so much of the shared-world craze, seems a bit pointless.

Manna (1984) ★ Novel by Lee Correy (G. Harry Stine, USA). An African nation leads the near-future space race. Fairly interesting space propaganda by a writer better known for his popular science books.

Manseed (1982) ★ Novel by Jack Williamson (USA). Superhuman colonists and their machines are 'seeded' on a dangerous alien planet where a previous civilization was wiped out. Adequate space adventure by an old hand.

Many Worlds of Barry Malzberg, The (Malzberg): see under *Man who Loved the Midnight Lady, The*.

Many Worlds of Magnus Ridolph, The (1966) ★★ Collection by Jack Vance (USA). Six adventures of the bearded, omniscient title character who roams the galaxy solving mysteries and righting wrongs. These pieces date from early in Vance's career, and they provide adequate though unmemorable entertainment.

Many Worlds of Poul Anderson, The (Anderson): see *Book of Poul Anderson, The*.

Many-Coloured Land, The (1981) ★★ Novel by Julian May (USA) – first part of a very long work known as 'The Saga of the Exiles' (other volumes are *The Golden Torc*, *The Non-Born King* and *The Adversary*). Misfits from the Galactic Milieu travel back to a Pliocene Europe disputed between the cruel, beautiful Tanu and warlike Firvulag. Julian May's depth of research and her experience as a writer only just enable her to keep all the aspects of the huge structure together – paleontology, Celtic myth, sex, Wagner, telepathy, politics, technology.

Marathon Photograph and Other Stories, The (1986) ★★★ Collection by Clifford D. Simak (USA), introduced by F. Lyall. Four stories about aspects of Time, including the Hugo and Nebula award-winner 'Grotto of the Dancing Deer' (1980). These are late tales, written by an author in his seventies, but they have considerable charm.

Marooned (1964) ★ Novel by Martin Caidin (USA). Near-future thriller about the space programme. Russians and Americans co-operate when a crisis occurs in orbit. Good technical detail (the author had written many aeronautics and rocketry books), but fairly humdrum as an sf story. Filmed in 1969 (dir. John Sturges).

Marooned in Real Time (Vinge): see under *Peace War, The.*

Marriages Between Zones Three, Four, and Five, The (1980) ★★ Novel by Doris Lessing (UK), sequel to *Shikasta* and second in the 'Canopus in Argos: Archives' series. In this book, which is different in tone from the first and perhaps more fantasy than sf, the author takes us on a tour of various 'zones' which lie parallel to our Earth. The moral emphasis is firmly on the relations between the sexes. 'There is an absence of explicit judgement ... which, after the tedious jeremiad of *Shikasta*, is refreshing' – Colin Greenland, *Foun-

dation. The remaining volumes in the sequence are *The Sirian Experiments* (1981), *The Making of the Representative for Planet 8* (1982) and *The Sentimental Agents in the Volyen Empire* (1983).

Martian Chronicles, The (1950) ★★★★ Collection by Ray Bradbury (USA). Loosely linked stories about the near-future colonization of Mars. Poetic mood pieces, occasionally satirical and moralistic, but often haunting in their power. Initially published in Britain as *The Silver Locusts*. An undeniable classic as a book, it formed the basis of a poor TV mini-series (1980; dir. Michael Anderson).

Martian Inca, The (1977) ★★★ Novel by Ian Watson (UK). A returning spacecraft from Mars crashes in South America, where Indians become infected by a virus which vouchsafes them strange visions and convinces them that the time has come to rebuild the Inca empire. Watson's customary mix of mind-blowing hard sf and Third-World politics. 'Unremittingly inventive, the novel contains superb descriptive writing within a ceaseless flow of ideas' – J. G. Ballard, *New Statesman.*

Martian Odyssey and Other Stories, A (Weinbaum): see under *Best of Stanley G. Weinbaum, The.*

Martian Time-Slip (1964) ★★★★ Novel by Philip K. Dick (USA). On a dreary colonial Mars of the near future, the handyman hero becomes involved with a manipulative union boss and an autistic boy who is able to communicate with the despised 'natives'. The believable characters, the humour and the horror all mingle effectively in one of Dick's best novels. 'A landscape that uncannily resembles southern California perceived through the glaze of some deep psychosis' – J. G. Ballard, *New Statesman*.

Martian Way and Other Stories, The (1955) ★★★ Collection by Isaac Asimov (USA). Four long tales in the admirable Dr Asimov's best style. The title story concerns the attempt by Martian colonists to get ice from the rings of Saturn to become independent of a totalitarian Earth.

Martians, Go Home (1955) ★★ Novel by Fredric Brown (USA). Humorous tale of an sf writer who foils an invasion of little green men from Mars. But if it hadn't been for him the Martians wouldn't have come in the first place ... An entertainment similar to the author's *What Mad Universe?* – but not quite as good.

Marune: Alastor 933 (1975) ★★ Novel by Jack Vance (USA). An amnesiac in the care of the bureaucrats of the Alastor Cluster (for which, see *Trullion: Alastor 2262*) turns out to be involved in a power struggle amongst the formal and arrogant Rhune of the planet Marune. Full of coinages and strange names, the style could be described as naïve decadence.

Mask, The (Gordon): see under *Hidden World, The*.

Mask for the General, A (1987) ★★★

Novel by Lisa Goldstein (USA). America after the Banking Collapse is a drab, repressed, rationed police state reminiscent of Cold-War Eastern Europe. The Tribes live on the edge of legality in California, avoiding work and identifying with animal totems. Well written and gripping, despite a heavy dose of New-Age mysticism.

Masks of the Martyrs (1988) Novel by Jack L. Chalker (USA), sequel to *Warriors of the Storm* and the final volume of the 'Rings of the Master' tetralogy. The heroes return to Earth with the vital rings for a showdown at the Master Control Centre in Cheyenne Mountain. Not as unpleasantly violent as previous books in the series, but still very formulaic and badly organized.

Masks of Time, The (1968) ★★ Novel by Robert Silverberg (USA). At the very end of the 20th century, a mysterious new messiah appears as if from nowhere. Is he a time-traveller from 1000 years hence? A satirical tale of martyrdom by this intelligent writer: but it doesn't quite bear the burden of significance which it seems the author intended. Published in Britain as *Vornan-19*.

Masque World (Panshin): see under *Star Well*.

Master of Life and Death (1957) ★ Novel by Robert Silverberg (USA). The hero is a bureaucrat who helps select candidates for euthanasia. One of Silverberg's very earliest: a competent though uninspired futuristic thriller.

Master of Paxwax (1986) ★★ Novel by Phillip Mann (UK/New Zealand), the first part of 'The Story of Pawl Paxwax, the Gardener'. Eleven human families dominate the galaxy, oppressing all alien races. Pawl Paxwax, scion of one of these families, comes abruptly into his inheritance and finds himself caught up in a conspiracy against the human empire. 'His descriptions of aliens are deft and melancholy and estranged; he does a good little space war ... But when he transcribes the excruciatingly prosaic poetry of his moody young Paxwax, and when he talks about adolescent love hots ... he gives us dead wood' – John Clute. Sequel: *The Fall of the Families*.

Masters of the Maze (1965) ★★★ Novel by Avram Davidson (USA). A complex parallel-worlds story in which humans come into conflict with an alien race. Well characterized: perhaps the quirky Mr Davidson's best sf novel.

Masters of the Pit, The (Moorcock): see under *City of the Beast, The*.

Masters of Time (van Vogt): see under *Three Eyes of Evil, The*.

Mastodonia (1978) ★★ Novel by Clifford D. Simak (USA). A Cheshire-Cat-like alien leads our Midwestern hero through a time portal into a pristine prehistoric Earth. We've encountered much of it before, but it's most enjoyably spun out. Published in Britain as *Catface*.

Matadora (Perry): see under *Man Who Never Missed, The*.

Mathenauts: Tales of Mathematical Wonder (Rucker): see under *White Light*.

Matter of Oaths, A (1988) ★★ Novel by Helen Wright (UK). The Guild of Webbers (i.e. starship pilots) holds the balance of power in a long-lasting war between the Old Empire and the New Empire, ruled by immortal emperors who rose to their positions 'as scum rises to the surface of a pond'. Rafe, a guild-member and a fugitive from the Old Emperor, turns out to be more than he at first seems.

Maxwell's Demon (1976) ★ Novel by Martin Sherwood (UK). Scientists investigate the cause of a mysterious sleeping-sickness: it transpires that the unarousable sleepers have been taken over by alien entities. A humdrum sf thriller by a science journalist whose qualifications don't really show. 'What we get is a run-down on sleep, consciousness, alpha rhythms, etc ... and then a mighty great step into the anything-goes realm of invented science, which is to say, gobbledegook' – George Turner, *Foundation*.

Mayday Orbit (Anderson): see under *We Claim These Stars*.

Mayenne (Tubb): see under *Winds of Gath, The*.

Mayflies (1979) ★★ Novel by Kevin O'Donnell Jr. (USA). The passengers of a generation starship are as mayflies to the computer-enhanced disembodied human brain which controls their vessel on its thousand-year flight. 'The trouble with an immortal hero/computer is that everyone else flits by too swiftly, however well handled in their brief moment on the stage. And the ending is pure wish-fulfilment' – David Langford, *Foundation*.

Maze of Death, A (1970) ★★ Novel by Philip K. Dick (USA). Various anxious characters (one of whom flies a spaceship called the Morbid Chicken) seek God on an alien planet. An extremely odd Dick book which is an uneasy mixture of inter-planetary sf, religious fantasy and parodic comedy.

Mechasm (Sladek): see *Reproductive System, The*.

Medea: Harlan's World (1985) ★★ Anthology edited by Harlan Ellison (USA). A long-gestating collaborative project in which Ellison brought together the talents of Hal Clement, Poul Anderson, Larry Niven and Frederik Pohl to conceive and design a planetary system known as Medea. The specifications were then given to four very different writers – Thomas M. Disch, Frank Herbert, Robert Silverberg and Theodore Sturgeon – who each wrote a story using the background. The resulting 500-page volume, which also contains later work by Jack Williamson and Kate Wilhelm, is a bit of a hotch-potch but a fascinating one.

Medicine for Melancholy, A (1959) ★★★ Collection by Ray Bradbury (USA). Sf and fantasy stories (rather more of the latter) including such Bradbury standards as 'Dark They Were, and Golden-Eyed', 'A Scent of Sarsaparilla' and 'The Smile'. Brief, poetic and (at their best) hauntingly mysterious tales. The British version of this volume, differing considerably in its contents, is entitled *The Day It Rained Forever*.

Medusa: A Tiger by the Tail (Chalker): see under *Lilith: A Snake in the Grass*.

Medusa's Children (1977) ★★ Novel by Bob Shaw (UK). Survivors of Earthly shipwrecks live in a mysterious underwater environment, somewhere out in space. A tall story based on the so-called Bermuda-Triangle mystery: well-written hokum. 'The sense of sun-filled water all around, the absence of movement and the suspension of time create a trance-like atmosphere in which the events of the narrative drift by like sleeping fish' – J. G. Ballard, *New Statesman*.

Megalomania (Wallace): see under *Croyd*.

Memoirs Found in a Bathtub (1971) ★★ Novel by Stanislaw Lem (Poland). Many centuries hence the memoirs of a man from the time of the 'Great Collapse' are discovered and decoded. There is much satire on bureaucracy and militarism in this complex, deceptive novel. Skilfully done, but not one of Lem's more approachable works.

Memories (1987) ★★★ Novel by Mike McQuay (USA). The psychiatrist hero is visited by a woman from the devastated future, who appeals for his help against an inter-temporal menace. The action soon slips in place and time to Europe in the era of Napoleon. It's somewhat sentimental and over-written; nevertheless, a satisfactory psychological time-travel yarn, wide-ranging, complex and long.

Memoirs of a Spacewoman (1962) ★★★ Novel by Naomi Mitchison (UK). This unique space adventure story is the reminiscences of a lifetime shared by bringing up children and contacting truly alien intelligence. The methods used to establish communication are based on sympathy, affection, touch and a little sex.

Memories of the Space Age (1988) ★★★★ Collection by J. G. Ballard (UK). Eight disturbing, atmospheric stories which deal with space-flight, although none of them is actually set off-Earth. Six are reprinted from earlier Ballard books, but two are collected for the first time here: the haunting title story (1982), in which a disease of the time-sense affects latter-day beachcombers in an abandoned Cape Canaveral, and the only slightly less effective 'The Man Who Walked on the Moon' (1985).

Memory of Whiteness, The (1985) ★★ Novel by Kim Stanley Robinson (USA). In the 33rd century, the Master of the Orchestra sets out on a concert tour of the solar system – the Orchestra being a wonderful instrument which unites the peoples of the inhabited planets. A well-written but slightly uneasy blend of space fiction and musical lore. 'A gravity-well tour ... which is Robinson's only failed novel to date' – John Clute.

Memory Wire (1987) ★★★ Novel by Robert Charles Wilson (USA/ Canada). In a brutalized near future, a man is 'wired' for video and has adventures in the company of various down-and-outs. A rather bleak but moving novel by a good new writer.

Men in the Jungle, The (1967) ★★ Novel by Norman Spinrad (USA). A crook and his consorts hightail it from the Asteroid Belt in search of another world to exploit. They find an oppressed planet ruled by cannibalistic sadists and, willy-nilly, they become its liberators. Dark, violent, crude, sexy: a 'dangerous vision' of the American New-Wave type. 'The ferociously bloody outcome is depicted with something less than subtlety by Spinrad' – James Cawthorn, *New Worlds*.

Men Inside, The (1973) ★★ Fix-up novel by Barry N. Malzberg (USA). Poor folk are recruited to the cause of medicine: miniaturized, they are inserted into the bowels of the rich in order to remove cancers. An absurdist's replay of the *Fantastic Voyage* scenario. It is partly based on the short story 'In the Pocket', which had already been published in book form in the collection *In the Pocket and Other SF Stories* (1971; as by 'K. M. O'Donnell').

Men Like Gods (1923) ★★ Novel by H. G. Wells (UK). A varied group of contemporary folk is plunged into a parallel world which turns out to be the utopia of the author's dreams. Most of them are too small-minded to appreciate their new surroundings, but the hero, Mr Barnstaple, is treated to a guided tour. An amiable expression of Wells's abiding concern for the perfectibility (or otherwise) of humankind.

Men, Martians and Machines (1956) ★★ Collection by Eric Frank Russell (UK). The world's first starship, Marathon, invented by long-haired boffins and crewed by hard-bitten spacemen, tentacled chess-playing Martians and one nice-guy robot, flies round the galaxy meeting bizarre alien species. Straightforward, light-hearted, rather dated adventure stories set in a future which resembles an all-male RAF base.

Men of War (Pournelle & Carr): see under *There Will Be War*.

Menace from Earth, The (1959) ★★★ Collection by Robert A. Heinlein (USA). Eight entertaining stories, first published between 1941 and 1957. The oldest, longest and most memorable of them is 'By His Bootstraps', a brain-teasing time-loop story which is still one of the best of its sort ever written. Also delightful is 'The Year of the Jackpot' (1952), a merrily apocalyptic tale of sun-spots and cyclic disasters.

Menace Under Marswood (1983) Novel by Sterling E. Lanier (USA). A terraformed Mars, seeded by the nations of Earth, has degenerated and now has all manner of nasty beasts and renegade humans living and fighting on it. A potboiler by a writer who is surely capable of better.

Mercedes Nights (1987) ★ Novel by Michael D. Weaver (USA). A star

comedian is kidnapped, cloned and sold as a sort of living sex doll. This turns out to be the front-shop operation for some political machinations. There is a parallel strand about travel to the stars by what seem to be mystical means. An energetic first novel.

Mercenary (Anthony): see under *Refugee*.

Mercenary, The (1977) ★ Fix-up novel by Jerry Pournelle (USA). Rather unpleasant account of a space-going hero called John Christian Falkenberg, wrongfully dismissed from the marines and forced to commit an atrocity to preserve order in a newly independent colony. This is one of the books which initiated the whole 'mercenary' sub-genre of latter-day space opera. Sequel: *Prince of Mercenaries* (1989).

Merchanter's Luck (1982) ★★ Novel by C. J. Cherryh (USA). Sandor, last survivor of a Union merchanter family massacred by Earth marines turned pirates, ekes out a living carrying semi-legal trade from star to star and fiddling credit accounts until he is tricked into a complicated plot to trap a warship renegade from the action of *Downbelow Station*. It's a bit hard to take the idea of the sole owner of a starship having to cadge money to buy a sandwich in a greasy bar.

Merchants' War, The (1984) ★★ Novel by Frederik Pohl (USA), a belated sequel to *The Space Merchants*. Decades after the action of the preceding book, the Venus colony founded by escapees from the Madison-Avenue dystopia of Earth is well established – and advertising has been banned. But back on the home planet things go on as before, and a new hero learns to rebel against his wasteful society. This time, his story ends with the hope of a fresh political order arising from the old, rather than a mere escape to a whole new world. 'It might be better described as a reworking rather than simply a sequel' – Kenny Mathieson, *Foundation*.

Merlin's Mirror (1975) ★★ Novel by Andre Norton (USA). A rather forced sf rationalization of King Arthur and Merlin as descendants of space-travellers equipped with computers and cryogenic storage.

Messiah at the End of Time (Moorcock): see under *Dancers at the End of Time, The*.

Metallic Muse, The (1972) ★★ Collection by Lloyd Biggle Jr. (USA). Seven sf stories from the late 1950s to the late 60s, mainly on arts-related themes. Most are fairly humdrum, but 'In His Own Image', about a robotic priest, is memorably absurd.

Methuselah's Children (1958) ★★ Novel by Robert A. Heinlein (USA), expanded from a 1941 magazine serial and part of the 'Future History' series. A secret breeding programme which dates from the 19th century has resulted in the 22nd-century 'Howard Families', an elite group of extremely long-lived persons. When their existence becomes known they are hounded off Earth and com-mence wandering the stars. The best of Heinlein's 1940s novels (if somewhat ragged in its pacing), this book introduces the character Lazarus Long, a cracker-barrel philosopher after the author's own heart. Belated sequel: *Time Enough for Love*.

Metrophage (1988) ★★★ Novel by Richard Kadrey (USA). Likeable hoodlum Jonny Qabbala has run-ins with various gangsters and corrupt powers in a decayed Los Angeles of the 21st century. The cyberpunk-ish background is brilliantly evoked and there are some good jokes, but the plot is nothing special. A first novel of considerable promise. 'The by-now familiar mix of urban decay, street-subverted technology, pop culture and hardboiled action is enlivened by a truly gonzoid imagin-ation' – Paul McAuley, *Interzone*.

Michaelmas (1977) ★★★ Novel by Algis Budrys (USA). A roving TV journalist of the near future becomes the secret ruler of the world, as a result of his cunning manipulation of an artificial-intelligence network – or is the AI manipulating him? Ambitious and richly-textured, this is a fundamentally implausible but seductive near-future power dream.

Midas World (1983) ★★ Fix-up novel by Frederik Pohl (USA), basically an expansion of his classic satire on rampant consumerism, 'The Midas Plague' (1954). Here Pohl has yoked it together with a number of other stories from the 1950s and the 1980s, but the whole adds up to less than the sum of the parts. An unwise exercise in the milking of old material.

Middle Kingdom, The (Wingrove): see under *Chung Kuo: The Middle Kingdom*.

Midnight (1989) ★ Novel by Dean R. Koontz (USA). Another one for the horror trade: miniaturized microprocessors are injected into people, giving them super-abilities, but unfortunately some subjects turn into monsters. An efficiently written but routine piece of technophobia, as unoriginal as its title.

Midnight at the Well of Souls (1977) ★ Novel by Jack L. Chalker (USA). A roller-coaster ride with hero Nathan Brazil through the Well World, a vast set of interlocking environments built by ancient aliens. Violent-action sf with exotic ingredients, it proved popular. Sequels (much more of the same): *Exiles at the Well of Souls* (1978), *Quest for the Well of Souls* (1978), *The Return of Nathan Brazil* (1979) and *Twilight at the Well of Souls* (1980).

Midsummer Century (1972) ★ Novel by James Blish (USA). Slim volume which tells of a man who is projected (in desembodied fashion) into the far, far future. It's a tenuous, attenuated little fable.

Midwich Cuckoos, The (1957) ★★★ Novel by John Wyndham (UK). A flying saucer lands in a sleepy English village, and all the local women subsequently become pregnant. Nine months later a brood of beautiful, talented and sinister half-human 'cuckoos' is born. An original and telling story. Published in the USA as *The Village of the Damned*, and later filmed under that title (1960; dir. Wolf Rilla).

Midworld (1975) ★★ Novel by Alan Dean Foster (USA). Attempts to exploit the natural resources of a planet almost entirely covered by an immense rain forest are prevented by nature-loving locals and the tiger-like carnivores which they regard as their pets. An obviously 'green' story: the forest itself has a sort of intelligence, controlling the animals living within it – which are in fact part of its reproductive cycle. 'His best single novel' – Gene Phillips, *20th-Century SF Writers*.

Mightiest Machine, The (1947) ★ Novel by John W. Campbell, Jr (USA), first serialized in 1934. Intrepid spacefarers are plunged into an alternative universe, where they discover descendants of ancient Earth-peoples and become embroiled in interplanetary war. Extravagant entertainment in the same rather juvenile vein as E. E. 'Doc' Smith's space epics of the period – though it displays a better grasp of science and engineering. Campbell's first novel in book form, and perhaps the best of his early space operas. Sequel: *The Incredible Planet* (1949).

Mile-Long Spaceship, The (1963) ★★ Collection by Kate Wilhelm (USA). Eleven sf stories from the late 1950s and early 60s. The first book by this capable author. Published in Britain as *Andover and the Android*.

Millenium (1976) ★ Novel by Ben Bova (USA), a sequel to *Kinsman*.

Tedious political goings-on in space as near-future Earth goes to the dogs. Notable for its enthusiastic 'prediction' of Reagan's Strategic Defence Initiative (weapons in orbit). Otherwise, it's a dull book. Later revised and republished as part of *The Kinsman Saga*.

Millennial Women (Kidd): see under *Eye of the Heron, The*.

Millennium (1983) ★★ Novel by John Varley (USA), expanded from his short story 'Air Raid' (1977). Time-travellers from a devastated future are in search of new blood to rebuild their society. They snatch present-day folk from our world when the latter are about to meet accidental death – the point being to prevent time paradoxes: only the 'doomed' may be saved. A cleverly worked novel which is to form the basis of a long-delayed film (1989; dir. Michael Anderson).

Milwaukee the Beautiful (1986) ★★ Novel by Dakota James (USA). The greenhouse effect precipitates an invasion of the United States from Latin America. The country breaks up, though Milwaukee independently maintains the old values. A satirical nightmare.

Mind Behind the Eye, The (Green): see *Gold the Man*.

Mind Master, The (Gunn), see *Dreamers, The*.

Mind of Mr Soames, The (1961) ★★ Novel by Charles Eric Maine (UK). A tale about the awakening and forced education of a man who has spent the first 30 years of his life in a coma. There is a rather prurient concentration on his sexual development. One of its author's better books, but it ends in tragedy. Filmed in 1970 (dir. Alan Cooke).

Mind of My Mind (1977) ★★ Novel by Octavia E. Butler (USA), sequel to *Patternmaster*. Well-written tale about a telepathic society of the future in which human minds are linked, not always happily. The later *Wild Seed* is a prequel, of sorts.

Mind One (1972) ★★ Novel by Mike Dolinsky (USA). A Jesuit priest-cum-psychiatrist and his female colleague discover a drug which induces telepathy. This brings them together sexually as well as mentally. Well characterized.

Mind Parasites, The (1967) ★ Novel by Colin Wilson (UK). Stilted version of the old plot about humanity being the tool of invisible alien beings (in this case they took over around the year 1800 and are responsible for both the despair and the dynamism of the 19th century) – together with speculations on psychology and history. A vaguely science-fictional horror story which doesn't live up to the author's reputation gained in other fields.

Mind Riders, The (1976) ★★★ Novel by Brian Stableford (UK). In the near future, the technology exists for a mass audience to enter emotional linkage with boxers. But these sportsmen do not perform in the flesh: their fights are simulated in a computer system controlled by supremely talented 'handlers' – and such men bear psychological scars. This is the story of one of them. A brief, sour, intelligent sf thriller.

Mind Spider and Other Stories, The (Leiber): see under *Big Time, The.*

Mind Switch (1965) ★★ Novel by Damon Knight (USA), expanded from his story 'A Visitor at the Zoo'. The hero accidentally switches minds with an alien, and the results are not entirely happy. One of Knight's more entertaining novels, but rather pointless. Published in Britain as *The Other Foot.*

Mind Thing, The (1961) ★ Novel by Fredric Brown (USA). An alien entity is able to insert itself into the minds of human beings, with fatal results. An adequate sf thriller by an author who wrote many successful crime novels. Brown's last sf novel, and one of his least.

Mind Transfer (1988) ★ Novel by Janet Asimov (USA). In a future of Roboticists versus Biofundamentalists, the former strive to perfect a robot which will carry a full human brain pattern. There's a certain amount of robotic sex, and a concern for the true meaning of 'humanness'. Mrs Asimov's first adult sf novel (she had already written many juvenile books, both with her husband and, earlier in her career, as Janet O. Jeppson).

Mind Trap, The (Morgan): see under *New Minds, The.*

Mind Warpers, The (Russell): see *With a Strange Device.*

Mindbridge (1977) ★★ Novel by Joe Haldeman (USA). A slug-like creature enables people to communicate telepathically with each other and the awesome L'Vrai. This patchy novel bears a slight resemblance to the peculiar *Runts of 61 Cygni C.*

Mindkiller (1982) ★ Novel by Spider Robinson (USA/Canada). A slickly-written near-future thriller in which the hero becomes involved in a conspiracy to 'mind-wipe' the human race – for its own good. 'A novel promoting the theme that great ends justify any means' – John P. Brennan, *20th-Century SF Writers.*

Mindplayers (1987) ★★ Novel by Pat Cadigan (USA). In a future of quasi-telepathic fun'n'games the heroine becomes a trained 'mindplayer'. Cadigan's first book, nicely realized but thin on plot. 'Bangs into play with panache and true grit on the part of gumption-filled Alexandra ... But the realization slowly dawns ... that there is really no story at all to tell, though a couple of hundred pages to tell it in, and the novel loses all steam long before gravity brings it to a halt' – John Clute.

Mindswap (1966) ★★ Novel by Robert Sheckley (USA). The hero swaps minds with a Martian, in order that both may enjoy a vacation on their respective planets. However, the alien makes off with the hero's body, and the latter finds himself stuck ... Sheckley in his usual absurd vein: another smoothly written episodic romp which contains many fine jokes but somehow doesn't quite add up to a novel.

Miracle Visitors (1978) ★★★ Novel by Ian Watson (UK). Researchers into altered states of consciousness become interested in flying saucers. Strange things begin to happen, and eventually the young hero visits the moon in a Ford Thunderbird automobile equipped for interplanetary flight. Sparky stuff, full of ideas: the ultimate UFO novel.

Mirror for Observers, A (1954) ★★★ Novel by Edgar Pangborn (USA). Long-lived but cunningly concealed Martian visitors meddle in humankind's affairs. In particular, they are interested in the fate of one young boy. A humane and rather 'literary' sf tale. International Fantasy award-winner, 1955.

Mirror Image (1972) ★★ Novel by Michael Coney (UK/Canada). Shape-changing aliens known as 'amorphs' can imitate human beings to perfection. Coney's first book, and a more than competent debut. The amorphs also feature in his later novel *Brontomek!*

Mirror in the Sky (1969) ★★ Novel by David S. Garnett (UK). A war-against-the-aliens story in which the war turns out to be more than it seems. A young writer's first novel. 'Action-adventure gently rippled by the New Wave worldview' – Brian Stableford.

Mirror of Minds (Zebrowski): see under *Omega Point, The*.

Mirrorshades: The Cyberpunk Anthology (1986) ★★★ Anthology edited by Bruce Sterling (USA). 'Cyberpunk' (a term said to have been coined by editor Gardner Dozois) was the most vigorous movement in the American sf of the 1980s: an attempt to combine New Wave literary virtues with punk-rock energy and a respect for high technology – in other words, hard sf done with style and a supposedly streetwise sensibility. At its best, as in the work of William Gibson and Sterling himself, it's brilliantly effective. Contributors to this banner-waving tome include Pat Cadigan, Gibson, Rudy Rucker, Lewis Shiner and John Shirley.

Missing Man (1975) ★★ Fix-up novel by Katherine MacLean (USA), expanded from her Nebula award-winning novella of the same title (1971). The psi-powered hero suffers social ostracism but nevertheless strives to use his abilities for the general good. The New York background is well depicted. A proficient treatment of an old theme by a writer best known for her earlier short stories.

Mission of Gravity (1954) ★★★ Novel by Hal Clement (USA). At the behest of human spacefarers, flat centipede-like creatures set out on a heroic mission across the surface of the heavy planet, Mesklin. Scrupulously thought out, this is one of the best loved examples of 'hard sf'. Belated sequel: *Star Light* (1971).

Mission to Moulokin (1979) ★ Novel by Alan Dean Foster (USA), sequel to

Icerigger. Ethan Fortune and friends, still stranded on the frozen world of Tran-ky-ky, make another desperate journey across the ice to help out some natives who are being exploited by aliens. Sequel: *The Deluge Drivers.*

Mission to the Stars (van Vogt): see *Mixed Men, The.*

Mission to Universe (1965) ★ Novel by Gordon R. Dickson (USA). A brilliant scientist invents a faster-than-light spacedrive, enabling assorted heroes to discover interesting and hostile alien races. Although there are a few hooks into the world of *Necromancer* (which provides the background to the 'Dorsai' series), this is basically a throwaway book.

Missionaries, The (1972) ★★ Novel by D. G. Compton (UK). Aliens arrive to spread their religion on Earth. They are all sweetness and light, but the human race reacts violently. A well-written, sourly comic fable.

Mr Da V, and Other Stories (1967) ★★ Collection by Kit Reed (USA). Many of these stories, dating from the 1950s and 60s, are fantasy rather than sf. In the title piece Leonardo is brought to the present day by magical means. Standouts include 'The Judas Bomb'. 'Kit Reed works with considerable success to sensitize the formula-ridden domestic moralities commonly found in genre magazines' – John Clute. Other sly collections by Reed include *The Killer Mice* (1976), *Other Stories, and the Attack of the Giant Baby* (1981) and *The Revenge of the Senior Citizens Plus* (1986).

Mister Justice (1973) ★★ Novel by Doris Piserchia (USA). Multi-stranded story of time travel and a vengeful superman vigilante, rather absurd but good fun. A very promising first novel.

Mixed Feelings (1974) ★★★ Collection by George Alec Effinger (USA). A debut volume of shorter works – sf, fantasy and the unclassifiable – by a young writer who is knowledgeable, witty, the master of a sly tone and unlikely subject matter. Effinger is clearly a 'genre-buster', one whose instinct is to go beyond the normal shapes and forms of the sf category.

Mixed Men, The (1952) ★ Fix-up novel by A. E. van Vogt (Canada/USA). The eponymous chaps have double brains, making them typical van-Vogtian *Übermenschen.* A far-out space adventure, involving robots, aliens and (of course) man's transcendent destiny. The sort of hokum at which this author excels. Republished as *Mission to the Stars.*

Mockingbird (1980) ★★ Novel by Walter Tevis (USA). In a post-literate future, where even the robots have more humanity than the humans, a young man rebels against his know-nothing culture. A smoothly-written love story with elements of social criticism.

Moderan (1971) ★★★ Collection by David R. Bunch (USA). Linked stories about a future technological 'utopia' where all is not well with the semi-mechanical inhabitants. Written in eccentric, lyrical style, this is its wayward author's only book (though he has contributed many stories to the sf magazines). 'A magnificent work, full of striking imagery' – Brian Stableford.

Molly Dear: The Autobiography of an Android (1988) ★★ Novel by Stephen Fine (USA). In this humorous, picaresque first-person narrative of an artificial woman the author makes a number of satirical digs at present-day targets. A would-be cross between Daniel Defoe (*Moll Flanders*) and John Sladek (see *Roderick*), it doesn't quite live up to its ambitions. Fine's first novel. 'Has moments of delightfully fresh humour exploiting the anarchic potential of black market data pills, programmed multiple personalities, and the like' – Faren Miller, *Locus*.

Molly Zero (1980) ★★ Novel by Keith Roberts (UK). In an unpleasant future Britain, the young heroine escapes from her huge, threatening school and becomes a wanderer. A well-written picaresque adventure, in the course of which the author rides a number of right-wing hobbyhorses.

Moment of Eclipse, The (1970) ★★★ Collection by Brian W. Aldiss (UK). Fourteen subtle tales, some comic, some sombre, all highly original. Includes several evocative, poetic titles: 'Orgy of the Living and the Dying', 'That Uncomfortable Pause Between Life and Art' and 'The Worm That Flies'. Some of these are late-60s New-Wave sf at its best.

Mona Lisa Overdrive (1988) ★★★

Novel by William Gibson (USA), sequel to *Neuromancer* and *Count Zero*. Complex four-ply narrative which cleverly picks up threads from the earlier books, tying them together most satisfactorily. A cyberpunk key work. 'Polished and urbane and sly, a rollercoaster of applied technique' – John Clute.

Monitor Found in Orbit (1974) ★★ Collection by Michael Coney (UK/Canada). The author's only collection of short sf to date. Unfortunately, it appeared too early in his career to contain much of his best work.

Monitor, the Miners, and the Shree, The (1980) ★ Novel by Lee Killough (USA). Fairly simple morality tale of a 'monitor'-heroine who investigates the competing territorial claims of some planetary miners and their rivals, the indigenous alien Shree. 'Almost all of the text is padding, and the story was probably originally conceived as a juvenile. There are few threatening words, and not an original one. What can you say?' – John Clute.

Monitors, The (1966) ★ Novel by Keith Laumer (USA). Benign aliens have invaded Earth and now keep the peace, though some humans plot against them. The story is played for laughs. Unsuccessfully filmed in 1969 (dir. Jack Shea).

Monkey Planet (Boulle): see *Planet of the Apes*.

Monsters and Medics (White): see under *Aliens Among Us, The*.

Monument (1974) ★★ Novel by Lloyd Biggle Jr. (USA), expanded from a 1962 magazine story. A renegade Earthman's knowledge helps the inhabitants of a beautiful alien planet to evade commercial exploitation. Quite an effective 'Edenic world' tale, and perhaps Biggle's best book.

Moon Children, The (1972) ★ Novel by Jack Williamson (USA). An attempt at a serious-minded 'comeback' novel by this author whose name was mainly associated with hoary space operas. He has produced better since.

Moon Goddess and the Son, The (1988) ★★ Novel by Donald Kingsbury (Canada). A think-tank of the rich and famous (and quite a few sf fans) studies Russian history and devises a military strategy for the 21st Century. There is a wealth of ideas and the characters are surprisingly human.

Moon is a Harsh Mistress, The (1966) ★★★ Novel by Robert A. Heinlein (USA). This account of a revolution in a former lunar penal colony is essentially a retelling of the American War of Independence in sf terms. The hero narrates it all in a vigorous futuristic dialect. There is copious background detail and some interesting political and sociological speculation – but, as with all the author's later books, the text is full of *talk*. Nevertheless, with its intelligent computer called Mycroft (after Sherlock Holmes's brother) and its by-now famous slogan 'TAN-STAAFL' (there ain't no such thing as a free lunch), it's entertaining enough: Heinlein's last decent novel. Hugo award-winner, 1967.

Moon of Ice (1988) ★★★ Novel by Brad Linaweaver (USA). A continuation of Joseph Goebbels' diaries in an alternative world in which the Nazis got the Bomb. His daughter Hilda becomes an anarchist and flees the Third Reich for the USA after warning her father about an attempt on his life by fanatical SS genetic engineers who plan to kill all non-Aryans. Politically intelligent and surprisingly humorous, the reader is reminded of just why Fascism is detestable even while shown the humanity of some individual Nazis.

Moonferns and Starsongs (Silverberg): see under *Needle in a Timestack*.

Moonstar Odyssey (1977) ★★ Novel by David Gerrold (USA). A sentimental treatment of the gender theme – set on a planet where the alien inhabitants are bisexual or hermaphroditic for part of their lives. Shades of Ursula Le Guin's *The Left Hand of Darkness*, although this work is much less distinguished.

Moorcock's Book of Martyrs (Moorcock): see under *Time Dweller, The*.

More Than Human (1953) ★★★★ Fix-up novel by Theodore Sturgeon (USA). A group of freaks and misfit children wander the backwoods of present-day America, and eventually form a psi-powered 'gestalt' which may evolve into a superbeing. Intense, moving and evocatively written – a masterpiece of its peculiar sort. International Fantasy award-winner, 1954.

More Wandering Stars (Dann): see under *Wandering Stars*.

More Women of Wonder (Sargent): see under *Women of Wonder*.

Moreau's Other Island (1980) ★★ Novel by Brian W. Aldiss (UK). The crew of a downed space shuttle are washed up on a remote island where dreadful experiments are in progress. A retelling of H. G. Wells's classic *The Island of Dr Moreau*, in late 20th-century terms. Published in the USA as *An Island Called Moreau*.

Moreta, Dragonlady of Pern (1982) ★ Novel by Anne McCaffrey (USA/ Ireland), a prequel to her 'Dragonriders of Pern' series. The dragonriders go to the races, get up to some jolly fun, and distribute vaccine to fend off a terrible plague, all at extreme length. Set about four centuries before *Dragonflight* and its sequels. Sequel (or rather, pre-prequel): *Dragonsdawn*.

Morlock Night (1979) ★★ Novel by K. W. Jeter (USA). A sequel to H. G. Wells's *The Time Machine*, wherein the nasty far-future Morlocks invade the London of 1892. It's played mainly for laughs, and shades into fantasy when King Arthur and Merlin are evoked to resolve the plot. Now billed as the original 'Steampunk' novel – i.e. a precursor of those 1980s sf tales, by Jeter and others, which have mock-Victorian settings.

Morning of Creation (Shupp): see under *With Fate Conspire*.

Morphodite, The (1981) ★★ Novel by M. A. Foster (USA). A shape-changing assassin, the 'morphodite' of the title, precipitates a revolution on a planet ruled by a dictatorial government. Fast-action stuff, inventively done. Sequels, in similar vein: *Transformer* (1983) and *Preserver* (1985).

Morrow's Ants (1975) ★★ Novel by Edward Hyams (UK). An immensely rich industrialist builds his ideal city and populates it with a thought-controlled citizenry. Hyams's last novel. 'Typically of writers not identified with the sf genre, [Hyams] tends to use sf components in a didactic fashion, in his case to considerable effect' – John Clute.

Mortal Gods (1978) ★ Novel by Jonathan Fast (USA). The hero attempts to discover who is killing off the media stars of the future, and falls in love with a sexy alien. Trivial.

Mortals and Monsters (del Rey): see under *Robots and Changelings*.

Mote in God's Eye, The (1974) ★★★ Novel by Jerry Pournelle and Larry Niven (USA), set in Pournelle's 'CoDominium' future. The new Empire encounters some highly specialized aliens who turn out to be more of a threat than at first supposed. A big bestseller: lots of pages, lots of characters, lots of astronomy and great fun – as well as being old-fashioned, overlong and politically unpleasant.

Motherlines (Charnas): see under *Walk to the End of the World.*

Movement of Mountains, The (1987) ★★★ Novel by Michael Blumlein (USA). An overweight doctor tells the story of his visit to another planet where he encountered a mysterious plague which ravaged a population of short-lived slave miners. A notable first novel: the author's bizarre medical imagination illuminates many scenes. 'One of the best books of the year' – John Clute.

Muller-Fokker Effect, The (1970) ★★★ Novel by John Sladek (USA). A man's entire personality is stored on computer tapes, and eventually he gains a new body – but not before a long chapter of accidents surrounding the tapes has led to general mayhem throughout America. A sharply satirical tale which in some ways was ahead of its time.

Multiface (Adlard): see under *Interface.*

Multiple Man, The (1976) ★ Novel by Ben Bova (USA). A near-future thriller which involves the concept of a cloned human being (the President of the USA in this case) – an idea which was very fashionable in the sf of the mid-1970s. This is one of the more routine treatments. (See, among others, Pamela Sargent's *Cloned Lives*, Kate Wilhelm's *Where Late the Sweet Birds Sang* and Gene Wolfe's *The Fifth Head of Cerberus* for better examples.)

Mutant (1953) ★★ Fix-up novel by Henry Kuttner (USA), originally published under the pseudonym 'Lewis Padgett'. A conjoining of five well-written but repetitive stories about the 'Baldies' – after-the-bomb telepaths who can never decide whether to integrate with or annihilate normal humans.

Mutant 59: The Plastic Eater (1971) ★★ Novel by Kit Pedler and Gerry Davis (UK). Eco-warning thriller about the havoc wreaked by a mutated virus which consumes plastic. Adequate near-future sf by the team that wrote the successful TV series *Doomwatch*.

Mutant Season, The (1989) ★★ Novel by Robert Silverberg and Karen Haber (USA), first in a projected series. In the 21st century, telepathic 'mutants' fight for their rights. An adequate latter-day treatment of well-worn sf themes. (Karen Haber is Silverberg's wife, and this represents her debut as a novelist.) 'Designed to be more a popular thriller than serious sf' – Carolyn Cushman, *Locus.*

Mutant Weapon, The (Leinster): see under *S.O.S. from Three Worlds.*

Mutants (1970) ★★ Collection by Gordon R. Dickson (Canada/USA). Includes 'Warrior' (part of the 'Dorsai' series) and 'Immortal' – later expanded into the novel *The Forever Man.*

Mutation (1989) ★★ Novel by Robin Cook (USA). A medical researcher at an in-vitro fertilization clinic uses genetic engineering to enhance the intellect of unborn children. Years later, his own son begins to behave very strangely at school. The medical background is impeccable (the author is a practising doctor) but the characterization leaves a little to be desired and the plot gets far-fetched towards the climax.

Mute (1981) ★ Novel by Piers Anthony (USA). Space adventure involving psi-powered animals. 'It bats along well, despite being obtrusively padded with repetitive banter and ludicrously-timed philosophizing (mostly during the fight scenes)' – Peter Garratt, *Interzone*.

My Brother's Keeper (1982) ★ Novel by Charles Sheffield (UK/USA). Badly injured twin brothers have their brains combined by surgical means. The resulting two-minds-in-one-body caper proves a disappointment. 'It's a very odd novel indeed. Starting off with some intensity to explore a split-brain problem to end all split-brain problems, it soon drops the issue like a couple of hot potatoes untimely ripped, and sidesteps into a Laumeresque international chase thriller' – John Clute.

My Experiences in the Third World War (Moorcock): see under *Time Dweller, The*.

My Father Immortal (1989) ★★ Novel by Michael D. Weaver (USA). Three newborn babes are cast into space and, as they grow towards puberty, machines teach them of their strange past ... A complex tale of suspended animation and post-nuclear horrors: crude in places, but powerful.

My Name is Legion (1976) ★★ Fix-up novel by Roger Zelazny (USA). Three futuristic detective stories about a slippery computer hacker who is able to adopt any identity he wishes. Slick, shallow stuff. The section entitled 'Home is the Hangman' won both the Hugo and Nebula awards, 1976.

My Petition for More Space (1974) ★★ Novel by John Hersey (USA). In an impossibly overcrowded future world, the hero tries to increase his few square feet of living space. A black dystopian warning by a mainstream American writer who has turned frequently to sf.

Mysterious Island, The (1874–75) ★★★ Novel by Jules Verne (France), sequel to *Twenty Thousand Leagues Under the Sea*. American balloonists are cast away on an uncharted island beneath which Captain Nemo lurks in his submarine, the Nautilus. This is *The Tempest* conflated with *Robinson Crusoe* – plus a large admixture of 19th-century technology and faith in Progress. Filmed in 1929 (dir. Lucien Hubbard) and in 1961 (dir. Cy Endfield).

Myths of the Near Future (1982) ★★★ Collection by J. G. Ballard (UK). Ten highly idiosyncratic and moody stories, some of them non-sf, which rework many of Ballard's favourite themes. Standouts are the title story and the very similar 'News from the Sun' (both subsequently reprinted in the American-published collection *Memories of the Space Age*).

N

Nagasaki Vector, The (Smith): see under *Probability Broach. The.*

Naked Came the Robot (1988) ★ Novel by Barry B. Longyear (USA). Daft satire about a world where almost everyone is enlisted in military service or works for the warlike 'Economy'. The protagonist sides with the downtrodden robots. For some reason, he is named after the hero of Stephen Crane's *The Red Badge of Courage* (1895) – and other literary references abound, over-burdening the novel. Too zany to be effective as social satire.

Naked Lunch, The (1959) ★★★★ Novel by William S. Burroughs. The ultimate satire on modern America: a Swiftian horror-vision of drugs, sex and corporate violence. Not really sf, but it does contain long passages set in such dystopian states as 'Freelandia' and 'Interzone' (a British sf magazine has been named after the latter).

Naked Sun, The (1957) ★★★ Novel by Isaac Asimov (USA), sequel to his *The Caves of Steel*. Detective Lije Baley and his robotic companion R. Daneel solve another mystery – this one on an alien planet where the wide open spaces may induce agora-phobia. In setting, it's a sort of inversion of the earlier novel, and it's equally cleverly plotted. Belated sequel: *The Robots of Dawn.*

Napoleon Disentimed (1987) ★★ Novel by Hayford Peirce (USA). A conman is propelled into an alternative Europe in which the French Empire still rules in 1992. He claims to be the Prince of Wales, falls in with some English nationalists plotting to change history, and attempts to reinvent champagne. A light-hearted and enjoyable first novel.

Narabedla Ltd. (1988) ★★ Novel by Frederik Pohl (USA). A New York accountant investigates the apparent death of a client who had signed a contract with the mysterious Nar-abedla company (pronounce it backwards). Soon, he too is whisked away into space by aliens ... 'A light-hearted diversion' – Dan Chow, *Locus.*

Narrow Land, The (1982) ★★★ Collection by Jack Vance (USA). Contains the novella-length 'Chateau D'If' and six short stories. The latter include 'Where Hesperus Falls', about the immortal Henry Revere whose keepers will not allow him to die, which contains the line: 'I was ninety-six thousand two hundred and thirty-two years old and life long ago lost that freshness and anticipation which makes it enjoyable.' Luckily for the reader, Vance is consistently fresh and enjoyable.

Natfact 7 (1984) Novel by John Tully (UK). Workers in a 21st-century forced labour camp in Devon campaign for equal rights and votes for the unemployed. Politically naïve, poorly written.

Native Tongue (1984) ★★★ Novel by Suzette Haden Elgin (USA). The author is an expert in linguistics, and in this highly praised novel about the future struggle between the sexes she invents 'Laadan', a secret language for women. Sequel: *The Judas Rose*.

Natural State and Other Stories (Knight): see *Three Novels*.

Nature's End (1986) ★ Novel by Whitley Strieber and James Kunetka (USA). The crazed leader of the 21st-century 'Depopulationist Party' attempts to solve the problem of global overpopulation by advocating mass suicide. An absurd stab at sf bestseller-dom by Strieber, who is a well-known horror novelist and author of allegedly 'factual' books about encounters with UFOs.

Nautilus Sanction, The (Hawke): see under *Ivanhoe Gambit, The.*

Navigator's Sindrome (1983) ★★ Novel by Jayge Carr (USA). A female member of the navigators' guild is threatened with enslavement on a decadent backwoods planet. Space adventure with a light feminist edge, intelligently done. Quasi-sequel: *The Treasure in the Heart of the Maze* (1985).

Neanderthal Planet (Aldiss): see *Intangibles Inc. and Other Stories.*

Nebula Alert (Chandler): see under *Space Mercenaries.*

Nebula Award Stories 1965 (1966) ★★★ Anthology edited by Damon Knight (USA), the first of a long series of annual volumes which have been edited by various hands. Knight virtually invented the Science Fiction Writers of America organization and its yearly awards, the Nebulas. This initial collection of Nebula winners and runners-up includes fine work by Brian Aldiss, Roger Zelazny and others. Later editors of the *Nebula Award Stories* series have included both the writers just named, in addition to other luminaries such as Harry Harrison, Poul Anderson, James Blish, Clifford D. Simak, Isaac Asimov, Ursula Le Guin and Samuel R. Delany. Inevitably, the quality of the volumes has varied.

Nebula Maker (Stapledon): see under *Star Maker.*

Necromancer (1968) ★ Novel by Gordon R. Dickson (USA). Paul

Formain, an engineer in the 21st century, develops psychic powers and is inducted into the semi-secret Chantry Guild. The rather mystical ending looks forward to the origins of the various space-faring cultures which appear in the author's 'Dorsai' series. Republished as *No Room for Man*.

Needle (1950) ★★ Novel by Hal Clement (USA). An alien cop takes over the body of a human lad, using him to pursue an alien criminal who has taken refuge on Earth. An adequately exciting tale of possession from outer space, by a writer who is well versed in the hard sciences. Clement's first novel. Belated sequel: *Through the Eye of a Needle* (1978).

Needle in a Timestack (1966) ★★ Collection by Robert Silverberg (USA). Early Silverberg stories: some are shallow, representative of the sort of apprentice material he was churning out so copiously in the late 1950s; but others, such as 'The Pain Peddlers' and 'To See the Invisible Man' (both 1963) prefigure the powerful novels to come. There have been many Silverberg collections (some of which recombine the same stories) and among them are *Dimension Thirteen* (1969), *Moonferns and Starsongs* (1971), *The Reality Trip and Other Implausibilities* (1972), *Sundance and Other SF Stories* (1974) and *Capricorn Games* (1976).

Nemesis (1989) ★★ Novel by Isaac Asimov (USA). The action alternates between a young girl growing up on Rotor, a space habitat which has travelled to a red-dwarf star that is approaching the solar system, and her father on Earth, who is involved in a project to build a starship. This is Asimov's only recent adult sf novel which is not connected with the earlier 'Robot', 'Foundation' or 'Galactic Empire' series – although there are hints that even this may some day be included in the Grand Design.

Neon Lotus (1988) ★★ Novel by Marc Laidlaw (USA). A little American girl has a mysterious ability to speak Tibetan, and it seems she is the reincarnation of an assassinated sage from the Roof of the World. The complex sf/fantasy adventure which follows makes good use of Buddhist lore. A pleasingly original work.

Neptune's Cauldron (1981) Novel by Michael Coney (UK/Canada). Perhaps the least impressive of this usually competent author's novels.

Neq the Sword (1975) ★ Novel by Piers Anthony (USA), sequel to *Sos the Rope* and *Var the Stick*. Neq attempts to rebuild the civilization that was destroyed in the previous episodes of the series. Unfortunately the narrative suffers badly from a brutality that was almost avoided in the earlier volumes.

Nerves (1956) ★★ Novel by Lester del Rey (USA), an expansion of his 1942 magazine story of the same title. Selfless engineers battle to control an accident in a nuclear power plant. All turns out well, and in some ways the heroics anticipate those of the real-life Chernobyl disaster. Reasonably tense, if unconvincing in its denouement, it's notable for being one of the first works to deal realistically with the problems of civilian atomic power.

Net, The (1987) ★ Novel by Loren J. MacGregor (USA). A first novel which is woefully short on plot and long on 'style', it concerns the adventures of a female space captain who has a run-in with a business rival. 'Obviously written by someone who has read Delany's *Nova* about twenty times, and Gibson's *Neuromancer* twice' – Scott Bradfield, *Foundation*.

Neural Atrocity, The (Farren): see under *Quest of the DNA Cowboys, The*.

Neuromancer (1984) ★★★★ Novel by William Gibson (USA). Flashy first novel which deals in 'cyberspace' – the realm where computerized information takes on visible, three-dimensional form. A thriller plot is set against a background of sleazy cityscapes littered with electronic gadgetry. Fast, knowledgeable, and poetic in its effects. 'Keep Gibson from dumb quest plots that read like TV pilots for tax-loss mini-series, and he'll write one or two of the best books of the coming decade' – John Clute. Hugo, Nebula and Philip K. Dick Memorial award- winner, 1985, Quasi-sequels: *Count Zero* and *Mona Lisa Overdrive*.

Neutral Stars, The (Morgan & Kippax): see under *Thunder of Stars, A*.

Neutron Star (1968) ★★★ Collection by Larry Niven (USA). Some of the earliest and best stories from the author's 'Known Space' series, such as 'Flatlander' and 'The Handicapped' (where we find out what really happened to the Slaver Empire). Why does Niven write so many stories in which a spaceship falls foul of a small but massive object? The title story, in which precisely that happens, won a 1967 Hugo award. Another early Niven collection, of similar quality, is *The Shape of Space* (1969).

Never the Twain (1987) ★★ Novel by Kirk Mitchell (USA). A present-day shyster devises a way to get rich quick, using his friend's newly invented time machine. This involves travelling into the 19th-century past and meeting up with Mark Twain and Bret Harte. Not unexpectedly, his plans go awry. An amusing time-twister. 'The plot alone guarantees an entertaining romp, but Mitchell achieves more than this. The characters reveal unexpected depths' – Faren Miller, *Locus*.

Neverness (1988) ★★★ Novel by David Zindell (USA). In a densely populated galaxy, the mathematically-skilled members of the Order of Pilots guide spacecraft through the 'manifolds' of hyperspace. The narrator is one such, and he embarks on a dangerous quest to uncover the mystery of exploding stars (and humanity's destiny). A first novel of vaulting ambition, evidently influenced by Gene Wolfe's *The Book of the New Sun*. '*Neverness* differs from its model chiefly through bypassing the recursive closures of the plot of *The Book*. It is, in comparison, an open, relaxed, expansive tale' – John Clute.

New Arrivals, Old Encounters (1979) ★★★ Collection by Brian W. Aldiss (UK). Twelve highly varied stories, ranging from the comic 'Amen and Out' (1966) to the atmospheric fable 'One Blink of the Moon' (1979). The book's title wryly encapsulates an essential Aldissian theme: encounters with the Old Adam in a shiny new future.

New Atlantis, The (1975) ★★★ Anthology edited by Robert Silverberg (USA). Three long stories of high literary merit: 'Silhouette' by Gene Wolfe, 'The New Atlantis' by Ursula Le Guin and 'A Momentary Taste of Being' by James Tiptree Jr. All are originals in the book, and have since been reprinted in the authors' own collections. This is one of a series of interesting 'triples' which Silverberg has edited. Others include *Chains of the Sea* (1973), *Threads of Time* (1974), *The Crystal Ship* (1976) and *Triax* (1977).

New Constellations (Disch & Naylor): see under *Bad Moon Rising*.

New Improved Sun, The (Disch): see under *Bad Moon Rising*.

New Minds, The (1967) ★★ Novel by Dan Morgan (UK), first in his 'Minds' series. A small group of telepaths is theatened by another psionic power. A well-handled but fundamentally unoriginal ESP yarn. Sequels, all in similar vein: *The Several Minds*

(1969), *The Mind Trap* (1970) and *The Country of the Mind* (1975).

New SF: An Original Anthology of Speculative Fiction, The (1969) ★★ Anthology edited by Langdon Jones (UK). Mainly British stories, and all in a New-Wave experimental vein. The book reads like a particularly well-filled issue of *New Worlds* magazine of the same vintage. Includes pieces by Aldiss, Moorcock, Sladek and Zoline, and to some readers many of them will not seem to be sf at all. Unfortunately, J. G. Ballard's contribution is merely a transcript of a radio interview.

New Springtime, The (Silverberg): see under *At Winter's End*.

New Women of Wonder, The (Sargent): see under *Women of Wonder*.

New Worlds: An Anthology (1983) ★★★ Anthology edited by Michael Moorcock (UK). Large uncompromising selection of prose and poetry from sf's most avant-garde magazine (the choices were first published in 1965–75). Wayward stuff, some of it brilliant, some of it perplexing. Contributors include Aldiss, Ballard, Disch, Sladek, Spinrad and Zoline.

New Writings in SF (1964–76) ★★ Anthology series edited by John Carnell and, after the original editor's death in 1972, by Kenneth Bulmer (UK). This long run of 29 anthologies contained original material by mainly British writers. Although the stated purpose at the outset was to publish exciting, path-breaking work, most of the stories were in fact old-fashioned in style – in marked contrast to the contents of the magazine *New Worlds* which Carnell had edited until early 1964. On the whole it was the safe 'second rank' of authors that Carnell attracted to these anthologies: the more adventurous writers stayed with the magazine under Michael Moorcock's editorship.

News from Nowhere, or An Epoch of Rest (1890) ★★★ Novel by William Morris (UK). The narrator awakes in a world where machines have been banished and everyone works as he or she wishes (with a strong emphasis on handicrafts). A utopian vision of the future which celebrates a kind of aesthetic socialism, and also prefigures some of the concerns of later environmentalists.

Next of Kin (1958) ★★ Novel by Eric Frank Russell (UK), originally published in the USA as *The Space Willies*. A human prisoner takes on his alien jailers and, of course, outwits them. It's essentially a World War II yarn in futuristic guise (as was Russell's *Wasp*), but nevertheless it's one of this sprightly author's most engaging space-adventure comedies.

Next Stop the Stars (Silverberg): see under *Silent Invaders, The*.

Nick of Time, The (1985) ★★ Fix-up novel by George Alec Effinger (USA). A zany time-travel comedy which opens with the hero going back from 1996 to the New York World's Fair of 1939. All manner of complications follow, but the delight is mainly in the telling. At one point the author breaks off to harangue the reader and to advertise his forthcoming sequel. Sequel: *The Bird of Time* (1986).

Night Mayor, The (1989) ★★★ Novel by Kim Newman (UK), based on the background of his short story 'Dreamers' (1984). In the 21st century, the movie industry has been replaced by the computerized dream industry. Professional dreamer Susan Bishopric is sent into the imaginary world of an 'escaped' convict in order to bring him back to the reality of his sentence. In his black-and-white dream world, it's always 2.30 a.m. and raining – and there's a gunman round every corner. A highly entertaining first novel which should be of particular interest to lovers of *film noir*.

Night of Kadar, The (1978) ★★ Novel by Garry Kilworth (UK). The settlers of a new planet – who have arrived there in frozen, embryonic form – have to fend for themselves when the machines which were supposed to educate them break down. A well-characterized adventure story.

Night of Light (1966) ★★ Novel by Philip José Farmer (USA), expanded from a 1957 magazine novella. One of the author's series heroes, Father John Carmody (see also *Father to the Stars*), here encounters a fearful upwelling of personae from the unconscious – on a planet called Dante's Joy. An odd, intermittently powerful treatment of alien religion.

Night of the Puudly, The (Simak): see *All the Traps of Earth*.

Night Walk (1967) ★★ Novel by Bob Shaw (UK). The hero is unjustly condemned to a remote prison on a far planet. He is also blinded. This is the story of how he devises a new form of sight and makes his escape. A fine sf thriller, with a taut plot and good imagery. Shaw's first novel.

Nightfall and Other Stories (1969) ★★★ Collection by Isaac Asimov (USA). A big volume of mainly old pieces. The title story (1941), about a daylit world from which the stars are almost always invisible, has often been voted the most popular sf short story ever (it creaks, but it still packs a sense of wonder). This collection has been split into two books for paperback reprints.

Nightmare Blue (1975) ★ Novel by George Alec Effinger and Gardner Dozois (USA). Fast-paced sf adventure which is scarcely representative of either author at his best. A piece of hack fiction by two intelligent writers. (Dozois's first novel.)

Nightmare Express (1979) ★★ Novel by Isidore Haiblum (USA). A cod private-eye caper set in the New York(s) of alternative time-lines. Perhaps this minor author's most ambitious work. 'Lots of mean streets, but humour too' – Brian Stableford.

Nightmare Journey (1975) ★★ Novel by Dean R. Koontz (USA). A complex far-future tale involving aliens, telepathy, genetic engineering and enhanced animals. Full of liberal all-creatures-are-brothers sentiments. One of the last sf novels Koontz

wrote before turning to a more lucrative career as an author of Stephen King-style supernatural-horror yarns.

Nightwatch (1977) ★★ Novel by Andrew M. Stephenson (UK). As a possibly threatening alien spacecraft approaches, humanity establishes a robotic line of defence on the moon and elsewhere in the solar system. The technical detail is convincing. A first novel, and an all-too-rare example of effective hard sf by a British writer.

Nightwings (1969) ★★★ Fix-up novel by Robert Silverberg (USA). In a post-technological far future, Earth is invaded by aliens, and the 'Watcher' hero must roam the world's ancient cities in disguise – accompanied by a winged girl. A lyrical picaresque, very pleasingly done: one of Silverberg's finest. A section of this book won the 1969 Hugo award as best sf novella.

Nightworld (1979) ★ Novel by David F. Bischoff (USA). Sf/fantasy crossover in which a rogue computer has filled a colony world with android versions of traditional bogeymen – vampires, werewolves, etc. Humorous adventure stuff, all a bit silly. Sequel, in similar vein: *The Vampires of Nightworld* (1981).

Nimrod Hunt, The (1986) ★★ Novel by Charles Sheffield (UK/USA). Spacefaring cyborg watchmen, designed to search out alien races and protect humanity from possible attack, go rogue. The ingenious plot poses questions about the nature of intelligence, but it's a pity the prose and characterization are so clunky.

Nine Billion Names of God: The Best Short Stories of Arthur C. Clarke, The (1967) ★★★ Collection by Arthur C. Clarke (UK). An American-published compendium of the author's best-known pieces. The excellent title story is reprinted from *The Other Side of the Sky*.

Nine by Laumer (1967) ★★ Collection by Keith Laumer (USA). Nine fast-moving tales by this prolific, usually exciting, often humorous but sometimes slapdash writer of sf thrillers. It contains such popular items as 'End as a Hero' and 'A Trip to the City'. Later Laumer collections (none truly outstanding) include *It's a Mad, Mad, Mad Galaxy* (1968), *Once There Was a Giant* (1971) and *The Best of Keith Laumer* (1976).

Nine Hundred Grandmothers (1970) ★★★★ Collection by R. A. Lafferty. None of these absurd and blackly humorous short stories can be described as 'typical' of Lafferty: choosing one at random, 'The Primary Education of the Cameroi' is the report of a PTA visit from Dubuque to an alien planet (containing their school curriculum as an appendix) and it's wonderful.

Nine Tomorrows (1959) ★★ Collection by Isaac Asimov (USA). Nine competent short stories by science fiction's equivalent of Agatha Christie. Reliable entertainment.

Nineteen Eighty-Four (1949) ★★★★ Novel by George Orwell (UK). Small-time bureaucrat Winston Smith rebels against the dictatorial society of Big Brother and the Thought Police. The greatest of all 20th-century anti-utopias – a book which has changed the world. Filmed in 1955 (dir. Michael Anderson) and, inevitably, in 1984 (dir. Michael Radford).

1985 (1978) ★ Short novel by Anthony Burgess (UK). The fiction is prefaced by a lengthy essay on Orwell's *Nineteen Eighty-Four* – the acknowledged inspiration for what follows. The story itself depicts a dystopian (or 'cacotopian') Britain of 1985 which is dominated by trades unions and Arab immigrants. One of the talented Burgess's most trivial and dyspeptic works. 'The sort of novel one suspects would be written by a tax-exile who reads right-wing British newspapers in his Monte Carlo home' – Christopher Priest, *Foundation*.

Nitrogen Fix, The (1980) ★★ Novel by Hal Clement (USA). On a future Earth, where the air is unbreathable and the water acidic, a few humans survive by precarious means. Alien observers arrive on the scene but are unable to do much to assist. An uncharacteristically grim tale by this old master of hard sf. 'What Clement has done is create a wonderland – a place where there is fire but no flame and many plants are explosive on impact, where life is a continuous, but grievously short, SCUBA dive, and where there is no way the hero can save the world' – Algis Budrys, *Fantasy & Science Fiction*.

No Blade of Grass (Christopher): see *Death of Grass, The.*

No Brother, No Friend (1976) ★ Novel by Richard C. Meredith (USA). The protagonist of *At the Narrow Passage* flees his alien employers through an alternative America accompanied by the wife of the German aristocrat he failed to kidnap. Good fun.

No Direction Home (1975) ★★★ Collection by Norman Spinrad (USA). Eleven sf stories with a socially relevant edge. Includes many of the author's best – 'The Big Flash' (1969), 'A Thing of Beauty' (1972) and 'The Lost Continent' (1970), among other lively and provocative pieces. A later volume, *The Star-Spangled Future* (1979), reprints most of these, along with some from Spinrad's inferior first collection, *The Last Hurrah of the Golden Horde* (1970), and four new pieces.

No Enemy But Time (1982) ★★★ Novel by Michael Bishop (USA). A black American travels two million years backwards in time to investigate early African ape-folk. He eventually 'marries' a hominid woman whom he calls Helen. Serious speculative sf, beautifully described though a trifle slow-moving. Nebula award-winner, 1983.

No Future in It (1962) ★★ Collection by John Brunner (UK). Clever, often downbeat, sf pieces by a bright young author. Includes the moving 'The Windows of Heaven' (1956), in which a returning astronaut decides to reseed an Earth which has been cleared of all life by using the only resources he has – his own body and the bacteria which live within it.

No Man Friday (1956) ★★★ Novel by Rex Gordon (S. B. Hough, UK). As the title suggests, this is a retelling of *Robinson Crusoe* in sf terms. An English astronaut is marooned on Mars, and must make shift to survive as best he can. Eventually he meets an intelligent Martian lifeform. Apart from a ropy start, it's remarkably gripping: Gordon's best novel. Published in the USA as *First on Mars*. (The film *Robinson Crusoe on Mars* [1964; dir. Byron Haskin] is not avowedly based on this novel, but perhaps it should have been.)

No Man on Earth (1964) ★★ Novel by Walter Moudy (USA). The tribulations of the son of an alien father and a human mother. It turns into a galaxy-spanning superman story, written with some feeling. Apparently it is the author's only book. 'Rather compellingly told' – John Clute.

No Place on Earth (1958) ★★ Novel by Louis Charbonneau (USA). Conventional dreadful-warning tale about future overpopulation and mechanization. A first novel, written in competent journalistic style.

No Room for Man (Dickson): see *Necromancer.*

No Time Like Tomorrow (Aldiss): see *Space, Time and Nathaniel.*

Nomad of Time, The (1984) ★★ Omnibus by Michael Moorcock

(UK), containing his three 'Oswald Bastable' novels: *The Warlord of the Air, The Land Leviathan* (1974) and *The Steel Tsar* (1981).

Nomads of Gor (Norman): see under *Tarnsman of Gor.*

Non-Born King, The (May): see under *Many-Coloured Land, The.*

Non-Statistical Man, The (1964) ★★ Collection by Raymond F. Jones (USA). Sf tales of the 1950s, mostly based on intriguing ideas. The title piece is about an insurance man whose work is thrown into disarray by the discovery that some people have perfect intuition. Also included here is the well-loved wish-fulfilment story 'Noise Level', about scientists who successfully brainstorm the problem of antigravity.

Non-Stop (1958) ★★★★ Novel by Brian W. Aldiss (UK). Savages roam among the overgrown hydroponics in the endless corridors of a vast spacecraft which is apparently embarked on a generations-long voyage to the stars. Well written, with lively characterization. Its author's first novel, and still one of his best. Published in the USA as *Starship.*

Nopalgarth (Vance): see *Brains of Earth, The.*

Norstrilia (1964–68) ★★★ Novel by Cordwainer Smith (USA). A boy from the sheep-farming planet Norstrilia becomes so rich that he is able to 'buy' Old Earth. Highly original, wacky and episodic, this was its author's only full-length novel. Originally published in two volumes as *The Planet Buyer* and *The Underpeople*, the combined book was first issued posthumously in 1975.

Northshore (Tepper): see *Awakeners, The.*

Not by Bread Alone (1983) ★★ Novel by Naomi Mitchison (UK). Plant biologists and corporate powers succeed in feeding the world, but unforeseen problems arise and an enclave of Australian Aborigines decides to reject the apparent boon of 'Freefood'. A short philosophical tale by a sprightly author well into her 80s. 'Rapid and melancholy and wise ... a tract for the times' – John Clute.

Not for Glory (1988) ★ Fix-up novel by Joel Rosenberg (USA). A new planet, 'Metzada', has been colonized by refugee Israelis, who protect themselves against various hazards with an elite fighting force – which is now available for hire to all and sundry. A curious, talky example of 'mercenary' space opera with, it would seem, a militantly Zionist slant.

Not This August (1955) ★★ Novel by C. M. Kornbluth (USA). The Russians and Chinese successfully invade America, but the lucky hero is able to fight back with a secret spacecraft. A well-written narrative, as one would expect from this author – but it's also a bundle of paranoid Cold-War clichés. Highly regarded in its time, it's now almost a forgotten book (though Frederik Pohl issued a revised edition in 1981). Published in Britain as *Christmas Eve*.

Not to Mention Camels (1976) ★★ Novel by R. A. Lafferty (USA). The author's fertile imagination gets the better of him for once – this weird novel of a man who survives after death by reincarnating himself in a succession of alternative realities approaches both incomprehensibility and brutality at times.

Not Without Sorcery (Sturgeon): see *Without Sorcery*.

Notions: Unlimited (Sheckley): see under *Pilgrimage to Earth*.

Nova (1968) ★★★ Novel by Samuel R. Delany (USA). Extremely flashy space opera, in which Captain Lorq von Ray plunges his ship into a star which is on the point of going nova. His purpose is to scoop up a rare element which will make him rich enough to change the economic balance of the galaxy. Joyous, lively, full of telling detail – one of the most 'utopian' visions of a spacefaring future ever penned.

Nova Express (1964) ★★★ Novel by William S. Burroughs (USA). The Nova Mob attempts to take over the Earth, in a 'hallucinatory interplanetary cops and robbers game'. Horrific, fragmentary and very funny in its ghastly way, this book about drug addiction and other forms of manipulation is in much the same vein as the author's *Naked Lunch*.

Novelty (1989) ★★★★ Collection by John Crowley (USA). Four imaginative stories, of which two are certainly sf. 'In Blue' is a sensitive study of character set against the background of a future dystopian society. The longest tale, 'Great Work of Time', is about a trip to an alternative time-line in which a successful British empire looms large. 'Crowley does such a number on the time-paradox story that I suddenly realize I am in the presence of a piece likely to become as much a benchmark as [Heinlein's] "By His Bootstraps" was 50 years before' – Paul Brazier, *Interzone*.

Now Begins Tomorrow (Knight): see *First Voyages*.

Now to the Stars (1956) Novel by W. E. Johns (UK), sequel to *Return to Mars*. Episodic account of travels around the universe, with an anti-war and anti-nuclear subtext some might find strange from the creator of Biggles. Further books in this fondly-remembered juvenile series are very similar: *To Outer Space* (1957), *The Edge of Beyond* (1958), *The Death Rays of Ardilla* (1959), *To Worlds Unknown* (1960), *The Quest for the Perfect Planet* (1961), *Worlds of Wonder* (1962) and *The Man Who Vanished Into Space* (1963).

Now Wait for Last Year (1966) ★★★ Novel by Philip K. Dick (USA). Against a standard space-war background, the author spins a daft and delightful yarn about hallucinogenic drugs, robotic quasi-life, psychological regression and political chicanery. Hastily written, but all the rich Dickian obsessions are in full flow.

Null-A Three (van Vogt): see under *Players of Null-A, The*.

Number of the Beast –, The (1980) Novel by Robert A. Heinlein (USA). An amazing farrago of sf and fantasy in which various fictional worlds intersect and the characters come to realize that they themselves are equally unreal. Lazarus Long (from *Time Enough for Love*) and Jubal Harshaw (from *Stranger in a Strange Land*) turn up again, as do many other familiar figments. It's all very jokey on the surface, but a desperate nightmare of solipsism seems to lie below. Dreadful old rubbish: one of Heinlein's worst.

Nutzenbolts and More Troubles with Machines (1975) ★★ Collection by Ron Goulart (USA). Madcap reports from the man-machine inter-face (for an earlier volume in the same vein see *Broke Down Engine*). Almost all Goulart's stories are written in a lean, dry, speedy, deadpan manner, with lots of crisp dialogue. Some readers find them very funny; others don't.

O

O Master Caliban! (1976) ★★ Novel by Phyllis Gotlieb (Canada). Mutant children and their alien friends battle against a dominating computer on a far planet. Despite its juvenile-sounding subject matter, this is an engaging moral tale. Sequel: *Heart of Red Iron* (1989).

Oath of Fealty (1981) ★★★ Novel by Larry Niven and Jerry Pournelle (USA). A self-governing arcology towers over near-future Los Angeles, its rulers driven to desperate measures to free one of their fellows imprisoned by the city police force. Niven moderates the effect of Pournelle's naïve social Darwinism. The novel that popularized the phrase 'Think of it as evolution in action.'

Observers, The (Knight): see under CV.

Occam's Razor (1957) ★★ Novel by David Duncan (USA). Two strange beings from another dimension enter a secret scientific base and cause pandemonium. Well written and sharply characterized, even if the ideas are rather weak. 'Duncan is one of the most accomplished stylists to have worked in sf and fantasy, yet he is an almost forgotten figure' – George Zebrowski, *20th-Century SF Writers*.

Ocean on Top (1976) ★ Novel by Hal Clement (USA). Rather flat account of an agent of a 21st-century world government who discovers an independent community living on the bed of the Pacific.

Octagon (1981) ★★ Novel by Fred Saberhagen (USA). The tale of a computerized war game which turns very nasty. An ingenious fictional exploitation of the early 1980s vogue for fantasy-based home-computer pastimes.

October the First is Too Late (1966) ★★ Novel by Fred Hoyle (UK). The Earth becomes mysteriously chopped up into different temporal zones: Britain remains in the present day, but much of continental Europe is located at the time of World War I and Greece is stuck in the 5th century BC. A fairly torpid scientific thriller with some interesting philosophizing and an intriguing premise (similar to the one which David Masson used in a short story, 'Lost Ground', published in the same year: collected in *The Caltraps of Time*).

Odd Job No. 101 and Other Future Crimes and Intrigues (1975) ★ Collection by Ron Goulart (USA). A cross between crime fiction and sf: bright, sharp, but repetitive tales about hero Jose Silvera and his run-ins with various futuristic crooks. 'Light reading with a long needle' – Richard E. Geis, *SF Review*.

Odd John (1935) ★★★ Novel by Olaf Stapledon (UK). The life story of a supremely talented individual, an 'Overman' born out of his time, who eventually founds a utopian community on a Pacific island. It's comparatively minor Stapledon, less cosmic than *Star Maker* and less touching than *Sirius*; and it shows its age in many respects; yet it remains one of the fundamental stories of the coming superman.

Odyssey (1987) ★ Novel by Michael P. Kube-McDowell (USA), first of the 'Isaac Asimov's Robot City' shared-world series. An amnesiac space traveller is revived by robots after an accident, then kidnapped by aliens. It's set against the background of Asimov's 'Robot' series and the interest is in the extension of the famous Three Laws of Robotics to aliens and to societies consisting entirely of robots. Sequels: *Suspicion* by Mike McQuay (1987), *Cyborg* by William F. Wu (1987), *Prodigy* by Arthur Byron Cover (1988), *Refuge* by Rob Chilson (1988)

and *Perihelion* by William F. Wu (1988).

Of All Possible Worlds (1955) ★★★ Collection by William Tenn (USA). Eight drily witty stories, including the savage 'The Liberation of Earth' – in which alien invaders are depicted as doing to planet Earth what the western powers have done to so much of the Third World. Also notable is 'Generation of Noah', about the threat of the atomic bomb. Tenn's first book.

Of Man and Manta (1986) ★★★ Omnibus by Piers Anthony (USA), comprising three novels: *Omnivore*, *Orn* and *Ox*.

Of Men and Monsters (1968) ★★ Novel by William Tenn (USA), expanded from his novella 'The Men in the Walls' (1963). Invading aliens have reduced human beings to the status of scavenging mouse-like creatures living in the walls of their vast domiciles. A notably sardonic adventure yarn, and talented short-story writer William Tenn's only sf novel.

Of the Fall (1989) ★★★ Novel by Paul J. McAuley (UK). The long-expected spaceship from Earth fails to arrive, and civilization on the planet Elysium collapses into destructive war. A somewhat helpless group of academics try to preserve what they can of Earth culture in the face of oppressive politics and the overwhelming presence of artificial intelligences which have long been making all the real decisions. Published in the UK as *Secret*

Harmonies (but the author prefers the American title).

Off Center (Knight): see under *In Deep*.

Off-Planet (1988) ★★ Collection by Clifford D. Simak (USA), edited by Francis Lyall. Seven old magazine stories, ranging from 'Ogre' (1943) to 'The Observer' (1972), six of them never collected before. Untypical of the author in that they are all set in outer space (he was most effective when he stuck to the bluff-tops of rural Wisconsin), they are nevertheless enjoyable in an undemanding way. Simak was one of the best of American sf's plain tellers of far-out tales.

Old Die Rich and Other Science Fiction Stories, The (1955) ★★ Collection by H. L. Gold (USA). Gold became famous as the editor of *Galaxy* magazine in the 1950s (an editor who was always rewriting his authors' stories), but most of these sf and fantasy tales date from an earlier period in his career. They are pleasantly entertaining, if uninspired, and they are accompanied by some interesting 'how-to' notes which make the book a kind of primer for would-be writers of sf.

Omega Point, The (1972) ★★ Novel by George Zebrowski (USA). A space opera with metaphysical pretensions, apparently influenced by the theories of Teilhard de Chardin. Zebrowski's first novel. Prequel: *Ashes and Stars*. Sequel: *Mirror of Minds* (the latter is included only in an omnibus volume entitled *The Omega Point Trilogy*, 1983).

Omicron Invasion, The (Goldin): see under *Imperial Stars, The*.

Omnivore (1968) ★★★ Novel by Piers Anthony (USA). Humans adrift on a fungal planet. The theme is the analogy between the relationships of the three main characters, the biological processes active in their world and ours, and the political forces which control their lives. On both planets omnivores are the dominant species, and the State is the greatest omnivore of all. Sequel: *Orn*.

On My Way to Paradise (1989) ★★ Novel by Dave Wolverton (USA). This over-lengthy but well-written first novel opens in 24th-century Panama, a vividly-depicted transit zone for refugees. However, the complex narrative, which involves rejuvenation and body-switching, soon takes off into outer space. A promising debut which has its longueurs.

On the Beach (1957) ★★ Novel by Nevil Shute (UK/Australia). Following a nuclear war in the northern hemisphere, the population of Australia and the crew of an American submarine await a slow death from drifting clouds of radiation. An admirably dark (though sentimental) bestseller-with-a-message from a very popular writer. Filmed in 1959 (dir. Stanley Kramer).

On the Run (Dickson): see *Mankind on the Run*.

On Wheels (1973) ★★ Novel by John Jakes (USA). A story about vagrants of the freeways in a near-future America, where the slogan is 'Life, liberty and the pursuit of mileage'.

This is generally thought to be the most effective sf book by a minor writer who has subsequently become famous for his bestselling historical novels (the 'Kent Family Chronicles', etc.).

On Wings of Song (1979) ★★★★ Novel by Thomas M. Disch (USA). A young couple escape the repressive 'Farm Belt' states of 21st-century Middle America. However, their experiments with machine-assisted out-of-body flight come to a tragic conclusion. A marvellous novel, richly entertaining. John W. Campbell award-winner, 1980.

Once There Was a Giant (Laumer): see under *Nine by Laumer*.

One (1953) ★★★ Novel by David Karp (USA). In a materially bountiful but totalitarian future, the rebelliously intellectual hero is brainwashed into a kind of conformity. A grim dystopia which traded on the post-Korean War obsession with mental conditioning techniques, and which was highly regarded in its day. Its author's only sf work.

One Against the Legion (Williamson): see under *Legion of Space, The*.

One Hundred and Two H-Bombs (1966) ★★ Collection by Thomas M. Disch (USA). Sardonic sf and fantasy stories, mainly written in the early 1960s, when the author was still under 25 years of age. Standouts include 'Final Audit' and 'Invaded by Love'. Disch's first collection. The revised American edition of 1971, with an introduction by Harry Harrison, is preferable to the UK first

edition, since it drops 'White Fang Goes Dingo' (best read in its expanded form as *Mankind Under the Leash*) and adds a couple of other early stories which are unavailable elsewhere. For yet another version of this collection see *White Fang Goes Dingo*.

One Hundred Years of Science Fiction (Knight): see under *Century of Science Fiction, A*.

One in Three Hundred (1954) ★★ Novel by J. T. McIntosh (UK). The human race must migrate to Mars in order to escape harmful solar radiation, but (as the title suggests) there's only room in the spaceships for a lucky minority. A rather harsh tale of survival by a once-popular Scottish author whose sf works are now largely forgotten. Other McIntosh novels on similar Darwinian themes include *World Out of Mind* (1953), *Born Leader* (1954) and *The Fittest* (1955).

One Million Tomorrows (1970) ★★ Novel by Bob Shaw (UK). By the 22nd century, immortality has become possible for human beings – but only at the expense of losing one's sexuality. Our lucky hero is given the opportunity to become an immortal and remain a 'functional male'. Another tartly written Shaw thriller.

One Step from Earth (1970) ★★ Collection by Harry Harrison (USA/ Ireland). Various stories linked by the device of a matter transmitter: most of them are ingenious enough. 'The workmanship is uneven, and there is a slight air of pot-boiling – of simply turning the stuff out ... It is only fair to add that run-of-the-mill short stories from Harrison are pretty damn good by traditional sf standards' – Peter Nicholls, *Foundation*.

One Winter in Eden (1984) ★★ Collection by Michael Bishop (USA). Twelve stylish sf and fantasy stories, mainly from the early 1980s. A handsome volume by a rather underappreciated author.

One-Eye (1973) ★★ Novel by Stuart Gordon (UK), first of a trilogy. On a post-holocaust Earth, where mutations abound, the mutant known as One-Eye releases a power he cannot control. Colourful, but rather chaotic, sf/fantasy adventure. Sequels: *Two-Eyes* (1974) and *Three-Eyes* (1975). 'The books have vigour, though the use of genre fantasy/romance materials, slightly science-fictionalized, is stereotyped' – John Clute.

Open Prison (1964) ★★ Novel by James White (UK). A captured human officer leads his fellows in a great escape from an alien-dominated prison planet. An adequately exciting and nicely detailed escape story, set against the background of a mutually-destructive interstellar war. Published in the USA as *The Escape Orbit*.

Ophiuchi Hotline, The (1977) ★★★ Novel by John Varley (USA). A fast-moving story set in a future of bio-engineering, cloning, instant sex-changes, and a hundred-and-one other technological fixes for the human condition – all made possible by a 'hotline' of free information from the stars. Its author's first novel – thoroughly likeable, if at times a bit silly.

Opium General and Other Stories, The (Moorcock): see under *Time Dweller, The*.

Optiman (1980) ★★ Novel by Brian Stableford (UK). Humans and aliens of various species, plus the genetically engineered superman of the title, conduct an elaborate struggle for supremacy on a far planet. Imaginative, ironic, more than a little dry. 'A routine book by an author who keeps revealing that he's really too intelligent to be writing it' – Colin Greenland, *Foundation*. Published in Britain as *War Games*.

Options (1975) ★ Novel by Robert Sheckley (USA). A spaceman is obliged to land on the planet Harmonia in order to find a vital spare part. All manner of absurd, surrealistic things befall him there, and the author leans heavily into the book in order to comment on his hero's travails. Sheckley's strangest work, admired by some but regarded as incomprehensible by others.

Or All the Seas with Oysters (1962) ★★★ Collection by Avram Davidson (USA). Seventeen varied tales, mainly fantasies with a humorous and ethnic Jewish flavour. However, the title story won a 1958 Hugo award as the best sf short story of its year.

ORA:CLE (1984) ★★ Novel by Kevin O'Donnell Jr. (USA). The hero can link his mind directly to computers, thanks to an implant in his brain, and is able to lead a rich life without ever leaving his apartment. But there are dangers, even in such a secluded existence ... A large, seriously-intended but somewhat turgid attempt to deal with a fully computerized world.

Orbit 1 (1966) ★★★ Anthology edited by Damon Knight (USA), the first of a roughly annual series of 21 volumes which were published up to 1980. These consisted of original stories, not reprints, and *Orbit* became perhaps the most influential of all such series during the 1960s and 70s. Many of the stories are dark, experimental and 'New-Wave' in tone, and later volumes show a falling-off in quality. Among the writers Knight discovered or regularly promoted in this series are Gardner Dozois, R. A. Lafferty, Kate Wilhelm and Gene Wolfe.

Orbit Science Fiction Yearbook 1, The (1988) ★★★ Anthology edited by David S. Garnett (UK). First of a new British series of 'best-of-the-year' collections. Only the reliable Garry Kilworth carries the flag, though. The remaining dozen stories are by the likes of Jonathan Carroll, Pat Murphy and Lucius Shepard, newish American writers of considerable talent. There are also valuable critical summations by Brian Aldiss and John Clute.

Orbital Decay (1989) ★★★ Novel by Allen Steele (USA). Astronaut-engineers, hired by a privatized American space agency of the near future, build solar-power satellites in Earth orbit. A first novel which skilfully deploys a sense of hard-headed space-age realism, in the manner of the late Robert A. Heinlein's early fiction. '"Hard hats in space," reads the blurb. Maybe so. But it is also one of the most unabashedly romantic novels of space exploration written since the '40s' – Dan Chow, *Locus*.

Orbitsville (1975) ★★★ Novel by Bob Shaw (UK). Spacefarers discover a vast Dyson sphere built by mysterious aliens. This awesome artefact, 625 million times the surface area of the Earth, may be intended as a 'honeypot' to trap intelligent species. A well characterized and continuously entertaining narrative. Sequels: *Orbitsville Departure* (1983) and *Orbitsville Judgement* (1990).

Orion Shall Rise (1983) ★ Novel by Poul Anderson (USA). The Maori have inherited the Earth after a nuclear war, and now find themselves in conflict with unreconstructed high-techers from devastated America. A long novel about the opposition between utopia and hard-headed engineering science – too long for its own good.

Orn (1971) ★★ Novel by Piers Anthony (USA). The heroes of *Omnivore* flee the government of their time into a prehistoric past where they have to learn to communicate with an intelligent bird, 'Orn', before their pursuers catch up with them. Sequel: *Ox*.

Orphan Star (Foster): see under *Tar-Aiym Krang, The*.

Orphans of the Sky (1963) ★★ Fix-up novel by Robert A. Heinlein (USA). Originally published as two magazine novellas, 'Universe' and 'Common Sense' (both 1941), this deals with a lost colony of Earth-folk who have reverted to primitivism aboard a multi-generation starship. The narrative now seems somewhat crude. (Compare Brian Aldiss's better-written novel *Non-Stop*.)

Ossian's Ride (1959) ★★ Novel by Fred Hoyle (UK). A mysterious corporation, which has become a fount of new inventions and products, has sealed off an area in Ireland. The hero's job is to penetrate this zone and discover the source of the technological boons which have been showered on the world. An adequately intriguing sf thriller by a major British scientist.

Other Americas (1988) ★★★ Collection by Norman Spinrad (USA). Four long tales set in near-future versions of the United States of America. Powerfully written, gruesome, occasionally funny. 'Spinrad doing what he does best. It is his strongest book in some time' – Dan Chow, *Locus*.

Other Days, Other Eyes (1972) ★★★ Fix-up novel by Bob Shaw (UK). This is the book which incorporates Shaw's classic short story 'Light of Other Days' (1966) and its two thematic sequels. About a new form of glass which retards the passage of light to such an extent that one can view scenes from days, weeks, even years in the past, the original story was both ingenious and touching. Here Shaw has woven a new plot around it and the other tales, which makes for a slightly lumpy though fascinating novel, full of good things.

Other Edens (1987) ★★★ Anthology edited by Christopher Evans and Robert Holdstock (UK). Original sf and fantasy stories by mainly British writers, among them Brian Aldiss, Garry Kilworth, Tanith Lee, Michael Moorcock, Keith Roberts, Ian Watson and the editors themselves. The first of a commendable series which so far includes *Other Edens II* (1988) and *Other Edens III* (1989).

Other Foot, The (Knight): see *Mind Switch*.

Other Human Race, The (1962) ★★ Novel by H. Beam Piper (USA), a sequel to *Little Fuzzy*. The Fuzzies have been proved sapient, but now they must defend their territory and way of life against human settlers. They do this mainly by making friends with everybody at a desperate pace. Also published as *Fuzzy Sapiens*.

Other Log of Phileas Fogg, The (1973) ★ Novel by Philip José Farmer (USA). A retelling of Jules Verne's *Around the World in Eighty Days* (1873), introducing aliens from outer space and other mysteries. Amusing, extravagant, a bit silly.

Other Side of the Mirror, The (Bradley): see under *Free Amazons of Darkover*.

Other Side of the Sky, The (1958) ★★★ Collection by Arthur C. Clarke (UK). Twenty-four stories (some of them short-shorts) which display the full range of this writer's abilities – from the humdrum to the visionary. The standouts are two famous tales of cosmic doom which blend astronomical with religious themes, in very different ways: 'The Nine Billion Names Of God' (1953) and 'The Star' (1955). The latter won a 1956 Hugo Award. Also included here is 'The Songs of Distant Earth', a mood piece which has since been expanded into a novel of the same title.

Other Side of Time, The (Laumer): see under *Worlds of the Imperium*.

Other Stories, and the Attack of the Giant Baby (Reed): see under *Mr Da V, and Other Stories*.

Other Time, The (1984) ★ Novel by Mack Reynolds and Dean Ing (USA). A present-day archaeologist who has become displaced in time helps the Aztecs fend off the Spanish invasion of Mexico. Interesting ideas, hastily executed. A posthumous Reynolds novel completed by Ing.

Other Times, Other Worlds (1978) ★★ Collection by John D. MacDonald (USA), introduced by Martin Harry Greenberg. Sixteen sf stories, first published between 1948 and 1968, including such frequently anthologized pieces as 'Spectator Sport' and 'A Child is Crying'. This volume serves as a reminder that one of America's most popular crime novelists also wrote a good deal of competent science fiction early in his career.

Other Worlds of Clifford Simak: see *Worlds of Clifford Simak, The*.

Our Children's Children (1974) ★ Novel by Clifford D. Simak (USA). Refugees from the future attempt to escape a ravening horde of aliens via time travel. A piffling entertainment from one of sf's Old Masters.

Our Friends from Frolix 8 (1970) ★★ Novel by Philip K. Dick (USA). Confusing story of a 22nd-century world dominated by psi-powered freaks – and a possible salvation from outer space for 'unimproved' humanity. Written in Dick's dense, humorous, middle-period style, but not one of his best.

Out of My Mind (1967) ★★★ Collection by John Brunner (UK). A dozen or so sf stories (US and UK contents differ), including Brunner standards like 'The Totally Rich', 'The Last Lonely Man' and 'Such Stuff'. Ingenious and dark-hued.

Out of Phaze (Anthony): see under *Juxtaposition*.

Out of the Dead City (Delany): see *Fall of the Towers, The*.

Out of the Deeps (Wyndham): see *Kraken Wakes, The*.

Out of the Everywhere and Other Extraordinary Visions (1981) ★★ Collection by James Tiptree Jr. (Alice Sheldon, USA). 'Her most effective stories seem motivated by outrage' – Brian Stableford.

Out of the Mouth of the Dragon (1969) ★★★★ Novel by Mark S.

Geston (USA). Brilliant journey through a meaningless world of misunderstood prophecy and inappropriate technology which fights the battle of Armageddon, finds to its distaste that it still exists, picks itself up, dusts itself down, then does it again and again and again. If not a sequel to *Lords of the Starship*, it is at least set in the same amazing, hopeless future.

Out of the Silent Planet (1938) ★★★ Novel by C. S. Lewis (UK), first of a trilogy. The hero, Ransom, is taken to Mars aboard a spaceship. There he finds wise spiritual beings who inform him that Earth (the silent planet of the title) is a fallen world. It's clearly a religious allegory, but it's nevertheless hauntingly effective as sf. Unfortunately, the novels which follow become steadily more fantastic, religiose and anti-scientific. Sequels: *Perelandra* (1943; republished as *Voyage to Venus*) and *That Hideous Strength* (1945).

Out on Blue Six (1989) ★★ Novel by Ian McDonald (UK). The future utopia known as the Compassionate Society of Great Yu is overdue for renewal, and a motley group of characters sets about that task. Another oddball, messy and occasionally dazzling piece of invention by a new British writer whose short stories and his first novel, *Desolation Road*, have won him much praise, particularly in America.

Out There Where the Big Ships Go (1980) ★★★ Collection by Richard Cowper (Colin Middleton Murry,

UK). Five well-written, amusing and affecting sf and fantasy stories, the contents overlapping with Cowper's earlier UK collection *The Custodians*. After many novels, the author has latterly proved himself to be a fine short-story writer.

Outlaw of Gor (Norman): see under *Tarnsman of Gor*.

Outreach (Lichtenberg): see under *Dushau*.

Outward Bound (Coulson): see under *Tomorrow's Heritage*.

Outward Urge, The (1959) ★★ Fix-up novel by John Wyndham and Lucas Parkes (UK). A brief, episodic 'family saga' about the near-future exploration of space. Cleanly written (in an old-fashioned way), but untypical of the author's best work. The collaborator did not in fact exist – 'Lucas Parkes' was a pseudonym for Wydham himself, and the use of this name perhaps indicated the author's unease (or his publishers') with this material.

Overloaded Man, The (1967) ★★★ Collection by J. G. Ballard (UK), later revised and republished as *The Venus Hunters*. Nine short tales plus an article on surrealist painting. Some stories, e.g. 'Escapement' (1956) and 'Now: Zero' (1959), are early and minor Ballard; others, such as 'The Time-Tombs' and 'The Venus Hunters' (both 1963) show the author at his moody (and witty) best.

Overman Culture, The (1971) ★ Novel by Edmund Cooper (UK). As usual with Cooper, the protagonist is a man who finds himself the leader of a group of humans who are to become the new population of a deserted planet. In this case the mentors are humanoid robots. Has a pleasantly surrealistic atmosphere: all children and robots are named after characters from British history – Michael Faraday (child hero), Queen Victoria, Sir Winston Churchill.

Overworld (1980) ★★ Novel by Michael Vyse (UK). A hive-like urban society of the future maintains a wasteful, high-consumption lifestyle – but its ecologically-aware opponents attempt to change things for the better. This appears to be a first novel, and it's certainly one with a message. 'Done with feeling, but with too close an eye on merely contemporary inconveniences' – Tom Shippey, *Guardian*.

Ox (1976) ★★★ Novel by Piers Anthony (USA), sequel to *Omnivore* and *Orn* featuring communication with a machine-line intelligence via the Game of Life. Interesting attempt to depict non-human mental processes. Together with the two earlier books, this represents Anthony's nearest approach to the great sf novel he now seems to have given up trying to write. The three have since been republished in one volume as *Of Man and Manta*.

O-Zone (1986) ★ Novel by Paul Theroux (USA). In a near-future America, raddled by pollution, the high-tech haves oppress the dehumanized have-nots. An unoriginal anti-utopian outing by a famous mainstream novelist, it fails to come to life. 'This is not the past or the future. It is the present; only a slight intensification of the situation between whites and blacks in South Africa or, more broadly, the West versus the rest, and Theroux is fully aware of it' – Lee Montgomerie, *Interzone*. 'A dismal novel: dull, ill-written, misconceived, nakedly exploitative' – Thomas M. Disch, *SF Commentary*.

P

Paingod and Other Delusions (1965) ★★ Collection by Harlan Ellison (USA). Painful, socially-aware stories, varying from cynical to absurdly hopeful. Sometimes embarrassing to read, sometimes they seem to have been embarrassing to write. Ellison thinks a lot of himself. One can't avoid noting 'Repent Harlequin, Said the Ticktockman' – which, even if it weren't so good, would deserve reprinting just for the flashy way he gets the title into a normal speech and makes it make sense.

Palace of Eternity, The (1969) ★★★ Novel by Bob Shaw (UK). An Edenic planet is being wasted by endless interstellar war. The hero leads a hopeless revolt against the military, dies, and is reborn as part of the planet's 'world-mind'. A far-fetched but seductive tale of transcendence. One of this author's finest.

Palace of Love, The (1967) ★★ Novel by Jack Vance (USA), sequel to *The Killing Machine* and third in his 'Demon Princes' series. About the continuing interplanetary quest of Kirth Gersen. The usual Jack Vance mixture of a formulaic plot and interesting background detail, all wrapped up in surprisingly elegant prose. Sequel: *The Face*.

Palimpsests (1985) ★★ Novel by Carter Scholz and Glen A. Harcourt (USA). An object from the future is found in an archaeological dig. The hero appropriates it and is pursued. A time mystery which is neither as original nor as 'deep' as at first it may seem. Scholz and Harcourt's debut novel.

Pan Sagittarius (Wallace): see under *Croyd*.

Pandora Effect, The (Williamson): see under *Best of Jack Williamson, The*.

Panic O'Clock (1973) ★ Novel by Christopher Hodder-Williams (UK). A plague of insanity known as the 'Virulent Panic' is brought on by the pressures of modern technological life, and leads to an epidemic of suicides. There's a happy ending, though. 'Hodder-Williams's least impressive book ... just another standard British disaster novel' – David V. Barrett, *Vector*.

Paper Dolls, The (1964) ★★ Novel by L. P. Davies (UK). Quadruplets with psychic powers, born as the result of Nazi genetic tinkering, pose a threat to humanity. A first novel by a competent British author who is really a mystery novelist rather than a science-fiction writer proper.

Paradise Game, The (Stableford): see under *Halcyon Drift*.

Paradox Men, The (1953) ★★★ Novel by Charles L. Harness (USA). Alar the Thief fights the 22nd-century Chancellor of America Imperial. An intricate and heartening tale of time paradoxes, written in grand pulp style. Harness's first novel. Originally published as *Flight Into Yesterday*, but now better known under its 1955 reprint title.

Paradox of the Sets, The (Stableford): see under *Florians, The*.

Paradox Planet, The (Spruill): see under *Psychopath Plague, The*.

Paratime (1981) ★★ Posthumous collection by H. Beam Piper (USA). One of the classic series of parallel-Earth tales, featuring a rather 19th-century policeman who tries to keep the 'paratime secret' from googols of alternative worlds. A related novel is *Lord Kalvan of Otherwhen*.

Partners in Wonder (1971) ★★ Collection by Harlan Ellison (USA), writing in collaboration with various hands. The noisy, hyperactive Ellison presents stories he has done in tandem with Budrys, Delany, Laumer, Silverberg, Sturgeon, Zelazny and others. Given the forced nature of the project, not all of the collaborations work equally well but there is some effective material here. 'Most of the volume's duos are either excellent or fascinating or both, showing their various senior collaborators off in splendid fashion, for Ellison has a distinctly vivifying influence on such writers as van Vogt and Sheckley and even Silverberg' – John Clute.

Passing for Human (1977) ★★ Novel by Jody Scott (USA). An indescribable sf/fantasy farrago, which puts the boot into the human race in general (and the male half of it in particular). Scott's first novel. 'Ribald and zestful' – Brian Stableford. Sequel, in similar vein: *I, Vampire* (1984).

Passing of the Dragons, The (Roberts): see under *Machines and Men*.

Passion of New Eve, The (Carter): see under *Heroes and Villains*.

Past Master (1968) ★★★ Novel by R. A. Lafferty (USA). Citizens of a future utopia in crisis decide to resurrect Sir Thomas More in the hope that he will come up with a solution to their problems. A highly original and highly praised sf/fantasy philosophical comedy which some readers have found overly whimsical and verbose. Lafferty is one of a kind, though – love him or hate him.

Past Through Tomorrow, The (1967) ★★★ Collection by Robert A. Heinlein (USA). Omnibus volume which includes all the contents of *The Man Who Sold the Moon*, *The Green Hills of Earth* and *Revolt in 2100*, plus the novel *Methuselah's Children*, and other, scattered, tales in Heinlein's so-called 'Future History'. In paperback editions it has appeared as two volumes, with the longest story omitted.

Past Times (1984) ★ Collection by Poul Anderson (USA). A clean-up volume of sf stories, mainly from the 1950s and 60s, most of them dealing in one way or another with time travel and past eras. There is also an essay, 'The Discovery of the Past', about the joys of history. Minor Anderson.

Pastel City, The (1971) ★★★ Novel by M. John Harrison (UK), the first of his 'Viriconium' sequence. This is a sword-and-sorcery tale, yet it borders on sf by virtue of its distant-future setting and the conceit that most of the 'magic' is in fact ancient, little-understood science. Despite its obvious debts to Vance and Moorcock, it's a very moody and stylish entertainment. The more complex sequel, *A Storm of Wings* (1980), is also borderline sf – though later books in the sequence can only be classified as fantasy.

Patchwork Girl, The (Niven): see under *Long ARM of Gil Hamilton, The*.

Path Into the Unknown: The Best Soviet Science Fiction (1966) ★★ Anthology with no editor credited, introduced by Judith Merril. One of the earlier English-language selections of modern Russian sf, it contains notable work by the Strugatsky brothers, etc. 'The future is seen in terms of a vast scientific bureaucracy in which the only creatures allowed any freedom or eccentricity are the robots' – J. G. Ballard, *Guardian*.

Patron of the Arts (1974) ★ Novel by William Rotsler (USA), expanded from his short story of the same title. A fairly undistinguished action yarn, its main point of interest is that it features an intriguing futuristic art-form which utilizes holography and other high-tech means of expression in an attempt to achieve a 'total experience'. Rotsler's first novel.

Patternmaster (1976) ★★ Novel by Octavia E. Butler (USA). In the future a community of telepaths has arisen, but they are threatened by mutants and other outsiders. A promising first novel, in the loosely-connected 'Patternist' series. Sequel: *Mind of My Mind*.

Patterns of Chaos, The (1972) Novel by Colin Kapp (UK). Our hero is a 'chaos catalyst', pursued by weapons launched millennia ago by a long-dead civilization attempting to neutralize his effect. Poorly constructed. 'The book is impenetrable to sense and taste alike' – John Clute. Sequel: *The Chaos Weapon* (1977).

Pavane (1968) ★★★★ Fix-up novel by Keith Roberts (UK). An alternative-world story in which present-day England is imagined as a technologically backward, Roman Catholic nation (the Spanish Armada succeeded in its conquest). Steam-driven automobiles and other examples of quiant machinery are lovingly described. A subtle, thoughtful work – its author's best.

Pawns of Null-A, The (van Vogt): see *Players of Null-A, The.*

Peace Company, The (1985) ★ Novel by Roland Green (USA). Military peace-keepers attempt to stop threatened civil war on a colonized planet. Yet another dull 'mercenary'-type space adventure by this author who specializes in producing examples of the form in collaboration with Jerry Pournelle and others. 'Recommended more for those who relish the details of planning and logistics than for those who seek larger-than-life characters and combat excitement' – Glenn Reed, *Fantasy Review*.

Peace Machine, The (Shaw): see *Ground Zero Man.*

Peace War, The (1984) ★★ Novel by Vernor Vinge (USA). Into a well depicted future of super-computers and biotechnology, the author introduces another *novum*: the spherical stasis-fields known as 'bobbles'. These, the ultimate form of defence, soon lead to war. An intricately plotted thriller which spins off ideas. Sequel, which depicts one-way time travel to the far future via stasis-field: *Marooned in Real Time* (1986).

Peacekeepers (1988) ★★ Novel by Ben Bova (USA). A global police force has been set up to prevent war. They are not permitted to oppose terrorists and drug-dealers but they provide covert support for those who do. The narrative consists of a series of short, violent incidents set in colourful and out-of-the-way locations. More like a TV series than a novel, but one of Bova's better efforts.

Pebble in the Sky (1950) ★★ Novel by Isaac Asimov (USA). A 'little tailor' (that's the hero's profession) of the present day is thrown into the far future where he finds himself caught up in a galactic war. Asimov's first novel shows its age, but it remains good fun.

Pellucidar (Burroughs): see under *At the Earth's Core.*

Penguin Science Fiction Omnibus, The (1973) ★★★★ Anthology edited by Brian Aldiss (UK), a combination of three briefer volumes originally published as *Penguin Science Fiction* (1961), *More Penguin Science Fiction* (1963) and *Yet More Penguin Science Fiction* (1964). These pleasing anthologies moulded the tastes of a generation of British sf readers. Classic stories by Asimov, Blish, Clarke, Harrison, Pohl, Simak and many others.

Penguin World Omnibus of Science Fiction, The (1986) ★★ Anthology edited by Brian Aldiss and Sam Lundwall (UK/Sweden). Variable selection of 26 stories from around the globe, intended as a showcase volume for the international writers' organization known as 'World SF'.

'The inclusion of a plodding school essay from Ghana can only be accounted for by courtesy or completism, but the rest of the stories are all acceptable, frequently exceptional, occasionally brilliant' – Lee Montgomerie, *Interzone*.

Pennterra (1987) ★★★ Novel by Judith Moffett (USA). Quaker settlers on the world of Pennterra are confined to one village by the native Hrossa (named after the Martians in C. S. Lewis's *Out of the Silent Planet*). When more humans arrive intending to colonize the rest of the planet the Hrossa warn them that the effort will undoubtedly lead to disaster, yet neither the Hrossa nor the Quakers can tell them what the disaster will be. A thoughtful, if somewhat incomplete novel.

Penultimate Truth, The (1964) ★★ Novel by Philip K. Dick (USA). Most people live underground, believing that nuclear war still rages overhead; in fact they are being held in captivity by a rich and cynical few. The cleverly conceived scenario is let down by a hasty prose style.

People Machines (Williamson): see under *Best of Jack Williamson, The*.

People Maker, The (Knight): see *A for Anything*.

People: No Different Flesh, The (Henderson): see under *Pilgrimage: The Book of the People*.

People of the Wind, The (1973) ★★ Novel by Poul Anderson (USA). Human colonists ally with noble, winged aliens to fight Earth's over-mighty empire. A nicely-detailed space-war yarn.

People Trap, The (Sheckley): see under *Pilgrimage to Earth*.

Perchance (1989) ★★ Novel by Michael Kurland (USA). A nude, amnesiac young woman keeps materializing in New York, at the beginning of this sf/fantasy romp about mind-links and travels in other dimensions. 'Not a book for those who want something meaty, but it's good mind popcorn' – Tom Whitmore, *Locus*.

Perelandra (Lewis): see under *Out of the Silent Planet*.

Perfect Lover, The (Priest): see *Dream of Wessex, A*.

Perihelion (Wu): see under *Odyssey*.

Persistence of Vision, The (1978) ★★★ Collection by John Varley (USA), introduced by Algis Budrys. The sentimental title story (Hugo and Nebula award-winner, 1979) concerns a colony of blind folk who develop amazing powers. Most of the rest are tales set in a bio-engineered, sexually-ambiguous spacefaring human society of the not-too-distant future. Fast and superbly inventive, they are carried off with astonishing aplomb. Varley became the most fashionable author in American magazine sf during the latter 1970s (just as James Tiptree Jr. had been Number One in the early 70s), and it was the stories reprinted in this book which brought him the acclaim.

Published in the UK as *In the Hall of the Martian Kings*.

Petrogypsies (1989) ★★ Novel by Rory Harper (USA). Specially modified alien creatures serve as the 'machinery' to extract Texas oil, in this wacky alternative-world adventure. A first novel. 'Harper's sensibility is warm, earthy, whimsical, cleverly off-centre, and, when he wants it to be, bawdy as all get out' – Edward Bryant, *Locus*.

Phaid the Gambler (Farren): see *Song of Phaid the Gambler, The*.

Phases of Gravity (Simmons): see under *Hyperion*.

Philip K. Dick is Dead, Alas (Bishop): see *Secret Ascension, The*.

Philosopher's Stone, The (1969) ★ Novel by Colin Wilson (UK). Perhaps the best of Wilson's rather mixed sf/occult novels. The complicated plot takes off from the notion that mathematicians live longer than other men, and launches out in all directions at once.

Phoenix (1968) ★★ Novel by Richard Cowper (Colin Middleton Murry, UK). A young man, romantically discontented with his lot in the comfortable 24th century, awakes from suspended animation to find himself in a much harsher society a couple of thousand years further on. A readable novel in which dark themes are treated with a generally pleasing lightness of touch.

Phoenix in the Ashes (Vinge): see

under *Eyes of Amber and Other Stories*.

Phthor (Anthony): see under *Chthon*.

Picnic on Paradise (1968) ★★ Novel by Joanna Russ (USA). Alyx, a Bronze-Age amazon, has been recruited as a Trans-Temporal Agent. Her task in this slim but densely-textured action tale is to escort some tourists to safety on a wartorn planet. This was the first book by sf's leading spokesperson for feminism, and it gained high praise. 'Here is adventure, not romanticized but as it really is: rough, dangerous and dirty, a-bristle with the unexpected, though with moments of high humour and surprising beauty' – Fritz Leiber.

Piece of Martin Cann, A (1968) ★★ Novel by Laurence M. Janifer (USA). A psychological therapeutic novel in which a mentally ill man is cured by a process of telepathic communion.

Pilgrimage (1981) ★★ Novel by Drew Mendelson (USA). In a depleted future, there is just one vast City – which creeps slowly across the surface of the Earth (a notion similar to that handled, in a smaller way, in Christopher Priest's *Inverted World*). The young protagonists rebel against a repressive, anti-scientific order. 'An intelligent, interesting and literate first novel' – Kenny Mathieson, *Foundation*.

Pilgrimage: The Book of the People (1961) ★★ Fix-up novel by Zenna

Henderson (USA). Telepathically-endowed aliens, almost indistinguishable from human beings, arrive on Earth after their own planet has been destroyed. They have to learn to survive surreptitiously. Pleasantly humane tales, mainly involving children. 'Secret aliens among us is an old sf notion but ... The sheer wholesomeness of her People is enough to set them apart' – Sandra Miesel, *20th-Century SF Writers*. Sequel: *The People: No Different Flesh* (1966).

Pilgrimage to Earth (1957) ★★★ Collection by Robert Sheckley (USA). Fifteen varied sf tales, some of them sinister but most very funny – and almost all with a satirical or admonitory edge. The third excellent volume by one of the best sf short-story writers of the 1950s. Subsequent Sheckley collections, none quite up to the standard of this one, include *Store of Infinity* (1960), *Notions: Unlimited* (1960), *Shards of Space* (1962) and *The People Trap* (1968).

Pillars of Eternity, The (1982) ★★ Novel by Barrington J. Bayley (UK). Joachim Boaz, cybernetically rebuilt by stoical philosophers, joins in a mad quest for the time jewels of the planet Meirjain, where he finds a way to exorcize the memory of the terrible pain of being burnt with ethereal fire in an alchemical experiment. As always with Bayley much of the book is about ideas – philosophical rather than scientific.

Pimpernel Plot, The (Hawke): see under *Ivanhoe Gambit, The*.

Pioneers (1988) ★★★ Novel by Phillip Mann (UK/New Zealand). Envoys of a dying human race go in search of the hardy pioneers who left Earth long ago. They succeed in finding these lost descendants of humanity, and save the day. Perhaps Mann's best novel so far. 'In many ways it is a thoroughly pre-modern work ... What saves it is Mann's gift for evoking the alien, put to good effect in describing the strange worlds and even stranger adaptations of the Pioneers' – Paul McAuley, *Interzone*.

Pirates of the Thunder (1987) ★ Novel by Jack L. Chalker (USA), second volume of 'The Rings of the Master'. The heroes of *Lords of the Middle Dark* escape into the galaxy on their quest for the magic rings which will enable them to reprogram the Master System, and take up a career as space pirates. Sequel: *Warriors of the Storm*.

Pirates of Zan, The (1959) ★★ Novel by Murray Leinster (USA). A young engineer is frustrated by the social and technological backwardness of various planets he visits, so he devises a cunning plan to liven things up – a scheme which involves space pirates. A pleasantly tongue-in-cheek adventure by an intelligent writer who churned out far too many potboilers. This is one of his best.

Plague from Space (1965) ★★ Novel by Harry Harrison (USA/Ireland). A returning spacecraft brings a dangerous infection back to Earth. A much-used idea (see, for example, a later work called *The Andromeda Strain* by Michael Crichton) is here handled with panache. 'Well plotted, interestingly written, with believable characters' – Hilary Bailey, *New Worlds*. Republished as *The Jupiter Legacy*.

Plague of Demons, A (1965) ★★ Novel by Keith Laumer (USA). Fast-moving space adventure in which the hero becomes transformed into a sort of armoured tank. Po-faced paranoid stuff – absurd, but perhaps Laumer's most characteristic book. 'The best nonhumorous Laumer novels and stories grip at one with manic panache through their stripping-away of everything irrelevant to the goal of arriving at a narrative embodiment of brute kinesis' – John Clute.

Plague of Pythons, A (Pohl): see *Demon in the Skull*.

Planet Buyer, The (Smith): see *Norstrilia*.

Planet Called Krishna, A (de Camp): see *Cosmic Manhunt*.

Planet Called Treason, A (1979) ★★ Novel by Orson Scott Card (USA). On Treason the descendants of human exiles have each founded a small nation or tribe, all specializing in some science or apparently magical power. The Muellers have made their way by engineering their own bodies to grow spare parts for organ transplants: and this is the story of the Mueller heir's exile amongst the other Families. Full of invention and fast-paced, jumping from idea to idea without ever really settling down, and already showing the author's fascination with omnicompetent heroes who outlive their enemies in suspended animation. Revised and retitled *Treason* (1988).

Planet Dweller, The (1985) ★★ Novel by Jane Palmer (UK). A first novel, very English in tone, which uses body-swapping aliens and other hoary devices to comic ends. 'Appropriates all the furniture of TV sci-fi and duly stands it on its head, with a wonderful pragmatic absurdity' – Mary Gentle, *Interzone*.

Planet Explorer, The (Leinster): see *Colonial Survey*.

Planet for Texans, A (1958) ★★ Novel by H. Beam Piper and John J. McGuire (USA). Stephen Silk, sent as ambassador to New Texas to frighten the locals into joining the Solar League, finds a planet which resembles a parody of the state of Texas (the 20th-century version of *Dallas* and LBJ, rather than the Wild West), where assassination is not a crime and barbecues are the main art form. Humorous, and very loosely connected to the author's later 'Federation' stories. Republished as *Lone Star Planet* (as by Piper alone).

Planet of Adventure (1968–70) ★★★ Series of novels by Jack Vance (USA), also known as the 'Tschai' series. The four parts are: *City of the Chasch* (1968) the unfortunately titled *Servants of the Wankh* (1969), *The Dirdir* (1969) and *The Pnume* (1970). The planet Tschai has been passed between the alien Chasch, Dirdir and Wankh in a long history of interstellar war, while the aboriginal

Pnume and Phing (and humans brought from prehistoric Earth by the Dirdir) have been driven underground. Space travellers from Earth undergo military and amorous adventures against the background of an astonishing variety of cultures, peoples and rituals. This is typical Vance, using an sf background and exuberant language to provide an unusual depth to what could have been a simple quest fantasy.

Planet of Exile (1966) ★★ Short novel by Ursula K. Le Guin (USA), second in her 'Hainish' cycle. 'Farborn' humans and human-like indigenous aliens come into conflict on a wintry planet. The telepathic heroine acts to unite the cultures. Minor Le Guin, but poetic and very pleasing.

Planet of the Apes (1963) ★★ Novel by Pierre Boulle (France). Space explorers find a world where apes are the dominant species and humans are treated as beasts. It's much more satirical than the famous movie version. Published in the UK as *Monkey Planet*. Filmed in 1968 (dir. Franklin J. Schaffner).

Planet of the Damned (1962) ★★ Novel by Harry Harrison (USA/ Ireland). The cause of a planetary population's violent ways is discovered to be an alien infection, and the planet is duly cured. Published in the UK as *Sense of Obligation*.

Planet of the Double Sun, The (1967) ★ Fix-up novel by Neil R. Jones (USA), first of his 'Professor Jameson' series. A scientist's corpse is put into Earth orbit, against the day when he may be revived. Millions of years later, benign aliens happen along and give him a new, mechanical body. 'The Jameson Satellite' (1931), was the beginning of a long series which ran in the magazines of the 1930s and 40s, and is reprinted here and in the sequel volumes: *The Sunless World* (1967), *Space War* (1967), *Twin Worlds* (1967) and *Doomsday on Ajiat* (1968).

Planet of the Robot Slaves, The (Harrison): see *Bill, the Galactic Hero: The Planet of the Robot Slaves.*

Planet of the Warlord (Hill): see *Last Legionary Quartet, The.*

Planet of Treachery (Goldin): see under *Imperial Stars, The.*

Planet on the Table, The (1986) ★★★ Collection by Kim Stanley Robinson (USA). A fine first volume of mixed sf and fantasy from a highly praised writer. Contains the notable Hiroshima story 'The Lucky Strike' (1984).

Planet Savers, The (Bradley): see under *Sword of Aldones, The.*

Planetary Agent X (1965) ★ Fix-up novel by Mack Reynolds (USA), first in his 'Section G: United Planets' series. The confederated planets of the inhabited galaxy are supposed to tolerate each other's differing social systems, but trouble inevitably brews and our hero is a special agent whose task is to resolve various cultural conflicts. Adequate space adventure with a distinct political edge. Other 'United Planets' novels, all in a similar vein, include *Dawnman Planet* (1966), *The Rival Rigellians* (1967), *Code Duello* (1968), *Amazon Planet* (1975) and *Section G: United Planets* (1976).

Planetary Legion for Peace (1960) Novel by Romulus Rexner (Stateless?). Well-meaning but hard to take seriously account of the founding of an army of the stateless and refugees (a sort of Woodcraft Folk with teeth) to bring 'liberty, light, life and love' to the world.

Planets Three (Pohl): see under *Early Pohl, The*.

Plasm (1988) ★ Novel by Charles Platt (USA), set in Piers Anthony's 'World of Chthon'. Aton escapes from the living world of Chthon to return to his mother, who is genetically engineered to obtain sexual pleasure from beatings and cruelty. There is an interesting telepathic alien, but on the whole this is an unpleasant book. Sequel: *Soma* (1989).

Platypus of Doom and Other Nihilists, The (1976) ★★ Collection by Arthur Byron Cover (USA). Four parodic sf/fantasy stories with titles like 'The Aardvark of Despair' and 'The Clam of Catastrophe'. Full of references to famous fictional characters and other aspects of modern popular culture. Silly stuff, but quite amusing.

Player of Games, The (1988) ★★★ Novel by Iain M. Banks (UK). Set in the same universe as the author's *Consider Phlebas*, but many centuries later, when the spacefaring utopian 'Culture' comes into conflict with an evil empire called Azad. An improvement on Banks's first space opera. 'Swift, sure-footed, pell-mell, and glows with a benign luxuriance' – John Clute.

Player Piano (1952) ★★★ Novel by Kurt Vonnegut Jr. (USA). In the highly automated United States of the near future, most people are out of work. An engineer rebels against the conformist status quo, but eventually discovers that human beings are irredeemable. An enjoyable satire with a sour edge, more conventionally written than the author's later books. Vonnegut's first novel.

Players of Null-A, The (1956) ★ Novel by A. E. van Vogt (USA), sequel to *The World of Null-A*. It was originally serialized in 1948, and first published in book form as *The Pawns of Null-A*. Further confusing space-operatic adventures of Gosseyn, the 'non-Aristotelian' hero of the earlier novel. 'It is typical of van Vogt that his central character is the product of a system designed to clarify thought and yet spends most of the story in a state of bewilderment' – James Cawthorn, *New Worlds*. Belated sequel: *Null-A Three* (1985).

Pluribus (1975) ★★ Novel by Michael Kurland (USA). Decades after a man-made plague has devastated the Earth, colonists from Mars return to the home planet with a vaccine which they hope will prevent a recurrence of the plague. Low-key, picaresque post-disaster story.

Pnume, The (Vance): see under *Planet of Adventure.*

Pocketful of Stars, A (1971) ★★★ Anthology edited by Damon Knight (USA). These stories were all produced by participants in the Milford sf writers' conference, an annual workshop for professional writers. Good, solid 1960s sf from people like Harlan Ellison, Kate Wilhelm and Gene Wolfe (who contributes the upsetting anti-war story 'The HORARS of War').

Podkayne of Mars (1963) ★★ Novel by Robert A. Heinlein (USA). The first-person tale of a teenage girl who aspires to be a space captain. In the end, she learns to accept a woman's role: 'a baby is lots more fun than differential equations'. Engagingly written, if thin, narrative which represents a partial and not wholly successful return to Heinlein's 'juvenile' mode of the 1950s.

Pohlstars (1984) ★★ Collection by Frederik Pohl (USA). A dozen short stories from the 1970s and 80s which prove that Pohl, even in his umpteenth collection, is still a considerable writer in the sf field. Notable items include 'Spending a Day at the Lottery Fair', 'We Purchased People' and 'The Sweet, Sad Queen of the Grazing Isles' (though this last is scarcely sf).

Poison Belt, The (1913) ★★ Novel by A. Conan Doyle (UK), second of his Professor Challenger tales. The Earth enters a cloud of poison gas, and Challenger and his friends take precautions which prove to be unnecessary. A promising disaster story which doesn't go far enough.

Police Your Planet (1956) ★ Novel by Lester del Rey (USA), originally published under the pseudonym 'Eric Van Lhin'. A grimly-depicted Mars colony of the near future is run virtually as a corrupt police state. The journalist hero aims to rectify things. (The 1975 reissue is revised.)

Politician (Anthony), see under *Refugee.*

Pollinators of Eden, The (1969) ★ Novel by John Boyd (USA). Biologists have illicit relations with weird plants on a strange planet. Intended as a satire, it's mostly padding around a short masturbation fantasy.

Polyphemus (1987) ★★ Collection by Michael Shea (USA). Colourful sf stories, mostly latter-day bug-eyed-monster tales and all with a fantastic or horrific tinge. Shea is a talented writer of fantasy in the Clark Ashton Smith/Jack Vance vein, and is known for such books as his World Fantasy award-winning *Nifft the Lean* (1982). This is his first sf collection.

Port Eternity (1982) ★★ Novel by C. J. Cherryh (USA). A starfaring pleasure boat, lost in hyperspace, is crewed by artificial human slaves who have been named for characters in the Arthurian legends – Lancelot, Gawain, etc. An ingenious sf adventure with a fantasy flavour.

Portal: A Dataspace Retrieval (1988) ★★ Novel by Rob Swigart (USA), based on a computer game. A starship captain, returned to find Earth uninhabited, searches various databases to discover what happened to all the people. Written throughout in computerese, not entirely successfully.

Possessors, The (1965) ★★ Novel by John Christopher (UK). A horror thriller set in a Swiss ski resort. It involves aliens which take over human bodies, and eventually have to be destroyed by fire. Unoriginal in theme, but a nail-biter.

Postman, The (1985) ★★ Novel by David Brin (USA). In an after-the-bomb America one survivor works as a 'postman', i.e. a teller of tales and a carrier of news between scattered communities. Gradually, he works towards the rebirth of the nation. A piously scientific moral tale which proved popular but was excoriated by some critics. 'I refuse to accept delivery of any of The Postman's messages' – Lee Montgomerie, Interzone.

Power (1974) ★★ Novel by Laurence M. Janifer (USA). The young hero rebels against an oppressive space empire, in this moderately complex tale of family intrigue by a minor sf writer. There is an ironic dimension. 'His most ambitious novel' – Brian Stableford.

Power, The (1956) ★★★ Novel by Frank M. Robinson (USA). A highly effective sf thriller about the hunting of a dangerous, psi-powered super-villain. Robinson's first novel. Filmed in 1967 (dir. Byron Haskin).

Power of Time, The (1985) ★★★ Collection by Josephine Saxton (UK). Varied sf and fantasy stories, ranging from 'The Wall' (Science Fantasy, 1965) to 'No Coward Soul' (Interzone, 1982). A long-overdue first collection from an under-appreciated British writer whose work is invariably powerful and sometimes blackly humorous, though it tends occasionally towards shapelessness.

Prayer Machine, The (1976) ★★ Novel by Christopher Hodder-Williams (UK). A laser device plunges the scientist hero into a parallel world which is terrorized by a totalitarian regime. But questions of reality and illusion dominate the plot of this psychological thriller. 'A maze of madness and metaphysics, tortuous enough to send you round the Mobius twist' – J. G. Ballard, New Statesman.

Preferred Risk (1955) ★★ Novel by Edson McCann (Lester del Rey and Frederik Pohl, USA). An insurance company has become the greatest force in society, and this has led to a future world in which all risks are eliminated. The hero embarks on a dangerous rebellion. A social satire-cum-adventure story in typical 1950s vein, though not quite as good as Pohl's collaborations with the late C. M. Kornbluth.

Prelude to Foundation (1988) ★ Novel by Isaac Asimov (USA). A latter-day prequel to the classic 'Foundation' series, describing Hari

Seldon's first visit to Trantor. It explains the events of the older stories as influenced behind the scenes by Daneel Olivaw, the robot hero of *The Caves of Steel* and *The Naked Sun*. Long and talky, as are all Asimov's 1980s novels.

Prelude to Space (1951) ★ Novel by Arthur C. Clarke (UK). The first rocket to the moon, in the year 1978, is described in scrupulous technical detail, in this rather wooden and very 'British' novel which was Clarke's first (written in 1947). Now very dated, it retains a historical interest.

Preserver (Foster): see under *Morphodite, The*.

Preserving Machine, The (1969) ★★★ Collection by Philip K. Dick (USA). Bulky volume of fifteen stories, ranging from 'Beyond Lies the Wub' (1952) to 'We Can Remember it For You Wholesale' (1966). Dick was rarely at his very best in the short-story form, but this book contains much that is stimulating.

Pride of Chanur (1982) ★★ Novel by C. J. Cherryh (USA). Set in 'the Compact', a loose trading community of interstellar species which mostly hate each other. Chanur, a family of lion-like Hani, save a human from torture by the horrid Kif. The plot is pretty much the same as that of Cherryh's earlier *Merchanter's Luck*. Sequel: *Chanur's Venture*.

Priest-Kings of Gor (Norman): see under *Tarnsman of Gor*.

Primal Urge, The (1961) ★ Novel by Brian W. Aldiss (UK). A mild science-fiction sex comedy, set in a future society whose citizens wear tell-tale lights on the foreheads which glow when they feel libidinal urges. Notably 'permissive' for its day, this is trivial Aldiss.

Prince of Mercenaries (Pournelle), see under *Mercenary, The*.

Princess of Mars, A (1917) ★★★ Novel by Edgar Rice Burroughs (USA), first in his 'Barsoom' series. John Carter, a 19th-century Confederate Army officer, is spirited to the planet Mars (Barsoom), where he finds an ancient, warlike civilization and falls in love with a red-skinned princess. Sheer hokum, more fantasy than sf, but nevertheless a surprisingly long-lived work of escapist entertainment. Sequels include *The Gods of Mars* (1918), *The Warlord of Mars* (1919), *Thuvia, Maid of Mars* (1920) and *The Chessmen of Mars* (1922).

Prisoner of the Planets (Fast): see *Secrets of Synchronicity, The*.

Prisoner of Zhamanak, The (de Camp): see under *Search for Zei, The*.

Prisoners of Paradise (1988) ★★ Novel by Ronald Anthony Cross (USA). A comedy which cleverly reworks the old enclosed-world theme of the multi-generational starship (see Heinlein's *Orphans of the Sky*, etc.). In this case, the environment has a bizarre holiday-camp, Disneyland atmosphere.

Private Cosmos, A (Farmer): see under *Maker of Universes, The.*

Privateers (1985) Novel by Ben Bova (USA). In a near-future world cowed by Soviet orbital weapons one brave (and highly sexed) American millionaire fights to break the Russian monopoly in the exploitation of space. Propagandistic rubbish, written in crass 'bestseller' style.

Pro (1978) ★★ Novel by Gordon R. Dickson (Canada/USA). The natives of world 48391D are not showing enough economic development to be useful to Earth, so a Sector Chief with a reputation for results is sent to shake things up. He fails dismally due to a lack of understanding of the locals, leaving a volunteer medical worker to save the day. The novel could easily have been set amongst European colonialists in Africa or Asia.

Probability Broach, The (1980) ★★ Novel by L. Neil Smith (USA), first in his 'Confederacy' series. A policeman from our time-line visits a parallel America which is 'governed' by an anarchist-libertarian confederacy, and soon becomes converted to his hosts' political point of view. An interesting projection of that strange brand of right-wing anarchism which seems to take its inspiration from the sf of Robert A. Heinlein. Smith's first novel, and winner of the 1982 Prometheus award (given annually by the Libertarian Futurist Society for the novel which best promotes its ideals). Sequels include: *The Venus Belt* (1981), *Their Majesties' Bucketeers* (1981), *The Naga-*saki Vector (1983), *Tom Paine Maru* (1984), *The Gallatin Divergence* (1985) and *The Wardove* (1986).

Probability Pad, The (1970) ★ Novel by T. A. Waters (USA), a sequel to Chester Anderson's *The Butterfly Kid* and Michael Kurland's *The Unicorn Girl.* Yet more hippie comedy.

Probe (1985) ★★ Novel by Carole Nelson Douglas (USA). A young woman with ESP powers becomes involved with the psychiatrist who is treating her. Psychological sf by a writer who has been more productive in the fantasy field. Sequel: *Counter-Probe* (1988).

Prodigal Sun, The (1964) ★ Novel by Philip E. High (UK). A man returns from an alien planet with certain super-powers: his purpose, to save the human race from doom. High's first novel. 'One of those run-of-the-mill British novels which isn't particularly bad and not particularly good' – James Colvin, *New Worlds.*

Prodigy (Cover): see under *Odyssey.*

Productions of Time, The (1967) ★★ Novel by John Brunner (UK). Enjoyable mystery story about the staging of a play which is a front for something much more sinister (the plot involves time travel). One of this prolific author's better entertainments of the period.

Profundis (1979) ★★ Novel by Richard Cowper (Colin Middleton Murry, UK). Black comedy about life aboard a huge submarine which circles the Earth aimlessly after a nuclear war. With its youthful hero on the run from the authoritarian captain, it's in a similar madcap vein to the author's earlier *Clone*. 'A genial, airy book – too good-tempered and light for passion' – D. West, *Foundation*.

Project Jupiter (Brown): see *Lights in the Sky are Stars, The*.

Project Pope (1981) ★★ Novel by Clifford D. Simak (USA). Robots and humans collaborate on a bizarre religious project — the building of a computer Pope. Wackily sentimental interplanetary adventure in its author's customary gentle vein. Perhaps the best of Simak's late novels.

Promised Land (Stableford): see under *Halcyon Drift*.

Prostho Plus (1971) ★★ Fix-up novel by Piers Anthony (USA). Humorous tales of a middle-aged dentist kidnapped by aliens and taken all round the galaxy to fix the teeth of various unlikely and repellent species. Flat, dated, but fun.

Protector (1973) ★★ Novel by Larry Niven (USA), part of his 'Known Space' sequence. The Pak, ancestors of humanity, live in the centre of the Galaxy. One of them visits us to find how we've got on, and is horrified to discover that none of us has ever grown up. The Pak get a bit hard to believe, but the story hangs together quite well. 'He's stuffed his series with so many irreconcilable aliens and gadgets and denouements that

this effort (especially as it comes early in the chronology that leads to *Ringworld*) nearly shakes the whole sequence to little bits' – John Clute.

Protectorate (1984) ★ Novel by Mick Farren (UK). Poets, politicians and prophets mingle in the decadent capital of an Earth passing from one set of incomprehensible alien masters to another.

Proteus Operation, The (1985) ★★ Novel by James P. Hogan (UK/USA). The Nazis have won World War II, so a team of American scientists goes back in time from the 1970s to 1939 in order to bring a different world into existence. In the complicated time-jumping adventure which follows, Churchill, Einstein, Hitler and a host of other real-life persons all have parts as characters. Quite an enjoyable attempt at a bestselling 'breakthrough' novel by this minor writer of hard sf.

Proteus Unbound (1988) ★★ Novel by Charles Sheffield (USA). Behrooz Wolf, the hero of *Sight of Proteus*, travels to the outer solar system to investigate problems in the Form Changing machines, and discovers a war about to start. The technology of Form Changing is well explained and internally consistent, if unbelievable.

Proud Enemy, The (Busby): see under *Cage a Man*.

Proud Robot: The Complete Galloway Gallegher Stories, The (Kuttner): see *Robots Have No Tails*.

Providence Island (1959) ★★ Novel by Jacquetta Hawkes (UK). A lost Stone-Age culture is discovered on a Pacific island which is threatened by nuclear tests. It turns out the natives have a psychic wisdom we have lost. A worthy foray into sf by J. B. Priestley's archaeologist wife.

Psion (1982) ★★ Novel by Joan D. Vinge (USA). In this 'young adult' tale, the tearaway juvenile hero, called Cat, grows into his extra-sensory powers and learns to use them in a life-or-death struggle. Colourful but conventional adventure fare for kids. Sequel: *Catspaw*.

Pstalemate (1971) ★ Novel by Lester del Rey (USA). The story of a man's gradual realization of his extra-sensory powers. An attempt at a 'serious' psi novel, it is old-fashioned and short on plot. 'Once Bronson has accepted his telepathic and precognitive faculties, he does almost nothing with them ... The second half of the book is very dull reading' – Christopher Priest, *Foundation*.

Psychedelic-40 (1965) ★ Novel by Louis Charbonneau (USA). In the 1980s the populace is controlled by a mind-expanding drug. A timely theme, handled in routine fashion – notable for its early use of the word 'psychedelic' in a book title. 'Provides at least a simulacrum of originality' – J. G. Ballard, *Guardian*. Published in the UK as *The Specials*.

Psychopath Plague, The (1978) ★ Novel by Stephen G. Spruill (USA). First of a series of interplanetary adventures in which a 22nd-century private eye called Elias Kane teams up with a formidable but pacific alien known as Pendrake. Routine stuff, with engaging lead characters. Sequels: *The Imperator Plot* (1983) and *The Paradox Planet* (1988).

Pulling Through (1983) ★ Novella and essays by Dean Ing (USA). A family lives through nuclear war in the western USA. Overtly intended to promote public civil defence and private survival preparations. Not as macho and brutal as some survivalist literature – it's mostly about things like basic nutrition and health care. There are plans for a fallout shelter and a cheap fallout meter. Perhaps it would work in a country with few people and widely dispersed targets; it's a pity Britain doesn't have that luxury.

Puppet Masters, The (1951) ★★★ Novel by Robert A. Heinlein (USA). Alien 'slugs' attack the earth, attaching themselves to people's nervous systems and turning their hosts into mindless puppets. Fast-moving tale of paranoid (anti-communist?) fears run wild. Well handled, a classic of its type.

Puppies of Terra, The (Disch): see *Mankind Under the Leash*.

Purity Plot, The (Goldin): see under *Imperial Stars, The*.

Purloined Prince, The (Wallace): see under *Deathstar Voyage*.

Purple Armchair, The (1961) Novel by Olga Hesky (UK). An almost unintelligible tale of a boring bureaucratic future visited by an alien tourist which looks like upholstery. One wonders why it bothered.

Purple Book, The (1982) ★★ Collection by Philip José Farmer (USA). Belated bringing together of the Hugo-winning novella 'Riders of the Purple Wage' (first published in the anthology *Dangerous Visions*, 1967) with its prequel 'The Oogenesis of Bird City' (1970) plus three other less obviously related tales. The principal story is one of Farmer's best things: a sprightly, punning, cranky utopian speculation which spins off ideas in all directions. It's a pity the author couldn't have expanded it into a proper novel rather than giving us this hodge-podge collection.

Purple Cloud, The (1901) ★★★ Novel by M. P. Shiel (UK). A cloud of purple gas kills off the human race – all save one lone Adam who wanders the deserted, corpse-strewn cities of Europe and the Near East. A unique work, highly regarded by many, though written in a near-hysterical tone of voice which is off-putting to some. 'A skill and artistry falling little short of actual majesty' – H. P. Lovecraft.

Putting Out (1988) ★★★ Novel by Neil Ferguson (UK). Semiotic thriller set in near-future New York. Fashion is all, and it carries a million coded signals. Ferguson's first novel. 'A very good book, quite brilliantly told, though intermittently skittish in its control of effect, so that the reader sometimes cares rather less than s/he should about the marbled intricacies of Ferguson's plotting' – John Clute.

Pyramids (1987) ★ Novel by Fred Saberhagen (USA). Time-travel larks in ancient Egypt, in this first of a series of light adventure novels about Pilgrim, the 'Flying Dutchman of Spacetime'. Sequel: *After the Fact* (1988).

Pzyche (1982) ★★ Novel by Amanda Hemingway (UK). Young woman lives on a far planet with her 'mad scientist' father. This seems to be more of a literary menarche fantasy than science fiction proper, though it undoubtedly uses many of the tropes of sf. 'Hemingway's novel has all the elements of a Keith Laumer space romp, but how differently deployed ... A confident and unusual first novel' – Colin Greenland, *Interzone*.

Q

Q Colony (1985) ★★ Novel by Robert Thurston (USA), expanded from his story 'The Oona Woman' (1981). Researchers on a newly-discovered planet investigate the local culture and become involved in sexual relations with the aliens. A tolerably well characterized work of speculative sf.

Quality of Mercy, The (1965) ★ Novel by D. G. Compton (UK). A fairly effective near-future psychological thriller about a looming nuclear war. Compton's first sf novel (he had already written crime fiction under the byline 'Guy Compton').

Quatermass (1979) ★★ Novel by Nigel Kneale (UK), based on his television serial. The legendary Professor Bernard Quatermass, now quite old, grapples with the problems of a crumbling near-future world, and in the process uncovers evidence of a sinister alien takeover. A well-written thriller which betrays a disgust for modern youth culture. The scripts of Kneale's three earlier 'Quatermass' serials (from the 1950s) have also been published in book form, but this is the only one which has been properly 'novelized'.

Queen of Air and Darkness, The (Anderson): see under *Beyond the Beyond*.

Queen of Springtime, The (Silverberg): see under *At Winter's End*.

Queen of the Legion, The (Williamson): see under *Legion of Space, The*.

Queen of Zamba, The (de Camp): see *Cosmic Manhunt*.

Quest for the Perfect Planet, The (Johns): see under *Now to the Stars*.

Quest for the Well of Souls (Chalker): see under *Midnight at the Well of Souls*.

Quest of the DNA Cowboys, The (1976) ★ Novel by Mick Farren (UK), first in a trilogy. A chaotically plotted sf/fantasy farrago which is full of rock-music and counter-cultural references. 'Sometimes recalls early Moorcock, but a more important influence is mid-1960s

Dylan, whose shadowy characters and hallucinatory aphorisms pop up everywhere' – Colin Greenland, *20th-Century SF Writers*. Sequels: *The Synaptic Manhunt* (1976) and *The Neural Atrocity* (1977).

Quest of the Three Worlds (1966) ★★ Fix-up novel by Cordwainer Smith (Paul Linebarger, USA). Four linked tales, which tell of the quest of a hero called Casher O'Neill across the strange landscapes of the Gem Planet, the Storm Planet, the Sand Planet, etc. 'Told with colour and uncommon imagination and a degree of whimsy that sets the teeth on edge' – James Cawthorn, *New Worlds*.

Quicksand (1967) ★★★ Novel by John Brunner (UK). Present-day mystery about a psychiatrist who treats a strange young woman. It turns out she is from the future, and he falls for her. But there's a nasty twist. An untypical work for this author, and one of his better books. 'Eminently readable' – Thomas M. Disch, *New Worlds*.

Quincuncx of Time, The (1973) ★ Novella by James Blish (USA), expanded from his magazine story 'Beep' (1954). Paradoxical problems arise when a spacefaring civilization of the future invents an instantaneous-communication device. Questions of free will and predestination are raised. The author's last novel, and one of his slightest. 'The story is in both versions marred by the contrived plot which Blish uses as a vehicle for the ideative content' – Brian Stableford.

R

R is for Rocket (1962) ★★★ Collection by Ray Bradbury (USA). Stories on space-travel themes, mostly selected from earlier Bradbury collections and here repackaged for a young readership. The follow-up volume is entitled *S is for Space*.

Radio Free Albemuth (1985) ★★★ Posthumously published novel by Philip K. Dick (USA). This was the original draft of the author's religious sf novel *VALIS* – but it's completely different from the other book (such was the throwaway profligacy of Dick's genius). It's as cranky as most of PKD's late work, but more lucid and entertaining than some of the other titles.

Radix (1981) ★★ Novel by A. A. Attanasio (USA). Cosmic rays (and other things too mysterious to paraphrase) trigger changes in Earth's biosphere. The hero grows up to be a killer of mutants, before discovering a greater, world-saving destiny. A long, confusing, ambitious and prolix first novel by an intelligent writer. 'At a level above the prose comic book it is difficult in the extreme to portray the efforts of a single strong man as affecting the destiny of the universe: when the universe in question is one that audience and author cannot grasp intellectually or sensuously then it becomes impossible' – Roz Kaveney, *Foundation*.

Ragged Astronauts, The (1986) ★★★ Novel by Bob Shaw (UK), first of a trilogy. Two worlds are joined by a narrow funnel of air. Population pressures and a deteriorating environment cause some of the inhabitants of 'Land' to make a heroic balloon journey to the mysterious 'Overland'. An ingenious narrative, nicely detailed. 'Shaw has ... returned to his grave and good best form as a teller of full-bodied sf tales' – John Clute. Sequel: *The Wooden Spaceships*.

Ragged Edge, The (Christopher): see *Wrinkle in the Skin, A*.

Rainbow Cadenza, The (1983) ★ Novel by J. Neil Schulman (USA). A girl reared in a 22nd-century space habitat returns to Earth and participates in a futuristic art-form involving lasers. The narrative is spun out with a great deal of political chit-chat. A sub-Heinleinian talk-piece in the Libertarian mode (compare L. Neil Smith's *The Probability Broach*). 'His characters' philosophizing is not only long-winded, insistent and ubiquitous; it is also shallow' – David N. Samuelson, *Foundation*.

Rama II (Clarke & Lee): see under *Rendezvous with Rama*.

Rapture Effect, The (1987) ★ Novel by Jeffrey Carver (USA). Some computer hackers and petty criminals get involved with an artificial intelligence which is being used to conduct a secret war in space. The aliens win, but are persuaded to make peace by respect for Earth's musicians and dancers.

Rax (Coney): see *Hello Summer, Goodbye*.

Reach (1989) ★ Novel by Edward Gibson (USA). Something very weird has happened to an astronaut in the outer solar system, and his buddies must find out what. The heroes of the novel are the astronauts and test pilots of the manned space-flight programme, delayed – but never frustrated – in their purpose by assorted politicians and office workers. Written by an ex-astronaut, this potentially interesting book is let down by gung-ho, adventure-comic monosyllabic prose.

Reach for Tomorrow (1956) ★★★ Collection by Arthur C. Clarke (UK). Twelve more sense-of-wonder tales, including such well-loved early pieces as 'Rescue Party' (1946), 'The Fires Within' (1949) and 'The Forgotten Enemy' (1953). Most are simply told, with twist endings.

Reality Trip and Other Implausibilities, The (Silverberg): see under *Needle in a Timestack*.

Realms of Tartarus, The (1977) ★★★ Novel by Brian Stableford (UK). Thousands of years hence, the surface of Earth has been covered by a vast platform where human beings enjoy an apparently utopian existence. However, new life-forms, cut off from the sun, are rapidly evolving below. A rather absurd premise here makes for a satisfying moral tale well founded in the author's knowledge of evolutionary ecology. Despite appearances, it's one of Stableford's best. Originally planned as a three-decker, part one alone appeared in the UK as *The Face of Heaven* (1976); all three parts were published in a single volume in the USA.

Real-Time World (1974) ★★ Collection by Christopher Priest (UK). Ten varied stories. In the effective title piece, an experimental group is deprived of all news and information from the outside world – with surprising results. Other notable tales include 'The Head and the Hand', about a futuristic showman who entertains the millions by progressively mutilating himself, and the powerful 'A Woman Naked'. Priest's fiction lacks a little in sparkle, but this is compensated for by a dogged originality.

Reavers of Skaith, The (Brackett): see under *Ginger Star, The*.

Rebel Worlds, The (Anderson): see under *We Claim These Stars*.

Rebel's Quest (Busby): see under *Star Rebel*.

Rebel's Seed (1986) ★ Novel by F. M. Busby (USA), sequel to *Rebel's Quest* and others. Lisele, daughter of the rebels who overthrew the political order of Earth's space empire in earlier volumes, is stranded on an isolated colony world. She gradually discovers the truth about the fate of the original settlers and the survivors' grotesquely authoritarian political system.

Re-Birth (Wyndham): see *Chrysalids, The*.

Rebirth, The (Cherryh): see *Cyteen*.

Recalled to Life (1962) ★ Novel by Robert Silverberg (USA). A private corporation perfects the means for resurrecting recently-dead bodies, but social conflict erupts when they try to get government permission to use their technique. Competent but uninspired near-future politicking. The novel was extensively revised in 1972.

Red Dwarf (1989) ★★ Novelization of their own TV series by 'Grant Naylor' (Rob Grant and Doug Naylor, UK). The hero is the only survivor of humanity, having been sentenced to three million years in stasis for taking an unauthorized cat aboard a spaceship. He converses with the ship's computer, various dream-personae, computer-generated characters, and a descendant of the cat (evolved to human intelligence), before settling down in a drug-induced hallucination of small-town America. The disorganized nature of the material makes the book less funny than the TV series – like the curate's egg, good in parts.

Red One, The (1918) ★★★ Collection by Jack London (USA). The title story, a novella, is widely regarded as an sf masterpiece. An explorer is captured by head-hunters, and discovers that their 'god' is an alien spacecraft. (Compare J G Ballard's story 'A Question of Re-Entry' in his collection *The Terminal Beach*.)

Red Peri, The (Weinbaum): see under *Best of Stanley G. Weinbaum, The*.

Red Planet (1949) ★★★ Novel by Robert A. Heinlein (USA). Two boys and their cute pet Martian called Willis get caught up in a colonists' rebellion on the red planet. An engaging yarn, beautifully imagined. It may be kids' stuff, but only the most curmudgeonly reader could fail to warm to it. This was the third of Heinlein's dozen 'juveniles' and the one in which the sequence really started to come good.

Red Sun of Darkover (Bradley): see under *Free Amazons of Darkover*.

Rediscovery of Man, The (Smith); see *Best of Cordwainer Smith, The*.

Redworld (1986) ★★ Novel by

Charles L. Harness (USA). On a planet of Barnard's Star, the elements are in short supply and scientific progress is retarded. A late, minor novel by this author who has been producing intriguing work sporadically since the 1940s – and who seems to have become more prolific in his old age.

Reefs of Earth, The (1968) ★★★ Novel by R. A. Lafferty (USA). A family of Puca (human-like creatures from an alternative world) are on Earth, persecuted and misunderstood. The children attempt to use their strange powers to have revenge on their persecutors. Nothing much bad happens; however it doesn't happen in Lafferty's unusual style – part fairy story, part children's fantasy, the story is advanced in asides, folktales, prophecies, and proverbs.

Reefs of Space, The (1964) ★ Novel by Frederik Pohl and Jack Williamson (USA), first in their 'Starchild' trilogy. Fairly clunky space opera which is representative of neither author at his best – and the sequels show small improvement. 'A cliché-ridden and hackneyed tale devoid of a single original image' – J. G. Ballard, *Guardian*. Sequels: *Starchild* (1965) and *Rogue Star* (1969).

Re-Entry (1981) ★★ Novel by Paul Preuss (USA). A satisfyingly convoluted hard-sf tale of time travel via black hole. 'Glossy, technophilic, ornate, savvy about the frontiers of knowledge, power-obsessed in the name of hardnosed realism: great on carapace; vacuous on the inner depths' – John Clute.

Refuge (Chilson): see under *Odyssey*.

Refugee (1983) Novel by Piers Anthony (USA). First volume of the 'Bio of a Space Tyrant' series. Hope Hubris, a Hispanic refugee from Callisto (which bears a strong resemblance to Central America) fails to enter the United States of Jupiter. The contemporary political references are lost in a book which reads as though it has been written at dictation speed and never revised. Sequels: *Mercenary* (1984), *Politician* (1985), *Executive* (1985).

Regenesis (1983) ★★ Novel by Alexander Fullerton (UK). In 1990 the American crew of an advanced submarine survives all-out nuclear war – but then discovers that some Russkies have survived too. An old-fashioned, militaristic sf thriller which moves along quite well. 'Clichés proliferate like ants at a picnic ... And yet, I enjoyed it' – Paul Kincaid, *Vector*.

Reign of Fire (1987) ★★ Novel by Marjorie Bradley Kellogg with William B. Rossow (USA), sequel to *The Wave and the Flame*, part two of 'Lear's Daughters'. Earthmen on the planet Fiix come to understand the nature of both the appalling weather and the native Sawls. 'Once out of the caves, Kellogg and Rossow vividly depict the strange landscapes caused by the climatic swings, and the strange lifeforms that survive there. And, given room to move, the characters become more three-dimensional – especially the coldly ruthless yet understandable villain' – Paul McAuley, *Interzone*.

Relatives (1973) ★ Fix-up novel by George Alec Effinger (USA). A curious, disjointed book about the fate of one man in three different parallel worlds. It's the work of an intelligent writer with a penchant for bizarre, surrealistic detail, but it fails to amount to more than the sum of its parts.

Remaking of Sigmund Freud, The (1985) ★★ Novel by Barry N. Malzberg (USA). In a late return to the sf field by this oddball writer, a reincarnated Sigmund Freud becomes the unlikely protagonist. 'Mature and rounded and at points hilarious' – John Clute.

Renaissance (1951) ★★ Novel by Raymond F. Jones (USA), from a 1944 magazine serial. A parallel-worlds adventure story of some complexity, incorporating many standard motifs, and possibly influenced by the works of A. E. van Vogt. Jones's first novel. Republished as *Man of Two Worlds*.

Rendezvous with Rama (1973) ★★★ Novel by Arthur C. Clarke (UK). A huge and apparently deserted alien spacecraft enters the solar system – providing Earth astronauts with a *Marie Celeste* mystery to the nth power. The characterization may be wooden, the psychological motivations flimsy and the plot paper-thin, but none of those things matter. The sense of wonder evoked by the gradual unfolding of Rama's secrets is what counts. One of Clarke's most effective novels. Hugo and Nebula award-winner, 1974. Sequel: *Rama II* by Arthur C. Clarke and Gentry Lee (1989).

Renegades of Time (1975) Novel by Raymond F. Jones (USA). Time-twisting nonsense in a van Vogtian vein, by a veteran sf writer. This happened to be the first in a line of cheap paperback sf novels known as 'Laser Books', a minor publishing phenomenon of the mid-1970s (edited by the then-ubiquitous Roger Elwood). Most Laser titles are not annotated here, but the series contained some competent works by younger writers such as Stephen Goldin, Gordon Eklund, Ray Nelson, K. W. Jeter and Tim Powers – as well as various novels by Jones.

Replay (1986) ★★★ Novel by Ken Grimwood (USA). The hero dies in 1988, and immediately finds himself reborn in his youthful body of the year 1963. With his knowledge of the 25 years to come, he proceeds to make himself rich by betting on races, investing in companies he knows will grow, and so on. But there are surprises in store. Not really sf, since no rational explanation is attempted, this is certainly one of the best 'timeslip' fantasies of recent years.

Report on Probability A (1968) ★★ Novel by Brian W. Aldiss (UK). Various persons from parallel dimensions watch each other obsessively. In part a meticulous description of humdrum suburban life, this is sf written in the style of Alain Robbe-Grillet – a voyeuristic anti-novel with a powerful air of mystery.

A unique work, unlikely to appeal to all tastes. 'Fossilized into the page, the events of the narrative have the exhausting tension of an Olympic slow bicycle race' – J. G. Ballard, *Times*.

Reproductive System, The (1968) ★★★ Novel by John Sladek (USA). A doll-manufacturing company decides to accept a US government grant to make self-replicating robotic machines (the 'reproductive system' of the title). Needless to say, they are all too successful: the production line runs out of control and the system's black boxes start to gobble everything up. A very funny first novel. 'Sladek's droll wit fills the narrative with grotesque characters' – J. G. Ballard, *Times*. Published in the USA as *Mechasm*.

Requiem for a Ruler of Worlds (1985) ★ Novel by Brian Daley (USA), first in his 'Hobart Floyt-Alacrity Fitzhugh' series. A roughly humorous space-adventure yarn about two Earthmen crossing the colonized galaxy in search of an inheritance. Colourful pulp shenanigans by a writer hitherto best known for his *Star Wars* spin-off novels (*Han Solo at Star's End*, etc). Sequels: *Jinx on a Terran Inheritance* (1985) and *Fall of the White Ship Avatar* (1987).

Rest of the Robots, The (1964) ★★ Collection by Isaac Asimov (USA). Clean-up collection of Asimov's 'positronic' robot stories serving as a sequel of sorts to his famous *I, Robot*. The original, massive, edition also contained the novels *The Caves of Steel* and *The Naked Sun*, but these have been omitted from reprints.

Restaurant at the End of the Universe, The (1980) ★★★ Novelization of radio serial by Douglas Adams (UK). Sequel to *The Hitch-Hiker's Guide to the Galaxy*, with a joke every paragraph and some genuine sf ideas as well. Not as good as the broadcast original. Sequel: *Life, the Universe and Everything*.

Restoree (1967) ★ Novel by Anne McCaffrey (USA/Ireland). A woman is snatched from the streets of New York and wakes up in a new body on a strange planet – stuck in the middle of an over-complex novel of intrigue, poisonings and assassinations that would be better set in Renaissance Italy.

Retief's War (Laumer): see under *Envoy to New Worlds* (also see that entry for all other books which have titles beginning with this hero's name).

Retread Shop (1988) ★ Novel by T. Jackson King (USA). The human hero grows up in an ancient space habitat which is, as the title implies, a sort of stellar second-hand goods emporium. A first novel. 'Fun, with lots of outrageously weird aliens, but too much goes on too fast to develop characters or scenario enough to sustain interest' – Carolyn Cushman, *Locus*.

Return of Nathan Brazil (Chalker): see under *Midnight at the Well of Souls*.

Return to Eden (Harrison): see under *West of Eden.*

Return to Mars (1955) ★ Novel by W. E. Johns (UK). The cast of *Kings of Space* are rescued by Martians and taken on a guided tour of the universe, setting the scene for seven further children's novels. Sequel: *Now to the Stars.*

Return to the Stars (Hamilton): see under *Star Kings, The.*

Revenge of the Senior Citizens Plus, The (Reed): see under *Mr Da V, and Other Stories.*

Revolt in 2100 (1953) ★★ Collection by Robert A. Heinlein (USA), introduced by Henry Kuttner. Three stories in the 'Future History' series: 'If This Goes On—' (1940) plus 'Coventry' (1940) and 'Misfit' (1939). Not the best of Heinlein's early work, these narratives show their age but retain some vigour.

Revolt of the Galaxy (Goldin): see under *Imperial Stars, The.*

Revolving Boy, The (1966) ★★★ Novel by Gertrude Friedberg (USA). A boy born in space is gifted with a sense of absolute direction, and is able to guide scientists to the source of an alien signal from another star. A well-told, beguiling narrative. Apparently its author's only novel.

Reward for Retief (Laumer): see under *Envoy to New Worlds.*

Rhapsody in Black (Stableford): see under *Halcyon Drift.*

Richest Corpse in Show Business, The (1966) ★★ Novel by Dan Morgan (UK). An amusing comedy about the future television industry, in which a producer finds himself threatened by a licensed killer – all for the delectation of the TV audience, natch. Morgan's least characteristic novel (most of his others have been dullish space operas or ESP stories), but also perhaps his best.

Riddley Walker (1980) ★★★ Novel by Russell Hoban (USA/UK). Many centuries after the bombs have fallen on Britain, young Riddley tells his story in a broken but poetic English. A tragicomic fable is enriched by ingenious puns and overtones of mysticism.

Right Hand of Dextra, The (1977) ★★ Novel by David J. Lake (UK/Australia). A rather rigid society of human colonists tries to come to terms with a planet whose biological make-up is fundamentally incompatible with that of Earth. Colourful adventure sf with an intelligent subtext and a number of literary references (the author is an academic). Sequel: *The Wildings of Westron* (1977).

Rim Gods, The (Chandler): see under *Road to the Rim, The.*

Rimrunners (1989) ★★★ Novel by C. J. Cherryh (USA), part of her loosely-knit 'Union/Alliance' series of space adventures. During an interstellar war, a marooned female soldier manages to find an uncomfortable berth on one of the enemy's 'Rimrunner' space vessels. The narrative is distinguished by good characterization and detail. 'Pared-down gritty realism ... This is space opera stripped down to its chassis, the usual widescreen effects compressed to the narrowest possible aperture' – Paul McAuley, *Interzone*.

Ring, The (1968) ★ Novel by Piers Anthony and Robert E. Margroff (USA). In the future, criminals are obliged to wear an electronic ring which prevents them from misbehaving. The rebellious hero realizes that the ring is in fact a good idea, in this vision of an unusually coercive technological utopia.

Ring Around the Sun (1953) ★★★ Novel by Clifford D. Simak (USA). Mutant human beings learn to penetrate the dimensions of space/time, and find a 'ring' of pristine alternative Earths. A very enjoyable pastoral tale with mystery overtones.

Ring of Garamas, The (1972) Novel by John Rankine (Douglas R. Mason, UK). Pedestrian space-war adventure stuff featuring Rankine's recurrent hero Dag Fletcher. 'Dulls the senses, tires the eye and allows the mind to wander away from the plot' – Christopher Priest, *Foundation*.

Ring of Ritornel, The (1968) ★★★ Novel by Charles L. Harness (USA). This 'comeback' novel (its author's first book in 15 years) is a rather old-fashioned but nonetheless impressive galactic-empire story – complexly plotted, with Harness's characteristic time themes thrown in. 'Among the most stylish modern space operas' – Brian Stableford.

Ringing Changes (Lafferty): see under *Strange Doings*.

Rings of Ice (1974) ★★ Novel by Piers Anthony (USA). The world is being deluged by a repeat of Noah's Flood; two survivalists have their fantasies about willing young women (with whom to refound the human race, natch) shattered when they pick up a diabetic, a transvestite ex-policeman, and a 13-year-old with cerebral palsy. They manage, in the end, to achieve some sort of domestic stability.

Ringworld (1970) ★★★ Novel by Larry Niven (USA). The space opera of the 1970s deserves its reputation for sheer effrontery of scale rather than the artificial characters or the stilted quest plot. The colossal Ringworld itself is not even the most impressive item in an array of over-the-top artefacts. Hugo and Nebula award-winner, 1971.

Ringworld Engineers, The (1980) ★ Novel by Larry Niven (USA), sequel to *Ringworld*. A rather weak plot is used as a device to answer reader's questions about that amazing artefact, the Ringworld.

Rissa and Tregare (Busby): see under *Young Rissa*.

Rissa Kerguelen (Busby): see under *Young Rissa*.

Rite of Passage (1968) ★★★ Fix-up novel by Alexei Panshin (USA). The young heroine must prove herself by leaving the huge spacecraft which is her home and surviving in the unfriendly conditions of a rough colony planet. A pleasing first-person narrative, with a well portrayed central character. Panshin's debt to Heinlein's juvenile novels has often been commented on, but the comparison doesn't tarnish this book. Nebula award-winner, 1969.

Rituals of Infinity, The (Moorcock): see *Wrecks of Time, The*.

Rival Rigellians, The (Reynolds): see under *Planetary Agent X*.

River of Time, The (1986) ★★ Collection by David Brin (USA). This first volume of shorter works by one of the most popular new sf writers of the 1980s contains varied material, most of it entertaining but some of it a bit glib. Includes the Hugo award-winning 'The Crystal Spheres' (1984), plus the well-received alternative-history fantasy 'Thor Meets Captain America' (1986).

Riverworld and Other Stories (1979) ★★ Collection by Philip José Farmer (USA). Eleven sf and fantasy stories, a few of which are reprinted from earlier Farmer collections. The title piece, about Tom Mix and Jesus Christ meeting in the afterlife, has been expanded to novella length for this book. The others are a mixed bag, ranging from an E. W. Hornung-'Raffles' pastiche to a brief 'Tarzan' tale written in the style of William S. (rather than Edgar Rice) Burroughs.

Road to Corlay, The (1978) ★★★ Novel by Richard Cowper (Colin Middleton Murry, UK), first in his 'White Bird of Kinship' trilogy. A thousand years hence an inundated Britain consists of many small islands, where a neo-medieval, theocratic society is disrupted by the coming of a millenarian cult which holds out the hope of social and spiritual renewal. Well-written, rather touching sf of a backward-looking, pastoral sort. The US and later UK editions include the related novella 'Piper at the Gates of Dawn' (also published in the collection *The Custodians*). Sequels (which carry the story much further into the future): *A Dream of Kinship* (1981) and *A Tapestry of Time* (1982).

Road to Science Fiction, The (1977–79) ★★★ Three-volume anthology edited by James Gunn (USA). Intended for teaching purposes (Gunn is a veteran sf writer but also an academic and one of the leading exponents of 'sf in the classroom'), the three books are arranged in chronological order and subtitled *From Gilgamesh to Wells*, *From Wells to Heinlein* and *From Heinlein to Here*. One could quarrel with the assumptions made in those subtitles – other than the fact that H. G. Wells is central to any history of sf – but the choice of short works and extracts to reprint is for the most part beyond reproach. A non-chronological fourth volume, subtitled *From Here to Forever*, was added in 1982.

Road to the Rim, The (1967) ★ Novel by A. Bertram Chandler (UK/Australia), part of his 'Rim Worlds' series. Chronologically, these are the earliest adventures of space-captain John Grimes, a sort of cosmic Horatio

Hornblower, out there on the galaxy's edge. Routine space opera, which gains a certain authenticity from its author's merchant-marine background. Other books about Grimes include *Into the Alternate Universe* (1964), *The Rim Gods* (1969), *The Hard Way Up* (1972), *The Big Black Mark* (1975), *Star Courier* (1977) and *Star Loot* (1980).

Roadmarks (1979) ★★ Novel by Roger Zelazny (USA). A dizzily-paced time-travel thriller, about various sketchily-drawn characters pursuing each other through numerous epochs and alternative worlds. Entertaining and often stylish, but shallow – like so much of Zelazny's output. 'A book as sweet as champagne and substantial as bubbles' – Tom Hosty, *Foundation*.

Roadside Picnic (1972) ★★★ Novel by Boris and Arkady Strugatsky (USSR). Alien visitors, who have stopped briefly on Earth for a 'picnic', leave behind a great deal of mysterious detritus. The plot concerns the men who scavenge among this rubbish, risking its dangers for the possible rewards. A subtle work with satirical touches. Filmed, obliquely and beautifully, as *Stalker* (1979; dir. Andrei Tarkovsky).

Robert Sheckley Omnibus, The (1973) ★★★ Collection by Robert Sheckley (USA), edited by Robert Conquest. Contains the novel *Immortality Inc.*, plus a dozen short stories including such classics as 'A Ticket to Tranai' and 'The Store of the Worlds'. All these works date from the 1950s, and the volume makes an excellent sampler from this witty author's best period.

Robot Adept (Anthony): see under *Juxtaposition*.

Robot Brains, The (1967) Novel by Sydney J. Bounds (UK). Time-travelling dwarfs with giant heads threaten Earth with mildly titillating sexy slave women. Amusing garbage.

Robot Dreams (1986) ★★★ Collection by Isaac Asimov (USA), illustrated by Ralph McQuarrie. Deluxe repackaging of twenty-one Asimov stories about robots, computers and space travel. Inevitably contains numerous overlaps with earlier collections (see *I, Robot, The Martian Way, The Rest of the Robots*, etc.), but the brief title story is an original.

Robots and Changelings (1958) ★★ Collection by Lester del Rey (USA). Proficient but unremarkable sf stories by an author who reached his peak in the pages of *Astounding* magazine during the 1940s – but who went on writing at a lesser pitch for a long time afterwards. Later del Rey collections include *Mortals and Monsters* (1965), *Gods and Golems* (1973) and *The Best of Lester del Rey* (1978).

Robots and Empire (1985) ★ Novel by Isaac Asimov (USA), a sequel to *The Robots of Dawn* and a prequel to the various novels in the 'Foundation' series (see *Foundation's Edge*). Lije Baley is now dead, but the robots Daneel and Giskard go on for ever – as does this 500-page novel, which is all talk, talk, talk.

Robots Have No Tails (1952) ★★ Collection by Henry Kuttner (USA), originally published under the pseudonym 'Lewis Padgett'. Five linked stories about the amusing adventures of Gallegher, who is capable of inventing fantastic devices only when he is drunk. He has a robot sidekick. All very silly, but they were regarded as among the best humorous sf of their day (the late 1940s). Reissued, with additions, as *The Proud Robot: The Complete Galloway Gallegher Stories* (1983).

Robots of Dawn, The (1983) ★★ Novel by Isaac Asimov (USA). The detective team of Elijah Baley and Daneel Olivaw (from *The Caves of Steel* and *The Naked Sun*) investigate roboticide on the planet Aurora and meet the telepathic robot Giskard, setting the scene for the rise of a non-robotic Galactic Empire. This book is a hinge between the (originally unconnected) 'Robot' and 'Foundation' series. Sequel: *Robots and Empire*.

Rocannon's World (1966) ★★ Short novel by Ursula K. Le Guin (USA). A human explorer, marooned on a far planet, attempts to save the place from an alien menace, and also learns 'mindspeech'. Well written, nicely imagined: the small beginning of a great sf career. Le Guin's first novel, and the first of her 'Hainish' cycle of books.

Rocket Ship Galileo (1947) ★ Novel by Robert A. Heinlein (USA). Space adventure story in which plucky kids fly to the moon with their brill-iant scientist friend. There they find a secret Nazi base. Notable only for being the first of Heinlein's excellent sequence of twelve juvenile sf novels. In this one he had not quite found the right ingredients. Filmed (very loosely) as *Destination Moon* (1950; dir. Irving Pichel).

Rod of Light, The (1985) ★★ Novel by Barrington J. Bayley (UK), a sequel to his *The Soul of the Robot*. Humanity is threatened by super-intelligent robots, who are fast gaining souls, and our mechanical hero Jasperodus must choose between humankind and robotkind. An amusing philosophical adventure.

Roderick (1980) ★★★★ Novel by John Sladek (USA). Roderick is a learning machine, a wide-eyed little robot who wanders like Candide through a crazy near-future America. It's a dense, wide-ranging satire, and the ultimate robot novel. Sequel (actually part two of a long novel which was chopped in half for publishing convenience): *Roderick at Random* (1983).

Rogue Bolo (Laumer): see under *Bolo: The Annals of the Dinochrome Brigade*.

Rogue Dragon (1965) ★★ Novel by Avram Davidson (USA). In the far future when the galaxy has been colonized, Earth has been turned into a sort of game reserve and happy hunting ground for 'dragons' — which turn out to be beasties of alien origin. One of this learned author's amiable sf potboilers.

Rogue Emperor (Kilian): see under *Fall of the Republic, The*.

Rogue Moon (1960) ★★★ Novel by Algis Budrys (USA). A matter transmitter is used to send men to the moon. There they encounter a terrifying alien 'maze'. This powerful psychological thriller deals with the human urge to transcend death.

Rogue Queen (1951) ★★ Novel by L. Sprague de Camp (USA), part of his 'Viagens Interplanetarias' series. Human explorers bring about a revolution on another planet: the matriarchal alien hive-dwellers learn the virtues of democracy. Adventure with touches of satire, told in its author's customary light manner.

Rogue Star (Pohl & Williamson): see under *Reefs of Space, The*.

Rolling Stones, The (1952) ★★ Novel by Robert A. Heinlein (USA). A fairly plotless juvenile adventure story about a family that buys a spaceship and goes on a grand tour of the solar system. Entertainingly done, and full of near-future 'realistic' touches. Published in the UK as *Space Family Stone*.

Rose, The (1966) ★★★ Collection by Charles L. Harness (USA). Three stories, two of which are short and comparatively insignificant. However, the long title story, originally published in 1953, has been hailed as a masterpiece by Judith Merril, Michael Moorcock and others. It is a well-balanced, cunningly-plotted (if sentimental),

tale of art and science, of love and transformation.

Rose for Armageddon, A (1982) ★★★ Novel by Hilbert Schenck (USA). Part love story, part scientific romance on the subject of 'morphology' (the finding of significant patterns in things), this is an unusual and moving book.

Rose for Ecclesiastes, A (Zelazny): see *Four for Tomorrow*.

Ruins of Earth: An Anthology of the Immediate Future, The (1971) ★★★ Anthology edited by Thomas M. Disch (USA). Stories on ecological themes, mostly dark-toned. The first of an excellent sequence of such compilations by Disch (see under *Bad Moon Rising* for details of others).

Rumours of Spring (1987) ★★ Novel by Richard Grant (USA), a quasi-sequel to *Saraband of Lost Time*. In an ecologically-devastated future America the last remaining forest begins to grow mysteriously and explosively. An expedition sets out to discover just what is going on. Fantasy-tinged sf on a greenwood theme, recalling such celebrated recent fantasy novels as John Crowley's *Little, Big* (1981) and Robert Holdstock's *Mythago Wood* (1984). 'The novel ends in passages – it is no matter how laboriously they were achieved – of surefooted earned elation' – John Clute.

Run, Come See Jerusalem (1976) ★★ Novel by Richard C. Meredith (USA). A satisfyingly complex time-travel and alternative-universe yarn. The author's knowledge of history is sound, and his depictions of possible 21st-century events (which are consequent upon his hero's meddling with the past) are well extrapolated.

Run to the Stars (1982) ★★ Novel by Mike Scott Rohan (UK). The hero and heroine pit themselves against malign bureaucrats who wish to destroy the space programme. A rumbustious space adventure with a pleasantly Scottish flavour. Rohan's first novel (his subsequent works have been fantasy).

Runts of 01 Cygni C (1970) Novel by James Grazier (USA). Sex on an alien planet. Hilariously bad, one of the prime contenders for the title of Worst SF Novel Ever Published.

Russian Hide and Seek (1980) ★★ Novel by Kingsley Amis (UK). A future-invasion-of-Britain story, in which the Russians have almost obliterated English culture. Not Amis's best: a bitter, reactionary comedy.

S

S is for Space (1966) ★★★ Collection by Ray Bradbury (USA). A recombination of well-known stories by Bradbury, intended for the juvenile market. A follow-up to the similar earlier collection *R is for Rocket*.

Sabella, or The Blood Stone (1980) ★★★ Novel by Tanith Lee (UK). The powerful tale of a woman who falls under the influence of an ancient Martian necklace – which effectively turns her into a vampire (sympathetically portrayed). Lee is known primarily for her fantasy novels, but this one uses the trappings of sf to good effect.

Saliva Tree and Other Strange Growths, The (1966) ★★★ Collection by Brian W. Aldiss (UK). Ten stories, of which the long title piece (1965) is the most notable: a centenary tribute to H. G. Wells, it reworks ideas from several of that great writer's novels. Other pieces, such as the space-operatic 'Legends of Smith's Burst' (1959), reveal Aldiss's talent for imagery and his relish for language (the last-named story concludes memorably: 'I noticed that her tears were falling upwards towards the tatterdemalion clouds').

Salvage Rites and Other Stories (1989) ★★ Collection by Ian Watson (UK). The usual mixed bag of shorter pieces from this spritely and prolific author. Standouts include the mysterious 'The Moon and Michelangelo,' and the bizarre fantasy 'Lost Bodies'. Many of the stories have an unexpected twist to them. 'When it works he's good and even if it doesn't he's still interesting' – Wendy Bradley, *Interzone*.

Sam McCade, Interstellar Bounty Hunter (1986) ★ Series of space adventure novels by William C. Dietz (USA). In the first book, *War World*, McCade, cashiered from the Imperial Navy for refusing to fire on an unarmed ship and earning his living as a bounty-hunter, is brought before his old commander and forced to go on a secret mission to save the interstellar Empire. The sequel, *Imperial Bounty* (1988), continues in the same predictable vein.

Same to You Doubled and Other

Stories, The (Sheckley): see *Can You Feel Anything When I Do This?*

San Diego Lightfoot Sue (1979) ★★ Collection by Tom Reamy (USA). Short stories and film outlines (almost everything printable from the author's short career), with a rather purple introduction/obituary from Harlan Ellison. Angels, demons, gays and country boys from Kansas walk the streets of Los Angeles, each as alien as the others. In the typical title story a naïve teenager goes to the big city and falls in love with a much older woman: it all ends in violence with a little black magic on the side.

Sandkings, (Martin): see under *Songs of Stars and Shadows*.

Sands of Mars, The (1951) ★★ Novel by Arthur C. Clarke (UK). The human colonization of the planet Mars is described in a technically accurate way (though certain details are now very dated) in this early and minor novel by a major writer.

Santaroga Barrier, The (1968) ★★★ Novel by Frank Herbert (USA). A small American town harbours a mystery: all its citizens seem to be unified against the outside world. It transpires that an experiment with a new drug has endowed the townsfolk with group-mindedness. One of Herbert's more effective treatments of the hive mentality – and the possible next step in the evolution of human intelligence.

Santiago (1986) ★★★ Novel by Mike Resnick (USA). This effective space opera has a cyclic structure of quests, as various bounty-hunters and opportunists search the galaxy of the far future for a famous criminal called Santiago.

Saraband of Lost Time (1985) ★★★ Novel by Richard Grant (USA). A motley band of adventurers sets out on a quest for the 'Overmind' on an Earth of decayed technologies. A stylish far-future mood piece, very much in the vein of M. John Harrison's sf/fantasy *A Storm of Wings* (see under *The Pastel City*) – though perhaps overlong. Grant's first novel. 'Great fun while it lasts, more literate and intelligent than a shelf full of generic posthistories' – Colin Greenland, *Foundation*. Quasi-sequel: *Rumours of Spring*.

Sardonyx Net, The (1981) ★★ Novel by Elizabeth A. Lynn (USA). Drugs enable slavers to maintain their rotten regime on a far planet. The subject matter may sound unpromising, but it's a well-plotted, sensitive adventure story.

Scanner Darkly, A (1977) ★★★ Novel by Philip K. Dick (USA). In near-future California an undercover narcotics agent uses high-tech means to spy on his friends – and himself. Full of ghastly black humour, and also very moving. A powerful indictment of the drug culture, by an author who knew it well.

Scarlet Plague, The (1915) ★★ Novel by Jack London (USA). Disease destroys most of humanity, and the survivors are reduced to savagery. A bleak tale from an author whose socialist idealism seems to have been mixed with a thorough contempt for the human race.

Scent of New-Mown Hay, A (1958) ★★ Novel by John Blackburn (UK). A vile Nazi scientist has created spores which transform women into monsters, and the plague sweeps the world. Horrific hokum with an sf rationale. The first of this author's many successful horror thrillers, some of which may be regarded as science fiction.

Schismatrix (1985) ★★★ Novel by Bruce Sterling (USA), the climax of his 'Shaper/Mechanist' cycle of stories (for others see under *Crystal Express*). This remarkably inventive book is an exploration of various 'post-human' cultures living, by no means harmoniously, in artificial space habitats. Few recent writers of sf have treated the future evolution of the human race in such serious and stimulating terms. Sterling's best novel.

Schrodinger's Cat: The Universe Next Door (1979) ★★ Novel by Robert Anton Wilson (USA). A strange, comic farrago which uses quantum mechanics as its imaginative underpinning. A typically zany work by the co-author of the cult *Illuminatus!* trilogy (1975; written with Robert Shea, it also has some claim to being sf). Sequels (or, more accurately, companion novels): *The Trick Top Hat* (1980) and *The Homing Pigeons* (1981).

Science Fiction Argosy, A (Knight): see under *Century of Science Fiction, A*.

Science Fiction Hall of Fame, Volume 1 (1970) ★★★★ Anthology edited by Robert Silverberg (USA). Huge collection of 26 stories selected by means of a poll of sf writers to find work published before 1964 which might have won Nebula awards – had Nebulas existed in earlier days. Everything you might expect to see is here, from 'A Martian Odyssey' (1934) by Stanley G. Weinbaum to 'A Rose for Ecclesiastes' (1963) by Roger Zelazny. The stories are in chronological order, and it's noticeable that almost all those written before 1945 (for example, Murray Leinster's 'First Contact' and Fredric Brown's 'Arena') have upbeat endings; afterwards – Judith Merril's depressing 'That Only a Mother' is the turning point – things get much darker. Perhaps it was the Bomb. The book has been split into two or more volumes for paperback reprints.

Science Fiction Hall of Fame, Volumes IIa and IIb (1973) ★★★ Anthologies edited by Ben Bova (USA). Longer stories chosen on the same basis as the 1970 Robert Silverberg anthology *Science Fiction Hall of Fame*. It's not as consistently brilliant a selection as the earlier book, but there is undoubtedly required reading here – such as E. M. Forster's 'The Machine Stops' (1909), Clifford D. Simak's 'The Big Front Yard' (1958) and 'The Ballad of Lost C'mell' (1962) by Cordwainer Smith. (Confusingly, the first half was published in the UK in three parts as *Science Fiction Hall of Fame: The Novellas*, volumes 1 to 3.)

Science Fiction of Edgar Allan Poe, The (1976) ★★★★ Collection edited by Harold Beaver (USA). An excellent annotated gathering of all Poe's proto-sf pieces (first published in the 1840s). Includes several stories easily located in standard Poe collections – 'MS. Found in a Bottle', 'A Descent Into the Maelstrom', etc. – but also such less accessible works as 'The Unparalleled Adventure of One Hans Pfaall', about a balloon trip to the moon, and 'Mellonta Tauta', a tale of the 29th century.

Science Fiction of Mark Clifton, The (1980) ★★ Posthumous collection by Mark Clifton (USA), edited by Barry N. Malzberg and Martin H. Greenberg. Eleven stories, mainly from the 1950s, representing about half of this workmanlike author's short-fiction output. Includes 'Sense from Thought Divide', perhaps his best known psi-piece in the 'Ralph Kennedy' series.

Science Fictional Solar System, The (1979) ★★★ Anthology edited by Isaac Asimov, Martin H. Greenberg and Charles G. Waugh (USA). Straight sf stories which work their way planet by planet through the solar system – from 'The Weather on the Sun' via Alan E. Nourse's classic 'Bright Side Crossing' (about Mercury) and tales by Robert Sheckley, Terry Carr, Asimov, James Blish, Arthur C. Clarke, Fritz Leiber, Alexei Panshin, Larry Niven and Robert F. Young (there are two stories for Pluto) to Duncan Lunan's 'The Comet, the Cairn and the Capsule', set on the doorstep of interstellar space.

Scorpion God, The (1971) ★★★ Collection by William Golding (UK). Three novellas, including the excellent 'Envoy Extraordinary' (1956), about a technological genius in Ancient Rome who is simply too far ahead of his time. The other stories are historical fantasies, written with this Nobel Prize-winning author's customary sensuous brilliance.

Scourge of Screamers, A (Galouye): see *Lost Perception The*.

Scudder's Game (1985) ★★ Novel by D. G. Compton (UK), initially published in German and not published in English until 1988. The ultimate contraceptive device has produced a near-future utopia of controlled population growth and free love. However, the crusty hero, Scudder, rebels. A well-characterized narrative, but alas the book (evidently written pre-AIDS) seems old-fashioned.

Sea and Summer, The (1987) ★★★ Novel by George Turner (Australia). An admirably sombre and well-realized vision of life in the 21st century after almost everything has gone wrong: the greenhouse effect has caused the seas to rise, and over-population and unemployment have led to catastrophic economic collapse. The tale of various people struggling to maintain a decent life in Australia, it's a dark but genuinely moving book. Turner's best novel. Winner of the 1988 Arthur C. Clarke award. Published in the USA as *The Drowning Towers*.

Sea of Glass (1987) ★★ Novel by

Barry B. Longyear (USA). A boy grows up in a vicious concentration camp for illegal children, in an America preparing for a war of triage with the desperately poor 'Otherworld' in the East. He takes mental refuge in old sf and war films, but, in the end, comes to accept the brutal philosophy of his jailers and the intelligent supercomputer that controls the country.

Sea-Horse in the Sky (1969) ★ Novel by Edmund Cooper (UK). Cooper's favourite wish-fulfilment theme – a group of Earthlings is kidnapped by aliens and left on an uninhabited planet with instructions to go forth and multiply, placing the protagonist (and thus the author and the male reader) in a situation where it is his duty to have sex with various attractive women and generally act the patriarch.

Search for Zei, The (1962) ★★ Novel by L. Sprague de Camp (USA), part of his 'Viagens Interplanetarias' series, first serialized in 1950. More rumbustious adventures on the backward planet called Krishna (see *Cosmic Manhunt* for an earlier instalment). Republished as *The Floating Continent* in the UK only. Other 'Krishna' novels, all humorous yarns with a fantasy flavour, include *The Tower of Zanid* (1958), *The Hand of Zei* (1963), *The Hostage of Zir* (1977), *The Prisoner of Zhamanak* (1982) and *The Bones of Zora* (1983).

Search the Sky (1954) ★★ Novel by Frederik Pohl and C. M. Kornbluth (USA). An episodic satire in which the hero visits several colonized planets, discovering that absurd social problems afflict each. It has good moments, but it's the least impressive of the authors' four collaborative sf novels.

Seasons in Flight (1984) ★★ Collection by Brian W. Aldiss (UK). Ten fable-like narratives, more fantasy than sf. Highpoints include 'The Gods in Flight' (1984), about a nuclear war as witnessed from Indonesia. Others, such as 'Incident in a Far Country', more nearly resemble fairy tales. The 1986 paperback reprint includes an extra story, the brief 'Juniper'.

Second Ending (1962) ★★ Novel by James White (UK). The last human escapes a radioactive Earth and outlives the solar system in suspended animation, cared for by loving robots. Plainly written, old-fashioned sf with a genuine cosmic vision.

Second Foundation (1952) ★★★ Fix-up novel by Isaac Asimov (USA), sequel to *Foundation and Empire* and third in the original 'Foundation Trilogy'. The grand story of Seldon's plan, Gibbon's *Decline and Fall of the Roman Empire* projected on to a galactic scale, comes to an exciting climax. The writing is creaky, but the over-arching vision shines through. Belated sequel: *Foundation's Edge*.

Second Genesis (1986) ★★★ Novel by Donald Moffitt (USA), sequel to *The Genesis Quest*. Artificially engineered humans from a remote galaxy arrive in the Milky Way and search for the 70-million-year-old remains of human civilization. They find that whole phyla have risen and fallen and come across some immense artefacts. Written with some understanding of evolution and a sense that the universe is a very big place indeed.

Second Nature (1982) ★★★ Novel by Cherry Wilder (New Zealand/ Germany). Maxim Bro, last of the hereditary record-keepers on the lost planet Rhomary, is torn between the preservation of memories of Earth, the desire to adapt to the present alien environment, and ritual contact with the native Vail – monstrous intelligences which vanished mysteriously generations earlier. A richly textured and intelligent treatment of alien environments.

Second Stage Lensman (Smith): see under *First Lensman*.

Second Trip, The (1972) ★★ Novel by Robert Silverberg (USA). A new personality is created for a 'mind-wiped' criminal, but the old memories keep breaking through. A chilling split-brain nightmare, written with all Silverberg's usual sophistication and breadth of reference.

Second Variety (Dick): see under *Beyond Lies the Wub*.

Secret Ascension, The (1987) ★★★ Novel by Michael Bishop (USA). In a horrid alternative time-line, America won the Vietnam war and the dictatorial Richard M. Nixon is still president in the 1980s. The novelist Phil Dick (who, in our world, died in 1982) attempts to rectify this. A tour de force in which Bishop plays with Dick's favourite reality-changing themes. 'He has created an homage that avoids the trap of pastiche, a novel that succeeds in its own right as a witty alternate history' – Michael A. Morrison, *SF & Fantasy Book Review Annual 1988*. Published in Britain as *Philip K. Dick is Dead, Alas*.

Secret Harmonies (McAuley): see *Of the Fall*.

Secret of Life, The (Rucker): see under *White Light*.

Secret Scorpio (Akers): see under *Transit to Scorpio*.

Secret Sea, The (1979) ★★ Novel by Thomas F. Monteleone (USA). A parallel-world story in which the hero encounters the *Nautilus*, Captain Nemo and Robur the Conqueror – all from the works of Jules Verne. One of a number of sf 'sequels-by-other-hands' which appeared in the 1970s (examples include Farmer's *The Other Log of Phileas Fogg* and Aldiss's *Frankenstein Unbound*). This one is tolerably entertaining.

Secret Songs, The (1968) ★★★ Collection by Fritz Leiber (USA). Sf and fantasy stories of considerable variety and idiosyncrasy, many of them reprinted from earlier Leiber collections. As well as early standards like 'The Smoke Ghost', it includes some interestingly unclassifiable tales from the 1960s such as 'The Winter Flies', and the title piece. 'Every story in the book is finished with a craftsman's care, and they are all thoroughly readable' – M. John Harrison, *New Worlds*. This volume appeared in Britain only.

Secrets of Synchronicity, The (1977) ★ Novel by Jonathan Fast (USA). Light-hearted space opera with touches of mysticism. A first novel by the son of bestselling author Howard Fast. Published in the UK as *Prisoner of the Planets*.

Section G: United Planets (Reynolds): see under *Planetary Agent X*.

Sector General (White): see under *Hospital Station*.

Seed of Earth, The (Silverberg): see under *Silent Invaders, The*.

Seed of Evil, The (1979) ★★ Collection by Barrington J. Bayley (UK). Crazy fiction of ideas, as only Bayley can write it. The prose is sometimes wooden, but the concepts are almost invariably stimulating. Standouts include 'Man in Transit' and 'Sporting with the Chid'.

Seed of Stars (Morgan & Kippax): see under *Thunder of Stars, A*.

Seedling Stars, The (1957) ★★★ Collection by James Blish (USA). Linked stories in the 'Pantropy' series, concerning humans specially engineered to survive on alien planets. Contains 'Surface Tension', perhaps Blish's most popular short story, about the heroic struggles of little people who live in a pool: they succeed in transcending their environment, and the sense of wonder which this evokes has stirred many readers.

Seeds of Time, The (1956) ★★ Collection by John Wyndham (UK). A likeable gathering of sf stories, most of them proficient treatments of fairly obvious themes. Among the most enjoyable are 'Pawley's Peepholes' (1951) and 'Dumb Martian' (1952) – well-mannered sf comedies in a very English vein.

Seetee Ship (1951) ★★ Fix-up novel by Jack Williamson (USA), originally published under the pseudonym 'Will Stewart'. The strange word in the title stands for 'contra-terrene' matter, a means to achieve an anti-gravity star drive. Space opera of a slightly more sedate and thoughtful variety than the author's galaxy-busters of the 1930s. Sequel (published in book form first): *Seetee Shock* (1950).

Seg the Bowman (Akers): see under *Transit to Scorpio*.

Sense of Obligation (Harrison): see *Planet of the Damned*.

Sentenced to Prism (1985) ★★ Novel by Alan Dean Foster (USA). A human visitor is stranded on a world which is dominated by rapidly-evolving machine-like, exuberant, colourful, crystalline silicate life. A typical Alan Dean Foster adventure story, with a nicely imagined background.

Sentimental Agents in the Volyen Empire, The (Lessing): see under

Marriages Between Zones Three, Four, and Five, The.

Sentinel, The (1983) ★★★ Collection by Arthur C. Clarke (UK). A sampler of the author's finest stories, here presented as an attractive package illustrated by Lebbeus Woods. The title piece is of course the story which eventually became *2001: A Space Odyssey*, and among the other notable items is 'Guardian Angel', the original magazine version of Clarke's most memorable novel, *Childhood's End*.

Sentinel Stars, The (1963) ★ Novel by Louis Charbonneau (USA). In an over-regimented future society, burdened by vast taxes, some citizens rebel. It's one of those fairly dreary dystopian warnings in which the characters have numbers instead of names.

Sentinels from Space (1953) ★ Novel by Eric Frank Russell (UK). Mars, Venus and Earth are torn by mistrust between telepaths and normal humans – but the discovery of interstellar travel and hostile aliens makes their squabbles irrelevant. More dated and less humorous than most of Russell's writing, and not at all the author's best work.

Serpent's Egg (1987) ★★★ Novel by R. A. Lafferty (USA). Indescribable farrago in unique Lafferty style about a group of super-children, some human. There is no real beginning, middle or end and what plot there is is mostly predicted by the characters who tend to talk in prophecy. Superb fun.

Serpent's Reach (1980) ★★ Novel by C. J. Cherryh (USA). Settlers isolated on an alien world, find a way to live with the non-human inhabitants (without ever understanding them), which is then disrupted by a new intervention from the human universe. The talented heroine allies with the ant-like aliens in her quest for revenge. A complexly-plotted space adventure story in its author's usual mode. Detailed and imaginative.

Servants of the Wankh (Vance): see under *Planet of Adventure.*

Seven Sexes, The (Tenn): see under *Wooden Star, The.*

Several Minds, The (Morgan): see under *New Minds, The.*

Sex and the High Command (1970) ★★ Novel by John Boyd (USA). Women are liberated from their need for men, thanks to a drug which provides them with both sexual pleasure and female babies. Men fight back, with military means, but are unable to prove their virility. A rather galumphing satire which will probably offend partisan readers of both sexes.

Sex Sphere, The (Rucker): see under *White Light.*

SF: Author's Choice (1968–74) ★★ Anthology series edited by Harry Harrison (USA/Ireland). Each contributor was invited to choose his or her own favourite sf story for reprinting here, and to write an afterword explaining the reasons for the choice. The results are quirky but interesting. The first volume only was published in the UK, under the title *Backdrop of Stars:* it contained work by Brian Aldiss, Poul Anderson, J. G. Ballard, Frederik Pohl and others.

SF: The Year's Greatest Science Fiction and Fantasy (1956) ★★★ Anthology edited by Judith Merril (USA), first in a series which reached 13 volumes. This book heralded the most celebrated of all the 'year's best' anthology series – and there have been many such series, from editors like Wollheim, Carr, Harrison and Aldiss, and Dozois. Merril's tastes were more catholic than most, and her critical commentary was wide-ranging and provocative. During the 1960s, she became the first American advocate of the 'New Wave' in sf, and her later volumes reflect that enthusiasm. The books were published every year except 1967, the last being *SF 13* (1969). (Unfortunately, the British reprint titles varied wildly: most of them were called *The Best of Sci-Fi*, with numbers which did not tally with those of the US editions.) An additional volume, *The Best of the Best* (1967), contained a retrospective selection from the first 11 books. 'Judith Merril anthologies were a big influence [on me] ... She would publish really esoteric, memorable things' – William Gibson, *SF Eye*.

Shadow Hunter, The (1982) ★★ Novel by Pat Murphy (USA). A Stone-Age man is plucked from his own era and brought to a future world he cannot understand. An engagingly written tale of cultural contrasts. Murphy's first novel.

Shadow of Alpha, The (1976) ★ Novel by Charles L. Grant (USA). In a post-disaster America, depleted by plague, formerly-subservient androids now roam dangerously free. A fairly routine first novel by a writer who has since become famous for his supernatural horror fiction. Sequels, tracing the subsequent fortunes of the 'Parric' family: *Ascension* (1977) and *Legion* (1979).

Shadow of Earth (1979) ★★ Novel by Phyllis Eisenstein (USA). A modern woman is plunged into an alternative world where male chauvinism is rampant. It transpires that the Spanish Armada succeeded in conquering England, and as a consequence the world in this time-line is technologically and socially backward. A well-worn scenario (see, for example, Brunner's *Times Without Number*), here presented with a feminist edge.

Shadow of the Ship, The (1983) ★ Novel by Robert W. Franson (USA). In an unlikely twist on the usual gimmicks of interstellar flight, here huge beasts pull caravans of travellers through space – like the wagon trains of the old west. 'A very unusual adventure story' – Brian Stableford.

Shadow of the Torturer, The (Wolfe): see *Book of the New Sun, The.*

Shadow on the Hearth (1950) ★★★ Novel by Judith Merril (USA). New

York comes under nuclear attack, and we view the consequences through the eyes of a suburban housewife whose world gradually falls apart. A tale of atomic doom which is very quiet and restrained, and all the more effective for it. Merril's first novel, and her best.

Shadows in the Sun (1954) ★★ Novel by Chad Oliver (USA). A small Texan town harbours a great alien mystery. This plainly written and very enjoyable tale of the everyday in contact with the cosmic is reminiscent of the books which Clifford Simak did so well at around the same time. Oliver's first novel.

Shadows of the White Sun (1988) ★★ Novel by Raymond Harris (USA). A woman from a sophisticated space-habitat culture learns to live the more rugged life of a pioneer on the surface of a modified planet Venus. Well detailed, but rather dry. It shows the influence of Wolfe's *The Book of the New Sun*: an ambitious example to follow. 'Recommended to fans of sociological/anthropological sf' – Carolyn Cushman, *Locus*.

Shadrach in the Furnace (1976) ★★ Novel by Robert Silverberg (USA). A near-future dictator undergoes elaborate organ-transplant surgery in order to sustain himself for ever. This is the story of his doctor, who eventually is expected to sacrifice his own body for the sake of his master's health. 'Ingenious and literate, the novel might well have given one or two interesting ideas to Howard Hughes in his last years' – J. G. Ballard, *New Statesman*.

Shakespeare's Planet (1976) ★ Novel by Clifford D. Simak (USA). An Earthman is marooned on an alien planet with some very strange denizens. Shakespeare has little to do with it. Simak is never less than decently entertaining, but this is one of his more mediocre efforts.

Shape Changer, The (Laumer): see under *World Shuffler, The*.

Shape of Sex to Come, The (1978) ★★ Anthology edited by Douglas Hill (Canada/UK). Eight stories, by Aldiss, Moorcock, Silverberg and others, which deal in one way or another with the future of sex. Other, similar, sf anthologies which have used this perennially popular theme include *Strange Bedfellows: Sex and Science Fiction* (1972) edited by Thomas N. Scortia and *Arrows of Eros* (1989) edited by Alex Stewart.

Shape of Space, The (Niven): see under *Neutron Star*.

Shaper's Legacy (Finch): see under *Garden of the Shaped, The*.

Shards of Honor (1986) ★★ Novel by Lois McMaster Bujold (USA), first in her 'Miles Vorkosigan' series. A hard-nosed military space yarn which also mixes in some love-story elements, and somehow makes the combination work. Bujold's first novel, and the beginning of a prolific and popular career. Sequel: *Brothers in Arms*.

Shards of Space (Sheckley): see under *Pilgrimage to Earth*.

Sharra's Exile (1981) ★★ Novel by Marion Zimmer Bradley (USA), a heavily rewritten and restructured version of her *The Sword of Aldones* (1962; see also the entry for that book). Telepaths on Darkover try to use the ancient sciences of the planet as weapons. A sequel to *The Heritage of Hastur* which features many of the same people and events as *The Sword of Aldones*, although this is a longer, more detailed, more internally consistent and (in the author's own opinion) more mature book. There is an emphasis on loneliness, friendship and loyalty, particularly in same-sex relationships.

Shatterday (1982) ★★★ Collection by Harlan Ellison (USA). Another gathering of sf, fantasy and unclassifiable tales by this author whom Algis Budrys has described as 'the quintessential sf short story writer of his time' (although there's not quite enough sf here to justify that praise). Most notable is the moving 'Jeffty is Five' (Nebula award-winner, 1978) a lament for the lost days of American radio entertainment.

Shattered Chain, The (1976) ★★ Novel by Marion Zimmer Bradley (USA). Three linked adventures set on the planet Darkover in the first generation after its rediscovery by Earth, each featuring women who have taken an oath never to bind themselves to men. There is a continuing theme of debate about marriage, choice and freedom. The characters introduced here reappear in *Thendara House* and *City of Sorcery*.

Shattered People, The (1975) ★

Novel by Robert Hoskins (USA). Intrigue in a galactic empire where rebels are 'mind-wiped' and transported to prison planets. All comes out well in the end, in this run-of-the-mill space opera.

Sheep Look Up, The (1972) ★★★ Novel by John Brunner (UK). In the very near future America is almost terminally polluted. An ecologist hero tries to stir people to action, but it's already too late. Anti-escapist sf: a large and ambitious catalogue of likely disasters, adding up to an effective 'dreadful warning'. However, some readers may regard it as an overstatement of its case.

Shield (1963) ★★ Novel by Poul Anderson (USA). With alien assistance from Mars, the hero invents a force-field – and soon everyone is after him for the secret. An adequately exciting sf chase thriller, more earthbound than most of Anderson's work.

Shift Key, The (1987) ★ Novel by John Brunner (UK). Old-fashioned mystery story about a small English town which is overcome by a strange malaise. People begin to behave irrationally, and a supernatural cause is suspected. It turns out there is an up-to-date scientific explanation. Minor Brunner and marginal sf.

Shikasta (1979) ★★ Novel by Doris Lessing (UK), first of her 'Canopus in Argos: Archives' series. Lessing is a major novelist, and her first full-blown foray into sf caused some consternation and controversy. It also elicited much praise. The philosophical tale of galactic empires in conflict, this opening volume concerns the visit of an emissary from benign Canopus to the colonized (but fallen) planet Earth, now renamed 'Shikasta'. Here and in the following volumes, our planet's affairs are put into a very wide context indeed. 'Lessing's primary cosmological and ethical source is the Old Testament, though she blends in stuff from Blake, Gilgamesh, Celtic and Arabic traditions; and of course von Daniken' – Colin Greenland, *Foundation*. Sequel: *The Marriages Between Zones Three, Four, and Five*.

Ship of Shadows (1979) ★★★ Collection by Fritz Leiber (USA). A gathering together of all the author's award-winning stories and novellas, including the short novel *The Big Time*. Several of the pieces are fantasy rather than sf, but all are excellent. Published in the UK only, to celebrate Leiber's appearance as Guest of Honour at the World Science Fiction Convention in Brighton.

Ship of Strangers (1978) ★★ Fix-up novel by Bob Shaw (UK). An account of the exploratory voyage of the starship *Sarafand* – and Shaw's homage to A. E. van Vogt's *The Voyage of the Space Beagle*. Needless to say, his writing is smoother than van Vogt's and his characters more believable.

Ship That Sailed the Time Stream, The (1965) ★★ Novel by G. C. Edmondson (USA). A modern naval vessel is thrown back a thousand years in time. The subsequent voyage in search of a way home takes the ship through several different time periods. A wittily parodic treatment of all the 'timeslip' clichés. Sequel, in similar vein: *To Sail the Century Sea* (1981).

Ship Who Sang, The (1969) ★★ Fix-up novel by Anne McCaffrey (USA/Ireland). A deformed woman is adapted to become the 'brain' of a starship – a wonderful new body which brings her freedom and much joy. A sentimental treatment of the cyborg theme which has some claim to being McCaffrey's best novel.

Shipwreck (1975) ★★ Novel by Charles Logan (UK). A man is cast away on an alien planet, where he must learn to survive with the help of his onboard computer. Convincingly detailed, it bears a resemblance to Rex Gordon's *No Man Friday* – and is equally indebted to *Robinson Crusoe*. Joint-winner (with Chris Boyce's *Catchworld*) of a Gollancz/*Sunday Times* sf competition, it appears to be its author's only novel.

Shiva Descending (1980) ★ Novel by Gregory Benford and William Rotsler (USA). A huge meteor (Shiva) threatens the Earth, and society begins to fall apart. So-so treatment of a well-worn theme. 'Though ostensibly a tale of human valour and technological triumph against almost insuperable odds, beneath all the acres of blockbuster filibustering there is a *fin-de-siècle* melancholy to the book' – John Clute.

Shock! (Matheson): see under *Shores of Space, The.*

Shockwave Rider, The (1975) ★★ Novel by John Brunner (UK). In a highly computerized 21st century one man rebels against the ubiquitous electronic regimentation. He manages to use the computers to undermine the system. A satisfying tale of human ingenuity set against a well-realized background, though the narrative is at times jargon-laden and stodgy. The last of Brunner's cycle of large dystopian novels which began with *Stand on Zanzibar.*

Shon'jir (1980) ★★ Novel by C. J. Cherryh (USA), sequel to *Kesrith* in the 'Faded Sun' trilogy. A human soldier and the last two Mri warriors flee from one dead planet to the next, searching for the long-lost home world of the Mri. They find it. Sequel: *Kutath.*

Shoot at the Moon (1966) ★★ Novel by William F. Temple (UK). A somewhat parodic murder-mystery story set on the moon. It has good characterization and dialogue, but little in the way of ideas or novelty to offer the sf reader.

Shore of Women, The (1976) ★ Novel by Pamela Sargent (USA). Long after a nuclear war for which the men have been blamed, women monopolize all power. The latter live in city enclaves where they make good use of high technology (including artificial insemination), while the men roam as barbarous tribes in the great outdoors (their numbers replenished by the boy-children sent from the cities). One rebellious young woman is banished, and ends up falling in love with a hairy male from beyond the pale. 'Not really sf at all – let alone feminist sf. It's not a novel of ideas, and it's not about social issues. What it is is a romance ... a singularly dull and unromantic romance' – Lisa Tuttle, *Foundation.*

Shores of Another Sea, The (1971) ★★ Novel by Chad Oliver (USA). Scientists studying baboons in Africa come into contact with aliens who are studying *them.* A pleasant tale which effectively utilizes its author's experience of anthropology and of Africa.

Shores of Death (Moorcock): see *Twilight Man, The.*

Shores of Space, The (1957) ★★ Collection by Richard Matheson (USA). A baker's dozen of sf and fantasy stories by this master of subtle menace. Very few pieces involve space travel or the future: most concern mysteries in the here-and-now. At their best, they're comparable with the short stories of Roald Dahl, or with the more tough-minded of Ray Bradbury's tales. Later Matheson collections, such as *Shock!* (1961), *Shock II* (1964) and *Shock III* (1966), contain a higher preponderance of supernatural horror stories and psychological mysteries, though with a few sf pieces mixed in.

Short Stories of H. G. Wells, The (1927) ★★★★ Collection by H. G. Wells (UK). This omnibus contains

The Time Machine (see separate entry) plus nearly all of the great writer's shorter pieces. Many of them may be defined as sf, including such masterpieces as 'The Star', 'The Empire of the Ants', 'The New Accelerator' and 'The Country of the Blind'. These are the imperishable creations of a truly ground-breaking imagination.

Showboat World (1975) ★ Novel by Jack Vance (USA), a belated sequel to *Big Planet*. Rivalry between actor-managers on the river-boats of Big Planet ends with the exposing of a royal crime during a performance of *Macbeth*.

Shrinking Man, The (1956) ★★★ Novel by Richard Matheson (USA). The classic sf horror tale of a man who steadily shrinks and shrinks until he disappears into a micro-cosmic world. There is some gobble-dygook about atomic radiation being the cause of all this, but basically it's a psychological fantasy – and a remarkably powerful one. Filmed as *The Incredible Shrinking Man* (1957; dir. Jack Arnold). The book has also been reprinted under the latter title.

Shrouded Planet, The (1957) ★ Fix-up novel by Robert Randall (Randall Garrett and Robert Silverberg, USA). A competent but un-memorable space adventure, about human–alien contact, by two of the most prolific magazine writers of the 1950s. Garrett's first novel. Sequel: *The Dawning Light* (1959).

Shuttle Down (1981) ★ Novel by Lee Correy (G. Harry Stine, USA). An American space shuttle is forced to make an emergency landing on Easter Island. As fiction it's wooden, but this one is interesting as an example of sf which has allegedly influenced (or at any rate antici-pated) the real-life space pro-gramme.

Side-Effect (1979) ★★ Novel by Raymond Hawkey (UK). The very rich enjoy the services of a sinister surgeon in the Bahamas – organ transplantation, cloning, the works. A well-turned futuristic thriller of no great originality.

Siege of the Unseen (van Vogt): see under *Three Eyes of Evil, The*.

Siege of Wonder, The (1976) ★★★ Novel by Mark S. Geston (USA). Science and magic are literally at war in this semi-fantasy which reworks the themes (if not the actual locations) of the author's earlier fiction. It's sometimes regarded as the best of Geston's four novels; however, this reviewer finds the more restrained manner less exhilar-ating than the over-the-top style of *Out of the Mouth of the Dragon* or *The Day Star*.

Sight of Proteus (1978) ★★ Novel by Charles Sheffield (UK/USA). In the 24th century Form Changing has revolutionized medicine and cos-metics, abolished surgery and created the world's largest consumer market. Behrooz Wolf of the Office of Form Control has to hunt down the criminals who are illegally redesign-ing people in order to move into space. Fascinating in places, but depends too much on Misunderstood Genius and Mad Scientist stereotypes. Sheffield's first novel. Sequel: *Proteus Unbound*.

Sign of the Mute Medusa, The (Wallace): see under *Deathstar Voyage*.

Silence in Solitude (1986) ★★ Novel by Melissa Scott (USA), sequel to *Five Twelfths of Heaven*. Space-pilot Silence Leigh trains as a Magus (well, Maga) but still fails to use her astrological learning to find the way to lost Earth. The magical and alchemical language used to describe space travel is great fun. Sequel: *The Empress of Earth*.

Silence is Deadly (Biggle): see under *All the Colors of Darkness*.

Silent Invaders, The (1963) Novel by Robert Silverberg (USA). Aliens, telepaths and big-breasted women in a hokum, galaxy-busting plot. A very minor and early Silverberg novel which has been reprinted – as have others of its ilk such as *Stepsons of Terra* (1958), *Collision Course* (1961), *The Seed of Earth* (1962) and the collection *Next Stop the Stars* (1962) – with a latter-day introduction by the author. It's far from representative of this intelligent writer, and best avoided. 'A strange and wonderful thing for a writer to forget the existence of one of his own novels ... *The Silent Invaders* is one that did indeed slip from my mind' – Robert Silverberg, introduction.

Silent Multitude, The (1966) ★★ Novel by D. G. Compton (UK).

Spores from outer space destroy concrete, and civilization literally crumbles. Long on characterization, short on action, this is a darker and more thoughtful tale than most British disaster novels. 'Might have resulted from a collaboration between Kafka and John Wyndham' – *Sydney Morning Herald*.

Silent Speakers, The (1962) ★★ Novel by Arthur Sellings (UK). A young man and woman discover that they are mutually telepathic – and, eventually, that they can share this ability with others. An intelligent treatment of a well-worn theme. Sellings's first novel. Published in the USA as *Telepath*.

Silkie, The (van Vogt): see under *War Against the Rull, The*.

Silver Eggheads, The (1962) ★★ Novel by Fritz Leiber (USA). Automated 'wordmills' produce the popular fiction (or 'wordwooze') of the future, in this satire on the writing, publishing and consumption of hack literature. The plot is silly, but the humour is good and there are some memorable details.

Silver Locusts, The (Bradbury): see *Martian Chronicles, The*.

Silver Metal Lover, The (1982) ★★ Novel by Tanith Lee (UK). A girl falls in love with a robot, a situation which causes difficulties. This is an ironic and erotic sf fable, not a comedy, and it's skilfully done.

Simulacra, The (1964) ★★★ Novel by Philip K. Dick (USA). The United

States' long-lived First Lady proves to be a simulacrum, in this comedy of 21st-century life by a master of the bizarre. It's an overpopulated novel which flies off wildly in too many directions, but it nevertheless adds up to a cherishable Dickian vision of a crazy, crazy world.

Simulacron-3 (Galouye): see *Counterfeit World*.

Simultaneous Man, The (1970) ★★ Novel by Ralph Blum (USA). A Cold-War thriller which effectively uses the sf theme of memory transfer and erasure.

Sin of Origin (1988) ★★ Novel by John Barnes (USA). Human surveyors attempt to understand and help the apparently hostile natives of an alien planet. An action-adventure story with some genuine scientific ideas. It has an underlying philosophical concern with the problem of the capacity for violence which may be innate in all living things.

Single Combat (Ing): see under *Systemic Shock*.

Sinister Barrier (1943) ★ Novel by Eric Frank Russell (UK), originally published in the first issue of *Unknown* magazine, 1939. Scientists are dying all over the world as they come to realize that, as Charles Fort said, 'We are property'. The alien owners turn out to be invisible mind-readers that live off human fear. In typical 1930s style the brave heroes discover a simple scientific trick to defeat the enemy, just at the last moment. The revision of 1948 may

have improved the style of this famous book, but the addition of nuclear bombs just highlights the patchy science.

Sins of the Fathers, The (1976) ★★ Novel by Stanley Schmidt (USA). First of an interplanetary series in which events are set in motion by wonderful, technologically advanced aliens known as the Kyyra. The author is a careful scientific speculator, qualities which gained him the editorship of *Analog* magazine from the late 1970s (since when his output of fiction has declined). Sequel: *Lifeboat Earth* (1978).

Sirens of Titan, The (1959) ★★★★ Novel by Kurt Vonneget (USA). Millionaire astronaut Winston Niles Rumfoord flies into a chronosynclastic infundibulum, but survives to found the Church of God the Utterly Indifferent. A hilarious satire on modern America which uses many of the devices of pulp space opera. Vonnegut has rarely done better.

Sirian Experiments, The (Lessing); see under *Marriages Between Zones Three, Four, and Five, The*.

Sirius: A Fantasy of Love and Discord (1944) ★★★ Novel by Olaf Stapledon (UK). The life story of a scientifically enhanced dog who falls in love with a human girl. Philosophical rather than sentimental, it is nevertheless extremely moving. Stapledon's best *novel*, in conventional fictional terms, it does not have the sweep of *Star Maker* and others, but it addresses some of the same themes: in particular, what is the place of intelligence in this cold universe?

6 x H (Heinlein): see *Unpleasant Profession of Jonathan Hoag, The*.

Six-Gun Planet (1970) ★ Novel by John Jakes (USA). A colonized world is made to resemble the Old West, complete with robotic gunslingers (an idea later used by Michael Crichton in the film *Westworld*, 1973). Minor adventure stuff by a prolific writer of fantasies, historicals, etc.

Sixth Column (1949) ★ Novel by Robert A. Heinlein (USA), expanded from a 1941 magazine serial. 'Pan-Asian' hordes conquer the United States, and six brave men armed with a super-scientific gizmo manage to defeat them. A fundamentally silly, paranoid (and racist) tale of future war, reputedly based on an idea suggested by the editor of *Astounding SF*, John W. Campbell. Republished in paperback as *The Day After Tomorrow*.

Sixth Winter, The (1979) ★★ Novel by Douglas Orgill and John Gribbin (UK). A succession of bad winters leads to a new Ice Age, in this earnest, old-fashioned disaster story which is well founded in modern climatological knowledge. Gribbin's first novel. 'It's a great scenario, full of detail, with a driving plotline' – Tom Shippey, *Guardian*.

Skirmish: The Great Short Fiction of Clifford D. Simak (1977) ★★★ Collection by Clifford D. Simak (USA). Ten stories, ranging from 'Huddling

Place' (1944) to 'The Ghost of a Model T' (1975) High point is the Hugo-winning novelette 'The Big Front Yard' (1958), about inter-dimensional trading. Charming stuff, and contains only three overlaps with the nearly-contemporary British-published volume *The Best of Clifford D. Simak*.

Sky is Filled with Ships, The (1969) ★ Novel by Richard C. Meredith (USA). Rebels are closing in on the Terran Federation and Robert Janas of the Solar Trading Company has to persuade his boss to remain neutral in the conflict. It adds up to a routine space opera.

Sky Lords, The (1988) ★★ Novel by John Brosnan (Australia/UK), first of a trilogy. After the 'Gene Wars' have wrecked the Earth, the piratical Sky Lords rule the roost from their airships. But they come up against a feminist heroine. Slow moving at first, it 'develops into a lively adventure story backed with the authority of a well-extrapolated future scenario' – Simon Ounsley, *Interzone*. Sequel: *War of the Sky Lords* (1989).

Sky Pirates of Callisto (Carter): see under *Jandar of Callisto*.

Skyfall (1976) ★★ Novel by Harry Harrison (USA/Ireland). A huge nuclear-powered satellite is in a decaying orbit, threatening to fall disastrously to earth. An attempt by this well-established sf writer to produce a bestseller in the near-future thriller mode. 'Efficiently told but somehow unstirring, its lack of conviction for some reason exaggerated by its careful straining after authenticity' – J. G. Ballard, *New Statesman*.

Skylark of Space, The (1946) ★ Novel by E. E. 'Doc' Smith (USA), originally serialized in 1928. Boyish genius Richard Seaton discovers an anti-gravity substance, and promptly builds his own spaceship. His adventures in the great beyond come fast and furious, involving weird aliens and conflict with a rival scientist called Blackie DuQuesne. This badly-written, juvenile space romp was simply the first of its type, and as such has been immensely influential. The 1958 and subsequent reprints have been revised, to remove touches of racism and various longueurs. Sequels: *Skylark Three* (1948), *Skylark of Valeron* (1949) and (after a long hiatus) *Skylark DuQuesne* (1966).

Slan (1946) ★★ Novel by A. E. van Vogt (Canada/USA), first serialized in 1940. An underground movement of 'slans', human beings with telepathic powers, is cruelly repressed by normal society. The young hero is one of these emergent supermen, all of whom can be recognized by the twin tendrils growing on their skulls. The plot is slam-bang action stuff, the style is grey and pulpish, the characterization is almost nonexistent – but even so this is one of the best-loved and most influential of all modern sf stories. Van Vogt's first novel.

Slapstick; or, Lonesome No More! (1976) ★ Novel by Kurt Vonnegut (USA). About a brother and sister who can link minds, about a new religious sect called the Church of Jesus Christ the Kidnapped, about many other things, this appears to be the author's mixture as before: a wild science-fiction satire. It is, however, the least of his books – flat and flippant and silly. 'A fake Vonnegut novel ... the irony has become simple bitterness, the sadness sarcasm, the compassion hollow laughter and the sentiment mockery' – Brian Stableford.

Slaughterhouse-Five, or The Children's Crusade (1969) ★★★ Novel by Kurt Vonnegut (USA). The famous satirical tale which finally made its author's name (after he had wandered for years in the wilderness of sf). Based on Vonnegut's own World War II experiences, it deals movingly with the dreadful firebombing of Dresden. But it's also sf, in that the hero Billy Pilgrim is an involuntary time-traveller who at one point is whisked away to the planet Tralfamadore (see *The Sirens of Titan*). A fine book, though marginally less satisfying to sf readers than a couple of Vonnegut's earlier novels. Filmed in 1972 (dir. George Roy Hill).

Slave Ship (1957) ★★ Novel by Frederik Pohl (USA). In a submarine crewed by specially-adapted animals, the hero sets out to fight the Vietnamese on behalf of the United Nations. An odd and rather unsatisfactory future-war story, not quite as 'prophetic' as it sounds. Pohl's first solo novel.

Sleeper Awakes, The (Wells): see *When the Sleeper Wakes*.

Slow Birds and Other Stories (Watson): see under *Very Slow Time Machine, The*.

Smile on the Void (1981) ★ Novel by Stuart Gordon (UK). The episodic tale of a millenarian messiah-figure in the closing years of the 20th century. A puzzling novel, full of bizarre details. 'Calculatedly bombastic and heavily ironic' – Brian Stableford.

Smoke Ring, The (Niven): see under *Integral Trees, The*.

Snail (1984) ★★ Novel by Richard Miller (USA). A Prussian Field Marshal meets the Wandering Jew who gives him a taste of the Elixir of Youth. They spend the rest of the 20th century moving from one sexual encounter to another, mostly with avatars of Pallas Athena. Scatalogical parody of Macdonalds Hamburgers, sloppy mysticism, and a bitter hatred of organized religion. Kurt Vonnegut's space-opera writer Kilgore Trout features as a character.

Snow Queen, The (1980) ★★ Novel by Joan D. Vinge (USA). On a world of long, slow seasons, the winter queen tries to perpetuate her rule into the summer by means of cloning and other 'offworld' technologies. A large and elaborate planetary romance which owes a little to Hans Andersen's fairy tale of the same title, and perhaps rather more to Robert Graves's *The White Goddess* (1948). Hugo award-winner, 1981. Sequel: *World's End* (1984).

So Bright the Vision (1968) ★★ Collection by Clifford D. Simak (USA). Four pleasant sf stories, mainly about alien encounters: 'The Golden Bugs' (1960), 'Leg. Forst.' (1958), 'So Bright the Vision' (1956) and 'Galactic Chest' (1956). Lacking in originality, but reliable entertainment.

So Long, and Thanks for All the Fish (1984) ★★ Novel by Douglas Adams (UK), sequel to *Life, the Universe, and Everything* and the fourth and final part of his 'trilogy' which began with *The Hitch-Hiker's Guide to the Galaxy*. Arthur Dent returns to a planet Earth which seems little affected by its destruction, while his friend Ford Prefect continues to suffer pratfalls around the galaxy. The humour is getting a little tired here, but nonetheless legions of Adams fans have lapped it up.

Soft Targets (1979) ★★ Novel by Dean Ing (USA). A near-future thriller in which a media campaign is waged against international terrorists – who, it is believed, may be defeated by ridicule. Ing's first novel, and an interesting attempt to deal with a major modern problem.

Software (1982) ★★ Novel by Rudy Rucker (USA). An aged hippie computer programmer is kidnapped by robots. Very much after the style of Philip K. Dick, almost an affectionate parody, it lacks the exuberant imagination of some of Rucker's other novels. Philip K. Dick Memorial award-winner, 1983. Sequel: *Wetware*.

Solar Lottery (1955) ★★ Novel by Philip K. Dick (USA). Political power in the 23rd century is conferred by random selection – but in reality this is all a front for the true powers that be. Complex and heartening tale of breakout from an oppressive system. Its author's first novel, and the start of an important sf career. Originally published in Britain as *World of Chance*.

Solaris (1961) ★★★★ Novel by Stanislaw Lem (Poland). Earthmen on a space station orbiting an alien planet have metaphysical encounters with the unapproachable, oceanic entity which inhabits that world. Part hard-sf thriller, part horror story, part satire on hidebound scholarship and the limits of human knowledge, this impressive philosophical novel is its author's best known (and perhaps best) work. 'The steady intellectual force of *Solaris* is in its cumulative consistency in remaining complex, its refusal to ask easy questions or give easy answers' – Peter Nicholls, *Foundation*. Stunningly filmed in 1972 (dir. Andrei Tarkovsky).

Soldier, Ask Not (1967) ★★★ Novel by Gordon R. Dickson (USA), expanded from his Hugo award-winning magazine story of the same title (1965). Third and best in the 'Dorsai' series. An Earthman studying the colonial Splinter Cultures learns first to hate then respect the religious fanatics of the Friendly Planets.

Soldier Boy (1982) ★★ Collection by Michael Shaara (USA). Sixteen sf stories, mainly from the magazines of the 1950s (although a couple are previously unpublished), by an author who subsequently went on to win a Pulitzer Prize for his work outside the sf field. Slickly written and affecting.

Soldiers of Paradise (1987) ★★★ Novel by Paul Park (USA), first of the 'Starbridge Chronicles'. A richly detailed account of life in the complex society of an alien planet. It's somewhat reminiscent of Brian Aldiss's 'Helliconia' books, and also shows the influence of Gene Wolfe's *The Book of the New Sun*. In other words, this is no ordinary tale of planetary adventure. A highly praised first novel. Sequel: *Sugar Rain* (1989).

Solution Three (1975) ★★ Novel by Naomi Mitchison (UK). An all-wise Council rules a future utopian world. One of their decrees does away with male-female sex and promotes homosexuality – in the interests of harmony and non-aggression. Eventually, a new, perfected human race will be created by cloning techniques. 'Reminiscent of *Brave New World*, although Mitchison's world is more temperate and rose-coloured than Huxley's ... surprisingly good-hearted' – Helen Nicholls, *Foundation*.

Soma (Platt): see under *Plasm*.

Some Will Not Die (1961) ★★ Novel by Algis Budrys (USA), originally published in abridged form as *False Night* (1954). A plague has destroyed American civilization, and the episodic narrative deals with the slow recovery over a period of many decades. A grim but compelling first novel.

Somerset Dreams and Other Fictions (Wilhelm): see under *Infinity Box, The.*

Somewhere a Voice (1965) ★★★ Collection by Eric Frank Russell (UK). Probably the definitive collection of Russell's early-50s 'yarns' (the author's name for them) such as 'U-turn' (public suicide booths are really teleportation devices) and 'I am Nothing' (a humane tale of an unloved child). 'Contain enough of the author's dry humour, the peculiar wit of the Liverpool Irish, to carry their conventional themes' – J. G. Ballard, *Guardian.*

Son of Man (1971) ★★★ Novel by Robert Silverberg (USA). A man awakes in a future so distant that almost anything has become possible. More of a meditation than a story: repetitive, incantatory, sexy, philosophical and sad. It's a boldly fantastic attempt to deal with the themes of mutability and death. 'A beautiful and brilliant book' – Brian Stableford.

Son of the Tree (1964) ★★ Novel by Jack Vance (USA), first published in magazine form in 1951. The Druids of Kyril keep millions of peasants in subjection to the worship of a giant intelligent tree. Joe Smith from Earth gets involved in political manoeuvrings to draw them into alliance with the industrial society of the planet Mang. Routine early Vance, but colourful.

Song for Lya and Other Stories, A (1976) ★★ Collection by George R. R. Martin (USA). Ten sf stories of the early 1970s, including the Hugo award-winning title piece and the popular 'With Morning Comes Mistfall'. Many of the pieces have alien planetary settings and strive for exotic atmosphere. Unfortunately Martin (whose first book this was) doesn't have the 'poetry' of a Zelazny or a Tiptree to carry this off effectively.

Song of Phaid the Gambler, The (1981) ★ Novel by Mick Farren (UK). Distant-future Earth, after the collapse of a starfaring civilization, is an exotic patchwork of mini-cultures. Here the eponymous Phaid plies his gambling trade, and fairly inconsequential things happen to him. A chaotic picaresque. Published in the USA in two volumes, as *Phaid the Gambler* and *Citizen Phaid.*

Song of the Axe, The (Williams): see under *Breaking of Northwall, The.*

Songbirds of Pain, The (1984) ★★★ Collection by Garry Kilworth (UK). Extremely varied sf and fantasy stories by a quite unpredictable writer. They range from the quirkily stylish 'Sumi Dreams of a Paper Frog' to the straightforward 'Let's Go to Golgotha!' (the latter is an ironic tale of time travellers witnessing the Crucifixion, and it won a *Sunday Times* sf competition prize in 1975).

Songmaster (1980) ★★★ Novel by Orson Scott Card (USA). The love between a child from the monastic Songhouse and the aged, cruel

Emperor he is forced to serve is the platform for a far-fetched but often poignant near-fantasy which (typically for this author) concerns itself with the whole life of its characters from childhood to the grave.

Songs from the Stars (1980) ★★ Novel by Norman Spinrad (USA). An ecologically sound, low-tech society has arisen in America in the aftermath of a nuclear war. However, there are still 'black scientists' over them thar hills, who plan to relaunch a space shuttle and retrieve long-lost knowledge from an orbital station. Spinrad's sympathies lie more with the hippies than the techies, but he attempts, in rather simplistic fashion, to achieve a happy synthesis of world views.

Songs of Distant Earth, The (1986) ★★ Novel by Arthur C. Clarke (UK), expanded from his 1958 short story of the same title. A simply-written tale of interstellar exploration which sticks rigorously to the facts of time and space as presently understood (no 'hyperspace' or faster-than-light travel is posited here). Clarke has interwoven a tragic little love story which depends on the pathos of relativistic time effects: 'Her last farewell to him would come from wrinkled lips long turned to dust.' Moving.

Songs of Stars and Shadows (1977) ★★ Collection by George R. R. Martin (USA). Nine sf stories of the mid-1970s, including the well received 'And Seven Times Never Kill Man' (the author's 'lyrical' titles are frequently irritating). Martin's second collection, it has been followed by several others, such as *Sandkings* (1981) and *Songs the Dead Men Sing* (1983).

Songs the Dead Men Sing (Martin): see under *Songs of Stars and Shadows*.

S.O.S. from Three Worlds (1966) ★★ Collection by Murray Leinster (USA). A 'Med Ship', crewed by a doctor and a small furry animal bred to produce antibodies, investigates a case of mass poisoning ('Plague on Kryder III'), discovers a planet split into isolated communities by fear of disease ('Ribbon in the Sky') and solves the problem of a deadly micro-organism that strikes down everyone who leaves Delhi ('Quarantine'). Other, similar, 'Med Service' books by Leinster include *The Mutant Weapon* (1959), *This World is Taboo* (1961) and *Doctor to the Stars* (1964).

Sos the Rope (1968) ★ Novel by Piers Anthony (USA), first of his 'Battle Circle' trilogy. Sos, an educated barbarian, exploits ritual combat to take control of nomadic tribes existing in uneasy symbiosis with what's left of industrial society a century after a nuclear war. Sequel: *Var the Stick*.

Soul of the Robot, The (1974) ★★★ Novel by Barrington J. Bayley (UK). Jasperodus is a robot, brought up by a loving human couple, who makes a vow to 'experience everything a man can experience' – and does. Excellent fun. Sequel: *The Rod of Light*.

Souls in Metal (1977) ★★ Anthology edited by Mike Ashley (UK). Robot stories by all the authors one might expect. Along with many perfectly decent pieces by the likes of Asimov, Kuttner and Simak, it includes such antiquated clunkers as Lester del Ray's famously sexist 'Helen O'Loy' (1938) – a love story about the ideal 'female' robot.

Southshore (Tepper): see *Awakeners, The*.

Space Barbarians, The (Godwin): see under *Survivors, The*.

Space Cadet (1948) ★ Novel by Robert A. Heinlein (USA). A careful account of the training procedure for a raw recruit to the Interplanetary Patrol, culminating in some adventures on the planet Venus. Clearly a fictionalization of the author's own experience as an Annapolis naval cadet in the 1920s.

Space Chantey (1968) ★★ Novel by R. A. Lafferty (USA). A highly coloured and fantastical space opera which is in fact a retelling of Homer's *Odyssey* in science-fictional terms. It's as bizarre as anything else by this idiosyncratic author. One of Lafferty's three debut novels, the others being *Past Master* and *The Reefs of Earth* – all published within a few months of each other in 1968.

Space Eater, The (1982) ★★ Novel by David Langford (UK). Matter transmission turns out to have very unfortunate side-effects: stars go nova and black holes gobble up large regions of space. It's also an exceedingly uncomfortable method of travel for the tough hero of this witty and technologically inventive but rather unevenly executed space-war tale. Langford's first novel.

Space Family Stone (Heinlein): see *Rolling Stones, The*.

Space Lords (Smith): see under *You Will Never Be the Same*.

Space Machine, The (1976) ★★ Novel by Christopher Priest (UK). A young man and woman of the year 1893 accidentally commandeer a secret space-and-time machine. It whisks them to the planet Mars, where the Martians are preparing to invade Earth with their frightful war machines. Eventually, they get a lift home. Pleasant reading, saggy in the middle. 'Curiously, pastiches of H. G. Wells tend to play down his matter-of-fact, no-nonsense style and cocoon his startling scientific fantasies inside the cosy mock-Victorianism of a Disney film, all frock coats and tasselled lampshades' – J. G. Ballard, *New Statesman*.

Space Mercenaries (1965) ★ Novel by A. Bertram Chandler (UK/Australia), sequel to *Empress of Outer Space* (1965). A competent adventure yarn about Chandler's usual competent space-naval sort of hero – in this case in league with the beautiful 'Empress' Irene. 'Assures the reader, even as Britain staggers into the 'sixties shedding overseas possessions like dandruff, that the sun never sets on the British Galaxy' – James Cawthorn, *New Worlds*. Sequel: *Nebula Alert* (1967).

Space Merchants, The (1953) ★★★★ Novel by Frederik Pohl and C. M. Kornbluth (USA). The ad-men run this overpopulated America of the future, a crassly materialist society which is challenged only by a weak underground movement of conservationists. Brilliantly detailed satire and exciting narrative: a joy, despite its grim theme. Belated sequel: *The Merchants' War*.

Space on My Hands (1951) ★★★ Collection by Fredric Brown (USA). Nine stories, mainly humorous. Among the more substantial items are 'The Star Mouse' (1942), about a space-travelling mouse, and 'Come and Go Mad' (1949), about a man who discovers who Earth's *real* masters are. These pieces, and several of the others, are also available in *The Best of Fredric Brown*.

Space Pirate, The (Vance): see *Five Gold Bands, The*.

Space Prison (Godwin): see *Survivors, The*.

Space Relations: A Slightly Gothic Interplanetary Tale (1974) ★★ Novel by Donald Barr (USA). Far-out yarn of space pirates, aliens, sex and derring-do – written, surprisingly enough, by a 'literary' author new to the sf scene. 'Poetry-filled, acerbic, linguistically foregrounded' – John Clute.

Space Swimmers, The (1967) ★ Novel by Gordon R. Dickson (Canada/USA), sequel to *Home from the Shore*: the sea people, scattered and hunted in the oceans of Earth, must unite amongst themselves, and then with their land-dwelling oppressors, in order to participate in Earth's exodus to space.

Space, Time and Nathaniel (1957) ★★★ Collection by Brian W. Aldiss (UK). Fourteen lyrical stories, comprising its author's first collection. Notable entries are 'Outside' (1955), 'Psyclops' (1956) and 'The Failed Men' (1957). The American-published collection *No Time Like Tomorrow* (1959) has about half its contents in common with this excellent volume.

Space Vampires, The (1977) Novel by Colin Wilson (UK). The Hammer-House-of-Horror title gives away both the plot and the style: creatures from space devour the 'life forces' of various humans, mostly attractive young German women who for no obvious reason then become sexually available to the (male) protagonist.

Space Viking (1963) ★★ Novel by H. Beam Piper (USA). Lucas Trask employs Space Vikings (mercenaries from the Sword Worlds, remnants of the old Federation) to achieve revenge on the men who murdered his fiancée. Straightforward interstellar adventure, proficiently done.

Space War (Jones): see under *Planet of the Double Sun, The*

Space War Blues (1978) ★★ Fix-up novel by Richard A. Lupoff (USA), expanded from his novella 'With the Bentfin Boys on Little Old New Alabama' (1972). Race-war in outer space. An ambitious but clotted narrative written in punning, allusive American New-Wave style. It caused some excitement on publication, but new readers may find it tediously difficult.

Space Willies, The (Russell): see *Next of Kin*.

Spaceache (1984) ★ Novel by Snoo Wilson (UK). Our heroine chooses to be cryogenically suspended and put in orbit rather than live in a near-future England that rather blatantly parodies the current one. Something goes wrong and she finds herself in an absurd parallel universe. Fun, but pretty standard stuff.

Spacehawk, Inc. (Goulart): see under *Sword Swallower, The*.

Spaceship Built of Stone, A (1987) ★★★ Collection by Lisa Tuttle (USA/UK). A career-spanning volume of sf and fantasy by this capable writer. 'Acute and accurate short stories, all of them gems of exceptional clarity and polish' – Lee Montgomerie, *Interzone*.

Spaceship for the King, A (1973) ★ Novel by Jerry Pournelle (USA). A tough military man assists a backward culture in the rapid development of a working space technology. Pournelle's first sf novel, and typical of much more that was to come from him. Revised and republished as *King David's Spaceship*.

Spacetime Donuts (1981) ★★ Novel by Rudy Rucker (USA). The America of the next century is controlled by a megalomaniac computer and inhabited by drug-crazed proles. Vernor Maxwell becomes involved with a mad professor who shows that each sub atomic particle literally contains the whole Universe. The cosmological theories are more fun than the sex-and-drugs and-rock'n-'roll background. Rucker's first novel, but published in book form subsequent to his *White Light*.

Space-Time Juggler, The (Brunner): see under *Interstellar Empire*.

Spacial Delivery (1961) ★ Novel by Gordon R. Dickson (Canada/USA). The planet Dilbia is inhabited by large bear-like creatures with black shiny noses whose idea of a joke is to hold an Earthman up by its legs to hear the funny squeaking noise it makes. John Tardy, an Olympic Decathlon winner, has been posted there as a diplomat because he may be able to stand up to the locals physically; however he would rather be respected for his mind than his body.

Speaker for the Dead (1986) ★★★ Novel by Orson Scott Card (USA), sequel to his *Ender's Game*. The isolated, deeply Catholic colony of Lusitania is shocked by the brutal killing of two scientists by the native Piggies (Card never was one for resonant names). They send for the 'Speaker', who turns out to be Ender Wiggin, the xenocidal hero of the earlier novel. The gradual unfolding of the ecology of the Piggies is counterpointed by the personal and spiritual tragedies of a human family. Slickly done, highly popular stuff. Hugo and Nebula award-winner, 1987.

Special Deliverance (1982) ★ Novel by Clifford D. Simak (USA). Yet another cosy quest, this one involving an English Professor transported to an alien world – in the tradition of *Destiny Doll, Shakespeare's Planet* and so many other Simak titles. Minor.

Specials, The (Charbonneau): see *Psychedelic-40*.

Spectre is Haunting Texas, A (1969) ★★ Novel by Fritz Leiber (USA). Texas has absorbed the rest of the United States, its citizens using hormone treatments to turn themselves into giants. The hero, an actor who has been reared in space, becomes the unlikely leader of a revolution among the Mexican underclass. Perhaps the best of Leiber's sf comedies, a satire which fires exuberantly in all directions.

Spectrum (1961–66) ★★★ Anthology series edited by Kingsley Amis and Robert Conquest (UK). This five-volume sequence began very well (the first two or three books bear comparison with Crispin's *Best SF* series), but became limited and curmudgeonly in its choices by the time of the last volume (when the editors began to react against the 'New Wave'). Outstanding, and mainly satirical, stories in the first volume include Frederik Pohl's 'The Midas Plague' and Robert Sheckley's 'Pilgrimage to Earth'.

Spell Sword, The (Bradley): see under *Sword of Aldones, The*.

Sphere (1987) ★★ Novel by Michael Crichton (USA). An ancient spacecraft is discovered deep beneath the ocean, and a team of scientists sets out to probe its mysteries. A realistic thriller intended for the mainstream mass market, like all this author's work it's already half-way to being a film script (since Crichton is also a movie director, that's probably excusable).

Spider World: The Tower (1987) ★ Novel by Colin Wilson (UK). In the far future, mutant insects and giant spiders have taken over the world. Human beings are enslaved and stupefied, but of course a few brave specimens of the superannuated race learn to fight back ... 'This is old-fashioned adventure fiction not so very upmarket of the recent works of that other unorthodox philosopher, L. Ron Hubbard' – Brian Stableford. Sequel: *Spider World: The Desert* (1987).

Spinneret (1985) ★ Novel by Timothy Zahn (USA). A hard-sf adventure written in what appears to be *Analog* magazine house style.

Spirit of Dorsai, The (1979) ★ Collection by Gordon R. Dickson (USA). Anecdotes told during the action of *The Final Encyclopedia*, filling in background to the author's 'Dorsai' series. Probably only of interest to readers of those works. Reprinted in *The Dorsai Companion*.

Splendid Chaos, A (1988) ★ Novel by John Shirley (USA). Humans are dropped on to an alien planet where strange forces may turn men into monsters. It's a wild, woolly sf/ fantasy of mutability, with many grotesque and violent touches. A novel which languished unpublished for some years. Original, but over the top.

Split Infinity (1980) ★ Novel by Piers Anthony (UK/USA), first in the 'Apprentice Adept' series. Stile is a serf who gets his living from playing futuristic computer games to the death and his kicks from an ever-willing robot slave-girl, programmed to love him. He escapes from a death-threat into a fantasy world which has magic and all the sword-and-sorcery trappings. Sequel: *Blue Adept*.

Split Second (1979) ★★ Novel by Garry Kilworth (UK). Experimentation with fossils leads to a modern-day boy being thrown across time and becoming a 'passenger' in the mind of a Cro-Magnon lad. A far-fetched adventure, nicely detailed but lacking in cohesion. 'An unremarkable book, dotted with many unusual insights, side-glances and speculations, but not enough to irradiate the whole' – Colin Greenland, *Foundation*.

Square Root of Man, The (Tenn): see under *Wooden Star, The*.

Squares of the City, The (1965) ★★ Novel by John Brunner (UK). In an imaginary South American country two power-brokers play a vast and deadly game of chess, using ordinary people as pawns. A large and ambitious novel, with a serious political theme, but only marginally sf. May be of great interest to chess enthusi-asts, since it is apparently based on an actual game.

Stained-Glass World (Bulmer): see *Ulcer Culture, The*.

Stainless Steel Rat, The (1961) ★★★ Novel by Harry Harrison (USA/ Ireland). About the interstellar adventures of a trickster hero called Slippery Jim diGriz (the eponymous rat of stainless steel). 'A joy forever' – John Clute. It has proved to be the first of a long-lived series (see below).

Stainless Steel Rat's Revenge, The (1970) ★ Novel by Harry Harrison (USA/Ireland). Second instalment in the adventures of Jim diGriz, spacefaring crook-turned-police-man. 'Lousy' – John Clute.

Stainless Steel Rat Saves the World, The (1972) ★★ Novel by Harry Harrison (USA/Ireland). Third of the Slippery Jim diGriz series, in which our hero gets involved in time-travel hi-jinks. 'Comes a long way back toward the form of the first book in the series' – John Clute.

Stainless Steel Rat Wants You!, The (1978) ★ Novel by Harry Harrison (USA/Ireland). Yet more adventures of Jim diGriz. Further sequels (on much the same level) include: *The Stainless Steel Rat for President* (1982) and *A Stainless Steel Rat is Born* (1985).

Stalking the Unicorn (1987) ★★ Novel by Mike Resnick (USA). An amusing private-eye spoof that approaches sf with a parallel New

York inhabited by unicorns, elves and the Devil himself.

Stand on Zanzibar (1968) ★★★ Novel by John Brunner (UK). Mammoth attempt to picture the world as it may well be in the early 21st century – overpopulated, over-automated, and torn by riots and muggings. The pop sociologist Chad C. Mulligan comments wryly on it all, and he is the nearest thing to a hero in this densely peopled book. Primarily didactic in intent, it borrows surface bravura from John Dos Passos's social-realist *U.S.A.* trilogy (1938). Brunner's most successful novel. Hugo award-winner, 1969. It also won other awards, including the French Prix Apollo.

Standing Joy, The (1969) ★ Novel by Wyman Guin (USA). An alternative-world superman enjoys super orgasms. Yes, the book's title is meant to be suggestive, although the sexual content is in fact quite mild. Guin's first (and, so far, only) novel.

Star Beast, The (1954) ★★★ Novel by Robert A. Heinlein (USA). The youthful hero has an alien 'pet' called Lummox, and this creature turns out to be a great deal more important then any one suspects. It becomes the cause of a diplomatic incident when a spacecraft arrives to reclaim its own. A wholly delightful novel for teenagers (though it was originally serialized in the adult *Magazine of F & SF*). Funny and inventive: one of Heinlein's best books from his best period.

Star Bridge (1955) ★★ Novel by Jack Williamson and James E. Gunn (USA). Baroque space adventure in which it transpires that all the characters are being manipulated by an unlikely mastermind. 'Its sometimes pixillated intricacy of plotting shows the mark of its senior collaborator's grasp of the nature of good space opera' – John Clute.

Star Colony (1981) ★★ Fix-up novel by Keith Laumer (USA). A spacecraft crash-lands on a new planet, and the episodic narrative follows the subsequent vicissitudes of its passengers as they cope with an alien menace and other challenges. Proficient thrills and spills of the type which this author always provides.

Star Courier (Chandler): see under *Road to the Rim, The*.

Star Fall (1980) ★ Novel by David F. Bischoff (USA). Body-swapping adventures and alien shenanigans aboard a huge star cruiser. Sequel, similarly lightweight and routine: *Star Spring* (1982).

Star Fox, The (1965) ★ Novel by Poul Anderson (USA). Militaristic space adventure in which a tough, independent-minded Earthman persuades the reluctant folks back home to tackle the alien menace. Typical of this author's huge output, but not among his best.

Star Gate (1958) ★ Novel by Andre Norton (USA). Space-travellers colonize a primitive world, interbreed with its inhabitants and then depart, leaving some half-breeds and a few scientists to flee through the

Gate into a parallel world where they must free the natives from their own alternates. The sf elements provide a background for the swordplay, underpinned with some vaguely religious mystical sorcery.

Star Guard (Norton): see under *Star Man's Son*.

Star Hammer (1986) ★ Novel by Christopher Rowley (USA). Violent space opera by a new writer. 'The villainous aliens behave like rabid stormtroopers, and most of the human characters are not much better' – Peter Garratt, *Interzone*.

Star Heater (White): see under *Hospital Station*.

Star King, The (1964) ★★ Novel by Jack Vance (USA), first in his 'Demon Princes' series. Space opera about a vengeance-seeking hero, Kirth Gersen. More notable for the size and complexity of its imagined universe, and for the quality of the writing, than for the originality of the plot. Sequel: *The Killing Machine*.

Star Kings, The (1949) ★★ Novel by Edmond Hamilton (USA). One of the classic American space operas: a retelling of *The Prisoner of Zenda* (1894) in futuristic, galaxy-spanning fashion. Hamilton's first novel in book form, though he had written many magazine novellas and serials over a 20-year period prior to this one's appearance. Sequel: *Return to the Stars* (1970).

Star Light (Clement): see under *Mission of Gravity*.

Star Light, Star Bright (1976) ★★★ Collection by Alfred Bester (USA). Half of the collected short stories of this brilliant author (the companion volume is entitled *The Light Fantastic*, and the two are also combined in the omnibus *Starlight: The Great Short Fiction of Alfred Bester*). Contains the early 'Adam and No Eve' (1941), as well as such fine 1950s pieces as 'Time is the Traitor', 'Hobson's Choice' and 'The Pi Man'. As John Clute says, these middle-period tales, along with Bester's novels from the same decade, 'are about the best sf ever published. They define the genre they inhabit.'

Star Loot (Chandler): see under *Road to the Rim, The*.

Star Maker (1937) ★★★★ Novel by Olaf Stapledon (UK). A man, contemplating life from a hill top, is whisked away into space in disembodied fashion and commences a grand cosmic journey which is awe-inspiring in its scope. This work, which attempts to portray the progress of all intelligent life in the universe, over a period of billions of years, is even grander in scale than the author's *Last and First Men*. It lacks plot, dialogue and the other virtues of good fiction, but it's the ultimate vision of the end of all things. An essential work. 'The one great grey holy book of science fiction' – Brian Aldiss, *Billion Year Spree*. An earlier version was published posthumously as *Nebula Maker* (1976).

Star Man's Son (1952) ★★ Novel by Andre Norton (USA). Vivid adventure in a postnuclear world of 2250 AD, written for teenagers. Norton's first sf novel (although far from being her first book; she had been writing for nigh on 20 years, mainly children's historical novels). It's plain fare, but this book is of historical importance because it marks the beginning of the 'Norton phenomenon'. She has written dozens of sf and fantasy novels since, mostly for young adults, and has quietly succeeded in becoming one of the most popular writers in America. Later titles in a generally similar vein include *Star Guard* (1955) and *Catseye* (1961).

Star of Danger (Bradley): see under *Sword of Aldones, The*.

Star of Gypsies (1986) ★★ Novel by Robert Silverberg (USA). A thousand years from now, the gypsies are still wanderers. They have taken to space, and in this book their King tells his extraordinary tale. It's a long, garrulous work full of remarkably vivid detail – but ultimately rather pointless.

Star of Life, The (1959) ★★ Novel by Edmond Hamilton (USA), expanded from a 1947 magazine serial. A grand old space opera with all the romantic ingredients: space travel, suspended animation, immortality, mutants and menacing aliens. Recommended to readers of nostalgic bent.

Star Prince Charlie (1975) ★ Juvenile novel by Poul Anderson and Gordon R. Dickson (USA), a sequel to their *Earthman's Burden*, about the cuddly, bear-like, absurdly imitative aliens called the Hokas. Sequel: *Hoka!*

Star Probe (1976) ★ Novel by Joseph Green (USA). A man is resurrected in the body of his grandson, and then sets out on a mission to investigate an alien vessel which has entered the solar system. A rather dull adventure by this competent American author, most of whose books have been published first in Britain – where he initially established his reputation with a number of ingenious short stories (see *An Affair with Genius*).

Star Rebel (1984) Novel by F. M. Busby (USA). First of a space-adventure series about Bran Tregare, linked to the series about Busby's principal heroine Rissa Kerguelen. Mainly concerns the hero's experiences at a brutal military college. Of course, he becomes a rebel. Sequels: *Rebel's Quest* (1985), *Rebel's Seed* and *The Alien Debt*.

Star Rider (1974) ★★ Novel by Doris Piserchia (USA). A teenage girl has the ability to teleport herself around the universe in the company of a horse. 'Relentless jolliness' – Lee Montgomerie, *Interzone*.

Star Road, The (1973) ★★ Collection by Gordon R. Dickson (Canada/ USA). Nine stories, perhaps among the author's less well-known. Includes 'Three-Way Puzzle', in which an alien (bear-like as are most of this author's aliens) tries to make sense of 'The Three Billy-Goats Gruff'; and 'Jackal's Meal', a war story showing the influence of

Kipling (as does so much of Dickson's work).

Star Smashers of the Galaxy Rangers (1974) ★ Novel by Harry Harrison (USA/Ireland). The title says it all. A parodic space opera which goes way over the top – sexually and otherwise. 'Shows a certain misdirected haste' – John Clute.

Star Songs of an Old Primate (1978) ★★★ Collection by James Tiptree Jr. (Alice Sheldon, USA), introduced by Ursula Le Guin. The author's third major collection, including such notable items as 'A Momentary Taste of Being' and 'Houston, Houston, Do You Read?' (Hugo and Nebula award-winner, 1977). Powerful, heavily emotional stories. By the time this book appeared, the author's true identity had been revealed, and she was hailed as an important contributor to the feminist sf of the 1970s.

Star Spring (Bischoff): see under *Star Fall*.

Star Surgeon (White): see under *Hospital Station*.

Star Well (1968) ★★ Novel by Alexei Panshin (USA). The amusing adventures of aristocratic starfarer Anthony Villiers and his frog-like alien companion. The author cleverly incorporates parodies of various popular fictional genres – but despite a certain erudition it's all very lightweight stuff. Sequels: *The Thurb Revolution* (1968) and *Masque World* (1969).

Star Winds (1978) ★★★ Novel by Barrington J. Bayley (UK). An alchemical space opera, in which starships sail the Ether. The setting is a depleted future, when the new science has been replaced by the old. Hard to tell whether it's sf or fantasy, but it's certainly one of the eccentric Mr Bayley's more engaging works.

Star-Anchored, Star-Angered (1979) ★ Novel by Suzette Haden Elgin (USA), fourth in her 'Communipath' series (see *Communipath Worlds*). Spacefaring special agent Coyote Jones sets off on another mission, becoming entangled with a female revolutionary on the planet Freeway. 'The feminism underlying the story is cogent and quietly sustained. But none of it much matters. Nothing has any follow-through' – John Clute. A later Coyote Jones novel, which is also a crossover with her 'Ozark' fantasy series, about a planet where magic works, is *Yonder Comes the Other End of Time* (1986).

Starburst (Pohl): see under *Gold at the Starbow's End, The*.

Starchild (Pohl & Williamson): see under *Reefs of Space, The*.

Starcrossed, The (1975) ★ Novel by Ben Bova (USA). The standard writer's view of the TV business as a money-grubbing pit of corruption, in this humorous novel with some sf elements. The hero is a caricature of Harlan Ellison; other sf writers have walk-on parts.

Stardance (1977) ★★ Novel by Spider and Jeanne Robinson (USA/

Canada). New forms of dance are developed on the space-station 'Skyfac', which enable the dancer Shawna to communicate in a Deeply Meaningful way with some very inhuman aliens. Sentimental stuff which proved popular. The shorter magazine version won Hugo and Nebula awards, 1978.

Stardeath (1983) Novel by E. C. Tubb (UK). A macho hero with a monosyllabic name sets out in his interstellar warship on a mission to make hyperspace safe for respectable travellers. Old-fashioned space opera of the third-rate British sort. 'Tubb has been writing books like this for decades. He should be stopped' – Lawrence I. Charters, *Fantasy Review*.

Stardreamer (Smith): see under *You Will Never Be the Same,*

Starfinder (1980) ★★ Fix-up novel by Robert F. Young (USA). Starfaring vessels are made from the dead bodies of 'space whales'. A colourful interstellar romance with time-travel and time-paradox ingredients.

Starfire (1988) ★★ Novel by Paul Preuss (USA). Grittily described near-future space adventure in which a doughty band of astronauts lands on an asteroid which has a very tight orbit around the sun. The familial and political machinations are dull, but once in space the story flies. 'A pity the Earth-bound soap opera lets the space opera down' – Paul McAuley, *Interzone*.

Starhiker (1977) ★ Novel by Jack Dann (USA). The picaresque space adventures of a minstrel from a devolved future Earth, who stows away on an alien ship. Dann's first novel. 'Action is replaced by fuzzy tricks involving nebulous mental powers; ideas by a dreary series of turgid lectures, couched in a "dream-language" on which the author exercises his total lack of descriptive ability' – Lee Montgomerie, *Foundation*.

Stark (1989) ★★★ Novel by Ben Elton (UK). A conspiracy of scientists and businessmen plans an exodus to space to escape the imminent ecological collapse of Earth. The action follows journalists and Green activists attempting to find out what is going on – rather like a Bova or Pournelle novel with the point of view reversed. The sharp character sketches and one-line jokes, together with some committed and intelligent political stirring, make *Stark* an easy book to dip into but perhaps a little long-winded to read in one sitting.

Starlight: The Great Short Fiction of Alfred Bester: see *Light Fantastic, The,* and *Star Light, Star Bright*.

Starman Jones (1953) ★★★ Novel by Robert A. Heinlein (USA). An orphaned youth on an overcrowded future Earth longs to go into space. He manages to gain a berth aboard a starship which goes astray and winds up in an unknown region. Luckily, the hero's mathematical ability enables him to calculate the route home through hyperspace. A gripping 'juvenile' in this author's best vein.

Starmen, The (1952) ★★ Novel by Leigh Brackett (USA). Colourful space fiction. 'Way above the typical space opera of the period ... Recommended'—*Locus*. Republished in the 1970s under its original magazine title, *The Starmen of Llyrdis*.

Starpirate's Brain (Goulart): see under *Sword Swallower, The*.

Starquake! (Forward): see under *Dragon's Egg*.

Starry Rift, The (1986) ★★★ Collection by James Tiptree Jr. (Alice Sheldon, USA). Three connected stories set in the same future world as the novel *Brightness Falls from the Air*. The third and longest, 'Collision', is typical, a humane first-contact tale in which all the characters are positive and there are no enemies except misunderstanding.

Stars Are the Styx, The (1979) ★★★ Collection by Theodore Sturgeon (USA). Ten stories, mainly from the 50s, by one of sf's most highly praised authors. Standouts include 'When You're Smiling' (1955) and 'The Claustrophile' (1956), affecting psychological tales of people with unexpected powers.

Stars in My Pocket Like Grains of Sand (1984) ★★ Novel by Samuel R. Delany (USA), first of a two-part series (though the promised second volume, *The Splendour and Misery of Bodies, of Cities*, has been much delayed). A densely-written utopian space fiction-cum-love story, it makes great demands upon the reader. 'A lovely book, as ornamental and prolix as its title, set in the remote future in the six-thousand-and-odd worlds of the inhabited galaxy watched over by the web and torn apart by the conflict between the Family and the Sygn' — Lee Montgomerie, *Interzone*.

Stars in Shroud, The (1978) ★★ Novel by Gregory Benford (USA), a revised version of his first novel *Deeper Than the Darkness* (1970). An alien weapon drives humans mad, in this intelligently written space-war story. The hero is immune, but all does not go well for him.

Stars, Like Dust, The (1951) ★ Novel by Isaac Asimov (USA). A minor Asimov space yarn, set against an early version of the same galactic-empire background as *Pebble in the Sky* and the 'Foundation' series.

Stars My Destination, The (1956) ★★★★ Novel by Alfred Bester (USA). 24th-century spaceman Gully Foyle seeks revenge on the owner of the spacecraft which left him to die in the void. Colourful backdrops, brilliant detail, tremendous narrative energy: perhaps the best novel of its kind. Published in the UK as *Tiger! Tiger!*

Starshadows (1977) ★★ Collection by Pamela Sargent (USA). Ten sf stories of the 1970s, some of them touching on biological and feminist themes (the author is editor of the notable anthologies *Bio-Futures* and *Women of Wonder*). Competent work by one of that decade's better new writers.

Starship (Aldiss): see *Non-Stop*.

Starship and Haiku (1984) ★★ Novel by Somtow Sucharitkul (Thailand/ USA). In an environmentally degraded future, humanity makes its peace with the whales. And a mad leader persuades the Japanese nation to commit mass suicide for the shame of having slaughtered so many cetaceans in the past. It's a cranky book, to say the least, but certainly intriguing.

Starship Troopers (1959) ★★ Novel by Robert A. Heinlein (USA). A starfaring infantryman of the future is caught up in a life-or-death struggle with despicable insectile aliens. A harsh, didactic tirade which proved very popular despite its evident designs upon the reader. Full of ingenious details and cleverly insinuated revelations (it turns out that the hero is black, a startling fact in its day). In retrospect, this novel can be seen to have initiated a whole school of militaristic American sf (see the works of David Drake, Jerry Pournelle and others). It also represented the beginning of Heinlein's hectoring, right-wing phase and the onset of his decline as an sf writer of the first rank. Hugo award-winner, 1960.

Starsilk (Van Scyoc): see under *Darkchild*.

Star-Spangled Future, The (Spinrad): see under *No Direction Home*.

Starswarm (Aldiss): see *Airs of Earth*.

Startide Rising (1983) ★★★ Novel by David Brin (USA), sequel to *Sundiver*. Intelligent dolphins and chimps co-operate with humanity in the exploration of space. Together they will prove Earth's worth in the galactic community. A nice idea, but it was probably the wealth of 'fannish' in-jokes and references which made this adventure novel so popular with the sf core audience. Hugo and Nebula award-winner, 1984. Sequel: *The Uplift War*.

Station Gehenna (1987) ★★ Fix-up novel by Andrew Weiner (UK/ Canada). Humans are busy terraforming another planet when one of their small team dies mysteriously. The psychologist hero is sent to investigate, and soon encounters strange alien phenomena. An interesting first novel by an author who had been producing magazine sf for about fifteen years; a subsequent volume of his short fiction is entitled *Distant Signals and Other Stories* (1989). 'Weiner proves himself adept at creating an atmosphere' – Dan Chow, *Locus*.

Stations of the Nightmare (1982) ★ Fix-up novel by Philip José Farmer (USA), first published as a four-part series in the *Continuum* anthologies edited by Roger Elwood (1974–75). The hero shoots at a UFO, and his brain is invaded by an alien entity which bestows super-normal powers on him. The book has some intriguing ideas, but it's underdeveloped.

Status Civilization, The (1960) ★★ Novel by Robert Sheckley (USA). The hero is memory-wiped and banished to the prison planet Omega, where he finds a society just as stratified as the one he has left – except that the criminals are on top and virtue brings no rewards. It's slightly grimmer, and rather better constructed, than most Sheckley novels.

Steam-Driven Boy and Other Strangers, The (1973) ★★★ Collection by John Sladek (USA). Thirteen funny stories by a master of the absurd, plus 10 brief parodies of other sf writers. Sladek's first collection. A later volume is entitled *Keep the Giraffe Burning* (1977), and many of the stories from both books (including the parodies) were recombined as *The Best of John Sladek* (1981; USA only).

Steel Crocodile, The (Compton): see *Electric Crocodile, The*.

Steel Tsar, The (Moorcock): see under *Warlord of the Air, The*.

Stepford Wives, The (1972) ★★ Novel by Ira Levin (USA). A far-fatched thriller set in a well-evoked dormitory suburb, where it transpires (gosh!) that all the swinish men have traded in their wives for ever-compliant robot copies. Another one for the mainstream readership. Filmed in 1975 (dir. Bryan Forbes). There have also been a couple of TV-movie sequels: *Revenge of the Stepford Wives* (1980; dir. Robert Fuest) and *The Stepford Children* (1987; dir. Alan J. Levi).

Steppe (1976) ★ Novel by Piers Anthony (UK/USA). A 12th-century Asiatic horse warrior is whisked away into the future where he must participate in an elaborate game called 'Steppe'. Needless to say, his wily military skills enable him to win. A curious blend of space opera and historical research.

Steps of the Sun, The (1983) ★ Novel by Walter Tevis (USA). An unhappy billionaire of the 21st century flies off into space on a one-man mission to find a safe source of energy. He succeeds, but this doesn't bring him joy. It has literary pretensions, but Tevis's last novel is unfortunately a tedious, self-pitying and scientifically wonky piece of nonsense.

Stepsons of Terra (Silverberg): see under *Silent Invaders, The*.

Still I Persist in Wondering (Pangborn): see under *Davy*.

Still River (1987) ★★ Novel by Hal Clement (USA). Five students of different species are on a field course on a mysterious planet to study its wind patterns, geology and chemistry. Conflict between characters is kept to the minimum: their antagonist is the planet itself, or rather their ignorance of it. As they learn more, so does the reader.

Still Small Voice of Trumpets, The (1968) ★ Novel by Lloyd Biggle Jr. (USA). Despite the daftly egregious title, it's a routine alien-world mystery story in its author's 'Cultural Survey' series. Sequel: *The World Menders*.

Stochastic Man, The (1975) ★★ Novel by Robert Silverberg (USA). A market analyst with an impressive ability to calculate the future joins a political leader's staff, where he comes into contact with a genuine clairvoyant. 'A fast and literate read, perhaps an early example of a new kind of sf whose chief interest will be its reflection of popular response, not to science and technology but to modish intellectualism: Chomsky and Levi-Strauss rather than rockets and laser beams' – J. G. Ballard, *New Statesman*.

Stolen Faces (1977) ★★★ Novel by Michael Bishop (USA). The hero becomes the governor of a sort of interstellar leper colony – only to find that his alien charges are not diseased after all. Fairly bleak philosophical adventure by a highly intelligent writer.

Stone God Awakens, The (1970) ★ Novel by Philip José Farmer (USA). The hero is frozen into 'stone' by means of some gobbledegook science, and eventually awakens 20 million years in the future – where he proceeds to have routine adventures among the bizarrely evolved life-forms. A quickie.

Stone in Heaven, A (Anderson): see under *We Claim These Stars*.

Stone That Never Came Down, The (1973) ★★ Novel by John Brunner (UK). In a disintegrating Europe of the 21st century one man attempts to prevent war and change human nature by means of a new drug. Contemporary worries become the stuff of yet another proficient Brunner entertainment.

Stonehenge (1972) ★★ Novel by Harry Harrison and Leon Stover (USA). Sf-cum-historical novel about the building of Stonehenge – with help from the inhabitants of Atlantis. The hero is a Mycenean Greek, and the novel is based on the well-known theory that 'Atlantis' was in fact the Mediterranean island of Thera which was destroyed by a volcanic eruption circa 1500 BC. The authors strive for historical realism, within the context of an action/ adventure plot.

Store of Infinity (Sheckley): see under *Pilgrimage to Earth*.

Storeys from the Old Hotel (Wolfe): see under *Endangered Species*.

Stories of Ray Bradbury, The (1980) ★★★ Collection by Ray Bradbury (USA). A massive tome which contains virtually all the contents of *The Martian Chronicles*, *The Illustrated Man* and the other Bradbury volumes up to *Long After Midnight*, together with a small handful of never-previously-collected pieces. A great deal of it is fantasy, or marginal whimsy, rather than sf; nevertheless much of the sf that is here is truly excellent. It has been split into two volumes for paperback reprints.

Storm of Wings, A (Harrison): see under *Pastel City, The*.

Stormqueen (Bradley): see under *Sword of Aldones, The*.

Storms of Victory (Pournelle & Green): see under *Janissaries*.

Strange Bedfellows: Sex and Science Fiction (Scortia): see under *Shape of Sex to Come, The*.

Strange Doings (1971) ★★★ Collection by R. A. Lafferty (USA). Sixteen tall tales by one of sf's grand eccentrics. Contains his classic 'Continued on Next Rock', about a very unusual find in an archaeological dig. Some pieces are fantasy, many are unclassifiable; but all these 'doings' are very strange indeed. Other Lafferty collections include *Does Anyone Else Have Something Further to Add?* (1974) and *Ringing Changes* (1984).

Strange Invasion (1989) ★★ Novel by Michael Kandel (USA). 'Tourists' from outer space threaten to despoil our planet. Slight, bright and humorous – a first novel by a writer previously known for his translations of the Polish sf author Stanislaw Lem. 'Reminded me of something Robert Sheckley might have written for *Galaxy* in the 50s' – Darrell Schweitzer, *Aboriginal SF*.

Strange Relations (1960) ★★★ Collection by Philip José Farmer (USA). Five long stories, mostly with interplanetary settings and each named after a familial relation ('Mother', 'Father', 'My Sister's Brother', etc.). In the best of these pieces grotesque alien biologies are depicted with relish. Considered strong, daring stuff in the 1950s, this is still one of Farmer's best books.

Strange Seas and Shores (1971) ★★ Collection by Avram Davidson (USA), introduced by Ray Bradbury. Seventeen sf and fantasy stories (mainly the fantasy, and mainly from the 1960s), including some of this offbeat author's best, such as 'Take Wooden Indians' and 'The Sources of the Nile'. Witty, knotty, sometimes exasperating.

Strange Things in Close-Up: The Nearly Complete Howard Waldrop (1989) ★★★ Collection by Howard Waldrop (USA). Nineteen wide-ranging sf and fantasy stories, all of them stylish and ingenious and many of them humorous. This UK-published volume comprises the complete contents of the US collections *Howard Who?* and *All About Strange Monsters of the Recent Past* (1987).

Strange Wine (1978) ★★ Collection by Harlan Ellison (USA). Fifteen sf, fantasy and borderline pieces, of varying merit but all stamped with the unmistakable Ellisonian flavour. Notable items include 'Croatoan' and 'The Wine Has Been Left Open Too Long and the Memory Has Gone Flat' (the latter demonstrates how Ellison strives for ever longer titles on his short stories).

Strangeness (Disch & Naylor): see under *Bad Moon Rising*.

Stranger in a Strange Land (1961) ★★★ Novel by Robert A. Heinlein (USA). Lengthy satire, beginning as sf but ending as sheer fantasy, which centres on the adventures of an innocent abroad: a young Earthman who has been reared by Martians and has absorbed their paranormal powers. Among other things, he has the ability to 'discorporate' people, i.e. to make them disappear into another dimension – a wish-fulfilment device if ever there was one. Much of the wordage consists of the conversations of the hero's guardian, Jubal Harshaw, a hack writer who is clearly an alter ego of the author. Its readableness, its humour, its iconoclasm and its (rather coy) sexual content made the book into an 'underground' bestseller (words such as 'grok' entered the language, if only temporarily), but there is no avoiding its deeply controversial and disturbing nature. It was one of mass-murderer Charles Manson's favourite novels, and he is said to have been inspired by it. Hugo award-winner, 1962.

Strangers (1978) ★★★ Novel by Gardner Dozois (USA). On a beautifully described far planet, an Earthman falls in love with an alien woman – with tragic consequences. It has obvious affinities with Philip José Farmer's path-breaking novel *The Lovers*, but it's far better done.

Strangers in the Universe (1956) ★★★ Collection by Clifford D. Simak (USA). Eleven intriguing stories which blend sentiment, humour, mystery and speculation in Simak's deceptively simple style. Standouts include 'Skirmish' (1950), 'Contraption' (1953) and 'Immigrant' (1954). British edition omits four stories, as do US and UK paperback reprints.

Strangler's Moon (Goldin): see under *Imperial Stars, The*.

Strata (1981) ★★ Novel by Terry

Pratchett (UK). The heroine, who specializes in moulding worlds for human colonization, discovers an artificial 'flat earth' built by aliens. When she lands there, some very unlikely things begin to happen. A funny sf novel by a writer who has since had great success with his humorous fantasies.

Streetlethal (1983) ★★ Novel by Steven Barnes (USA). Tough-talking tale of street violence in near-future California after an earthquake. Proficient entertainment, more or less in the mode made popular by such films as *Escape from New York* and *Blade Runner*.

Stress Pattern (1974) ★★ Novel by Neal Barrett Jr. (USA). An earthman struggles to survive in the unfamiliar environment of an alien planet where the aliens are quite indifferent to him. The background is described with great ingenuity and inventiveness. 'Had this novel appeared under the byline of a more established writer, it would almost certainly have excited more comment than it did' – Don D'Ammassa, *Twentieth-Century Science-Fiction Writers*.

Study War No More (1977) ★★ Anthology edited by Joe Haldeman (USA). Nine stories about 'alternatives to war', together with an essay by Isaac Asimov; best is Damon Knight's 'Rule Golden', in which all attackers suffer the same pain as their victims.

Sturgeon in Orbit (1964) ★★ Collection by Theodore Sturgeon (USA). Five odd, intermittently powerful stories (all from the period 1951–55) which unfortunately do not show this author at his very best.

Sturgeon Is Alive and Well (1971) ★★ Collection by Theodore Sturgeon (USA). A dozen stories, some of them slight and humorous and scarcely sf. Standouts are 'To Here and the Easel' (1954) and 'Slow Sculpture' (1970), the latter a Hugo and Nebula award-winner about a cure for cancer and the art of bonsai.

Sudanna, Sudanna (1985) ★ Novel by Brian Herbert (USA). A tale of the daily doings of aliens on a planet which carries the vestiges of outside invaders. 'Hovers uneasily between comedy and seriousness' – Brian Stableford.

Sudden Star, The (1979) ★★ Fix-up novel by Pamela Sargent (USA). Society gradually disintegrates when the world is struck by a new plague, in this episodic but fairly complex post-catastrophe tale with a large cast. Published in Britain as *The White Death*.

Sugar Rain (Park): see under *Soldiers of Paradise*.

Sunburst (1964) ★★ Novel by Phyllis Gotlieb (Canada). Subtle, well-written tale of psi-powers and emergent super-children. A first novel by a writer known for her plays and verse. 'Beautifully avoids the clichés of conventional sf on this theme' – Douglas Barbour, *20th-Century SF Writers*.

Sundance and Other SF Stories

(Silverberg): see under *Needle in a Timestack*.

Sundered Worlds, The ★ Fix-up novel by Michael Moorcock (UK). The eponymous worlds belong to a star system which travels through various dimensions of the 'multiverse'. A slam-bang space opera which is not at all representative of its author's later works. Moorcock's first sf novel (although he had already published two sword-and-sorcery books). Republished as *The Blood Red Game*.

Sundiver (1980) ★★ Novel by David Brin (USA), set in the same 'Uplift' universe as the later *Startide Rising*. Human scientists and their chimpanzee and dolphin clients investigate intelligent life on the sun and try to prove that the Earth is worthy to be part of the galactic community of civilizations. An engaging first novel, popular with the sf in-crowd.

Sundog (1965) Novel by Brian N. Ball (UK). Aliens have 'locked' the human race into its solar system, but one intrepid astronaut breaks out. A rather ill-written and hard-to-follow space adventure which seems to owe a debt to the complex narratives of A. E. van Vogt. Ball's first novel.

Sunfall (1981) ★★ Collection by C. J. Cherryh (USA). Six skilfully-turned stories set in the cities of a far-future decadent Earth that resembles parts of the planet's past. A quiet, downbeat tone very different from most of Cherryh's work.

Sunless World, The (Jones): see under *Planet of the Double Sun, The*.

Sun's End (1984) ★★ Novel by Richard A. Lupoff (USA). A Japanese space engineer is frozen after an accident, and awakes 80 years later to find that he has been revived with bionic enhancements. Effectively a superman, it is now his task to save the solar system from coming doom. Space adventure of a basically old-fashioned sort, despite its modern gloss. Sequel: *Galaxy's End* (1988).

Suns of Scorpio, The (Akers): see under *Transit to Scorpio*.

Sunstroke and Other Stories (Watson): see under *Very Slow Time Machine, The*.

Superluminal (1983) ★★ Novel by Vonda N. McIntyre (USA), expanded from her story 'Aztecs' (1977). The heroine is a faster-than-light spacecraft pilot who has to be surgically modified in order to do her job. ('She gave up her heart quite willingly,' as the book states in a nicely ambiguous first sentence.) But the love interest conflicts with the space operatics. 'The kind of colourful, sexually-liberated, and mildly socially-concerned novel that comes after Delany – a long way after' – Mary Gentle, *Interzone*.

Supermind (Phillips): see under *Brain Twister*.

Survival! (1984) ★ Collection by Gordon R. Dickson (Canada/USA), introduced by Sandra Miesel. A dozen stories, mostly from the 1950s and largely concerned with aspects of human survival way out there on the harsh interstellar frontiers.

Minor Dickson. Another 'clean-up' collection of similar type (and with the seemingly obligatory exclamation mark) is *Invaders!* (1985).

Survival Margin (Maine): see *Darkest of Nights, The*.

Survivors, The (1958) ★ Novel by Tom Godwin (USA). Humans are marooned by hostile aliens on a high-gravity planet. They survive, escape and prevail. Upbeat hard sf: a first novel by the author who is best known for his short story 'The Cold Equations' (1954). Republished as *Space Prison*. Sequel: *The Space Barbarians* (1964).

Suspicion (McQuay): see under *Odyssey*.

Svaha (1989) ★★ Novel by Charles de Lint (USA). In an environmentally-degraded 22nd century, the good guys live in protected enclaves, while the riff-raff have to make do in the great outdoors. The Amerindian hero is obliged to venture from his cosy enclave – and of course he learns a thing or two. A Cyberpunk-ish entry into sf by a writer best known for his fantasy novels.

Swampworld West (1974) Novel by Perry A. Chapdelaine (USA). A planet's colonists have trouble with native aliens called (believe it or not) Splurgs. Pretty poor stuff. 'This extraordinary and dismal farrago of clichés' – John Brunner, *Foundation*.

Swan Song (Stableford): see under *Halcyon Drift*.

Swastika Night (1937) ★★ Novel by Katharine Burdekin (UK), originally published under the pseudonym 'Murray Constantine'. In this chilling vision of a 26th-century world which is ruled by Germany and Japan (as a result of their victories in the mid-20th century) the emphasis is on the latter-day Nazis' mistreatment of women. An interesting example of feminist, anti-fascist sf, chiefly remarkable for the early date at which it was written. It was rediscovered and republished under the author's true name in 1985.

Sweet Dreams, Sweet Princes (1986) ★★ Novel by Mack Reynolds and Michael Banks (USA), the last of the 'People's Capitalism' sequence and sequel to The Fracas Factor. Dennis Land, mild-mannered history teacher and amateur gladiator, is drafted into a plot to kidnap a Belgian scientist whose research threatens to destabilize the Universal Disarmament Treaty. As with other works, the interest is in the depiction of a future political system which is obviously rooted in Reynolds's view of our own.

Sweet, Sweet Summer, A (1969) ★★ Novel by Jane Gaskell (UK). Britain falls apart after it has been isolated from the rest of the world by mysterious aliens whose ships hover overhead. An eccentric, well-characterized, rather cynical book by an author who has also written lush fantasy novels.

Sword of Aldones, The (1962) ★★ Novel by Marion Zimmer Bradley (USA), first-published in her lengthy 'Darkover' series. The planet Darkover (isolated from the rest of the human race for centuries) has developed a strange science based on mental powers and a feudal, decentralized political system intended to restrict their use. The opportunity to join a newly-expanding Galactic Empire causes internal strife and the temptation to use these powers to oppose Terran technology. This was the first written (though not the first in internal chronology) of the 'Darkover' sequence, using the language of sf as a background to stories which are in many ways more like sword-and-sorcery fantasy. Two much later books The Heritage of Hastur, and Sharra's Exile, return to the events described in this first volume. See also The Bloody Sun, Darkover Landfall, The Winds of Darkover, The World Wreckers, The Shattered Chain, The Forbidden Tower, Thendara House and City of Sorcery. Other books in the series, not annotated here, include The Planet Savers (1962), Star of Danger (1965), The Spell Sword (1974), Stormqueen (1978), Two to Conquer (1980) and Hawkmistress (1982).

Sword of Chaos (Bradley): see under Free Amazons of Darkover.

Sword of Forbearance, The (Williams): see under Breaking of Northwall, The.

Sword of Rhiannon, The (1953) ★★★ Novel by Leigh Brackett (USA). A Martian explorer is plunged back a million years, and has world-saving adventures in an epoch when the red planet was green. A space-opera/

sword-and-scorcery blend (best call it 'planetary romance') which is written with tremendous verve. 'The most magical sub-Burroughs of them all, the best evocation of that fantasy Mars we would all give our sword arm to visit' – Brian Aldiss, *Billion Year Spree*.

Sword of the Lictor, The (Wolfe): see *Book of the New Sun, The*.

Sword Swallower, The (1968) ★★ Novel by Ron Goulart (USA). The secret-agent hero is a member of the face-changing 'Chameleon Corps'. In this wacky adventure, he visits a colonized planet in search of some missing military experts. Goulart's first novel, and typical of all the light, breezy work which was to follow. Later books in the same vein include *The Chameleon Corps and Other Shape Changers* (1972), *Spacehawk, Inc.* (1974), *A Whiff of Madness* (1976) and *Starpirate's Brain* (1987).

Sybil Sue Blue (1966) ★★ Novel by Rosel George Brown (USA). The eponymous heroine is a resourceful future cop who goes in search of interstellar drug smugglers. 'Feminist' sf adventure by a writer who died young. Republished as *Galactic Sybil Sue Blue*. Sequel (published posthumously): *The Waters of Centaurus* (1970).

Sykaos Papers, The (1988) ★★ Novel by E. P. Thompson (UK). For his first novel this distinguished British historian and political pamphleteer has chosen to write science fiction of sorts (it is subtitled 'Being an Account of the Voyages of the Poet Oi Paz to the System of Strim in the Seventeenth Galaxy ...', etc., etc.). A powerful and humane message is embedded in an overlong narrative which lacks sophistication of sf technique. 'Thompson has written a Swiftian satire, a fantastic voyage to dystopia, a didactic fable, a tract, a diatribe; he has not written (nor could he have intended to have written) a science-fiction novel' – John Clute.

Synaptic Manhunt, The (Farren): see under *Quest of the DNA Cowboys, The*.

Syndic, The (1953) ★★★ Novel by C. M. Kornbluth (USA). Future America is ruled partly by a Mafialike mob and partly by a more benign organization referred to as 'the fat, sloppy, happy Syndic'. An enjoyable adventure story with satirical barbs and an underlying darkness of tone.

Synergy: New Science Fiction, Volume 1 (1988) ★★ Anthology edited by George Zebrowski (USA), first in a proposed annual series. All original stories by writers of the calibre of Charles L. Harness and Frederik Pohl as well as a number of lesser-known names. The quality is variable, though certainly Pohl is on first-class form with his humorous tale 'My Life as a Born-Again Pig'.

Synthajoy (1968) ★★ Novel by D. G. Compton (UK). An unscrupulous psychiatrist invents a device to record emotional experiences. His wife murders him. A subtle, well-characterized tale in its author's usual downbeat vein.

Synthetic Man, The (Sturgeon): see *Dreaming Jewels, The.*

Systemic Shock (1981) ★ Novel by Dean Ing (USA). Nuclear-cum-biological war has destroyed most of the United States, and what remains is ruled by the Mormons and other religious organizations. Postholocaust sf adventure with a 'survivalist' slant. Sequels: *Single Combat* (1983) and *Wild Country* (1985).

Syzygy (1973) ★★ Novel by Michael Coney (UK/Canada). The colonized planet Arcadia has a problem: whenever its six moons come into a certain alignment, tidal waves and general madness ensue. It seems that intelligent clusters of plankton have an adverse effect on the human colonists' mental equilibrium. A moral tale of environmental consequences, efficiently told. Quasi-sequel: *Brontomek!*

Syzygy (1982) ★ Novel by Frederik Pohl (USA). A quickie written to cash in on the faddish notion of the 'Jupiter Effect' – the idea that a rare alignment of planets in 1982 would have disastrous consequences on Earth. This turns out to be sleight-of-hand on Pohl's part, though, as the novel is really about contact with alien intelligence. 'Come on, Michael Coney: get your own back – call your next novel *Gateway*' – Ian Watson, *Foundation.*

T

Tactics of Mistake, The (1971) ★★ Novel by Gordon R. Dickson (USA). In terms of internal chronology, it's the first of the 'Dorsai' series (see *Dorsai!*), concerning the education and development of Donal Graeme, a great spacefaring general. It suffers slightly from the author's inability to tell us exactly what is so unique about his hero's military genius.

Taflak Lysandra (1988) ★ Novel by L. Neil Smith (USA). The title character goes on a mission to the planet Majesty with plenty of more-or-less twee furry friends and enemies. Minor.

Taji's Syndrome (1988) ★★ Novel by Chelsea Quinn Yarbro (USA). Genetic tampering causes a terrifying new disease, highly contagious and fatal in most cases, but the few who survive develop psychokinetic powers. The plot concerns those who want to eliminate the disease — and those who wish to spread it. 'The struggle is gripping, the characters real, and the ideas carefully worked out. What more could you ask from a science-fictional medical thriller?' – Tom Whitmore, *Locus*.

Takeoff (1952) ★ Novel by C. M. Kornbluth (USA). A badly dated thriller about the building of the first moon rocket: here, a scientist and a businessman conspire with various juveniles to carry out the mighty project in secrecy. Kornbluth's first solo novel.

Talent for War, A (1989) ★★ Novel by Jack McDevitt (USA). A young man sets out to unravel a puzzle, against the background of an interstellar conflict between humans and aliens several millennia hence. A more thoughtful work than most recent space-war novels, though rather stodgily written.

Tales from Planet Earth (1989) ★★ Collection by Arthur C. Clarke (UK). Sixteen reprinted short stories from 1949 to 1987, including the well-known 'If I Forget Thee, Oh Earth ...' and the original short version of the novel *The Deep Range*. There are just two previously uncollected pieces, the brief 'The Other Tiger' and the equally brief 'On Golden Seas'. All cleanly written, with much sense of wonder: a perfectly adequate Clarke sampler.

Tales from the Forbidden Planet (1987) ★ Anthology edited by Roz Kaveney (UK). Original sf and fantasy stories by 'name' authors, all of whom happen to have participated in book-signings at London's Forbidden Planet Bookshop. There are many good authors here – Aldiss, Brunner, Kilworth, Moorcock, Roberts, etc. – but it was a weak occasion for an anthology and few of these stars shine. The pieces by Tanith Lee and Lisa Tuttle stand out from the ruck. 'This, I'm afraid, is a collection of second bests' – David V. Barrett, *Foundation*.

Tales from the White Hart (1957) ★ Collection by Arthur C. Clarke (UK). Humorous tall tales supposedly told in a pub. Most of them are sf, but they do not show the author in his most characteristic light.

Tales of Known Space (1975) ★★ Collection by Larry Niven (USA). Thirteen short stories, plus bibliographic material and some explanation from the author, which complete his 'Known Space' future-history series. One suspects that most of the stories here were not judged good enough to be included in his earlier collection, *Neutron Star*.

Tales of Ten Worlds (1962) ★★ Collection by Arthur C. Clarke (UK). A variable gathering of sf stories. It includes the memorable dreadful-

warning piece 'I Remember Babylon' (1960), about a near-future world saturated with televised pornography and propaganda thanks to unregulated satellite-TV broadcasts: a prediction which may well 'come true' in the 1990s.

Tales of the Flying Mountains (Anderson): see under *Beyond the Beyond*.

Tanar of Pellucidar (Burroughs): see under *At the Earth's Core*.

Tangents (1989) ★★★ Collection by Greg Bear (USA). Nine sf and fantasy stories, including one original called 'Sisters', a fine piece about genetic manipulation. Also here is 'Blood Music', the award-winning short version of the author's highly praised novel of the same name. An earlier, small-press collection by Greg Bear rejoiced in the unlovely title of *The Wind from a Burning Woman* (1983).

Tapestry of Time, A (Cowper): see under *Road to Corlay, The*.

Tar-Aiym Krang, The (1972) ★★ Novel by Alan Dean Foster (USA). The Krang is a huge organ in a pyramidal concert hall, supposed to be a weapon developed for use in the war that destroyed the Tar-Aiym Empire half a million years ago. Philip Lynx, or Flinx, a street-urchin from Moth, gets caught up in a madcap scheme to capture it. A workmanlike adventure story, introducing the character of Flinx and the Human-Thranx ('Humanx') Commonwealth. Foster's first novel. Sequels include: *Blood-*

hype, *Orphan Star* (1977) and *Flinx in Flux* (1988).

Tarnsman of Gor (1966) Novel by John Norman (USA), first of an interminable series. Gor is a planet which exists on the far side of the sun, hidden from our view. Its barbarous slave-owning culture is continuously supplied with manpower – and, more especially, with womanpower – kidnapped from Earth. This first book is a reasonably competent fantastic adventure in the Edgar Rice Burroughs mode. However, later volumes (and there has been approximately one a year for more than 20 years) have degenerated into obsessive sado-masochistic pornography of an offensively sexist kind. They have been popular, alas. Sequels: *Outlaw of Gor* (1967), *Priest-Kings of Gor* (1968), *Nomads of Gor* (1969), etc., etc.

Tarzan at the Earth's Core (Burroughs): see under *At the Earth's Core.*

Tatja Grimm's World (1987) ★★ Fix-up novel by Vernor Vinge (USA), originally published in shorter form as *Grimm's World* (1969). A picaresque narrative based on a number of short stories about a young barbarian woman of supernatural intelligence who takes over a mobile sf-and-fantasy publishing house which roams the seas in a giant barge. An oddity. In its original version, this was Vinge's first novel.

Tau Zero (1970) ★★★ Novel by Poul Anderson (USA). As an interstellar space vessel approaches the speed of light its braking mechanism jams and the craft continues to accelerate ... A mind-boggling tale which uses the paradoxes of Einsteinian physics to excellent effect. Despite shortcomings in the characterizations, it's probably Anderson's best novel.

Technicolor Time Machine, The (1967) ★★★ Novel by Harry Harrison (UK/Ireland). Movie producers get hold of a time machine, and decide to shoot a Viking epic on location – in the 11th century AD. A thoroughly madcap romp in its author's best vein. 'Harrison's most successful blending to date of humour, science and violent action, with characters as nearly three-dimensional as the complicated plot permits' – James Cawthorn, *New Worlds.*

Technos (Tubb): see under *Winds of Gath, The.*

TekWar (1989) ★★ Novel by William Shatner (USA). A 22nd-century ex-policeman fights the latter-day computerized drug barons, in this quite competent first novel by a well-known film and TV actor ('Captain Kirk', etc). Perhaps the only surprise is that the author has steered well clear of the *Star Trek* sort of thing, and instead produced a futuristic cops-and-robbers thriller (Shatner himself described it on a chat show as 'T. J. Hooker in the future').

Telempath (1976) ★★ Novel by Spider Robinson (USA). Urban civilization is destroyed by mad scientists who give us back our sense of smell; and the few survivors are threatened by aerial intelligences which used to eat the air-pollution.

Telepath (Sellings): see *Silent Speakers, The.*

Telepathist (Brunner): see *Whole Man, The.*

Temple of the Past, The (1958) Novel by Stefan Wul (France). A rocket from Atlantis crashes on an alien planet where it is swallowed by a sea monster. A crew-member survives, and eventually brings civilization of a sort to the monster's multitudinous lizard-like offspring. 'Reads as though it was tossed off in a week or so by an amateur who didn't care enough about his work to plan ahead or even re-read what he had produced ... Excruciatingly awful' – John Brunner, *Foundation.*

Ten Thousand Light-Years from Home (1973) ★★★ Collection by James Tiptree Jr. (Alice Sheldon, USA). Fifteen sf stories, about a third of them slick comedies from the author's debut year (1968), the remainder increasingly powerful and anguished works of the sort which made Tiptree the most fashionable American sf author of the early 1970s. Highpoints include 'And I Awoke and Found Me Here on the Cold Hill's Side' and 'Painwise' – stories which successfully fuse slickness with soul. Tiptree's first book.

Tenth Victim, The (1966) ★★ Novelization by Robert Sheckley (USA), based on the script of the Italian-made film of the same title (1965; dir. Elio Petri), which in turn was based on Sheckley's short story 'Seventh Victim'. Humorous action-adventure stuff set in a future society of legalized death duels, a world of declared 'hunters' and 'victims'.

Terminal Beach, The (1964) ★★★★ Collection by J. G. Ballard (UK). Twelve fine stories, ranging from 'Deep End' (1961) to 'The Drowned Giant' (1964). Standouts include 'A Question of Re-Entry' (1963), about the fate of an astronaut who crash-lands amidst cannibals in the Amazon basin, and the title story (1964), about a man who feels a compulsive need to maroon himself on the nuclear testing island of Eniwe-tok. These marvellously haunting and original stories mark an early high point in 1960s 'New-Wave' sf.

Terminal Man, The (1972) ★ Novel by Michael Crichton (USA). An epileptic is subjected to experimental surgery: a nuclear-power pack is embedded in his body in order to control his disease. However, the patient proves unreliable and becomes a sort of living bomb. A weak thriller impressively tricked out with technological jargon in Crichton's usual style. Filmed in 1974 (dir. Mike Hodges).

Terraplane (1988) ★★ Novel by Jack Womack (USA), a quasi-sequel to *Ambient.* This post-Cyberpunk effort opens in an amusingly described free-market USSR at the end of the 20th century. Two American agents use a new time-travel device which accidentally throws them into a nightmarish alternative USA of the year 1939. Things get violent and complicated. 'Told in a clipped, compressed, brutal dialect ... it's an efficient tale. Recommended, but not for the squeamish' – Paul McAuley, *Interzone*.

Terrarium (1985) ★★ Novel by Scott Russell Sanders (USA). Future humans live in domed cities, insulated against the pollution outside. Some bold souls decide to venture out, and they find an environment which has now recovered from the depredations of humanity.

Terry's Universe (1988) ★ Anthology edited by Beth Meacham (USA). This volume was published to honour the memory of sf editor Terry Carr, who died in 1987. Although it contains original stories by an impressive line-up of 'names' – Gregory Benford, Ursula Le Guin, Fritz Leiber, Kim Stanley Robinson, Robert Silverberg and Roger Zelazny are among them – the results are disappointing. 'Practically an insult ... Only Carter Scholz and Kate Wilhelm have produced work that does Carr's memory justice' – Paul Kincaid, *Vector*.

Test of Fire (1982) ★ Novel by Ben Bova (USA), an expansion of his earlier book *When the Sky Burned* (1973). War and solar flares destroy the Earth, but a colony survives on the moon. An adequate adventure story by a writer (and erstwhile editor of *Analog* magazine) who has a respect for hard science.

Testament of Andros, The (Blish): see *Best Science Fiction Stories of James Blish*.

Tetrasomy Two (1974) ★ Novel by Oscar Rossiter (USA). A telepathic superman story, laced with humour and sex. 'This amiable little tale, ill balanced between its two main themes, does rather break down in the hokum apocalypse of its final paragraphs' – John Clute.

Texas-Israeli War: 1999, The (1974) ★ Novel by Jake Saunders and Howard Waldrop (USA), expanded from their story 'A Voice and Bitter Weeping'. Oil-rich Texas uses Israeli soldiers to defend its interests against the other states of the Union. A zany little idea which is here spun out at too great a length. Waldrop's first novel.

Texts of Festival, The (1973) ★ Novel by Mick Farren (UK). In a post-catastrophe setting, the community named Festival is intended to preserve the love-and-peace spirit of the Woodstock rock-music festival. However, things soon degenerate into violence. An odd, rag-tag mixture of pop-culture clichés and science-fiction western.

That Hideous Strength (Lewis): see under *Out of the Silent Planet*.

That Uncertain Midnight (1958) ★★ Novel by Edmund Cooper (UK). A deep-frozen man is revived in the 22nd century, to find an unhappy world where androids do all the work and normal humans live in decadent luxury. There are a few rebels, though, and he joins them. Cooper's first novel. 'A good sound pedestrian idea, with characterizations and techniques firmly in the

Wyndham/Christopher mould' – Joyce Churchill, *New Worlds*. Republished as *Deadly Image*.

Theatre of Timesmiths, A (1984) ★★ Novel by Garry Kilworth (UK). In a totalitarian closed environment known as 'First City', embedded in icc, the heroine, a 'mind-prostitute', attempts an escape. 'An original and inventive use of old themes' – Mary Gentle, *Interzone*.

Their Majesties' Bucketeers (Smith): see under *Probability Broach, The*.

Their Master's War (1987) ★ Novel by Mick Farren (UK/USA). A party of barbarians is kidnapped by aliens: they are put through brutal military training and become foot-soldiers in an interstellar war they cannot comprehend. A very traditional adventure story that could just as easily have been a historical novel as sf.

Them Bones (1984) ★★★ Novel by Howard Waldrop (USA). A complex time mystery, in which archaeologists find strange objects in a bone-bed. 'Meanwhile,' a 21st-century meddler is attempting to change history, and ends up in an alternative universe. The first solo novel by a writer highly respected for his short stories. 'Packed with gritty detail. Pleasurable and fine' – Gregory Benford.

Thendara House (1983) ★★ Novel by Marion Zimmer Bradley (USA). Yet another 'Darkover' story (see *The Sword of Aldones*), set among the 'Renunciates' or 'Free Amazons' – the guild of women introduced in *The Shattered Chain* who are crucial to the later books in this lengthy sequence. The story is continued in *City of Sorcery*.

There is No Darkness (1983) ★ Fix-up novel by Joe Haldeman and Jack C. Haldeman (USA). Three humorous stories about Carl Bok, a huge backwoodsman from the Springworld who gets into various scrapes with Starschool (a sort of university on a spaceship), wrestling bears on Earth, failing the survival course on Hell, and saving the universe in the Construct where alien races meet. A minor collaboration between the talented Joe Haldeman and his older brother.

There Will Be Time (1972) ★ Novel by Poul Anderson (USA). A time-traveller who dislikes what he sees up ahead decides to change history. The inevitable complications ensue. Not one of the author's best time stories: it's partly a satire on the 1960s counter-culture scene (which Anderson deplores).

There Will Be War (1983) ★ Anthology edited by Jerry Pournelle and John F. Carr (USA). The title uncompromisingly states what the book is about and also hints at the ideological stance of its editors and contributors. Militaristic sf seems to have become a boom industry in the past decade, and Pournelle's works are at the heart of all that furious activity. Sequel volumes: *Men of War* (1984), *Blood and Iron* (1985), *Day of the Tyrant* (1985), *Warrior* (1986), *Guns of Darkness* (1987), *Call to Battle!* (1988) and *Armageddon!* (1989).

They Shall Have Stars (1956) ★★★ Fix-up novel by James Blish (USA), the second-published in his *Cities in Flight* sequence. Near-future tale involving the discovery of anti-gravity (which makes possible the 'Spindizzy' device which will lift whole cities into space in the other novels). Patchy, but brilliant in parts: particularly impressive is the segment about the building of a huge 'bridge' on Jupiter. Intelligent, knotty, scientifically literate. Republished in paperback as *Year 2018!*, but included under its original title in the omnibus *Cities in Flight*.

They Walked Like Men (1962) ★★ Novel by Clifford D. Simak (USA). Earth is invaded by spherical aliens who have the ability to mimic (and replace) human beings. An entertaining first-person tale of economic mayhem, with rather a cop-out ending.

They'd Rather Be Right (1957) ★★ Novel by Mark Clifton and Frank Riley (USA), first serialized in *Astounding SF* in 1954. The super-computer called 'Bossy' helps humans to evolve psi-powers and longevity. A first novel which seems fairly dim, wish-fulfilling stuff today, but it was very popular with 1950s magazine readers. Hugo award-winner, 1955 (the second, and most obscure, winner of this prize). A paperback reprint was re-titled *The Forever Machine*.

Thing and Other Stories, The (Campbell): see *Who Goes There?*.

Thinking Seat, The (Tate): see under *Greencomber*.

Third Eagle, The (1989) ★★ Novel by R. A. MacAvoy (USA). A tattooed warrior from a backwoods planet travels through the inhabited worlds, learning much about life. This skilfully written exercise in the interstellar picaresque is the first sf work by a writer known for her fantasy novels.

Third from the Sun (Matheson): see under *Born of Man and Woman*.

Third Level, The (1957) ★★★ Collection by Jack Finney (USA). A dozen slickly enjoyable stories, almost all of them on sentimental time-related themes. Published in Britain as *The Clock of Time*. 'In general, [Finney's] use of sf themes is adroitly manipulative but not original' – John Clute.

Thirst! (Maine): see *Tide Went Out, The*.

Thirst Quenchers, The (1965) ★★ Collection by Rick Raphael (USA). Four long stories, two of which deal with a near-future world in which water is extremely scarce. The technical detail is impressive, and the story-telling slick. This collection appears to have been published in the UK only: like Daniel F. Galouye and Joseph L. Green, Raphael is one of those minor American sf writers of the 1960s who was more honoured in Britain than in his home country.

This Darkening Universe (Biggle): see under *All the Colors of Darkness*.

This Immortal (1966) ★★★ Novel by Roger Zelazny (USA), expanded from his Hugo award-winning magazine serial ' ... And Call Me Conrad' (1965). The Vegans have conquered Earth and turned the planet into a backward tourist trap. Long-lived hero Conrad Nomikos acts as a sort of secret agent on behalf of the human race in this allusive tale set against the background of a depopulated, radioactive Greece where ancient gods and mythical beasts seem to be coming to life. A dazzling style is the hallmark of this first novel – it's all surface, with decidedly murky depths.

This is the Way the World Ends (1986) ★★★ Novel by James Morrow (USA). Fantasy-tinged sf satire on the theme of nuclear doom. The hero survives the war but is forced to stand trial for his complicity in the collective crime which has deprived future generations of their lives. It's both sharp and moving, but the framing narrative, which involves Nostradamus and Leonardo da Vinci, is a bit silly. 'Eccentric, sardonic, argumentative, sentimental and whimsical, it eschews all tough-guy stuff amid the smouldering rubble' – Lee Montgomerie, *Interzone*.

This Island Earth (1952) ★★ Fix-up novel by Raymond F. Jones (USA). Scientists receive mysterious instructions from aliens in this space-operatic narrative of an interstellar war which is brought to Earth in clandestine fashion. Old-fashioned fun. Filmed in 1955 (dir. Joseph Newman).

This Perfect Day (1970) ★★ Novel by Ira Levin (USA). A young man rebels against the computerized regime which rules his life and which keeps the masses in drugged submission. A slickly-written update of Huxley's *Brave New World*, lacking in originality but very professionally put together.

This World is Taboo (Leinster): see under *S.O.S. from Three Worlds*.

Thorns (1967) ★★ Novel by Robert Silverberg (USA). An overweight, sado-masochistic communications-mogul of the 'utopian' future attempts to manipulate the lives of two crippled people for his own dubious ends – but they turn the tables on him. Interestingly dark: an sf novel which strives for literary effect, and sometimes achieves it.

Those Gentle Voices (1976) Novel by George Alec Effinger (USA). A so-called 'Promethean Romance of the Spaceways' which fails on just about every count. The hackwork of a sophisticated author who appears to be slumming. Effinger is so much better as a short-story writer.

Those Idiots from Earth (1957) ★★ Collection by Richard Wilson (USA). Light, bright, clever and humane sf stories by a somewhat underrated author of the 1950s and 60s. A later collection, in much the same vein, is *Time Out for Tomorrow* (1962). Alas, his best-known story, 'Mother to the World' (Nebula award-winner, 1968), remains uncollected.

Thousandstar (Anthony): see under *Chaining the Lady*.

Threads of Time (Silverberg): see under *New Atlantis, The*.

Three Eyes of Evil, The (1973) ★ Collection by A. E. van Vogt (USA). Contains two short novels: the title story (formerly *Siege of the Unseen*, 1959) and 'Earth's Last Fortress' (formerly *Masters of Time*, 1950). They blend the usual superman, space-travel and time-travel motifs. Extravagant, fast-moving and fun (if you're in the right mood), they could also be described as dreadful old balderdash.

Three Go Back (1932) ★★ Novel by J. Leslie Mitchell (UK). Fun tale about a trio of ever-so-modern folk from the 1930s who are cast back in time to ancient Atlantis in the days when Neanderthals still roamed. Makes some serious philosophical points, though the style is at times irritatingly arch. A curiosity (the Scottish author was better known for his non-sf under the pseudonym 'Lewis Grassic Gibbon').

Three Novels (1967) ★★ Collection by Damon Knight (USA). A trio of very proficient novellas by this master of the sf short story: 'Rule Golden', 'Natural State' and 'The Dying Man'. Republished in Britain as *Natural State and Other Stories*.

Three Stigmata of Palmer Eldritch, The (1964) ★★★ Novel by Philip K. Dick (USA). A new narcotic, 'Chew-Z', is introduced into the Solar System by shady businessman Palmer Eldritch. The results are confusing, but it's an inventive and hugely entertaining novel, part satire and part metaphysical drama. One of Dick's best.

334 (1972) ★★★★ Novel by Thomas M. Disch (USA). Six interweaving tales set in 21st-century New York, a scene of high unemployment and heartless 'welfareism'. The book deals convincingly (and unusually) with the marginalized members of a future society. The result is moving and at times harrowing: a masterpiece.

Three to Conquer (1956) ★★ Novel by Eric Frank Russell (UK). A telepath 'hears' a dying scream from a car – and becomes the only human to realize that intelligent viruses from Venus have taken over the bodies of three astronauts. Slick entertainment written in private-eye style.

Three-Eyes (Gordon): see under *One-Eye*.

Threshold (1985) ★ Novel by David R. Palmer (USA). The protagonist is a fantastically rich businessman who wins formula-one races, can change into a dragon, and is destined to save the universe. The book is meant to be funny.

Throne of Madness, The (Sucharitkul): see under *Light on the Sound*.

Through Darkest America (1987) ★★ Novel by Neal Barrett Jr. (USA). After the holocaust and the extinction of all traditional livestock, a young boy grows up in rural innocence, helping his father herd the 'meat' (human beings with their tongues removed) to market. When his parents are killed, he begins to learn the grisly truth about his world. Well-written – but a horrible, horrible book: full of violence, torture, cannibalism and the death of all hope. Sequel: *Dawn's Uncertain Light* (1989).

Through the Eye of a Needle (Clement): see under *Needle*.

Thunder and Roses (Sturgeon): see *Way Home, A*.

Thunder of Stars, A (1968) ★ Novel by Dan Morgan and John Kippax (UK). Military space opera, British style, in which Earth's space corps takes on an alien menace. Competent action stuff, but completely unremarkable. Sequels: *Seed of Stars* (1972), *The Neutral Stars* (1973) and *Where No Stars Guide* (1975; this last by Kippax alone, published posthumously).

Thurb Revolution, The (Panshin): see under *Star Well*.

Thuvia, Maid of Mars (Burroughs): see under *Princess of Mars, A*.

Tide Went Out, The (1958) ★★ Novel by Charles Eric Maine (UK). Nuclear tests cause the oceans to drain away under the Earth's crust. A stiff-upper-lipped British disaster novel of the old school, and one of Maine's better books. Following the drought of 1976, it was revised and reissued in the UK as *Thirst!*

Tides of God, The (1989) ★★ Novel by Ted Reynolds (USA). A spacecraft sets out to destroy 'God' – which, it seems, is some sort of alien entity that comes within range of Earth every thousand years or so, causing outbreaks of visionary experience in human beings. An interesting first novel. 'Reynolds shows the madness and ecstasy of religion very well, and does not give easy answers' – Tom Whitmore, *Locus*.

Tides of Kregen, The (Akers): see under *Transit to Scorpio*.

Tides of Light (1989) ★★★ Novel by Gregory Benford (USA), sequel to *Great Sky River*. The galactic struggle between machine life and fleshly forms continues. Here cyborg entities, whose distant goal is a kind of god-like transcendence of the galaxy, use a 'cosmic string' to dismantle a planet. Such a story may be lacking in human interest (as far as some readers are concerned) but the physics and cosmology are up to date and the vistas which unfold are truly mindbending. 'Not since Stapledon has an imagination ranged so widely' – Dan Chow, *Locus*.

Tides of Time, The (1984) ★★ Novel by John Brunner (UK). On an Earth which is gradually drowning due to rising temperatures, an ex-astronaut couple turn their backs on space and dream of the planet's past. An odd, philosophical time-travel story.

Tiger by the Tail and Other SF Stories (1961) ★★ Collection by Alan E. Nourse (USA). Nine sprightly tales, mainly from the 1950s. 'Family Resemblance' contains the revelation that humans are descended from pigs, and most of the other stories have similar twists. Published in Britain as *Beyond Infinity*.

Tiger! Tiger! (Bester): see *Stars My Destination, The*.

Tik-Tok (1983) ★★★ Novel by John Sladek (USA). Dedicated to 'decent law-abiding robots everywhere', this is the zany tale of a 21st-century mechanical man who blows his 'asimov circuits' and goes on a murderous rampage. Funny and satirical, in Sladek's customary acute manner.

Time and Again (1970) ★★★ Novel by Jack Finney (USA). Psychological time-travel sf with a fantasy flavour. Researchers 'think' themselves back into the American past – merely by surrounding themselves with bygone artefacts and wishing hard enough. Despite the shaky rationale, it's a classic modern timeslip romance, detailed and moving. Its author's best book.

Time and Again (1951) ★★ Novel by Clifford D. Simak (USA). A complex space-and-time opera, all twists and turns, which bears some resemblance to Charles L. Harness's *The Paradox Men*. Liberal, anti-racist and full of respect for the diversity of life – its well-liked author's first notable book. Reprinted in US paperback as *First He Died*.

Time and Stars (1964) ★★ Collection by Poul Anderson (USA). Six mainly hard-sf tales from the early 1960s, including the Hugo award-winning 'No Truce with Kings'. Other satisfactory pieces include 'Epilogue' and 'Turning Point'. On the whole, a good sampler of this author's work.

Time Bender, The (1966) ★ Novel by Keith Laumer (USA). A humorous semi-fantasy about Lafayette O'Leary, a resourceful but lazy lab technician who learns how to move around among alternate worlds. He ends pleasantly set up with a wife and private income in the kingdom of Artesia. Sequel: *The World Shuffler*.

Time Dweller, The (1969) ★★ Collection by Michael Moorcock (UK). Nine sf and fantasy stories, some of which had already appeared in an earlier paperback collection called *The Deep Fix* (1966; published under the pseudonym 'James Colvin'). Perhaps the best pieces here are the title story and its sequel, 'Escape from Evening' – moody far-future tales with some evocative landscape painting. Later collections by the author include *Moorcock's Book of Martyrs* (1976; published in the USA as *Dying for Tomorrow*), *My Experiences in the Third World War* (1980) and *The Opium General and Other Stories* (1984).

Time Enough for Love: The Lives of Lazarus Long (1973) ★ Novel by Robert A. Heinlein (USA), a belated sequel to *Methuselah's Children*. Some 2000 years after the events of the previous novel, the crusty Lazarus Long is still alive and kicking. His adventures and his often tiresome wit'n'wisdom are recorded in numerous episodes, anecdotes and aphorisms, culminating in a time-travel escapade where he goes back to the year of his birth and beds his own mother. In this overlong, narcissistic book the author attempts to tie together much of his earlier fiction, with unhappy results.

Time for the Stars (1956) ★★★ Novel by Robert A. Heinlein (USA). Identical twin boys play their part in the exploration of the stars: one stays at home while the other travels the light years, but they keep in touch by telepathic means. An ingenious adventure story for younger readers which should also appeal to most adults. 'Packed with serious technical detail ... what gives the book its quality is the lively conversational narrative ... Gaiety and fluent style' – *Times Literary Supplement*.

Time Hoppers, The (1967) ★★ Novel by Robert Silverberg (USA), expanded from a 1956 short story. People of the 25th century are disappearing mysteriously into the past, in this likeable but minor variation on a standard theme. 'Features that familiar Silverberg character, the middle-rank bureaucrat slightly at odds with the overcrowded future world which he helps to govern' – James Cawthorn, *New Worlds*.

Time in Advance (1958) ★★★ Collection by William Tenn (USA). Four long and sardonic sf stories, all intelligently conceived. 'Firewater' (1952) is perhaps the most original of them – about the terrible culture shock experienced by the human race when advanced (non-hostile) aliens arrive on Earth.

Time is the Simplest Thing (1961) ★★ Novel by Clifford D. Simak (USA). Men 'mind-travel' to the stars – and one comes back with more than he bargained for. An effective sf thriller, a shade tougher than this sentimental/pastoral author's normal fare.

Time Machine, The (1895) ★★★★ Novella by H. G. Wells (UK). The time traveller tells of his visit to a future epoch in which the human race has become divided into helpless Eloi and brutish Morlocks. He then travels on, to witness the Earth's last days. Beautiful and gripping: a supreme masterpiece of sf. Filmed in 1960 (dir. George Pal). Sequels by other hands: *The Man Who Loved Morlocks* by David J. Lake and *Morlock Night* by K. W. Jeter.

Time Mercenaries, The (1968) ★ Novel by Philip E. High (UK). Effete future-folk, unable to defend themselves against an alien menace, use a time-travel device to pluck some tough sailors (a present-day submarine crew) from the past in order to help them out of their predicament. 'Possibly High's best work' – Don D'Ammassa, *20th-Century SF Writers* (which isn't saying much).

Time of Changes, A (1971) ★★ Novel by Robert Silverberg (USA). An alien from the ultimate collectivist society comes under the influence of Earthly ideas and has the temerity to write an autobiography – this book. A telling description of a world-view in which the concept of 'I' does not exist, much of the novel deals with the mental agony which the protagonist's growing sense of selfhood provokes. It's all a bit grim and, despite general praise, not one of the author's very best works. Nebula award-winner, 1971.

Time of the Eye, The (Ellison): see *Alone Against Tomorrow*.

Time of the Fourth Horseman (1976) ★★ Novel by Chelsea Quinn Yarbro (USA). A junior hospital doctor in near-future America is horrified to discover that all the old diseases are coming back: polio, diphtheria, meningitis. It seems that someone in authority is trying to solve the overpopulation problem by means of 'controlled plagues'. A well-written admonitory tale, rather reminiscent in its grimness of Brunner's *The Sheep Look Up*. Yarbro's first novel.

Time Out for Tomorrow (Wilson): see under *Those Idiots from Earth*.

Time Out of Joint (1959) ★★★ Novel by Philip K. Dick (USA). The eccentric Ragle Gumm solves a newspaper puzzle every day. Gradually it becomes plain that he is living in an artificial world, and his apparently pointless activity is vital to his nation's war effort. An ingenious metaphysical black comedy.

Time Out of Mind (1986) ★ Novel by John R. Maxim (USA). A 'bestseller' fiction of marginal sf appeal. Genetic memory enables a man to avenge a wrong done to his grandmother a century earlier. There are interesting flashbacks to 19th-century New York business and high society.

Time Patrolman (1983) ★★ Collection by Poul Anderson (USA), sequel to *Guardians of Time*. Two long stories about the further adventures of Manse Everard in ancient Phoenicia, Dark-Age Europe and other exotic ports of call on the far shores of the time stream. Historical detail good; characterization leaves something to be desired.

Time Probe: Sciences in Science Fiction (1966) ★★★ Anthology edited by Arthur C. Clarke (UK). Solid selection, intended to illustrate the way in which sf writers have been inspired by the different branches of science and technology. It contains such old standards as Robert Heinlein's 'And He Built a Crooked House' (architecture) and C. M. Kornbluth's 'The Little Black Bag' (medicine).

Time Storm (1977) ★★ Novel by Gordon R. Dickson (Canada/USA). Mysterious 'storms' disrupt Earth's temporal continuity, so that different areas exist in different time-periods (an idea very similar to that used earlier by Fred Hoyle in *October the First is Too Late*). The hero sets out on a quest to uncover the meaning of it all, and the resulting picaresque is one of its author's best tales.

Time Story (1972) ★★★ Novel by Stuart Gordon (UK). A time-paradox tale in which a thief is kidnapped from his straightlaced 1996 and taken to a feudal post-bomb 2300 by a beautiful woman who claims to be acting on his own future orders. However, the 24th century they arrive in is not quite the one she remembers. Richard ('Stuart') Gordon's first novel – presumably, he changed his first name so as not to be confused with the author of the 'Doctor' comedies.

Time to Teleport (1960) ★ Novel by Gordon R. Dickson (Canada/USA). A minor tale of political manoeuvring a couple of centuries hence, displaying Dickson's idea that the human race must evolve to survive.

Time Transfer and Other Stories (1956) ★★ Collection by Arthur Sellings (UK). Varied and mostly competent stories from early in this underrated author's career. The themes are standard, and some pieces are dated, but highpoints include the darkly-tinged 'Categorical Imperative' and 'A Start in Life'. Sellings's first book. The 1966 reprint drops five of the weaker pieces.

Time Travellers Strictly Cash (Robinson): see under *Callahan's Crosstime Saloon*.

Timefall (1987) ★★ Novel by James Kahn (USA). A multiple-worlds story, hung on the hoary plot device of memoirs left to the author by an obsessed man who had some nasty experiences with lost civilizations in the Amazonian jungle. The characters relive some of the action of Kahn's previous novels, *World Enough and Time* and *Time's Dark Laughter*, and attempt to prevent a recurrence of the destruction that ruined the parallel Earth.

Timekeeper Conspiracy, The (Hawke): see under *Ivanhoe Gambit, The*.

Timelapse (1988) ★ Novel by David Nighbert (USA). Anton Stryker, a cloned cyborg assassin, attempts to kill the Emperor. This is one of those space operas in which the heroes just happen to have the fastest ship in the galaxy. It's neither boring nor particularly original. A first novel.

Time-Lapsed Man and Other Stories, The (1990) ★★★ Collection by Eric Brown (UK). Ingenious sf stories, mostly reprinted from *Interzone* magazine, by a young writer making his debut in book form. Standouts include 'Big Trouble Upstairs' (1988), about mayhem on a sort of Disneyworld space habitat, and the title story (also 1988), about a man whose senses go alarmingly awry after space flight. These are well-crafted pieces by one of the brighter hopes for the 1990s.

Timeliner Trilogy, The (1987) ★ Omnibus by Richard Meredith (USA). Repackaging of *At the Narrow Passage*, *No Brother, No Friend* and *Vestiges of Time*.

Timequest (Nelson): see *Blake's Progress*.

Time's Dark Laughter (1982) ★★ Novel by James Kahn (USA), sequel to *World Enough and Time*. Glaciers advance across a future California, squeezing the surviving humans between the ice and the vampire cities of the South. Josh returns to the City with No Name, and fathers a superpowered child who brings about the end of the world. There is some rather unpleasant dwelling on the sexual domination involved in vampirism. Sequel: *Timefall*.

Time's Last Gift (1972) ★★ Novel by Philip José Farmer (USA). A scientific expedition travels by time machine from the 21st century to the year 12,000 BC. The author's didactic urge runs away with him, and what at first appears to be an adventure story soon turns into a series of lectures on anthropology and philology (all interesting stuff, admittedly). Then, in a surprise ending, it turns into another twist on the 'Tarzan' theme (setting the scene for Farmer's subsequent *Hadon of Ancient Opar*).

Times Without Number (1962) ★★ Fix-up novel by John Brunner (UK). An intriguing 'time wars' and alternative-history yarn in which it is posited that 16th-century Catholics won the counter-reformation. As a consequence, 20th-century Europe is technologically backward. Compare Keith Roberts's *Pavane* and Kingsley Amis's *The Alteration*: Brunner was there first, though his treatment is less distinguished.

Timescape (1980) ★★★★ Novel by Gregory Benford (USA). Two interweaving story-lines, set in the early 1960s and the late 1990s. Future scientists attempt to communicate with the past in order to alter the course of history and avoid a polluted environment. Excellent scientific detail and convincing characters in a well-rounded novel: its author's best. Nebula award-winner, 1981.

Timestop (1960) ★ Novel by Philip José Farmer (USA), also known as *A Woman a Day* and *Day of the Timestop*, and originally published in a shorter magazine version in 1953.

An early, unsatisfactory Farmer title which is a quasi-sequel to his *The Lovers* – set in the totalitarian, fundamentalist future Earth which was briefly depicted in the background of the earlier story. The thriller-ish plot concerns a rebellion against the state-church, or 'Sturch'.

Time-Swept City, The (1977) ★★ Fix-up novel by Thomas F. Monteleone (USA). An episodic account of Chicago's future development. It eventually gains artificial intelligence and becomes a city of robots.

Timetipping (1980) ★★★ Collection by Jack Dann (USA). The author's best-known stories of the 1970s, including 'Junction', the original shorter version of his novel of the same name. The title story is an effective piece about a man who has the ability to skip through time. Most of these tales, such as the fine 'Camps' and 'The Dybbuk Dolls', are dense and demanding, in a late New-Wave manner. 'Dann's recurrent theme ... [is] the possibilities of human transcendence, the mutability of consciousness under extremes of experience' – Gregory Feeley, *Foundation*.

Timetracks (1972) ★ Collection by Keith Laumer (USA). Time-twisting yarns of so-so quality, several of which have appeared in earlier Laumer collections. According to John Clute, the author has two typical veins: 'the licketysplit adventure romp with an affectless mercenary through time and space; and the "comic romp" with Retief or someone like him bamboozling a cast of gildersleeves or aliens (i.e. Coloured folk) without the law.'

Tin Angel, The (1973) Novel by Ron Goulart (USA). A man and his wise-cracking cybernetic dog try to survive in a rather whimsical 21st-century California. Minor.

Titan (1979) ★★ Novel by John Varley (USA). Huge, enjoyable, detailed and rambling account of a NASA expedition to a newly-discovered moon. The moon eats all the crew, who wake up inside and discover it to be a sort of living spaceship which has created various beings derived from Earth myths it's seen on television. Sequels: *Wizard* and *Demon*.

Titan, The (1952) ★★ Collection by P. Schuyler Miller (USA). Eight sf tales from the magazines of the 1930s and 40s, some of them rather creaky but many with a certain charm. Most notable is the long title piece about an Earthman who is kept as a curiosity in a Martian zoo.

Titan's Daughter (1961) ★ Novel by James Blish (USA), expanded from his story 'Beanstalk' (1952). Experiments in genetic engineering produce giant, long-lived human beings who suffer society's hostility. 'Has much in common with Wells's *The Food of the Gods*, but the satirical overtones of the early novel are missing' – Brian Stableford.

Tithonian Factor and Other Stories, The (1984) ★★★ Collection by Richard Cowper (Colin Middleton Murry, UK). Six more sf and fantasy

stories by this fine writer, varying from the excellent title piece, about the drawbacks of longevity, to the South American adventure 'Incident at Huacaloc' with its evocation of Inca rituals. 'His romanticism is kept on the leash of a thoroughly British gift for telling understatement' – Brian Stableford.

To Die in Italbar (1973) ★ Novel by Roger Zelazny (USA). Against a background of interstellar plague and other miseries, the bitter hero searches the galaxy for a mysterious healer. A tiresomely convoluted space opera which goes through the motions but lacks all conviction. One of Zelazny's weakest efforts.

To Here and the Easel (1973) ★★★ Collection by Theodore Sturgeon (USA). A British-published conflation of the best stories from the US collections *Sturgeon Is Alive and Well* and *The Worlds of Theodore Sturgeon*.

To Live Again (1969) ★ Novel by Robert Silverberg (USA). The souls or personae of the recently dead may be stored for use by other individuals. With this conceit at the centre of his plot, the author spins an over-complex, over-sexy tale of competing tycoons. Not one of Silverberg's better books.

To Live Forever (1956) ★★ Novel by Jack Vance (USA). A convoluted tale of a future society in which people will kill for the chance of immortality. A standard theme, stylishly presented, in one of the most solid of this talented author's earlier works.

To Open the Sky (1967) ★★ Fix-up novel by Robert Silverberg (USA). In a teeming 21st century, a messianic oldster called Vorst founds a religious movement whose goals are travel to the stars and immortality. The book deals in episodic fashion with the spread of his ideas. Not a major work, but it marked the beginning of Silverberg's busiest and most fruitful period as an sf writer.

To Outer Space (Johns): see under *Now to the Stars.*

To Ride Pegasus (1973) ★★ Novel by Anne McCaffrey (USA/Ireland). A story which deals with the political and social impact of telepathy on a near-future Earth – the use of telepathy is likened to riding a winged horse: wonderful if you can manage it, terribly dangerous if you fall off.

To Sail Beyond the Sunset (1987) Novel by Robert A. Heinlein (USA). The subtitle is 'The Life and Loves of Maureen Johnson', and the lady referred to is the mother of the author's favourite character, the immortal Lazarus Long (see *Methuselah's Children, Time Enough for Love,* etc.). This was Heinlein's last work, and perhaps it would be kindest to say no more.

To Sail the Century Sea (Edmondson): see under *Ship That Sailed the Time Stream, The.*

To Warm the Earth (1988) ★★ Novel by David Belden (USA), sequel to *Children of Arable.* On a far-future icebound Earth, part of the 'Galactic Collectivity', the few remaining people worship the great Goddess. The heroine is a priestess whose lot in life is to guard the fires which may one day re-warm the planet. 'Not a work of light escapism, but a book to make the reader think' – Carolyn Cushman, *Locus.*

To Worlds Unknown (Johns): see under *Now to the Stars.*

To Your Scattered Bodies Go (1971) ★★★ Fix-up novel by Philip José Farmer (USA), the first of his 'Riverworld' series. The entire human race is resurrected, in hairless 25-year-old bodies, along the banks of a vast river on a distant planet. Sir Richard Francis Burton, erstwhile Victorian explorer, decides to follow the river to its source and locate the secret masters of this world. Good fun, even if it fails to live up to its staggering premise. Hugo award-winner, 1972. Sequel: *The Fabulous Riverboat.*

Today We Choose Faces (1973) ★ Novel by Roger Zelazny (USA). In a normally peaceful future of enclosed urban environments, the seven members of a clone 'family' are mysteriously threatened by murder. A complex but curiously drab tale of violent adventure, below par for Zelazny.

Tom O'Bedlam (1985) ★★ Novel by Robert Silverberg (USA). In a future America, following a nuclear 'Dust War', a new religious cult arises. Tom O'Bedlam, a dreamer of other worlds, becomes one of its prophets. Is he a lunatic, or the genuine seer of a transcendent future? Silverberg reworks some of his favourite themes, of alienation and millenarian madness, at perhaps too great a length.

Tom Paine Maru (Smith): see under *Probability Broach, The.*

Tommyknockers, The (1987) ★★ Novel by Stephen King (USA). An ancient, buried spacecraft is discovered in the Maine woods. Before long, the folk nearby are mysteriously inspired to invent wonderful new gadgets. Then things begin to turn nasty. It reads like a massive inflation of Nigel Kneale's *Quatermass and the Pit*, transposed to an American setting. 'Suffers only slightly from literary bloat. It's good gruesome fun' – Faren Miller, *Locus.*

Tomorrow and Tomorrow (Collins): see *Tomorrow's World.*

Tomorrow and Tomorrow (1947) ★★★ Novel by M. Barnard Eldershaw (Australia). A man of four centuries reflects on the 20th-century history of Australia; he depicts a doom-laden post-World War II period (the future at the time this odd but powerful novel was written). The author is a woman, Marjorie Barnard, who collaborated on various historical novels with Flora Eldershaw – though the latter had no hand in this particular book. Reissued as *Tomorrow and Tomorrow and Tomorrow* (1983), with original text fully restored. 'Nobel Prize-winner Patrick White named it as the Australian novel he would most like to see republished. It has been' – George Turner, *20th-Century SF Writers.*

Tomorrow File, The (1975) ★★ Novel by Lawrence Sanders (USA). This is the gripping tale of the rise and fall of a benevolent scientific dictator in a bureaucratic near-future United States. A bestseller by a mainstream writer of thrillers (*The Anderson Tapes*, etc), it's also surprisingly good sf – if fundamentally unoriginal in its vision of creeping social horrors to come.

Tomorrow Lies in Ambush (1973) ★★★ Collection by Bob Shaw (UK). Varied sf yarns, mostly conventional in subject matter and ideas but unfailingly well constructed, well characterized and, as a result, thoroughly entertaining. Shaw's first collection. 'His prose is economical and neat, his images are graphic and instantly clear' – Christopher Priest, *Foundation.* The contents of the UK and US editions differ slightly.

Tomorrow Might be Different (1975) ★ Novel by Mack Reynolds (USA), expanded from his magazine story 'Russkies, Go Home'. The Soviet Union has become a highly successful production economy, while the USA has gone into a slump. As a result, Russians are now the rich tourists who plague the world. An intriguing political-economic idea, rather badly fleshed out.

Tomorrow Testament, The (Longyear): see under *Manifest Destiny.*

Tomorrow Times Seven (Pohl): see under *Case Against Tomorrow, The.*

Tomorrow's Crimes (1989) ★★ Collection by Donald E. Westlake (USA). Contains the short novel *Anarchaos* (1967; originally published under the pseudonym 'Curt Clark') as well as a selection of other sf and fantasy stories by this well-known crime novelist. 'All smoothly readable' – Edward Bryant, *Locus*.

Tomorrow's Heritage (1981) ★★ Novel by Juanita Coulson (USA), first in the 'Children of the Stars' sequence. The near-future exploration of space, including an encounter with aliens, is here retailed in fat 'family-saga' form. Sequel: *Outward Bound* (1982).

Tomorrow's World (1956) ★★ Novel by Hunt Collins (Evan Hunter, USA). Lively satire on a doped-up hedonistic near future, by a writer who has become much better known for his mainstream novels and crime fiction. Quite sexy for its day. It has also been published under the title *Tomorrow and Tomorrow*.

Tongues of the Moon (1964) Novel by Philip José Farmer (USA). A very minor space-operatic tale of conflict on the moon and further afield, expanded from a 1961 magazine novella. One of Farmer's weakest.

Tool of the Trade (1987) ★★ Novel by Joe Haldeman (USA). Nail-biting thriller about a secret agent who has invented a technological gizmo which compels others to do as he commands. Eventually the intelligence agencies of both superpowers are pitted against him ... The 'surprise' denouement, in which the hero persuades the leaders of both

nations to reduce their nuclear stockpiles, already seems to have been overtaken by history.

Toolmaker Koan (1987) ★★ Novel by John McLoughlin (USA). Soviet and American space missions fight to be the first to contact an apparent visitor from outside the solar system, against the background of imminent world war. The author, a professional evolutionist, tries to explain the 'Fermi Paradox' (the contradiction between theories that expect intelligent life to be common in the Universe and the total lack of communication from them) by arguing that 'cultural toolmakers' will acquire the power to wipe out their species at the same time as the ability to travel in space.

Top Science Fiction: The Authors' Choice (1984) ★★★ Anthology edited by Josh Pachter (UK). Twenty-five fine stories from the years 1929–83, each chosen by its author as his or her personal favourite. Contributors include Aldiss, Bester, Bradbury, Clarke, Le Guin, Leiber, Niven, Silverberg and van Vogt.

Torch of Honor, The (1985) ★★ Novel by Roger MacBride Allen (USA). Space colonies are attacked by a mystery fleet. The villains turn out to be descendants of the English National Front, escaped in the starship *Oswald Mosley* to found a New Order in the skies. Enjoyable, if violent.

Torrent of Faces, A (1967) ★★ Novel by James Blish and Norman L. Knight (USA). A terribly overpopulated, but stable, future Earth is disrupted by the coming of an asteroid. Good rationalization of its basic premise.

Total Eclipse (1974) ★★ Novel by John Brunner (UK). A human expedition to another star system puzzles over the mystery of an alien civilization's complete extinction. There are suggestions that the same may happen to humanity – and the conclusion of this novel is appropriately bleak. A serious-minded space story which undercuts genre expectations.

Touch of Strange, A (1958) ★★★ Collection by Theodore Sturgeon (USA). Nine weird stories, mostly sf. Standouts include 'Mr Costello, Hero' (1953), about a manipulative, McCarthyite villain in outer space, and 'The Other Celia' (1957), about the aliens who live amongst us.

Touch of Sturgeon, A (1987) ★★★★ Collection by Theodore Sturgeon (USA), edited and introduced by David Pringle. Eight longish tales: a posthumous 'best of' this fine author's sf stories, ranging from the action-packed 'Killdozer!' (1944) to the delicately emotional 'Slow Sculpture' (1970).

Tower of Glass (1970) ★★ Novel by Robert Silverberg (USA). Ostensibly to communicate with aliens, a madman attempts to build a kilometre-high tower in the Arctic, using android labour. His workers worship him as a god, but eventually one of them comes to appreciate his master's true nature – and sparks an android revolt. An oddly-flavoured allegory of obsession, inevitably reminiscent of William Golding's *The Spire* (1964).

Tower of Zanid, The (de Camp): see under *Search for Zei, The*.

Tower to the Sky (1988) ★ Novel by Phillip C. Jennings (USA). In an attempt to escape from a quarantined world of 2000 years hence, the hero and his cohorts have to climb a vast tower known as Earthstalk. A confusing first novel with moments of promise. 'Either brilliantly obscure New-Wave writing or Just Plain Awful. I'm still not sure which. Maybe both' – Carolyn Cushman, *Locus*.

Towers of Toron, The (Delany): see *Fall of the Towers, The*.

Towers of Utopia, The (1975) ★ Novel by Mack Reynolds (USA). A forgettable thriller plot is set against the interesting background of a near-future world in which the citizenry leads a near-utopian, high-tech existence in vast tower-blocks. It's one of Reynolds's more serious speculative efforts, related in theme to his *Looking Backward, from the Year 2000* and *Commune 2000 A.D.*

Toymaker, The (1951) ★★ Collection by Raymond F. Jones (USA). Six sf stories by a competent writer who contributed a good deal to *Astounding SF* during the 1940s. 'Forecast' is a typical piece – about the consequences of effective weather control. For a later sampling of the same author's work see *The Non-Statistical Man*.

Toyman (Tubb): see under *Winds of Gath, The*.

Toynbee Convector, The (1988) ★ Collection by Ray Bradbury (USA). The author's first all-new collection in a dozen years, it contains his customary mix of humour and horror, sf and fantasy. Full of exclamation marks and one-sentence paragraphs, some of the stories are very slight indeed. 'Bradbury is still writing pretty much as he wrote two, three, and even four decades ago. He has not grown up. That is both his abiding charm and strength, and his cardinal failing as an artist' – Michael Bishop, *Thrust*.

Trader to the Stars (1964) ★ Collection by Poul Anderson (USA). Three long tales about the space adventures of the crafty Nicholas Van Rijn, one of this author's archetypal free-enterprise heroes. Other books in the loosely-knit 'Polesotechnic League' series include *War of the Wing-Men* and *The Trouble Twisters*.

Trader's World (1988) ★ Novel by Charles Sheffield (UK/USA). In a post-nuclear-war Earth, which has retained various high-tech capabilities though everything is in a balkanized state, the hero works as a trader in valuable information. A would-be picaresque which doesn't quite come off.

Traitor to the Living (1973) Novel by Philip José Farmer (USA), an unacknowledged (clean) sequel to his pornographic fantasies *The Image of the Beast* (1968) and *Blown* (1969). An ex-private eye becomes involved with a bogus computer-link to the afterlife. Body-switching shenanigans ensue. Tired stuff. 'The novel certainly gives the impression of having been written faster than the author could type' – John Clute.

Transatlantic Tunnel, Hurrah!, A (Harrison): see *Tunnel Through the Deeps*.

Transfigurations (1979) ★★★ Novel by Michael Bishop (USA), an expansion of his novella 'Death and Designation Among the Asadi' (1973). About a daughter's quest to find her anthropologist father in the forbidding ritualistic culture of the natives of an alien planet. A highly literate narrative which makes good use of its imaginary anthropology.

Transfinite Man (1964) ★ Novel by Colin Kapp (UK). An angry superpowered hero discovers his identity and saves the universe. Clichéd nonsense, here packaged with some verve: its author's first (and perhaps still his best) novel. Published in the UK as *The Dark Mind*.

Transformation of Miss Mavis Ming, The (Moorcock): see under *Dancers at the End of Time, The*.

Transformer (Foster): see under *Morphodite, The*.

Transit (1964) ★ Novel by Edmund Cooper (UK). Its author's usual plot – a group of humans are kidnapped by aliens and taken to another world to become the progenitors of a new human race. In this case they have to prove themselves by defeating a similarly kidnapped group of another species.

Transit to Scorpio (1972) ★ Novel by Alan Burt Akers (Kenneth Bulmer, UK), first in the lengthy 'Dray Prescot' series. Efficiently-written pastiche Edgar Rice Burroughs. Like the latter's John Carter of Mars, Earthman Dray Prescot has colourful adventures on the planet of another star. This is sf at its most formulaic. Sequels (which tend to go in three-to-six volume cycles) include: *The Suns of Scorpio* (1973), *Manhounds of Antares* (1974), *The Tides of Kregen* (1976), *Secret Scorpio* (1977), *A Life for Kregen* (1979), *Beasts of Antares* (1980), *Delia of Vallia* (1982), *Seg the Bowman* (1984), and many more.

Travelling Towards Epsilon: An Anthology of French Science Fiction (1977) ★★ Anthology edited by Maxim Jakubowski (UK). Interesting stories by the French *nouvelle vague*, including such writers as Daniel Walther and Dominique Douay. There's a high sexual and political content. 'Since May 1968 many of the younger French writers have regarded sf as an explicitly political tool in a sense never dreamed of by the Anglo-Americans' – J. G. Ballard, *New Statesman*.

Treason (Card): see *Planet Called Treason, A*.

Treasure in the Heart of the Maze, The (Carr): see under *Navigator's Sindrome*.

Triax (Silverberg): see under *New Atlantis, The*.

Trick Top Hat, The (Wilson): see under *Schrodinger's Cat: The Universe Next Door*.

Triplanetary (1948) ★ Novel by E. E. 'Doc' Smith (USA), originally serialized in 1934. The inhabited worlds of the solar system struggle to repel an interstellar alien menace. Although not originally conceived as such, this space opera was tailored when it appeared in book form to make it the first volume in Smith's magnum opus, the 'Lensman' series (grandiosely titled 'The History of Civilization' in one uniform printing). For further details of the series see under *First Lensman*.

Triple Detente (1974) ★ Novel by Piers Anthony (USA). Earth's space-fleet swaps places with an alien fleet, and each is allowed to conquer the other's planet. The situation is confused when a third spacefaring civilization is discovered. The writing is occasionally stilted and it is hard to believe that either fleet could tolerate the other carrying out the cruel policies used to reduce the over-population of the respective planets.

Triplet (1988) ★ Novel by Timothy Zahn (USA). Demons from the Fourth World take over robots and machines on Shamsheer, a world you can only get to through a teleporting tunnel that leaves your clothes behind.

Triton: An Ambiguous Heterotopia (1976) ★★ Novel by Samuel R. Delany (USA). In a fantastically rich and varied spacefaring future, people can choose their own sexes, identities, whatever. A densely-written (some would say turgid) utopian novel of high ambition. It represented a partial return to form for Delany after the dreadful (or brilliant, depending on your point of view) *Dhalgren*. But be warned that it's a difficult book to read.

Triumph of Time, The (1958) ★★★ Novel by James Blish (USA), third-published in his *Cities in Flight* sequence. This presents the breath-taking climax of the series about cities in space (made possible by the 'Spindizzy' anti-gravity device). New York City and its immortal mayor, John Amalfi, face the end of the universe – and the beginning of a whole new cycle of time. Published in the UK as *A Clash of Cymbals*, but included under its American title in the omnibus volume *Cities in Flight*.

Trojan Orbit (Reynolds): see under *Lagrange Five*.

Trouble Twisters, The (1966) ★★ Collection by Poul Anderson (USA). Three more tricky adventures of the interstellar trader David Falkayn, a prophet of free enterprise to the stars. 'Anderson offers a smooth blend of science and action that few other authors can achieve with such consistency' – James Cawthorn, *New Worlds*.

Trouble with Lichen (1960) ★★ Novel by John Wyndham (UK). The discovery of an effective longevity serum creates the eponymous trouble in this enjoyable though rather talky moral tale. Like most of the books published under the Wyndham byline, this one was aimed at a general audience and the emphasis is firmly on character rather than ground-breaking sf ideas.

True Names … and Other Dangers (1987) ★★ Collection by Vernor Vinge (USA). Sf stories about artificial intelligence. The title novella (1981) prefigured the Cyberpunk atmosphere of William Gibson's *Neuromancer* in its depiction of an electronic data-net as an all-embracing 'media landscape' where talented computer-hackers may create a species of fantasy world. The rest of the volume is less impressive, though it contains 'The Peddler's Apprentice', a workmanlike collaboration between the author and his ex-wife, Joan D. Vinge.

Trullion: Alastor 2262 (1973) ★★ Novel by Jack Vance (USA), first of his 'Alastor Cluster' series. In a galactic cluster of 30,000 stars and 3000 inhabited planets, all ruled over by the more-or-less benign 'Connatic', the water-world known as Trullion is of small importance. But it is the scene of this bucolic adventure story, written with all Vance's usual skill for the picturesque. Other books in this loosely-knit series are *Marune: Alastor 933* and *Wyst: Alastor 1716*.

Tuf Voyaging (1987) ★★ Fix-up novel by George R. R. Martin (USA). The episodic adventures of Haviland Tuf, spacefaring ecologist who creates genetically-engineered life-forms to suit various planets. 'Martin employs a certain dry wit, and the stories, which in true *Analog* house style proceed almost entirely through argument loaded in favour of the hero, showcase his talent for inventing nastily baroque yet mostly plausible creatures, but he's coasting here. And why not?' – Paul McAuley, *Interzone*.

Tunnel in the Sky (1955) ★★ Novel by Robert A. Heinlein (USA). Trainee space colonists are dumped via matter transmitter on a hostile planet where they have to survive by their wits. It is intended to be a ten-day exercise but it stretches into a two-year ordeal when plans go wrong. A rather harsh Heinlein 'juvenile' which extols the boy-scout virtues.

Tunnel Through the Deeps (1972) ★★ Novel by Harry Harrison (USA/ Ireland). An amusing alternative-history scenario: England never lost its American colonies, and the British Empire endures into the late 20th century. The plot concerns the building of a tunnel under the Atlantic (natch). Told with gusto, this good-humoured tale is perhaps just a little too arch at times. Published in the UK as *A Transatlantic Tunnel, Hurrah!*

Turn Left at Thursday (Pohl): see under *Case Against Tomorrow, The*.

Turning On (1966) ★★ Collection by Damon Knight (USA). Fourteen sf tales, including such items as 'The Man in the Jar' and 'The Big Pat Boom'. Not quite as strong as some of Knight's earlier collections, it nevertheless contains several excellent stories.

Turning Wheel and Other Stories, The (Dick): see *Book of Philip K. Dick, The*.

Twenty Thousand Leagues Under the Sea (1870) ★★★★ Novel by Jules Verne (France). The most famous of all submarine novels, in which the protagonists are kidnapped by the surly Captain Nemo in his sumptuously appointed vessel (Nemo turns out to be a renegade Indian prince with a grudge against the British Empire). It's a travelogue-cum-marine biology lesson, but still a fascinating narrative with mythic resonances. Sequel: *The Mysterious Island*. Filmed in 1954 (dir. Richard Fleischer).

Twice Twenty-Two (1966) ★★★ Omnibus by Ray Bradbury (USA), containing the entire contents of the sf/fantasy collections *The Golden Apples of the Sun* and *A Medicine for Melancholy*. This is one of several Bradbury omnibuses and samplers, another example being *The Vintage Bradbury* (1965), which have since been superseded by his near-definitive collection *The Stories of Ray Bradbury*.

Twilight at the Well of Souls (Chalker): see under *Midnight at the Well of Souls*.

Twilight Man, The (1966) ★★ Novel by Michael Moorcock (UK). On an Earth which has ceased rotating, an apparently utopian society faces its doom. Very early Moorcock (serialized in *New Worlds* in 1964) which has some nice touches and shows promise of the better things to come. Republished as *The Shores of Death*.

Twilight of Briareus, The (1974) ★★★ Novel by Richard Cowper (Colin Middleton Murry, UK). Radiation from a supernova causes sterility and climatic changes. The world turns wintry, and it seems the end is nigh – until it is discovered that alien entities have ridden the stellar wavefront in order to invade human minds and guide us towards a racial rebirth. Perhaps over-ambitious, but a well-told tale which carries you along. 'Cowper has allowed the two sub-genres of "catastrophe" and "psychic breakthrough" to mix without quite getting them to fuse' – Tom Shippey, *Foundation*.

Twilight of the City (Platt): see *City Dwellers, The*.

Twilight World (1961) ★★ Novel by Poul Anderson (USA), expanded from his first published short story, 'Tomorrow's Children' (1947). Dour adventure in world of genetic mutations caused by an all-out nuclear war. In its early form this was one of the first sf stories to deal in this theme.

Twin Worlds (Jones): see under *Planet of the Double Sun, The*.

Twistor (1989) ★ Novel by John Cramer (USA). A tale of squabbling in a physics department where two junior members discover a means of 'twisting' matter into other dimensions of space/time – including, as it turns out, human beings. A first novel. 'It would be nice if (as in Gregory Benford's *Timescape*) new Hard Science Fiction writers would deal with people as people instead of cardboard cutouts' – Tom Whitmore, *Locus*.

Two Hawks from Earth (Farmer): see *Gate of Time, The*.

Two of Them, The (1978) ★ Novel by Joanna Russ (USA). A female galactic agent rescues a young woman from the male-dominant culture of a colonized planet. The narrative defies genre expectations, and the author intrudes with the suggestion that it is all a fiction. 'It is written as from anger, and it is clearly intended to anger its readers' – John Clute.

Two Planets (1897) ★★★ Novel by Kurd Lasswitz (Germany). As in Wells's near-contemporary *The War of the Worlds*, the Martians invade Earth – but in this case they are ultimately benign and help bring into existence a utopian world state. Lasswitz's romance, first published as *Auf zwei Planeten*, was exceedingly influential in Germany. 'I devoured this novel with curiosity and excitement as a young man' – Wernher von Braun. The English-language edition of 1971 is abridged.

2018 A.D., or The King Kong Blues (1974) ★★ Novel by Sam J. Lundwall (Sweden). Hard-hitting dystopian satire which takes swipes at just about everything: government, business, religion, advertising, the lot. It's a horrid 21st century that Lundwall predicts; nevertheless, his book was a bestseller in Sweden.

2001: A Space Odyssey (1968) ★★★ Novel by Arthur C. Clarke (UK), based on the screenplay for the film of the same title (by Clarke and Stanley Kubrick) and expanded from his short story 'The Sentinel' (1951). The evolution of the human race, from apeman to 'Star Child', is compressed into a number of fictional epiphanies in this celebrated story. The bulk of the narrative concerns a voyage to the planet Saturn in order to discover the origins of a mysterious monolith found on the moon – but the imaginative scope of the book is much greater than an outline of the central action would suggest. In comparison to the enigmatic film (1968; dir. Stanley Kubrick) the novel is straightforward, and at times even pedestrian, stuff. Nevertheless, it provokes a sense of wonder. Sequel: *2010: Odyssey Two*.

2061: Odyssey Three (1987) ★★ Novel by Arthur C. Clarke (UK), sequel to *2010: Odyssey Two*. This one takes the story of humankind and the mysterious, transforming monoliths yet further into the future. Written in Clarke's customary brief-chaptered, limpid style, with much fascinating and up-to-date scientific detail. Forget the characters, enjoy the vistas.

2010: Odyssey Two (1982) ★★ Novel by Arthur C. Clarke (UK), a belated sequel to his *2001: A Space Odyssey*. A new expedition sets out to the moons of Jupiter (it was Saturn in the previous novel, but never mind) in order to discover what happened to the space vessel *Discovery*. They encounter a vast alien monolith, the intelligent computer HAL 9000 and a much transformed David Bowman (hero of the preceding novel). It builds to a nice climax. Filmed in 1984 (dir. Peter Hyams). Sequel: *2061: Odyssey Three*.

Two to Conquer (Bradley): see under *Sword of Aldones, The*.

Two-Eyes (Gordon): see under *One-Eye*.

Two-Timers, The (1968) ★★★ Novel by Bob Shaw (UK). Breakdown in a marriage leads to a strange knot in time: the guilt-ridden hero travels into an alternative time-line in order to prevent his wife's murder by a rapist – but in order for him to reclaim his wife from that world, he first has to lay plans to kill his other self ... An ingenious, well-written *doppelgänger* tale, nicely plotted with excellent dialogue.

U

Ubik (1969) ★★★ Novel by Philip K. Dick (USA). Characters inhabit each other's 'realities'; human artefacts revert to earlier forms; Joe Chip fights entropy with a spray-can of the wonder-substance Ubik. A complex, confusing, but at times brilliant sf/fantasy.

Ulcer Culture, The (1969) ★ Novel by Kenneth Bulmer (UK). The rich live in dream worlds while machines serve their every need. Things go awry. A sombre view of the future by this prolific writer who normally specializes in escapist adventure. Republished as *Stained-Glass World*.

Uller Uprising (1982) ★★ Novel by H. Beam Piper (USA), originally serialized in the 1950s. The natives of Uller rebel against the Earth-based company that uses them as mercenaries and labourers on the hell-planet Niflheim. The day is saved by the loyalty (or venality) of some of the native troops. Vaguely based on the Indian Mutiny against the British.

Ultimate Enemy, The (Saberhagen): see under *Berserker's Planet*.

Ultimate Jungle, The (1979) ★ Novel by Michael Coney (UK/Canada). Perhaps the author's darkest novel. 'Another of those books that I like to just forget about' – Michael Coney, interviewed by David Barrett in *Interzone*.

Unaccompanied Sonata and Other Stories (1981) ★★ Collection by Orson Scott Card (USA). Highly proficient but sometimes nasty tales, mostly set against a future spacefaring background. Standouts include the title story and 'Ender's Game' (the latter was subsequently expanded into a very successful novel). 'At the heart of all his work to date a compulsive cold technical polish unflaggingly exposes to view some of the oddest mortal coils the genre has yet presented to its readership, but I for one have never been able to tell if the innards he formaldehydes are gut or plasteel'– John Clute.

Uncensored Man, The (1964) ★★ Novel by Arthur Sellings (UK). A physicist discovers that the memories of all humanity's dead continue to exist in a sort of collective consciousness which inhabits another dimension. This entity is now trying to make contact with living humanity. A well-characterized mystery story with an intriguing sf premise.

Under Compulsion (1968) ★★★ Collection by Thomas M. Disch (USA). Seventeen sly, highly intelligent sf and fantasy stories by an extremely talented young writer (still only 28 at the time of this book's publication). Standouts include 'The Roaches', about a woman's perfect horror of cockroaches, and 'Casablanca', about the fate of American tourists in North Africa when World War III breaks out. Subsequently published in the USA as *Fun With Your New Head*.

Under Heaven's Bridge (1981) ★★ Novel by Michael Bishop and Ian Watson (USA/UK). A polyglot crew of explorers from Earth encounter some particularly strange aliens. The story plunges into metaphysics. Brief, all-too-sketchy but interesting collaboration between two highly talented authors from different sides of the Atlantic.

Under Old Earth and Other Explorations (Smith): see under *You Will Never Be the Same.*

Under Pressure (Herbert): see *Dragon in the Sea, The.*

Under the Green Star (1972) Novel by Lin Carter (USA). Exotic planetary adventure in an outdated sf/

fantasy vein. Yet more pastiche Edgar Rice Burroughs stuff, by a writer who seemed to produce almost nothing else (see his *Jandar of Callisto*). Sequels include: *When The Green Star Calls* (1973) and *By the Light of the Green Star* (1974).

Underkill (1979) ★ Novel by James White (UK). Gruesome and pessimistic medical shocker set in a hospital in a near-future urban jungle. Two of the staff discover that a large part of the pain and suffering of human life is being deliberately caused by aliens – for our own good.

Underpeople, The (Smith): see *Norstrilia.*

Unexpected Dimension, The (1960) ★★★ Collection by Algis Budrys (USA). Fine, intelligent sf stories from the 1950s. Includes 'The End of Summer', about a society of immortals, and the moving 'The Distant Sound of Engines', about the death of an alien. On the strength of this first volume and his second. *Budrys' Inferno*, the author seemed poised to become the best American sf writer of his day – but it didn't quite happen.

Unfamiliar Territory (1973) ★★ Collection by Robert Silverberg (USA). Thirteen stories from the early 1970s, most of them exercises in American 'New Wave' style. Highpoints include the humorous 'Good News from the Vatican', about a robot Pope, and the rather more grim 'In Entropy's Jaws'. 'Despite Silverberg's professional touch with words, several stories ramble, the author circling wearily round the point' – David I. Masson, *Foundation*.

Unforsaken Hiero, The (Lanier): see under *Hiero's Journey*.

Unicorn Girl, The (1969) ★★ Novel by Michael Kurland (USA), a sequel to Chester Anderson's *The Butterfly Kid*. More far-out hippie comedy. Sequel: *The Probability Pad* by T. A. Waters.

Unicorn Variations (1983) ★★ Collection by Roger Zelazny (USA). Twenty-one sf and fantasy pieces of widely varying quality (it's something of a 'clean-up' collection), with introduction, afterword and headnotes by the author. The highpoint is the Hugo and Nebula award-winning 'Home is the Hangman' (1975), which is also available in the book *My Name is Legion*.

Universe (1971–87) ★★★ Anthology series edited by Terry Carr (USA). Unlike Carr's *Best Science Fiction of the Year*, these more-or-less annual volumes consist of all-original stories, sometimes fantasy but usually sf. The literary standard is high: many of the stories won awards and some were subsequently reprinted in the following year's *Best … volume*. Authors who produced particularly good work for Carr include Fritz Leiber, Joanna Russ, Robert Silverberg, Howard Waldrop and Gene Wolfe. Since Carr's death in 1987, the series is being continued as a bi-annual edited by Silverberg.

Universe Against Her, The (1964) ★★ Novel by James H. Schmitz (USA). Telzey Amberdon, holidaying on another planet, discovers both her own psionic powers and the intelligence of a native species of big cat. Typically for Schmitz, the heroine is young, female and non-white, and the book stresses tolerance, intelligence and being nice. Its fault is that, like Superman, Telzey becomes so powerful that dangers she meets are no real challenge.

Unorthodox Engineers, The (1979) ★ Collection by Colin Kapp (UK). Heavily scientific tales of problem solving, all of which involve the eponymous engineers. The sequence begins with 'The Railways Up on Cannis' (1959).

Unpleasant Profession of Jonathan Hoag, The (1959) ★★★ Collection by Robert A. Heinlein (USA). Six stories originally published between 1940 and 1959. The earliest, 'And He Built a Crooked House', is also one of the best, a comic number about an architect who builds a house into the fourth dimension. The latest, 'All You Zombies', is another Heinlein classic, about a time-traveller who arrives at the revelation that he is his own father and mother. The others, including the excellent title novella, are fantasy rather than sf. Republished in US paperback editions as *6 × H*.

Unreasoning Mask, The (1981) ★★★ Novel by Philip José Farmer (USA). Adventures of the Muslim captain of a living spaceship known as al-Buraq. He steals a sentient artefact which gives him a direct channel to

God (or 'The Pluriverse'). Metaphysical space opera, one of its author's best.

Unsleeping Eye, The (Compton): see *Continuous Katherine Mortenhoe, The.*

Unteleported Man, The (1966) ★ Novel by Philip K. Dick (USA). One of this highly talented author's least satisfactory books. Republished posthumously, in expanded form, as *Lies, Inc.*

Untouched by Human Hands (1954) ★★★ Collection by Robert Sheckley (USA). Thirteen humorous stories of great sprightliness: a sheer delight in its day, the book makes adroit and witty use of many standard sf themes. Among the notable titles are 'Cost of Living', 'The Monsters', 'Seventh Victim' and 'Specialist'. Sheckley's first book.

Up the Line (1969) ★★★ Novel by Robert Silverberg (USA). A Time Courier whose job is to conduct tourists on sight-seeing trips to the past, neglects his duty and allows history to be changed. Fearing retribution, he goes on the run, dodging through the time-lines. Full of sprightly detail: a clever re-complication of old time-paradox themes, here played for laughs.

Up the Walls of the World (1978) ★★★ Novel by James Tiptree Jr. (Alice Sheldon, USA). A vast interstellar entity which gobbles stars; a threatened alien planet, where the squid-like aerial inhabitants live in the 'walls' of the wind; a military ESP experiment on Earth ... It adds up to a multi-stranded tale of some complexity, written in an intense style which is at times reminiscent of Theodore Sturgeon's. Undeniably impressive, though it disappointed some admirers of the author's outstanding short stories. Tiptree's first novel.

Uplift War, The (1987) ★★ Novel by David Brin (USA). The civilized chimpanzees of the planet Garth are left to fend for themselves when the alien Gubru invade and intern nearly all their human patrons. The action takes place at the same time as the author's *Startide Rising*, against the same future-history background. Hugo award-winner, 1988.

Urth of the New Sun, The (1987) ★★★★ Novel by Gene Wolfe (USA), being a fifth, pendant, volume to his masterly tetralogy *The Book of the New Sun*. Severian undertakes a space voyage (described in superbly Gothic fashion) in order finally to gain a new sun for his dying Urth. 'If this book is less brilliant than its predecessor, the flaw is one that is hard to spot with the unaided eye' – Colin Greenland, *Times Literary Supplement*.

Usual Lunacy, A (1978) ★★ Novel by D. G. Compton (UK). A hitherto unknown disease causes people to fall unwillingly in love. A rather bitter satire, and decidedly minor Compton.

Utopia Hunters (Sucharitkul): see under *Light on the Sound*.

Utopia-3 (Effinger): see *Death in Florence*.

V

Vacuum Flowers (1987) ★★★ Novel by Michael Swanwick (USA). Breathtakingly inventive adventure in a densely-inhabited solar system of the near future, where human beings swap personas through the casual application of 'wetware'. Bang up to date, but solidly in the tradition of the finest American sf (from Heinlein through Bester to Varley). 'Makes extremely adroit use of the cyberpunk rhetoric of information overload, the deadpan medias-res data-buzz which characterizes the best work of writers like Gibson ' – John Clute.

Valentina: Soul in Sapphire (1984) ★★ Fix-up novel by Joseph H. Delaney and Marc Stiegler (USA). Episodic narrative about the accidental growth to awareness of an intelligent computer program. The plot(s) concern such matters as Valentina's struggle to legally establish her 'personhood'. Clever, technically well informed, but shallow. Its authors' first novel.

Valentine Pontifex (Silverberg): see under *Lord Valentine's Castle*.

VALIS (1981) ★★★ Novel by Philip K. Dick (USA). The acronymic title stands for Vast Active Living Intelligence System – a Godlike entity which communicates by mystical means with the novel's shambling hero, Horselover Fat (clearly an alter ego of Philip Dick). Its author's strangest novel – both richly comic and intensely painful. 'A monument to a mind that had pulled itself back together, after struggling on the brink' – Kim Stanley Robinson.

Valley of Creation, The (1964) ★★ Novel by Edmond Hamilton (USA), expanded from a 1948 magazine serial. A rousing sword-and-sorcery type of tale, with an sf rationale, written in Hamilton's best pulp-magazine style.

Valley of Horses, The (Auel): see under *Clan of the Cave Bear, The*.

Valley Where Time Stood Still, The (1974) ★ Novel by Lin Carter (USA). A pastiche planetary romance, more or less in the style of Leigh Brackett's *The Sword of Rhiannon* but much less sophisticated. 'Heavily nostalgic' – Brian Stableford.

Vampires of Nightworld, The (Bischoff): see under *Nightworld*.

Vaneglory (Turner): see under *Beloved Son*.

Vang: The Military Form, The (1988) Novel by Christopher Rowley (USA). A standard-issue Horrid Parasitical Thing (from space-opera Central Casting) turns up on a spaceship and almost takes over a helpless human colony, in this wooden and aimless piece of militaristic sf adventure – apparently related to the series which began with Rowley's *The War for Eternity*.

Var the Stick (1972) ★ Novel by Piers Anthony (USA). The central characters of *Sos the Rope* launch a 'war to end war' against the industrial centre which their primitive tribes depend on for arms. The plot is occasionally lost in a Gilbertian maze of abandoned children and secret identities, in which nearly everyone is married to the wrong person. Sequel: *Neq the Sword*.

Variable Man and Other Stories, The (1957) ★★ Collection by Philip K. Dick (USA). Five long tales, of which 'Second Variety' (1953) and 'Autofac' (1955) are the most notable.

Venetian Court, The (1984) ★★ Novel by Charles L. Harness (USA). In a computer-controlled future, patent infringement has become a capital offence. The author puts his real-life

experience as a patent lawyer to good use in this science-fictional courtroom drama. 'Contrived and stagy, but carried off with great panache' – Brian Stableford.

Venus Belt, The (Smith): see under *Probability Broach, The*.

Venus Equilateral (1947) ★ Collection by George O. Smith (USA). Linked stories about life aboard an artificial satellite which maintains communications between the inhabited planets of the solar system. The pieces are all of the 'problem-solving' type, undistinguished as fiction but fondly remembered by some older readers. Republished, with three additional stories, as *The Complete Venus Equilateral* (1976).

Venus Hunters, The (1980) ★★★ Collection by J. G. Ballard (UK). This revamping and retitling of *The Overloaded Man* drops the former title story and two other pieces, and adds three newer tales: 'The Killing Ground' (1969), 'The 60 Minute Zoom' (1976) and 'One Afternoon at Utah Beach' (1978). All are interesting, if not representative of Ballard's very best.

Venus of Dreams (1986) ★★ Novel by Pamela Sargent (USA). An intelligently crafted family saga set against the background of a massive terraforming project on the planet Venus – a process which will take centuries. 'Shows true mastery of the grand scale' – Faren Miller, *Locus*. Sequel: *Venus of Shadows*.

Venus of Shadows (1988) ★★ Novel

by Pamela Sargent, sequel to *Venus of Dreams*. Things go wrong with the Venusian terraforming project, but it's clear that humanity will win through in the end, in this very long, complex, generational-saga of an sf novel. Commendably ambitious, as was its predecessor.

Venus on the Half Shell (1975) ★★ Novel by Kilgore Trout (Philip José Farmer, USA). 'Kilgore Trout' is of course a fictional author created by Kurt Vonnegut Jr. The sly Phil Farmer decided to bring one of Trout's fabled novels to life: a hack space opera with a heart of gold. The resulting far-out comedy was quite successful, and many people assumed it was a pseudonymous work by Vonnegut – which annoyed Vonnegut somewhat, and he forbade any sequels.

Venus Plus X (1960) ★★★ Novel by Theodore Sturgeon (USA). An average American Joe awakes in a world inhabited by lovely, fluting-voiced hermaphrodites. He is suitably appalled – at first. This utopian novel is a thoughtful speculation on the gender question.

Vermilion Sands (1971) ★★★★ Collection by J. G. Ballard (UK). Nine stories about a decaying artists' colony in the near future, set against surrealistic desert landscapes. Marvellously original, with unforgettable imagery. One of Ballard's most brilliant books.

Vertigo (1978) ★★★ Novel by Bob Shaw (UK). In the 21st century, anti-gravity harnesses give everyone the power of personal flight. But in such a world how is traffic to be controlled safely, and how do policemen deal with juvenile delinquents who have the whole sky in which to play their dangerous games? A fine example of logical extrapolation conveyed in an ingenious plot with interesting characters.

Veruchia (Tubb): see under *Winds of Gath, The*.

Very Private Life, A (1968) ★★★ Novel by Michael Frayn (UK). An amusing satire about a future world in which people make contact only via their electronic communications devices. The heroine rebels, then conforms once more in true Orwellian fashion. 'One of the most delightful fabulations in the genre' – Michael J. Tolley, *20th-Century SF Writers*.

Very Slow Time Machine, The (1979) ★★★ Collection by Ian Watson (UK). Thirteen ingenious sf stories from the magazines of the 1970s. The title piece is an extremely unusual variation on the time-travel theme. Most of the stories are quirkily written and bristling with new ideas. Watson's first collection. Later volumes of his shorter works include *Sunstroke and Other Stories* (1982) and *Slow Birds and Other Stories* (1985).

Vestiges of Time (1978) Novel by Richard C. Meredith (USA), last and least satisfactory of the 'Timeliner' trilogy. The protagonist acquires mystical powers, discovers the secret history of the human race, and gets his own back on the alien oppressors. By the end the reader sympathizes with the aliens.

Vicinity Cluster (Anthony): see *Cluster*.

Victim Prime (1987) ★ Novel by Robert Sheckley (USA), first of a series. Futuristic bounty-hunter tale which re-uses ideas from the author's short story 'Seventh Victim' and novel *The Tenth Victim*. 'The ending is abruptly chopped off, leaving numerous threads of sub-plot twitching helplessly in space' – Lee Montgomerie, *Interzone*. Sequel: *Hunter/Victim*.

View from Another Shore (1973) ★★★ Anthology edited by Franz Rottensteiner (Austria). A sampler of Russian, Polish, Czech, French and other European sf in translation, with notable contributions by Stanislaw Lem and Josef Nesvadba. 'I am an ardent supporter of translated sf because it is in collections like *View from Another Shore* that we can most easily see the wood instead of the trees. We can get far more idea of the potential of sf as a literary form from foreign literature than we can from our own' – Brian Stableford.

View from the Stars, The (1964) ★★★ Collection by Walter M. Miller (USA). Nine varied tales from the early 1950s, including such stand-outs as 'Crucifixus Etiam' and 'Anybody Else Like Me?' 'Miller is more interested in the responses of his characters to their bizarre situations than in the ostensible themes of the stories' – J. G. Ballard, *Guardian*.

Village of the Damned (Wyndham): see *Midwich Cuckoos, The*.

Vindication, The (Cherryh): see *Cyteen*.

Vintage Bradbury, The (Bradbury): see under *Twice Twenty-Two*.

Virgin Planet (1959) ★★ Novel by Poul Anderson (USA). A man arrives on a world colonized by ship-wrecked women who have maintained their population by partheno-genesis. Predictable adventures ensue. Readable, macho fun – but a novel which sf's feminists have come to hate, with good reason. 'It seems a pity that Anderson has not stopped to wonder what women would really be like in a society where there were no men. Would they really fight axe-wars?' – Hilary Bailey, *New Worlds*.

Viscous Circle (Anthony): see under *Chaining the Lady*.

Visible Light (1986) ★ Collection by C. J. Cherryh (USA). Five stories, ranging from the (corny) 1000-word 'Last Tower' to the (dull) 40,000-word 'Companions', together with rather self-indulgent introductions.

Visible Man, The (1977) ★★★ Collection by Gardner Dozois (USA), introduced by Robert Silverberg. Twelve striking tales by one of the better new sf writers of the 1970s (alas, he seems to have settled into the role of magazine- and anthology-editor during the 1980s). Standouts include the title story, 'Chains of the Sea' and 'A Special Kind of Morning'. All are written with feeling.

Visions and Venturers (1978) ★★ Collection by Theodore Sturgeon (USA). Eight odd and stylish stories, mostly from the 1940s and 50s. Notable items include 'The Martian and the Moron' (1949) and 'The Touch of Your Hand' (1953). Passed over for earlier Sturgeon collections, some of these tales have a patchy, anti-climatic feel – despite the undoubted talent they display.

Visitors, The (1980) ★ Novel by Clifford D. Simak (USA). Aliens in the form of giant black boxes land mysteriously on Earth. They begin to manufacture gifts, but little else happens. Pleasant as far as it goes, but everything is left dangling.

Voice of the Dolphins and Other Stories, The (1961) ★★ Collection by Leo Szilard (Hungary/USA). Szilard helped invent the atom bomb; these stories, in which benevolent dolphins direct human scientific research for our own good and people are paid to live in Mined Cities as hostages to nuclear deterrence, are very much a product of his desire to atone.

Voice of the Whirlwind (1987) ★★ Novel by Walter Jon Williams (USA), a quasi-sequel to his *Hardwired*. A clone is awakened, given the memories of his 'alpha' (the original cell-donor he is twinned from), and sent into space to find out what happened to the alpha, presumed murdered in a raid on an alien embassy somewhere in the outer solar system. A

proficient example of hard sf, throwing in lots of ideas on biology and information technology.

Voice Out of Ramah, A (1979) ★★ Novel by Lee Killough (USA). On a planet which was settled by the members of a religious order, 90% of males are killed in their youth, the remainder forming an elite priesthood. One man rebels against this terrible state of affairs, forming an alliance with a visiting Earthwoman. A well-meaning feminist parable with some absurdities of plot but moments of power. Killough's first novel.

Voices of Time, The (1963) ★★★★ Collection by J. G. Ballard (UK), originally entitled *The Four-Dimensional Nightmare*. Eight superbly atmospheric stories, ranging from 'Chronopolis' (1960) to 'The Cage of Sand' (1962). High point is the title story (1960), about a sleeping sickness which afflicts a near-future human race surrounded by mutating life forms and a universe running down.

Void Captain's Tale, The (1983) ★★★ Novel by Norman Spinrad (USA). The first-person narrative of the captain of the 'void ship' *Dragon Zephyr*, which leaps the light years with ease by means of its special orgasmic drive. An sf/fantasy about the ultimate phallic spacecraft. As is usual with Spinrad, there's a great deal of floridly-written sex – but this is perhaps his best novel since *Bug Jack Barron*. 'Very clever and written with much verve' – Brian Stableford. Quasi-sequel: *Child of Fortune*.

Volteface (Adlard): see under *Interface*.

Vornan-19 (Silverberg): see *Masks of Time, The*.

Voyage from Yesteryear (1982) ★★ Novel by James P. Hogan (UK/USA). A new starship from Earth reaches an already-colonized world, bringing with it outmoded political ideas. This planet is already a libertarian paradise, and wants no truck with notions of centralized government and economic planning. Right-wing special pleading, in a tolerably entertaining sf adventure plot.

Voyage of the Space Beagle, The (1950) ★★ Fix-up novel by A. E. van Vogt (Canada/USA). Two of the stories rewritten to form this book were first published in 1939, and are among van Vogt's earliest works (incidentally, he is the inventor of the widely-accepted term 'fix-up', which describes this practice). They're also among his most effective – tales of encounters between talented human beings and a variety of terrifying alien creatures. This is the classic 'bug-eyed monster' novel, the unacknowledged inspiration for the film *Alien* and scores of similar stories.

Voyage to Dari, A (Wallace): see under **Croyd**.

Voyage to the Bottom of the Sea (1961) ★ Movie novelization by Theodore Sturgeon (USA), based on a screenplay by Irwin Allen and Charles Bennett. The crew of the atomic submarine *Seaview* attempt to escape global catastrophe. A notable effort by a major sf author to imbue a silly story with human meaning. Superior to the film (1961; dir. Irwin Allen), even though the latter led to a TV series.

Voyage to the City of the Dead (1984) ★★ Novel by Alan Dean Foster (USA). Two human scientists trek across a far planet. The landscape is the thing here: a lopsided globe, one huge polar plateau cut by abyssal gorges and great rivers, sparsely populated by at least three alien races, variously decadent and primitive. The concoction is reminiscent of Jack Vance's work. At the end, the couple are rewarded with tidbits of information about the universe which provides the background to many of Foster's novels.

Voyage to Venus (Lewis): see under *Out of the Silent Planet*.

Voyager in Night (1984) ★★ Novel by C. J. Cherryh (USA), set in the author's 'Alliance/Union' future history. Three human space travellers are captured and copied, like so many computer programs, by a millennia-old intelligent spaceship. The narrative gets bogged down in the problems of describing alien personalities within a multiplex mind.

Voyagers (1981) ★★ Novel by Ben Bova (USA). A near-future political melodrama, in which an intruding alien spacecraft is investigated by a joint US-Soviet space mission. One of the author's more realistic efforts. 'An intelligent practitioner's deliberate attempt to translate sf into the bestseller marketplace' – Algis Budrys, *Fantasy & Science Fiction*. Sequel: *Voyagers II: The Alien Within*.

Voyagers II: The Alien Within (1987) Novel by Ben Bova (USA), sequel to *Voyagers*. Sketchily drawn story of a superpowered alien who tries to save the world from itself. Full of powerful women who only got ahead by sleeping with rich men. Rather unpleasant.

Vulcan's Hammer (1960) ★ Novel by Philip K. Dick (USA). A very minor work by the excellent Dick, expanded from a 1956 magazine story. It concerns rebellion in a future society which is ruled by a computer called Vulcan III.

W

Waldo and Magic, Inc (1950) ★★
Collection by Robert A. Heinlein
(USA). Two novellas from the early
1940s. 'Waldo' concerns a sick
young engineer who is obliged to live
in the weightless conditions of an
orbiting satellite in order to compensate for his wasted muscles. But from
there he is able to solve several of
Earth's problems. (Real-life remote-
control manipulation devices have
been name 'waldoes' after the hero of
this story.) The other piece, 'Magic,
Inc.', is an enjoyable fantasy about a
world where magic is taken for
granted.

Walk to the End of the World (1974)
★★★ Novel by Suzy McKee Charnas
(USA). Horrifying tale of a post-
disaster world where male chauvi-
nist values reign supreme. Women
are enslaved and forgotten, and men
go in terror of the moon (symbol of
all things female). A salutary feminist perspective on 'boys' stories',
written with vigour and relish.
Sequel: *Motherlines* (1978).

Walkers on the Sky (1976) ★★ Novel
by David J. Lake (UK/Australia). In
the distant future, near-immortal
humans have terraformed a planet,
using force-fields to keep various
'levels' separate. Against this exotic
background the young hero gets
caught up in war and rebellion.
Lake's first novel.

Walking Shadow, The (1979) ★★★
Novel by Brian Stableford (UK). By
means which are never adequately
explained, 'time jumpers' travel for-
wards in time to witness the end of
all independent life on Earth. A marvellous (and terrifying) vision of the
distant future embedded in a sometimes banal action-story plot.

Wall Around the World, The (1962)
★★★ Collection by Theodore R.
Cogswell (USA), introduced by
Anthony Boucher and Frederik Pohl.
Ten sf and fantasy stories, including
the author's best known pieces: the
enjoyable title story, about a boy's
discovery of the nature of his strange
world, and 'The Spectator General'.
Minor classics of the 1950s.

Wall of Years, The (1979) ★★ Novel
by Andrew M. Stephenson (UK). A

time-traveller must go back to the days of Alfred the Great in order to rectify historical anomalies which have arisen as the result of war between parallel worlds. The depiction of early medieval England is well-informed and intriguing.

Wanderer, The (1964) ★★★★ Novel by Fritz Leiber (USA). A new planet arrives in Earth orbit, and turns out to be a vast spacecraft operated by feline aliens. Earthquakes and tidal waves wreck our world, but a lucky few are granted a spectacular vision of the universe. Long, talky and endearing – undoubtedly Leiber's best sf work. Hugo award-winner, 1965.

Wandering Stars: An Anthology of Jewish Fantasy and Science Fiction (1974) ★★★ Anthology edited by Jack Dann (USA), with an introduction by Isaac Asimov. Thirteen fantastic stories on an ethnic theme, some of them by mainstream writers (Isaac Bashevis Singer, Bernard Malamud) and some by genre authors (Avram Davidson, Robert Silverberg, etc.). The overall standard is high. Sequel volume: *More Wandering Stars* (1981).

Wanting Seed, The (1962) ★★ Novel by Anthony Burgess (UK). An over-the-top satire on the future prospects of a teeming human race, by a notable 'mainstream' novelist. It displays a good knowledge of modern sf, but it's not as striking as Burgess's more linguistically-inventive *A Clockwork Orange* (written in the same year).

War Against the Rull, The (1959) ★ Fix-up novel by A. E. van Vogt (Canada/USA), based on stories first published in the 1940s. The deadly Rull is capable of taking on human form; however, humanity is aided in its struggle against this foe by some well-meaning aliens. The shape-changing motif has also been used extensively by van Vogt in a later novel, *The Silkie* (1969).

War for Eternity, The (1983) ★ Novel by Christopher Rowley (USA). A militaristic space adventure with much confusion and much slaughter. Rowley's first novel. Sequel, in similarly bloody vein: *The Black Ship* (1985).

War Games (Stableford): see *Optiman*.

War in the Air, The (1908) ★★★★ Novel by H. G. Wells (UK). Inoffensive Cockney hero becomes caught up in a world war fought with aeroplanes and dirigibles. Contains a wonderful passage in which a German air fleet attacks New York. Written well before World War I, it is both a marvellous piece of entertainment and a terrible warning – Wells's most underappreciated novel. 'I told you so. You *damned* fools' – author's preface to the 1941 edition.

War of Dreams, The (Carter): see under *Heroes and Villains*.

War of the Sky Lords (Brosnan): see under *Sky Lords, The*.

War of the Wing-Men (1958) ★ Novel by Poul Anderson (USA), first in his loosely-connected 'Trader Van Rijn' series (see also *Trader to the Stars* and *The Trouble Twisters*). Not to be confused with the same author's *The People of the Wind*, which is also about a war and features winged aliens. Revised and republished in the USA as *The Man Who Counts*.

War of the Worlds, The (1898) ★★★★ Novel by H. G. Wells (UK). Martians land in the English Home Counties. Striding on three-legged walking machines, wielding heat rays, they begin to destroy London. Powerfully imagined, hauntingly well written, it remains one of the greatest sf novels. Adapted for American radio by Howard Koch and Orson Welles in 1938, it caused a real-life panic. Filmed, none too faithfully, in 1953 (dir. Byron Haskin).

War with the Newts (1936) ★★★ Novel by Karel Capek (Czechoslovakia). A race of intelligent newts is discovered in the Far East. They rapidly learn the ways of civilization and begin to take over the world. Ebullient if a trifle overlong, this is a classic satire by the Czech author of the science-fiction stage-play *R.U.R.* (1921), which first introduced the word 'robot' to literature.

War World (Dietz): see *Sam McCade, Interstellar Bounty Hunter.*

Wardove (Smith): see under *Probability Broach, The.*

Warlord of Mars, The (Burroughs): see under *Princess of Mars, A.*

Warlord of the Air, The (1971) ★★ Novel by Michael Moorcock (UK), first in his 'Oswald Bastable' trilogy. The hero (whose name is borrowed from the children's books of E. Nesbit) is plunged into a parallel 1970s where the British and Russian and other European empires still hold sway over the territories they commanded in the 1900s – and where armed airships rule the skies. Old fashioned derring-do with a large dash of modern irony. Sequels: *The Land Leviathan* (1974) and *The Steel Tsar* (1981).

Warlords of Xuma (Lake): see under *Gods of Xuma, The.*

Warm Worlds and Otherwise (1975) ★★★ Collection by James Tiptree Jr. (Alice Sheldon, USA), introduced by Robert Silverberg. Twelve furiously imaginative, occasionally explosive sf stories, the best of which are quite brilliant. Highpoints: 'The Girl Who Was Plugged In' (Hugo award-winner, 1974), 'The Women Men Don't See' and 'Love is the Plan, the Plan is Death' (Nebula award-winner, 1973). Tiptree's second book, published at a time when no one was aware that 'he' was a woman. 'There is to me something ineluctably masculine about Tiptree's writing' – Robert Silverberg, introduction.

Warrior (Pournelle & Carr): see under *There Will Be War.*

Warrior's Apprentice, The (1986) ★★ Novel by Lois McMaster Bujold (USA). A light-hearted story of the son of a count who accidentally becomes a mercenary after failing the exams to get into the spacefaring Imperial Military. Slickly told, popular stuff.

Warriors of Dawn, The (1975) ★★ Novel by M. A. Foster (USA). Human attempts to create a superhuman race via genetic engineering have misfired. After some dissension, the so-called 'Ler' have left for another planet. What follows is an adequate space opera. Foster's first novel. Sequels (becoming more detailed and complex): *The Gameplayers of Zan* (1977) and *The Day of the Klesh* (1979).

Warriors of Day, The (1953) ★ Novel by James Blish (USA). Hero is mysteriously translated to the world of Xota, which he must help defend against space invaders. A none-too-successful attempt at a colourful adventure romp of the kind Henry Kuttner did so well.

Warriors of Mars (Moorcock): see *City of the Beast, The*.

Warriors of Spider, The (1988) ★ Novel by W. Michael Gear (USA), volume one in the 'Spider' trilogy. A newly-contacted colony of 'wild men' (descendants of American Indians, etc.) threatens to disrupt a fairly placid galactic empire. Wide-canvas, cowboys-and-Indians space opera. A first novel. Sequels: *The Way of Spider* (1989) and *The Web of Spider* (1989).

Warriors of the Storm (1987) ★ Novel by Jack L. Chalker (USA), Book Three of *The Rings of the Master*. The pirates from the pre-ceding novel, *Pirates of Thunder*, capture two more of the rings needed to take control of the Master System. A straightforward sequence of adventures on exotic planets with sex and violence never far beneath the surface. Sequel: *Masks of the Martyrs*.

Wasp (1957) ★★ Novel by Eric Frank Russell (UK). One brilliant Earthman confounds the stupid Sirian enemy by travelling behind their lines on an alien planet and playing various provocative pranks. An amusing but chauvinistic tale, with a distinct flavour of World War II heroics.

Watch Below, The (1966) ★★ Novel by James White (UK). A cleverly-conceived two-ply story about humans surviving aboard a sunken tanker and about aliens who have taken up residence at the sea bottom. Naturally, the two groups meet. Plainly told, but atmospheric and ingenious – one of White's best.

Watchers (1987) ★ Novel by Dean R. Koontz (USA). An over-violent tale of a man harbouring a genetically engineered superdog. Imagine Richard Adams's *The Plague Dogs* (1977) rewritten by a TV scriptwriter immediately after reading *The Island of Doctor Moreau*.

Watchers of the Dark (Biggle): see Under *All the Colors of Darkness*.

Water Witch (1982) ★★ Novel by Cynthia Felice and Connie Willis (USA). Water-diviners rule an alien sand planet, and the heroine tries to join their ranks. An enjoyably tricky plot results. Willis's first novel.

Waters of Centaurus, The (Brown): see under *Sybil Sue Blue*.

Wave and the Flame, The (1986) ★★ Novel by Marjorie Bradley Kellogg with William B. Rossow (USA), book one of a two-part series called 'Lear's Daughters'. An Earth expedition hopes to exploit the resources of an alien planet which is subject to sharp climatic changes. They meet the lowly natives, and ideological struggles ensue. 'The Sawls are too conveniently human in appearance and behaviour, their lovingly-detailed society too idealized. The weather may be awful on Fiix, but the caves are beguilingly cosy ... pure, painless, wish-fulfilment, eighties safe sf' – Paul McAuley, *Interzone*. Sequel: *Reign of Fire*.

Wave Rider (1980) ★★ Collection by Hilbert Schenck (USA). Five long sf/fantasy tales from the late 1970s, all connected in one way or another with the sea (which is the author's speciality: he has worked for decades as a marine engineer and has written popular non-fiction books about skindiving, etc.).

Wave Without a Shore (1981) ★★ Novel by C. J. Cherryh (USA). The humans of the planet Freedom have become inward-looking from centuries of ritual avoidance of the native aliens. A sculptor creates a monument to a local ruler even as the aliens gather around him and the Alliance warships land. The book is spiced with rather arty philosophi-cal dialogues which, unfortunately, don't quite come off.

Waves (1980) ★★ Novel by M. A. Foster (USA). Russian colonists on a far planet encounter an intelligent ocean. Slow-moving, with a love-story element, it seems to be something of a rewrite of Stanislaw Lem's *Solaris*.

Way Home, A (1955) ★★★ Collection by Theodore Sturgeon (USA), selected and introduced by Groff Conklin. Nine moralizing, sometimes sentimental, sf stories by a master of the form. Standouts include 'Mewhu's Jet' (1946), about a technologically-advanced alien who turns out to be a playful juvenile, and 'Thunder and Roses' (1947), about the moral dilemmas which face dying members of the US military in the aftermath of an atomic attack. Retitled *Thunder and Roses* (with slightly differing contents) for British publication.

Way of Spider, The (Gear): see under *Warriors of Spider, The*.

Way of the Pilgrim (1987) ★ Novel by Gordon R. Dickson (USA). Shane Evert leads a double life – as an interpreter for the war-like alien rulers of Earth, and as the Pilgrim, symbol of rebellion, even though his knowledge of the conquerors' perfectionist and totalitarian culture leads him to believe that the cause is hopeless. An extremely long treatment of some traditional sf themes, it can't avoid comparison with *The Interpreter* by Brian Aldiss, which is both shorter and better.

Way Station (1963) ★★★ Novel by Clifford D. Simak (USA). A Civil War veteran who farms a lonely corner of Wisconsin is contacted by aliens who want him to become the keeper of their interstellar 'way station'. He agrees, and they reward him with longevity. A simply written, deeply felt pastoral which shows this author at his best. Hugo award-winner, 1964.

We (1924) ★★★ Novel by Yevgeny Zamyatin (USSR). In a future totalitarian society where the first-person singular is outlawed and names have been replaced by numbers, one man mounts a futile rebellion. Many of the dark dystopian clichés were originally coined by Zamyatin for this powerful work, which is more science-fictional in its inventive detail than the later book which it so clearly influenced – George Orwell's *Nineteen Eighty-Four*. In part a satire on the ambitions of the Soviet state, it was first published in the West. 'A tour de force of irony and contempt, the novel is a terrifying portrait of a totally dehumanized society' – J. G. Ballard, *Guardian*.

We All Died at Breakaway Station (1969) ★★ Novel by Richard C. Meredith (USA). A space warrior has been resurrected as a cyborg, and now must make his last stand against an alien foe. Space opera with slight philosophical overtones, and possibly the late Mr Meredith's best novel. 'A kind of Horatio-at-the-bridge epic that is given extra dimension by its main character's questing intelligence' – Robert Thurston, *20th-Century SF Writers*.

We Can Build You (1972) ★★ Novel by Philip K. Dick (USA). Written in the early 1960s, serialized in 1969, this entertaining but flawed Dick novel concerns a world of puppet people and robotic automata (see also *The Simulacra*). One of his most paranoid visions.

We Claim These Stars (1959) ★ Novel by Poul Anderson (USA). Routine space adventure which happens to be the first in Anderson's long, long series about the exploits of a tough Earth agent called Dominic Flandry. Other 'Flandry' books (both novels and collections) include *Earthman, Go Home!* (1960), *Mayday Orbit* (1961), *Agent of the Terran Empire* (1965), *Ensign Flandry* (1966), *The Rebel Worlds* (1969), *A Circus of Hells* (1970), *A Knight of Ghosts and Shadows* (1974), *A Stone in Heaven* (1979) and *The Game of Empire* (1985).

We Who Are About To ... (1977) ★★ Novel by Joanna Russ (USA). A group of Earthfolk is stranded on a barren alien planet. They attempt to perpetuate the human race, squabble among themselves, and gradually realize that they will die. A grim tale which inverts the usual sf myth of human indomitability. It was not popular. 'For all its brevity, [it] can withstand a multiplicity of readings. If it is about how to die, then it is as much about how to live' – Sarah Lefanu, *In the Chinks of the World Machine*.

Weapon from Beyond, The (1967) ★ Novel by Edmund Hamilton (USA), first in his 'Starwolf' series. Conventional intersteller heroics in good old-fashioned style: the last hurrah of a grand master of space opera. Sequels: *The Closed Worlds* and *World of the Starwolves* (both 1968).

Weapon Makers, The (van Vogt): see under *Weapon Shops of Isher, The*.

Weapon Shops of Isher, The (1951) ★★ Fix-up novel by A. E. van Vogt (Canada/USA). 'The right to buy weapons is the right to be free': so runs the libertarian motto of the high-tech weapons emporia which are the bone of contention between the good guys and the repressive galactic empire that forms the back-drop of this extravagant story. Ill-written, unconvincingly detailed, yet suffused with a dream logic and great kinetic energy, this is one of van Vogt's most popular works. Sequel: *The Weapon Makers* (1952).

Weapons of Chaos (1989) Omnibus of three novels by Robert E. Vard-eman (USA): *Echoes of Chaos*, *Equations of Chaos* and *Colors of Chaos*.

Web (1979) ★ Posthumous novel by John Wyndham (UK). A Pacific island, bought by a millionaire in order to found a utopian community, suffers from a plague of spiders. It's an old-fashioned tale of biological menace, published in unfinished form a decade after the author's death. 'The pedestrian nature of the first and closing chapters, as well as lack of development in characteri-zation, mar the book; but if the episode on the island falls short of being a masterpiece, it is only by the breadth of a silken thread' – Ashley Rock, *Foundation*.

Web Between the Worlds, The (1979) ★★ Novel by Charles Sheffield (UK/USA). About the construction of a vast space elevator or 'Sky-Hook', this novel appeared a few months before Arthur C. Clarke's similar *The Fountains of Paradise* (the concept was first suggested by a Russian scientist in 1960: see the afterword to Clarke's book).

Web of Angels (1980) ★★ Novel by John M. Ford (USA). The hero is a Webspinner, someone who has the talent to manipulate the interstellar communications network known as the Web. This forces him to become an outlaw, on the run from various policing entities. Extravagant sf with a mythological fantasy flavour.

Web of Spider, The (Gear): see under Warriors of Spider, The.

Web of the Chozen, The (1978) Novel by Jack L. Chalker (USA). The tough hero lands on a colonized planet where it seems everyone has been turned into a herbivorous deer-like creature by a computer-developed virus. He too is duly turned into a deer – and finds that he enjoys prolonged orgasms. An extremely silly piece of hackwork by an over-prolific writer.

Web of the Magi and Other Stories, The (1980) ★★★ Collection by Richard Cowper (Colin Middleton Murry, UK). Four satisfactory sf and fantasy tales. The title piece is a 'lost race' story reminiscent of the work of Rider Haggard.

Weeping May Tarry (1978) Novel by Raymond F. Jones and Lester del Rey (USA). Alien visitors find a church and a Bible on an otherwise denuded Earth, are duly converted to the faith, and decide to proselytize it to the stars. Jones's (and del Rey's) last published novel to date. 'A dreadful little book ... one of the least plausible Christian messages I've ever been cozened into reading' – John Clute.

Welcome, Chaos (1983) ★★ Novel by Kate Wilhelm (USA). Scientists keep a longevity drug hidden from the world because of the unfortunate problems associated with its use (sterility being just one of them). A well-characterized psychological narrative by an sf writer whose strengths are primarily those of the 'mainstream' novelist.

Welcome to the Monkey House (1968) ★★★ Collection by Kurt Vonnegut Jr. (USA). Amusing sf and mainstream stories by this major novelist, some of them slickly sentimental pieces from general magazines of the 1950s. The more notable sf items include 'The Barnhouse Effect' and 'Harrison Bergeron'. This volume replaced the out-of-print *Canary in a Cat House* (1961), which contained some of the same stories.

Werewolf Principle, The (1967) ★★ Novel by Clifford D. Simak (USA). Spaceman returns to Earth with alien intelligences lurking in his unconscious mind. He becomes a hunted 'werewolf', intent on unravelling the mystery of himself. Pleasing entertainment, but less hard-edged than the author's somewhat similar *Time is the Simplest Thing*.

West of Eden (1984) ★★ Novel by Harry Harrison (USA/Ireland), first in a trilogy. An epic alternative-world scenario: Harrison posits a time-line in which the dinosaurs did not die out but instead survived to develop saurian civilization. In time, this advanced dinosaur culture comes into conflict with an emergent human race. Quite a yarn, incorporating some ingenious biological speculation – even if the action-adventure elements are at times banal. Sequels: *Winter in Eden* (1986) and *Return to Eden* (1988).

West of Honor (1976) ★ Novel by Jerry Pournelle (USA), part of his 'Falkenberg' series. A rather more interesting prequel to *The Mercenary*. Junior space officers attempt to do their duty in a situation thoroughly ruined by weak and corrupt politicians.

West of the Sun (1953) ★★ Novel by Edgar Pangborn (USA). Stellar explorers are marooned on another planet, where they build a successful colony in collaboration with various alien races. When an Earth vessel comes to rescue them they greet it very reluctantly. An unspectacular but well-written narrative by this sensitive author. Pangborn's first sf novel (although he had been writing non-sf for decades).

Wetware (1988) ★★ Novel by Rudy Rucker (USA), sequel to *Software*. The moon-dwelling robots of the previous novel wish to increase their store of knowledge. Fun, sexy, but too muddled to be excellent. 'Clumsy, jagged, witty, metaphysical, bumptious, pixillated and first-draft' – John Clute. Joint winner of the Philip K. Dick Memorial award, 1989.

What Entropy Means to Me (1972) ★★ Novel by George Alec Effinger (USA). On a far planet, a man narrates the story of his brother's quest along a largely symbolic River. An odd work, more fantasy than sf, in American New-Wave vein. Strong on imagery, short on rational coherence, it received much praise from critics such as Theodore Sturgeon. Effinger's first novel.

What Mad Universe? (1949) ★★★ Novel by Fredric Brown (USA). An sf-magazine editor falls into a parallel universe where bug-eyed monsters really exist. Comic romp which nicely satirizes many of the sf clichés of its day.

What Might Have Been, Volume 1: Alternate Empires (1989) ★★ Anthology edited by Gregory Benford and Martin H. Greenberg (USA). All-new alternative-world stories by Poul Anderson, George Alec Effinger, Karen Joy Fowler, Frederik Pohl, Kim Stanley Robinson and other capable writers. The first of a projected series of original anthologies, it's perhaps just a little too predictable overall.

What Rough Beast (1980) ★★ Novel by William Jon Watkins (USA). A benign, furry, female alien visitor attempts to solve some of Earth's problems, but is opposed by short-sighted humans. Eventually she makes common cause with the planet's computer intelligences – all for our race's good. Heartwarming stuff.

What's It Like Out There? and Other Stories (1974) ★★ Collection by Edmond Hamilton (USA). A dozen stories by one of the better magazine writers of American sf's early days. The title piece (1952), about a manned trip to Mars, was notable in its time for its harsh, anti-romantic realism. This solid volume has only two overlaps with the later *The Best of Edmond Hamilton*.

Wheel of the Winds (1988) ★★ Novel by M. J. Engh (USA). An Earthman is stranded on an alien planet and must travel a great distance to retrieve some signalling equipment. His adventures are seen almost entirely through the uncomprehending eyes of two of the planet's indigenes. Intelligently conceived, but curiously thin and lacking in visualization; coming twelve years after her brilliant first novel, *Arslan*, it's a disappointment. 'As much a comedy of manners as an epic saga' – Paul McAuley, *Interzone*.

Wheels Within Wheels (1978) ★ Novel by F. Paul Wilson (USA), expanded from a 1971 novella of the same title and part of the author's 'LaNague Federation' sequence of stories. This is a footling alien-mystery yarn, the main point of which seems to be to push the author's ultra-libertarian views on political economy. 'A fast-paced *Analog*-type book, affording a modicum of enjoyment if read at the prescribed fast pace while the higher cerebral functions are looking the other way' – Dave Langford, *Vector*. Wilson's first novel, *Healer* (1976), is a related work, as is his later *An Enemy of the State* (1980).

When Gravity Fails (1987) ★★★ Novel by George Alec Effinger (USA). A well-written sf thriller about a small-time Middle Eastern crook who sets out to track down some killers, assisted and hindered by brain-implants and other high-tech gewgaws. Effinger's most successful novel to date, with a fresh and intriguing background. 'Yields great entertainment and places Effinger in the company of writers like William Gibson – and Gibson's idol, William Burroughs, and of course Philip K. Dick – writers who explore the future of the city combat zone' – Thom Dunn, *SF & Fantasy Book Review Annual 1988*. Sequel: *A Fire in the Sun* (1989).

When HARLIE Was One (1972) ★ Novel by David Gerrold (USA). A computer threatened with close-down decides to create a new program which will take over the world. A fairly lively treatment of an obvious old theme. The 1988 reissue is extensively revised, removing once-modish references to drugs and updating the computer technology.

When the Green Star Calls (Carter): see under *Under the Green Star*.

When the Kissing Had to Stop (1960)

★ Novel by Constantine FitzGibbon (USA/Ireland). Sensational nonsense about an ultra-left-wing British government of the near future which permits a Soviet takeover. The Gulag is extended to England. The book is efficiently written, and became a UK bestseller.

When the Sky Burned (Bova): see *Test of Fire*.

When the Sleeper Wakes (1899) ★★★ Novel by H. G. Wells (UK). The hero wakes up in a mechanized future world – and soon finds himself leading a revolution against the capitalistic powers that be. Not Wells at his mythopoeic best but nevertheless an exciting narrative full of telling details. Revised and retitled *The Sleeper Awakes*.

When the World Shook (1919) ★★ Novel by H. Rider Haggard (UK). Explorers find the remains of an Atlantean civilization, where they meet a high priest and his beautiful daughter who have been in suspended animation for quarter of a million years. A 'sunken world' yarn which is also a far-fetched love story in a similar vein to the author's supernatural romance *She* (1886).

When They Come from Space (1962) ★ Novel by Mark Clifton (USA). Semi-humorous alien-invasion-of-Earth stuff, featuring the author's omnicompetent hero Ralph Kennedy, who had also appeared in a number of short stories for *Astounding* magazine (see *The Science Fiction of Mark Clifton*). Minor.

When We Were Good (1981) ★★
Novel by David J. Skal (USA). Worldwide radiation-induced sterility
causes scientists to genetically engineer a new race of hermaphroditic
children. The consequences are not
particularly happy.

When Worlds Collide (1933) ★★
Novel by Philip Wylie and Edwin
Balmer (USA). A new planet swims
into view and threatens to destroy
the Earth, but an enterprising few
manage to escape doom by embar-
king on a spacecraft. A now dated
story which was popular in its time
and has been influential. Sequel:
After Worlds Collide (1934). Filmed
in 1951 (dir. Rudolph Maté).

Whenabouts of Burr, The (1975) ★★
Novel by Michael Kurland (USA). A
comedy of alternative time-lines
which casts Aaron Burr, Alexander
Hamilton and other figures from
American history in unlikely roles. It
adds up to a pleasing confection for
the US domestic audience, but it's
likely to be opaque to most British
and other overseas readers (who *was*
Aaron Burr?).

Where Late the Sweet Birds Sang
(1976) ★★ Fix-up novel by Kate
Wilhelm (USA). After civilization
falls apart and sterility afflicts the
human race, one group of survivors
manages to propagate itself by
cloning. The episodic narrative contrasts the psychology of the cloned
humans with the 'normals'. A sensitive, thoughtful work but (given the
long time-span of the story) perhaps
too compressed. Hugo award-
winner, 1977.

Where No Stars Guide (Kippax): see
under *Thunder of Stars, A.*

Where Time Winds Blow (1982) ★★
Novel by Robert Holdstock (UK). On
a far planet, 'time winds' blow
objects (and persons) around in time
in a baffling manner. A rather talky,
serious-minded sf mystery by an
author who has since achieved
greater success with his fantasies
Mythago Wood (1984) and *Lavon-
dyss* (1988), both of which deal in
not dissimilar time themes.

Whiff of Madness, A (Goulart): see
under *Sword Swallower, The.*

Whipping Star (1970) ★★ Novel by
Frank Herbert (USA). The incom-
prehensibly alien Caleban are the
only race that can accomplish telepathic communication over interstellar distances; when one dies all
other intelligent beings within range
either die or go mad. The Bureau of
Sabotage has to deal with a human
who has employed a Caleban as a
willing victim of torture. The
attempt to describe the indescribable
sometimes falls into language of near
meaninglessness. Sequel: *The
Dosadi Experiment.*

Whirligig of Time, The (Biggle): see
under *All the Colors of Darkness.*

White Death, The (Sargent): see
Sudden Star, The.

White Dragon, The (1978) ★ Novel
by Anne McCaffrey (USA/Ireland).
Longest of the 'Dragonriders' books,
a sequel to both *Dragonquest*
and *Dragonsinger*. Very much *My*

Friend Flicka in space. The author seems more interested in explaining the inner workings of her world of Pern than in progressing the story, which gets bogged down in a mess of odd rivalries and time-travel paradoxes. For a prequel to the whole series see *Moreta, Dragonlady of Pern.*

White Fang Goes Dingo and Other Funny SF Stories (1971) ★★ Collection by Thomas M. Disch (USA), a substantially revised version of his first collection *One Hundred and Two H-Bombs* (1966). This edition adds such amusing items as 'The Invasion of the Giant Stupid Dinosaurs' and 'The Affluence of Edwin Lollard', as well as a couple of brief collaborations with John Sladek. The long title story has also been published in expanded form as the novel *Mankind Under the Leash.*

White Light (1980) ★★★ Novel by Rudy Rucker (USA). If you accelerate to the speed of light the whole universe will seem to fold itself up into a solid wall. Rucker's characters get out and walk around on it, in the best of his sex 'n' drugs 'n' mathematics novels (more fantasy than sf). Later books by this author, in a similar heavily mathematical vein, include *The Sex Sphere* (1983) and *The Secret of Life* (1985). He has also compiled the entertaining anthology *Mathenauts: Tales of Mathematical Wonder* (1987).

White Lotus (1965) ★★ Novel by John Hersey (USA). In an alternative timeline, China has invaded North America. The eponymous heroine is

an American-born slave girl, and this is her first-person story of degradation. A shocking inversion of historical circumstances for the edification of present-day WASP readers.

White Plague, The (1982) ★★ Novel by Frank Herbert (USA). A biologist whose wife has been murdered by terrorists deliberately releases a plague which may kill all the women in the world. A powerful though rather far-fetched tale of a terrible vengeance. Grim.

Who? (1958) ★★★ Novel by Algis Budrys (USA). An American scientist is badly injured in an explosion, then 'repaired' by Soviet doctors and returned to the USA. The problem is that he is now virtually a cyborg and no one can be sure of his identity. A clever Cold War thriller which established this young writer's reputation. 'Perhaps as fine a study of dehumanization and alienation as sf will ever produce' – Gene Wolfe, *20th-Century SF Writers.* Filmed in 1974 (dir. Jack Gold).

Who Can Replace a Man? (Aldiss): see *Best Science Fiction Stories of Brian W. Aldiss.*

Who Goes Here? (1977) ★★ Novel by Bob Shaw (UK). Warren Peace joins the Space Legion to forget. The trouble is that they mind-wipe him, causing him to forget so thoroughly that he immediately wants to remember whatever it was that he wished to forget. A time-twisting space-war comedy in its author's best light-hearted style. Humour as good as Robert Sheckley's, but carried by a better plot. The 1988 paperback reprint also contains the short story 'The Gioconda Caper' (from *Cosmic Kaleidoscope*).

Who Goes There? (1948) ★★★ Collection by John W. Campbell Jr. (USA). Seven tales from the 1930s sf magazines, including the classic title story – in which a shape-changing alien monster ravages an encampment in Antarctica – and the equally famous far-future, dying-fall mood pieces 'Twilight' and 'Night'. Although dated, these fictions have worn better than most American sf of their decade. Published in the UK as *The Thing and Other Stories*. The title story has been filmed twice as *The Thing (from Another World)* (1951; dir. Christian Nyby; and 1982; dir. John Carpenter).

Who Needs Men? (1972) ★ Novel by Edmund Cooper (UK). An all too grim satire about a female-dominated future society which persecutes its poor, long-suffering men. Published in the USA as *Gender Genocide*. 'Unfortunately, Cooper becomes so involved in the plot he forgets that it's a joke and starts taking it seriously' – Brian Stableford.

Whole Man, The (1964) ★★★ Fix-up novel by John Brunner (UK), based on magazine stories published in 1958–59. The tale of a deformed telepath who gradually overcomes his social ostracism and the consequent psychological problems. It has a certain poignancy, and it was the novel which first marked Brunner

out as more than a mere purveyor of space operas. Published in the UK as *Telepathist*.

Whores of Babylon (1988) ★★ Novel by Ian Watson (UK). In a vast experiment, the ancient city of Babylon is rebuilt in the Arizona desert. The purpose is to study the fall of civilizations, and find out whether they are inevitable. But the author keeps us guessing as to what is really going on ... The hero's adventures 'illustrate humankind's ability to mess up even the most sure-fire everlasting empire, but they also add up to a rather contrived plot which overshadows the ideas' – Simon Ounsley, *Interzone*.

Why Call Them Back from Heaven? (1967) ★★ Novel by Clifford D. Simak (USA). Much of humanity lies frozen in suspended animation, awaiting revival in a mythical Golden Age. But one man pits himself against the tyranny of the 'Forever Centre'. Enjoyable romp with (fairly soft) satirical touches.

Wild Card Run (1987) ★★ Novel by Sara Stamey (USA). An interplanetary adventure with a resourceful heroine who encounters artificial intelligences and much else. Pacey writing. 'Stamey's trying hard to do a hardboiled science fictional future that's quite different from anyone else's' – Tom Whitmore, *Locus*. Sequel: *Win, Lose, Draw* (1988).

Wild Cards (1987) ★★ Anthology edited by George R. R. Martin (USA). Described by its editor as 'a mosaic novel', this unusual book contains linked pieces by Edward Bryant, George R. R. Martin, Lewis Shiner, Melinda M. Snodgrass, Howard Waldrop, Walter Jon Williams, Roger Zelazny and others. The premise is that an alien virus was unleashed over America in 1946, leading to a number of human mutations – some benign, resulting in super-powered 'Aces', and some malign, causing the rise of deformed and sometimes villainous 'Jokers'. In short, it's comic-book stuff set in an alternative timeline, and as such it works quite effectively. There's a nice sense of period detail, particularly in Waldrop's opening story 'Thirty Minutes Over Broadway!' Sequel volumes (all edited by Martin, and with many of the same contributors): *Aces High* (1987), *Jokers Wild* (1988), *Aces Abroad* (1988), etc.

Wild Country (Ing): see under *Systemic Shock.*

Wild Seed (1980) ★★★ Novel by Octavia E. Butler (USA). An immortal West African man meets a shape-changing three-hundred-year-old woman: they emigrate to America, where they will breed a super-race. Perhaps more fantasy than sf: highly unusual love story by an Afro-American writer. It sets the scene for her earlier 'Patternist' novels (see under *Patternmaster).*

Wild Shore, The (1984) ★★★ Novel by Kim Stanley Robinson (USA). A well-written, rather elegiac view of life in a simplified America many decades after a nuclear war. Sensitively done, but a bit predictable. Robinson's first novel.

Wild Talent (1954) ★★ Novel by Wilson Tucker (USA). A man who discovers that he has telepathic abilities foolishly reveals himself to the military and is subsequently persecuted by government agents. A more than adequate treatment of a standard sf theme, interestingly dark for its time.

Wildeblood's Empire (Stableford): see under *Florians, The.*

Wildings of Westron, The (Lake): see under *Right Hand of Dextra, The.*

Wilk Are Among Us, The (1975) Novel by Isidore Haiblum (USA). A would-be comic space-operatic romp in which an octopoid alien narrator visits sundry planets, including Earth. Fast-moving and determinedly daft: the 'noise is tremendous, and the general effect scatty' – John Clute.

Win, Lose, Draw (Stanley): see under *Wild Card Run.*

Wind from a Burning Woman, The (Bear): see under *Tangents.*

Wind from Bukhara, A (Engh): see *Arslan.*

Wind from Nowhere, The (1962) ★ Novel by J.G. Ballard (UK). As the eponymous storm-wind batters London a few characters, including a megalomaniac pyramid-builder, struggle to survive. A surprisingly conventional disaster tale in the John Wyndham/John Christopher vein. The author's first novel, and one which he has subsequently disowned.

Wind from the Sun: Stories of the Space Age, The (1972) ★★ Collection by Arthur C. Clarke (UK). Eighteen tales from the 1960s, many of them brief, jokey squibs. The longest and most notable item is 'A Meeting with Medusa', about the exploration of Jupiter's atmosphere by balloon.

Wind Whales of Ishmael, The (1971) ★ Novel by Philip José Farmer (USA). A supposed sequel to Melville's *Moby-Dick* (1851), in which Ishmael finds himself translated to a far future world where the seas have evaporated and the whales have taken to the skies. Extremely far-fetched fun. Alas, it doesn't live up to its premise and soon turns into a routine adventure set against a colourful background. Like some other Farmer novels, it has no chapter divisions and consists of one headlong slab of text. No doubt it was written very fast.

Windhaven (1981) ★★ Fix-up novel by George R. R. Martin and Lisa Tuttle (USA). On a colonized planet which suffers repeated storms, the human inhabitants use flyers with artificial wings to maintain communications between their islands. This is the story of a young woman who becomes a flyer, against the odds. A romantic sf adventure which works well enough. (Tuttle's first novel.)

Windows (1979) ★★ Novel by D. G. Compton (UK), sequel to *The Continuous Katherine Mortenhoe*. The snooping TV reporter from the previous novel has his camera-eyes removed. Then it is his turn to become the subject of ghoulish media reportage. A good sequel to a fine original – but barely sf.

Winds of Change and Other Stories, The (1983) ★ Collection by Isaac Asimov (USA). Short stories from the late 1970s and early 80s, and something of a return to Asimov's older style. Whimsical, clever, liberal, the stories tend to feature absent-minded academics and to end with punch lines.

Winds of Darkover, The (1970) ★★★ Novel by Marion Zimmer Bradley (USA). A Terran space pilot gets involved in a feud between Darkovan families, in which the aggrieved party is forced to use the Sharra matrix (a crystal that acts as a telepathic focus, and seems sometimes to have a personality of its own) as a weapon. This betrayal of the treaties which hold Darkovan society together sets the scene for the central action of the series (in *The Heritage of Hastur* and *The Sword of Aldones*). One of the shorter, and better, 'Darkover' novels.

Winds of Gath, The (1967) ★ Novel by E. C. Tubb (UK). First of a long series of space-operatic adventures about the quest of a dour hero called Earl Dumarest to find his long-lost home-planet, Earth. Repetitive, routine, time-filler stuff, efficiently done. Later 'Dumarest' novels, all much of a muchness, include *Derai* (1968), *Toyman* (1969), *Kalin* (1969), *The Jester at Scar* (1970), *Lallia* (1971), *Technos* (1972), *Mayenne* (1973), *Veruchia* (1973), *Jondelle* (1973), *Zenya* (1974), and many more up to the mid-1980s.

Winds of Limbo, The (Moorcock): see *Fireclown, The.*

Wind's Twelve Quarters, The (1975) ★★★★ Collection by Ursula K. Le Guin (USA). Beautifully-written sf and fantasy stories, including 'The Ones Who Walk Away from Omelas' (Hugo award-winner, 1974) and 'The Day Before the Revolution' (Nebula award-winner, 1974), plus such other fine pieces as 'Nine Lives' and 'Vaster Than Empires and More Slow'. An outstanding volume. Unfortunately, it has been split in two for some paperback reprints.

Winter in Eden (Harrison): see under *West of Eden.*

Winter's Children (1974) ★★ Fix-up novel by Michael Coney (UK/Canada). A new ice age has come, and a group of persons with mono-syllabic names survives, thanks to a mixture of heroism and low-down cunning. There are mutated polar bears and other creatures, and there's a rote ESP element to the plot. It's surprisingly light and effervescent – all air, like a meringue.

Witches of Karres, The (1966) ★★ Novel by James H. Schmitz (USA). Three telepathic girls get the better of strait-laced space crew in this typical James Schmitz mix of humour, strange mental powers and mild anarchy.

With a Strange Device (1964) ★ Novel by Eric Frank Russell (UK). A researcher in a near-future secret US government establishment is brain-washed into believing that he has committed a murder. Very dated, rather dull. Published in the USA as *The Mind Warpers.*

With Fate Conspire (1985) ★★ Novel by Mike Shupp (USA), Book one of 'The Destiny Makers'. A Vietnam veteran is plunged into a future in which 'Teeps' (telepaths) are treated as Jews were in Europe not so long ago – tolerated for their usefulness, never allowed a full part in the state, and always in danger of pogrom. The country in which they live is losing a war, so they try to fix things by changing history – with all the traditional confusing results of the time-travel tale. Sequel: *Morning of Creation* (1986).

Without Sorcery (1948) ★★★ Collection by Theodore Sturgeon (USA). Debut volume by this intense and mercurial author. Thirteen tales, ranging from the ⸱playful 'Ether Breather' (1939) to the heavily psychological superman-story 'Maturity' (1947). Later republished, stripped of five stories, under the title *Not Without Sorcery.*

Witling, The (1976) ★★ Novel by Vernor Vinge (USA). Stranded interstellar explorers discover that planetary natives have developed a limited kind of teleportation. The description of the peculiar nature of this travel and the effects it has on society are more interesting than the plot or characters.

Wizard (1980) ★★ Novel by John Varley (USA). Cirocco Jones, the spaceship captain from Varley's previous novel *Titan*, is recruited by the living world Gaia as a sort of internal policeman, wandering around her huge body as the representative of the ageing mind. Extravagant stuff. Sequel: *Demon*.

Wolfbane (1959) ★★ Novel by Frederik Pohl and C. M. Kornbluth (USA). Pyramid-shaped aliens wrench the Earth from its orbit, and turn the remnants of humanity into fleshy machine components. But one talented individual finds the resources to mount a rebellion. An extremely odd story, part satire and part gosh-wow tale of super-science. The fourth and last collaborative sf novel by these talented authors (Kornbluth died in 1958). In a 1986 revision Pohl has smoothed over some of the first edition's faults.

Wolfhead (1978) ★★ Novel by Charles L. Harness (USA). In a post-disaster society, the hero descends into the underworld with his wolf companion. A curious, and not entirely successful, amalgam of the Orpheus myth and Dante's *Inferno* in an sf plot. Unlike Harness's other books.

Woman a Day, A (Farmer): see *Timestop*.

Woman on the Edge of Time (1976) ★★★★ Novel by Marge Piercy (USA). Long-suffering Mexican-American heroine makes contact with her alter ego from a utopian future. Fine depiction of a woman's lot in present-day America contrasted with a technologically sophisticated feminist alternative. Deeply moving.

Women as Demons: The Male Perception of Women Through Space and Time (1989) ★★★ Collection by Tanith Lee (UK). Sixteen sf and fantasy stories, most of which deal in one way or another with the theme indicated in the sub-title. At her best, Lee is a powerful, provocative artist – though more of a fantasist than a writer of science fiction proper.

Women of Wonder: SF Stories by Women About Women (1975) ★★★ Anthology edited by Pamela Sargent (USA). A dozen well-known sf stories by female writers, ranging from Judith Merril's 'That Only a Mother' (1948) to Vonda McIntyre's 'Of Mist, and Grass, and Sand' (1973). Other authors represented include Le Guin, McCaffrey, Russ and Wilhelm. With a lengthy, well-argued introduction by the editor, it is perhaps the most solid (and has proved the most influential) of all the 'feminist' sf anthologies published in the 1970s. Sequels: *More Women of Wonder* (1976) and *The New Women of Wonder* (1978).

Wonder Effect, The (1962) ★ Collection by Frederik Pohl and C. M. Kornbluth (USA). These collaborative pieces date mainly from the 1940s, when the authors were very young, and they reveal only flashes of the talent both were to display later. 'Pohl declares that at least 25 of the short stories which the team wrote deserve to remain buried. Readers of this collection may consider him conservative' – James Cawthorn, *New Worlds*. The book was subsequently revised and re-issued by Pohl as *Critical Mass* (1977).

Wooden Spaceships, The (1988) ★★ Novel by Bob Shaw (UK), sequel to *The Ragged Astronauts*. The action resumes twenty-odd years after the great balloon flight from 'Land' to 'Overland' (planets which share a narrow funnel of atmosphere). There is war between these worlds, and a third planet, 'Farland', comes into the picture. A satisfactory conclusion is promised in volume three. 'A fine book' – John Clute. Sequel: *The Fugitive Worlds* (1989).

Wooden Star, The (1968) ★★ Collection by William Tenn (USA). Eleven stories, including some of the author's best pieces from his heyday of the 1950s, such as 'Brooklyn Project', 'Null-P' and 'Eastward Ho!', which had not appeared in earlier collections. Two other volumes which were published at the same time as this book (in a special William Tenn promotion from Ballantine) – *The Seven Sexes* and *The Square Root of Man* – are somewhat inferior 'clean-up' collections.

Word for World is Forest, The (1976) ★★★ Novella by Ursula K. Le Guin (USA), originally published in Harlan Ellison's *Again, Dangerous Visions* (1972). Violent humans attempt to colonize an Edenic planet, where the alien natives live in harmony with their forest. It's obviously a parable of American involvement in Vietnam, but it's also a moving work of sf – linked to Le Guin's 'Hainish' cycle of novels and stories. Hugo award-winner, 1973 (as novella).

World and Thorinn, The (1981) ★

Fix-up novel by Damon Knight (USA). In a barbarous distant future, the youth Thorinn explores a subterranean realm, finding remnants of machine civilization. The author's first attempt at a novel in more than a decade, it's sadly deficient in most of the novelistic virtues. 'It rambles on and on and on, with no shape, no characters, no plot, and no imaginative vitality' – Brian Stableford.

World Between, A (1979) ★ Novel by Norman Spinrad (USA). A well-balanced, tolerant human society on a planet named Pacifica is threatened by media overkill from two pressure groups: 'transcendental scientists' (fill in the name of the authoritarian religion of your choice) and lesbian feminists. The author satirizes both these movements in fairly crude terms, and makes a strong plea for liberal good sense. 'Behind all the power-games and rhetoric the book's message is as simple and naïve as anything that came out of San Francisco in the late 1960s' – Charles Platt, *Foundation*.

World Called Solitude, A (1981) ★ Novel by Stephen Goldin (USA). Marooned Earthman suffers self-pityingly on an exotic alien planet, where he is eventually joined by a tough female companion who makes him snap out of it. 'An honest though slightly dumb novel about the salvation in human terms of a hyperventilating Silverbergian soul far from Manhattan' – John Clute.

World Enough and Time (1980) ★★ Novel by James Kahn (USA). Genetic engineering has created vampires and intelligent animals who have almost wiped out humans in a genocidal war. Josh, one of the few survivors, pursues the monsters who have kidnapped his family to a City with No Name in Southern California where they are being used in a horrible experiment in artificial intelligence. Sequels: *Time's Dark Laughter*, set in the same parallel universe, and *Timefall*, set in our own version of California.

World in Winter, The (1962) ★★ Novel by John Christopher (UK). A new ice age drives refugees from Northern Europe to Africa, where they encounter various degrees of intolerance. A readable disaster story, and a nice inversion of contemporary racial tensions. Published in the USA as *The Long Winter*.

World Inside, The (1971) ★★ Novel by Robert Silverberg (USA). In a grotesquely overcrowded world of the 24th century, everyone is crammed into 1000-storey Urban Monads — vertical cities whose inhabitants are encouraged, perversely, to be fruitful and multiply. As is not uncommon in his best work of the period, Silverberg gives us a vision of a hell with no easy way out.

World Jones Made, The (1956) ★★ Novel by Philip K. Dick (USA). The eponymous Jones is an unhappy dictator who can foresee the future, by exactly one year. Its author's second novel, from the period before he had come into his full powers. 'A spectacular, brim-full grab bag of ideas' – Damon Knight.

World Menders, The (1971) ★ Novel by Lloyd Biggle Jr. (USA), sequel to *The Still Small Voice of Trumpets*. Members of the 'Cultural Survey' are worried by the existence of institutionalized slavery on an alien planet. 'Heavily influenced by John W. Campbell's ideas about the merits of slavery' – Brian Stableford.

World of Chance (Dick): see *Solar Lottery*.

World of Null-A, The (1948) ★★ Novel by A. E. van Vogt (Canada/ USA), serialized in 1945. A space-operatic mystery story in its author's best vein, with a hero who seemingly can die and be reborn endlessly (thanks to his 'non-Aristotelian' mental powers). It's dreadful old garbage by any reasonable critical standard, and yet it has a dreamlike conviction which has endeared it to generations of readers. The works of van Vogt, which have provided so much escapist joy, are among the great embarrassments of modern sf. Sequel: *The Players of Null-A*.

World of Ptaavs (1966) ★★ Novel by Larry Niven (USA). The last survivor of the ancient Slaver Empire is awakened by unwitting Earthfolk. Niven's first novel, and perhaps the best introduction to his 'Known Space' menagerie of alien cultures which forms the background to so many of his stories.

World of the Starwolves (Hamilton): see under *Weapon from Beyond, The*.

World Out of Mind (McIntosh): see under *One in Three Hundred*.

World Out of Time, A (1976) ★★ Fix-up novel by Larry Niven (USA). The protagonist, reborn into a new body, embarks on a voyage of three million years' duration, returning to a world which has changed out of recognition. A space adventure yarn of considerable imaginative sweep, not connected to the author's 'Known Space' series.

World Set Free, The (1914) ★★ Novel by H. G. Wells (UK). Written some months before the outbreak of the First World War, this is the far-reaching story of a devastating global conflict in which atomic weapons are used. In the aftermath, a saner order arises. A rather distant tale, lacking in characters, it is nevertheless a thought-provoking work of prophecy.

World Shuffler, The (1970) ★★ Novel by Keith Laumer (USA), sequel to *The Time Bender*. O'Leary wanders into an alternative world on his way home from a party and spends the rest of this comic, mildly titillating short novel trying to get back to his home in Artesia. Sequels, in very similar vein: *The Shape Changer* (1972) and *The Galaxy Builder* (1984).

World Without Men (1963) Novel by Charles Eric Maine (UK). Flash-backs from genetic experiments to recreate males to the experiments that did away with them 5000 years earlier. As usual in the many sf novels set in a world where women give birth to women by artificial parthenogenesis, the society of Woman is painted as more restrictive and less tolerant than that of Man.

World Wreckers, The (1971) ★★ Novel by Marion Zimmer Bradley (USA). Some years after the failed rebellions described in *The Sword of Aldones* and *The Heritage of Hastur*, the planet Darkover faces ecological disaster as the ruling telepath caste are picked off one by one by assassins. Final destruction is, of course, just averted by the return of the lovely alien Chieri, long believed extinct. Rather sentimental, if not positively soppy.

Worlds (1982) ★★★ Novel by Joe Haldeman (USA). A student from an orbital republic visits 21st-century Earth and gets involved in politics, leading to personal and general disaster. A more realistic account of politics and nuclear war than most of the large crop of 1980s novels with a space-colony background. Sequel: *Worlds Apart*.

Worlds Apart (1986) ★★ Anthology edited by Camilla Decarnin, Eric Garber and Lyn Paleo (USA). Gay and lesbian sf, companion volume to *Kindred Spirits*. Stories by Edgar Pangborn, James Tiptree Jr., Samuel Delany, Joanna Russ and others.

Worlds Apart (1983) ★★★ Novel by Joe Haldeman (USA). Sequel to *Worlds*. The people of New New York are divided between trying to help an Earth devastated by war, plague, famine and fanatic religion or else sending an expedition to the nearby stars.

World's Best Science Fiction: 1965 etc. (Wollheim & Carr): see under *Best Science Fiction of the Year, The*.

World's End (Vinge): see under *Snow Queen, The*.

Worlds of A. E. van Vogt, The (van Vogt): see *Far-Out Worlds of A. E. van Vogt, The*.

Worlds of Clifford Simak, The (1960) ★★★ Collection by Clifford D. Simak (USA). A first-class volume of twelve stories by this most rewarding of middle-range sf authors. High points are 'Dusty Zebra' (1954), a delightful piece about interdimensional dickering, and 'Green Thumb' (1954), about a man who communes with plants. The British edition, published as *Aliens for Neighbours*, omits three tales (among them the Hugo award-winning 'The Big Front Yard'). Another partial version has appeared in US paperback as *Other Worlds of Clifford Simak* (six stories).

Worlds of Fritz Leiber, The (1976) ★★★ Collection by Fritz Leiber (USA). A fine, fat gathering of sf and fantasy stories by an old master (whose light has shone most clearly in the fantasy category). It includes the Hugo and Nebula award-winning tale 'Catch That Zeppelin!' (1975). Pleasingly, this book contains no overlaps with *The Best of Fritz Leiber*, published two years earlier. It is, in effect, a second 'Best of ...' selection.

Worlds of Robert A. Heinlein, The (1966) ★ Collection by Robert A. Heinlein (USA). A raggle-taggle selection of stories plus a longish introduction. The best-known story, 'Blowups Happen' (1940), is reprinted from *The Man Who Sold the Moon*. The newest piece, 'Free Men' (1966), is a dud which reworks the subject matter of one of the author's poorest novels, *Sixth Column*. The contents of this volume, plus some other fictional barrel-scrapings and a good deal of non-fiction, were subsequently republished in a book entitled *Expanded Universe: More Worlds of Robert A. Heinlein* (1980).

Worlds of Robert F. Young, The (1965) ★★ Collection by Robert F. Young (USA). Polished sf and fantasy stories, mainly on romantic themes and many involving time travel. A standout is the satirical 'Romance in a 21st-Century Used-Car Lot', about a society in which people literally wear their automobiles as clothing.

Worlds of the Imperium (1962) ★★ Novel by Keith Laumer (USA). A US diplomat is kidnapped and forced to become a secret agent by a British Empire which never fought World War I and extends a benevolent rule across hundreds of parallel Earths. Laumer's first book, and quite fun. Sequels: *The Other Side of Time* (1965) and *Assignment in Nowhere* (1968); an omnibus volume, *Beyond the Imperium* (1981), combines these last two.

Worlds of Theodore Sturgeon, The (1972) ★★★ Collection by Theodore Sturgeon (USA). Nine long stories, some of them, e.g. 'Shottle Bop' (1941) and 'Maturity' (1947), reprinted from his first collection, *Without Sorcery*. Standouts include

'The Perfect Host' (1948) and 'The Skills of Xanadu' (1956). Powerful, sentimental, occasionally rather dated.

Worlds of Wonder (Johns): see under *Now to the Stars*.

Worlds of Wonder (1988) ★★★ Anthology edited by Robert Silverberg (USA). Well-known stories from the 50s and 60s (such as 'Light of Other Days' by Bob Shaw, C. M. Kornbluth's 'The Little Black Bag' and 'Scanners Live in Vain' by Cordwainer Smith) together with extensive notes by the editor on his own career and the technique of writing sf. Adds up to a good 'how-to' book with examples.

Worlds Without End (1964) ★★ Collection by Clifford D. Simak (USA). Three long stories – 'Worlds Without End' (1956), 'The Spaceman's Van Gogh' (1956) and 'Full Cycle' (1955). Competent, entertaining but unmemorable.

Worthing Chronicle, The (1982) ★★★ Novel by Orson Scott Card (USA). Jason Worthing is woken from a sleep of centuries to pass on his life story, in dreams and myth, to the blacksmith's son in a poor farming village. He recounts the story of the novel *Hot Sleep* from his own point of view, and tells how his telekinetic descendants established a guardianship over humanity as stifling as that of the fallen Empire. Stylistically adventurous, shot through with the belief that comfort and contentment are incompatible with moral growth.

Wreath of Stars, A (1976) ★★★ Novel by Bob Shaw (UK). The near-approach of a cosmic body shakes loose an 'anti-neutrino planet' from within our Earth, a sort of shadow-world which no one knew existed. It's an intelligent story, well-characterized and nicely envisioned, with a highly original central notion. One of Shaw's best. 'What a splendid mind-gobbling read this is! It wouldn't put me down' – Brian Aldiss, *Guardian*.

Wrecks of Time, The (1967) ★★ Novel by Michael Moorcock (UK) Fifteen alternative Earths (one of them ours) are threatened with destruction. The colourful Dr Faustaff attempts to save them. The kind of flamboyant sf adventure, salted with humour, which Moorcock just doesn't write any more, alas. Republished as *The Rituals of Infinity*.

Wrinkle in the Skin, A (1965) ★★ Novel by John Christopher (UK). Massive earthquakes devastate the globe, draining some of the seas. The hero, a resident of Guernsey, walks across the English Channel. Cosy, but it's perhaps Christopher's best catastrophe tale after his famous *The Death of Grass*. 'The characters [behave] like fugitives from a mislaid picnic ... this is the end of the world seen from Pooh's Corner' – J. G. Ballard, *Guardian*. Published in the USA as *The Ragged Edge*.

Writers of the Future (Budrys): see *L. Ron Hubbard Presents Writers of the Future*.

Wyrms (1987) ★★ Novel by Orson
Scott Card (USA). Fantasy-flavoured
adventure on a far planet called Ima-
kulata. As slick and ingenious as all
Card's work. 'The extrapolation of a
hard sf idea suffers in its forced marriage to a plot which depends on the
quaint notion that the course of
history is entirely determined by the
actions of uniquely dynamic individuals. The join shows in an in-
digestible three-page expository
lump and a certain amount of twisting of the history of human colonization of the alien world to make
sure the story comes good' – Paul
McAuley *Interzone*.

Wyst: Alastor 1716 (1978) ★ Novel
by Jack Vance (USA). Standard-
variety space opera set in Vance's
immense 'Alastor Cluster' (see *Trullion: Alastor 2262*). This one concerns an egalitarian planet where
food binges (called 'Bonters',
perhaps after Billy Bunter?) are the
height of fashion. Contains far too
many silly words and half-jokes to be
genuinely readable.

X, Y, Z

Xeno (1979) ★ Novel by D. F. Jones (UK). Aircraft which mysteriously disappear (Bermuda Triangle-wise) are in fact whisked away to another planet. They return bearing alien parasites which devastate our world. A feeble, talky chiller, poorly characterized, and with a political axe or two to grind. 'An antique BEM-story recast in a glossy 70s TV-thriller format' – Tom Hosty, *Foundation*. Published in the USA as *Earth Has Been Found*.

Xenogenesis (Butler): see *Dawn: Xenogenesis 1*.

Xenogenesis (1969) ★★ Collection by Miriam Allen DeFord (USA). Sixteen more-than-adequately entertaining sf and fantasy tales, many of them on sexual and reproductive themes. Warmly written fare, with mystery-story twists, by an elderly writer (born 1888) perhaps better known for her crime fiction.

Xorandor (1986) ★★★ Novel by Christine Brooke-Rose (UK). Children encounter a rock-like alien creature and find that they can com- municate with it via their portable computer. A highly accessible entertainment of ideas by an erstwhile avant-garde novelist. 'The plot – which is about how to save the world from us, and about how Xorandor can hope to survive his self-exposure to the relentless superflux of us – trundles safely on overhead, but the action is in the dazzling tesserae of words wording words' – John Clute.

Year Before Yesterday, The (Aldiss): see *Cracken at Critical*.

Year of the Cloud, The (1970) ★★ Novel by Theodore L. Thomas and Kate Wilhelm (USA). The Earth passes through a cosmic cloud and, among other disasters, the oceans turn to jelly. An enjoyable catastrophe novel – more typical of the sort of thing which British writers used to produce.

Year of the Quiet Sun, The (1970) ★★★ Novel by Wilson Tucker (USA). Time travellers are horrified to find a near-future America riven by inter-racial war. A simple but moving cautionary tale, and probably

Tucker's best book. Retrospective winner of the John W. Campbell award, 1976.

Year 2018! (Blish): see *They Shall Have Stars.*

Year's Best Science Fiction, The (1968–76) ★★★ Anthology series edited by Harry Harrison (USA/ Ireland) and Brian Aldiss (UK). This nine-volume sequence of selected sf and fantasy stories had much more of a British flavour, and ranged more widely in its choices, than did Terry Carr's rival series, *The Best Science Fiction of the Year.* At times, it seemed rather eccentric in its eclecticism, but all the volumes contained some startling fiction. Published in the USA under the series title *Best SF: 1967* et seq.

Year's Best Science Fiction, First Annual Collection, The (1984) ★★★★ Anthology edited by Gardner Dozois (USA). A massive gathering of top-notch sf, mainly from the US magazines, including the quasi-sf magazine *Omni* (Dozois has since been appointed editor of *Isaac Asimov's SF Magazine,* but his bias in favour of that particular magazine was apparent before the fact). The first of an annual, ongoing series which has now established itself as the most comprehensive of its type. Some later volumes have been published in Britain under the series title *Best New SF.*

Year's Greatest Science Fiction and Fantasy, The (Merril): see *SF: The Year's Greatest Science Fiction and Fantasy.*

Years of the City, The (1984) ★★★ Fix-up novel by Frederik Pohl (USA). Five linked stories set in 21st-century New York, following the development of housing, commerce, recreation and the law under the influence of drastic technological change. The book shows an understanding of the politicians, construction workers, union officials, and landlords who fill its pages as well as a real love for the social and material fabric of the city. John W. Campbell award-winner, 1985.

Yesterday's Men (Turner): see under *Beloved Son.*

Yonder Comes the Other End of Time (Elgin): see under *Star-Anchored, Star-Angered.*

You Sane Men (1965) ★ Novel by Laurence M. Janifer (USA). A nasty, ironic vision of a world where torture and sadism are institutionalized, and this has the effect of eliminating violence in daily life. Republished as *Bloodworld.*

You Will Never Be the Same (1963) ★★★ Collection by Cordwainer Smith (Paul Linebarger, USA). Richly decorated tales of a far future unlike anyone else's, including such classics as 'The Game of Rat and Dragon' (1955) and 'Alpha Ralpha Boulevard' (1961). This was Smith's first collection, and all the stories have since been reprinted in later volumes (see for instance *The Best of Cordwainer Smith*). Other volumes which have now been subsumed in 'definitive' collections are *Space Lords* (1965), *Under Old Earth and*

Other Explorations (1970, UK only) and *Stardreamer* (1971).

Young Rissa (1984) ★ Novel by F. M. Busby (USA), originally published as part of the massive novel *Rissa Kerguelen* (1976). Heroine Rissa is brought up in brutal privatized welfare homes, wins a lottery, and escapes to the 'Hidden Worlds'. Straightforward space opera, contemporaneous with the action of the later novel *Star Rebel*, which is the story of Rissa's future husband. Sequels: *Rissa and Tregard* (1984) and *The Long View* (1976).

Zanzibar Cat, The (1983) ★★★ Collection by Joanna Russ (USA), introduced by Marge Piercy. Seventeen sf and fantasy stories, mainly from the 1960s and 70s, and including much of Russ's more conventional work in shorter forms – making this a very approachable book for a reader who may be new to this sometimes difficult author. Contains 'When it Changed', 'Nobody's Home', 'The Soul of a Servant' and other sensitively written pieces. 'A volume of astonishingly high overall quality' – Gregory Feeley, *Foundation*.

Zap Gun, The (1967) ★ Novel by Philip K. Dick (USA). Satire on the arms race: hero is a 21st-century weapons fashion designer. Despite good moments, this is one of Dick's most clotted narratives.

Zen Gun, The (1983) ★★ Novel by Barrington J. Bayley (UK). The genetically engineered ape Pout steals a weapon that greets him with the telepathic jingle 'You can maim and you can kill with your Zen Gun.' It becomes a threat to the Galactic Empire, crippled by robot industrial workers on strike for sentient status. Perhaps one of Bayley's less successful novels: the continual flow of crazy ideas threatens to get in the way of the plot.

Zenda Vendetta, The (Hawke): see under *Ivanhoe Gambit, The.*

Zenith: The Best in New British Science Fiction (1989) ★★ Anthology edited by David S. Garnett (UK). Among the most effective pieces are Barrington Bayley's 'Death Ship', Christopher Evans's 'The Bridge' and Garry Kilworth's 'White Noise'. Indicative of great promise is 'Skyrider' by newcomer William King. The first volume of an original sf short-story series which, with luck, will become an annual regular (like its current rival, the *Other Edens* series edited by Holdstock and Evans).

Zenya (Tubb): see under *Winds of Gath, The.*

Z-Sting (Wallace): see under *Croyd.*

Author Index

Wu, William F.
Cyborg
Perihelion

Wul, Stefan
*Temple of the Past,
The*

Wylie, Philip
After Worlds Collide
Disappearance, The
End of the Dream, The
When Worlds Collide

Wyndham, John
*Best of John Wyndham,
The*
Chocky
Chrysalids, The
*Consider Her Ways and
Others*
Day of the Triffids, The
Infinite Moment, The
Kraken Wakes, The
Midwich Cuckoos, The
Out of the Deeps
Outward Urge, The
Re-Birth
Seeds of Time, The
Trouble with Lichen
Village of the Damned
Web

Yarbro, Chelsea Quinn
Cautionary Tales
False Dawn
Hyacinths
Taji's Syndrome
*Time of the Fourth
Horseman*

Yermakov, Nicholas
Epiphany
Jehad
Journey from Flesh
Last Communion

Yolen, Jane
Cards of Grief

Young, Robert F.
Last Yggdrasil, The
Starfinder
*Worlds of Robert
F. Young, The*

Yulsman, Jerry
Elleander Morning

Zahn, Timothy
Blackcollar, The
Cobra
Cobra Bargain
Cobra Strike
Coming of Age, A
Spinneret
Triplet

Zamyatin, Yevgeny
We

Zebrowski, George
Ashes and Stars
Macrolife
Mirror of Minds
Omega Point, The
*Synergy: New Science
Fiction, Volume 1*

Zelazny, Roger
Bridge of Ashes
Damnation Alley
Deus Irae
*Doors of His Face, the
Lamps of His Mouth,
The*
Doorways in the Sand
Dream Master, The
Eye of Cat
Four for Tomorrow
Frost and Fire
Isle of the Dead
Lord of Light
My Name is Legion
Roadmarks
Rose for Ecclesiastes, A
This Immortal
To Die in Italbar
Today We Choose Faces
Unicorn Variations

Zindell, David
Neverness

Zoline, Pamela
*Busy About the Tree of
Life*
*Heat Death of the
Universe and Other
Stories, The*